THE PRINCE

THE

PRINCE

The Secret Story of the World's Most Intriguing Royal
PRINCE BANDAR BIN SULTAN

WILLIAM SIMPSON

REGAN
An Imprint of HarperCollinsPublishers

Insert photographs courtesy of the personal collection of His Royal Highness Prince Bandar bin Sultan bin Abdul Aziz Al-Saud, with the following exceptions:

Insert pages 1 and 2 (top) courtesy of Ron McGaffin; pages 4 (top), 5 (bottom), and 7 (bottom) courtesy of the National Archives and Records Administration; page 9 (top) by permission of the Associated Press; page 11 (top) courtesy of Gerald Scarfe; page 12 (bottom) by Eric Drapper-White House/Getty Images; page 13 (bottom) courtesy of William Burrell; page 14 (top right) by the author.

Interior photographs courtesy of the personal collection of His Royal Highness Prince Bandar bin Sultan bin Abdul Aziz Al-Saud, with the following exceptions:

Photos on pages vi, 19, 26, 27, and 30 by permission of the AOC and Commandant of RAF College Cranwell; page 21 courtesy of Robert Elliott Deacon; pages 34, 37, and 40 courtesy of Rob McGaffin; pages 35, 75, 244, 342, 347, 363, and 386 courtesy of Joe Ramsey; pages 78, 370, 374, 375, 377, 383, 384, and 392 (right) courtesy of Bob Lilac; pages 80, 111, 161, 205, 251, 256, 259, 337, and 348 courtesy of the National Archives and Record Administration; pages 97 and 359 by David Hume Kennerly/Getty Images; pages 101 and 131 courtesy of Qorvis Communications, LLC; page 103 by Ramzi Haidar/AFP/Getty Images; page 116 by Terry Ashe/Time Life Pictures/Getty Images; page 121 by Consolidated News Pictures/Getty Images; page 139 by Johnny Eggitt/AFP/Getty Images; page 151 by Crown Copyright/MOD, image from www.photos.mod.uk, reproduced with the permission of the Controller of Her Majesty's Stationery Office; pages 175 and 184 by Karim Sahib/AFP/Getty Images; page 188 by Kevin Larkin/AFP/Getty Images; page 196 by Time & Life Pictures/Getty Images; page 198 courtesy of James Baker; page 231 by Christophe Simon/AFP/Getty Images; page 275 by Getty Images/Staff; page 279 by Steve Snowden/Getty Images; page 287 by Shaun Heasley/Getty Images; page 294 by Amr Nabil/AFP/Getty Images; pages 296 and 306 courtesy of the Saudi Information Office; page 307 by David Silverman/Newsmakers; page 314 by Spencer Platt/Getty Images; page 316 by Chris Kleponis/AFP/Getty Images; page 326 by Thomas Hartwell/Time Life Pictures/Getty Images; page 329 by STR-AUSAF Newspaper/AFP/Getty Images; page 343 by the author; page 345 courtesy of Tarek Shawaf; page 399 courtesy of John Veltri; page 417 courtesy of Robert Hunter; pages 422 and 425 by Win McNamee/Getty Images; page 423 by Imagno/Getty Images.

HarperCollins books may be purchased for educational, business, or sales promotional use. For information please write: Special Markets Department, HarperCollins Publishers Inc., 10 East 53rd Street, New York, NY 10022.

FIRST EDITION

Designed by Kris Tobiassen

Library of Congress Cataloging-in-Publication Data

Simpson, William.
    The prince : the secret story of the world's most intriguing royal, prince Bandar bin Sultan / William Simpson.
        p. cm.
    ISBN-13: 978-0-06-089986-8
    ISBN-10: 0-06-089986-7
    1. Bin Sultan, Bandar, Prince.   2. Princes—Saudi Arabia—Biography.   3. Ambassadors—Saudi Arabia—Biography.   4. Saudi Arabia—Foreign relations—United States.   5. United States—Foreign relations—Saudi Arabia.   I. Title.   II. Title: Bandar bin Sultan.

DS244.526.B55S56   2006
327.538073092—dc22
[B]   2006050357

06 07 08 09 10 WBC/RRD 10 9 8 7 6 5 4 3 2 1

To my wife Wendy, daughter Anna and son Michael;
for me, their love and unqualified support
over many years has been vital.

CONTENTS

Foreword by Nelson Mandela ix

Foreword by Baroness Margaret Thatcher xi

A Note on Sources xiii

Prologue xv

Introduction 1

ONE Who Is Prince Bandar? 9

TWO Fighter Pilot Prince 33

THREE The Tip of the Iceberg 63

FOUR The Years of Intrigue 95

FIVE Bandar the Arms Dealer 133

SIX A New World Order 169

SEVEN The Gulf Explodes 187

EIGHT Peace in the Middle East 241

NINE The Invisible Ambassador 271

TEN 9/11 Cataclysm 313

ELEVEN Friends and the Traveling Court 341

TWELVE The Private Prince Bandar 373

THIRTEEN Bandar: The Enigma Revealed 403

FOURTEEN A New Life 429

Acknowledgments 437

Notes 441

Index 469

FOREWORD

by Nelson Mandela

In the world of politics, friendships can all too often be transient or diplomatic and thus measurable only in terms of expediency or necessity. For Prince Bandar bin Sultan and I, that was certainly not the case: I have enjoyed a lasting and intensely personal friendship with Prince Bandar, an individual of extraordinary warmth, intellect, and loyalty. Bandar has given me his unhesitating support over the years in many ways; throughout, he has been honest and generous, no less than I would expect from this statesman of such great stature.

In writing Prince Bandar's biography, William Simpson has met a massive challenge, as he has captured the essence of the man—the enigma—that is Bandar. Addressing the twists and turns in this amazing life is a feat in itself, as is identifying those factors that have created the charismatic and accomplished individual that I am proud to know as a close friend.

Prince Bandar has had a quite astonishing influence during the past two decades as a roving international peacemaker, operating mainly in the background, never seeking public recognition and rarely accepting the plaudits of his peers. The remarkable respect accorded to Prince Bandar by so many heads of state and government and statespersons and opinion makers around the world should come as no surprise to those of us who know him well, but until now his central role has remained largely unheralded.

Prince Bandar is an outstanding man—a charming, eloquent, and nonetheless humble figure, who has so often guided the pattern of world events. I am delighted that I could contribute to an account that I know is vibrant and humorous, punctuated by Bandar's own stories—always larger than life and full of fun—for he is a storyteller without equal.

In conclusion, Prince Bandar's achievements deserve international recognition. He has worked relentlessly in the cause of peace, and I unconditionally applaud him as a man of principle, a diplomat of astonishing caliber, and one of the great peacemakers of our time.

—NELSON MANDELA

FOREWORD

by Baroness Margaret Thatcher

I have witnessed the outstanding talents of Prince Bandar as a diplomat and man of action for over twenty years. As a former fighter pilot he is bold and decisive, a man after my own heart. He makes things happen rather than waiting upon events. He has of course played a central role in the relations between the Kingdom of Saudi Arabia and the United States, as well as with the United Kingdom. His extraordinary ability to win the respect and confidence of world leaders has equipped him to serve his government in many other no less sensitive tasks in the Middle East, in China, and in Russia. I recall particularly the crucial part he played in building the coalition to resist Saddam Hussein's occupation of Kuwait in 1990. This book tells the story of a man for our time, who has been at the very heart of world events for two decades, and whom I am proud to call a friend.

—MARGARET THATCHER

A NOTE ON SOURCES

Though he stressed this would be an "unofficial biography," Prince Bandar nonetheless gave me unrestricted access to his family and friends. In doing so, he allowed me to tap directly into the collective memory of his closest friends. As those who know him will attest, Bandar is a remarkable raconteur and over the years has recounted to these friends, many times over, amazing diplomatic episodes. By interviewing those acquaintances, I was able to assemble, often under the strict caveat of anonymity, detailed personal accounts and anecdotes. Unless otherwise sourced, all direct quotes, dialogue, conversations and stories were gathered from this circle of friends. Accepting the request for secrecy from some sources, in this biography the conversational accounts of meetings and events attributed to Bandar are thus often unreferenced; they are nonetheless accurate.

PROLOGUE

In 1986, I found myself sitting around the campfire one night in the Arabian Desert; the Milky Way shone brilliantly across the dark. The fire crackled and burned.

My companions, sitting cross-legged in the sand with me, were all young officers and NCOs of the Royal Saudi Air Force. We had eaten our fill of fresh roasted goat and rice and now the cardamom-flavored coffee was being passed around in small cups.

We all knew each other well; everyone was relaxed and at ease, and for some reason the conversation turned to Prince Bandar. My colleagues had no idea of my past connections with Prince Bandar, and what I heard surprised me. They showed a warmth of affection and respect for him that was genuine and heartfelt. His exploits, many doubtless exaggerated, were recounted; they took pride in his achievements. This was not just for show—there was no need under the circumstances. Prince Bandar was clearly highly respected and loved, not just as a soldier and an airman, but also for his character as a man.

Bandar had somehow managed to reach out and touch all those men seated around the campfire that night, even though none had ever met him. It was a testament to the man I shall not forget, and which but for a twist of fate would have remained forever unrecorded.

—MARTIN SHEWRY,
96D Squadron, RAF Cranwell
(a Regiment officer who trained
Royal Saudi Air Force personnel
in the kingdom)

INTRODUCTION

"And in the end, it's not the years in your life that count. It's the life in your years."

ABRAHAM LINCOLN (1861–1865)

"I love my insecurities. If you cut me, I bleed. If you say something nasty to me, I get hurt. If I have to face danger or a challenge, we are all trained that our character will come through and we will do what needs to be done . . . I am not secure, I am insecure; I just don't allow my insecurity to stop me doing what needs to be done."

PRINCE BANDAR BIN SULTAN BIN ABDUL AZIZ AL-SAUD

In March 1949, the cry of a hawk, soaring high above the desert floor, heralded the birth of a Bedouin prince, one who was to have a profound impact on the world some decades later. As a child, however, this young boy would struggle simply to gain an audience with his father. For while he would eventually be recognized by the Saudi royal family, Prince Bandar bin Sultan was illegitimate, the progeny of a liaison between his father, Prince Sultan bin Abdul Aziz Al-Saud, the Saudi defense minister, and a young servant girl named Khizaran.

For the first eight years of his life, Bandar had little contact with his father. It was his influential grandmother, Princess Hussa bint Ahmed Al-Sudairi, a favorite wife of King Abdul Aziz bin Abdul Rahman Al-Saud, often known as Ibn Saud, the founder of Saudi Arabia, who saw the promise of the young boy and sought to bring him into the royal household. It was she who recognized the precociousness of this cheerful, clever, resourceful young boy, and effected the subsequent reconciliation with his father.

The passage of time saw the young prince aspire to become a pilot. Motivated by an innate drive to prove himself—particularly to his father—Bandar lied about his age and gained admittance to the British Royal Air Force College Cranwell, the RAF's premier military academy. At Cranwell, the prince's dreams of becoming a fighter pilot crystallized. It was there that he learned to prosper on his own merit, casting aside the title of prince, and absorbing a strange new world, though continuing to hold fast to Arab traditions and his Bedouin culture. In this alien environment, he mastered a new language, earned the unqualified respect of his peers, and learned to traverse the cultural chasm that separates East and West. He also surrounded himself with a group of fellow cadets, including myself, whose friendship, thirty-nine years later, remains undiminished.

Following his graduation from Cranwell, the next decade saw Bandar mature as a fighter pilot in the Royal Saudi Air Force (RSAF), during which time he embarked on successive training assignments with the United States Air Force. It was the ultimate culture clash—a Saudi prince, raised in the deserts of the Saudi peninsula, educated in the Lincolnshire countryside, now immersed in the American ethos in Texas. But it presaged a cultural rounding in the young prince. He readily embraced this new way of life, becoming an ardent fan of the Dallas Cowboys, making new friends, developing a profound understanding of American society, while assiduously improving his linguistic skills, and enthusiastically embracing the colloquial, frequently punctuated by jet jockey allegories.

Appointed to command an F-5 squadron and then the F-5 Operational Conversion Unit, Bandar would go on to train many of the current generation of Saudi Air Force fighter pilots. His flying days, however, were cut short in 1977 when he attempted to land an F-5 aircraft that had suffered undercarriage problems. Left with permanent spinal problems, the flying career he had counted on and trained for, was over. His next career, however, one that would consume the next twenty-four years of his life and make him a legend on the global diplomatic stage, was about to begin.

Fate reached in once again and took the controls of the prince's life when, in 1978, Prince Turki Al-Faisal, then in Washington lobbying for the sale of sixty F-15 aircraft to Saudi Arabia, and aware of Bandar's expertise as a pilot, his proficiency in English, and his embrace of the American culture, asked for his assistance. It was a task that Bandar relished and he quickly helped a hard-pressed President Jimmy Carter, not only to force through a reluctant Senate the sale of aircraft to Saudi Arabia, but also to secure passage through Congress of Carter's Panama Canal Treaty Bill.

Throughout, the young prince thrived in this unfamiliar political arena. Bandar's enthusiasm, professional knowledge as an experienced pilot, and a hitherto unseen inherent talent for diplomacy, persuaded many senators and resulted in the resounding defeat of the previously invincible American Israel Public Affairs Committee (AIPAC). He would later downplay this achievement and similar episodes with the often-used aphorism, "I'd rather be lucky than smart any day."[1]

Success in overcoming fierce resistance from a hostile pro-Israeli Jewish lobby during the 1978 F-15 battle, and his later success during the passage of the contentious sale of AWACS aircraft, together with his skilled involvement in brokering a ceasefire in Lebanon soon thereafter, earned him the deep respect and gratitude of King Fahd. In short succession, following his success on Capitol Hill, Bandar was appointed military attaché in Washington, became a special envoy for the king, and finally, at the astonishingly young age of just thirty-four, was named Saudi Arabia's ambassador to the United States.

In the twenty-three years following his appointment as ambassador, Bandar arguably became the essential bridge between the Middle East and Washington for Presidents Jimmy Carter, Ronald Reagan, George H. W. Bush, Bill Clinton, and George W. Bush. President Carter was to observe, ". . . of all of the Eastern people that I have ever known, he is the most natural bridge between our culture and the culture of the Middle East."[2] He operated as the natural "go-to" man[3] for all matters concerning Saudi Arabia; his influence was soon unassailable. As a uniquely powerful dean of the Diplomatic Corps, he held court in Washington as the virtual "fifth estate."[4] Presidents would come and go, but Bandar would remain as the dominant diplomatic figure embedded deeply inside the Beltway.

Yet he did not confine his relationship to Washington. King Fahd's decision to award the United Kingdom with the massive Al-Yamamah project, an ongoing contract, worth a stupendous $60 billion, for the acquisition and maintenance of a whole range of aircraft, ships, and other equipment—was an arms deal engineered and negotiated by Bandar. It was a deal, ironically, that had been requested originally by Ronald Reagan, was sanctioned by the United States Air Force, but ultimately rejected by Capitol Hill. The innovative structure Bandar devised to finance the Al-Yamamah project was masterly and cemented his rapport with Prime Minister Margaret Thatcher. The financial mechanics of the deal, which drew great media criticism, provided amazing scope for flexibility and deception, greatly benefiting both Saudi Arabia and Great Britain. From Al-Yamamah grew a relationship between Bandar and Thatcher, which was one of mutual admiration; it would be of inestimable value during the Gulf War in 1990.

In their rejection of the sale of additional fighters to the Saudi kingdom, the U.S. Congress effectively forced the Saudis to go abroad for their military hardware. Nonetheless, it did not impair Saudi Arabia's affiliation with the United States. Its relationship with President Reagan, in particular, would continue to strengthen. The decade of the 1980s saw the Saudis and the Americans collaborate over and over again to give teeth to American foreign policy, specifically to the anti-Communist program known as the Reagan Doctrine. In Afghanistan, Chad, Nicaragua, and Italy, the Saudi partnership was essential to American success.

The role played by Saudi Arabia, while recognized by a grateful Reagan administration, scarcely entered the public view. In the time-honored tradition of the Middle East, Bandar operated below the horizon, acting as the essential liaison between the kingdom and the White House.

Such success, however, was not without controversy, and Bandar became heavily embroiled in the Iran-Contra affair. Indeed, while the full extent of his involvement in covert CIA activities can only be guessed at, the scope of his diplomatic activities was astonishing: the negotiation of a ceasefire in Lebanon; an end to the Iran-Iraq war; the Soviet withdrawal from Afghanistan; the prosecution of the Gulf War; the resolution of the Lockerbie bombings—all show evidence of Bandar's fingerprints.

Perhaps most meaningful to Bandar—though its outcome in the current climate seems far from certain—are his efforts to bring peace to the Middle East, particularly between Israel and the Palestinians. In doing so, Bandar has cast an indelible shadow on the world stage as an architect of peace and war and a formidable force for moderation in the Middle East.

As President Bill Clinton worked to establish his place in history by achieving a breakthrough in the Palestinian-Israeli issue during the dying days of his administration, Bandar worked assiduously at persuading an intransigent Yasser Arafat to accept a deal that had hitherto been unthinkable.

The proposals made by Israeli Prime Minister Ehud Barak at Camp David and finally at Taba gave the Palestinian leader 98 percent of what he had hoped for; still, Arafat walked away. Unable to say publicly what he felt privately, a frustrated Bandar admitted to me, "It was not a tragedy—it was a crime!"

When approaching this biography, I had to ask myself the question: How do I accurately portray a man who is in essence an enigma? Is he a man of peace—as President Mandela was quick to declare—a man of principle, conscience, and moral correctness? Or, as some would have it, given his covert, behind-the-scenes art of diplomacy, is he to be depicted as a Machiavellian Prince—*destitute of political morality, ruled by expediency only; crafty, perfidious and amoral in conduct and activity*[5]—a man of whom it could be argued both precipitated the Gulf War and facilitated the Bush Administration's preemptive efforts and the invasion of Iraq? The following pages will, in providing some remarkable insights into the enigmatic Prince Bandar, allow the reader to establish the answer to these questions.

I came to this biography in an unusual manner. Three years ago, I received an intriguing invitation from Bandar to join some old military buddies for a reunion. The prospect of renewing old friendships was compelling. With growing anticipation at seeing old Cranwell friends, I ventured across the Atlantic to Bandar's ranch in Aspen—a fifty-five-thousand-square-foot luxury pad in the Rockies that defies description. Together with fifteen others, we enjoyed a wonderful weekend reminiscing about old times. Bandar and I were in the same entry and squadron—96D. We also shared a mutual love of fencing; he sporting the saber, I favoring the épée. When the weekend was over, we said our farewells and returned to the day-to-day pressures of our own lives.

Two years later, after several alarming health scares, I resigned as CEO of an Internet company and took stock of life. Astounded at the stories I had heard at Bandar's ranch in Aspen, and with an interest in writing, I wondered if his biography had yet been penned. It had not. Excited about the possibilities, I contacted Rob Deacon Elliott, a fellow Cranwell colleague who was very close to Bandar. I explained what I was considering, and asked whether he thought the prince might agree.

I was unaware that, at that very moment, Deacon Elliott was actually staying with Bandar in Rabat, Morocco. By chance, my e-mail arrived as both were set to depart. "As Bandar was getting on his aircraft going one way, and I was heading off in another direction," Deacon Elliott later explained, "I didn't get a chance to discuss it with him. So I gave him this e-mail from you verbatim and I said, 'Bill Simpson sent me this e-mail; have a safe flight and read this sometime.' I saw Bandar a few weeks later and I asked, 'What do you think?'"

Bandar said, "I think Bill should join us on our round trip of America. We haven't seen each other properly for over thirty years. Let's see how we all get on."

And so it was that I joined Bandar on a speaking tour of American states during which time we discussed my ideas for the book for barely forty minutes. Our old friendship, however, was quickly rekindled. When we finally returned to Washington, Bandar introduced me to his wife, Princess Haifa bint Faisal bin Abdul Aziz Al-Saud, who was enthused by the idea of the biography. What I did not know at the time was that Bandar was considering resigning as the Saudi ambassador to the United States: the timing of my approach was fortuitous.

As I engaged in researching Bandar's life story, interviewing world leaders, politicians, and statesmen, I was astounded. "It's a fascinating story—it's a great story," said Louis Freeh, former director of the FBI.[6] Freeh's comments were to be echoed by others, over and over again. Yet little did I realize the extent of the prince's influence on the international stage. Time and again I was stunned by new revelations. It became clear that he wielded power lightly and covertly, effectively charting the direction of world events from behind the scenes.

Such power, however, cannot be exercised without drawing fire, and while many of the world's leaders praise Bandar's work, others respond to the influence he exerted with cynicism. Speaking to his capacity and talent for intrigue, observing on the prince's involvement in many murky CIA episodes worldwide, Canadian reporter Matt Welsh wrote, "This enthusiasm, selective discretion and access to a medieval governing system make Bandar an all-too-tempting bagman when a U.S. president feels handcuffed by such pesky irritants as laws, journalists or decency."[7] Bandar has also been harshly criticized by former CIA operative Robert Baer, who griped, "Bandar could wander into the White House and around Congress for a chat anytime he liked. It took me weeks to get an appointment with a low-ranking staffer in the National Security Council, and I'd be lucky to get even a few minutes. Forget the crap about democracy, about the capital of the free world. Washington was a company town, and Bandar had a seat on the board. If you wanted to move into even the outer reaches of his orbit, you had damn well better play by his rules."[8]

Yet he has impressed even his harshest critics with his straightforward style. Various Jewish groups in the United States, while intent on undermining his position and the Arab cause at large, grudgingly described Bandar as "everything a diplomat is expected to be: Charming. Gracious. Witty. Opaque."[9] Even within the Jewish community, which suffered defeat on not one but two occasions as Bandar first shepherded the sale of F-15 fighter aircraft to Saudi Arabia during the Carter administration and later the sale of Airborne Warning and Control System (AWACS) technology during the Reagan administration, there was an open respect for Bandar. Henry Siegman, then the executive director of the American Jewish Congress, said, "He does not fall into the trap of arguing the old polemics of the Arab-Israeli dispute. He is a refreshingly different diplomat—non-ideological, highly pragmatic."[10]

During Bandar's time in Washington, the media assembled a lexicon of descriptions and analogies, ironically reinforcing the mirage of deception that surrounds him. Many see him as a political chameleon, while others are intrigued by his vast wealth and generosity. For some, his talent for wielding power in Washington and his unparalleled access single him out as someone to be envied and feared. Others focus on his devotion to peace. Still others point to his association with scandal and conspiracy. Early in the writing of this book, it was Bandar's life story, his rise from an inauspicious beginning as son of a slave girl to fighter pilot and statesman that fascinated me. In the end, however, it was the elusive and Byzantine nature of his character that most compelled me.

It is these complexities, I believe, that make him such a powerful and successful statesman. Yet it is his loyalty, warmth, and generosity that make him a truly remarkable man. I consider Bandar a friend, and I count myself lucky to be part of his life and he a part of mine. He is a fascinating and charismatic personality, and I am convinced that even those who do not know him will be riveted by the incredible trajectory of his life and the extraordinary reach of his accomplishments.

—BILL SIMPSON
October 2006

ONE

WHO IS
PRINCE BANDAR?

"All men dream, but not equally. Those who dream by night in
the dusty recesses of their minds wake in the day to find that it
was vanity: but the dreamers of the day are dangerous men, for
they may act their dream with open eyes, to make it possible."

T. E. LAWRENCE,
"THE SEVEN PILLARS OF WISDOM"[1]

Fifty-seven years ago, inside a traditional Bedouin tent, a young servant girl
gave birth to her only child, a boy. But for one detail, the birth of a child to a
young mother of indifferent, even insignificant status, deep in the desert,
would be of import to very few. That singular detail, however, was important,
for the father of the infant boy was Prince Sultan bin Abdul Aziz Al-Saud, a
member of the royal family and son of the founder of Saudi Arabia, King Abdul Aziz bin Abdul Rahman Al-Saud—known in the West as Ibn Saud.

At the time, Saudi Arabia itself was still in its infancy, for not until 1932
did Ibn Saud unify the diverse tribal regions in the center of the Arabian
peninsula, rename the country the Kingdom of Saudi Arabia, and name
himself as its first king.*

Ibn and *bin* both mean "son of."

The formation of modern Saudi Arabia did not come about easily. In the early nineteenth century, members of the Al-Saud tribe ruled Najd, a central and physically isolated region, which included the holy cities of Mecca and Al Medina. In 1811, the Ottoman sultan asked Muhammad Ali, ruler of Egypt, then part of the Ottoman Empire, to depose Al-Saud. Ali sent two of his sons to invade Najd, and in 1818, his second son, Ibrahim Pasha, captured Dir'iyyah, the capital. Its ruler, Abdallah ibn Saud, was sent into exile, first to Cairo and then to Constantinople, where he was beheaded. With his death, so too died the first Saudi state.

A second Saudi state emerged in 1824, when Turki bin Abdallah bin Saud bin Abdul Aziz bin Muhammad Al-Saud, ousted the Egyptians from Najd and established Riyadh as his capital. Although this second state prospered initially, internal disputes saw the leadership change hands within the family until Faisal bin Turki took charge in 1843. Under Ibn Turki's leadership, order prevailed. Yet his death in 1865 marked the return of disorder and strife. In 1891, the Ottoman Rashidi tribe defeated that of the Al-Saud, forcing its leader, Abdul Rahman—grandfather of the present King Abdullah and great grandfather of Prince Bandar—to flee into what is now Kuwait. He was exiled with his family, including his son Abdul Aziz. With Rahman's exile, the second Saudi state came to an end.

Abdul Aziz, who would become known as Ibn Saud, spent the remainder of his childhood in Kuwait, where he attended the daily governing councils, *majlis* of the emir of Kuwait,* from whom he learned about the wider world. Seeking to restore the kingdom to the Al-Saud, Abdul Aziz set out in 1901 with a small number of warriors intent on recapturing Riyadh. Luck and audacity favored him when, on the night of January 15, 1902, he scaled Riyadh's walls with only twenty men and laid in wait for the Rashidi governor, Ajlan. The following morning, Abdul Aziz and his raiding party attacked, killing Ajlan and launching a campaign that would ultimately give rise to the third Saudi state. Over the next thirty years, Ibn Saud would gradually seize control of each of the tribal regions. In 1932, the Kingdom of Saudi Arabia was born.

Though born into the royal family of Ibn Saud, Bandar bin Sultan's fu-

---

Majlis is an Arabic term used to describe various types of formal legislative assemblies in Islamic countries. It also stands for the term *parliament* in some Islamic states. Finally, the term *majlis* can also be used to describe a room in a private home used to entertain family and guests. The seating is usually arranged around three walls of the room. In some homes there is a women's *majlis* and a men's *majlis*.

ture was far from certain. His mother was Khizaran, a dark-skinned sixteen-year-old commoner from the province of Asir, located at the southern end of Saudi Arabia. It was a desolate place of vast plains and salt marshes, hostile mountains, and deep ravines. Its seaports, however, had allowed centuries of interaction with both Yemen and the Horn of Africa.

Though his father, Prince Sultan, was one of the Sudairi Seven,* the seven sons of Ibn Saud and Princess Hussa bint Ahmed al-Sudairi, one of King Abdul Aziz's favored wives, the boy's birth was inauspicious. Bandar is now quite blunt about his place in the Saudi royal family, saying, "I was conceived out of wedlock and my mother was a concubine."

Although his dark-skinned mother was but a servant in his father's household and they were unmarried, Islamic law protects illegitimate children if recognized by their father, and Bandar's father acknowledged the birth. "My father recognized the pregnancy of my mother before I was born," recounted Bandar. "That is the reason why I was born in King Abdul Aziz's tented camp in Taif. He personally, King Abdul Aziz, named me with four other kids." That naming by the king effectively established the boy's pedigree as royal. Yet there was still a separation—a distancing of the prince from the other sons born to Prince Sultan's many wives.

The birth of a child to an Arab prince and a concubine, though perhaps romantic, was not without pathos. Bandar's mother had been a servant girl before becoming a concubine to the twenty-year-old Prince Sultan, who had been appointed governor of Riyadh in 1947. Bandar remembers, "My mother was not related to any tribal leader that would provide me with power, nor was she from a royal family." Having lived in the Asir Province of Saudi Arabia, which nestles across from Africa, Khizaran was darker skinned, a feature she passed on to her son Bandar, who is noticeably darker than his brothers. It has been a common misconception in the U.S. press that the prince's mother was African. Bandar often derives curious enjoyment from knowing the truth of a situation while the media speculates endlessly and wrongly about him, and he has made no attempt to explain the

---

*The Al Sudairi clan, better known as the Sudairi Seven (also spelled *Sudeiri* and *Sudayri*) are seven full brothers, all sons of Saudi Arabia's founder King Abdul Aziz bin Saud and Princess Hussa bint Ahmad Al Sudairi, which is where the name comes from. Since Fahd's ascent to the throne in 1982, they have become the most powerful alliance within the ruling Saudi royal family. The Sudairi Seven include: King Fahd bin Abdul Aziz Al-Saud, Prince Sultan bin Abdul Aziz Al-Saud, Prince Nayef bin Abdul Aziz Al-Saud, Prince Abdel-Rahman bin Abdul Aziz Al-Saud, Prince Turki bin Abdul Aziz Al-Saud, Prince Salman bin Abdul Aziz Al-Saud, and Prince Ahmed bin Abdul Aziz Al-Saud.

geographical background to his mother's heritage. He confessed, "I coyly let that stand for a long time, because as you know by now, I enjoy knowing something that the whole world is talking about mistakenly and I know that it is not true."

Though the press insists that Bandar was not recognized by his father, he insists otherwise. "Not being recognized by my father," he says, "is a matter of not having access to my father." Recognition of his status had occurred when he was named by the king. "Anytime that a royal child was born in those days, he had a salary," he explained. "I think it was about $10 or so back then. That salary came from the Ministry of Finance; so the minute that the king christened the kid, the Royal Court informed the minister of interior to start a salary for him and his mother. My mother received that salary. So that was an official acknowledgment of my status at that point—and, indeed, was recognition by my father. The fact that I did not live with my father does not mean that he did not recognize me." There was, however, little contact between Bandar and his father, a reality that he acknowledged to be a problem that took years to overcome because, physically, he wasn't with him.[2] Bandar's daughter, Princess Reema, explained, "They [the media] tried to make it seem like a deliberate exclusion and it wasn't. It was just a matter of fact. The woman who is married and is in the house, her children by nature are closer to the father; the women living out of the house or divorced from the man do not therefore have the same contact."[3]

Bandar's father, Prince Sultan—the long-serving minister of defense—became crown prince in 2005 at the death of King Fahd, his brother. Sultan is also half-brother to King Abdullah and is unquestionably a powerful and influential figure in the House of Saud. Bandar has never taken lightly his father's recognition of him—and, with that, his legitimacy—saying with great deliberation, "Something that I will never forget about my father is that he did not let me come to earth with doubts as to who my father was."[4] Yet behind this bold statement, the distance between the young prince and his father would provide a fundamental element of his character, a facet of his personality that has driven his unremitting desire to achieve and thereby prove himself to his father. It is, perhaps, understandable against this backdrop—one in which, although he was born into the royal family, he was not on an equal footing with his brother princes.

As Bandar explained, "Under Islamic Sharia law, if you have a slave or a concubine and you make love to her, and she doesn't have any children, she stays a slave." As a servant girl, his mother clearly had been a slave; slavery wasn't abolished in the kingdom until 1962. Yet, Bandar continued, "The minute she gets pregnant and you acknowledge it before she has the baby, then it is automatic freedom from slavery. But you still have to deal with the cultural realities; you'll always be the kid who's a different color, a kid whose parents never got married.[5] Bandar's plain words were echoed by David Ottaway, of the *Washington Post*, who said, "Bandar had grown up an only child in his mother's home in Riyadh, but with thirty-two half-brothers and half-sisters, children of Sultan's various wives. He was a dark skinned one with the nappy hair, the awkward loner."[6]

For the first eleven years of his life Bandar was brought up by his mother and his Aunt Loulou in a home with one light and one toilet. Although Bandar's mother never went to school, she nonetheless taught herself to read and write. Khizaran's spirit and strength of character have been passed on to her son. "A major factor for Bandar is his mother," Princess Haifa, Bandar's wife, has stressed. "He takes after her, in his wanting to succeed. She is very intelligent and she instilled everything in him. If it wasn't for her bringing him up the way she did, he wouldn't be the Bandar we know—that is very important."[7]

During these years, Bandar had little or no relationship with his father, except to see him on weekends and to kiss his hand at family gatherings. Yet Bandar has often remarked, "It taught me patience, and a defense mechanism, to not expect anything. I thought that if I didn't expect anything and I didn't get anything, then I didn't get disappointed."[8]

Although removed from the Royal Court, the young Bandar regarded the elusive, aloof man who was his father with an earnest caring. He tells the story of hearing of an illness suffered by his father, and his own fretting. "When I was about nine years old," he said, "I was living with my aunt and I heard from the women in the house that my father was sick. I didn't understand how sick or how serious it was

Bandar at age six—the earliest known photo of the prince

and I was a little too proud to ask people or to show people I didn't know." Being aware that his father had a chauffeur, the prince explained, "I saw him call at the house so I called to him and asked, 'Sir, how is my father?'"

The driver was clearly moved by the young boy and he relayed the conversation to Sultan, who promptly asked for his son. Bandar's aunt got him cleaned and dressed in readiness for a journey to visit his father. It was the first time that he had seen his father in bed. Sultan beckoned him over and held him close. Bandar vividly remembers, "I was on top of the world—in fact, I felt like he gave me the whole world."[9]

The prince's isolation from the family ended soon after this visit. King Abdul Aziz had died several years earlier, and it was decided that Bandar and his mother should live in the palace with his grandmother, Princess Hussa. "It was a practical decision, but it completely altered my life," said Bandar. Each day at 5 A.M., Hussa would wake up her grandson for prayers, after which she imbued him in the history and folklore surrounding the House of Saud. "She was not educated, but she had learned the Koran by heart," Bandar recalled. He worshiped her, and she returned the affection, making him feel special. "She was the most influential figure in my life," he said without hesitation, reflecting, "It was fascinating to sit with this woman who was the wife of the founder of Saudi Arabia, who had known all those big and mighty men, like King Faisal, as children. She would wake me up before dawn prayers every day to go to pray with her. That usually meant I had at least an hour or so before I was ready to go to school and I had nothing to do. So I would sit with her and she would start telling me stories."[10]

Gen. Faisal Mifgai, a close friend of Bandar's since childhood, has said that when the Prince was a young boy, he showed a tremendous interest in the history of the Al-Saud family. "He would like to sit in the majlis, listening to the old men telling stories about his grandfather, and he would ask them questions in a way which would surprise the old men. He had a fascination about his grandfather, King Abdul Aziz, which bordered on obsession; by listening to his elders he became an expert on his grandfather, whom he admired very much." Mifgai added, "He showed a maturity and a thirst for knowledge well beyond his years."

Once Bandar was living in the palace, a closer relationship with his father became possible. Mifgai recalled that as a child Bandar would make expeditions into the desert on horseback with Prince Sultan. "He taught him about hunting with falcons and how to shoot. His father was keen for Bandar to learn the Bedouin skills for surviving in the desert. They would spend all day together in the desert, leaving at first light in the cold of the morning, returning late into the evening, and sometimes they slept the night in Bedouin tents."[11]

Bandar recalled one hunting trip when he and his brothers had to select a falcon. He was the last to choose, and after all the attractive birds had been selected, he was left with a scruffy, black and dark brown–feathered bird that everyone had laughed at. However, he remembered with pride that that same falcon had showed a hunting prowess that eclipsed any of the proud birds on show that day. Bandar, perhaps, was seeing a similarity between himself and his falcon.

Gen. Mifgai and Bandar met as schoolchildren while attending school at the Institute of Riyadh. According to Mifgai, Bandar was one of the most distinguished students at the Institute. "He had a superb academic record. He was also a very popular student . . . charming, outgoing, and was fun to be around. He was a mature, placid, and well-balanced young man. He was slow to anger and never lost his temper, choosing instead to ignore someone and walk away." Mostly, though, Mifgai remembered Bandar's love of flying; how, when they were both at school and an aircraft passed overhead, the prince would turn to him and say, "One day I will be a pilot!"[12]

When Bandar was thirteen, his father was named defense minister. Three years later, determined to become a pilot, Bandar faked his age on his application, and was selected for officer and flying training at Royal Air Force College Cranwell in England. Many have speculated that this was a move intended to please his father; it also was a reflection on his status within the family; a close friend of the prince's confided, "He wasn't sent to Eton—he was sent to military school." Coincidentally—or perhaps by design—Bandar has since sent three of his sons to Eton.

Bandar had learned self-reliance from a young age and did not expect anything

Bandar at thirteen

of his father. Having spent his early life outside of the family, he was rather uncomfortable with his position as a prince; he had always felt somewhat uncertain of the attention people showed him, "I didn't feel I did anything to earn it except by happenstance, circumstance. Just because my father is a prince, I became a prince. I never worked a day in my life to be one. Compare that with my feeling when I got commissioned a second lieutenant. I was so proud."[13]

And so it was that in March 1967, Bandar was enrolled into RAF College Cranwell, where I was first introduced to the cocky, story-telling joker whom I then knew simply as "Ben."

The transformation from prince to officer cadet at the RAF's primary military academy, RAF Cranwell, was bewildering. The familiar sounds of home and the easy, privileged pace of life as a young boy had now been replaced by the harsh reality of a military boot camp—a hostile and confusing setting where status counted for nothing and survival in this alien machine was a growing imperative. The familiar comfort of an Arab *thobe** and sandals and the warmth of the sun were gone, replaced by a choking, starchy collar, and the abrasive, ill-fitting, and thoroughly uncomfortable "hairy blue" uniform that was the standard RAF jacket and trousers. His feet were now clad in "unyielding instruments of torture," the heavy black RAF leather boot, the sole of which was almost an inch thick and was shod with metal tips, heels, and studs. Unaccustomed to the British climate, the incessant drizzle and the chill of Lincolnshire mornings, Bandar later would say that he was cold for six months straight.

To be selected to attend RAF Cranwell was a great achievement, in much the same way a British army officer would view his selection to Sandhurst, or an American would view selection to West Point or the Air Force Academy at Colorado Springs. And it was his desire to fly—"I was dying to join the Air Force," Bandar enthused—that prompted him to fake his date of birth. The prince has admitted that although his official date of birth is March 2, 1949, it is a sham. Bandar had to be seventeen to join the Air Force, and he disclosed that he convinced his doctor to change his birth

---

*A *thobe* is an ankle-length garment similar to a robe, worn by men in the Arabian Peninsula and surrounding countries.

certificate. So when Bandar joined the Air Force, he was actually sixteen, not seventeen, making his date of birth late 1950.

This was later confirmed by his wife, Princess Haifa. Following this confession, Bandar observed, "This was the funny part about it; my uncle was the king, my other uncle was the crown prince, my third uncle was the second deputy premier, and my father was the minister of defense. So why would the date be a problem? Because I could not join the Air Force if my birth certificate said that I was not seventeen years old." Expectations of young cadets were high, and the rigorous training program placed significant demands on any individual. For someone handicapped by a limited knowledge of English, just being able to complete the course, let alone achieve a sound performance, was an accolade in itself. This was especially true of a sixteen-year-old.

Bandar's life, and those of his colleagues in D Squadron, 96 Entry, was to be ruled by their immediate superior, Sgt. Ken Adams. In a scene that doubtless would be familiar to military men around the world—no matter the service, no matter the country—Bandar's first day at Cranwell was brutal.

Standing in front of his misbegotten collection of trembling youths, Sgt. Adams marched swiftly up to the young prince and, with his face just inches from His Royal Highness Prince Bandar bin Sultan bin Abdul Aziz Al-Saud, screamed, "When I say halt, Mr. Sultan, I mean halt in my time, not yours; I mean today, not tomorrow! You are not in the ruddy desert now, you horrible little man—now sharpen up or you will double round this parade ground until I say stop. Get it!"

"Yes sir," responded Bandar.

"I didn't hear that," yelled Sgt. Adams.

"Yes sir," shouted a sodden prince, desperately hoping that his tormentor would focus on another cadet, any other cadet.

But Sgt. Adams was not to be distracted. "Don't call me sir, I'm too smart to be called sir; call me sergeant!"

Eventually dismissed from the parade ground, Bandar and his fellow cadets marched off briskly, not to the splendors of College Hall, but to the antiquated huts known as the South Brick Lines that were to be his home for the next six months. These huts comprised some toilet and shower accommodations immediately inside the entry door that led through to the bedroom accommodation. Each individual had a locker, bedside unit, and bed. At the end of the hut was a very spartan sitting room.[14]

Frozen to the core, the young men now faced an hour of "bull"—cleaning the hut and preparing their personal equipment for inspection by Sgt. Adams, ironing vests, shirts, and sportswear into perfect nine-inch squares. All this and not a servant to be seen—no wonder Bandar saw this as a hostile environment. Even as he attempted to apply his bulling skills to his gear, his peers had begun to clean the hut, to ensure that windows would be gleaming, all surfaces would be dusted and spotless, floors polished to a mirror finish, and the white enamel of showers, toilets, and communal bath cleaned until glistening. Every man was expected to pull his weight; there were no exceptions.

Like the Air Force itself, each activity at Cranwell was measured against the clock, part of a rigid program that dictated every second of the young officer cadet's time for a full three months. His presence was demanded on the parade square for drill practice, then at the gym for rigorous physical training or a cross-country run across Lincolnshire's plowed fields, an exercise that saw the participants return exhausted, sweaty, and caked in mud. Studies in Whittle Hall included current affairs, strategic studies, the whole range of math and sciences, and English. Indeed, academics would become a welcome respite from the grueling physical regimen.

The initial emphasis on drill, constantly marching up and down the same gravel-covered square, combined with detailed gear and hut inspections, was designed to encourage a sense of discipline and unwavering respect for military commands. It was also an attempt to take the officer cadets to the limit of their physical and mental reserves, while at the same time introducing some form of cohesion among the disparate collection of recruits that had been selected from all corners of the former colonial globe: Singapore, Rhodesia, South Africa, Malta, Kenya, and Ceylon, and from all over the British Isles. Add to this a smattering of foreign cadets, and the resultant Babel of voices must have sounded like bedlam to the young Saudi who only recently had begun to learn the "Queen's English."

John Waterfall, a fellow cadet, when asked how Bandar handled the transition to military life, responded, "He had some adjusting to do, but we all did. That was part of the Cranwell thing—taking all these blokes from diverse backgrounds and grinding them down."[15] Martin Shewry, another of Bandar's fellow 96 Entry D Squadron contemporaries, said about the early days, "What I didn't realize was the degree of culture shock that Prince Bandar must have experienced when he arrived at Cranwell. In saying that you need to know what Saudi Arabia was like in 1966—cars were very infrequent there—it was still a very basic society compared with the

U.K. We didn't have an easy time at Cranwell, and Prince Bandar had even further to go than everyone else."[16]

During the early weeks of training, after arrival, Sgt. Adams would castigate the young cadets in a range of expletives of varying degrees of intensity to put these inexperienced young men under pressure and to ensure that he had a firm grip on discipline. Yet Bandar would come to harbor great affection for his drill sergeant. This in spite of repeated transgressions.

Sgt. Adams laughed as he recalled, "As you know, he [Bandar] got a bit naughty at one stage." The Saudi cadets in the senior entries had taken to calling Bandar and inviting him to join them for meals in Lincoln—strictly forbidden for young novice cadets during the early weeks of training. Bandar simply disappeared and left his mates to cover for him. However, Adams soon was tipped off that even though everyone was confined to barracks in those early weeks of training, Bandar was skipping out for meals with his fellow Saudis. Adams would later learn that a naive young Bandar had informed his cadet colleagues, "I have nothing to do with this domestic rubbish; the rest of you can do what you want, but I'm only here to fly." Adams related, "The other guys were doing his job as well as their own, and were saying nothing so as to protect him." He explained, "Having received a nudge, I walked in on Prince Bandar's hut one evening." When Adams asked where he was, everything went quiet; there was no answer. He left instructions that Bandar was to report to him first thing in the morning for extra duties—duties which saw Bandar cleaning toilets for weeks.

"He had a great sense of humor," Adams said, "I'll always remember that you could have a go at him about anything and he would still laugh." After he crossed swords with the prince over domestic chores, the sergeant enlisted the help of a very responsible fellow Saudi, Prince Mugrin. Adams briefed Mugrin on the problem with Bandar and the adverse influence of other Saudi

Being inspected at RAF Cranwell

cadets; that fellow Saudi made it abundantly clear to the young prince exactly how he should behave. The transition, Adams said, was remarkable and occurred almost overnight. Bandar became the ideal cadet. Adams observed, "As you know, he did exceptionally well after that, and was always extremely smart and well turned out—and a handsome bastard to boot! I used to say to him, 'With your looks and my money, you could go far!' "[17] In fact, in his final term, Bandar was selected to be a color warrant officer of the College Color Party, a prestigious position for those cadets chosen to guard the Queen's Color for RAF Cranwell—positions demanding the highest standards of personal turnout and parade drill.

Prior to entering RAF Cranwell as an officer cadet, Bandar spent time improving his spoken English, initially with a Mrs. Genham, a Royal Navy officer's widow, and her daughter Sarah at their home in Maidstone in Kent. Bandar continued English language training at RAF Upwood before joining his contemporaries at Cranwell, where his father bought him his first car, a white Mercedes. It was the beginning of a lifelong love of cars. Within weeks, though, he had rolled it into a ditch.

In those days, young officers weren't allowed to meet with fellow lady officers in the mess. Bandar recalled, "One day this really sweet young lady took my eye and I wanted to take her out." The prince therefore took her to the American officers' club at RAF Alconbury, a much more relaxed environment than the officers' mess at Upwood. How-

ever, while driving home along the narrow lanes of Cambridgeshire, Bandar accidentally hit the ignition, and the steering wheel on the Mercedes promptly locked. They came upon a bend in the road at speed, and the car went up a bank and flipped over. In a bit of a daze, Bandar struggled from the car but suddenly realized that his date hadn't moved. He looked through the open door—the car was still on its roof—to see the girl hanging upside down in her seat. Without

Bandar dressed in an unofficial RSAF cadet uniform he designed while undergoing English language training at RAF Upwood.

thinking, he released her seat belt and she fell straight onto her head. As he was later to observe with a laugh, "She wasn't injured until I rescued her!"

The Mercedes wrecked, Bandar moved on, this time to an Aston Martin. As Sgt. Adams recalled, "Prince Bandar would use this car to drive to London at weekends, and if the police picked him up, he would produce a Saudi driving license and claim he had diplomatic immunity." Adams added, "He also had a drawer for parking tickets picked up in London, which were never paid, and had a set of CD plates* which he used to stick on the car for weekends."[18]

Fellow cadet John Waterfall recalled, "I remember coming back from London with him; Robbie [Hunter] and I were in his Aston Martin. We pulled in about two o'clock in the morning to get some gas and right behind us was a police car."

John exclaimed, "They hadn't pulled us over for speeding or anything; they were just admiring the car."

Bandar recalled asking one of the policemen, "Officer, would you like to drive my car?"

The constable replied, "Bloody hell—yes!"

So he got into the prince's car and drove it away. So Bandar went over to the policeman's colleague and said, "Look, your mate took my car; can I drive your car?"[19]

*Corps Diplomatique license plates for foreign diplomats that enable the owners to claim diplomatic immunity.

Bandar's first car—which he crashed soon after.

Confirming this story, Bandar recounted how he ended up chasing his Aston Martin in a police car, with Robbie Hunter and John Waterfall in the back. After several miles, they caught up with his car and a very elated policeman. Episode over, they continued their journey back to Cranwell.

Despite having the ability to escape from Cranwell at weekends, vacations were more problematic. There was, however, a group of cadets who were known as the "orphans" because their parents lived overseas. Like Bandar, they were unable to get away from Cranwell to rejoin their families. A close friendship he had developed with one of these orphans enabled Bandar to escape to Malta with his friend Rob Deacon Elliott, whose father, an air vice marshal (AVM), was air officer commanding (AOC). He recalled, "So I joined them in Malta, where we stayed at the Hilton Hotel."

When I spoke with Mrs. Grace Deacon Elliott about the prince's trip to Malta, she recalled, "The first time that I met Ben, Robert came out from Cranwell sometime in 1967, and he arrived with this little boy—Ben." She continued, "We took him out on my husband's launch—he was AOC at the time—right out to the middle of Island Bay. The children used to dive in because they were all brilliant swimmers, and they swam over to the rocks, which were a long way away. I don't think Ben could swim, but the children all dived in and started swimming. So Ben jumped in and he sort of dog-paddled all the way there. When I saw this, I asked the crew to keep a special eye out for him." She added that perhaps it was the presence of the commander's daughters that prevented Bandar from admitting that he couldn't swim.[20]

Rob Deacon Elliott was keen to emphasize the close relationship that developed between Bandar and his parents during his time at Cranwell. "Not only did Bandar respect my father, Air Vice Marshal Deacon Elliott,* but my mother as well; she was quite a significant person in his life—in a sense they were like adopted English parents."[21] Mrs. Deacon Elliott confirmed this, saying, "He used to call us his mother and father; I think he felt relaxed with

---

*AVM Robert Deacon Elliott (1914–1997); joined RAF 1937; 72 Fighter Sqn, Dunkirk, France, and Battle of Britain, 1939–1941; headquarters, Fighter Command, 1942–1943; Second Allied Tactical Air Force, Northwest Europe, 1944–1946; Air Ministry 1946–1948; commander, Flying Wing and 26 Armament Practice Centre, Cyprus, 1948–1951; headquarters, Fighter Command, 1951–1954; instructor, Army Staff College, 1954–1956; commander, RAF Station Leconfield, 1956–1957; commander, RAF Station Driffield, 1957–1958; Air University, USAF, Maxwell AFB, United States, 1958–1961; commandant, Officer & Air Crew Selection Centre, Biggin Hill, 1962–1965; air officer commanding RAF Gibraltar and commander Maritime Air Gibraltar, NATO, 1965–1966; air officer commanding RAF, Malta, and deputy commander-in-chief (Air), Allied Forces, Mediterranean, 1966–1968; retired 1968; bursar, Civil Service College, 1969–1979.

us and he just fell into the family pattern. I always thought of him as a little boy just starting out in life. It was like a family; I loved it and so did my husband."[22]

Thirty years later, in a remarkable gesture, Bandar would arrive unannounced to pay his respects to the family following AVM Deacon Elliott's death on June 5, 1997. "He made a special journey from Washington on the day of the funeral, just to show his respects in person," said Rob Deacon Elliott. "He then turned around and made his way all the way back to Washington."[23] Having traveled so far, by aircraft, helicopter, and car, the Prince did not wish to intrude on what was a private family occasion; but he had paid his personal tribute to a friend in a unique way that was indicative of the nature of the man and his loyalty to friends.

Once Bandar had endured the military boot camp element of training at Cranwell, the college focused on training this young man as an officer, influencing the development of his character, and that of his contemporaries, with a mixture of camaraderie, discipline, academics, field craft, sport, and, finally, flying.

All cadets at Cranwell took part in an exercise in Germany involving field craft training, canoeing, rock climbing, abseiling,* and escape and evasion—this was known as Exercise King Rock.† Bandar participated in this exercise in 1968 and was subjected to the same fitness, endurance, and field training techniques that all cadets were obliged to experience. Throughout the grueling exercise, cadets were allowed to carry only barely adequate field rations; hence, hunger was the order of the day. The canoeing was particularly onerous, as it involved white-water skills over a twelve-mile stretch of water, endurance tests on the Eder and Möhne Dams of Dambuster fame,‡ together with capsizing techniques.

---

*Abseiling, which stems from the German *abseilen,* "to rope down," is the process of descending on a fixed rope.

†King Rock was a demanding field exercise that took place in Germany and required stamina and fitness from all cadets. It allowed directing staff to assess cadet leadership qualities and determine their courage in a range of strenuous activities. It was an extremely challenging exercise.

‡Led by Squadron Leader Guy Gibson, 617 Squadron—the Dambusters—flew Lancaster bombers from RAF Scampton in Lincolnshire, in an attack on the Möhne, Eder, and Sorpe dams in the German Ruhr valley on May 16, 1943. These dams in the Ruhr were attractive yet daunting targets, providing Germany with much-needed hydroelectric power, industrial and domestic water, and maintaining levels in the canals which fed materiel between German factories and war depots. It was believed that destroying these targets would reduce the enemy's capacity to wage war, and the psychological impact of success was of immense importance to Great Britain at that time. Using bouncing bombs specially designed by the brilliant, if eccentric,

All of this training culminated in a three-day escape-and-evasion exercise in which cadets were abandoned in small groups in "enemy territory," simulating a downed pilot situation. Armed only with basic maps and a twenty-four-hour ration pack, the teams of three were given instructions to proceed to a rendezvous by a given time, avoiding capture by army units that had been given the task of catching them. Bandar led his team. Deciding to play the game by his own rules, he secreted a one-hundred-deutsche mark note into his cap. The prince recalled, "Our attempt to find that location nearly came to grief as I blundered into an electric fence and I received an electric shock. As I floundered around a field in the dark, I lost my footing and ended up with my face in a cow pat." Beyond annoyed, he said to his colleagues, "Look, I've had enough; I am not going to walk forty kilometers back to the camp. After all, this is an escape-and-evasion exercise and we have to use our brains."

Bandar promptly led his group to the nearest highway and hitched a ride to the rendezvous point. They then found a German *gasthof*, where they quickly tucked into a huge meal of grilled chicken and potato salad. Now replete, the team realized that it was too early to report into the RV, so they walked to within a mile of it and bedded down with their ponchos until a reasonable time had elapsed for them to have made the journey on foot. They duly reported in and were congratulated on their achievement by the directing staff. Years later Bandar was to recall that Rob Deacon Elliott—whom he refers to as his conscience—never forgave him for cheating. The rest of the exercise went largely without incident and he avoided capture. The squadron commander's report stated, "There was evidence of courage, stamina, and the ability to lead."[24]

As a young cadet, Bandar initially adopted soccer as his preferred sport, having acquired the basic skills while at school in Riyadh. But early in his first year at Cranwell he became intrigued by the sport of fencing and, in time, he became a passionate and reasonably competent sabreur. As his skills developed, he was selected as a member of the Cranwell fencing team, with whom he traveled to the French Air Academy at Salon en Provence, properly

---

scientist and aircraft designer, Barnes Wallis, the Dambusters flew against lethal defenses, at heights below sixty feet and at a constant speed of two hundred fifty miles per hour, the optimum speed for the bombs to be effective. The raid was fairly successful, with the Möhne Dam being attacked first; it was completely destroyed, and a rectangular wedge two hundred fifty feet wide and one hundred twelve feet deep was torn away from a fifty-foot-thick wall, flooding the valley below. The Eder Dam was also breached; little damage was done to Sorpe. Eight Lancaster bombers and fifty-six men did not return to Britain.

known as L'Ecole de L'Air. I was also selected for that team, fencing with the epée.* This annual event was always hotly contested; it involved the sports of rugby union† and fencing. Rivalry between the rugby and fencing teams was fierce; victory was deemed essential for honor of the College.

After a long trip from Cranwell to Salon in a lumbering Britannia military aircraft, the Cranwell teams were shown to their rooms and encouraged to change for dinner. The hospitality was excellent, and the hosts made sure that the British teams had plenty of wine before, during, and after the meal. A surfeit of wine, however, soon prompted a drinking song competition, with the losers drinking full glasses of red wine. Casualties were high as the wine took its toll of British and French officer cadets alike.

During this now raucous gathering, Bandar recalled, "I asked one of my hosts if he was on the fencing team or the rugby team."

The French cadet replied, "Neither." Bandar then asked if he could meet any of the French fencing team. A perplexed prince was informed that none of the fencing or rugby teams were there: they were all in bed asleep. The next morning, most of the Cranwell team woke up much the worse for wear, many still fully dressed from the evening before.

Wilson (Wils) Metcalfe, a member of the rugby team and a fellow cadet at the time, described how, on the morning after arriving in Salon and the aforementioned dinner, everyone had to rise early after their heavy night to watch the raising of the French Tricolor and RAF Ensign—"all with intense hangovers."[25] The rugby team, after a very hard-fought competition, surprised everyone by winning its match against a much fresher French team. Meanwhile, Bandar and the fencing team were trying to recover from the previous evening before the fencing match later that afternoon. The Cranwell cadets already were considered the underdogs, and it was expected that the superior French team, aided by their unfair sabotage tactics the previous evening, would quickly demolish the RAF team.

Much to our surprise, however, an inspired Cranwell fencing team secured a clear victory that owed much to the anger over the unscrupulous

---

*An epée is a modern version of the dueling sword. It is similar to a foil, but has a stiffer, V-shaped blade and is heavier. *Epée* is French for sword.

†Rugby union is a team sport that, according to legend, developed from the rules used to play football at Rugby School in England. Two teams, each of fifteen players, have the task of outscoring the opposing team. Players clutch a ball similar in shape to an American football in their hands or arms, and may pass it backward or laterally across the pitch, or kick it in any direction. The opposing players attempt to halt the ball carrier by tackling him with their arms and bodies.

deception of the previous evening. Bandar recollected that he was still angry and launched himself at the opposition, slashing wildly with his saber at his French victims. French finesse was no match for his blind fervor, and Bandar took the match.

It is clear from the college records that Bandar was determined to be an outstanding pilot, and his total focus was on flying; the other activities at Cranwell, particularly those relating to the academic environment, were distractions from that primary goal. He was, nonetheless, capable of being an exemplary cadet when he put his mind to it. Thus, Sgt. Adams wrote in his drill report, "When he tries, he is one of the best in the squadron. On occasions he is immaculate. He could reach great heights, if only he would realize that he is not here for the flying only."[26]

But for Bandar, the desire to fly, and above all, to become a fighter pilot, was overarching. This was his only goal in life. In practice, he showed promise. Bandar was the first pilot in the entry to go solo after only nine hours flying, having never flown before. But in the early months his performance was erratic. He was also overconfident, a trait that almost resulted in catastrophe on several occasions. Hence, when talking about the prince's ability as a pilot, John Waterfall, a fellow pilot, was blunt—as only a friend can be, "He was pretty shit at Cranwell you know."[27] Robbie Hunter confirmed the prince's shaky start in the air when he told of one occasion when Bandar

The Cranwell fencing team with Bandar (back row, second from right) and author Bill Simpson (front row, left).

joined the airfield circuit in the wrong direction, and flew against the prevailing pattern of traffic, putting the fear of God into the rest of his fellow students. The analogy would be that of driving against oncoming traffic in the fast lane of a freeway. The actual comment on his flying record by his flying instructor, Tony Yule, was somewhat more muted and diplomatically suggested that "Sultan flies with spirit and enthusiasm. He has had a problem in the circuit, but was coping quite well by the end of the course."[28]

The prince later confided that his flying instructor, Tony Yule, always told him that he would never make a fighter pilot. He admitted, "I almost resigned, thinking to myself that if I'm not going to be a fighter pilot, then I don't want to be a pilot." But three years after he left Cranwell, Bandar located Yule and, with evident satisfaction, recalled that he was flying tankers—VC10s. The prince told him, "I have been flying fighters ever since I left Cranwell. Goddammit, now I know why you said I wouldn't make a fighter pilot—you didn't know what you were looking for."

Air Chief Marshal Sir Richard Johns was a squadron commander of No. 2 Squadron at RAF Cranwell in 1969, and the Prince's flying instructor. He recalled, "I remember Prince Bandar Sultan very well. First of all, he was a prince of the royal family of Saudi Arabia and the only Arab on his course. He was so incredibly cheerful; I can't remember ever seeing him down at the squadron, when he wasn't buzzing around with the most infectious smile on him . . . he entered into the spirit of everything with 100 percent enthusiasm. That's what I really recall about him—his sense of humor and his enthusiasm."

Reflecting on the prince's performance during his flying training, Johns observed, "I cannot recall any doubts being raised at all about Bandar Sultan's capacity to complete that phase of his flying training, or indeed, of his capability. He was looked upon as being a "good egg," but also as someone who, if you remember the initial language difficulties, had made the move across to the United Kingdom

Before his first solo Jet Provost flight

comfortably." Johns stressed, "He had accepted the challenges and had risen to every one. He was quite clearly going to graduate with his wings."

There was one incident, however, that almost ended his career and his life. Johns related, "Anyone who's had a fairly long flying career has had moments in it when you think: my God that was close. I can remember one such incident with Bandar Sultan. We were coming back to base and were doing controlled descents through cloud, so there was no other option but to come down through cloud, and in the process we had to do an inbound turn to the airfield. I was trying to fly at my absolute smoothest on instruments, and I started the inbound turn. However, I looked out and saw the chap on the starboard side, Bandar Sultan, start to slide out again."

Analyzing this maneuver, Johns explained, "It's not unusual; it's difficult, particularly when you're learning to hold formation in cloud, because you start to get disorientated. What should have happened in those circumstances is that he [Bandar] should level his wings and fly away; but he didn't. He actually tried to come back in again and in the process overbanked towards me. I'm not quite sure what happened up there afterwards, but I remember thinking, 'Oh shit, that was bloody close.' I certainly pushed quite hard on the pole to get out of his way. I think by then his instructor had also taken control and we split up in cloud."

Still agitated, Johns described how the aircraft recovered to Cranwell, where instructors and pilots discussed precisely what happened. Bandar was blithely unaware that he had almost collided with several Jet Provosts, including one flown by his friend Rob Deacon Elliott, and would certainly have taken out Sir Richard, the future chief of the Royal Air Force, as well as his 96 Entry colleagues. He was just inches away from disaster. "The interesting thing," said Johns, "is it didn't affect him: a lot of cadets would probably have gone back into their shell. Certainly not with him, he just got on with it."[29]

Despite a somewhat checkered flying history at Cranwell, Bandar did learn to fly; he gained his wings and graduated successfully. His report stated, "His officer training has generally been satisfactory, and during leadership training in the field, he has been prepared to assert himself showing courage and stamina in good measure." Indeed, in his commissioning report on July 21, 1969, in his all-important training as a pilot, it was said of the prince, "Sultan is a determined and competent pilot who can produce very good results when the need arises. His aerobatics are spirited but lack finesse. He inclines towards overconfidence when things are going well. With a little more effort, Sultan will make a very good pilot of above average potential and a sound aircraft captain."[30]

Bandar was to experience an incident that would have a lasting impact on him, an episode that he related during a reunion of 96 Entry and which would influence his attitude in later life. While at RAF Alconbury one evening, Bandar met with an American friend who later introduced him to another pilot and to his wife. "He was still dressed in a flying suit, as he had just been night flying," the prince reflected. "I thought he must be an American pilot, but I noted that he had no nametag or rank tabs which I thought was a little strange." When he discovered that the officer's wife was from California, it reinforced his assumption that her husband was an American officer. The evening went well and the prince enjoyed himself, dancing with the pilot's wife.

Later that evening Bandar asked the pilot, "Are you Californian, too?" He replied, "No, I am from Israel." Apparently, the officer thought that the prince was English and he asked, "Where are you from?" His reply, "I am from Saudi Arabia," saw the atmosphere suddenly turn very chilly as the two men looked at each other in complete silence. Bandar recalled, "Suddenly I felt a hatred for this man, who up until now was an individual that I liked immensely."

As Bandar reflected on the situation, he began to realize the impact of that moment, where a change of circumstances or perceptions had occurred, simply out of the recognition that one was Israeli and the other Arab. "Over time," said the prince, "it gave me hope that if we got to know each other better, we could break the stereotype." However, as a result of the recognition of their respective identities, the prince said, "The Israeli officer agreed to shake hands and forget we had ever met."

That evening Bandar had unwittingly stumbled across a covert military operation run on a U.S. Air Force base in England. At that time, Israel was unable to buy military equipment from the United States because the U.S. government had placed an embargo on all military sales to the Middle East after the 1967 Six Day War. However, the U.S. administration covertly agreed to sell Phantom F-4 airplanes to Israel, and President Johnson decided that it should be kept a secret. Thus, it was agreed that the training should be completed, not in the United States, but at RAF Alconbury which is a U.S. Air Force base in the United Kingdom. The irony is that during that evening, as a raw young officer cadet, by sheer chance, Bandar was to stumble on a well-protected and potentially explosive secret.

Toward the end of the thirty months of training at Cranwell, the focus increasingly centered on graduation and commissioning. For pilots, Bandar included, there was also the promise of the prized pilot's wings. But for the officer cadets, a final hurdle was the graduation parade. Sgt. Adams recalled the cadet practice of performing various stunts during the final rehearsal for that parade one Saturday morning. By tradition, cadets would introduce various unscheduled events during that rehearsal, and 96 Entry arrived on a double-decker bus, before forming up in their positions on the parade ground. As Sgt. Adams reflected, "Great fun, great spirits, and no harm done!"

Bandar recalled another piece of innocent fun enjoyed by the Color Party—or, as he refers to it, the Colored Party—for which he was the warrant officer. His close friend, Dick Calder, was the color bearer. About midnight the night before, they got some planks of wood to lay on the college steps, and backed an old MG convertible sports car up the steps and into the college. They then removed the planks.

The next morning, the whole college was called to parade. Suddenly, the planks leading down the College Hall steps were put in place again. The "Colored Party"—the English members of which had painted their faces black (Bandar had painted his face white)—was called on to the parade

ground by the parade commander, who yelled, "March on the Colored Party." To everyone's surprise, instead of marching in from the left wing of the parade ground as was usual, the Colored Party drove down the College Hall steps and took up their normal position, dismounting from the MG, which was promptly driven away.

A week later, on August 2, 1969, Bandar graduated from RAF Cranwell. A much more

Marching with the colors as
Color Warrant Officer

mature young man, the next phase of the prince's life would see him integrate even more deeply into Western cultures. As a pilot in the Royal Saudi Air Force, he would next undertake extensive training in the United States, translating his still embryonic flying skills into those of a seasoned fighter pilot.

TWO

FIGHTER PILOT PRINCE

"Don't 'over-control' like a novice pilot. Stay loose enough
from the flow that you can observe it, modify, and improve it."

DONALD RUMSFELD,
U.S. SECRETARY OF DEFENSE

Sir Richard Johns, Bandar's flying instructor at RAF Cranwell, said of Bandar's flying, "Quite clearly, he was made in the Cranwell mold to become a fighter pilot; he would never be anything else but a fighter pilot if he was going to go to the Royal Saudi Air Force, and of course, he did. He became a Lightning pilot . . . and that band of pilots were the elite of the Air Force at that time. They were quite a special group of people and all of them went on to do quite exceptional things."[1]

After graduating from RAF Cranwell in 1969, Bandar returned to Saudi Arabia as a second lieutenant, stationed at Royal Saudi Air Force (RSAF) Dhahran Air Force Base (AFB). There he flew the T-33 training aircraft—"the T Bird"—to develop his flying prowess. But as a "green" young officer, he was also expected to add to his skills as an officer and leader of men, and was thus appointed company commander of fifty students at the RSAF Technical Training Institute (TTI). A United States Air Force (USAF) flying instructor, Lt. Col. Keith Phillips, then training Saudi pilots as part of the Saudi-USAF Peace Hawk training program, observed in awe, "His charisma and leadership was just phenomenal—absolutely phenomenal! Those kids in his flight were miles ahead of the others; there was simply no contest."[2] Unlike his royal contemporaries, Bandar did not insist on being addressed as a prince when he worked in the RSAF. Said one of his airmen, "He was just called Captain Bandar, simple as that. He did not carry his title until he became ambassador. We just called him Captain Bandar or Major Bandar. That's all, nothing more."[3]

Early in 1970, after settling into the RSAF, Bandar was posted to Lackland AFB in Texas, where he received advanced English language training, an essential prerequisite to the advanced flying training he required. After Lackland, Bandar was posted to Myrtle Beach AFB in South Carolina, where he flew the AT-33 aircraft as lead-in fighter training, before moving on to Perrin AFB in Texas to complete air defense training on the F-102 aircraft. He then progressed on to Williams AFB in Arizona to begin tactical fighter training on the F-5A/B aircraft that were being introduced into the RSAF. This training was part of the Peace Hawk modernization program. Peace Hawk was a U.S. and British-supported program, designed to enhance Saudi Arabia's military capability so as to enable the Kingdom to counter the growing menace posed by Soviet-supported nations on its borders. USAF Col. Bob Lilac, chief of the Peace Hawk F-5 test program and an F-5 flying instructor observed, "It was the F-5 program that planted the seed that bore fruit in the relationship between the Saudi military and the U.S. military."[4] It was that bond that would prove a vital asset in coming years when the Gulf exploded into conflict.

On the day Bandar arrived in Lackland to begin his training, by his own admission, he learned his first lesson in humility.

"I was a cocky fighter pilot," he recalled, "a second lieutenant. My first day in America was in San Antonio, Texas, and I decided to call home. In those days you could not dial direct, so I called the operator. 'I would like to put a call through to Saudi Arabia,' I said."

Beside an F-5

The operator passed Bandar through to the international operator. Once again, he said, "I would like to put a call through to Saudi Arabia."

The operator asked him, "Where is it?"

"In the Middle East," he replied.

"Where? Mid-east?"

"No," Bandar said, "Middle East."

"Huh?"

"Listen madam," Bandar asked, "do you know where Israel is?"

"Yes," she replied.

"Well," he explained slowly, "just a little south of there."[5]

It was at Lackland AFB in 1970 that Col. Joe Ramsey first met Bandar. Ramsey, who was then training commander, would go on to become a significant figure in Bandar's life and a lifelong friend. He explained, "When Prince Bandar arrived at Lackland, he joined other foreign students who were to be assessed for their command of English . . . just about all foreign military students went to the language school, even if they were English speakers, for U.S. terminology orientation."

Col. Ramsey recalled that when he arrived, Bandar needed a bank, so he introduced him to the president of his own bank just outside the base, where the prince promptly made a deposit of $5,000 in cash. The colonel related, "The president was impressed and offered to do anything he could for him. But only two days later, I get a call from the bank president to say the account is overdrawn. He told me, 'There was a deposit of $5,000, but

Bandar and Col. Joe Ramsey

I have got checks amounting to $6,000.' So I contacted Bandar and he said, 'Don't worry about it.'" The colonel continued, "The next day this guy flies in from the embassy and Bandar goes around to the bank and deposits $10,000. So the bank president rings me and says it is all a misunderstanding. Two days later he is back on the phone to say he is overdrawn again—'we can't deal with these people!'" The colonel called Bandar once again, and the prince said, "Don't worry about it." The colonel concluded, "So the next day a guy from the embassy in Washington comes with a suitcase full of cash for the bank president, opens it up, and says, 'How much do you need to keep him out of trouble?'"[6]

While in Texas, Bandar also ran up against the law. Driving from Dallas back to Perrin AFB, the Prince recalled, "I was late and there was nobody else on the highway, and I thought, Who would notice? I'll just belt it a little bit. Suddenly, out of the blue there was a flashing light, so I pulled over. This very nice old policeman came around and asked me to get out of my car. He told me that I was speeding and I apologized; but I told him that my English was really not that good—I'm a foreigner. He didn't know that I'd spent four years at college in England. I had a great time faking the accent, and I didn't have to try hard because to him, my accent—British—was fake anyway." However, the officer asked him for his driver's license and Bandar duly gave it to him.

The prince mimicked the officer turning the license over and over and examining it quizzically before saying, "Son, I want your driver's *license.*" Bandar replied, "Sir, this is my driver's license." The officer repeated again to him calmly, "I said—give me your driver's *license.*" Bandar said, "I thought I'd explain to him what the papers were, so I said, 'Officer, this is my driver's license, and it is called an international driving license.'" He then added, "I went further to explain to him; I said, 'Officer, you see, there is this international club and all countries that are members of this club, with this bit of paper, may drive in each other's countries. And sir, the United States of America is a member of that club.'" Bandar recalled with a grin, "He listened very carefully to me and very patiently—then he looked at me and said, 'Son, let me tell you something—the United States of America may be a member, but Texas ain't!'"[7]

Following his flying training at Perrin, Bandar immediately proceeded to Williams AFB to attend a course flying the F-5 aircraft, which would be the mainstay of the RSAF under the Saudi-USAF Peace Hawk training program. The additional training began to show in his flying, and he received the Top Gun award in 1971, winning all three awards: top academic, top air-to-air, and top ground-to-ground on the F-5 training course.

When Bandar returned to RSAF Dhahran AFB from the United States in late 1971, he and the other F-5 trained pilots discovered that it would be six months before the RSAF would take delivery of their American-made Northrop F-5E Tiger II aircraft; in the interim they had to fly the British-built Lightning supersonic interceptor jets. "Britain is a very small island," Bandar explained, "so this plane was designed to fly very high and very fast, but it couldn't go very far without refueling. Now Saudi Arabia is a continent compared to Britain, so operations were very disappointing—you'd fly out, launch your missiles, complete the operation, and then you must immediately turn back to refuel."

While at Dhahran, Bandar moved over from the Lightnings to become operations officer on the F-5 Operational Conversion Unit (OCU) working alongside Col. Joe Ramsey, who also had moved to Saudi Arabia. Ramsey confirmed, "I was there when they introduced the F-5 and Bandar turned out to be the lead pilot working on the F-5 Peace Hawk project with us."[8] USAF Lt. Col. Keith Phillips, who served in Saudi Arabia as an F-5 adviser, explained, "When we brought the F-5, Bandar showed up on the station in the fall after we had received the first six F-5B models. Part of our program was to get the rest of the Royal Saudi Air Force acquainted with the aircraft, so we flew them around to all the bases."

Amplifying his remarks, Phillips explained, "We put together a very watered-down aerobatic team. We had a flight of four and a single ship—it was all very, very basic. We had instructor pilots in the backseats and I was leading the flight of four." As for the first time he flew with Bandar, Phillips recalled, "I said to him, 'This is what you have to get used to.' We were flying at about one hundred feet and I rolled it upside down, which is a bit disconcerting if you've not done it before." Phillips confirmed, "As you know, he's quick to learn, and Bandar

"Top Gun" Bandar sweeps the board during F-5 training.

picked up on it very well, but he had a tendency to over-G the aeroplane. Suffice it to say, we checked him out."

After the other pilots were brought up to speed, the five aircraft gave flight displays at several Saudi airfields. Phillips said, "At Tabuk, we put on this Armed Forces Day for King Faisal, and he invited King Hussein of Jordan. That was when Bandar blew their *ghoutras* off."* He explained, "This armed forces show had tanks, paratroopers, and aircraft and took place on a large open desert maneuver area south of Tabuk. It was used to show off their military equipment, so they constructed this huge amphitheater-type facility with a large sunshade that was perhaps fifty to seventy feet tall." The colonel continued, "We practiced for several days and integrated the F-5s with the Lightnings in various formations. In the grand finale, we had the airplanes lined up to fly an F [formation] for King Faisal. Col. Behery was leading that bunch and was supposed to be at one thousand feet flying south to north. Bandar would come from the north, in the opposite direction, flying underneath them. Col. Abdullah was leading the second flight of F-5s which was then followed by a flight of Lightnings." Phillips recalled, "Each flight would fly in diamond formation. We did about four passes in all, with Bandar performing as a singleton aircraft; his final maneuver would be to fly underneath the massed formations."

Continuing, Phillips said, "That final formation flew at one thousand feet so that Bandar would have plenty of room. However, as the formation came forward it started to get lower and lower; I called Behery and said, 'Lead, watch your altitude!' I was in the backseat with Fahd bin Abdullah in the second flight, and I thought, 'Jesus, he's getting too low.' Bandar had to fly underneath, but he was a little bit late and had both reheats going.† He could see the formation ahead, but it kept getting lower, so Bandar kept going lower so he could fly underneath as planned."

Phillips recounted how Bandar "managed to tuck underneath; but he was very low when he passed over the dais. The vortices from his aircraft wreaked havoc: fancy rugs, flowers, chairs, and clothing flew all over the

---

*The head cloth worn by Arab men is called a *ghoutra,* used to keep the head cool in the summer and warm in the winter. Traditionally, it was a useful item of clothing for desert life, wrapped around the face to protect the eyes and mouth during sandstorms. The *ghoutra* is folded diagonally and is kept in place by wearing a double black cord called an *akal,* wrapped around the head. The *ghoutra* may be made of silk but normally is white or red and white checked cotton.

†In aviation terminology, to engage reheat, a pilot will active an afterburner—an additional component added to some jet engines—that provides significant additional power.

place; he blew the *ghoutras* off both kings. Seriously, he blew both their *ghoutras* right off! I didn't know that this had happened but I heard the controller say, 'Sweet Jesus—that was spectacular!' Then I heard in English, 'This is Gen. Zuhair—he was commander of the Air Force—stop the show! This is Gen. Zuhair—stop the show!' I thought, 'What the hell happened?' We had no way of knowing because we were in the air and the show was over anyway. So we all landed and the aircraft and crews lined up. Then the king came by in his open jeep with King Hussein in review and the crews all saluted as he passed."

Phillips continued, "When they got to Bandar's aircraft, they stopped and King Hussein got out and walked over to Bandar and shook his hand; he really took some pressure off him. Prince Sultan was in the crowd and he said to Bandar, 'You're court-martialed; you're grounded.'" Phillips recalled, "Immediately after the fly-past, Bandar knew he was in deep shit, and when I talked to him later about the incident, he joked, 'Well, I pulled up vertical and I went as high as I could go. I thought to myself, 'I'm going to punch out (eject) and if Allah is good to me, the winds will blow me into Israel.'" Laughing now, Phillips concluded, "He knew he had screwed up."[9] However, despite getting into hot water, the prince was tactfully selected for another course in the United States and the incident was simply forgotten in his absence.

While stationed at Dhahran, Bandar's first home was a small, one-story place he built with concrete blocks. But he employed an unusual building technique: the blocks were stacked vertically, steel piles were driven down to hold them in place, and, finally, concrete was pumped down in the holes in the blocks and they were capped over. Joe Ramsey observed, "The place could have withstood a nuclear attack."[10] In contrast to his palatial abodes in later years, this first home was small and modest, but sufficed for his lifestyle at that time, one of a young, recently married squadron pilot intent on establishing himself as a member of a close-knit team of fellow pilots. In December 1972, Bandar had married Her Royal Highness Princess Haifa bint Faisal bin Abdul Aziz Al-Saud, one of the daughters of the then Saudi ruler, King Faisal. Returning from their honeymoon already pregnant with their first daughter, Haifa quickly took on the traditional role of a Saudi wife, running the household and bringing up a growing brood of children.

During 1973, Bandar was promoted to captain. Following his flying training at Cranwell, advanced fighter pilot training in the United States, and retraining on the F-5 aircraft, he had thoroughly honed his flying skills.

He was now—in Saudi terms—a relatively experienced pilot and fully operational.

In October 1973, the Yom Kippur War brought widespread conflict to the Middle East, as Egyptian and Syrian forces threatened to overwhelm Israel in a surprise attack. With the onset of hostilities, unbeknownst to Western countries, including the United States, the Saudi Air Force agreed to support the Egyptian and Syrian offensive against Israel, and authorized a mission of ten "strike attack" F-5 aircraft; Bandar was a flight commander. At this time, Israeli forces were being driven back to the pre-1967 boundaries. An alarmed U.S. administration, led by Secretary of State Henry Kissinger, was frantically trying to negotiate a ceasefire to protect Israel within the 1967 boundaries.

The particular mission for which Bandar and his team had trained involved five experienced crews who were tasked with low-level napalm attacks on Israeli oil and refinery installations, followed by five less experienced crews that would follow up with fire bombs. Simulations of the mission concluded that only one pilot would return, although the mission should achieve its objective. Bandar and his fellow pilots rolled out onto the runway with the almost certain probability that all but one would not survive the mission.

Bandar described the operation, saying, "The ten of us who were qualified would take off and practice for our mission. There were five blast-bomb and five fire-bomb sorties which would fly behind Bahrain, turn around, and at thirty feet above sea level—that's tough—would get to the shore and drop napalm bombs on a target in Saudi Arabia simulating Elat." He gravely observed, "We expected the PPK (probability of kill) to be nine to one. So out of ten pilots, nine would be killed and one might return alive. So our plan was that if anyone got shot, he would turn hard right, count to ten and eject, because then we would be over Jordan—it was that close. Why Elat? Because Elat had a huge Israeli fuel depot—deny them that and it could cripple their

On Quick Reaction Alert during the Yom Kippur War.

war machine." Bandar explained that they practiced for this mission every night, but in the squadron, they didn't know when the actual real live mission was due to go. He said, "So that night, and every night, was live practice."

Prior to launch, Bandar said, "I was immensely scared, but nonetheless determined to complete the mission. I led my flight to the end of the runway and waited for the permission to launch. The moment seemed to last forever; I remember sweat rolling down my face, and my knees were shaking uncontrollably." The order to launch, however, never came. And not until thirty years later did Bandar learn why.

While on a speaking tour of the United States in September 2003, Bandar was reading Henry Kissinger's book, *Crisis: The Anatomy of Two Major Foreign Policy Crises*, about his efforts to achieve a ceasefire during the Yom Kippur War. Bandar recalled how the Nixon administration had said to the Egyptians, "If you continue the war, we will help the Israelis; we will never allow Israel to be defeated. We will put in an air bridge until they win." He then observed, "That was approximately the time when we were supposed to go on our mission. We had got as far as the end of the runway preparing to launch; it was the real attack when we received this eleventh-hour reprieve."

Ever the realist, Bandar remarked, "So we turned around and I must tell you we were all surprised, because in this kind of conditions—we were all huffing and puffing, sweating—there's no bravery in war, trust me, until after the fact, particularly if you've never tasted it and you think you're about to go. All this bullshitting you see in the movies is not true. When we got back to the squadron, we were told that the mission had been scrapped. I must tell you that there was not one person in that room who was unhappy."

When I interviewed Henry Kissinger, I posed the question, "Did you know that you once saved Prince Bandar's life?" I then revealed to him that Bandar was about to lead a potentially suicidal air attack on an Israeli oil installation with almost zero likelihood of returning from that mission. It was only because Kissinger had negotiated a ceasefire that the mission had been canceled.

Until then, Kissinger had been sitting

Henry Kissinger

back in an armchair, his heavy-lidded eyes closed as he listened intently, replying to my questions in his deep baritone voice. Suddenly, he sat bolt upright. His eyes flashed, and he was clearly shocked at my revelations. He exclaimed, "I was totally unaware that the Saudis had been on the verge of entering the war."[11] And so, too, was America.

Joe Ramsey left Saudi Arabia in August 1973, prior to the start of the Yom Kippur War. Before he left, however, Bandar had approached Ramsey and asked to arrange his return to the United States for additional training, specifically to fly the new F-5E aircraft then entering service with the RSAF. Ramsey recalled, "He said, 'You need to put a package together for me.' So I put together a proposed sequence of training for him. Anyway, they [Bandar and Haifa] came back to San Antonio." Thus, Bandar traveled back to the United States in 1974, where he attended squadron officer school (SOS) at Maxwell AFB in Alabama; pilot instruction training (PIT) at Randolph AFB in Texas; and finally, F-5E conversion training at Williams AFB near Phoenix, Arizona.[12] This is where he first encountered Col. Bob Lilac, now a very close friend, who was chief of the F-5E test program at Williams AFB.

Once his training was completed, the prince returned to Dhahran in 1975 as squadron commander of the F-5 Operational Conversion Unit (OCU), responsible for training Saudi pilots on the F-5 aircraft. He also was appointed Peace Hawk project officer for the F-5 activation at RSAF Khamis AFB, successfully liaising with the U.S. Peace Hawk personnel to introduce the new aircraft to the RSAF and train their pilots. He performed a similar role at Mustayat AFB from 1976 to 1977, developing his own flying skills while ensuring that the RSAF reached the highest operational standards.

During that time, he became involved in an unusual equipment purchase after a chance meeting with Lord Mountbatten in the VIP lounge at Heathrow Airport. Bandar recalled how an elderly man joined him in the lounge and he walked over to the prince and started interrogating him.

"Who are you? I am Mountbatten."

"I know you, your lordship," Bandar replied, "You gave a lecture at Cranwell when I was there."

When he discovered that Bandar was from Saudi Arabia, Mountbatten responded, "What relation are you to the royal family?"

The intimidated Bandar replied, "Well, I am one of them."

In his cultured British accent, Mountbatten said, "Good, good. I have been everywhere in the world, except Saudi Arabia."

"I am sure that you are welcome to visit Saudi Arabia," Bandar naively replied.

"Yes, that would be jolly good." Mountbatten responded, "Do you chaps have hovercraft? Well, you bloody should! Do you know that hovercrafts are British and that they have called a hovercraft Mountbatten? If I come to Saudi Arabia, I will talk to your people about buying hovercraft."

Bandar thought no more of the meeting until a couple of months later when he was instructed to fly back to the Ministry of Defense in Riyadh immediately. Thinking himself to be in trouble, Bandar duly returned to see his uncle, Prince Turki, then deputy minister of defense, who accused him of inviting Mountbatten to visit Saudi Arabia. "I didn't invite Lord Mountbatten," said the prince, only to be told, "The British Embassy has passed a message to the Royal Court saying that Lord Mountbatten wants to inform his majesty and the Royal Court that he accepts the invitation he was passed by his majesty through Prince Bandar of the Saudi Arabian Air Force." Despite the Prince's denials, Prince Turki said to him, "The damage is done. He is arriving next week as his majesty's guest in Riyadh; you are to escort him throughout his trip." Bandar responded, "Okay, but trust me, I didn't do anything."

Talking about that visit, Bandar recalled, "When Mountbatten arrived, I had a fun time; he was like a walking history book. You would say Eisenhower and he would say, 'Ike told me this . . .' and you would say Patton and he would say, 'Oh, George told me this . . .' and the same for Montgomery, Churchill, and so on. He taught me more about history in a day and a half than I had learned in my whole life."

As result of Mountbatten's visit, Saudi Arabia agreed to buy hovercraft.

From 1977 to 1978, Bandar became squadron commander of No. 3 Squadron

Mountbatten of Burma

at RSAF Taif AFB flying F-5s, during which he was awarded the RSAF Falcon Medal for flying and leadership. He was then appointed as squadron commander of No. 15 Squadron, also flying F-5s at RSAF Khamis Mustayat AFB, while still retaining his Peace Hawk project officer duties.

However, in 1977 Bandar suffered a flying accident that would lead to lifelong back problems. His last job had been commander of the OCU and as chief instructor he had very strict standards, insisting on following safety procedures to the letter. Every morning briefing saw him state to his pilots, "You are more valuable than a lump of hardware. Thus, when in doubt, pull it out—eject!"

In a general conversation over dinner with friends in McLean, Virginia, Bandar reflected on an incident in which he very clearly broke his own rules. He recalled that Ramadan had just finished and the squadron was performing routine patrols. Two of his pilots were instructed to fly over an air show at Abha and perform some aerobatics. He explained that it was simply a general display, buzzing the airfield and landing. However, one of the pilots fell ill and as the squadron was still under strength, the prince decided to fly the mission as "number two."

It was an uneventful trip, and after he returned, Bandar recalled, "I prepared for a running break and selected gear down; nothing happened, so I called in for a 'touch and go' landing and overshot. I then asked my number one to check the aircraft as I attempted to recycle my landing gear. Still nothing happened, and I was advised that my undercarriage doors were half open." A serious-looking Bandar related, "At this stage it is worth stressing that the aerodynamics of an F-5 are unforgiving, and it required landing with a high angle of attack. The flight safety rules were simple—if you couldn't get the gear down, then you had no option but to eject."

The prince explained, "With a high angle of attack, the aircraft would simply stall, and for that reason, for the past seven years, I had instructed everyone, 'Never land if the gear does not come down.'" As Bandar admits, "Ego got in the way. I thought to myself, 'I am an experienced instructor on the aircraft type and I am also the Saudi Air Force solo aerobatic pilot.' While I knew I should eject, I thought to myself, 'This landing cannot be done, but if ever it could be done, then I am the man!'"

Bandar instructed air traffic to lay foam on the runway, but just as they began the task, a Lightning aircraft returned and called finals. Given that the Lightning was critical on fuel, Bandar arbitrarily decided that that pilot needed to land first and instructed that the foam laying cease; the

Lightning landed without incident. However, Bandar explained, "I also was now out of fuel but still decided to go for a landing. I approached the runway at a higher speed than normal, thus allowing me to reduce the angle of attack. However, as I touched down, I cut the throttle and the aircraft landed very heavily in clouds of smoke and dust, skidding along the runway."

The impact was severe and Bandar tried to evacuate from the aircraft once it had ground to a halt, but he recalled ruefully, "I realized that my right leg had gone dead and I couldn't feel it. One of the first people to the aircraft was my crew chief, who pulled me out of the cockpit and helped me into an ambulance." Though he instructed the driver to take him to hospital, he was adamant that the staff should not be briefed on the heavy landing. He confided, "I was frightened that I might lose my flying category and insisted instead they check me out for lumbago; I still had no feeling in my right leg. I was subsequently released even though my leg was still numb. At the time my nightmare was that an injury would stop me flying."

Bandar's fears were correct: that heavy landing in 1977 would eventually end his career as a fighter pilot, though not immediately or directly. What transpired next would have far-ranging consequences, more than anything he might have done as a fighter pilot.

In 1978, Bandar returned to RSAF Dhahran AFB and was promoted to major, and became the squadron commander of 7 Squadron flying F-5s. Scarcely had he settled into this role when he unexpectedly became immersed in helping a Saudi team in Washington, D.C., working to provide assistance and information to the Carter administration in securing approval from Capitol Hill for the sale of sixty F-15 aircraft, then the world's most advanced fighter aircraft.

When Bandar first entered RAF Cranwell, by his own admission all he wanted was to become a fighter pilot. There are, however, some who see their path through life in tunnel vision: these are the workers. They have a role, be it in industry, commerce, society, or the armed forces. They are promoted from one rank to another, their focus being to reach the best possible position. There are others, however, who can see outside this box and are able to visualize the whole picture. They understand that it is only by assembling the disparate jigsaw pieces of the tunnel visioners that progress is made: these are the leaders. From company directors to statesmen, they use their ability to take command. Yet beyond these, there are just a handful of exceptional individuals who can influence events on a global scale. From the moment he joined the RSAF, Bandar was keen to gain as much experience as possible and he flew a number of aircraft types and attended various courses in the United States. He was not only increasing his knowledge, but was also developing a wide circle of friends in a very powerful country.

When Bandar came to head the Saudi team in Washington, D.C., working to acquire F-15 aircraft, it was his first tentative step into politics. And once he had stepped out of the cockpit, there was no turning back.

The history of U.S. arms sales to Saudi Arabia had been tumultuous. As Bandar explained, "Going back to Kennedy, we wanted to purchase F-104 Starfighters because the Egyptians and the Russians were in Yemen at that time and they had deployed MIG 21s there. We only had F-86 aircraft and we wanted a supersonic aircraft to combat them. However, Kennedy could not pass it through Congress. We were advised that if we made a deal with the British, America would not oppose it, hence the Lightning and the Hunter deal was negotiated." He continued, "The Americans said to the U.K., 'We will sell you the F-111s and C-130s in return for selling the Lightnings to the Royal Saudi Air Force.' So the U.K. got the F-111s and C-130s and Saudi Arabia got the Lightnings—called Magic Carpet— a package deal."

At that time, America was trying to sell F-111 strike and C-130 cargo aircraft to the United Kingdom, but the United Kingdom's adverse balance of payments meant it could not go ahead with the deal. However, the purchase of Lightning and Hunter aircraft by Saudi Arabia provided the United Kingdom with the cash necessary for the sale. A solution was devised against the knowledge that if the Saudis could not get what they wanted, then they would buy French Mirage 3s. Bandar said, "The British and the Americans didn't want that, so we ended up with everyone getting what they needed; we got our Mach 2 Lightning airplanes, and we also got our strategic objective in facing off the Russians. The British got their F-111s and C-130s, and

President Gerald Ford

the Americans got their deal." With a grin, he added, "And the French didn't get anything."

Recounting the pattern of events that placed Carter in a quandary— trying to reconcile Israel's interests with the interests of national security— Bandar said, "President Nixon had visited Saudi Arabia and Egypt in 1974, and he agreed to sell the kingdom F-15s. However, he then resigned—and because Nixon resigned, there was no deal. So President Ford took over and we approached him. Ford agreed, but asked that it be deferred until after the elections. He made a commitment, but it was only to be fulfilled if he was reelected. When Ford lost the election, we went to Carter, and we said, 'Ford promised, can you deliver?' and he said, 'Give me time.'" Unknown to the Saudis, the President's position was further complicated by a secret request from Israel in July 1977 for one hundred fifty F-16 and twenty-five F-15 aircraft.

The key to understanding the recurring obstacles, objections, and rejections encountered in attempting to sell advanced weapons to Saudi Arabia is the special relationship that exists between the United States and Israel. A thorough understanding of the workings of the American political system, and an immensely effective and well-organized lobby in the form of American Israel Public Affairs Committee (AIPAC),* provides Israel with considerable influence over U.S. foreign policy in the Middle East. This relationship has presented Israel with unequaled access to America's state-of-the-art weapons systems and technology. Historically, the United States has shared its advanced weapons systems with Israel, guaranteeing it overriding military supremacy in the Middle East. In spite of Israel's uniquely vulnerable position, the combination of its extraordinary military capability and American recognition of its political legitimacy has protected the Jewish right to resettle in their biblical homeland.

A clear example of this access to the best military hardware was the original development and distribution of the F-15 Eagle. Designed as the world's most advanced attack jet, the first purpose-built "dogfighter" since

---

*The American Zionist Committee for Public Affairs (AZCPA) was established on March 22, 1954. This organization, which was later renamed the American Israel Public Affairs Committee (AIPAC) in 1959, was assigned the task of "coordinating and directing public actions on behalf of the American Zionist movement, bearing upon relations with governmental authorities, with a view to maintaining the improving friendship and good will between the United States and Israel." AIPAC is the only American-based agency registered with Congress for lobbying and propagandizing in the field of American-Israeli relations.

the Korean War F-86 Saber, the F-15 not only set new records for speed and altitude, but also flew across the Atlantic nonstop without refueling.[13] Built by McDonnell Douglas and controlled by an IBM intelligence system, it was the first fully digitally controlled warplane ever made and was priced at a cool $30 million per plane. When the first F-15s rolled off the production line in 1976, they naturally were absorbed by the USAF; the second batch of twenty-five F-15s went directly to Israel.

However, Israel was not the only country in the Middle East to enjoy a special rapport with the United States. A surreptitious affiliation existed between America and the oil-producing, modern Arab states. Both Presidents Nixon and Ford were acutely aware of this harmony, which had its foundations in "oil for security," an equation that was the central tenet of the U.S.-Saudi relationship that provided tangible gains for all involved. Despite religious differences, consumer interests had forged a mutually beneficial bond between the United States and the Kingdom of Saudi Arabia.

When President Ford, however, decided to recommend the sale of advanced Maverick air-to-ground missiles to Saudi Arabia in 1976, intending to secure the kingdom's support within OPEC (Organization of Petroleum Exporting Countries) for lower oil prices, he faced strong opposition from AIPAC. His proposal just scraped through. While agreeing to support a Saudi request for F-15 aircraft should he be reelected, Ford chose to defer proposing the deal to Congress until the outcome of that election.

What made the proposed controversial sale of F-15s to Saudi Arabia so resonant was that it was the first time in U.S. history a president was obliged, not only to acknowledge openly and honor this friendship, but to act directly in its interests, despite the interests of Israel. Therein lay the true significance of the F-15 sale and the furious lobbying that took place in Washington during the run-up to the vote on that sale on Capitol Hill. As Seth P. Tillman candidly reflected, "The issue transcended the technicalities of the military balance; it had come to encompass the political and psychological aspects of the 'special relationships' between Israel and the United States and between Saudi Arabia and the United States."[14] The Saudi request to purchase F-15s precipitated an ensuing debate that would dramatically test American resolve in the Middle East. Yet the request was not a wild card played by the Saudi monarchy; successive administrations had given every indication that the sale would be approved. During a state visit to Saudi Arabia in 1976, President Ford's deputy secretary of defense, William P. Clements Jr., pledged that the United States would assist Saudi

Arabia to replace its outdated aircraft with whatever American fighter plane the Saudis requested. Immersed in the melting pot of Middle East conflicts, the wealthy, oil-rich kingdom unsurprisingly wanted the best. Interestingly, it has been suggested that America not only favored but had strenuously recommended the newly advanced F-15 as the first choice for the RSAF. The USAF pushed hard for the sale of the F-15s in order to lower production costs and accelerate procurement.[15] It was hardly surprising, therefore, that the principal Saudi expectation of the newly established Carter administration, other than an active U.S. resolve to promote peace in the Middle East, was permission to purchase the F-15.

Although the desire for peace may appear to conflict with the desire to arm, the desire for safety—national security—overrides both. Pro-Israel supporters, however, argued that the Saudi need to arm lacked legitimacy and that any Saudi-owned weapons posed a grave threat to Israel.

There was damning evidence to support the Israeli case. Two years prior to the F-15 debate, King Fahd had been quoted in the *New York Times* saying, "All our nations' armed forces are a force in the defense of the Arab nations and the Arab cause."[16] Similarly, Prince Sultan, the Saudi defense minister, had pledged to the Saudi people, "All our weapons are at the disposal of the Arab nations and will be used in the battle against the common enemy."[17]

Contributing to Israeli anxiety were whispers on Capitol Hill of a future Saudi request for AWACS (Airborne Warning and Control System)—a system so sophisticated and expensive that even Israel had not been able to add this advanced weapons system to its armory. Yet the topic at hand was the sale of F-15s, and from a U.S. policy perspective, despite strident Israeli arguments, Saudi Arabia's right to arm and its reasons for doing so could not be overlooked.

Sitting on its eastern borders was the increasingly volatile state of Iran, whose population of fifty million dwarfed that of Saudi Arabia's seven million. Threats from Israel, coupled with those of Soviet-supported Marxist regimes in South Yemen and Ethiopia, were highly valid reasons for the Saudi request to arm its nation with the latest technology. Sitting on the world's largest oil reserves and staunchly conservative in nature, the House of Saud was naturally apprehensive about national security. As London's *The Economist* aptly phrased it, "The Saudis have a good case for being nervous. They live in a tough neighborhood and own the world's largest oil reserves."[18]

The extent of the threat to Saudi Arabia prompted a Saudi-sponsored report released in the United States, which concluded, "In the last several years, Saudi Arabia has had to face developing Communist pressure to its north, south, and southwest. Because of its pro-Western policies and its great wealth, Saudi Arabia is and will remain the prime target for Soviet expansionism and political extremism in the Mid-East."[19] A map of the region graphically illustrated the threatening encirclement of Saudi Arabia by Communist-supported regimes. Contemporaneously, Henry Kissinger stated, "The Soviet purpose in Ethiopia is to outflank the Middle East, to demonstrate that the U.S. cannot protect its friends, to raise doubts in Saudi Arabia, Egypt, the Sudan, and Iran."[20]

Saudi arguments were crucially supported by President Carter, who saw a clear benefit to Israel in the development of the relationship between Saudi Arabia and the United States. In a speech given in May 1978, the president reiterated his concern that the United States "keep that sense in Saudi Arabia that we are their friends" and that "they can trust us when we make a commitment." He added, "I believe that it's best for Israel to have this good, firm, solid, mutually trustful, friendly relationship with the moderate Arab leaders."[21]

Coupled with security reasons for Saudi Arabia to arm itself was constructive evidence that Saudi intentions were defensive in nature, not offensive. In a letter written to the chairman of the House International Relations Committee by Secretary of Defense Harold Brown, firm assurances were made about Saudi Arabia's use of the F-15s for "legitimate self-defense" only if the Saudi kingdom agreed "not to transfer the planes to a third nation or allow nationals of another country to train, pilot, or gain access to the aircraft without consent from the United States."[22]

These guarantees were considerably enhanced by the long-standing relationship linking the desert kingdom to the United States—a relationship baldly based on oil and security. In return for U.S. military help in the defense of the kingdom, Saudi oil would be made available to the United States. Moreover, the fundamentally conservative principles displayed by the Saudi monarchy distinctly echoed the American approach to problems in the Middle East.

Aware of the enormity and complexity of the issues at stake in the sale of F-15s to Saudi Arabia, President Carter said he had "no apology at all to make for this proposal."[23] However, while running for the presidency, Carter had been highly critical of President Ford's pro-Arab foreign policy and had frequently voiced his robust backing for the Jewish cause. He had also delivered powerful statements against Ford's proposed sale of arms to Egypt and Saudi Arabia and stated in a speech on June 6, 1975, that "the survival of Israel is not just a political issue; it is a moral imperative."[24]

Early in his term in office, Carter reiterated, "Our number one commitment in the Middle East is to protect the right of Israel to exist, to exist permanently and to exist in peace."[25] Yet despite these campaign views on weapons sales to the Middle East, the newly elected president, after a brief stop in Riyadh between visits to Tehran and Aswan in January 1978, returned with the determination not to renege on the American commitment to the Saudis promised by President Ford.

During my interview with President Carter, he resolutely defended his decision on the issue, making it clear that this was both a personal and moral target for him, "One of the things that I wanted to do, as a matter of fairness and as a matter of strategic importance to the United States, was to help equip Saudi Arabia to defend itself." He added, "The sale of advance fighter planes, F-15s and later AWACS, to Saudi Arabia was a very important issue for me. This was strongly opposed by the Israeli lobby, which was then, and still is, the most powerful in Washington and no such proposal had ever been successful in passing through Congress which, as you know, is heavily influenced by AIPAC."[26]

It has been argued that Carter's support for the sale of arms to Saudi Arabia, and that of Reagan some years later (although advocating diametrically opposing strategies), was that these sales were crucial for national security. Their position reflects both the contextual position of Saudi Arabia as an ally and the realpolitik of the complex relationship between the United States and the oil-producing Arab states.[27] In short, the sales of both the F-15s and AWACS to Saudi Arabia would be symptomatic of a pragmatic approach to the complex equation embracing U.S. foreign policy, economics, and the fragile impression of trust and friendship that existed between Saudi Arabia and the United States.

During the late 1970s and early 1980s the Saudi Arabia-U.S.-Israel triangle was further complicated, as Saudi foreign policy was targeted at "encouraging a forceful U.S. role in promoting a comprehensive Middle East peace settlement."[28] Despite being initially reassured by President Carter's active interest in finding a peaceful Arab-Israeli resolution, America's continued vacillation in the region led to Saudi unease about the direction of American foreign policy. Having been promised F-15s by the Ford administration, the ruling Saudi elite had been hoping for Ford's reelection. Yet, with the inauguration of Carter, Saudi Arabia diplomatically upheld its promise to delay any official application to purchase arms from America during the election year and waited until May of the following year before submitting an application to purchase sixty F-15s.

The historic visit of Egyptian President Anwar Sadat to Jerusalem in November 1977, which eventually led to the Camp David Treaty,* contributed to Saudi fears that they might lose the window of opportunity to update their increasingly obsolete air force. Carter's stopover in Riyadh, however, in January 1978, answered any such concerns, and on February 14, 1978, the Carter administration announced its intention to sell sixty F-15s to Saudi Arabia, fifty F-5Es to Egypt,† and fifteen F-15s along with seventy-five F-16 fighter-bombers to Israel.

Perhaps Carter's best and yet most controversial move relating to the F-15 deal was his deliberate packaging of arms for Israel with arms for Arab states, a decision that was the result of a series of inauspicious and contradictory positions imposed on his administration. It was a package that reconciled his emotional and moral commitment to the right of the Jewish people to resettle in their biblical homeland, with an ethical obligation to support Palestinian rights as part of an overall duty to human rights, a central precept of his foreign policy.

Well aware of what was rapidly becoming a debt of honor to the Saudis left by President Ford, Carter had also to contend with the Senate's heightened sensitivity over arms sales to the Middle East and by the covert request made by Israel in July 1977 for one hundred fifty F-16 and twenty F-15 aircraft. Fortunately, the Pentagon's position that Israel had no pressing military need for these weapons provided the administration with justification for delaying action on Israel's request. With the Israeli request still on the table, President Carter was able to incorporate it into a complex system of leverage explicitly designed to pass the proposed Arab sale of arms through the Senate. The president astutely initiated the proposal by intentionally packaging all three requests for arms from Israel, Egypt, and Saudi Arabia

---

*The Egyptian President's peace-finding mission to Israel was greatly supported by the United States— so much so that many members of Congress and the Senate opposed any future arms sales to the Middle East in writing, even before they had been proposed by the president as a means of being seen to support Anwar Sadat's courageous trip to Jerusalem.

†The F-5E is an aircraft that is no longer used by the USAF but was widely sold to third-world countries. In this instance, Saudi Arabia was to pay for the Egyptian F-5Es.

into one bill. Furthermore, he delivered the bill to Congress on April 28, 1978, with the express warning that should any part of the package be rejected, then it would be his intention to withdraw the entire proposal.

The impact of the proposed arms sale on political Washington was colossal. It marked a watershed in the lobbying tactics, not only of AIPAC, but also the pro-Arab lobby, which for the first time threatened AIPAC's supremacy on Capitol Hill.

AIPAC was established in 1959 to act for the American Zionist movement, influencing relations with governmental authorities, so as to improve friendship and goodwill between the United States and Israel; it is a well structured and powerful lobby group that is registered with Congress and is focused exclusively on enhancing and protecting American-Israeli relations. However, AIPAC's involvement in the F-15 battle was huge, "The organization's level of activity and access to key decision makers was relatively great. However, the committee's policy objectives were perceived as essentially antagonistic, diffuse, and unconstructive; the principal goal was to eliminate the Saudi portion of the proposed arms deal."[29]

Yet, for the first time, AIPAC was actively challenged by an organized Arab lobby. Given its past record in Washington, the metamorphosis of pro-Arab lobbying took AIPAC by complete surprise. A quote by a Washington aide in Hoag Levins's book *Arab Reach* reflects the changed reality, "The Arabs just suddenly appeared in Washington in 1978. It was that quick. Boom! One day you didn't see them. The next day, there they were. The progress they made was incredible."[30]

This change coincided with the arrival of Bandar in Washington. Assisting Prince Turki bin Faisal, Bandar quickly made his mark in Washington's political circuit. President Carter recalled, "We were not making much progress on it [the F-15 sale] and then all of a sudden I became acquainted with Bandar through my chief of staff, Hamilton Jordan, completely bypassing the Saudi ambassador. He said that he had been recommended by his father, Prince Sultan, to help us with this project." The president continued, "I didn't know how a young Air Force major would be effective at all, but after I talked with him I saw that he was urbane, he was westernized adequately, he was eloquent, and he obviously had direct ties to the highest level of the royal family. I didn't see Bandar every day, but I had a feeling that Bandar was basically living in the White House. He was working intimately and almost persistently and constantly with my staff members."[31]

During the lobbying for the F-15 deal, Bandar would often be faced with a potentially hostile audience. Relating one exchange, Bandar said, "I am always reminded of the late Senator Church. We were debating the F-15 sale and we had lunch with the Foreign Relations Committee. He sat there in front of his colleagues and charged at me with a very passionate plea that a Saudi air base in the north of Saudi Arabia called Tabuk is only five minutes from an Israeli population center. 'Can't you feel, Mr. Prince?' he said, 'Can't you feel what they feel; they're nervous, they could be attacked within five minutes from your base.' "

"And what struck me was that he was so emotional: I thought Minnesota was going to be attacked. But I was surprised how little homework he had done; the reason there is emotionalism and the reason logic has not been a factor is because it has been always a one-way story—somebody tells it and people take it and believe it and go on. What we are trying to do is balance that story."

"I looked at the senator and in front of his colleagues said, 'Senator, I agree with you—if I was five minutes away from a potential adversary I would be very nervous; but can I remind you that five years before that Israel was ten minutes away.' " After a pause, Bandar then said, "Fifteen years before they were fifteen minutes away. I did not move my base north; they came closer to me. Now," he finished, "if you take them back fifteen minutes away where they were—we will all be happy."[32]

Despite the highly sensitive and volatile nature of the proposed F-15 sale in Washington, Carter refused to delay the vote, which had been set for May 16, 1978. However, he was adamant that it should not go ahead until after the completion of his work on the Panama Canal Treaty.*

"We needed one or two votes," he said, speaking of the Panama Canal Treaty, he recalled, "and there was a senator named James Abourezk who was Lebanese and who had well-known ties with Saudi Arabia and with the Arab world; he was very undecided." Abourezk was the first Arab-American to be elected to the U.S. Senate and had openly condemned AIPAC's vast influence in Congress as "dangerous." "So I called my new friend Bandar

---

*President Jimmy Carter and Panamanian Chief of Government Omar Torrijos signed the Panama Canal Treaty and Neutrality Treaty on September 7, 1977. This agreement relinquished American control over the canal by the year 2000 and guaranteed its neutrality. In 1903, U.S. military force had supported Panamanian revolutionaries in their quest for independence from Colombia. On May 4, 1904, Panama granted the U.S. the right to build and operate the canal and control the five miles of land on either side of the canal in exchange for annual payments. The Panama Canal Treaties of 1977–1978 were meant to rectify a long-term, contentious issue in U.S.–Latin American relations. By the 1960s, Panamanian calls for Canal Zone sovereignty saw U.S. relations with Panama deteriorate. President Carter saw the canal's return as the key to improving U.S. relations in the hemisphere.

and told him we needed Abourezk's vote," said Carter, who recognized that the senator would be open to, in his words, the "charming, attractive, intelligent, and very effective" Bandar. He was right. Within a few days of approaching the prince for his help in securing the senator's vote, Carter received word from James Abourezk that he would vote for the treaty. The president added, "And we passed it by a one-vote margin. So I've always appreciated Bandar's help, because it was a turning point in this hemispheric relationship. The United States was becoming almost unanimously condemned by Latin American countries because . . . Presidents Johnson and Nixon and Ford—all of them, Democrats and Republicans—had promised to modify the very unfair Panama Canal Treaty that had been consummated, despite the opposition of Panamanians. It was something that needed to be done. So we were finally successful."[33]

By securing this vital vote for the president, Bandar earned more than just President Carter's respect; it was to cement a personal friendship that endures to this day. Carter maintains, "The biggest political challenge I ever had, even transcending my campaign for president, was my approval of the Panama Canal treaties, which was a very necessary and important move. But it was highly unpopular with the general public, because Ronald Reagan and others who were outside government were constantly berating me for giving away our canal and for selling out to a 'tin-horn' dictator in Panama." Linking the F-15 and Panama Canal votes, Carter said, "[They were] two of the biggest votes that took place while I was president; but far more important to me was the Panama Canal Treaty."[34]

The successful passage of that treaty was also an essential prerequisite for the F-15 sale to Saudi Arabia—failure to secure the former would have almost certainly prohibited the presentation of the F-15 sale to Congress. Bandar's role in securing the safe passage of the F-15 vote was therefore actually eclipsed in importance by his conversion of Senator Abourezk, without whose vote the Carter administration could have suffered a damaging defeat over the Panama

Jimmy Carter thanks Bandar for his help with the Panama Canal Treaty and the F-15 votes.

Canal Treaty. Instead, the ratification of the Panama Canal Treaty meant that in opposing the F-15 sale, the Jewish–Israeli lobby was faced with the prospect of confronting a resolute administration, fresh from winning a major foreign policy victory and with the knowledge that no proposed arms sale had ever been vetoed by Congress.

It became clear at this point that Carter's initial reservations about Bandar's ability to influence Congress had quickly been set aside, so much so that the president exclaimed, "So this was a major commitment of mine and we had come to depend on Bandar to be a very effective spokesperson—I would use the word lobbyist—on Capitol Hill." With a clear sense of pride, he said, "This was the first time it had ever been done—to confront a powerful lobby successfully."[35]

It was not only with Senator Abourezk that President Carter drew upon Bandar's developing diplomatic talent. A complicating factor in the F-15 battle on Capitol Hill was the looming election campaign challenge from Republican nominee Ronald Reagan. In the struggle to secure a positive vote for the sale of F-15s to Saudi Arabia and in order to ease the deal's passage, the Carter administration found it necessary to secure Reagan's support to sway the F-15 vote in the Senate, for while Reagan had no vote, he had great influence over the conservatives in the Senate. Then in opposition, Reagan was clearly anxious not to be seen to support the incumbent Democratic president. However, Carter was all too aware of this and sent Bandar to persuade Reagan to declare his support for the sale.

Bandar rang Tom "T.V" Jones, then CEO of Northrop (manufacturer of the F-5 aircraft then being purchased by Saudi Arabia), who was also a member of Reagan's Kitchen Cabinet. Jones duly arranged an appointment for Bandar and Reagan to meet.

On being introduced to the future president for the first time, the prince was asked two direct questions: "Are you a Communist?" and "Does Saudi Arabia support the United States?" Bandar reassured Governor Reagan that the United States had a fiercely loyal and long-standing ally in the conservative monarchy of the Saudi kingdom. Bandar also affirmed that Saudi Arabia had no ties to Communism—in fact, it could not abide Communist regimes to such an extent that known Communist passengers stopping over in Saudi Arabia were not even permitted to disembark from their aircraft onto Saudi soil.

Having satisfied Reagan on these points, Bandar asked him if he would support President Carter's proposal on the F-15 sale to Saudi Arabia. The prince recalled Reagan's clipped response, "Okay, I'll support it; but get a reporter to ask me a question about it." The prince recounted how he told the *Los Angeles Times* that Reagan was going to support Carter's sale of the F-15 to Saudi Arabia. "And they didn't believe him, but they still sent a reporter to the airport where Reagan was leaving for Iran. He asked Reagan, 'Do you support President Carter's selling F-15s to Saudi Arabia?' Reagan said, 'I don't see why not; they are our friends. So I'll support that, but I disagree with Carter on everything else.' " Bandar recalled Reagan's insistence on the caveat, "but I do not support any of Carter's other policies."

In this first meeting between Bandar and the future president, the mutual interests shared by both up-and-coming personalities and the countries they represented were established. In just a few short years, the fiercely anti-Communist approach to foreign policy and steadfastly conservative attitudes shared by the future president and the future Saudi ambassador to the United States would materialize in the form of the momentous Reagan Doctrine and in a valuable personal friendship.

Bandar's work on behalf of the F-15 sale continued. While traveling around the United States trying to obtain Senate votes, he recalled, "I had to meet a senator from the south called Senator Long." After hearing Bandar's pitch, Senator Long looked him straight in the eye and said, "My vote will cost you $10 million!"

Thinking that he might have been set up Bandar said, "Sorry?"

Long repeated, "My vote will cost you $10 million."

"Senator, I'm not here to bargain with you about money," Bandar said. "I am just here to explain our position, and I hope I can convince you to vote."

"You silly young man, you don't understand," explained Senator Long. "I don't want the money for me; I want you to assure me that your government will deposit $10 million in a bank in my town. You keep your money in New York; why not move just a little bit to Louisiana? Before you do that, let me know so that I can tell the bank president that he's going to get Saudi money invested with his bank. He will then pay for my reelection. You can then draw your money back any time, once I have been reelected."

Such deals, Bandar found, were not unhelpful. In those days, the Saudis had a lot of cash in Chase Manhattan. Bandar recounted asking David Rockefeller to help persuade certain senators to vote for the F-15 deal. Despite repeated promises to help, however, nothing happened.

Convinced that Rockefeller was leading him on, Bandar called Crown Prince Fahd and explained the problem.

"What do you suggest?" Fahd asked.

"You could order the Finance Minister to move $200 million from Chase Manhattan to JP Morgan," the prince replied, "and give me the authority to move it back when I decide."

"Done," the crown prince said.

"The next day," Bandar recalled, "David Rockefeller called me at eight o'clock in the morning; I was asleep. He called me at nine; I was busy. He called me at ten; I was out. At four o'clock in the afternoon, Madison Hotel reception phoned me and said, 'Mr. Rockefeller is in the lobby and he wants to come up to see you.' I said, 'Tell him I have meetings and when I'm finished I will talk with him.'"

Bandar observed, "I kept him in that lobby until six o'clock in the evening." Even then, Bandar told Rockefeller that he was too busy to talk, as he was on his way to Capitol Hill to try to secure the votes that he had promised.

A flustered Rockefeller replied, "I am going to stay here in Washington until I get you all the votes you want."

"Every night for three days," the prince recalled, "he would call me and say, 'I've got Senator so-and-so or Senator so-and-so.' And about three days later when he had got all the senators that he had promised to deliver—and two more—I told our Finance Ministry to move the $200 million back to Chase Manhattan."

But while Bandar was employing his persuasive skills in high-level maneuvering for President Carter, the real battle for votes was taking place between the pro-Arab and pro-Israeli lobbies. The newly emerging and highly organized pro-Arab lobby inspired and spearheaded by Bandar, found its greatest support in business. Huge oil-based corporations including the Fluor Corporation,* Bechtel Corporation, the Computer Sciences Corporation, and, of course, Mobil—all Houston-based giants of industry—joined the campaign to support the F-15 sale to Saudi Arabia.

With no political experience and with little time to prepare, Bandar adopted the KISS philosophy—"keep it simple, stupid." He tasked his at-

---

*The Fluor Corporation builds factories for extracting, transporting, and refining and processing oil, gas, coal, and synthetic fuels. One of the largest corporations of its kind, its biggest single project—estimated at $5 billion—is with Saudi Arabia.

torney Fred Dutton, a former special assistant to President John F. Kennedy and arguably the most effective consultant lobbying for the Saudi F-15 sale, to prepare a simple two-page briefing for him on the AFL-CIO. Having analyzed the lobbying techniques conventionally employed by AIPAC, the prince reasoned that the F-15 proposal equated to Saudi Arabia's spending $5 billion largely with McDonnell Douglas and its subcontractors and that such a huge contract equated to U.S. jobs. He believed that this would lend huge weight to the Arab case. Feeling, in his words, like "the Lone Ranger," Bandar took the case to the unions at McDonnell Douglas, who in turn brought in their subcontractors. The result was phenomenal, and massive mailing campaigns were initiated, matching those of the pro-Israeli operation.

Of Bandar's operating style, Douglas Bloomfield, a former lobbyist for AIPAC, who met the prince during the F-15 battle, observed, "A lot of questions have been raised about how much he is a lone ranger, or a freelancer, operating beyond the instructions of his government. He has gotten in trouble; he has been recalled and told, 'You've gone too far.'" Bloomfield added, "But I think Bandar is a daring personality. And from my pro-Israel point of view, he has made a significant contribution to try to ease the tensions."[36]

With regard to bitter Arab-Israeli disputes and having been warned by his mentor, Prince Fahd, not to get tied down in rancorous debates, Bandar would simply deflect such questions by saying, "You want to talk about the Palestinians; you want to talk about the Middle East? I have nothing to do with that, I am a fighter pilot. I am telling you why, operationally, we need this F-15—full stop."[37]

During the F-15 campaign, Bandar was to be strongly influenced by advice from Tip O'Neill, the legendary Speaker of the House from Massachusetts. O'Neill always maintained that, "All politics are local politics. It doesn't matter what you take, the bottom line is—it's local politics." He warned Bandar that if he took the relationship between Saudi Arabia and the United States as a foreign policy issue, more often than not he would be disappointed with the American reaction. He counseled, "If, however, you consider yourself as a domestic issue and you make your judgment based on that—meaning I'm trying to sell something just like the farmers, or the motor industry, or the aviation industry—only then can you be sure that you can predict what the American reaction would be."

Bandar heeded that advice, explaining the Saudi strategy on Capitol Hill,

"So basically, what we did—and it didn't take a genius—we looked at what the Israelis had been doing and reversed it, with Saudi Arabia instead of Israel. We took the same plan and played it, but substituted worker's votes, union and labor votes, for Jewish votes—whoever would benefit from the sale." Bandar opined, "When we saw the votes from senators—not from the perspective of foreign policy strategic rationale, but from a domestic perspective—'You have fifty thousand workers, Senator, that will benefit from the sale, it's up to you; do you want to give your vote or not?' Now it's a pure domestic issue, not even national, state by state by state." He concluded, "Usually they count employment as every billion dollars spent creates or keeps fifty thousand jobs. A $5 billion contract would give two hundred fifty thousand jobs. Now that works regardless of what the subject is."

Saudi Arabia also enlisted the services of numerous law firms and the public relations industry to create advertising drives. Saudi Arabia, Iraq, Algeria, Libya, and the United Arab Emirates combined to enlist the services of twenty-five paid foreign agents to act on their behalf as opposed to Israel's twenty-one.

The Saudis, like Israel, saw the F-15 deal as a litmus test of American support. Initially refusing any conditions or modifications to the sale, the Saudis at one point informed U.S. officials that delay was as bad as rejection. Given their economic position, they had good reason to take this stance—the kingdom was in a position to actually pay for the planes they required, a unique scenario in the lucrative world of arms sales and which in any other business situation would be the only real point of negotiation. However, given the complex exigencies of the Middle East and the unique rules applicable to politics and weapons deals, there were many conflicting factors at play.

Among these were allegations of "oil blackmail," charges that have been vehemently denied by Saudi Arabia. Nonetheless, the issue could never have been far from the president's mind, particularly following the Saudi minister of petroleum's statement on May 1, 1978, that "enthusiasm to help the West and cooperate with the United States" would be severely undercut by a refusal, leading to the Saudi feeling that America was "not concerned with our security" and doesn't "appreciate our friendship."[38] Conversely, he also asserted, "Linking the F-15 with oil sales is not justified."[39] This statement was quickly supported by the kingdom, which reassuringly emphasized, "Saudi oil production and dollar prices were based solely on economic foundations and would be maintained or altered only on the basis of economic considerations."[40]

Whatever the case, the delicate economic balance between Saudi Arabia and the United States was founded on oil; it provided a convincing argument for maintaining the friendship in the interests of national security. John P. Richardson, director of public affairs for the National Association of Arab Americans, acknowledged this when he encouraged Americans to "face up to the fact that [American] interests include continuing access to the one commodity that makes the whole thing go."[41] Adding to this pressure, the administration was keenly aware of the fact that should the deal fail, Saudi Arabia had every intention of taking its wealth elsewhere, perhaps purchasing the French Mirage F-1, as well as possibly financing the development of an aircraft comparable to the F-15.

The protection of Saudi oil fields against a possible Communist threat was cited in a letter from King Khalid to President Carter, in which he highlighted the need to blunt "Communist expansion in the area." This argument would later influence the Reagan administration and was taken up by Harold Brown, secretary of defense during the Carter administration. However, former Secretary of State Henry Kissinger berated the administration for hypocrisy, saying, "One cannot say that they have no military impact on Israel but they can have a military impact on threats from the Soviet side."[42]

Henry Kissinger became heavily embroiled in the F-15 deal, acting in support of the sale, but favoring what could arguably be viewed as an attempt to bribe Israel in order to pacify AIPAC. He recommended to the Senate's Foreign Relations Committee the sale of twenty extra F-15s to Israel, which, together with those already delivered, would balance the number of F-15s owned by Israel and Saudi Arabia. He also proposed constraints on the deployment of the Saudi planes and the sale of follow-up equipment. President Carter eventually conceded, and on May 11, 1978, he promised to sell an additional twenty F-15s to Israel, and assured the Israelis that he would not sell auxiliary fuel tanks, bomb racks, or air-to-air missiles to the kingdom, or allow the planes to be based within striking distance of Israel. Most notoriously, he promised not to sell AWACS to Saudi Arabia.

During this particularly tricky period, it was speculated that Israel had negotiated arms transactions worth nearly $900 million and signed a Memorandum of Understanding accelerating the delivery of F-16s, as well as securing cooperative research and development projects with the United States. Despite these concessions, AIPAC's efforts to block the sale continued apace, considering, like the Saudis, that the real issue was not the military hardware at stake, but a test of the alliance.

Further evidence on the importance both factions attributed to the "litmus test" surfaced during the Senate debate on the sales of arms to Egypt, Israel, and Saudi Arabia on May 15, 1978. In closed session, Senator McClure reported a private conversation he had in Riyadh in January 1978 with the foreign minister of Saudi Arabia, who said, "Unfortunately, the plane sale has become symbolic in our minds. It is a symbol of whether or not the United States will remain a dependable friend of the Saudis."[43]

The F-15 debate, though already fierce, was soon to escalate. On March 11, 1978, Palestine Liberation Organization (PLO) guerrillas crossed into Israel by sea from South Lebanon and hijacked a coastal bus; thirty-seven people were killed. On March 14, Israel retaliated with the launch of Operation Litani—the invasion of South Lebanon up to the Litani River by almost twenty thousand troops, resulting in thousands of Lebanese fatalities and casualties. In Washington, the conflicting interests and savage determination of both lobbies increased, leading to a heated internal clash between the president and the Senate over control of foreign policy.

Carter's arguments for the sale of F-15s as a matter of national security were met with resolute opposition within the Senate. Nonetheless, on May 15, 1978, the Senate's Foreign Relations Committee made the unusual decision, after a deadlocked vote of eight to eight, to return the F-15 vote to the Senate without recommendation. Believing that internal conflict corrodes credibility abroad, an open fight on the Senate floor was something Carter hoped to avoid. Yet a fight it would be.

A telegram issued by the President's Conference to every member of Congress on May 10, 1978, aggressively opposed the sale as "harmful to the national interest, a threat to the security of Israel, and an impediment to peace negotiations."[44] A top congressional aide commenting on the situation on Capitol Hill at this time reported "arm-twisting like you wouldn't believe—on both sides."[45] Yet perhaps a greater indication of the strength of feeling generated by the debate and the ramifications of the eventual decision was the White House's unsubtle position that the outcome of the vote would reflect on who precisely was administering foreign policy—the prime minister of Israel and the Israeli lobby or the president of the United States?[46]

On May 16, 1978, within days of Israel's thirtieth anniversary as a state, the Senate voted 54–44 against the motion to block the proposed tripartite arms transfer. For the first time in U.S. history, the United States openly defended its friendship with an Arab nation in the face of severe Israeli objections.

THREE

THE TIP OF
THE ICEBERG

"One's reputation is like a shadow, it is gigantic when it precedes you, and a pigmy in proportion when it follows."

CHARLES-MAURICE DE TALLEYRAND

I am pleased to inform you that the Kingdom of Saudi Arabia has decided to appoint Air Force Lt. [Lieutenant] Colonel Bandar bin Sultan in charge of contact with the federal government since the issue of the arms package sale to Saudi Arabia has bypassed its political framework and entered its technical framework, now that agreement has been reached and the package has been sent to the Congress. Consequently, the most important aspect of the issue now is to coordinate fully the work of the U.S. government team, with that of the Saudi counterpart team headed by Lt. Colonel Bandar bin Sultan, in order to carry out the necessary contacts in a way guaranteeing progress and the best of results."[1]

This letter, written by Ambassador Faisal Alhegelan, the Saudi Arabian ambassador to the United States, introduced Bandar as the middleman between Saudi Arabia and the United States over the sale of a substantial arms package that included five AWACS aircraft.

The era of the late 1970s had witnessed a series of destabilizing events in the Middle East, which caused great alarm in both Washington and Riyadh.

The Iranian revolution, overthrow of the Shah, and subsequent taking of American hostages in Tehran, was followed in short order by the Soviet invasion of Afghanistan on December 26, 1979, and the start of the Iran-Iraq war on September 22, 1980.

The encroaching expansion of the Soviet Union was seen by the Saudis as a grave threat. In stark terms, the royal family was convinced that once the Red Army invaded Afghanistan and took up positions a few hundred miles from the kingdom, the Kremlin's grand design would call for a move on the Saudi oil fields.[2] A member of the Saudi royal family declared, "The Soviet military presence in Cuba is not nearly so serious a threat to Western security as the military presence of the Russians in the Gulf and in the Horn of Africa."[3]

The Saudi response was to seek to buttress their own position vis-à-vis the acquisition of sophisticated military equipment and technology, including their request to purchase five AWACS aircraft from the United States. Bandar's involvement in the AWACS sale began six days after the outbreak of the Iran-Iraq war. On September 28, 1980, Gen. David Jones, chairman of the Joint Chiefs of Staff, made an official visit to Saudi Arabia at Bandar's request. Upon his arrival he was greeted by the prince, who told him in blunt, forceful language, "We want AWACS immediately. We want AWACS for twenty-four-hour surveillance of the Gulf. We need it. We can't protect the kingdom without it. Can you get it for us?"[4]

This demand, and its intensity, was scarcely surprising. USAF Col. Bob Lilac, who would be a key player in the AWACS battle and had significant knowledge of the major Peace Hawk modernization undertaking of the RSAF, recalled, "We [the USAF] had done a major study that talked about the needs of the kingdom. One of these was a need for airborne surveillance; Saudi Arabia had all this coastal territory, and they needed earlier warning than they could get with their existing radars. At the time we were finishing the study, the U.S. Air Force decided, with the Department of Defense, the State Department, and the National Security Council, that we needed to help protect those oil assets and recommended that the Saudis buy AWACS."[5]

The report also recommended that the airbases constructed to accommodate these aircraft be designed and built by Americans so that they could be used (and were used during the Gulf War) by American planes in the event of a Middle East crisis.

Despite opposition from Carter's advisers, who warned of potential negative voter reaction as the 1980 election campaign neared its climax, Jones succeeded in persuading the president to address the Saudi need. Soon after his visit with Bandar, four American-manned AWACS landed in Saudi Arabia on a "temporary training mission." They subsequently operated around the clock, three hundred sixty-five days a year, and were still there some seven years later. To show its gratitude, Saudi Arabia stepped up oil production, thereby easing oil prices.

This AWACS technology, when coupled with other military capabilities, provided continuous radar coverage of the Gulf area and gave the Saudis between ten and fifteen minutes of warning time in the event of an air attack against their oil fields. Capable of tracking two hundred forty targets or hostile aircraft simultaneously and directing fighter aircraft to intercept them, it was the most advanced command-and-control radar system in the world, generations ahead of the best Soviet technology then in existence. The integration of AWACS into the Saudi command-and-control system made it possible for an F-15 fighter to make at least one pass on an attacker before the enemy hit its target. It also allowed the Saudis to vector the acquisition radars of their Hawk missile batteries, allowing them to engage an attacking aircraft effectively and even provide some backup coordination for their F-5E fighter aircraft.

These four temporarily loaned aircraft whetted the appetite of the Saudi military, and it was not long before the Saudi government posed the inevitable question: would the Carter administration sell Saudi Arabia five AWACS planes and seven KC-135 tankers—and, by the way, could we also have some F-15 jet fighter equipment and air-to-air missiles at a price tag of $8.4 billion?

That request was political dynamite: Israel had long feared a modern Saudi air force and Congress specifically had been promised by President Carter in 1978 that the Saudis would not be allowed to buy AWACS. Even so, Defense Secretary Harold Brown informed the Saudis that Carter was "favorably disposed" to sell AWACS to the kingdom.

After discussions between the White House, the Department of Defense, and the State Department, a package was prepared for submission to Congress. In addition to selling the Saudis five AWACS aircraft, this package also stipulated the sale of conformal fuel tanks,* multiple injection

---

*Conformal fuel tanks (CFTs) are additional fuel tanks that are fitted closely to the profile of an aircraft. They extend either the range of an aircraft or its time on station with fewer aerodynamic penalties than external drop tanks.

racks that would permit the F-15 fighter bombers to carry more bombs, KC-135 tankers for refueling the F-15s in mid-air, and advanced Sidewinder (AIM 9-L) air-to-air missiles.

The timing was inauspicious; mere weeks remained before Carter left office. In several meetings in December 1980 between outgoing President Carter and President-elect Reagan, Carter offered to grant Saudi Arabia the right to purchase the new weapons, thereby allowing Reagan to avoid being involved in an extremely contentious issue at the outset of his presidency. Reagan declined the offer, however, advising Carter that his administration would conduct its own evaluation of Middle East policy, including the thorny subject of arms for Saudi Arabia.[6]

It is worth recalling the difficulties Reagan faced when he came to office in 1981. The Middle East was in turmoil; America's standing on the world stage had been damaged by the Carter administration's handling of the American hostage crisis in Iran; the U.S. economy was staggering from the impact of oil prices that had jumped nearly sevenfold; and the Soviet Union had "progressed from a continental power to a global one."[7]

Ronald Reagan was elected on the promise that he would turn around the economic and military malaise the United States suffered in the 1970s. Yet his vision was constrained by acute budgetary restraints. America had been hit hard by the oil shocks of 1973 and 1979. In addition, following a decade of war in Vietnam, there was little public appetite for new military endeavors. Nonetheless, Reagan was determined to pursue his anti-Communist agenda, and abetted by CIA Director Bill Casey, he soon identified Saudi Arabia as a prospective "milk cow" for his planned campaign against the Soviet Union. Furthermore, by aiding the Saudis, the United States would ensure the stable flow of oil at reasonable prices. The sale of F-15s to the kingdom appeared to be a smart move.

Sensing the coming battle, the new administration was keen to gauge feelings on the Hill. In a test of likely reaction, Under Secretary of State James L. Buckley provided informal briefings on the proposed sale of arms to Saudi Arabia to the House Foreign Affairs and Senate Foreign Relations committees on February 26, 1981. Acknowledging Israeli fears about the sale, Buckley advised that Israel would be permitted to purchase fifteen more F-15s. In addition, the administration announced that Israel would receive $600 million in military credits to allow it to overcome any perceived military imbalance between it and Saudi Arabia. Crucially, in return,

Israel's government covertly advised the Reagan administration that it would not fight the sale, nor would it encourage the Israeli lobby in Washington, notably AIPAC, to block the sale.

On March 6, 1981, the Reagan administration announced that to meet a "growing threat" from the Soviet Union in the Middle East and Persian Gulf, it was ready to sell an F-15 enhancement package to Saudi Arabia. This sale was intended to be a purely defensive package and would not include bomb racks. Reaction on Capitol Hill was subdued.[8] Four weeks later, following a National Security Council meeting held on April 2, 1981, to discuss the sale of weapons to Saudi Arabia, it was agreed that Saudi Arabia would be provided with five AWACS aircraft and KC-135 tankers, as well as the F-15 enhancements package, including the conformal fuel tanks, bomb racks, and Sidewinder missiles.

What Reagan was proposing was by far the largest U.S. arms sale to date; estimates varied on the actual size of the deal, but it was arguably in the region of $7 to $9 billion, with the follow-on infrastructure and operational and training support eventually elevating that to about $85 billion. Through the provision of conformal fuel tanks, this planned new sale would give Saudi Arabia's sixty-two F-15s the endurance and range to maintain air combat patrol, increasing the effectiveness of their fighters. Because of their extended range, those fighters could also mass in the Gulf area for short periods, even if Saudi Arabia should lose the air base at Dhahran. The KC-135 tankers would further enhance the operational effectiveness of Saudi defensive fighters by making it possible to refuel the AWACS, F-15, and F-5E aircraft. Those airborne tanker aircraft would enable Saudi Arabia to accept reinforcements from U.S carriers or airbases outside the kingdom. Finally, the Sidewinder missiles with their all-aspect capability would give the F-15 and F-5E fighters a weapon for use in near "head-on" intercepts against low-flying attackers, without having to sacrifice the time and probable failure to execute an intercept when maneuvering into a long-stern or "dog fight" position—a valuable feature in view of the limited warning time the AWACS could provide.[9]

When discussing the logistics of the deal, Col. Lilac said very forcibly, "The tanker part of the deal was very important—right behind the AWACS aircraft. But the Hill didn't want to give tankers to Saudi Arabia; after all, why would Saudi Arabia want to go anywhere? That was a very controversial aspect of the sale." He observed, "It turned out later on that the

AWACS almost got to be the easier part of the deal, because conformal fuel tanks extended the range of the F-15, and the AIM 9-L gave you head-on capability, and the refuelers—they became very difficult."[10]

As Reagan had entered office with the reputation of being very pro-Israeli and cynical about the Arab nations, his staunch support for the AWACS sale was surprising. Prior to being appointed president, he had tended to disparage the significance of contact with any Arab country.

Yet his support for the sale recognized a simple economic truth—any threat to Saudi Arabia, and any consequent prolonged interruption in oil exports from the Persian Gulf, would almost certainly be a devastating blow to the global economy. The underlying political instability of the region, the huge economic and strategic stakes involved in the preservation of those oilfields, and their vulnerability to air attack, meant that Reagan's approval of the AWACS sale was a prudent foreign policy decision. It also established the United States as the prevailing military power in the Persian Gulf.

The true agenda behind the sale of AWACS to Saudi Arabia ran extremely deep, but the simple equation was the defense of Saudi Arabia by the United States in return for the secure provision of vital oil to the United States. Yet there was another factor in Reagan's decision to support the sale. The president had begun to construct a foreign policy that was devised from his affirmed passion to see a reversal of the growth of the Evil Empire* and the ultimate destruction of Communism.

President Reagan's right-hand man in the war against Communism, CIA Director Bill Casey, understood that Saudi disquiet about Soviet intentions made the desert kingdom a natural ally. Moreover, he was aware that oil was the indispensable lubricant of the Western economy and that stable, secure access to reserves was essential if there was going to be any economic recovery.

In truth, Reagan and Casey were pushing an open door; Saudi Arabia had its own reasons for helping America fight the Soviets. First, the United States already was actively helping with the protection of Saudi oilfields and the Saudi leadership was determined that the kingdom and the Americans should remain on good terms. Second, Saudi Arabia was increasingly concerned about the threat posed by Soviet hegemony in the region. Riyadh interpreted Moscow's Afghanistan exploits as part of a Soviet-directed drive

---

*President Reagan described the Soviet Union as the "Evil Empire" in a speech to the House of Commons on June 8, 1982.

to surround the Arabian Peninsula with Communist regimes and subvert the oil-rich monarchies; Soviet activities in Yemen and Ethiopia reinforced that assessment. Third, the kingdom was awash in petrodollars and the United States could easily find use for that money.[11]

In weighing up the prospect of a partnership with Saudi Arabia, Casey knew that President Reagan wanted not only to contain the Soviet Union, but also to "reverse the expansion of Soviet control and military presence throughout the world." These ambitions, articulated in what would become branded as the Reagan Doctrine, sought to inflate the cost of Moscow's foreign policy efforts by championing democracy, outspending the Soviets on defense, and supporting anti-Soviet rebellions in the developing world. However, within the administration, it became obvious that in order to roll back Communism, "You had to be able to fund it and we simply couldn't do that alone." CIA Director Bill Casey could see the real possibility of Saudi assistance for achieving Reagan's goals would be financial.[12]

Saudi Arabia was fervently anti-Communist, an ideologically compatible American partner in the battle against "godless Communism." However, oil was also a vital component of the coming campaign that had the Soviet Union in its sights. As the world's largest producer, Saudi Arabia could determine the outcome of a game in which the American economy could be reenergized, while the Soviet Union could find its hard currency income squeezed beyond breaking point, with disastrous consequences for its expansionist policies. Every time the price of oil fell by one dollar a barrel, it meant $2 billion a year less hard currency for Moscow from the sale of its oil. The issue of oil pricing and the U.S.-Saudi security relationship were aligned. As Secretary of Defense Caspar Weinberger recalled, "It was a critical element of Reagan's strategy. We wanted lower oil prices; that's one of the reasons we were selling them arms."[13]

It was this backdrop that precipitated a unique, unlikely, and often covert partnership, one that would endure for the next two decades. Reagan's was an era of unprecedented strength in U.S.-Saudi relations. Prince Bandar bin Sultan, the thirty-four-year-old ex–fighter pilot turned diplomat, would soon emerge as the essential link between the two nations.

Despite the obvious need for discretion, news of the massive and still unannounced deal leaked. On April 7, the House floor erupted as congressman after congressman, Republicans and Democrats alike, lambasted the administration's decision. While opposition to the sale of the F-15 enhancements package had remained relatively muted, the addition of

AWACS planes to the deal changed the climate at a stroke. Over one hundred congressmen made speeches opposing the sale; an Associated Press poll found only twenty senators willing to support it.[14] The debate on the Hill precipitated wholesale opposition to the sale and prompted a postponement of the administration's plan to place the arms package before Congress on April 27.[15]

Rather than force a conclusion to the AWACS sale and run the very real risk of its rejection, the Reagan administration went on spin control. Assistant Secretary of State for Congressional Relations Richard Fairbanks began massaging members of Congress, saying, "The proposal emphasizes this administration's commitment to counter the erosion in Middle East/Persian Gulf security, bolster our friends, protect vital Western interests, and block Soviet exploitation of regional tensions and vulnerabilities. . . . A more secure Saudi Arabia will help the Saudis promote stability in the region and expand their already great cooperation with us." Fairbanks also emphasized that the dynamics of the Persian Gulf had altered dramatically in the light of overriding political instability in the region since 1978 and the threat to the security of Saudi Arabia had been elevated to a dangerous level, driving home the Saudi need for AWACS and heightening the menace of Soviet penetration and exploitation. Fairbanks repeatedly highlighted the Soviet invasion of Afghanistan, the chaos of the Iranian revolution, the dangers posed by the Iran-Iraq War, and the Soviet presence in South Yemen and Ethiopia. Moreover, Fairbanks stressed, as a "swing producer" with great influence in OPEC, Saudi Arabia had tried to ensure oil market price stability after the disruption of Iranian oil exports.[16] The AWACS sale would persuade Saudi Arabia to continue to follow that policy.

While Reagan endeavored to keep the AWACS battle from entering the public domain more than it already had, Prime Minister Menachem Begin, who had previously agreed not to block it, now openly condemned it, unreservedly denouncing it as a potent threat to Israel. By late June, Senator Bob Packwood, an Oregon Republican and an ardent pro-Israel senator, teamed up with Tom Dine, AIPAC's executive director, announcing on June 25 that fifty-four senators—a majority in the Senate—had signed a bipartisan letter to the president opposing "the administration's intent to sell the F-15 enhancement and AWACS package to Saudi Arabia. It is our strong belief that this sale is not in the best interests of the United States and therefore recommend that you refrain from sending this proposal to Congress." Later that same day, a House resolution, signed by two hundred twenty-four members, was released disapproving of the sale. In July, AIPAC declared that its goal was "to keep the package from ever being submitted" to Congress for a required vote of approval—simple majorities in both houses could block the deal.[17]

A defiant President Reagan determined that he would press on. In a private and unannounced meeting with Bandar, he promised him that the formal AWACS package would be submitted to Congress during the autumn and vowed to do his utmost to secure passage of the deal. For their part, the Saudis thought that they could help the administration, as they had done in 1977 and again in 1979 with the Carter administration, by putting forward constructive ideas designed to bring about a peaceful settlement to the Israeli-Palestinian situation.

As was the case in the F-15 struggle in 1978, the Senate became the main battleground for the AWACS sale, but this time the White House was slow off the mark, focusing on tax and budget issues in the early months of the new administration. Asked about the difference between confrontations with AIPAC and Capitol Hill involving the F-15 and AWACS deals, Fred Dutton observed, "The Reagan AWACS deal was a tougher fight." He explained, "The F-15 deal got on stage in a hurry and got off stage in a hurry. Whereas the AWACS deal was a bloody protracted fight; AIPAC got wind of it early on and fought furiously against it. In effect, AIPAC started calling the shots."[18]

Opponents of the AWACS deal feared that the Saudi government would eventually use the planes to threaten the security of Israel, consistent with Riyadh's long history of unrelenting hostility toward the Jewish state. They also viewed the Saudi government as a corrupt and inefficient regime that could collapse at any time, placing the aircraft in the hands of another Islamic revolutionary regime modeled after the one that had surfaced in Iran.

Col. Lilac explained that another of the hurdles the Reagan administration was confronted with was the sensitivity concerning access to AWACS technology. "We never put a formal restriction on where the aircraft was based, but there were canards, as I called them—false excuses put forward by the Hill to block the sale—and this was one of the excuses that was put forward to try to prevent the sale, because the technology was so sensitive; the electronics and the software controlling the acquisition and tracking of two hundred forty targets, multiple inputs and communications. There were lots of fancy devices inside the black boxes. A lot of people were saying that access to these was fraught with peril; they could see them getting in the wrong hands and being handed over to the Soviets."[19] Ambassador Richard Murphy* remarked, "[Reagan's] whole pitch was that Saudi Arabia is an Arab country; but it's an Arab country that is not a front-line state and it has no ambitions to join an attack on Israel. In any case, it has ample need facing the new Iranian government." Murphy said, "We were very nervous throughout that period about Iran—and on the war itself—and I think I heard a former American official say that it was in our interest that the two of them, Iran and Iraq, bleed each other white. That was never my interest, because I was always nervous that the Iranians might just have the punch to move over against the smaller states of the Gulf and start another fire that we would need to resolve."[20]

Under the terms of the Arms Export Control Act, once Congress receives formal notification of an arms sale, it has thirty days to stop that sale by majority vote in both houses. In the event of a split vote, the president's proposal would go ahead. On September 14, 1981, in a personal effort by President Reagan to coax reluctant votes, twenty-seven senators were invited to the White House. His efforts met with little success: later that month, another bipartisan petition against the AWACS sale was signed by fifty-six senators.

It was during this phase of the debate that attempts were made to place restrictions and obtain concessions from the Saudis on the operation of the aircraft—whatever was necessary to secure a vote in the Senate. The Saudis quite naturally resisted those restrictions and indicated their willingness to obtain weapons systems from England or France if necessary. The administration, caught between the proverbial rock and a hard place, informed Congress that it would submit a formal notification of the sale by October 1.

On October 1, 1981, as required by the Arms Export Control Act, the

---

*Richard W. Murphy is a renowned Arabist who has followed Near Eastern developments for over forty years, thirty-four of which were spent as a career foreign service officer. After U.S. Army service, he joined the State Department and from 1955 to 1968 served in Salisbury, Southern Rhodesia (now Zimbabwe); Beirut, Lebanon; Aleppo, Syria; Jeddah, Saudi Arabia; and Amman, Jordan. He spent 1968–1971 in Washington, D.C., as country director for the Arabian Peninsula, and director of personnel for the Near Eastern Bureau. In 1971, President Nixon nominated him to serve as ambassador to Mauritania, and in 1974 he became ambassador to Syria. Later, he served as ambassador to the Philippines and Saudi Arabia. From 1983 to 1989, he was assistant secretary of state for Near East and South Asian affairs under President Reagan, and was particularly active in the Israeli–Arab peace process. Richard Murphy has received the President's Distinguished Service Award three times and the State Department's Superior Honor Award twice. In 1985, he was named career ambassador, a title held by only five officers serving at any given time. Retiring from government service in 1989, Mr. Murphy joined the Council on Foreign Relations in New York as senior fellow for the Middle East.

Pentagon Defense Security Assistance Agency sent the crisp document, transmittal number 81-96, for approval to the Senate and the House. This concise document stated that the Air Force had found no strategic reason to refuse Saudi Arabia's request to purchase five AWACS aircraft for $8.5 billion.[21] The package included five E-3A Sentry AWACS aircraft, eighteen related ground radar installations, six KC-135 tanker aircraft (with an option on two more), one hundred one conformal fuel tanks for the F-15 aircraft acquired in 1978, and 1,177 Sidewinder air-to-air missiles with an all-aspect guidance and control system. It was an air defense package with massive infrastructure support, which was actually worth $85 billion, ten times the nominal value of the AWACS sale.[22]

During the initial phase of the AWACS dispute from April to August 1981, the Saudi government stayed silent, relying on the Reagan administration to push the deal through Capitol Hill. However, as it became clear that the struggle was intensifying and that the Senate did not have faith in the guarantees that the Saudi government had given the president that the AWACS would be employed only in a defensive role, it began an open campaign, targeted at bringing around industry.

The House of Saud hoped that the diplomatic message it was sending with the appointment of Bandar, who could in effect speak for the king, would volubly demonstrate the importance the kingdom attached to the deal. He was a rising player for Saudi Arabia in Washington, son of Defense Minister Prince Sultan, and confidant of Crown Prince Fahd. The Saudi government clearly intended to transmit an unambiguous signal that Riyadh looked upon the AWACS sale as critical to Saudi Arabia's national security interests. Bandar was seen by the Saudi royal family as the natural person to make that case.[23]

Strangely, though, Bandar's assignment in Washington to help with Reagan's fight to sell AWACS to the

Bandar presents his credentials as Ambassador to President Ronald Reagan.

kingdom may also have been precipitated by Secretary of State Alexander Haig, who visited Saudi Arabia in April 1981. After he informed Crown Prince Fahd that President Reagan was willing to go with the AWACS deal, he asked, "And by the way, where is my friend Prince Bandar? We need him to do what he did with the F-15."

Fred Dutton, the Saudi's principal lobbyist, explained the choice of Bandar as emissary, "Crown Prince Fahd decided that Prince Bandar should come over to help ensure that the deal went through—Fahd was the Prince's sponsor and Bandar his protégée." Dutton had years of experience with Capitol Hill; he had been special assistant to President John F. Kennedy and later appointed secretary of state for congressional relations in the State Department. He knew the ropes and his contacts on the Hill were legion; so too were his contacts in the media. "When I first got to Washington, the media people were easier to get to know and Kennedy expected all of us who had roles in his administration to work the media. I think that that was one of the reasons that Kennedy brought me back to Washington, because I was such a strong advocate of 'work the media; work the press and TV.' "[24]

In Dutton, Bandar had a strong ally with the ability to employ a fully briefed and selectively focused prince almost like a point-and-shoot weapon. Thereafter, it was a question of the prince's reaching out and engaging senators, congressmen, and the media. Coached by Dutton, Bandar would provide lunch for the selected press in a Kalorama Park townhouse, lacing the conversation with well-timed and tasty news leads. Dutton would identify, invite, and prebrief the cream of Washington's reporters and journalists who were then panting at the prospect of inside information on the AWACS fight. In this way the Saudi behind-the-scenes AWACS campaign, in support of the main player, President Reagan, was begun.

Bandar's proficiency at reading Washington's complex and often very subtle political hieroglyphics is a skill that has allowed him to act decisively when the situation demands. It has also enabled him to understand how to exercise power. Bandar set up his headquarters in a six-room suite at the Fairfax Hotel in downtown Washington. Here, he communicated freely with pro-Arab groups and supporters as well as with key U.S. senators who had indicated their support for the sale. He worked with those same senators to develop a strategy that would persuade some of their more intractable colleagues to switch their allegiance. Despite being a comparatively junior lieutenant colonel, Bandar's aptitude and his ability to achieve results were becoming recognized, as was his special relationship with Crown Prince Fahd.

In undertaking this responsibility, Bandar acted as the facilitator, the conduit, and the emissary between the United States and Saudi Arabia. He could translate—not just between languages but between cultures; he was the glue between the two largely dissimilar dynasties and his stature grew as the relationship deepened.

Insofar as Saudi tactics during the AWACS debate were concerned, Fred Dutton confirmed that they were trying to make it look as though President Reagan was taking the lead. Yet a great deal of work was required to make that happen. Of Bandar's role, Dutton said, "He learned the political game here reasonably fast and he was always trying to work the backstage as hard as the front of the stage—and he did very well. As to the strategy or tactics, it was to keep the burden on Reagan. In the final days prior to the vote, Reagan had resorted to cajoling, persuading, and even threatening—he was doing everything necessary. He couldn't lose this one—it was too big—it was his first big foreign policy test." Dutton concluded, "Our tactic was to 'Keep Reagan on the hook.'"[25]

The Saudi strategy was twofold. With his wealth of contacts, Dutton worked the media hard. On the other side, Bandar worked to pull in America's industrial base, leading the corporate charge to back the AWACS sale by letting it be known, albeit diplomatically, that Saudi Arabia would assess the actions of those companies, or lack thereof, when determining future business agreements. David Sadd, executive director of the National Association of Arab Americans, helped the prince organize the support of U.S. industries with an interest in the AWACS purchase by Saudi Arabia. The oil industry lobbied fiercely for the sale, with Mobil

Bandar with his close friend and confidante, Fred Dutton.

spending more than a half million dollars on full-page newspaper advertise-
ments commending the merits of the economic alliance between the United
States and Saudi Arabia. The most intense lobbying effort was coordinated
by Boeing, the principle AWACS contractor, and United Technologies,
which had a $100 million contract at risk. Indeed, the presidents of Boeing
and United Technologies dispatched more than six thousand five hundred
telegrams to subsidiaries, vendors, and suppliers throughout the United
States, pressuring them to champion the sale.[26] Journalist Steven Emerson
reported that one midwestern senator was approached on behalf of AWACS
by every major CEO in his state.

The Saudi campaign on behalf of AWACS resulted in one of the most
successful manipulations of American business and American foreign policy
ever attempted by a foreign power. Bandar called for and received the uncompromising assistance of some of the most influential corporations in America:
Mobil Oil, Bechtel Corporation, Boeing, Westinghouse, United Technologies
Corporation. Likewise, scores of other business interests assisted the drive so
as to protect existing petrodollar contracts or to secure new contracts. Thousands of others were circuitously encouraged to join the crusade as a result of
pressure from their own domestic suppliers, purchasers, or even business partners. Many others with no commercial stake in the AWACS deal, or even in
Saudi Arabia, added their support to the lobbying effort simply because they
were convinced that not upsetting the Saudis was essential.

The Saudi strategy reflected an awareness of the leverage that could be
gained by soliciting and mobilizing the support of the American business
community. Hundreds of CEOs, corporate presidents, and vice presidents
were contacted and strongly urged to write or call their senators. The message that Saudi business was good business and meant jobs was rammed
home, especially in those states where senators were politically vulnerable.

During the six-week run-up to the vote, the pace of the business lobbying
effort increased. Scores of Washington representatives of major American
corporations were invited to attend receptions at the Saudi embassy in Washington. As the outcome of the vote looked more and more precarious, the
pressure was intensified and contracts were used as lures for hungry busi-
nesses. On September 19, 1981, Bandar met with former President Gerald
Ford in Palm Springs, California, during which time they discussed U.S.-
Saudi relations and the AWACS sale. A month later, President Ford would
telephone various senators and express his support for the AWACS sale.

Through the efforts of Bandar and the entire Saudi team, Reagan was able to call upon "the aggressive involvement of the entire spectrum of the American business community," an effort that has been described as "the most extensive business lobbying goal ever pursued by American business on a foreign policy issue."[27]

Bandar was later to say that the logic of allying their case with American industries and the need to hire the best lawyers (and lobbyists and PR experts) became very clear. "I have always believed that the Israelis had a lousy case, but good lawyers . . . and we the Arabs have always had a good case but lousy lawyers." The prince enthused, adding with a smile, "Why the hell do they whip us all the time in politics? [That is] until we began to learn the rules of the game and began to play [by] the same rules."[28]

Yet it was not only the business community that was pulled in. Other top officials who helped the Saudi lobby included Clark Clifford, President Johnson's defense secretary, Richard Kleindienst, President Nixon's attorney general, and William Rogers, Nixon's secretary of state. The prince pulled out the stops and added former Carter administration officials to his pro-AWACS political lobby, including former Secretary of Defense Harold Brown, former Secretary of State Edward Muskie and the former ambassador to Saudi Arabia, John West, as well as current Republican Senate leader, Howard Baker, and Senator John Tower, chairman of the Armed Services Committee.[29]

The prince recognized the need for and then cultivated influential and experienced experts in the Washington political arena; in short, he surrounded himself with the best money could buy, which allowed the Saudi team to compete effectively in the Washington power game in the face of the very strong opposition afforded by other major players and opponents.

The Reagan administration's AWACS effort was led by a special working team consisting of the White House, the National Security Council, the State Department, the Defense Department, congressional personnel, and the USAF, represented by Bob Lilac. Their progress was charted on a wall in the Scheduling Room, located in the basement of the West Wing of the White House. There was a similar chart back at the Saudi offices in the Fairfax Hotel. The degree of communication between the two teams, White House and Saudi, was extremely close.

That interaction was enhanced by the personal rapport that existed between Bandar and Lilac. As the AWACS campaign intensified, Lilac often became the link between the White House team and Bandar. He knew where

to find him—knew all of his regular haunts. Lilac recalled how one evening after a long meeting in the Situation Room in the White House they needed to
contact Bandar urgently to get a draft AWACS agreement signed off. "It was
suggested," said Lilac, "that one constraint that would bring a particular senator into [our] camp might be to deny access for Saudi-contracted Pakistani
technicians to particular AWACS software packages—the RSAF had a lot of
Pakistani technicians." A decision needed to be made quickly, and protocol and
courtesy demanded that the White House clear it with Bandar. Lilac said, "We
needed to get an answer, we had to get back to this senator that night or first
thing in the morning, so we needed to get the Saudis' agreement fast."

Unable to find the prince through the embassy, Rick Burt, then working
for Secretary of State Haig, and Lilac drove to Bandar's apartment, where
Lilac told the security staff, "It's Bob Lilac. I have got to see Prince Bandar."
He was informed that he was in a private meeting with the secretary of
state, but Lilac insisted, "You've got to let us bust in." Lilac and Burt were
eventually allowed to join the prince and Secretary Haig, who were quietly
enjoying a glass of whiskey and a cigar.

As they entered the room, Haig looked up to see Burt and Lilac, who
was still in uniform, and said to Bandar, "Gee, Bandar, we're in trouble—
we got the Air Force here. What in the hell are you guys doing here?"

Lilac replied, "I need Prince Bandar's signature on a restriction on
AWACS."

Bob Lilac briefs President Reagan on AWACS.

"Okay, let's look at it," said Bandar. After studying it briefly, he signed it, saying, "I don't think we'll have any trouble with that—I don't even need to go back home on that."

Laughing, Haig motioned to the door and said, "You guys get the hell out of here and get back to work."[30]

When Israeli Foreign Minister Yitzhak Shamir visited Washington in February 1981, he received an indication that President Reagan was likely to agree to a Saudi aircraft deal. Yet the details of the sale were largely glossed over; he was merely advised by the administration that the Saudis would be sold airborne surveillance equipment but its exact nature was unspecified.[31] It was intimated that the sale would include only the F-15 upgrade or enhancement package previously discussed with the Carter administration. Shamir was not told that it would include AWACS aircraft. From the viewpoint of Israeli air superiority, these modified Boeing 707 aircraft, complete with large radar dishes and sophisticated data processing equipment, would significantly erode Israel's military advantage; they were far more advanced than the Grumman E-2C Hawkeye aircraft that was in Israel's inventory.

By the time Prime Minister Menachem Begin visited Washington in September 1981, the addition of AWACS to the Saudi package had already been confirmed. Begin's reaction, and that of Tel Aviv, was fiercely antagonistic. Nevertheless, the administration thought they had persuaded Begin to limit his remarks on AWACS and not make a crusade of it in the media. They were wrong.

Reagan said, "I learned that almost immediately after he left the White House, Begin went to Capitol Hill and began lobbying very hard against me, the administration, and the AWACS sale—after he told me he wouldn't do that. I didn't like representatives of a foreign country—any foreign country—trying to interfere in what I regarded as our domestic political process and the setting of our foreign policy. I told the State Department to let Begin know that I didn't like it and that he was jeopardizing the close relationship of our countries unless he backed off. Privately, I felt he had broken his word and I was angry about it."[32] As such, despite President Reagan's pro-Israel leanings, the AWACS debate took place against a backdrop of mounting tension between the United States and Israel.

Begin's interference in U.S. relations with Saudi Arabia was widely viewed as improper. In his biography of Reagan, Lou Cannon notes, "Begin's tactics galvanized Reagan into an unusual display of political involvement. Encouraged by White House Chief of Staff James Baker, Reagan made the AWACS deal a test of his personal prestige, then sky-high among Republicans."[33] The Israeli government had inadvertently impaired its own cause. Whereas the Saudis were seen to be working in a positive manner with the U.S. administration—circulating a Middle East peace plan and providing more oil—in contrast, an angry Prime Minister Begin went on the attack. Begin was perceived to be using the authority and status of his office as leader of a foreign nation to sway Congress into preventing a third-party sale. Moreover, the diplomatic impunity of Begin was exacerbated because he was not just the leader of any nation, but of a nation that had exceptionally close ties with—and was the source of deep-seated emotional links with—the most politically well-organized cultural faction in the United States, the Jewish community. As prime minister, he was not just representing his government in its lobbying campaign against the AWACS sale, but was also perceived to be speaking for the American Jewish community.

Without a shadow of doubt, the empathy that existed between Israel and the American Jewish community enabled Begin to wield greater political influence on Capitol Hill than perhaps any other foreign leader in the world. The irresponsible use of that influence, in the eyes of both Reagan and the White House, explains why Begin's efforts to persuade Congress to block the AWACS sale caused both disquiet and resentment in the White House. No lobbyist for Saudi Arabia carried the same political clout, not even Bandar.[34] And Bandar, though leading the Saudi lobbying campaign, was a mere Air Force officer. His efforts were seen as a natural advocacy, while Begin's had begun to be perceived as sovereign interference.

At the news conference held on October 1, 1981, in the East Room of the White House during Begin's visit, Reagan defiantly announced that he was offi-

Menachem Begin

cially sending the AWACS package to Congress. In a barbed and transparent accusation directed at Begin, Reagan affirmed, "It is not the business of other nations to make American foreign policy. As president, it's my duty to define and defend our broad national security objectives. The Congress, of course, plays an important role in the process and while we must always take into account the vital interests of our allies, American security interests must remain our internal responsibility."[35]

The untimely intervention by a fiery Menachem Begin played right into Bandar's hands. Indeed, Bandar gave much of the credit for the Saudi lobbying success to the Israeli prime minister, saying, "Begin, of course, was our best ally in AWACS, because every time he talked we won some more people." He added, "I'm sure he did not intend it that way, but he was my biggest trump card—all I had to do was say, 'Did you hear Begin?' "[36]

What had originated as a question of Saudi defense following U.S. Air Force recommendations vis-à-vis their oilfields, became a matter of politics once Begin and AIPAC determined to prevent the sale. Bandar reasoned that should the Saudis lose the AWACS deal, then they would win the president, and if they won AWACS, they still won because the president wanted the AWACS sale. Thus, for Saudi Arabia, once Israel had engaged in the war of words, it was a "win-win" situation. To quote an exuberant prince, "What we were interested in was making sure the Israelis committed themselves to fighting us on AWACS. Once they did that, they were fighting the president and we disengaged. We left them alone because either way we would win. That's the only way I like to have it." The rewards of this Capitol Hill conflict were more profound than just the acquisition of military hardware—it was to mark a sea change in American public opinion.

On a tactical level, Prime Minister Begin's interference in the AWACS debate enabled Fred Dutton to frame the choice facing the Senate as "Reagan or Begin."[37] In truth, it has been reported that the most effective AWACS lobbyist was probably Fred Dutton and that "his most significant contribution was to transform the debate on AWACS from substantive issues to a personal one; that is, he was able to frame the issue as a fight between the president of the United States and the prime minister of Israel." As Dutton told the *New York Times*, senators who opposed the sale would have to explain, "How will they run foreign policy now that they have chosen Begin over Reagan?' "[38]

Though the House, as expected, shot down the sale with a vote of

301–111, Reagan unflinchingly undertook a personal lobbying campaign in the U.S. Senate that was almost unparalleled in modern history. He became the most prominent lobbyist of all and made dozens of phone calls to wavering senators inviting them to back the sale. Where necessary, he promised a multiplicity of budgetary and legislative favors. The president talked individually with forty-four senators, pressuring, convincing, and finally intimidating, trying to persuade them of the utter need for the AWACS deal to be approved.[39]

In the final days before the vote, Reagan's personal campaign was aided by pressure now being generated by the American arms and oil industries, encouraged by Bandar and his team of lobbyists. Saudi covert influencing of the media, a particular talent of Dutton's, together with the efforts of the White House team, gradually began to capture crucial votes. The gap in the Senate began to narrow.

To counter the threat posed by AIPAC, the president mustered a small army of officials, including the former secretaries of state and defense, to make the administration's case to Congress in formal hearings and informal briefings. Among the administration's lobbyists for the sale was Air Force Gen. Richard Secord, who had helped negotiate the terms of the deal with the Saudis. Gen. Secord was the highest-ranking military officer who assisted the White House in leading briefing teams to Congress. Three officers were assigned by the Pentagon to keep track of scheduling and issues, one of whom was a lively marine lieutenant colonel named Oliver North. From this meeting of Gen. Secord and the ultimately notorious North, the seeds were sown from which flowered the Iran-Contra affair.

Part of the infrastructure that supported Reagan's AWACS campaign included the Scheduling Room. Explaining its function, Lilac said, "Scheduling involved keeping a record of which congressmen or senators were being briefed by whom, plus they also kept track of scheduling briefings that we gave to groups. They would bring these [groups] or journalists into the Indian Treaty Room in the old Executive Office." Lilac quickly added, "We fairly regularly briefed the White House press corps, and I also briefed the senior staff such as Mike Deaver, Ed Meese, and so on. But the schedulers kept track of all these things; primarily they were there to keep track of who needed what in Congress."[40]

In his memoirs, Reagan called the AWACS debate "one of the toughest battles of my eight years in Washington. . . . With the exception of two or three votes on our tax and spending cut legislation, I spent more time in one-on-one meetings and on the telephone attempting to win on this measure than on any other."[41] Against a backdrop of this massively undeclared arms and infrastructure sale to the Saudi kingdom, with the attendant impact on his foreign policy and U.S. military capability in the Middle East, it is understandable that the president should show such personal resolve. James Baker said later, "The president would have done almost anything to avoid defeat on this one. He would have made himself available twenty-four hours a day if necessary. He felt that he absolutely had to win."[42] Outlining the extent of his personal involvement in lobbying the Senate, the president ascribed the acrimonious and hostile nature of the AWACS debate to the forceful and strident conflict organized by the pro-Israeli lobby. The fact that Reagan felt the need to orchestrate such a powerful bipartisan lobby for the AWACS sale, weeks ahead of the Senate vote, demonstrates the intensity of the AIPAC-led opposition and his perception of the threat to his iteration of U.S. foreign policy.

The truth was that over the years, AIPAC had developed from the embryonic pro-Israel public affairs forum of the 1950s with just a few thousand members into a large, highly influential and often threatening lobby to which dozens of senators and congressmen turned for direction. President Reagan recognized the reality of the threat posed by this highly effective lobby group, and he knew that plenty of senators and House members regarded AIPAC's political influence as nothing short of awesome. On the whole, AIPAC had "gathered strength and gained muscle by adapting to the new Washington politics: the spread of power in Congress, the potency of grass-roots lobbying, the need to be bipartisan, and the importance of throwing financial support to friends and against enemies and then advertising the results." In short, AIPAC was intimate with the new rules of the lobbying game and played to win.[43]

In this test of strength with the Israeli lobby, the determined president enlisted the support of former Presidents Nixon, Ford, and Carter, who publicly endorsed the sale.[44] Also vital to Reagan's strategy was the clear-cut support for the AWACS sale within the foreign and national security policy community, in particular former secretaries of state and defense, White House national security advisers and chairmen of the Joint Chiefs of Staff. The support of these former leaders succeeded in constructing a credible case that ultimately persuaded the Senate that the AWACS sale was crucial to U.S. national security interests, thereby making it politically impossible for the Senate to impede the deal.

Even Henry Kissinger, who had originally opposed the sale, ultimately stood with the phalanx of other former foreign policy leaders and statesmen in backing the sale. Speaking at a televised meeting, he said, "Mr. President, I'm aware of the intense debate that is going on over this issue and I can sympathize with many of the concerns that have been expressed. It is my strong conviction, however, that these concerns cannot be met by rejecting the sale of AWACS. I believe the sale is in the national interests of the United States; it is compatible with the security of Israel; it is essential for the peace process in the Middle East and it is important for the president's ability to conduct an effective and credible foreign policy. I would urge those who have legitimate concerns to meet them in conversation with the administration and to vote for the AWACS package without attaching conditions that are incompatible with the dignity of Saudi Arabia and with the effective conduct of our foreign policy."[45]

Reagan resorted to browbeating fellow Republicans, including Senator Bob Packwood, the man who introduced the Packwood Resolution, the legislative vehicle opposed to the AWACS sale. They met on September 11, 1981, in an exchange that was testy at best. Packwood headed up a campaign committee that raised funds for GOP Senate candidates, and he stressed that Jewish benefactors were unhappy with the AWACS plan. Recognizing that there was no hope of converting Packwood, the president neatly outflanked him by having the White House leak its own account of the meeting, thereby embarrassing Packwood. The leak focused on the debate on Dutton's clever characterization of the "Reagan versus Begin" theme, and thus the intrinsic merits of the arms proposal itself were no longer the issue, nor indeed was the tactical ground chosen by the president for the battle ahead.[46]

The pro-Israeli coalition in the Senate held a narrow majority of 54–46. One by one, against the Reagan/Saudi onslaught, senators were stolen away. Nonetheless, when President Reagan sent formal notice to Congress on October 1, Baker warned the president that the outlook was bad.

In a prepared statement read at the October 1 press conference, the president made it very clear that opponents of the AWACS sale served Tel Aviv, not Washington. AIPAC could no longer rely on its oft-quoted defense, "We are acting as patriotic Americans in the best interests of our nation." They now were being depicted by the president as an agent of Israel.

On October 4, White House representatives met with Senator John

Warner and Senator Sam Nunn to draft a resolution intended to reassure Congress that AWACS would be used only for defensive purposes and with a degree of American supervision. Warner and Nunn were chairman and ranking minority member, respectively, of the U.S. Senate Committee on Armed Services. For its part, the White House also wrote a presidential letter detailing conditions the Saudis would have to meet in order for the sale to go through. This document was shown to wavering senators and amended several times to meet some of their individual requests. One by one, opponents began to announce conversion to Reagan's side.

On October 6, 1981, Egyptian President Anwar Sadat was assassinated. In a grisly precursor of latter-day events, a mindless act of terrorism by anti-modern Muslim extremists threatened to shatter the hard-won moderate Arab progress with the West. Utah Senator Orrin Hatch used the murder of President Sadat to champion the need to help strengthen moderate Arab states. On October 7, President Reagan held a closed-door meeting with forty-three Republican senators, many of whom had already signed a resolution against the sale. Both in that session and in one-on-one meetings with Republicans, the president stressed the need for party loyalty and for credibility of the U.S. presidency in the conduct of foreign affairs. "Vote against me," he said privately on several occasions, "and you will cut me off at the knees."[47]

One of the most intense, protracted, and bitter political debates since the Vietnam War almost foundered on the pages of the *Washington Post*. Just days before the AWACS vote, an eleventh-hour unraveling of the White House strategy was avoided only by the timely intervention of Gen. Secord.

Though unknown to all but a few, the AWACS package was not limited to five military aircraft. It also established a network of advanced forward operating bases, airfields, military storage facilities, depots, naval installations, and elaborate command and control facilities inside the kingdom, and created a massive infrastructure in the Middle East, far beyond the immediate needs of the Saudi armed forces.

Just before Congress was to vote on the package, the Pentagon told *Washington Post* reporter Scott Armstrong that the AWACS planes cost about $110 million each. This puzzled Armstrong because when he did the math, he could see that five times $110 million must be $550 million—not the estimated $8.5 billion being talked about in Congress for the proposed Saudi purchase. He therefore began to suspect that the AWACS sale was about far more than just five airplanes and that what had been announced as a small arms deal was in fact the start of something much bigger. In a PBS *Frontline* documentary, Armstrong said the AWACS deal was to be "the linchpin to an elaborate electronic communications system that would be the equivalent of the heart of what we have in NATO. . . . It was creating a new theater of war."[48]

Realizing the scale of the proposed Saudi contract, Armstrong prepared an explosive *Washington Post* article claiming that the AWACS sale was just the start of a covert $50 billion plan to build U.S. proxy military bases in Saudi Arabia. But the White House got wind of the story. On Friday, October 23, only five days before the vote, Pentagon officials called the *Post*. As Gen. Secord recalled, they said to the editor, "You know, this guy's preparing this cockamamie story. You've got to give us a break on this. This is crazy."[49]

And the *Post* backed off, even though the story was accurate, only to run it four days after the vote.

The endless around-the-clock lobbying by the White House had begun to make inroads. Several senators announced that they were supporting the president after receiving "top secret" assurances regarding Israel's security. Closed-door "horse trading" was essential to the White House campaign. Senator Slade Gorton received a White House promise to support an appropriation to renovate a public health hospital in Seattle. Senator Charles Grassley found that his request for the appointment of his candidate for U.S. attorney in Iowa was being expedited. Montana's Senator John Melcher was enticed by support for a coal conversion facility near Butte.

The pressure on senators was immense. At the last moment, ostensibly because of pressure from farm manufacturing equipment companies, farm co-ops, and defense contractors, Senator Roger Jepsen (R-IA), who had been a staunch leader in the anti-AWACS coalition, switched his vote in favor of President Reagan. His defection was a hard loss, for Jepsen had been in the core of original anti-AWACS force. Racked by conflicting pressures, Jepsen literally broke down crying as he told other Republicans that "highly classified" White House information and his desire not to hurt Reagan's prestige had switched his vote. That broke loose others.[50]

On October 28, hours before the Senate vote, Reagan and his team pulled off a final masterstroke: at the last minute, the details of the inflexible, rigorous precautions imposed by the administration governing the use of the Saudi AWACS were revealed publicly. A letter was crafted to each senator offering Reagan's assurances that the aircraft would be used only by American and Saudi personnel—not by other Arabs; AWACS intelligence could not be shared with any other nation unless Washington approved, and, finally, AWACS would be protected against falling into hostile hands. "For wavering senators," said James Baker, "the letter gave them a legitimate out; an excuse to go along with the deal."[51]

The safeguards forced on the Saudis were so tough that few senators could employ the argument of misuse with any degree of credibility. Reagan had effectively destroyed the single most potent, influential, and compelling case that challengers of the AWACS sale had made against the deal: that it created a threat to the security of Israel. Without that, Reagan's opponents in the Senate were deprived of their central claim, the pivotal element of the case they had used against the agreement from the very outset of the debate. By making the details of those safeguards public only hours before the vote—depriving opponents of the sale time for rebuttal—Reagan won the final votes he needed to guarantee that a majority in the Senate would reject the Packwood Resolution.

As late as October 23, the *New York Times* had counted fifty senators opposed to the sale and only forty in favor, with the rest undecided. In the forty-eight hours before the decision, however, all the movement was toward the White House position. The day before the Senate vote, following the dramatic reversal by Roger Jepsen, eight other senators announced they would support the sale. At 5:03 P.M., on October 28, 1981, the Senate roll call began for the AWACS deal; minutes later it was over. After news of the successful vote in the Senate filtered through to the White House, it was reported that Reagan's instantaneous response when he heard the news in private was to exclaim, "Thank God!" In a later joke about his relief about the painful AWACS battle, President Reagan would say that the battle was "like shitting a pineapple."[52] In an outcome scarcely conceivable even a few weeks previously, the Senate rejected the anti-AWACS Packwood Resolution by a vote of 52–48.

The president had prevailed.*

On November 1, the *Washington Post* ran Armstrong's article outlining the details that had been hidden in the bill's language, which had never

---

*The United States conducts government-to-government transfers through the Defense Department's Foreign Military Sales (FMS) program. In an attempt to strengthen its powers against the "imperial presidency," in 1974, Congress gave itself the authority to review any proposed arms sale valued at more than $25 million. Under the terms of the 1976 Arms Export Control Act, originally enacted as part of the 1974 foreign aid bill, an arms sale proposal may be blocked by Congress if both houses pass a concurrent resolution of disapproval within thirty days of being formally notified of the sale by the executive branch. Although the House of Representatives rejected the AWACS sale, the vote of disapproval was rejected by the Senate, and hence the president could proceed with the sale.

been addressed in the congressional debate: that in return for an integrated package of highly sophisticated military technology, Saudi Arabia would build a massive network of naval and air defense facilities that could sustain U.S. forces should they ever be needed to protect the region against an aggressor.[53] Congress had been massively deceived by the White House.

The true extent of what document 81-96 allowed the Saudis to buy never underwent thorough public scrutiny. Indeed, senators and congressmen might have been advised to focus on paragraph three of the single-page addendum, for, in addition to the five aircraft, the Saudis were also getting approval for the future "design, construction, and supply of required AWACS-related ground-based command, control, and communications (C3) facilities and equipment, including an appropriate number of ground radar systems."[54] That package—of which much less than $10 billion was visible—would amount to an estimated $85 billion. This was the real AWACS bill.

Packwood would later say that the vote was "the battleship against the destroyers and we were outgunned."[55] In reality, though, the vote was never as close as it seemed. A surprise comment by Ambassador Richard Murphy revealed the extent of the power AIPAC had wielded on the Hill right up until the final votes were cast. Murphy said, "It was a terribly close vote in the Senate; it didn't have to be as close as it was." Certain senators, it seemed, had agreed to vote against the Packwood Resolution[56] and with President Reagan, but only if their votes were absolutely necessary. The reality, confirmed by U.S. Deputy Secretary of State Richard Armitage, was that there were several senators who had agreed to switch their allegiance to favor the president at the final vote if it were absolutely necessary. If not necessary, however, they would support the pro-Israeli Packwood Resolution.[57]

Col. Lilac concurred, saying, "That is my understanding of it also. I think there were at least two senators, but I don't know their names."[58] Fred Dutton also affirmed the situation, saying, "Yes, that's absolutely correct;

The chairman of Boeing presents Bandar with a solid silver model of AWACS and a KC-135 tanker refueling aircraft as Bandar takes delivery of the first Saudi AWACS aircraft.

we had about four more votes that were covert—they were an insurance pol-icy."[59] He concluded that those senators had feared the power of the Jewish lobby in their home states and, in the certain knowledge that the president already had the deal in the bag, voted against their conscience and in favor of the resolution.

AIPAC's Director, Tom Dine, described the AWACS debate as a ten-month marathon lasting from December 1980 until October 28, 1981. AIPAC's strategy, based on the provisions of the Arms Export Control Act, through which Congress either approved or rejected all proposed arms transfers, suc-ceeded in obstructing the AWACS sale at every stage in the legislative pro-cess except the last: the final vote in the Senate.[60]

Learning from these defeats on the F-15 and AWACS sales to Saudi Ara-bia, a resurgent AIPAC would soon regroup and reassert its supremacy. In an interview with Fred Dutton about the influence of AIPAC, he recalled, "The AIPAC defeats, first with the F-15 deal and then the AWACS deal, given that they had never been defeated before, caused a fundamental reor-ganization which left AIPAC much stronger. They started rebuilding at ground level; they have a much more effective operation."[61]

AIPAC unquestionably rose like the mythical phoenix in the wake of AWACS. That AIPAC fought the AWACS sale bitterly is an understatement. Its loss suggested to many that the political balance on Arab-Israeli issues had tipped. However, as Fred Dutton stressed, that was far from being the end of the story. Over the next four years, AIPAC transformed itself, en-hancing its power immensely. The AWACS vote shocked AIPAC into devis-ing a new political strategy, turning it, ultimately, into a superlobby. In just nine years, its budget shot up eight times and its membership exploded from nine thousand in 1978 to fifty-five thousand in 1987.[62]

By early 1988, AIPAC had again become a bastion of power within Washington. Former CIA analyst Kathleen Christison wrote that the Rea-gan years witnessed a distinct change in the lobby's influence on policy mak-ing and shrewdly said, "If in past administrations it [AIPAC] was thought to have a major limiting impact on policy formulation, the magnitude of its influence today is so great that it can no longer be considered merely a con-straint on policy,"[63] adding, "under Reagan, AIPAC had become a partner in policy making. The Reagan administration has elevated AIPAC to the level of a player in this game."[64]

Reflecting AIPAC's new power, the *New York Times* detailed the scale of the American largesse toward Israel, when it reported that though Israel anticipated receiving more than $2.6 billion in economic and military assistance in the fiscal year beginning October 1, 1983, the Senate Appropriations Committee, under pressure from the Israeli lobby, voted to allocate Israel significantly more money than the administration had asked for. The administration had asked for $1.7 billion in military credits, of which $500 million would not have to be repaid, and $800 million in economic grants (i.e., nonrepayable gifts). However, the committee voted instead to increase the credits that did not have to be repaid to $850 million and added $125 million to the $800 million in economic assistance.[65] The article stressed that Israel was the largest recipient of U.S. aid in both military and economic categories, receiving more than 20 percent of all assistance the United States gave to nations overseas.

The extent of Israeli support from the United States continued to accelerate. In 1992, the *Washington Post* would document that since the 1979 Egyptian-Israeli peace treaty was concluded, Israel had received a total of $40.1 billion, equal to 21.5 percent of all U.S. aid.[66] By 1995, this figure would rise to $60 billion.[67] By any standards, Israel is a costly ally, for these massive figures did not include a variety of special arrangements routinely granted to Israel, including large transfers of surplus military equipment, subsidies for Israel's foreign aid program, early lump-sum payments of aid, and refinancing of its debt.

Though the Senate had approved the AWACS sale, there remained still the need to get the contract signed. The administration understandably wanted this concluded as quickly as possible so as to avoid any further obstacles to the deal. Too much blood had been spilled on Capitol Hill, and too many senators were still sensitive to the unremitting pressure that had been applied personally by both Reagan and AIPAC. With press speculation that there wasn't a deal until the Saudis signed, the White House wanted the topic closed off as quickly as possible.

The key sale document was the Letter of Offer and Acceptance (LOA), and Col. Lilac had the task of getting this finalized. This document detailed the crucial contract constraints agreed to over the preceding months. These restrictions had been vital in swinging the final vote in the Senate. However, now all that remained "was for the Saudis to accept the deal with Prince Sultan's signature."

Lilac suddenly became "point man." As he wryly recalled, "This was about November 14. I got on an airplane and went to Riyadh." Almost inevitably, he met resistance to the caveats. In the face of severe Saudi pressure, he had to stand his ground. When pressed by Prince Fahd bin Abdullah (Director of Operations, RSAF), Lilac pushed back, saying, "Fahd, you can't change it—you cannot change an 'i' or uncross a 't' or put another comma—this is it!"

The whole deal was predicated on the restrictions, and Lilac recalled how he thought to himself, "This is going to be wonderful—Reagan has set his foreign policy on this and the Saudis aren't going to sign the contract!"

Instructed to have the contract signed by Defense Minister Prince Sultan and on Caspar Weinberger's desk by 9 A.M. on Friday morning, so that he could announce to the press that the deal had been closed, Lilac was in a bind. Prince Sultan was not in Riyadh, but in Dhahran with Bandar who was in the hospital with a recurrence of his back problems. Lilac said, "On Thursday we flew to Dhahran, but by the time we got to the hospital, it was ten o'clock in the evening. My scheduled commercial flight to New York, connecting to Washington, was due to leave at midnight. So I'm booked on this flight and I'm sitting [in the hospital] sweating because I still didn't have Prince Sultan's signature."

At the hospital, Bandar was indeed flat on his back, but his face broke into a broad grin as Lilac and Prince Fahd entered. Sitting in the corner of the room was Prince Sultan. Bandar said to him, "This is the guy who made this [the AWACS deal] all possible."

Yet in the ensuing polite conversation there was no mention of the contract. Lilac was beginning to despair. "It is now a quarter before midnight," he recounted, "and I thought to myself, 'That's it—I've failed; my aircraft will be gone in a few minutes. I'm done.'" He explained his dilemma to Bandar and Prince Sultan, who then left the room. At five minutes after midnight, Sultan returned, took the contract from Lilac, signed it with a flourish, and said, "Have a nice trip."

And so it was done. But Lilac nevertheless feared that he had failed.

"That's great," he said to Prince Fahd, "except I failed my mission. Weinberger is going to kill me."

Fahd replied, "What do you mean kill you? Let's go."

When he arrived at the airport, Lilac found that the Pan Am 747 was still there waiting, his U.S. Air Force "back of the aircraft" ticket torn up.

"Now I'm sitting in first class," Lilac laughed, "and all these people are muttering because we took off forty-five minutes late. I arrived in New York, made my connection, and was in Weinberger's office at nine o'clock to give him the signed LOA."[68]

The deal was done.

A world away from Saudi Arabia and extracted from the dash and discipline of his days as a fighter pilot, Bandar had been immersed in a brutal conflict between the Israeli and Arab lobbies. To his own amazement, he found that he excelled. He took great pride in his record of success over AIPAC, which heralded a new career for this able young Air Force pilot.

Prominently displayed for years among his other personal memorabilia downstairs at his McLean home was the headline taken from the front page of the *New York Daily News* of October 1, 1981. It read:

RON TO ISRAEL: BUTT OUT
Rips Jewish Anti-AWACS Lobby

His success in that protracted engagement was rewarded by an appointment to military attaché in Washington, D.C., in 1982. "I was suddenly transferred," he says, "into a different world."

In this new assignment he would work on various U.S.-Saudi military programs that he had experienced firsthand as a fighter pilot. As military attaché, he was all too aware that when the Saudis bought the F-15s, the caveats in the original LOA limited their operational capability. After all, he had had to clear them with Riyadh. However, Bandar and the Saudis adopted a pragmatic stance, saying, "We understand that they are screwing us, but let's do it anyway because we'll get a foot in the door."[69] In truth, each one of the programs had limitations, but the Saudis were astutely playing the long game.

Recognizing that his flying career had been curtailed through injury must have simplified the prince's decision to enter the political arena. He has been heard to observe philosophically, "It was easy for me to disengage," and reflecting on his love of flying, "I left it hungry—it was the right time to go." Bandar had managed to exit while still on top, and this allowed him to derive great satisfaction from his days as a fighter pilot. Talking about this dramatic period of change in his life, he said, "Suddenly I was in a different league and I looked in the mirror and I thought: I haven't changed. I am the same person; my environment has changed. The question became, am I capable of surviving in this new environment or not?"

As it turned out, he was more than capable of meeting the challenge of a new career. Bandar had a gift—not just for staying afloat in the turbulent waters of Washington, but for adapting to a new and changing political landscape. The timing of Bandar's arrival in Washington was propitious. He was lucky; not only did it coincide with the wider spread of power within the capital, but after the inauguration of President Reagan, a change in presidential approach was soon under way. Hedrick Smith captured this change when he wrote, "The urge of modern presidents is to engage in personal diplomacy—summit meetings, personal visits, and a flow of private correspondence with kings and prime ministers everywhere."[70] This new personal style of presidency was well suited to Bandar, who was well versed in the Saudi approach to ruling, very much a family affair where leisure and socializing go hand in hand with decisions on policy.[71] As his career in Washington and on the world stage progressed, the false projection of himself as frivolous socialite did much to disguise Bandar's true alter-ego—a Machiavellian prince.

Bandar's first appearances in the media began shortly after he emerged in the U.S. capital in the early 1980s, a supremely confident, cocky, young ex-fighter pilot, a thirty-year-old member of the Saudi royal family. However, this image was at juxtaposition to the real, unsure, and often insecure prince, who has himself been heard to admit of this time in his life, "As I succeeded with each task that I was assigned, I always asked myself the question, 'How long is this stroke of luck going to last?'" Despite his built-in insecurity, Bandar had his own philosophy and this helped him prepare himself for his next responsibility. He confided, "All I've wanted to be all my life is the best in what I am doing and not worry about the future. The future will come. There is no point in getting an opportunity only for people to find that you are lousy at it. As a lieutenant, I wanted to be the best lieutenant in the Air Force. When a job came for a captain and they wanted to select who was going to be the best lieutenant to be a captain, guess what? I was there, ready."

Bandar continued stoically, "You prepare yourself in advance to expect the unexpected or to be agile so you can quickly pull hard or pull many Gs, cut the power, and duck, turn around, and go the other way. You have to have that agility built in and then you have to look for the son-of-a-bitch who's better than you. You know, my instructor pilot, a fighter instructor pilot, told me you have to believe that you are the best fighter pilot in the world. Once you believe that, you then have to spend the rest of your life looking for that one 'son-of-a-bitch' who's better than you, who's just about to kill you, in order to stay alive."

That Bandar was accepted by Washington society following his appointment as military attaché was unequivocal. "As doyen of the diplomatic corps in Washington," noted the *Financial Times*, "the Saudi prince melted into the capital's political establishment with great ease, accumulating influential friends and entertaining celebrities."[72] Secretary Baker eloquently explained the prince's foundations for success in Washington when he wrote, "As King Fahd's nephew, Bandar had extraordinary influence with his uncle. He'd been educated in the States, had an idiomatic command of the English language, and understood the American psyche very well. Bandar exuded an aura of charming roguishness, but he possessed a first-rate intellect and was the most progressive of the king's closest advisers."[73] It was hardly surprising, as Americans could relate to this cigar-smoking, eloquent, and entertaining diplomat. Bandar spoke their language and then some—what other foreign diplomat could manage to weave "Monday morning quarterbacking" into a conversation with a natural ease? As David Plotz so succinctly expressed it, "He won over Americans with his irrepressible zing. He smokes cigars! He roots for the Dallas Cowboys! He speaks English like an American!"[74]

Downplaying his success, Bandar has said, "Like everything in my life, I'd rather be lucky than smart. I don't seek out things; I just find myself in the middle of things and I go from there. And because of that, throughout my life, I just continuously make myself ready for whatever it is that's not on the horizon now, whether it's knowledge, information, or contacts. Once my fate and my luck couple together, I hit the ground running, instead of starting from zero every time."[75] It is this admission that he deliberately primes himself for whatever is ahead that makes a truism of Colin Powell's perspicacious observation, "Luck tends to come to people that are well prepared."[76]

FOUR

THE YEARS
OF INTRIGUE

"Success is not final, failure is not fatal: it is the courage to
continue that counts."

WINSTON CHURCHILL (1874–1965)

In the early 1970s, the arrival in Lebanon of Yasser Arafat and thousands of
armed Palestine Liberation Organization (PLO) militants aggravated the increasingly strained relations between Lebanon's Christian and Muslim communities. The ruling Maronite Christians feared that PLO raids across the
Israeli border would provoke retaliation. Such fears were not unwarranted.

On April 13, 1975, gunmen killed four members of the Maronite party
militia, known as Phalangists, during an assassination attempt on Pierre
Gemayel, the president of Lebanon and leader of the Phalange party. Believing the assassins to have been Palestinian, the Phalangists retaliated, attacking a bus carrying Palestinian passengers, killing twenty-six of the
occupants. Immediately, fighting erupted in earnest, with Christians on one
side, and a PLO-led Muslim militia alliance on the other.

In June 1976, at the request of the Maronite Christian government, and
with Israeli and U.S. approval, Syrian President Hafez al-Assad sent forty
thousand troops into the Lebanon to contain the fighting. Four months
later, in October 1976, a League of Arab States (Arab League) summit conference was convened in Riyadh, Saudi Arabia, to resolve the Lebanese cri-

sis. The resulting multilateral agreement mandated a ceasefire and authorized the creation of the Arab Deterrent Force (ADF) to impose and super-
vise the ceasefire. In theory, the ADF—funded by the Arab League—was to
be a pan-Arab peacekeeping force under the supreme command of the
Lebanese president. In reality, only about five thousand Arab troops from
Saudi Arabia, the Persian Gulf states, Libya, and Sudan augmented the existing Syrian forces. The agreement effectively legitimized and subsidized
the Syrian occupation of Lebanon.

Speaking of this period and the political paradox it created, Bandar explained that the ADF achieved its goal of protecting the Christians, but in doing so produced a Lebanese Christian versus Lebanese Muslim civil war.
Unable to negotiate a resolution, the Arab forces eventually withdrew. Although the Palestinians had been militarily suppressed by the Syrians, the PLO
nonetheless continued to launch terrorist incursions into Israel from Lebanese
territory. Those attacks would soon provoke an Israeli military response.

On June 6, 1982, Israel invaded Lebanon, seeking to destroy the rem-
nants of the weakened PLO in Beirut. Israel's Defense Minister Ariel
Sharon led a massive force comprising eleven tank divisions and eleven infantry brigades supported by six hundred aircraft in an incursion called Operation Peace for the Galilee. The Israelis quickly brushed aside the Syrian
occupying forces and drove all the way to Beirut, surrounding an estimated
twelve to fourteen thousand PLO fighters and the Lebanese civilian population, and placing the city under siege. Israel justified its breach of the shaky
ceasefire that had been in place since July 24, 1981, citing the attempted assassination of the Israeli ambassador in London, continuing PLO cross-
border attacks on the Galilee settlements, and a buildup of PLO armaments
and troops in South Lebanon.

By June 15, Israeli forces were entrenched outside Beirut. Recognizing
that Israel's invasion of Lebanon was a bid to wipe out the PLO, Yasser
Arafat, with the support of Saudi Arabia, began to attempt a disengagement
and effect a retreat for his PLO fighters.

At the time, Bandar was still settling into his new role as military attaché
in Washington, D.C., unaware that he would be drawn into this conflict in
the role of mediator. Only days earlier, on June 13, 1982, following the
death of King Khalid, Bandar's mentor Crown Prince Fahd had ascended to
the throne. In one of his first decisions as king, Fahd instructed Bandar to
meet with Secretary of State Alexander Haig to broker a solution that
would permit PLO withdrawal from Lebanon.

Bandar knew Haig well—he had worked with him on the AWACS deal. Bandar had also been to Haig's house, and vice versa; they were on first-name terms. So when he went to meet with Haig to discuss the Lebanon issue, he expected a friendly welcome. Accompanied by Nicolas Veliotis, assistant secretary of state for Middle Eastern affairs, Bandar was escorted into Secretary Haig's office. Unlike other secretaries of state, Haig was seated behind a desk located at the end of a long, imposing anteroom in front of the smaller office where the secretary of state would normally have worked. Bandar said, "Secretary Haig's decision to have his desk at the end of the anteroom was a legacy of his four-star ego from his days as Supreme Allied Commander Europe."

Instead of the warm welcome that Bandar was expecting, Haig "started wagging his finger at me, saying, 'Prince Bandar, you must get the PLO out immediately before Sharon eats them alive. The only reason the PLO has not been totally destroyed is because we have been holding Sharon off. I can't hold him any longer.' By then he was shouting at me."

As he reached Haig's desk, Bandar thrust out his hand and said, "General Haig, in my country we say hello first." Haig immediately apologized, and walked around his desk to shake Bandar's hand. Together, the three of them, Bandar, Haig, and Nick Veliotis, who was taking notes during the meeting, sat down. Haig continued to rant about how Sharon would destroy the PLO. He had them surrounded, he said, and they had nowhere to go.

"Look," Bandar said, outlining the Saudi position, "King Fahd wants to solve this problem, but it is essential that four conditions must be fulfilled:

Alexander Haig

the PLO must leave with all the weapons that they can carry with them, basically side arms and light weapons; they must leave their heavy weapons to their allies in Lebanon; they must have naval military escorts for their ships until they reach their destinations—Egypt, Yemen, and Tunisia; and, lastly, they must keep political offices open in Beirut."

Sharon was insisting that the PLO leave Lebanon without anything, including all weapons, for a third country and close all its offices in the Lebanese capital. Haig immediately erupted, saying, "That's absolutely unacceptable! Sharon will never accept this and Begin would never accept this. I'm telling you, they are going to be destroyed."

Bandar explained that these were his instructions, and that was the only way that Saudi Arabia was going to help, and he directed Haig to pass this message to the Israelis, to see what their reaction would be.

Haig interrupted, "I know what the reaction will be. I can assure you that if that is the bottom line, the PLO will be destroyed by tomorrow, by Sharon."

"Well, you are not Sharon," Bandar countered. "Pass the message to the Israelis and let's see their reaction, Mr. Secretary. If Sharon could have overwhelmed and destroyed the PLO in Beirut, he would not be waiting for permission from you or anybody else. The reason he hasn't is because he can't. It's a death trap, a city of a million people, many of whom are armed. It would be a massacre and it would be at a huge cost to the Israelis. So please don't stop Sharon, tell him to go in. If he doesn't accept our conditions for intervening and solving the problem, then let him go in."

Secretary Haig replied, "Is that your view or is it your boss's view?"

An angry Bandar retorted, "Who do you think I speak for? I'm not here freelancing, speaking for myself."

Haig asked Bandar to return to Saudi Arabia to discuss their meeting with King Fahd. Bandar refused, explaining that he had already set out the Saudi position. He concluded testily, "If you doubt my word, you have an ambassador in Riyadh—tell him to go and meet with my boss."

By now the meeting had become very tense, and Nick Veliotis got up slowly and made to leave.

"Sit down, Nick," Bandar said. "I want a witness."

There was a long pause, as each man waited for the other to move. Finally, Haig asked, "This is the bottom line?"

"This is it," said Bandar.

"All right," Haig answered, "give me a few minutes."

Retreating into the office behind his desk, Haig got on the phone. When he returned he said simply, "We have a deal."

History records that to prevent civilian casualties, Israel agreed to a ceasefire so as to enable an American diplomat, Ambassador Philip Habib, to mediate a peaceful PLO withdrawal from Lebanon. Bandar's role is scarcely a footnote. On August 24, 1982, U.S. Marines went ashore in Beirut as part of a multinational contingent with French and Italian units. The PLO was subsequently provided with safe passage to Tunis, in a Saudi-inspired face-saving formula, along with their side arms. The PLO evacuation was completed without significant incident and the Marines withdrew to their ships on September 10.

After seeing Arafat and his followers safely ensconced in North Africa, and over the most strenuous objections of Secretary of Defense Caspar Weinberger, the Marines were ordered to return to Lebanon and resume their efforts as peacekeepers. That decision was to presage the horrific bombing of the U.S. Marine barracks in Beirut on October 23, 1983, that killed two hundred forty-one U.S. military personnel and precipitated the withdrawal of U.S. forces from Lebanon, amounting to the death knell of the Gemayel government and ultimately of Lebanese sovereignty itself.[1] But for Bandar, his first diplomatic engagement had been successfully concluded.

Despite his nominal position as military attaché, Bandar was to work with the CIA on behalf of Saudi Arabia to undermine a growing threat of Communism in Italy in the early 1980s. Allegedly, the CIA had first intervened in Italian elections in 1948, buying votes to prevent a Communist victory. Thirty-five years later, concerned about the potential resurgence of the Italian Communist Party, PCI (Partito Comunista Italiano), the CIA entered into a partnership with the Saudi government to again thwart Communist election prospects. The PCI was one of the most potent Communist parties in western Europe and became a major force in Italian politics. At the height of its popularity in 1976, the PCI captured more than one third of the votes in the national elections.

In the run-up to the 1983 Italian elections, the Christian Democrats looked set to lose to the PCI, which was showing very strong in the polls. This occurred during the eyeball-to-eyeball confrontation between Reagan and the Soviets. It would have been a disaster if, in this face-off at this time, a major western European country went Communist. According to Bandar, Prime Minister Thatcher, President Reagan, and Crown Prince Fahd determined that they would not allow this to happen and deliberately conspired to sway the outcome of the elections of a democratic sovereign state.

Bandar's role in the affair was first revealed by Bob Woodward, who disclosed that the prince contributed $2 million to assist in a secret operation to block the PCI's democratic ascent.[2] Woodward got it only partially right. Confirming that the money provided by the Saudis was $10 million, and not the $2 million alleged by Woodward, Bandar explained, "Basically, the Americans came up with a plan and Saudi Arabia came up with the financing, which we deposited in the Vatican Bank in Italy. From there, we didn't know what happened to it, but the Christian Democrats eventually won."

Following agreement to the plan by Thatcher, Reagan, and Fahd, Bandar flew directly to Rome with a suitcase full of money. He drove into the Vatican, where, at the Vatican Bank, a priest came out to meet him and took the suitcase containing $10 million. His working contacts on this mission were CIA Director Bill Casey and William A. Wilson, Reagan's personal envoy to the Holy See who, on March 7, 1984, became America's first ambassador to the Vatican. After staying in Rome for the night, the prince returned to Washington.

Commenting on the cash he had deposited in the Vatican Bank, Bandar said, "It was done with a deniability factor, because you would never see American fingerprints—or the British—on it. The money didn't come from them. They didn't authorize it through Congress or Parliament. Everybody could say, 'I had nothing to do with that; it's nothing to do with me,' but yet that's the way things got done." Bandar concluded, "This was a classic example of how strategic cooperation took place between Reagan, Fahd, and Thatcher in many, many ways."

Bandar later affirmed that the choice of the Vatican Bank for the deposit was intentional. Convinced that the Christian Democrats could lose the election, Giulio Andreotti, one of the most powerful politicians in postwar Italy, who served as the prime minister of Italy seven times and as foreign minister between 1983 and 1989, broached his concerns to Pope John Paul II, who agreed that Andreotti should contact CIA Director Bill Casey. Hearing of the Vatican's concerns, Casey immediately alerted Ronald Reagan.

The solution that Reagan and Casey devised, and which was supported by the pope and Andreotti, was, according to Bandar, "a repeat of the 1950s when de Gaulle was going to lose the election to the Communists and President Eisenhower decided to intervene; the CIA went there and intervened in the elections. That was how de Gaulle won." Bandar suggested that the Holy See's involvement in the conspiracy was prompted not only by its fear of religious restrictions in a Communist, atheist Italy, the center of the Catholic world, but also by its belief that defeating the Soviet Union would offer the opportunity for a resurgence of Catholicism in eastern Europe. American funding of the plan, of course, would be impossible, as it would have to be cleared by Congress. So Casey proposed the Saudi option and made the approach to Bandar, who briefed Fahd and soon received his agreement to provide the necessary $10 million. Because of the Vatican involvement in the conspiracy, the cash was deposited into the Vatican Bank.

And so it was that Bandar became the bagman for the pope.

Bandar quickly gained in experience working as military attaché. He had a flair for diplomacy and negotiation, and intimate insight into the clandestine activities of the CIA. Having made his mark on Middle East affairs by facilitating the withdrawal of the PLO from Beirut, he would again be drawn into the volatile Lebanese political scene.

The civil war in Lebanon had abated, but it was still a tinderbox waiting to explode into violence once again. The armistice signed on May 17, 1983, between Israel and Lebanon fell short of a full peace treaty. At the end of August 1983, fierce fighting again broke out between the Lebanese Shiite Amal militia and the Christian militia in Beirut. The Lebanese army intervened and after four days gained control of the heart of West Beirut. Yet tensions escalated on September 4, 1983, when the Israelis pulled back from their position in the Chouf Mountains outside Beirut. Without the Israeli presence as a buffer, fighting quickly broke out between Muslim and Christian militia members.

Pope John Paul II was prepared to undermine Italian democracy in the fight against communism.

Back in Washington, in a surprise move, King Fahd decided to promote Bandar to the position of ambassador. Recalled to Riyadh to be briefed by the king and to collect his accreditation documents, Bandar was asked by Fahd to travel to Damascus to give President Assad a letter. He recalled, "I didn't know what was in the letter, but it was sensitive enough that the king wanted it to go directly to Assad—he didn't want anybody to see it." He said, "I thought I would just transit through Damascus, give the letter to the president and then travel back to America via London." Though focused on returning to Washington, Bandar duly flew to Damascus and presented Fahd's letter to Assad. He recalled that Assad read the letter and then looked up and asked, "What do you think?"

Bandar was taken aback. He did not know the contents of the letter. He stressed to Assad that his job was simply to deliver the letter.

Assad said, "I would like you to spend the night here, because I want to respond to the letter and I want you to take it to Riyadh."

Attempting to disengage, Bandar suggested that one of Assad's officials could deliver it, but Assad was insistent. The next day, Bandar took Assad's reply back to King Fahd and was promptly tasked by him to work with Rafik al-Hariri,* to help the Lebanese and the Syrians to put an end to the war. He said, "For twenty-five days I stayed in Damascus, where I met and negotiated with the leaders of the different militias."

As Saudi Arabia was the one country on good terms with all the factions involved, the kingdom was able to adopt a critical behind-the-scenes peace-keeping role in collaboration with Syria and Egypt. During the crisis, Bandar and Hariri would frequently travel to the neutral ground of Cyprus in order to meet directly with leaders of the Lebanese parties. Bandar operated from Damascus as a base, but some of the warring factions did not trust the Syrians, and Cyprus was often used as an alternative meeting place. Bandar would fly from Damascus to Cyprus and the Christian Lebanese and Phalangists would fly there or take a boat. The negotiations would take place in Bandar's Gulfstream 3 private aircraft and once complete, the Prince would fly back to Damascus. He has frequently joked that at that time he became the most expensive postman in the world.

---

*Rafik Bahaa Edine Hariri was a Lebanese self-made billionaire and business tycoon, who was twice prime minister of Lebanon from 1992 to 1998 and again from 2000 to 2004. Hariri was assassinated on February 14, 2005, in Beirut, an attack that prompted Syrian withdrawal from Lebanon, and implicated the Syrian government in the assassination, which has since been the subject of a United Nations investigation.

Working in concert with Bandar, Robert "Bud" McFarlane, then special envoy to the Mideast, developed such a close friendship with the prince that many argue it clinched McFarlane's later appointment as national security adviser during the Reagan administration. It was reported of Bandar's activity level while he was working in Lebanon that "he bombarded McFarlane with so many cables that the team nicknamed them Bandar-grams."[3]

At the time, McFarlane described the situation in the Lebanon as "very near impossible."[4] Even Bandar admitted to Fahd that "there is no solution." Fahd replied simply, "There must be one." Bandar later bemoaned the absence of a detailed brief during this early diplomatic minefield, explaining, "That was the only instruction I got!" Of his efforts in Lebanon, Bandar said, "I soon got an agreement between all the parties that they should stop killing each other and should start talking. The tragedy was that it took three weeks more to get them to translate that into an acceptable format."[5] And then it all fell apart.

In an analysis of the respective positions of the key players at the time, Bandar said, "The Syrians wanted to look as though they were neutral, that Saudi Arabia and Syria were negotiating as neutrals. Of course, the Syrians were not neutral, but we were willing to play the game. They were supposed to deliver their allies, and the Americans were involved with Bud McFarlane going back and forth. They were supposed to bring to the table the voice of the Christians and the Israelis."

In Damascus, Bandar would meet with leaders who were friendly with Syria. Every now and then, however, he needed to meet with someone who refused to travel to either Syria or Cyprus. Because Fahd and Assad would not permit Bandar to go into Lebanon, Hariri would travel to Beirut with protection from the Syrians. After about fifteen days of negotiating, Bandar thought they finally had reached a solution.

He explained, "An important point here is the May 17 agreement, which was a U.S.-backed attempt to create peace between Lebanon and Israel agreed to ear-

Rafik al-Hariri, the Lebanese philanthropist who later became Prime Minister.

lier that year."* It had met strong opposition from Lebanese Muslims and the Arab world, where it was seen as an illegal agreement imposed while the country was under military occupation, essentially a compulsory surrender. Bandar stressed that the Americans had wanted to force the May 17 agreement through, but had been unsuccessful. Although the agreement was signed, it was never ratified due to strong Syrian opposition to the treaty. Bandar and Hariri proposed that if Saudi Arabia was to nullify the May 17 agreement, then the Syrians would first have to direct their Lebanese allies to agree to and sign a deal that would protect the Christians and the presidency. As Saudi Arabia was the host of the holy Muslim places, Fahd did not want it to be perceived that the kingdom was supporting the Muslims against the Christians. Bandar emphasized that the Saudi role was to support all the Lebanese people and to encourage peace and reconciliation. He admitted that an underlying influence had been the close friendship between Lebanese Christian political leaders and the leaders of Saudi Arabia ever since the creation of Lebanon as an independent state in 1943. Nevertheless, Bandar insisted, Saudi policy truly was neutral and in the interests of all Lebanese. "We wanted peace for everybody," he stated unequivocally, "we wanted to preserve their dignity and their rights."

In order to make headway in constructing a peace deal, Bandar recognized that it would, paradoxically, be necessary to upset his American allies. He explained, "I recommended to my boss that we should be willing to make America mad by defeating an agreement that they had mediated." The May 17 American agreement, Bandar believed, was fundamentally flawed because of Israeli participation. He was convinced that his proposed solution would provide a better peace that protected the Christians and the presidency while not destroying the whole Lebanese system. He described how the Syrians were shocked when they learned of the Saudi position, opposing the American-backed treaty. This stance added to Bandar's credibility and was to be reinforced by his statement, "We are America's friends; we are not America's puppets. We have interests and they have interests, but in

---

*Following Operation Peace for the Galilee, Israeli and Lebanese negotiators met to discuss a treaty between the two countries. The delegations held over thirty-five sessions alternatively in Khalde, Kiryat Shemona, and Netanya starting on December 28, 1982. The agreement was finally signed on May 17, 1983, following high-level U.S. involvement, including ten days of shuttle diplomacy by Secretary of State Shultz. The main features of the agreement include ending the state of war between Israel and Lebanon, and the development of a mechanism for cooperation and the establishment of an Israeli consulate in Beirut.

this case, we think that the Americans should be happy that we are protecting the people whom they are supporting."

Bandar recalled that after he got all the parties to agree to his proposal, he received a message that the president of Lebanon was unhappy. An aggrieved Gemayel was embarrassed that Bandar had met with all the factions except him. While he agreed with Bandar's solution, Gemayel was suffering severe loss of face. Bandar often has stressed the need in any difficult political situation, especially in matters of Mideast diplomacy, for all sides to be able to save face. The importance of this factor is perhaps greater within the Arab culture than in the West, but is vital to any diplomatic negotiations if there is to be a fair and lasting peace. Hariri requested that the prince meet with Gemayel in Beirut in front of the rest of the Christian militias, so that Gemayel could "look like an important player." But for Bandar to travel to Beirut was dicey. Of their machinations, Bandar explained that he and Hariri got together and decided that if they asked King Fahd for permission for Bandar to go to Beirut, he would refuse. Nor would Assad approve, as fighting in Lebanon was still intense.

So Bandar made a deal with the Americans, who agreed to provide two helicopters. Together, Bandar and Hariri flew to Cyprus, where they met up with McFarlane. That night, the three men climbed into the U.S. helicopters and flew to the presidential palace in Beirut. Bandar exclaimed, "I tell you, when we approached the coast of Lebanon, it looked like the Fourth of July, complete with fireworks; it was heartbreaking to see shells exploding everywhere."

As a precaution, Bandar had left a message to be passed to the Syrians after he had gone, informing them that he was going to Beirut and that they should tell their allies to be careful not to shoot him down. But there was panic when Fahd found out; he called Assad and kept calling every half hour, saying, "Are they back? Are they back?" Meanwhile, the helicopters landed in a Ministry of Defense garden in Beirut where two APCs* were waiting for them. As they landed, Bandar said to Hariri in Arabic, "We must look dignified from the helicopter until we get to the APC; let's just walk calmly over there." However, he admitted, "As soon as the Marine helicopter landed and we got out, I saw people running like crazy because shells were going off all over the place. Hariri and I looked at each other and we both thought, 'To hell with being dignified,' so we grabbed up our Arab *thobes* and ran like hell."

---

*Armored personnel carriers.

When the trio—Bandar, Hariri, and McFarlane—got to the presidential palace, the bombing was so intense that they could not hear each other talking. Down in a bunker, they met President Gemayel and the leader of the largest Sunni faction, former Prime Minister Saeb Salam, an ally of Saudi Arabia.* Salam's presence demonstrated to Bandar that the Christians were not isolated, that they had Sunni support. The prince acknowledged, "President Amine Gemayel† agreed with me that to save Lebanon and to save the presidency, if we could have a Syrian commitment that its allies would accept a ceasefire and that there would be no more massacres, the institution of the presidency would be respected and observed, then he would be willing to drop the May 17 agreement. It was a commitment that he had already given to me, but for protocol, for prestige, for political reasons, he had to show that we got it from him directly. So we got agreement to my proposals."

An elated Bandar flew back to Damascus via Cyprus, thinking that Gemayel had showed courage, for there had been opposition to this agreement from his own supporters. Arriving in the early morning, and following a thorough dressing down from Fahd over the phone for going into Beirut without his permission, he confidently told Fahd that he expected Damascus to agree to the deal and for the ceasefire to come into effect. However, as he pragmatically observed later, "Right then, we had the agreement; everyone had agreed to the document, then suddenly it all unraveled. The Druze leaders pulled out at the last moment, then the Shiites." He concluded that the Syrians were not committed. On the surface Assad had supported the Saudi positions with the different parties, but once Bandar left, things quickly came undone.

Awareness of Syrian duplicity was to be confirmed in a meeting shortly afterwards between Bandar, Hariri, and a senior Lebanese leader of whom Bandar asked, "What's your problem? Are you enjoying the deaths of so many of your people? We have produced a fair deal for everybody." The

---

*Saeb Salim Salam, Lebanese politician and statesman (b. January 17, 1905, Beirut; d. January 21, 2000, Beirut), was a prominent Sunni Muslim and Arab nationalist who served as his nation's prime minister six times between 1952 and 1973 (once for only four days) and worked for Muslim-Christian reconciliation during and after the Lebanese civil war (1975–1976).

†President Amine Gemayel, the eighth president of the Lebanese Republic, was born in Bikfaya, Lebanon, on January 22, 1942, into a Christian Maronite family. He is the son of Sheikh Pierre Gemayel, founder of the Phalange (Kataeb) party in 1936, and the brother of Bashir, who was elected president on August 23, 1982, and assassinated three weeks later on September 14, 1982.

leader started screaming at him in an unexpected tirade, saying, "This is an unacceptable agreement; this is selling out to the Israelis and the imperialists."

But then the Lebanese leader put his finger to his lips.

Hariri passed Bandar a note saying, "He cannot speak just in case the Syrians are listening to him."

So Bandar moved out onto his balcony and beckoned the Lebanese politician to join him, where he asked, "What's the problem?"

The leader replied, "I have no problem with the deal; the Syrians won't let me [sign the agreement]."

The next day, armed with the truth of the Syrian position, Bandar told his staff to prepare his aircraft for imminent departure. As a guest of the Syrians, he had been provided with a presidential protocol car, complete with security and police escort. As he didn't want the Syrians to know that he was leaving, however, Bandar decided to use the Saudi ambassador's car instead. Nevertheless, the Syrians soon realized what was happening and advised him that the foreign minister, Mr. Khaddam* wanted to speak with him.

Bandar demurred, explaining that he needed to return home. At the airport, he was again intercepted and again gave the same response, suggesting testily that unless they were prepared to arrest him, he was leaving. He then boarded his aircraft and returned to Jeddah.

When Bandar called Fahd to tell them that he was in Jeddah, the king was surprised and chastised him for leaving without consulting him. The prince explained that he had reached the conclusion that the Syrians had decided not to close the deal, that while on the surface they could not have been more helpful—supporting the presentations that he and Hariri made to the various factions—as soon as the meetings were over, it was "back to square one—someone backed out."

Once at home, Bandar saw on Saudi TV that the Council of Ministers

---

*Abdul Halim Khaddam. As one of the only Sunni Muslims in a regime dominated almost entirely by Alawites (an esoteric offshoot Islamic sect considered heretical in much of the Arab world), Syrian Vice President and Foreign Minister Abdul Halim Khaddam exercised a great deal of influence over Syria's foreign relations within the region for two decades. Once considered a possible successor to Syrian President Hafez Assad, Khaddam was a key player in Syria's intervention in Lebanon after 1976. His role in cultivating the Syrian regime's political control within Lebanon earned him the nickname "Lebanon's High Commissioner." His relationship with former Lebanese Prime Minister Rafik Hariri was very close.

was meeting in emergency session. He immediately was concerned that something serious had happened, but never thought that it was anything to do with his mission to Damascus. Soon after, though, he received a call from the Royal Court summoning him to the Council of Ministers meeting. The whole government had been convened, and the king asked Bandar to repeat to the assembly what he had told him earlier.

At the end of the meeting, the king consulted with the crown prince and other ministers, and it was decided that Bandar should not resume his mission. The king issued a public statement that Saudi Arabia had tried to mediate in this issue, but that it didn't believe that all of the parties, including Syria, were ready for a deal. Within half an hour of that statement being released, Assad sent a message to Fahd asking that Bandar come back to Damascus that night or he would personally fly to Jeddah. The next morning Bandar returned to Syria. On his arrival, he was taken directly from the airport to meet with Assad, who was concerned as to why Bandar had left so suddenly—had he been insulted, or had anyone misbehaved or insulted him?

Bandar explained that he had come to the conclusion that the Syrian government had decided not to close the deal and even if he had stayed another twenty days, he would still have failed to secure a deal. Bandar said to Assad, "So I decided to cut the mission short and take the blame for it, instead of waiting until it became apparent that you were not willing to conclude a deal. For then there would be a conflict between you and King Fahd and I could not allow that to happen."

Assad said, "That's a smart maneuver."

"No," countered Bandar, "I was just trying to protect the relationship between you and King Fahd. I could be dismissed—they could say that I failed, that I didn't do a good job and somebody else could come, or you could decide to change your mind. But if Fahd came to the conclusion that you were not being straight with him, then that could lead to a crisis between our two countries, and I couldn't allow that."

Assad smiled and said, "All right, go and see the foreign minister. You have a deal."

"I'm not going to see anybody," Bandar replied. Instead, he insisted that Assad call his foreign minister, Halim Khaddam, and tell him that not only was Bandar coming to see him, but that he was sitting with the president listening to what he was telling him.

Bandar's blunt stance worked. Assad laughed and picked up the phone and called his foreign minister. At the end of the conversation, Assad told Bandar, "Now you can go and see him."

Recalling this episode, Bandar explained that he entered the home of the foreign minister. Declining an invitation to eat, Bandar said, "No, I want to get the document ready to sign."

Khaddam replied, "Consider it done."

When Bandar asked Khaddam why he had told him on his last visit that they couldn't get the Lebanese factions to agree, the foreign minister smiled meaningfully and said, "Yes, but that was before the boss called me."

Bandar's persistence and unorthodox diplomacy paid off; it took just three days to get the deal signed by all parties. Working closely with Hariri and McFarlane, the prince was able to announce the Lebanon ceasefire at a press conference in Damascus on September 25, 1983, alongside Syrian Foreign Minister Halim Khaddam. Thereafter, an Arab committee from Algeria, Saudi Arabia, and Kuwait started working on the Taif Agreement, which, when signed in Saudi Arabia in September 1989, established the Lebanese political protocol ending the war in Lebanon, instituted special relations between Lebanon and Syria, and created a framework for the beginning of Syrian withdrawal from Lebanon.*

Reflecting on his role as King Fahd's personal emissary for peace, Bandar said, "I think they were convinced that I wasn't going to leave [the second time] without an agreement. They couldn't get rid of me, so they reached an agreement."[6] For all Bandar's modesty, U.S. officials gave the prince considerable credit for the ceasefire. He not only had provided access to the Syrians for U.S. Special Envoy Robert McFarlane, but also helped shape the agreement that emerged. Bandar also impressed his American colleagues with his "can do" attitude, releasing more pressure from the Lebanese stalemate through Arab diplomacy than the West's variously implemented foreign policies. Engaging in intense shuttle diplomacy, Bandar and McFarlane made six trips together to Damascus. Saeb Salam, the former Lebanese prime minister who was closely involved in the ceasefire negotiations, said

---

*General Aoun, head of the Lebanese government at the time, rejected the agreement, as Syria did not commit itself either to rapid or complete withdrawal from Lebanon. Instead, Syrian forces stayed in place for a full two years, ostensibly "assisting the Lebanese government to extend its authority." Even then, Syrian forces redeployed only as far as the Beqaa valley. The agreement gave no timetable for any further Syrian withdrawal, merely stipulating that "such withdrawals would be negotiated at the appropriate time by the governments of Lebanon and Syria." However, Syrian forces remained in Lebanon until 2005.

of Bandar, "Lebanon was very difficult terrain for him to cover, but he handled it very wisely."[7]

The formal ceasefire took effect at 6 A.M., on September 26, 1983. A day later, on September 27, Bandar was officially appointed as ambassador to the United States.

Although a relative newcomer to Washington and to the world of diplomacy, the prince quickly established himself as a significant Arab diplomatic figure. Shortly after his arrival as ambassador it was reported that, "Few ambassadors here are so much at the center of events or carry so much clout."[8] Beneath the glitz and excitement of the new Reagan era and behind the polished exuberance of the new Saudi ambassador, there lay furious and determined mutual diplomatic objectives for Washington and Riyadh, centered primarily on Reagan's approach to American foreign policy. His aggressive political stance was formally pronounced in the 1985 State of the Union address and became known as the Reagan Doctrine. President Reagan stated, "We cannot play innocents abroad in a world that's not innocent; nor can we be passive when freedom is under siege. We must not break faith with those who are risking their lives—on every continent, from Afghanistan to Nicaragua—to defy Soviet-supported aggression and secure rights which have been ours from birth. . . . Support for freedom fighters is self-defense."[9]

Reagan was supported in those aspirations by CIA Director William Casey. Casey was no ordinary director. He held full cabinet status, a seat at the table of every senior foreign policy decision-making body, and had an office in the White House as well as his formal office in Langley. Bandar

joked about Bill Casey's unique position within the Reagan administration and his White House office, saying, "He would use it to impress foreign visitors, because if he said, 'Come and meet me in the White House,' they thought, 'Oh my God, this guy is really close to the president; he's got an office there.' That was part of the showmanship of Casey."

President Hafez al-Assad of Syria

The Saudis, with their mix of wealth, secrecy, and avowed anti-Communism, would become a critical component of Reagan's strategic offensive against the Soviet bloc, augmented by the vision and resolve of Casey. "Saudi Arabia was one of the most important American allies for us in the 1980s," recalled Alan Hers, who ran operations for the CIA on the Arabian Peninsula at the time. "They were seen as a linchpin and we had an unabridged relationship with them. They were critical for a whole host of important objectives."[10]

Convinced that the United States had to counter Soviet expansion wherever it occurred in the world, Casey said, "The primary battlefield . . . is not on the missile test range or at the arms control negotiating table, but in the countryside of the third world." The Soviets were pursuing a strategy of "creeping imperialism" and they had two specific targets, "the isthmus between North and South America" and "the oil fields of the Middle East, which are the lifeline of the Western alliance."[11] Like the House of Saud, Casey believed that the Soviet invasion of Afghanistan was part of a strategy that threatened those oilfields.

During his time in office, Reagan regularly cited a list of countries of concern: Afghanistan, Angola, Cambodia, Ethiopia, and Nicaragua. What few people appreciated was that Saudi Arabia was either directly or indirectly involved in four of these five campaigns, Cambodia being the exception. The Reagan administration devised a strategy that would address Saudi Arabian global concerns and channel the Saudis' surplus cash into U.S. foreign policy. In order to destabilize Ethiopia's pro-Soviet Mengistu

CIA director William Casey and Ronald Reagan—the architects of the Reagan Doctrine.

government, Saudi Arabia funneled money into its neighbor, Sudan. In support of U.S. policy, Saudi Arabia also helped Angola's rebel leader, Jonas Savimbi, by providing Morocco with money for a UNITA (National Union for the Total Independence of Angola) training camp. In an episode that would ultimately threaten the president with impeachment, Saudi Arabia transferred $32 million to the Contras in Nicaragua. Together, Washington and Riyadh poured $3 billion into Afghanistan to undermine the Soviet occupation, the desert kingdom matching the United States dollar for dollar.

Speaking of the partnership between the United States and Saudi Arabia, Bandar confided, "If you knew what we were really doing for America, you wouldn't just give us AWACS; you would give us nuclear weapons."[12]

Saudi efforts to fight the Communists were not limited to oil and petrodollar contributions for CIA covert operations. Bandar maintains, "We didn't use East-West arguments or America's anti-Communism; we used religion. We said, 'The Communists are atheists; they don't believe in religion and we are fighting them for religious reasons.' We galvanized the Muslim world behind us, which fitted perfectly into Reagan's strategy for fighting the Soviet Union in an area where they could not influence it in a way that we could." The prince restated Saudi logic when talking with Muslim countries: "To hell with America—we are fighting the Communists because they are atheists." That assertion was repeated by the U.S. ambassador to Riyadh when he said, "The United States was a desirable partner for Saudi Arabia . . . there was a common interest in opposing godless Communism. That was seen by the Saudis as the principle threat to the kingdom and to Islam and to the region."[13]

Reinforcing the Saudi pitch to the Muslim world, Bandar explained that in some of his interviews during that time, when asked if Saudi Arabia was doing it because America asked them, he would say, "No. America has a Soviet embassy, and there is an American embassy in the Soviet Union. Saudi Arabia does not have a relationship with the Soviet Union, not because of America, but because they are atheists." The prince pointed out that Saudi Arabia was the only country in the world in those days that would not allow Communist nationals to even get out of an aircraft when it landed in Saudi Arabia; they had to stay in the aircraft until they left.

While there can be no doubting the strength of the Bush-Saud association in later years, it was arguably the covert, concerted, and coordinated partnership between Reagan's administration, the CIA, and Saudi Arabia that set the scene for subsequent relationships. This liaison would lead not only to the demise of the Soviet Union and the end of the Cold War, but also would establish the United States as the preeminent military power in the world.

It would be a considerable oversimplification to suggest that the complex global struggle for power played out by Russia and the United States in the 1980s and the outcome of the Cold War was ultimately dictated by wealth. Nevertheless, the Saudi-U.S. alliance was vital to the American Cold War victory. Frequently, the Cold War was not so much a test of military might, but a contest between the dollar and the ruble, and the funding of numerous rebel forces in countries such as Afghanistan, Nicaragua, and Angola lay at the heart of the U.S. Cold War strategy. The manipulation of the global oil price was just one way in which Saudi Arabia supported Reagan and the United States during the 1980s. By lowering the price of oil, not only did the Saudis considerably boost U.S. industry, but they effectively crippled the Russian economy, which was reliant on its oil revenue and hard currency receipts. Indeed, the intention of the Reagan Doctrine was to make Soviet intervention in third-world countries too costly to sustain. Within the decade, that strategy would succeed.

One of the mainstays of Machiavellian thought hinges on the undertaking of what must be done, even when such endeavors require a certain degree of secrecy and departure from the normal rules of conduct or moral codes. It would be difficult to find a case more closely adhering to such theory than the U.S.-Saudi dealings during the Iran-Contra affair. In 1985, via a Democratic initiative known as the Boland Amendment, Congress abruptly removed financial support for the Contra rebels fighting the Sandinista regime in Nicaragua. This decision precipitated what became known as the Iran-Contra affair, a scandal that was to dramatically mar the last years of Ronald Reagan's presidency.

The Iran-Contra affair actually comprised several separate operations. First, the United States secretly sold weapons to Iran, a terrorist state—a sale prohibited by American law. Indeed, these sales violated Reagan's own highly publicized Operation Staunch, an international campaign to stop all countries from selling arms to Iran. Second, the U.S. government violated the Boland Amendment by secretly aiding the Contra rebels in their war against the leftist Sandinista government of Nicaragua. These two covert ventures became entangled because National Security Council (NSC) staff members, especially Oliver North, a Marine lieutenant colonel, managed both operations. In due course, North would eventually secretly divert profits from the Iranian arms sale to fund the Nicaraguan Contras.[14]

Although the Boland Amendment didn't come into effect until February 1985, by early 1984, fearing that they would be unable to secure congressional support for further Contra funding, the White House began to consider other options. National Security Adviser Bud McFarlane testified to the joint congressional committees investigating the Iran-Contra affair that he was considering the possibility of farming out the whole Contra support operation to another country.[15] Without the knowledge of Secretary of State George Shultz, McFarlane met with Bill Casey to discuss his own ideas for securing aid for the Contras. Casey liked his ideas and sent McFarlane a memo saying, "I am in full agreement that you should explore funding alternatives with Israel and perhaps others."[16] Israel had been the natural first choice, as it was considered to have the military expertise needed to fuse the inexperienced Contra recruits into an effective fighting force.

Disappointingly, McFarlane's approach to the Israelis for cash was rebuffed, and Shultz, when he heard of the request from the U.S. ambassador in Tel Aviv, admonished McFarlane against making such solicitations. But by May 1984, the Contras were virtually out of funds and the administration's request for another $21 million in Contra aid from Congress was rejected. Meanwhile, McFarlane had been directed by the president to "keep the Contras together body and soul," an order that he could not fully execute without serious legal compromise.[17] McFarlane transmitted Reagan's instruction to Oliver North, an NSC staff aide, who was also the administration's principal liaison with the Contra forces.[18]

As Secretary Shultz had made clear his views about McFarlane's approach to Israel for assistance, he was excluded from the new, quiet efforts under way to secure external financial support for the Contras. As North reported, "Shultz didn't know it at the time, and neither did I, but the president had already authorized McFarlane to see Prince Bandar bin Sultan, the Saudi ambassador to Washington, to ask for a contribution from his government."[19]

The legality surrounding third-party funding of the Contras was a major issue in the White House. Shultz was advised by White House Chief of Staff James Baker that such solicitations would constitute an "impeachable offense." Vice President Bush maintained the position that the only problem in seeking third-country support would be "if the United States were to promise to give these third parties something in return." The deal then could be interpreted as an "exchange." However, it appears that little or no account was taken of James Baker's dictum that the government could not do indirectly what it could not do directly.[20]

The extreme sensitivity of third-party funding prompted McFarlane to caution against making any of the discussion public, saying, "I propose that there be no authority for anyone to seek third-party support for the anti-Sandinistas (Contras) until we have the information we need, and I certainly hope none of this discussion will be made public in any way." The National Security Planning Group (NSPG), however, agreed that a legal opinion should be sought from the Justice Department.[21] The day after the NSPG meeting, Bill Casey met with Attorney General William French Smith, who determined that third-country funding of the Contras was legally permissible as long as no U.S. funds were used for the purpose, and as long as there was not an expectation on the part of the third country that the United States would repay the aid.[22] Underscoring the extreme secrecy surrounding the matter, Reagan warned against leaks, stating, "If such a story gets out, we'll all be hanging by our thumbs in front of the White House."[23]

However, even before the NSPG meeting, McFarlane had reached out to Bandar. He told the prince that it was nearly inevitable that the administration would fail to win congressional approval for additional Contra aid. McFarlane also stated that the only real threat to a Reagan victory in the fall would be trouble in Central America.[24] For Bandar, that was the clincher; Saudi Arabia wanted to see Reagan returned for a second term.

According to McFarlane in his subsequent testimony, "In May or June 1984, a 'foreign official,' later identified as Bandar, offered to donate $1 million a month in ostensibly private funds for the Contras. In early 1985, that contribution was increased to $2 million a month."[25] The prince reportedly offered this contribution as a humanitarian gesture, saying that the donation signified King Fahd's gratitude for past Reagan administration support of the Saudi government.[26] In fact, the prince's confirmation that Saudi Arabia would provide the funds that the Contras so desperately needed brought with it its own short-lived concerns as to how it should be handled. The transaction was so unprecedented that neither McFarlane nor Bandar knew how to proceed. McFarlane reportedly went back to his office; informed his deputy, John Poindexter, of the situation; and then instructed Oliver North to find out from the Contra leaders into what bank account to put the money.[27] North directed Nicaraguan Democratic Force (FDN) leader Adolfo Calero to set up an offshore bank account for the Contras into which the Saudis could deposit the funds. The secret payments of $1 million a month began arriving in an offshore Cayman Island account in June 1984, ensuring that the Contras would remain a military presence in Nicaragua regardless of any action taken by Congress.[28]

A day or two after Bandar had agreed to provide the money, McFarlane informed Reagan and Vice President Bush. Several days later, he told Shultz and Weinberger. He did not, however, tell them who had done the providing, nor did they press him for details. Later, during the Iran-Contra investigation, McFarlane would testify that he had notified the president of the first Saudi contribution in June 1984, by putting the information on a card that he slipped into the president's daily briefing book so no other officials would know of the arrangement. Reagan wrote back, "Good news!"[29] McFarlane also said that he told the president, either in writing on the card or orally that "no one else knows about this," and Reagan had responded, "Good, let's just make sure it stays that way."[30]

Throughout, McFarlane maintained that he had not solicited the money—that he had done everything but actually ask for money. But it was the interpretation of the manner in which McFarlane's approach was framed that generated controversy at the height of the Iran-Contra investigations. McFarlane couched his answers during those investigations in terms designed to protect the administration, asserting that Bandar had volunteered the money and that he had made no solicitation. Bandar, however, steadfastly maintains that McFarlane made a direct request for financial support.

Although McFarlane tried to phrase his responses during the Iran-Contra investigations in a way that inferred that no solicitation had been made, he still managed to damn the administration when he alluded to a promise of something in return. "It became pretty obvious to the [Saudi] ambassador," McFarlane testified, "that his country would gain a considerable amount of favor, and

Bud McFarlane revealed Bandar's role during the Iran-Contra hearings.

frankly, they thought it was the right thing to do; they would provide the support when the Congress cut it off."[31] McFarlane's recognition of the Saudi expectation of downstream benefits seemed clear. But did it meet the definition of an "exchange" as pointed out by George Bush? It was certainly an extraordinarily fine line.

Bandar's public position during this period was evasive. During an interview on CBS, Bandar was asked, "There have been stories about your government and you and your relationship with the Reagan administration and money coming from a personal account of the king. Saudi Arabia understood very early that if you do things for the Americans as the Israelis have, you will therefore gain the American government's support in your time of need. Is that a fair appraisal of a general principle?" His couched response was, "I think the principle that treatment of people to each other always reflects on each other is a general principle in the world. Even God said, 'You do this, I'll send you to Heaven, you do that, I'll send you to Hell.' He didn't say, 'Whatever you do, I'll send you to Hell.' In relationships—any relationship—it has to be a two-way stream."[32]

North's account of his discussion with McFarlane indicates the secrecy with which the Iran-Contra agreements were deliberately veiled and of the awareness in the White House of the illegal nature of what they were orchestrating. North recalls McFarlane saying, "If you have to write everything down, you don't belong in this business. The money should go directly from a foreign account into Calero's offshore account. It shouldn't come into this country at all. Do it with a wire transfer."

North asked, "Why does it have to be an offshore account?"

"Two reasons," McFarlane replied. "First, all Nicaraguan bank accounts in the United States have been frozen. Second, the Treasury Department monitors large transfers of funds in and out of American banks. Someone was bound to notice these transactions and start asking questions."[33]

As two very different stories about how Saudi funding of the Contras came to be, the friendship between Bandar and McFarlane chilled.

"McFarlane was a close friend," Bandar said. "We had worked well together in Lebanon. One day he approached me to fund the Contras in Nicaragua." Outlining Saudi Arabia's involvement in the funding of the Nicaraguan Contras, the prince reiterated that their support was needed because the Boland cut-off had blocked the U.S. government from providing any further funds for the Contras. He added that the Soviets and Cubans had responded to that cessation of funds and the consequent denial of vital arms to the Contras by pouring arms into Nicaragua, giving the Sandinistas a clear advantage in a forthcoming major battle.

The Saudi cash was intended to allow the Contras to receive much-needed weapons until such time as the CIA could secure new funds. Support of the Contras was seen by the Saudis to be in the national interest of both America and Saudi Arabia. "We had no problem with that," Bandar said. "It was a sovereign operation outside the USA and so we were not breaking any laws. We were funding a number of anti-Communist operations in various parts of the world, and this was no different." Bandar informed McFarlane that the Saudi government was actually prepared to go public on their support for the Contras so that in the event of a leak no one would be embarrassed. McFarlane, however, indicated that the American line was still to keep the cash and Saudi support under wraps, insisting that there would be no leaks.

In February 1985, with the Boland cut-off in effect, McFarlane met with the prince to discuss King Fahd's upcoming visit. Again, they discussed the Contras. McFarlane told Bandar that the United States, despite Saudi contributions so far, was still facing a funding problem. When Fahd arrived, he and President Reagan met, as was customary, in the Oval Office. A less customary second meeting, however, took place on February 11 in the family residence of the White House.

That meeting between Fahd and Reagan resulted in a secret Saudi agreement to raise the level of funding for the Contras. "My Friend," North wrote to Calero, "Next week, a sum in excess of $20 million will be deposited in the usual account. . . . It should allow us to bridge the gap between now and when the vote is taken and the funds are turned on again." The money, North said, should be used to redeploy and hide Contra forces from an expected Sandinista offensive, outfit and train "the forces and volunteers," and develop a regular air resupply operation. "This new money," he continued, "will provide great flexibility we have not enjoyed to date."[34]

North later confirmed that it was a deal that was never supposed to be exposed to the light of day; nor was the fact that Saudi Arabia was the key financier. Although he was assured by U.S. officials that the ploy was legal, Bandar knew it was "politically dicey." North later testified that Bandar "had sought to keep under wraps his role in funneling millions through a Swiss bank account."* He added, "He was promised we were going to keep it secret, and we tried."[35]

---

*It was actually an account in the Cayman Islands.

The Contra funding secret didn't hold, however, and Bandar, who had diplomatic immunity, refused to cooperate with investigators. Though Mc-Farlane characterized the Contra funding as a transfer of a foreign official's "personal funds," Bandar simply denied the story and declined requests from the special prosecutor to explain his role. For the Saudis and for Bandar, it was just another anti-Communist joint venture hatched in secrecy with senior Reagan aides; part of the bonding of interests that marked his tenure as ambassador.[36] Later, Bandar confirmed that Fred Dutton had advised him to turn down the special prosecutor's request.

During the summer of 1986, reports began to appear in the press alleging that the Saudis had contributed money to the Contras as part of an informal arrangement connected with the sale of AWACS aircraft to Saudi Arabia. An article featured in the *San Francisco Examiner* on July 27, 1986, cited intelligence sources who stated that the Saudi contribution "was but the latest example of a long-standing practice of financing U.S. covert operations with money set aside from foreign military sales."[37] Caspar Weinberger went public, denying that there had been any Saudi contributions. The Saudi embassy issued a press release on October 21, 1986, in which Bandar stated, "Saudi Arabia is not and has not been involved either directly or indirectly in any military or other support activity of any kind for or in connection with any group or groups concerned with Nicaragua."[38]

At the time, one of Weinberger's principal concerns had been maintaining good relations with Saudi Arabia, whom he considered to be a pivotal ally in the Middle East. Weinberger's relationship with the prince was solid, and his denials of Saudi involvement with the Contras had consistently shielded not only the president, but also Bandar.[39]

Believing that he had the full support of the White House, Bandar watched in shock and fury as McFarlane testified during the hearings that Bandar had volunteered to provide funds. In trying to shield his president, McFarlane indicted Bandar, who had categorically denied any Saudi funding of the Contras in the press.

Speaking about this episode, Bandar emphatically underlined his disappointment in McFarlane, saying angrily, "He spilled his guts and let me down. The only time I lied to the media was that time when I said, 'We have nothing to do with it and America never talked to me about it'—because that is what he and I agreed to say. I said to him, 'Look, I don't care what the truth is; if you're going to tell some story, let's tell it together. If it's a lie, then let's lie together. If it's the truth, then let's tell the same story. But you're going to kill yourself or me if we tell different stories.'"

Acknowledging his complicity, Bandar said plainly, "And the press bought it from me because I always told the truth. I always leveled with the press. I would tell them either I'll tell you the truth or I will say that I cannot comment."

Bandar's anger and resentment was ill concealed as he continued his story, "And he [McFarlane] sits in front of the whole world in Congress and says, 'I must confess, Prince Bandar of Saudi Arabia called me one day and said, 'Come on over—we want to help you and the Contras—can we give you $25 million?'" Bandar irately continued, "He not only lied, because I didn't give a damn about the Contras—I didn't even know where Nicaragua was—but he came to me in the middle of the night saying, 'Look, we need help, etc., etc.' and I said, 'Fine, but has the president authorized this?' McFarlane said, 'He did and you can check with him yourself, but you can't talk to anybody else. I will take you there to see him and he will say, 'Thank you.' I said, 'Fine, that's all that I need.'" Bandar took McFarlane at his word.

"So not only did he lie at the hearing," Bandar continued, "but he made me lie saying we had nothing to do with it and then he said we did. Then he said that we initiated the contact, which is not true and that really hurt because he told me, 'Prince Bandar, I am a Marine and I will fall on my sword before I let down my friends and my president.' So I said, 'Well, that makes two of us. I'm not a Marine, but I will fall on my sword to protect my king and my friends.'" Bandar had made very clear to the national security adviser that Saudi Arabia would support whatever angle the Americans wished to take so long as they both had the same agenda and stuck to it. McFarlane had reassured the prince repeatedly that secrecy was the only option and had even affirmed that knowledge of the funding would never become public except, of course, if Bandar failed to uphold his side of the agreement.

Bandar was highly cynical about McFarlane's attempted suicide the night before he was due to provide his testimony. McFarlane overdosed on tablets and then had his stomach pumped. "The guy was an ex-Marine," Bandar exclaimed. "If he had really wanted to kill himself, then he could have come up with a more efficient and final way of doing it!" In the end, McFarlane's testimony was merely deferred. Bandar confirmed that he has not spoken with McFarlane since, saying, "He is no longer a friend."

As a footnote, I was to discover that although media coverage of the

Iran-Contra affair depicts Oliver North as the central character, strangely, Bandar and Colonel North have never met. The only time that Bandar was supposed to talk with North was just before the story broke. McFarlane called the prince, explaining that he was leaving for Russia and should the prince need anything or to talk to anyone, he should contact Col. North, who would pass a message to him wherever he was. McFarlane was surprised to learn that the prince had never met the colonel and suggested that North stop by and meet with him. Bandar, however, was recalled to Saudi Arabia and the planned meeting was canceled.

Given the significant backtracking involving McFarlane and North that took place during the investigation, Bandar's dealings with the media were naturally tense. Walking a tightrope between the official line of secrecy and denial originally laid down by McFarlane and the endless new discoveries and allegations in the U.S. press, the prince adopted what could be seen as a policy of deflection, saying, "I think it is not proper for a diplomat to make comments on the internal affairs of a host country." In other words, he left it to the Americans to put their own house in order.

Throughout this period of intense media speculation, Bandar stuck to his script: "People who say that we dance to the tune of America are mistaken because we both operate based on our mutual national interests; sometimes they meet, sometimes they don't. And I don't see what the novelty is of that."[40]

The almost masochistic delight that the U.S. media exhibited during the Iran-Contra hearings did little to tarnish Saudi Arabia's standing in the political eye. Seeing the situation for what it was, Washington recognized that when the United States president had asked for help, it was Saudi Arabia that had come to his aid in the fight against Communism. Somewhat later during

Oliver North testifies during the Iran-Contra hearings.

the extensive media attacks on Saudi Arabia following 9/11, one writer was prompted to recall, "While all of these operations—and many more—were necessarily kept secret at the time, when they became public during the Iran-Contra affair, the Saudis received accolades from those who now want them out, beginning with the *Wall Street Journal*."[41]

As Bandar came to be seen as a persona outside the normal pattern for Saudi diplomacy, he soon became the target of intense media scrutiny. One of the most extreme allegations to be leveled against him was his supposed involvement in the attempt on the life of Sheik Mohammed Hussein Fadlallah in 1985. Fadlallah was the spiritual leader of Hezbollah, the Lebanon-based, Iran-financed Party of God, and had been implicated in terrorist operations targeting U.S. interests in Beirut. After the 1983 truck bombing of a U.S. Marine Corps barracks near Beirut airport that killed two hundred forty-one servicemen, American officials accused Fadlallah of ordering the attack.[42]

The attempted assassination of the sheik took the form of a car bomb which exploded in front of Fadlallah's apartment, killing eighty bystanders and injuring another two hundred, though leaving the sheik unscathed. The finger of suspicion was quickly pointed at the CIA and the Saudis. Rumors that Saudi Arabia had provided $3 million to fund the assassination took root in the United States, culminating in Bob Woodward's book, *Veil*. Woodward wrote in explicit detail about an alleged meeting between Bandar and Casey, including descriptive accounts of covert conversations, the sharing and destruction of information, and even about a mysterious English ex-military man supposedly hired by the Saudis to orchestrate the operation.[43] Bandar categorically denies that this meeting ever took place. Woodward's allegations were to be repeated by Howard Blum,[44] Holly Sklar,[45] William Blum,[46] and Hala Jaber.[47] In his review of Woodward's book, however, Thomas Powers observed, "Woodward strongly suggests, but does not actually say, that this [Saudi] money was used to mount an attempt to assassinate Sheikh Mohammed Hussein Fadlallah."[48]

Woodward was less cautious during his *Frontline* interview on "Target America" with Bill Moyers when he said, "Casey, in 1985, worked out with the Saudis a plan to use a car bomb to kill Sheik Fadlallah, who they determined was one of the people behind not only the Marine barracks [bombing], but was involved in the taking of American hostages in Beirut. Casey had lunch with Prince Bandar . . . one of the most powerful figures, even to-day, in Washington." Woodward continued, "And they went for a stroll in the garden, and they said, 'We have to go off the books.' And they agreed that the Saudis would put up the money to hire some professionals to try to car-bomb Sheik Fadlallah. And it was so off the books, there's no evidence that Reagan knew about it or Weinberger or Shultz. It was Casey on his own, saying, 'I'm going to solve the big problem by essentially getting tougher or as tough as the terrorists, in using their weapon'—the car bomb."[49]

Over the years, Bandar has never attempted to contradict Woodward's revelations or the media reports and books covering this story. However, he has steadfastly maintained that allegations of Saudi involvement in the at-tempt on Fadlallah's life are completely without foundation, explicitly stat-ing that he played no part in this assassination attempt. Immediately after the attempt on Fadlallah's life, Bandar approached the Muslim cleric on be-half of King Fahd, who was anxious that the religious leader did not believe the accusations of Saudi involvement in the bombing. The sheikh assured Bandar that he held the United States and not Saudi Arabia responsible and the two shook hands as friends. Later, Bandar offered to pay Fadlallah $2 million in food, university scholarships, and other aid in exchange for an agreement not to attack U.S. targets in Lebanon.

It's possible that Woodward misinterpreted this gesture as an admission of guilt, subsequently writing about a conversation in which Bandar suppos-edly told Casey, "It was easier to bribe him than to kill him." Bandar dis-misses this report out of hand. In contrast to accepted Western practice, Bandar has always maintained that so long as he knows the truth regarding a situation and can justify his own and the Saudi position, then whatever is written in the press does not overly concern him.

It was later alleged that this operation was not carried out by the CIA at all, but by a highly secretive organization created by the Reagan administra-tion in 1982, called the Special Situations Group. The *New Statesman* went on to claim that one SSG plan evidently involved the creation of a preemp-tive counterterrorist force, which, after one false start, resulted in a group, organized by a former British Special Air Service (SAS) man, unsuccessfully attempting to assassinate Fadlallah with a car bomb in early 1985.[50]

There was some truth to this claim. Bandar later learned from Saudi in-telligence sources that the assassination attempt on Fadlallah was under-taken by an ex-SAS/CIA agent in a rogue operation. That action, however, was never financed by Saudi Arabia.

*   *   *

There is perhaps no better illustration of U.S.-Saudi covert cooperation in foreign policy than the defeat of Colonel Qaddafi's Libyan Armed Forces subsequent to the Libyan invasion of the northern province of Chad.

In 1980, after making a number of border claims, Muammar Qaddafi moved twenty thousand troops into the newly established country of Chad, a former French colony. With an undeveloped leadership, Chad was unable to repel the invading Libyan army. Qaddafi was exultant and boasted of his success on Libyan TV and in the press. However, under increasingly insistent pressure from other African countries and from political factions in Chad, the Libyans withdrew in November 1981.

A second Libyan incursion occurred between June and August 1983, when Qaddafi intervened in force, driving the Chadian army out of the one hundred-kilometer-wide Aouzou Strip. The subsequent intercession by three thousand French troops ended the Libyan successes and led to a de facto division of the country, with Libya maintaining control of all territory north of the sixteenth parallel. Although both France and Libya later agreed to a mutual withdrawal from Chad, the Libyans secretly dispersed, maintaining their control of the northern region.

While not directly allied with the Soviets, Qaddafi's anti-Western stance pleased Moscow, as they benefited from the profit in extensive arm sales to Libya, estimated by U.S. intelligence to be somewhere in the region of $1 billion annually. The ties between Libya and the Soviet Union, combined with Qaddafi's new acquired taste for "adventurism," was not well received in the White House. Adding to U.S. and Western concerns was the formidable Libyan-orchestrated terrorist threat to capitals such as London, Paris, Rome, Athens, Beirut, Tunis, and Madrid.

Saudi Arabia, too, was alarmed by Qaddafi's regime, which had been linked to the discovery of military hardware and explosives found in the suitcases of Libyan passengers traveling for the hajj.* Furthermore, Libya had

---

*The religion of Islam is founded on five cardinal pillars, of which the performance of the pilgrimage to Mecca is called the *hajj*. However, unlike the other four pillars, the hajj is incumbent upon the Muslim only if he can afford it. The annual hajj begins in the twelfth month of the Islamic year, and pilgrims wear special clothes: simple garments that strip away distinctions of class and culture, so that all stand equal before God. The rites of the hajj, which are of Abrahamic origin, include going around the Ka'bah in Mecca seven times, and going seven times between the hills of Safa and Marwa. The pilgrims later stand together on the wide plains of Arafat (a large expanse of desert outside Makkah) and join in prayer for God's forgiveness, in what is often thought to be a preview of the Day of Judgment.

signed a cooperation treaty with Ethiopia and South Yemen; together they represented three of the most volatile—and anti-Saudi—countries in Africa.

In the Middle East any overt action taken against Libya could have triggered highly undesirable repercussions, effectively elevating the Libyan colonel to the lofty status of Muslim martyr. Therefore, when the CIA approached Bandar for the funding of a covert operation against Qaddafi, the Saudis readily agreed to aid the strategy devised by Casey and Haig. Their goal was the careful and subversive bleeding of Qaddafi's weakest point—his military expeditions and invasion of Chad. According to Bob Woodward, Casey believed "that the Chad adventure was the Achilles' heel for Qaddafi."[51]

With Saudi and CIA funding, the inexperienced Chadian forces bolstered their army with well-equipped professional mercenaries, recruited and flown into Chad to support an attack on Libyan regular forces. Fred Dutton told me how Bandar enjoyed relating how the Libyan Army received a bloody surprise when it unexpectedly encountered fierce resistance from a supposedly inferior Chadian army.

"Saudi Arabia, in conjunction with the CIA, provided $10 million to support the rearming of the Chadian army and the recruitment of a mercenary army to support the Chadian forces on the ground. The Saudis were not involved in it; they just financed it. The Americans undertook the operational part, and the result was the defeat of Qaddafi and the withdrawal of Libyan forces from Chad. During the Libya-Chad operation, ground forces were supported by American air operations designed to soften up the Libyan Army, taking out the heavy equipment, tanks, etc., and interdicting the Libyan force's lines of retreat." Dutton described how Libyan forces were being hit from the ground and the air and in the ensuing chaos, the Libyans were unsure whether the aircraft would refuel, rearm, and return for further operations. While that panic was going on, the Chadian ground forces, supported by mercenaries, just swept on through. Beginning in December 1986 and stretching into early 1987, Qaddafi's forces were routed and pushed all the way back into Libya.

Highly satisfied with the outcome of this clandestine undertaking, Bandar said, "Indeed, after that bloody nose, Qaddafi never again moved his forces outside Libya."[52] Interestingly, the prince's turn of phrase directly echoed Haig's stated purpose in Chad, which was to "bloody Qaddafi's nose" and to "increase the flow of pine boxes back to Libya."[53] However, there was far more to the U.S-Saudi alliance and success in Chad than the media has reported.

According to Dutton, the extensive air support for the Chadian army was provided by the U.S. Sixth Fleet operating from the Gulf of Sirta. Flying at night, they actually flew over Libyan air space en route to their targets in Chad. More astoundingly, in order to disguise the nature of the operation and conceal any possible U.S. involvement, American carrier aircraft were loaded with Afghan Mujahideen-supplied Soviet bombs and ordnance.

Challenged on the veracity of this revelation, Dutton exclaimed, "You will not find anybody that is prepared to touch this story with a ten-foot pole—but it's true. A lot of people will debate it and some admit it and some will deny it!" He laughed, clearly amused by the impact that this story would have in Washington and Langley when it broke.[54] Dutton's account was later corroborated by Ambassador Ahmed Kattan, then deputy chief of staff at the Saudi embassy in Washington, and now Saudi ambassador to the Arab League in Cairo, in a private conversation.

In a similar episode, almost a year before, on April 15, 1986, in what could be deemed a rehearsal for the Chad operation, in retaliation for the Libyan bombing of a Hamburg nightclub, a massive precision night attack operation was mounted against Libyan targets by U.S. Navy A-6s and U.S. Air Force F-111s. The A-6 aircraft operated from the Sixth Fleet carriers, the USS *America* and the USS *Coral Sea*, and the F-111 aircraft operated from RAF bases at Mildenhall and Upper Heyford in the United Kingdom. Speaking of the widely reported American targeting of Qaddafi's home, Bandar observed bitingly, "France refused to allow American aircraft operating from the U.K. to fly over French air space. In contrast, Maggie Thatcher not only agreed to allow aircraft to overfly the U.K., but also permitted operations to be flown from bases located in the U.K."

Saudi involvement in the Libya-Chad conflict was to surface later during the Prince's delicate negotiations to secure agreement for the trial of the suspected Lockerbie bombers in 1999. During a lull in those talks, Qaddafi brought up the Libyan expedition into Chad, recalling the "valiant exploits" of his "brave army." Sitting beside Qaddafi and listening to this boast, the prince realized that the colonel was completely unaware of the Saudi support for Chad. Unable to refrain from speaking, Bandar said to Qaddafi, "Since now we're being frank with each other, Chad was our baby. We were in it and we checkmated you that time."[55]

* * *

One of the primary assets that contributed to Bandar's growing power during the Reagan years was his ability to forge influential friendships rapidly. He arguably had no greater partnership in those early years than his friendship with Nancy Reagan. It long has been acknowledged that throughout the Reagan era "the second most powerful person in the Reagan White House was the one the president loved most dearly. As first lady, Nancy Reagan wielded more influence over executive branch actions and policies than any presidential spouse in modern history."[56] As she admitted in her memoirs, "Did I ever give Ronnie advice? You bet I did. I'm the one who knows him best, and I was the only person in the White House who had absolutely no agenda of her own—except helping him." She said, "I gave Ronnie my best advice—for eight years I was sleeping with the president, and if that doesn't give you special access, I don't know what does!"[57]

Over two Reagan administrations, Bandar never underestimated Nancy Reagan. He held the first lady in highest esteem, while forging a special friendship that would have attendant political benefits. As Mrs. Reagan admitted, "I don't know much about economics or military affairs, but I have strong instincts about people, and I'm a good judge of character."[58] With Bandar, Nancy Reagan's sixth sense rang true—his loyalty to her, to her husband, and to the Reagan Doctrine was steadfast. Their relationship was to have a profound impact not only on world events, but also—and controversially—within the White House itself.

Nancy Reagan has been credited with the shift inside Reagan's cabinet away from hard-line conservatives toward those with more moderate approaches to foreign policy. Although she largely left policy to the Reagan men, the first lady was deeply involved in selecting who those men were. Significant changes attributed to Nancy included the replacement of Secretary of State Alexander Haig with George Shultz mid-

An extraordinarily close friendship existed between Bandar and Nancy Reagan.

way into Reagan's first term in office; Judge William Clark's replacement as national security adviser with Robert McFarlane.[59] Bandar's fingerprints can be found in both these appointments.

Inside the Beltway, Washington is a turbulent and frequently changing maelstrom of insecurity. It is a hostile place where the infidelity of power and the tenaciousness of the media are the only certainties. This is perhaps best illustrated by the "resignation" of Secretary Alexander Haig, the man who had requested Bandar's support for the Reagan administration's vital AWACS vote. On the afternoon of June 25, 1982, reporters were summoned to the White House Press Room for an unexpected briefing. At 3:04 P.M., President Reagan strode up to the microphone and said, "With great regret I have accepted the resignation of Secretary of State Al Haig." Reagan went on to announce, "I am nominating as his successor, and he has accepted, George Shultz, to replace him."[60] Reagan's remarks were broadcast live on nationwide radio and television.

The impression given was that Haig had resigned voluntarily. However, rumors of a White House coup surfaced almost immediately. Later that day, Secretary Haig was to make a statement to the State Department in front of an audience of around one thousand reporters and department employees. It had been scheduled for 4 P.M., but the outgoing secretary of state was nearly half an hour late. In fact, he had only learned of his resignation a few hours earlier, around noon. According to Haig, he had been compelled to compose a letter of resignation and pretend, for public consumption, that he had already given it to Reagan. His late arrival at the State Department press conference was due to the fact that he was still putting last-minute touches on his public statement. Haig had been ordered to keep his entire statement to a maximum of five minutes and he had been warned not to accept questions. During the speech, Haig spoke slowly; his attitude was one of resignation, his mannerisms were indicative of defeat. At one point he could hardly get the words out.[61]

Shortly after Haig's statement, Sam Donaldson of ABC News, said, "It may seem strange for people who know General Haig's background; but the hard-liners, from the standpoint of the Soviet-American relations, and the hard-liners when it comes to trying to curb what many people see as excessive violence by Israel in Lebanon, have won on this one."[62]

Coincidentally, Bandar was to host a dinner party at his home that evening. He explained that this dinner party had been planned for twenty guests, but during the week prior to the party, Haig came under pressure to resign. Because the news of Haig's resignation broke on the day of Bandar's party, Bandar contacted the secretary of state and asked if he should cancel it. He said to Haig, "I don't want it to appear that this was a dinner party held as a consequence of the resignation." Haig agreed that to hold the dinner with so many Washington personalities might be misread by the Inner Beltway, and suggested instead a more intimate dinner, just the two of them and their wives.

Secretary Haig and his wife duly arrived at Bandar's home in McLean, Virginia. Bandar had planned that Princess Haifa should take Mrs. Haig into the Morocco Room to allow him to talk privately with Haig in Bandar's study about his resignation. However, Mrs. Haig followed her husband into the study. As all four sat there, there was an extended and tangible silence. Bandar confessed, "No one knew what to say."

Eventually, he broke the silence, saying, "Well, Mr. Secretary—this has been a surprising day."

"What happened next," Bandar said, "was remarkable." To his amazement, Secretary Haig, ex-Supreme Allied Commander Europe and four-star general, broke down in tears. Sitting in Bandar's study, head in his hands, in a sustained emotional outburst, Haig wept in anguish. Bandar explained that he didn't know what to do. Apart from the sobbing Haig, everyone was silent. Eventually, Haig stopped crying, wiped his eyes with his handkerchief, and asked, "Can I have a scotch?"

In time, both couples retired to the dining room. During the meal it emerged that Haig had been pushed out of office, that he had had no intention of resigning. Furthermore, he regretted giving the "sons-of-bitches" the opportunity to force him out. When President Reagan had announced Haig's resignation to the media, saying that he had received his letter of resignation and that he had reluctantly accepted it, Haig had yet to write that letter. An increasingly concerned White House staff had been frantically contacting Haig's office to try to get the letter. Haig told Bandar angrily, "I delayed my reply for over three hours." Speaking with real venom, Haig explained, "It was my one last chance to stick it to them!"

Although Bandar played no role in the departure of Secretary Haig, he was nonetheless to influence other Reagan administration appointments. Nancy Reagan was widely credited in the U.S. press with selecting Robert McFarlane in 1983 for the job of national security adviser instead of Jeane Kirkpatrick.[63] However, Bandar says it was he who blocked Kirkpatrick's appointment, and that he did so because he did not believe that Kirkpatrick was the right candidate for Saudi Arabia. Instead, he was eager to recommend McFarlane, with whom he had worked closely to craft a ceasefire agreement to end the fighting in Lebanon. Bandar felt that McFarlane, not Kirkpatrick, would be most compatible with Saudi interests. Bandar admitted, "I kept telling her [the first lady], 'This guy is really loyal to your husband—a good supporter!' " Bandar concluded, "The result—McFarlane became national security adviser."

When asked to comment on media speculation about his relationship with the first lady and rumors that he had influenced the selection of senior administration officials by lobbying Mrs. Reagan, Bandar nodded an affirmation, and then explained that Mrs. Reagan had asked him to provide her with feedback on those administration appointees who were outside the Reagan Kitchen Cabinet and were therefore unknown quantities. He said, "Mrs. Reagan made it clear that she wanted only loyal supporters of the president within the administration." Bandar's advice allowed Nancy to construct her own "hit list" with which to influence her husband, a list carefully constructed by Bandar to match the best interests of the kingdom. Nancy Reagan asked Bandar for information on the loyalty, or otherwise, of her husband's cabinet. In making her request for information, Bandar recalled how Nancy Reagan had told him that she had an instinctive feel for disloyal members of the administration. She would wiggle her fingers animatedly from her forehead, insect-like, saying, "I have my antennae out," and look around furtively as if to sniff out wrongdoers.

When it was put to Bandar that by accepting his advice, Nancy Reagan was effectively soliciting the support of a foreign diplomat, he instantly responded, "But in her mind, she was not thinking of me as a foreign official; she was thinking of me as a friend of her husband. She knew that I admired him. Obviously, she knew that there was close cooperation between Ronald Reagan, Maggie Thatcher, and King Fahd. In her mind she was thinking, 'My husband likes this guy and trusts him. His boss and my husband are close to each other and Maggie Thatcher, so obviously I can trust him in trying to find out what other people say about my husband, other leaders and other officials, and which other American officials are presenting him in a good light to foreigners. Or do they laugh at him or do they joke about him?' To her, the world started and ended with her husband—period. She didn't care about the politics, vis-à-vis I'm protecting Ronnie; nobody should hurt him, not if I can help it."

Asked to comment on recurrent media speculation about the influence

Nancy Reagan had over her husband, Bandar was explicit. He affirmed that, as a very persuasive lady, she unquestionably manipulated Ronnie from time to time, and reiterated that she had sought his advice.

To illustrate this point, Bandar said, "There was a famous TV interview of both of them at their ranch. They asked Reagan a question and he said, 'Well,' and during that pause, Nancy looked across at him and said sharply, 'We'll have to think about it.' And President Reagan promptly echoed her words saying, 'We'll have to think about it.'" Bandar laughed and added, "And it was on tape—so people knew that she had influence!"

Bandar would again dabble in U.S. politics, just before Edwin Meese would go public with details of the Iran-Contra scandal in late November 1986, in what appeared to be an effort to accelerate the departure of Secretary of State George Shultz. It was reported that Bandar acted on behalf of Nancy Reagan.

Bandar confided that the president's wife had revealed to him that once the [Iran-Contra] scandal had blown over, "We're going to get rid of him [Shultz]." Armed with this information, Bandar met with Caspar Weinberger in his office and informed him that Nancy Reagan thought Shultz should go; the first lady was very upset with Shultz.[64] According to Bandar, Mrs. Reagan said that the secretary of state had been "a real weakling" and "disloyal" to her husband.

Weinberger subsequently disclosed that Bandar had recommended to the first lady that he, Weinberger, should be named secretary of defense. It

From left to right: Caspar Weinberger, George Shultz, Ed Meese, Don Regan, and Ronald Reagan at the White House. Shultz was soon targeted by Nancy Reagan with Bandar's support.

is more than coincidence that the proposed removal of Shultz, under whom the prince reportedly felt the State Department was too pro-Israel, coincided with the appointment of Weinberger, with whom the prince had already worked closely. The Saudis also felt that Weinberger would encourage a hard line when dealing with the Soviets.

The next day, Weinberger called his friend William Clark in California and relayed Bandar's comments; both men were shocked about the Saudi ambassador's maneuvering to select the secretary of state.[65]

Bandar's personal friendship with Ronald and Nancy Reagan, but particularly with the first lady, combined with Saudi support for the anti-Communist Reagan Doctrine; careful use of the oil weapon, and petrodollars; and his direct line of contact with King Fahd, furnished Bandar with extraordinary access within the White House. Washington operates on many complex and often opposing levels, and Bandar's spheres of influence were as diverse as the field on which he was playing. Throughout both Reagan administrations, he built a network of friendships with key administration figures, which allowed him to quietly wield unparalleled political influence within the White House.

Bandar's power in Washington was already the source of considerable media speculation. *Time* magazine attempted to capture his influence when it reported, "Prince Bandar's royal blood and his savvy about American ways have given him access in Washington unmatched by any other envoy, including the Soviet Union's twenty-one-year veteran Anatoly Dobrynin."[66] But little could *Time* imagine that through his close friendship with Nancy Reagan, Bandar, a foreign diplomat, could—and did—covertly determine the shape of both Reagan administrations.

FIVE

BANDAR THE ARMS DEALER

"If we are strong, our strength will speak for itself. If we are weak, words will be of no help."

JOHN FITZGERALD KENNEDY
(1961–1963)

"My friends, let me tell you, we are not masochists; we don't like to spend billions of dollars and get insulted in the process."[1] Speaking to a group of McDonnell Douglas executives, Bandar was referring to the rejection of Saudi Arabia's 1985 request for additional F-15 aircraft and Lance missiles. However, he could have been referring to any of a number of difficult and frustrating arms negotiations between the United States and Saudi Arabia.

After sealing the agreement to buy one hundred F-15s from the United States and successfully moving the deal through Congress in 1978, Saudi Arabia requested immediate delivery of the first sixty planes; the remaining forty, it was agreed, would be received at a later date—much later, as it turned out. After the initial delivery, the Saudi government would spend the next five years attempting to take possession of those remaining forty planes. Given the time already invested in the project and the close friendship that existed between the United States and Saudi Arabia—not forgetting the Saudi ability to actually pay for the goods requested, somewhat of a novelty for the U.S. arms industry—the congressional rejection of the new Saudi request for forty-two additional F-15s, helicopters, and anti-ship missiles was considered an insulting swipe at U.S.-Saudi relations.

This was not the first time that Saudi weapons interests in the United States were thwarted in the final hour. In 1976, congressional clearance was granted to Saudi Arabia to buy four thousand model B Maverick air-to-air missiles. Yet, because of the protracted time taken to clear the deal, the model B production line had been shut down before delivery. The manufacturer recommended that the purchase order be changed to model D missiles—then in production and much easier to find parts for than the older model. When the deal was returned to Congress for amendment to the model D, the entire deal was rejected.

Saudi Arabia's frustration at the seemingly illogical actions of Congress was understandable. And in a competitive consumer market, the Saudis' reaction was clear-cut; they simply took their business elsewhere. Nevertheless, despite the apparent congressional bias against Saudi Arabia's armaments requests, Bandar has always stressed, particularly to the American people he meets when speaking on the "shop floor" in U.S. industrial and military plants, that American weapons have always been, and always will be, Saudi Arabia's first choice when negotiating defense contracts. The Prince reiterated that it is through no fault on the Saudi side, or that of the American defense industry, that lucrative defense deals between Saudi Arabia and the United States have fallen through, but rather the fault of Congress. He observed, "We have always chosen as a first priority American defense weapon products for two reasons: number one, for the technology being simply the best, and number two, because fifty years of friendship has its own dynamics that makes you our first priority, our choice."[2]

Defense has always been crucial to the kingdom of Saudi Arabia. Sharing borders with seven volatile, militaristic countries, acting as the fulcrum of leadership for the Muslim world, and sitting on over one third of the world's oil supply, the stakes are enormous for Saudi Arabia. President Reagan's time in office spanned a period of uncertainty and upheaval in the Middle East. Ayatollah Khomeini, leader of the Iranian revolution, had called for the overthrow of the Saudi monarchy, viciously denounced the capitalist West, and entered into a costly eight-year war with Iraq. In response, a belligerent Iraq launched a massive offensive against Iran, firing Scud and Frog missiles into population centers in western Iran and targeting a series of intense chemical and gas attacks along the front lines.[3]

With such deadly high-tech weaponry operating between two of Saudi

Arabia's neighbors, the Saudis looked to enhance their own defensive arsenal. In late 1984, they asked America for approval to buy forty-two additional F-15 fighters, anti-aircraft missiles, Harpoon anti-ship missiles, and Blackhawk troop-carrying helicopters.

Yet Congress again proved intractable and rejected the request out of hand. In February 1985, a pragmatic President Reagan was burdened with the unenviable task of informing King Fahd and Prince Bandar that he would be unable to secure congressional approval for the weapons package.

Reagan told Fahd, "I support it, I agree with it; but Congress will not go with me. So, it's your call. If you want me to go with it, I'll go with it, but we will lose."

"No, no, no," Fahd immediately replied. "I don't want you to be humiliated or embarrassed because if you are, I will be embarrassed too. I appreciate your attitude, but you know, Mr. President, I support you. You believe in peace through strength, and I'm like you. The stronger you are, the less chance for war."

"If you were me," Fahd asked Reagan, "what would you do?"

The president responded quickly, "If I were you, I would go somewhere else and buy it."

With that, Fahd effectively secured Reagan's endorsement of a Saudi search for weapons outside the United States.

Once it became clear that the United States would not supply the F-15 aircraft, Saudi Arabia immediately did begin to look elsewhere: to France and their Mirage 4000 aircraft, still on the drawing board, and to Britain for the Tornado strike/attack aircraft then entering service with the Royal Air Force. Reciprocally, upon learning that Saudi Arabia was in the market to buy, France and Britain both eagerly sought to fill the gap,

Margaret Thatcher and Bandar

competing head-to-head to strike lucrative defense deals with the desert kingdom. The British government was determined to secure the deal, launching a powerful sales campaign personally headed by Margaret Thatcher.

"Hurrah," Thatcher is said to have exclaimed. "I want that contract! I want it to be British. I want to get my factories and manufacturers working!"

Mrs. Thatcher asked Bandar if he was sure that the Americans would not sell F-15s to the Saudis.

"I am sure," Bandar said.

Thatcher responded, "That's very stupid."

"Will you help us?" he asked the prime minister.

"Of course we will," Thatcher said. "But please tell his Majesty that nobody should know that we have talked. I'm going to call Ronnie. He will tell me he can't make the deal because Congress won't let him. Then I will go to Congress and lobby the chairman of the committee for the sale of F-15s and they will tell me they can't. And I will tell them, 'All right, but the Saudis might go to the Russians. We must do something to stop them. I'm going to sell them Tornados so they don't go to the Communists. I will rescue you from this embarrassment; I will sell you Tornados—so they don't go to Russia or China.'"

"The political genius of what she did," said Bandar, "is that she collected the benefit economically and she sold it to the Americans as though she was doing them a favor. And the Americans were grateful to her! When she went there, people in the Congress were telling her that they agreed with her, but they couldn't do it for political reasons—the Jewish lobby, etc."

He laughed, "Little did Congress know that she and I had already planned the whole thing—genius!"

Bandar had long known and respected Thatcher's political instinct and gamesmanship. "During the Falklands War," he recalled, "Margaret Thatcher instructed the admiral in charge of the Falklands Task Force (Rear Admiral Sandy Woodward) not to report victory, except to her directly; he was not to go through the command chain. When the admiral did report it to her, she said, 'Okay—wait half an hour, then you can declare it.'" Bandar continued, "She then rushed out of Ten Downing Street and went straight to Parliament, stood there, and made the declaration."*

---

*Mrs. Thatcher told the House of Commons on June 14, 1982, that land forces commander General Jeremy Moore had decided to press forward to the capital the previous night after a series of successful attacks on enemy troops.

Afterward, she drove back to Downing Street and met her husband Dennis. Bandar explained that as you enter Ten Downing Street there is a corridor, in which, when Margaret Thatcher was prime minister, hung a huge painting of Churchill.

As she drew alongside the painting, Prime Minister Thatcher stopped, looked up at Churchill, and said, "Thank you."

She then walked toward a door that opened to the stairs that led to her private quarters.

Her husband said to her, "Maggie, what are you talking about; who were you thanking?" "Churchill," she said. "I was thanking Churchill."

"You said 'thank you' to Churchill?"

"Oh—didn't you hear him?" Thatcher promptly replied, "He said, 'Well done, lass!' So I said, 'Thank you.'"

Margaret Thatcher's private secretary in 1985 was Lord Charles Powell (then Sir Charles Powell).* Commenting on his introduction to Bandar, Powell observed, "He came into our lives in Number Ten as a trusted emissary of the king and someone who was concerned about securing Saudi Arabia's air defense needs on behalf of his government following President Reagan's advice that he was unlikely to be able to secure Capitol Hill approval for the proposed F-15 package." In coming to Britain, Bandar told Powell, he planned to talk to a number of British companies, the Ministry of Defense (MOD), and its Defense Export Sales Organization (DESO) to discuss a possible arms purchase. Powell observed, "I think he came to Number Ten with a much more political message, wanting to know whether Saudi Arabia would have the top-level support of Margaret Thatcher for supply of aircraft from the U.K.; the answer was, very strongly, 'Yes it would.'" Powell continued, "That was reaffirmed when in March 1985 she stopped [in Saudi Arabia] on the way back from a visit to Asia. She spent a day or so in Riyadh and had long discussions with the king, with Prince Bandar present." Powell explained, "The sale itself was barely discussed in Number Ten; it was the political backing for it, the political framework for it. Were we dependable, reliable friends of Saudi Arabia who would ensure that there would be no political obstacles in the way of a deal if one was struck? And would we be there for the long term to support not just the sale of aircraft, but everything that went with it in terms of the support services and so on?"

---

*By coincidence, Lord Powell's father was Station Commander at RAF Upwood at the time that the prince was a student in an English language course before becoming an officer cadet at RAF Cranwell.

Powell emphasized, "That was very readily forthcoming." When asked whether there was a realization at that stage that the potential deal was very much larger than just the supply of aircraft, Powell responded, "It was certainly clear to me that this was a long-term deal which would start with a few aircraft. It went through a long, long life cycle to things other than aircraft and had to be backed up by training, support, maintenance, and construction." The pressing concern about French competition for the deal and the need for extraordinary flexibility provided a compelling setting to the deal. "At the back of our minds was the knowledge that the French were also very hot in the market, and were constantly claiming to have the deal locked up." Powell said, "Mrs. Thatcher, a great champion of British companies and British exports, was very keen that it should come to a British company, British Aerospace."*[4]

The way in which Bandar operated in the United Kingdom had distinct parallels with the freewheeling manner he used to such great effect inside the Beltway, working from the top down, bypassing the State Department in preference for the White House. In London, Bandar would breeze into Number Ten with uninhibited panache. From Margaret Thatcher to John Major to Tony Blair, Bandar's access was extraordinary. "It's remarkable how he is able to do that," said Tony Edwards, former head of the DESO. "Part of the enigma is how he is viewed in this country by the various parties; it's not consistent." Edwards was alluding to the differing perceptions of Bandar on Downing Street and in the Foreign Office. He believes that Bandar's habit of making contact from the top down caused ripples in the Foreign Office, which prefers to observe traditional protocols. "For example, we once had to get Robin Cook to write a telegram to the British ambassador in Saudi Arabia reminding him that British foreign policy is set in London and not in Riyadh; there is a whole history there which in the fringes involves Bandar."

When it was pointed out that Bandar similarly upsets the U.S. State Department in Washington by working directly with the White House, Edwards responded, "But, although Prince Bandar can do that, at the same time he is prepared to put himself out if it's important, to go to more junior meetings. He would go out of his way to come to something if he felt it was

---

*BAe Systems was created in 1999 by the merger of British Aerospace with Marconi Electronic Systems. Throughout this book British Aerospace will be used for both British Aerospace and BAe Systems.

critical, in the interests of his country and the two countries he says [Saudi Arabia] must keep close to—the United States and the United Kingdom." He stressed, "Bandar will do anything to make sure those three countries stay together. I have seen him do things, like make a trip over here—in one case just on my say-so, because I thought it was important at that time—in the event it turned out that it was pivotal."[5]

Sir Richard Evans, former chairman of British Aerospace, played a significant role in securing the weapons deal that would become known as the Al-Yamamah (Dove of Peace) contract. He believes that, although the problems and delays resulting from opposition in the American Congress may have provided a stimulus for Saudi Arabia's decision to turn to the United Kingdom for a range of military support, the decision to use British equipment stemmed from Britain's earlier involvement in providing military hardware such as the Lightning aircraft. He postulated, "I really believe that Al-Yamamah had its origins back in the very early days of the original Lightning deal, which was struck in 1965, before Bandar was admitted to RAF Cranwell. What the intergovernmental positions were between the Saudi and British governments—what they created—was very much a political bridge between the two countries. On the Saudi side, Fahd presumably recognized the value of maintaining the bridge."[6]

The political bridge referred to by Evans was a $280 million deal the Saudis made with the United Kingdom in 1965 for forty Lightnings, twenty-five Jet Provost trainers (Strikemasters), and eight Cessna 172 (CT-41) trainers, with the United States providing Raytheon Hawk missiles.

Sir Richard Evans *(foreground)* of British Aerospace.

Those Lightning aircraft were used by the RSAF for a long time. This sale was engineered at a time when the United Kingdom was undergoing a severe balance-of-payments crisis, placing in jeopardy its ability to purchase F-111 strike and Hercules C-130 transport aircraft from the United States.[7] In an endeavor to effect the F-111 sale, U.S. Defense Secretary Robert McNamara and British Air Minister Roy Jenkins agreed that America would facilitate a $400 million joint U.S.-British military air defense package to Saudi Arabia—Lightning interceptors, Strikemasters, and Cessna trainers—foregoing a previous U.S. offer to the kingdom of F-5 or F-104 fighter aircraft. In this way, Britain then had the money to pay for the aircraft it wanted from the United States. Announcing the sale to Parliament in December 1965, John Stonehouse, parliamentary secretary to the Air Ministry, admitted that it could not have been made without "American cooperation."[8] Nevertheless, it was an arrangement in which Britain got what it wanted and Saudi Arabia got second best.

Twenty years later, the Al-Yamamah deals would have a similar political impact and would not have happened without American agreement. Sir Richard Evans stressed that Bandar was key in ensuring that the United States would not block the Al-Yamamah deal, saying, "It could only have been done at the level of Reagan and Bandar. This required a clear understanding between the British and American administrations in relation to requirement. The Arabian approach to business, closely aligned with past friendships, trust, loyalty, and the foreign policies of the countries they deal with, clearly influences their armament decisions."[9]

On September 9, 1985, an exultant British government announced that two Memoranda of Understanding had been signed between the British and Saudi defense ministers, Michael Heseltine and Prince Sultan bin Abdul-Aziz. Prior to the announcement, in July 1985, the final negotiations had taken place at the residence of the honorary British consul in Salzburg where Mrs. Thatcher was on holiday.[10] The Memoranda of Understanding signed between Britain and Saudi Arabia granted Saudi Arabia the opportunity to transform each memorandum into a separate contract as and when required—it is these memoranda that were named the Al-Yamamah agreements.[11]

The announcement came as a surprise to the French defense industry, which had been working feverishly to secure the sale of their Dassault Mirage aircraft to Saudi Arabia, and they expected to clinch the contract; the Mirage was to be the F-15 substitute and it had the advantage of being 25 to 30 percent cheaper than the Tornado.[12]

Tony Edwards believes that the French government felt that its offer was the front-runner. He was told by his opposite number in France, "It was all lined up and the deal was done; it was going to be French."[13] A French spokesman later said of the U.K. deal that it was "unexpected, incomprehensible, and catastrophic" and that "this brutal change [was] of a political nature."[14]

"What influenced the whole deal was that the French were going to sell the Saudis the Mirage 2000 and the Mirage 4000," Bandar related to friends. "The structure of the RSAF always required a high-low combination, where you have an aircraft like the Hawk or the F-5 providing the low part and the F-15Cs and Ds providing top cover." Before the United States turned down the F-15Es, the Saudis were going to have the French aircraft as the low mix, and the F-15Es as the high mix.

With the rejection of the F-15E aircraft in February 1985 by Congress, Bandar explained, "the only way to get close to the F-15E was to get a strike aircraft." The Mirage was not a realistic option. Having made that decision, for compatibility, then it made sense for the Saudis to buy both strike and air defense Tornados.

The lack of strict rules on the use and deployment of the Tornado aircraft was also a strong selling point. Expanding on the Saudi acquisition strategy, Bandar added, "So we knew that if we were going to commit the Tornado [strike bombers] in combat—in areas restricted by the Americans as part of the original F-5 deal—we would immediately lose the cover of our F-15Cs as an interceptor. We would have to send our bombers in without cover." That was an unacceptable position and so operationally it made sense for Saudi Arabia to buy, in addition, twenty-four Tornado aircraft—the air defense variant.

But this was not the only reason why the French Mirage bid failed. At the time of the Saudi deliberation over the arms package, the French government decided to cut oil imports from Saudi Arabia by 50 percent. This decision, of which Aramco was notified in a brief telegram, annoyed King Fahd. He was even more incensed by the timing of the decision, which occurred during an oil crisis for suppliers. Oil prices were going down, and France had decided to switch from Saudi Arabia and to buy from Iran. Publicly, the king took a pragmatic stance, saying, "That is the prerogative of a sovereign nation; we can't tell them what to do."

Privately, however, Fahd would not forget the slight. When the French got wind that the contract with the British was about to be announced, President Mitterrand sent his brother on an urgent mission to see the king. Fahd, guessing that he wanted to talk about the Mirage deal, agreed to see him on a Thursday. Twelve hours before his scheduled meeting with Mitterrand, in an unsubtle political riposte, Fahd announced the deal between Saudi Arabia and the United Kingdom.

By the time Mitterrand's brother walked in, the deal was done. Yet Fahd played along, saying, "I welcome you. France is a good friend, and the president of France is a good friend of mine."

Gen. Mitterrand responded, "Well, the subject I wanted to see you about—it's already too late."

"Yes?"

"If I had had the chance," he explained, "I was to ask you to delay your decision until we had an opportunity to look at the package again."

"I know you say this with good intentions," Fahd responded, "but you see, my friend, we have come to a decision, a sovereign decision, and we don't take advice from anyone on a sovereign decision. In any case, Gen. Mitterrand, I am sure that President Mitterrand will understand my position. A few months ago, you decided to cut imports of oil from Saudi Arabia by 50 percent. I don't remember the president sending you to tell me about this, or to give us a 'heads up' beforehand or tell us why you were doing it. We only found out when a telegram came to our oil company, and to be honest, I didn't take kindly to that because that hit us in our bread-and-butter trade."

Fahd finished, saying, "But I said to myself that President Mitterrand must have done it because it was in France's national interest. I had no right to question his decision in sovereign matters and therefore I hope you are not questioning my decision now."

A flustered Gen. Mitterrand responded with a stutter, "No-no-no, Your Majesty. I was not aware of this story. Had I been aware of it, I would not have come on this mission."

Behind the foundation of the multibillion-dollar Al-Yamamah contracts was the rejection by the U.S. Congress of the Saudi request to buy forty-two F-15 jets. The actions of Congress in blocking the sale in 1985 were widely recognized as resulting from the unremitting pressure exerted on Capitol Hill by AIPAC. Following the Al-Yamamah deal, a British aviation official was quoted as saying, "The American Jewish lobby has done us a favor."[15] It is ironic and highly significant that of the seventy-two Tornados purchased by Saudi Arabia in the Al-Yamamah deal, only twenty-four were air defensive variant interceptor-fighters; the remaining forty-eight were the advanced-strike fighters. When the Saudis first approached the Americans for the F-15s, they did so with the knowledge, gained from previous negotiations, of the concomitant prohibitions and restrictions on the supply of fuel tanks and additional armament stations on the aircraft, together with restrictions on the deployment of the aircraft close to Israel. The F-15 purchase would have been one of a defensive nature. Denied the additional F-15s, the Saudis instead were able to buy British strike/attack offensive Tornados, with no deployment restrictions and full operational specifications. Similarly, the thirty Hawk aircraft ordered as part of the arms package could also have an attack role.[16]

Bandar has often questioned in public the convoluted logic of the congressional decision, one he clearly believes was a misguided attempt to support Israel and AIPAC. "I asked our friends in Washington again," he said. "Please explain to me, maybe I am dense, how is Israel safer by us going to Britain and buying one hundred twenty first-line-of-fire and strike airplanes, instead of buying forty airplanes from you? There was no answer."[17]

Although the British did impose restrictions concerning the Saudi resale of the Tornados, no restrictions were made concerning their use or deployment such as the restrictions imposed by the United States on the F-15 sale in 1978.[18] This is not insignificant, as the British press noted, "The main security concern surrounding Al-Yamamah has been Saudi Arabia's reputation as an unreliable end user of British weapons."[19]

Ironically, the dramatic increase in Saudi Arabia's arsenal through the purchase of British arms may have had a potentially more destabilizing effect on the Middle East military balance than Reagan's proposal to Congress on the kingdom's behalf. When viewed from a political perspective, America's rejection of the Saudi request was more than a simple arms issue—it was a signal to the Middle East that despite the strong personal relationship between Reagan and Bandar, the American commitment to Saudi Arabia as an ally was unstable. Rebuttal from such an influential ally left the Saudi kingdom feeling not only insulted but, more importantly, vulnerable.

The colossal revenues rumored to be generated by the British government through the resulting Al-Yamamah deals is frequently cited, angrily, by the American defense industry; in a competitive commercial market, someone will always be willing to meet demand. The same argument was employed by former British defense minister Michael Heseltine, in March 1989, in a reference to the Al-Yamamah deal when he was quoted as saying,

"It is of considerable significance that the Saudis should have a continuing relationship with this country. They want the kit and they are going to get it from somewhere. So why shouldn't we sell it?"[20]

Looking back on the Al-Yamamah deal, Bandar said, "When we first made the agreement, we had no contract. It was a handshake between me and Mrs. Thatcher in Ten Downing Street." Bandar later tried to contact the Prime Minister when the contracts were ready. It was suggested that he speak with Mr. Whitelaw, the Deputy Prime Minister as Thatcher was out of the country. The Prince declined saying, "I don't want to see him; I have nothing to discuss with him. But I'll come back when the Prime Minister is back.' Bandar then got a call saying, "Can you go to Austria?" So he went to Austria and met with Thatcher and her husband. Bandar recalled, "I told her specific numbers, shook hands, and the deal was done."

But there was one final act to come.

Several weeks after the completion of the deal, Mrs. Thatcher gave a dinner for Prince Sultan at Ten Downing Street. The following day, Sultan, along with Norman Tebbit, Secretary of State for Trade and Industry, was to visit the British Aerospace factory at Wharton. As Bandar was leaving Downing Street after that dinner, he said to Mrs. Thatcher, "Wouldn't it be fun tomorrow if I surprised my father by flying the Tornado display for him?"

Thatcher replied, "It would be wonderful—why not?"

Bandar explained that Prince Sultan would not approve it, and neither would British Aerospace or the Royal Air Force unless it was authorized.

Margaret Thatcher said immediately, "Good God—we would authorize it."

"If you're willing to do that for me, Prime Minister, do me one favor."

"Of course," she replied, "What is it?"

"Instruct everyone not to tell my father anything," said Bandar.

"Done," replied Thatcher crisply.

Bandar recalled, "I left a message with my father's staff to say that I was not feeling well and that I would not be going on the visit." Early the next morning he left for Wharton, where he was kitted out for the flight and took off in the aircraft with the test pilot just before his father arrived.

"After my father finished his tour of Wharton," Bandar explained, "he was taken to the stand to be shown what the Tornado could do. The aircraft duly completed its display—it was impressive—after which we landed and the aircraft taxied right in front of the stand and stopped."

Sir Richard Evans said to Prince Sultan, "Your Royal Highness, the crew would like to come and pay their respects to you."

The two pilots climbed out of the aeroplane and with their bone domes still on walked up to the stand. As they approached him, Bandar took his helmet off.

Prince Sultan turned to Gen. Behery of the Royal Saudi Air Force and said, "I cannot believe it. Who authorized this?"

Immediately, the general responded, "I knew absolutely nothing about this."

At this, Mr. Tebbit interjected, "The prime minister did."

Prince Sultan laughed. After Bandar had kissed his hand, he slapped him lightly on the cheek and said, "Don't dare do it again."

The Al-Yamamah contracts have always been shrouded in an incomparable degree of secrecy. In her resolute approach to the deal, Mrs. Thatcher left nothing to chance and her resolve was clearly conveyed to those in her government who were given the task of finalizing the structure.

In 1988, *The Economist* reported that, after running the gauntlet of U.S. congressional hearings, meddling reporters, and the Freedom of Information Act, Saudi Arabia welcomed the British climate of confidentiality in general, and the Official Secrets Act specifically.[21]

The U.K. government's effectiveness in enforcing such privacy despite frequent and persistent haranguing by the media is testimony to Thatcher's insistence to the deal's supreme sensitivity and value. The extent of the confidentiality blanketing Al-Yamamah was reinforced by the deliberate suppression of a National Audit Office (NAO) report into the deal on the grounds of national interest.[22] That NAO report remains the only report that has never been released to the public or members of Parliament. Prompted by sustained speculation in the press over the payment of huge commissions, the audit was undertaken by Sir John Bourn. However, it was suppressed in March 1992 by the House of Commons Public Accounts Committee (PAC). The decision to sit on the report was made by then Labour Chairman of the PAC, Robert Sheldon, who said there was "no evidence of corruption or of public money being used improperly."[23] Yet, most PAC members supported Sheldon's decision without ever being allowed to read the report themselves—an astounding situation. The PAC members merely accepted their chairman's assurances.[24]

Despite this apparent "clean bill of health" for Al-Yamamah, the British press continued to level accusations of bribery and corruption against the Saudi contracts. However, such accusations began to be explained by those familiar with Saudi Arabian customs. In his article for *The Times*, trade weapons analyst Anthony Sampson explained, "In the tradition of proper negotiation in Saudi Arabia, commissions have been an essential part of the process. Every big deal is seen as an opportunity to enrich members of the royal family and to spread favors to friends in the courts; the total price of any product is increased to allow for commissions."[25] Similarly, Chrissie Hirst, in a report for the Campaign Against Arms Trade (CAAT), supported Sampson's line of argument saying, "It is common knowledge that large contracts cannot be won from Saudi Arabia without payments which can be described as bribes or commissions." She pointed out that many Middle Eastern countries have laws in place to govern the commercial practice of paying commissions to agents or middlemen, and concluded, "It is extremely unlikely that Al-Yamamah was not arranged in accordance with this accepted practice."[26]

Despite being an arguably accepted Saudi practice, it is nonetheless illegal. Saudi law "does not permit commissions or brokerage fees on arms imports or other public sector contracts."[27] Not only is it illegal in Saudi Arabia to deal in commissions in the case of a contract between governments, "on February 14, 2002, it became illegal under U.K. law to pay foreign officials."[28]

The Guardian newspaper accused British Aerospace, by far the greatest benefactor of Al-Yamamah, of using a British Virgin Island company and offshore Swiss bank accounts to distance it from commission-related transactions, thereby removing its fingerprints from the deal. It was also alleged that British Aerospace used a Swiss bank to keep the only copy of the agreement outside British jurisdiction. In its defense, British Aerospace stated that it "rigorously denies any allegations of wrongdoing."[29]

But the unique barter deal developed for the Al-Yamamah contract—the Saudi government pays for the weapons, not with cash, but with oil—is an arrangement that added to speculation that it was created to screen commissions and backhanders, and has been heavily criticized. The financing structure, however, not only secured for the kingdom the weapons it required and a guaranteed market for its oil, but it also provided a useful mechanism that bypassed some of OPEC's restrictive quota guidelines.[30] Nonetheless, it also exposed the contract to the vagaries of the oil market, and for a time falling oil prices heightened pressure on the British Aerospace balance sheet. Tony Edwards confided that at one stage British Aerospace was running a contract deficit of $3 billion. Yet a guarantee premised on one quarter of the world's oil reserves makes for remarkably favorable, not to mention dependable, collateral.

Initially, Saudi Arabia contracted to provide six hundred thousand barrels of oil a day. This level dropped to four hundred thousand barrels a day in later years. Edwards admitted that for the Saudis the use of oil meant that the contract was effectively an off-balance-sheet transaction: it did not go through the Saudi treasury. Edwards also confirmed that one of the main attractions for the Saudis in this unique arrangement was British flexibility. "The British were much more flexible than the Americans," he said. "The Americans went through the Foreign Military Sales system, which has congressional law behind it. If the customers get out of line and they fail to pay the money, then they are cut off. In this country, it was quite flexible; sometimes the oil flow and the associated monies that were received by selling it were ahead, at other times it fell behind."

The phenomenal amount of money generated from the sale of oil comes through DESO, before being paid to British Aerospace. Edwards admitted that the government does charge a little commission for administering the contract, money that attracted the attention of the treasury as it built up a considerable surplus. That surplus proved highly significant when Britain signed the Ottawa Treaty on fragmentation weapons,* which impacted on the JP233, an airfield denial weapon that had been banned under the Convention.† The JP233 had been sold legitimately to the Royal Saudi Air Force, but Saudi Arabia didn't sign the Convention. This created a problem,

---

*The Ottawa Convention on the Prohibition of the Use, Stockpiling, Production and Transfer of Anti-Personnel Mines and on their Destruction, as the Protocol was properly known, went into effect on March 1, 1999. It was signed by nearly three quarters of the world's nations and came into force faster than any other multilateral global agreement. Participants include all of the Western hemisphere, except the United States and Cuba, and all NATO countries except the United States and Turkey.

†The Hunting JP233 airfield denial weapon was a bomblet dispenser that was originally developed as a means to destroy and prevent the repair of Warsaw Pact airfields. The pod was in two sections, each carrying a different submunition: the rear section carried SG357 anti-runway weapons, which penetrated the runway surface before exploding and cratering the runway. The forward portion carried HB876 area denial mines that were scattered around the damaged area and created a hazard for any repair teams. The JP233 submunitions were later proscribed under the Ottawa Protocol that bans the use of landmines. The weapon was used in the Gulf War in its intended role, airfield attack, and it was extensively used by RAF Tornado strike aircraft early in the air war to disrupt the operation of Iraqi airfields; two 6.5-meter-long JP233s could be fixed to the bottom of a Tornado. However, the strikes were at low level and were extremely hazardous to the Tornado crews.

because if British engineers supported the Saudi JP233, as was contracted under Al-Yamamah, then they could have gone to jail for supporting a country that was violating the agreement that Britain had signed. Edwards speculated that Bandar helped arrange the deal whereby Britain bought back the Saudi JP233s, which were destroyed and replaced with Paveway bombs."* The cost of this exercise was met by DESO, using the commission surplus accrued over the years.

The Al-Yamamah deal Mrs. Thatcher negotiated placed British Aerospace as the prime contractor for the provision of any other military equipment purchased for Saudi Arabia. "By supporting not just the British aircraft but the American aircraft too," said Edwards, "Al-Yamamah was an integral part of supporting the Saudi Air Force in total." He stressed that DESO and British Aerospace have thus ended up supporting all Saudi aircraft—the Peace Shield program—all funded through Al-Yamamah.† Edwards concluded, "In other words, the value of this stream of income and what it is used for has drifted a little bit over the years into things other than it was originally destined for."[31]

In effect, Al-Yamamah would become a backdoor method of covertly buying U.S. arms for the kingdom; military hardware purchases that would not be visible to Congress. It specifically had been structured to provide an unparalleled degree of flexibility whereby the Saudis could purchase military equipment under the imprimatur of DESO and British Aerospace.

The ingenious diversity of Al-Yamamah, together with the British government's discretion and liberal approach to a unique finance deal, largely founded on the undisputed collateral of the huge Saudi oil reserves, could explain the financial black holes assumed by a suspicious media to be evidence of commissions. Many press allegations were predicated on large discrepancies in the cost of military hardware; for example, the cost of ten helicopters may be X amount, yet when the balance sheets are examined it becomes apparent that a far greater amount has been spent in that financial

---

*The Paveway Laser Guided Bomb is essentially a one-thousand-pound general purpose bomb with a seeker head fitted to the nose and with movable guide fins fitted to the tail. It is sometimes referred to as a "smart" weapon as the precision-guidance package.

†The Peace Shield program was a U.S.-managed kingdom-wide command, control, and communications air defense system program for the Royal Saudi Air Force that was critical to the defense of Saudi Arabia.

year. This prompts the question: "Where is the money going?" Left to develop its own conclusions, the press assumed a gigantic Arab slush fund. Another explanation is that although the British sold the Saudis ten helicopters for X amount, they also purchased, on Saudi Arabia's behalf, technological and military hardware from other countries.

Although Al-Yamamah constitutes a highly unconventional way of doing business, its lucrative spin-offs are the by-products of a wholly political objective: a Saudi political objective and a British political objective. Al-Yamamah is, first and foremost, a political contract. Negotiated at the height of the Cold War, its unique structure has enabled the Saudis to purchase weapons from around the globe to fund the fight against Communism. Al-Yamamah money can be found in the clandestine purchase of Russian ordnance used in the expulsion of Qaddafi's troops from Chad. It can also be traced to arms bought from Egypt and other countries, and sent to the Mujahideen in Afghanistan fighting the Soviet occupying forces.

The strategic benefits of the Al-Yamamah off-balance-sheet transactions were crucial to the defense and protection of Saudi Arabia. Arguably, its consummate flexibility is needed because of inevitable opposition to Saudi arms purchases in Congress. Sources close to Bandar explained that, "As a nation, for example, if the Saudis wanted to buy ten Super Puma helicopters, and the Ministry of Defense budget is X amount, the Ministry of Finance will say this is what you've been allocated this year. It means that you have to defer this purchase until next year." Ordinarily, deferral would cause little difficulty, but when the U.S. Congress is factored into the equation, time suddenly becomes of the essence. Past experience shows that any delay would give AIPAC the time to organize a campaign against the sale.

The oil barter arrangement circumvented such bureaucracy. "What Al-Yamamah did, because it is oil for services, is to say: Okay. Al-Yamamah picks up the tab; Saudi Arabia will sign with the French or whoever, and Britain pays them on their behalf. So suddenly now the Saudis have an operational weapons system complete with its support that doesn't reflect on Al-Yamamah as a project. Therefore, if Saudi Arabia wants some services from the Americans, or some weapon systems that they have to buy now, otherwise Congress will object to it later, and they can't get it from their current defense budget, then they simply tell Al-Yamamah, 'You divert that money.'"

In a remarkable insight into the British government's desire to secure the Al-Yamamah deal, even at the expense of its own operational capability, it was revealed that the first airplanes given to the Saudis came directly from the Royal Air Force inventory. Downing Street evidently thought the Saudi deal was so important that an erosion of the RAF's front-line strength was perfectly acceptable. "They trained Saudi pilots and a small cadre of technicians, and within a few months the first Tornados were flying operational sorties in the kingdom. And the contract was signed a few months after that, once the details had been negotiated." The British attitude to the sale played a significant part in the Saudi decision. "That was another reason why the Saudi government went to the British, because they were willing to deliver, move fast, and be there."

Al-Yamamah was a utopian arrangement, under which everyone involved was a winner, but none more so than Saudi Arabia. Military requirements could now be met without the consent of the Saudi treasury, and American weapons could be purchased under the radar of Congress.

It is unfortunate that Saudi Arabia has had to resort to this subterfuge to circumvent Congress. Bandar has stressed the value of commercial relationships between nations, saying, "If you look at history, you find relationships between nations that have no commercial element to it will last an average of ten to fifteen years and then collapse. And you will find that relations between nations that have strong commercial aspects to them last for centuries; because commercial interests, particularly if they work both ways, make each side protect that relationship in order to improve it, add to it, and so on. If you have nothing to protect, then the first wind that comes— it will fall apart. So we are looking at a period, when the military requirement, the political requirement, and the commercial requirement all met at one point." This very strong message from Bandar clearly underpins Saudi Arabia's relationship with the United Kingdom, which saw its first sound commercial links constructed in the 1960s. In contrast, whereas the kingdom has always favored the United States as its prime defense contractor, and has worked assiduously at developing a bilateral relationship with it, resistance to contracts on Capitol Hill has shaken its foundations from time to time.

There is one final point concerning Al-Yamamah on which Bandar remains extremely clear. He feels very strongly that when the kingdom went to war in 1991 against Iraq, with the United States and the other allies, the strike capabilities of the RSAF were of critical importance to the Saudi contribution and the outcome of that war. The Tornados were at the heart of its offensive. The prince is convinced that eviction of Saddam Hussein from the oil fields of Kuwait and the removal of the menacing Iraqi presence from the borders of Saudi Arabia vindicate whatever allegations of corruption were propagated by Al-Yamamah.

Ultimately, the Kingdom engaged in its arms deal with the United Kingdom to secure its own defense; when it counted, when the kingdom was under threat, the Tornados came through for the RSAF.

The year 1985 saw significant developments in the Middle East. In the Iran-Iraq war, the two sides began to exchange indiscriminately launched missiles in what became known as the War of the Cities. Describing that period, Bandar explained that the Iranians were attacking Baghdad and the Iraqis were attacking Tehran. About the same time, the South Yemen government was given Scud missiles by the Russians, and the Russians and Cubans moved into Somalia, Ethiopia, and Aden. Saudi Arabia was being squeezed from every side.

A desire to acquire ballistic missiles can stem from either political or military needs, and even if they are never fired, ballistic missiles can confer strategic status on countries that possess them. By mid-1985, there were at least nine other countries in the Middle East with missile forces; even such small powers as South Yemen and Kuwait had missiles.[32] Saudi Arabia, however, had none.

With Reagan's message to King Fahd that he could not secure the 1985 Saudi request for F-15 aircraft and Lance missiles, Bandar's instructions from Fahd were brief—get them elsewhere. But where? The only country Bandar knew to be selling such weapons, apart from the Russians, was China.

The Tornado strike/attack bomber purchased by Saudi Arabia under Al-Yamamah.

Since the outbreak of the Iran-Iraq conflict, China had been supplying Iraq with weapons. By 1983, the value of the Chinese-Iraqi arms deals was approaching $3.6 billion. In support of its then ally Iraq, Saudi Arabia granted the People's Republic of China access to its territory as an indirect route for the delivery of Chinese weapons to Iraq.[33] By 1985, however, China was also selling arms to Iran.

Understanding perhaps better than most that a country's actions are dictated by national interests, the Saudis were quick to recognize that no amount of force or persuasion would deter China from selling its arms to Iran. It was all about economics and politics. Bandar saw his opportunity. He explained, "I went to Secretary of State George Shultz and said, 'Would it be okay if we go to China and make them an offer they can't refuse—that we will buy all the weapons they were going to sell to Iran and give them to Iraq?" Shultz thought that it was a great idea and unwittingly gave Bandar the cover he needed to go to China and deal with the Chinese. In effect, the prince successfully employed Operation Torch—a U.S.-Saudi operation designed to stop weapons going to Iran—as a subterfuge to mask his own approach to the Chinese to acquire an armory of Chinese DF-3A Dongfeng or "East Wind" ballistic missiles, known in the West as the CSS-2. The situation was not without a degree of irony, as Bandar was keen to point out. "I came and asked my friends, the Americans, for missiles—a ground-to-ground missile with an eighty-mile range called the Lance. But we were told no, because it's a threat to somebody [Israel]. So we went and got a sixteen-hundred-mile-range missile. Now is that a threat or isn't it?"[34]

Bandar decided to approach the Chinese ambassador in Washington, despite the fact that Saudi Arabia had no diplomatic relations with the Chinese and openly recognized Taiwan. "The ambassador was a little stunned," Bandar admitted. A month later the Chinese and the Saudis opened a dialogue. Numerous meeting places were suggested, including Beijing and Riyadh. In the end, the Saudis suggested Pakistan, which was accepted. Bandar and the Chinese ambassador agreed that the cover for their meeting would be the sale of petrochemicals, and the prince took with him a huge delegation of petrochemical specialists from Saudi Arabia's biggest company SAVAK. Under this guise, the Saudis and the Chinese met twice.

When Bandar told his Chinese opposite number that his objective was to buy both ground-to-ground missiles for the kingdom and those arms the Chinese were selling to Iran, the Chinese representative, the minister of foreign affairs, explained that he would need to consult with his leadership. The problem then became how to relay the answer to Bandar. Time was of the essence and secure communications were difficult. Bandar told them, "I cannot fly to Pakistan every time you want to talk." Finally, it was agreed that if the Chinese ambassador in Washington told Bandar, "You are invited to Beijing," it would mean that they were interested. However, if he told Bandar, "It's not the right time to come to Beijing," then that would mean no deal.

He soon received an invitation to the Chinese capital.

Arriving in Beijing, having first flown to Hong Kong, the prince was driven straight to the official guest houses. His delegation had been told not to open the curtains so as not to give away their presence. The next morning, however, Bandar opened the curtains to look at the garden. To his surprise, a couple of cars pulled up to the next villa. It was an Iranian delegation wearing mullahs' headgear. Bandar, of course, had known that the Iranians were getting weapons from the Chinese, but seeing the mullahs arriving next door was alarming nonetheless.

Bandar's initial negotiations involved intense interrogation. He was repeatedly asked, "How dare you ask us to sell you arms if you still have a relationship with Taiwan and no relationship with us?"

Late twentieth-century politics meant that to deal with the Chinese was to subjugate any relationship with Taiwan. You could not have a relationship with both countries. Yet despite the intransigence of the People's Republic, Bandar struck back candidly with the single right response. Saudi Arabia had a need that could not be fulfilled elsewhere. The only options were the Soviet Union or China. Saudi Arabia trusted China more than the Soviet Union.

"Need means opportunity and it depends on how big a vision you have," Bandar told the Chinese. "If you are looking at this as tit-for-tat, then I guess we are not going to have a deal, and I will have to leave. You should look at it as an opportunity; a friend in need is a friend indeed." Bandar intimated that by answering that need and helping Saudi Arabia, other developments might emerge, He insisted, however, that he had no authority to discuss anything other than weapons.

Bandar then resorted to a tactic over the seemingly intractable problem of Saudi relations with Taiwan that he was to employ consistently on both official and personal levels throughout his diplomatic career. "If we sold our friends cheaply," he said to his Chinese host, "why would you want to be our friends?"

Referring now to the separate, multibillion-dollar deal the desert kingdom was prepared to strike with China in order to redirect arms away from Iran and into Iraq, Bandar said, "By the way, I would also like to buy a couple of billion dollars worth of weapons that you are going to send to Iran." He explained to his hosts that if the Chinese agreed to this proposal, then they would be helping Saudi Arabia and the entire Arab world. He also stressed that both the Americans and the British would be happy with the arrangement. He concluded, "Plus, you will get hard currency and good politics out of it—therefore, everybody wins."

After a protracted ten-hour silence, the prince was asked to see the Chinese prime minister, Xao Zhiang. At that time Chairman Chao Ping was very concerned about the Chinese policy of nonalliance and the five principles of peaceful co-existence,* so the prince had taken pains to stress Saudi Arabia's agreement to those principles. Outlining Saudi Arabia's nonaggressive position, explaining the deterrent role missiles would play, Bandar pressed his case.

Yet the issue of Taiwan still loomed; it would have to be countered. Bandar took the offensive, stressing that this deal, if it was consummated, would enhance the possibility of improving Sino-Saudi relations. The prime minister, however, remained unconvinced, reiterating that China refused to normalize its relationship with America until and unless the United States broke its diplomatic relationship with Taiwan.

Agreeing that China had done the right thing because both the United States and China were superpowers, Bandar argued that Saudi Arabia was a small country; it was not a superpower, nor was it antagonistic. He reasoned that the kingdom should not be measured by the same standards, concluding, "In the final analysis I think you did the right thing with America, but that is not the way to deal with us."

This statement evidently impressed the Chinese. Bandar was informed that Chairman Chao Ping had approved the deal personally. China respected Saudi Arabia, he was told, and wanted to conduct business so long as Saudi Arabia kept in mind that they hoped to normalize their relationship and hoped it would influence the kingdom's relationship with Taiwan at the right time.

Bandar was stunned and speechless. He quickly returned to Saudi Arabia

---

*The five principles of peaceful co-existence that accord with the policy of nonalignment are: mutual respect for each other's territorial integrity and sovereignty; mutual nonaggression; nonintervention in the other's internal affairs; equality and mutual benefit, and peaceful co-existence.

to brief King Fahd. When Fahd had first instructed Bandar to acquire missiles for the kingdom, he said not to tell the Americans, but neither was Bandar to lie to them. With Fahd's approval, Bandar now informed Secretary of State Shultz of the agreement by which the Kingdom of Saudi Arabia would purchase Chinese weapons destined for Iran. Bandar maintains that he never lied to his American friends—he told them what he intended to do [buy weapons destined for Iran] and he did it. He simply omitted any mention of a further purchase of missiles for the kingdom.

While Bandar did not need the help of military specialists to ensure the smooth purchase of the weapons intended for Iran, he would need their help in assessing and negotiating for the missiles destined for the kingdom. Fearing that the presence of Saudi military experts might alert the United States to Saudi plans, Bandar preemptively suggested to the Americans that he did in fact need a specialist in air defense and another specialist in artillery to help with the purchase of missiles for Iran. The Americans quickly agreed.

According to Bandar, his second visit to China was semi-open, in the sense that he went with the petrochemical delegation and spent three days visiting plants and petrochemical installations, and receiving briefings. Eventually, he was taken with his two specialist officers to see the Terracotta Warriors. It was only then that they were able to discuss the missiles.

Hours of negotiation with the Chinese military followed, during which it soon became apparent to Bandar that the Chinese did not have a short-range missile or Scud-like equivalent. They did have medium-range missiles. He was stunned by their sheer size. But size was the least of it. He found it eerie, almost surreal, "I was in the middle of Communist officers and generals. And I had spent my life fighting Communism."

Chinese CSS-2
ballistic missiles

During these meetings, it became evident to Bandar and his team that the Chinese had designed this type of missile to carry nuclear warheads. Bandar maintains that they paid the Chinese to modify the missile to carry a conventional warhead. Thus, the Chinese converted a nuclear missile into a conventional weapon.

Once the negotiations were completed, Bandar had to address the problem of getting the missiles into the kingdom. Their transport and housing all had to be undertaken without the knowledge of the Americans, yet the Prince still had to meet King Fahd's explicit remit that the Americans should not be lied to. The Saudis recognized that the American reaction to news that the Saudis had brokered a deal with the Chinese would be explosive.

The decision was made that once the missiles had been safely installed in the desert, then, and only then, would an announcement be made. A media event would be created whereby Prince Sultan would announce that King Fahd had been to visit the strategic missile force that had just been acquired. Timing was everything. Only after the missiles were in place would it be prudent to publicize their purchase. It would be explained that the missiles were designed to form a major deterrent, contributing to peace in the region; no one would dare to attack the kingdom if they knew that its missiles could reach anywhere in response. Bandar was very clear on this, "That was the real value of the weapon; if no one knew about it, it could scarcely be a deterrent, and we certainly didn't want to use it for first strike."

Having purchased the missiles, there remained a fundamental question: how could the massive silos needed to house the weapons be built in the middle of the desert without arousing American suspicion? Bandar came up with an imaginative ruse: he reminded the Americans that the largest Saudi armament depot was very near to Riyadh. He then explained that King Fahd was concerned that should there ever be a military coup and the armaments depot fall into the wrong hands, it could be very dangerous. So it had been decided to move it as far away as possible from Riyadh. The Americans thought this was a very shrewd move and were happy to support it.

Foreseeing that the installation of the missiles would involve a huge influx of Chinese personnel into the kingdom, Bandar also needed to create a pretext for their presence. Yet again he approached the Americans, suggesting that just to make sure that the Chinese wouldn't go back on their promise not to sell weapons to Iran, Saudi Arabia was proposing to give them the contract to build the new armament depot. He reasoned that by building this facility, the extra hard currency and investment would help cement their support. Again, the Americans had no objection, and Bandar stressed that when the complex was built, sure enough, it contained depots for ammunition; he had fulfilled King Fahd's strict criteria to tell the truth—but not the whole truth.

One of the greatest risks of detection was the threat posed by American "eyes in the sky." Tasked with identifying the time scale of the orbit of any American satellites, Bandar admitted that the risk was that it might give away what the Saudis were doing, and he could not afford to expose his government to complicity in espionage. Bandar went to his contacts in the U.S. National Security Agency (NSA) and led them to believe that Iraq had passed information to Saudi Arabia about a huge buildup of Iranians south of Iraq, between Kuwait and Basra. Under the guise of needing urgent confirmation that this information was true, thus enabling a decision to be made on strengthening Saudi forces in that area, he told the agents that Riyadh was highly concerned and urgently required America's help.

The NSA told Bandar that he would have the information by the very next day.

The prince insisted that he needed the information immediately. When they still refused, Bandar feigned concern that if he told Riyadh that he had not been given the satellite intelligence information, they would think that the NSA was hiding something from them. After all, Iran was the common enemy.

It worked. An intelligence agent quickly explained, "The reason why it must be tomorrow has nothing to do with the strength of our resolve to help you, but it takes twelve hours for our satellites to go over that place, and they just passed, so we need another twelve hours, plus time to download." After thanking him for his candor, Bandar immediately passed this information back to Riyadh.

With this intelligence on U.S. satellites, the kingdom managed to keep the acquisition and delivery of the Chinese missiles under wraps for almost two years, no mean feat for any country, and especially one in which the United States has such a vested interest. However, the secret broke on March 4, 1988, when the *Washington Post* ran with a story that Saudi Arabia had purchased Chinese CSS-2 ballistic missiles with a range of over of fifteen hundred miles and that the missiles were capable of carrying nuclear warheads. The architect of that deal, Bandar, was now firmly in the hot seat.

The missiles had been detected after one of the Saudi transport trucks had broken down and, in the confusion, security forces had been sent to protect it. The movement of those security forces had attracted the attention of analysts poring over satellite pictures. When these images were cross-checked with American databases, it soon became evident that what they were seeing was a Chinese DF-3 missile.

Half of the missiles ordered from the Chinese were already in the country before this discovery was made. Unaware that the DF-3 missiles didn't carry nuclear warheads, the United States went into a state of high alert. The deal between Saudi Arabia and the Chinese had been struck at the same time that Russia and the United States had been negotiating final agreements for scrapping medium-range nuclear weapons. Embarrassment, resentment, and anger at the Saudi deception permeated Capitol Hill. William Safire wrote critically, "The Chinese-Saudi missile deal stunned Washington, which mistakenly thought that neither Beijing nor Riyadh would alter the balance of power in the Middle East without checking with the U.S."[35]

Even more embarrassing to the Americans was the involvement of the hitherto totally cooperative Bandar, who, after all, was so close to CIA director Bill Casey. As the Saudi ambassador to Washington, the prince's role in nurturing Sino-Saudi relations and getting the deal off the ground without informing the United States was as extraordinary as it was discomforting inside the Beltway.

Under U.S. law, the discovery that another country has acquired a nuclear capability must be reported to Congress within forty-eight hours. The sale of Chinese missiles with nuclear capability threw the administration into a panic. Secretary Shultz was outside the country on a major visit to Moscow, Europe, and the Middle East, and was not due to return until the weekend. The White House decided to start the forty-eight-hour countdown from that Friday, writing off Saturday and Sunday as the weekend. Monday then became the final twenty-four hour window before Congress had to be informed.

Coincidentally, perhaps, the Chinese foreign minister was due to visit Shultz on Monday. Having completed negotiations and passed responsibility for the missiles to his brother, Prince Khalid, Bandar was no longer involved in the deal. However, as a precaution against news of the missile deal breaking before installation was complete, the Prince had agreed with the Chinese ambassador that they should both adhere to the same line: "I understand your concern, but this is a military matter and I am only a diplomat. I will ask my government and come back to you with an answer."

That Sunday, March 6, 1988, Bandar received a call from Richard Murphy, assistant secretary of state for the Middle East. Murphy was brief. "I have something to discuss with you," he said. "Can I stop by for a few minutes?"

When Murphy arrived with his wife and children, Bandar said, he could see that "Ambassador Murphy looked unwell and was agitated."

Murphy asked, "Can we talk alone for a second?"

They adjourned to another room when suddenly Murphy exploded, "Nuclear weapons for f*** sake!?"

Angrily, he handed the prince a yellow envelope. Bandar recalled, "I felt an instant ulcer!"

The stress of the moment was intense. Bandar remembered saying to himself, *Think, think, think!* Trying to buy time and remember the statement he and the Chinese ambassador had agreed upon, Bandar blurted out, "What nuclear weapons?"

"Bandar, we've been friends for a long time," Murphy said, "Let's not B.S. each other."

Bandar replied calmly, "Of course I won't B.S. you; what are you talking about?"

"Look, we know you have DF-3 missiles in Saudi Arabia with nuclear warheads."

"Hold it," Bandar said. "I understand what you are saying and I will pass it to my government and ask for an explanation because I am not a military man, I am a diplomat. But I can assure you of one thing: whatever it is that you are talking about, Saudi Arabia didn't have nuclear weapons in the past, does not have them now, and does not plan to have them. About that, I can give you categorical assurance."

At this point the ambassador showed the prince the satellite images of the missiles. Yet Bandar held rigidly to the line he had agreed with the Chinese, saying, "I will have to consult with my government first, and I'll get back to you."

"Well, let me tell you something." Murphy replied, "As we are talking now, the Chinese foreign minister is having dinner with Secretary Shultz and he will ask him the same question, so you have until Monday morning. We need an answer before Monday morning; otherwise, the clock ticks and we'll have to inform Congress. I hope you realize how serious this issue is."[36]

Bandar later observed to friends, "The reason they changed the Chinese foreign minister's schedule was so that we couldn't talk to each other. They deliberately got the Chinese minister to Shultz's house at the same moment that Richard Murphy came to see me, and the Chinese foreign minister, bless him, said exactly the same thing, 'I am foreign minister; I will have to ask Beijing, and we'll get the answers back to you.'"

As soon as Murphy had left, Bandar made a preplanned call to King Fahd, informative, yet at the same time designed for the ears of the CIA. After the usual preliminaries, the prince casually told Fahd, "Our friends in America have some reports that we have nuclear weapons systems in Saudi Arabia. I assured them that we don't and they will have the formal answer from Your Majesty and the government."

There was a short pause while the king gathered his thoughts as to what his nephew needed before replying, "Nuclear weapons—I wish! But tell them if they are willing to sell any nuclear weapons for our defenses, then we would be very appreciative and we would be happy to negotiate immediately." Fahd then moved on to another topic altogether, adding, "By the way, there is something concerning Egypt and the Palestinians that I have to discuss with you. Why don't you come over and discuss it with me?"

No sooner had the prince organized his aircraft for immediate departure than U.S officials, having digested the content of his phone call, informed Bandar that the president needed to see him the next morning at 8:45—fifteen minutes before Reagan was to meet with the Chinese foreign minister. Unable to refuse the president, Bandar duly called his staff and delayed his flight.

That night, however, Bandar and the Chinese ambassador found time to have a quiet drink together.

Pointing to a photograph taken on the morning of his visit to the White House to meet with President Reagan, Bandar said, "President Reagan said to me, 'We understand that you people have acquired nuclear missiles. That is not acceptable to us, and by law I have to inform Congress. I would like an official answer on this issue, and I hope we can work out a way to defuse this crisis.'" Bandar again pointed to the photograph and said, "If you look at the picture, you will see that he had cards in his hand. I was looking at his cards, and because the print was big, I could read them. So I stopped him before he got to the last point that his staff had put for him, which read, 'Or else!' That solved the whole crisis."

Bandar explained, "They had outlined the points the president was to make, and the final point was: you have nuclear weapons and we want you to dismantle them, send them back, or destroy them. It was a clear demand, so I thought quickly that if I could stop him before he reached that final point, then I could prevent having to relay a powerful ultimatum to King

Fahd and also have the chance to get instructions from my government. So when I could see he was nearing this final point, I said, 'Mr. President, may I interrupt for a second?' He was such a genteel man that he paused and said, 'Yes.'"

Explaining that King Fahd had acquired the Chinese missiles purely as a deterrent, Bandar stressed, "I can assure you categorically that the kingdom does not have nuclear missiles." The prince then asked the president if he could return to Saudi Arabia so that he could bring back a letter from King Fahd confirming that Saudi Arabia didn't have nuclear weapons.

The president did not finish reading the rest of his briefing. He simply observed, "Well, I don't think we can ask for more than this from our friends."

As Bandar shook hands with the president, Secretary Baker interjected, saying, "Mr. President, I need to emphasize one thing. Prince Bandar, we have been friends for a long time, and this is very, very serious."

"I understand that," Bandar replied, "that is why I am going to leave right now to go to Saudi Arabia."

As he left the meeting, State Department officials attempted to reinforce the message it had provided in the president's notes, but the prince brushed them off, saying, "I met with the president and he gave me a message for his Majesty. I am not negotiating with anyone else; I will go back home, pass a message to my boss, and bring back an answer for the president—period."

En route to the airport, Bandar got calls from both Pentagon and State Department officials asking for urgent meetings with him, which he promptly declined. He flew to Saudi Arabia and later returned to Washington with a letter that categorically denied any purchase of nuclear weapons. It confirmed the purchase of ground-to-ground missiles from China as a result of the congressional decision not to sell the kingdom U.S. Lance missiles, but gave assurances that they were never intended to be used offensively. It was made clear, however, that if attacked, the kingdom would defend itself.

Reagan warmly greets Bandar—his Saudi ally in the worldwide fight against Communism.

American reaction was fierce and swift. The U.S. government directed Saudi Arabia to dismantle the missiles, send them back, or permit American access to them for inspections, which was unacceptable to the Saudis. A vexed Richard Armitage, assistant secretary of defense for international security affairs, seethed at Bandar, saying, "I want to congratulate you. This is the law of unintended consequences. You have put Saudi Arabia squarely in the targeting package of the Israelis. You are now number one on the Israeli hit parade. If the balloon goes up anywhere in the Middle East, you're going to get hit first."[37]

The administration issued a statement saying, "The acquisition of such a system is not in the interests of peace and stability in the region." Congressional reaction was sharper; fifty U.S. senators and 187 members of the House of Representatives signed a letter of protest, which stated, "Our government must make unequivocal its absolute opposition to the presence of Chinese missiles, which represents a new and grave threat to the peace of the region."[38] In essence, though, they were presented with a fait accompli.

The sense of shock in Washington at the time is perhaps best illustrated by a story related by Secretary of State Colin Powell just ten days before he announced his resignation in November 2004. Asked for any little cameo pieces or tales about Bandar, he recalled, "I have an anecdote about the day we caught him buying missiles in China."

Powell recalled how when the news broke—he was then assistant to the president for national security affairs (more commonly known as the national security adviser)—he immediately went over to Bandar's house and yelled, "What are you doing? Why are you doing this?" He told Bandar that they had maps and pictures of him in front of a Chinese military factory and said, "You guys have done something really stupid and you'd better hope the Israelis don't bomb it." But he added, "I don't think they will, because it's not a very good system you've bought, but nevertheless you bought it. Really dumb—but you got it! We hope you and your missiles will be very happy together!"[39]

Israeli Prime Minister Shamir was in the United States at the time the news broke and made a public statement that Israel would not wait to be attacked; if threatened, it would take preemptive measures. That very quickly got Saudi attention.

Saudi Arabia asked the United States to send a discreet message to Israel that the CSS-2s would not be directed against Israel.[40] In a separate conversation with Powell, Bandar made the Saudi position very clear, saying, "I'm just telling you, if you could pass this to the Israelis, the message is that we do not intend to use these for first strike."

This message about Saudi intentions, or lack thereof, went unheeded. Just weeks later, Bandar received a call from Prince Sultan explaining that Tabuk air base radars were picking up Israeli airplanes flying near Aqaba. It was believed that the aircraft might be grouping for an attack on Saudi Arabia, and Bandar was to ask the Americans to intercede quickly so that it did not get out of hand.

Bandar questioned Sultan about the Saudi position should they attack; his reply was grim. The king had ordered the whole Saudi Air Force to mobilize and to fly to the north, fully loaded and fully armed. He stressed that Saudi Arabia did not want to start a confrontation, but if attacked, it would have no option but to engage, and that would include using the Chinese missiles.

Bandar emphasized that the preparation and operational readiness of aircraft on Saudi air bases should not be hidden from the American pilots and advisers, as that would carry a much more convincing message than anything that he might tell the White House. Sultan confirmed that it was already being addressed.

Bandar immediately called Gen. Powell and went straight to his home. By the time he arrived, Powell had been informed by U.S intelligence of the Israeli movements and Saudi mobilization.

The general greeted Bandar, saying, "Didn't I tell you—you thought you were safer, now look what you've done to yourselves."

"General, we have been friends for a long time," Bandar replied. "Here is a very simple message from Saudi Arabia. We have no intention of attacking anybody with these missiles. We know Israel's capabilities. It would be suicidal for us to attack them and cause some damage, because then they would destroy everything we have. Why take us from the category of not wanting to engage to a category where we have no option but to?"

He concluded, "I can assure you that if we are attacked by the Israelis, Saudi Arabia will have no option but to retaliate—come what may. My government would not survive an attack by Israel without retaliating. So, for God's sake, tell the Israelis that."

Gesturing Bandar to wait, Powell disappeared into his study. When he returned, he said, "The Israelis are saying, 'Why are the Saudis jumpy? We are just doing night exercises.'"

Bandar cut him off, "Well, we are just doing night exercises, too!"

"Okay, let's cut the bullshit. The president wants Israel and Saudi Arabia to stand down; he doesn't want anybody to attack anybody."

"You have no doubt about it with me," Bandar responded. "But I want an assurance that the other side will not attack. I can give you an assurance that we are not going to do it unless we are attacked."

Convinced that this confrontation between Israel and Saudi Arabia had taken the kingdom to the brink of war, Bandar endeavored to assure his American allies that the Chinese long-range missiles were non-nuclear. He reiterated that they had been acquired for defensive purposes only, in response to the threat from Iran, and following America's rejection of its request for Lance short-range missiles. Israel reluctantly accepted the kingdom's assurances, doubtless reinforced by intelligence assessments of the missile's limited military effectiveness and lack of accuracy. The covert purchase of the missiles precipitated tensions in the U.S.-Saudi relationship, and the political impact of the introduction of the missiles into the region was significant. "The Saudi decision to purchase the Chinese missiles represented a significant break with past weapons procurement strategies and, in the proverbial single stroke, changed the strategic equation in the region."[41] Perhaps the greatest change to the strategic equation was the range of the CSS-2, which was estimated at two thousand miles. Even modified to carry a heavier conventional payload, they were reported to be the biggest and longest-range missiles outside the armories of the major nuclear armed nations,[42] bringing countries such as Israel, Iran, and the Soviet Union within easy reach of the Saudi capabilities, as well as Somalia, Ethiopia, Sudan, Turkey, Afghanistan, Pakistan, and western India.

The Chinese missile deal at once decreased the kingdom's reliance on the Western armaments umbrella, moved toward the creation of a level playing field between Arab and Israeli armaments, and increased access to the Persian Gulf for the People's Republic of China. More significantly, it marked a singular change to the way Saudis had traditionally operated in the West. In any event, the Saudis now possessed a powerful and relatively sophisticated missile, perhaps most valued for its psychological and prestige value. Bandar, the architect of the CSS-2 transaction, admits, "The psychology behind [the missile] was more important" than its capability.[43]

The surreptitious purchase of missiles with three times the range of the most advanced missiles operational in the region at that time, without so much as a furtive glance in America's direction for consent, was perhaps the most proactive and bold move made by the Saudi kingdom since the U.S.-Saudi friendship was first initiated. The press noted that "instead of quietly apologizing for deceiving Washington and then lying low, the Saudis are assertively taking credit for pulling off a coup."[44] Speaking more narrowly, Powell said, "Bandar, for his part, privately expressed glee at Washington's discomfort, indicating that such developments were the consequence of congressional interventions in arms sales."[45]

In an interview with Charlie Rose on CBS News *Nightwatch,* Bandar simply and doggedly defended Saudi Arabia's missile acquisition, saying, "I didn't go to China to thrill the Americans or to upset them either. Had we gotten American missiles from you, we would not have had to go somewhere else for them." Changing political message midstream, Bandar took a direct blow at Congress and their loyalties: "I think the mutual lesson for each of us is that we must be less emotional when we discuss those kinds of issues; be more logical and see what will serve our national interests."[46]

The Saudi refusal to dismantle or return the missiles, together with their decision not to permit an American inspection of the weapons, resulted in Secretary Shultz's cutting ties with Bandar. Instructions were issued that no American officials should contact, talk to, or deal with the prince; U.S. diplomatic ties were effectively frozen, the single exception being the desk officer for Saudi Arabia. Bandar's response was simple, "I'm sorry about that, but you guys have just given me a vacation," and he went off to Aspen.

Within two weeks, though, trouble had flared up in Lebanon, and Bandar was asked to return for talks in Washington. Shultz continued to shun Bandar, who admitted that he could understand why Shultz was hurt. But, from his perspective, Bandar felt that he hadn't lied to him. He said, "Everything I told him, I did; and what I didn't tell him, I didn't have to tell him." Aware that it was a fine line he had been treading, the prince confessed that it was sometimes pushing it to the limit.

The ambiguity of the Chinese missile deal remains to this day, evident particularly from the exaggerated disparity between accounts of the deal and, more importantly, in the numbers. According to various versions, the number of missiles purchased varies anywhere from twenty-five to one hundred. Similarly, the number of missile launchers bought was estimated between nine and fifteen. The cost of each missile was speculated to be about $100 million.[47] Very little is known about the quantity, cost, accuracy, or—perhaps most interesting—the location of the missiles. Israeli intelligence puts their deployment at al-Sulaiyil (500 kilometers south of Riyadh) and al-Jaffer (100 kilometers south of Riyadh).[48] Yet their exact location remains unconfirmed. So too does their effectiveness. Propelled by liquid fuel, which lengthens preparation times, the East Wind missiles require fixed hardened silos and are believed to have a relatively ineffective guidance system, with a CEP (Circular Error of Probability)* or accuracy of around two kilometers.[49]

When questioned as to the number of missiles purchased, Bandar indicated that it was still sensitive information, but confirmed that it was not a high number. This would tend to be supported by Bandar's disclosure that the cost of the deal, including the construction of the silos and armament depot was in the region of $3 billion. This would indicate that, unless the kingdom acquired the missiles at a lower unit cost than the $100 million predicted by the experts, Saudi Arabia purchased only twenty-five to thirty missiles. Bandar also confirmed that the accuracy of the missiles had since been improved by indigenous modifications.

Despite the shockwave that reverberated throughout Washington at that time, the rationale of the Saudi leadership could not be refuted. In King Fahd's own words, "It is not strange for the kingdom to purchase defense weapons to defend its beliefs and country."[50] This was particularly apposite given the turbulent events that had unfolded in the region: the year 1986 saw an Iranian plane, packed with explosives, land on Saudi soil, an incident the Iranian leadership subsequently "regretted"; the year 1987 witnessed the storming of the Saudi embassy in Tehran, followed a week later by the tragic deaths of four hundred two pilgrims, eighty-five of them Saudi citizens caught up in violence incited by Iranian radicals attempting to storm the Holy Mosque in Mecca during hajj. In an interview on American television at this time, Bandar stated unequivocally, "There are two things we don't compromise on: our faith and our security."[51] King Fahd observed acerbically, "We are buying weapons, not principles."[52]

Despite the strong independent stance taken by the Saudis during the Chinese missile deal, there is little reason to suspect that the missiles were intended for any purpose other than defense. The CSS-2, though having extensive range, was known to be highly inaccurate due to its size. Although the Chinese undoubtedly designed the CSS-2 for the specific purpose of

---

*The CEP is the diameter of a circle within which you expect half of your missiles to land, but for a nuclear blast, its power would compensate for such inaccuracies.

carrying nuclear warheads, Bandar has repeatedly stressed that the missiles bought by Saudi Arabia were adapted to carry conventional warheads. Reiterating this, King Fahd wrote to President Reagan, giving his personal assurance that the missiles would neither be fitted with unconventional warheads nor used in a first-strike mode. He further affirmed that Saudi Arabia would not obtain or use either nuclear or chemical warheads.[53] Further proof of the purely defensive role determined for the missiles was evidenced in the fact that although the missiles were considered to be fully operational by 1990, they were not used during the first Gulf War, probably due to their inaccuracy. Referring to their status, Bandar said, "King Fahd ruled out that option [launching missiles against Iraq] because of the fact that you cannot control them accurately. Our war was not with the Iraqi people; it was with Saddam Hussein and his clique."[54]

Despite its attention to creating a modern military, the kingdom has never resorted to external aggression. The long-standing friendship between Saudi Arabia and the United States may have lessened fears about Saudi intent with regard to Israel. Saudi Arabia's desire to see the Middle East become a region free of nuclear weapons is a position of long standing.

In defense of its repeated declarations that it has no nuclear aspirations, Saudi Arabia joined the coalition of countries that support making the Middle East nuclear free, becoming signatory to the Nuclear Non-Proliferation Treaty in October 1988. In May 1999, the permanent Saudi representative to the United Nations officially affirmed Saudi Arabia's interest in eliminating weapons of mass destruction from the Middle East.[55] However, while Israel maintains its suspected nuclear stockpile, this target remains decidedly unattainable.

SIX

A NEW WORLD ORDER

"I think when the true contribution that Bandar has made to Middle East and Western politics generally is revealed—it will be quite a surprise to a lot of people how wide an influence he had had and over how long a period."

SIR RICHARD EVANS, FORMER
CHAIRMAN OF BRITISH AEROSPACE

William Casey and Bandar worked closely together to implement the anti-Communist Reagan Doctrine. One of their most successful collaborations was in Afghanistan. Saudi financial support for the Mujahideen was, in the prince's words, "done with the knowledge of both parties; Congress knew about it, so there was nothing wrong with it, except it was secret." Recalling this period of particularly close cooperation between the United States and Saudi Arabia, Bandar recounted, "I remember walking into Congress and people were patting me on the shoulder and saying, 'Hey, thank you, Buddy, for helping us in Afghanistan. We understand and will keep quiet.'" Indeed, Congress had every reason to thank its Saudi allies, particularly since at this time they were co-funding the armament of the Afghan rebels dollar for dollar with the United States.

That money would win the war in Afghanistan.

In February 1988, tasked with persuading the Russians to withdraw from Afghanistan, Bandar flew to Russia to meet with Gorbachev. There, he presented the Russian leader with a clear-cut U.S.-Saudi message: get out of Afghanistan.

Recalling his role in securing the Soviet withdrawal from Afghanistan, Bandar explained that King Fahd and President Reagan had made a solid commitment that they would see this war through to a successful conclusion, that there would be no compromise. Nine years into the Soviet occupation, the Americans received intelligence that there might be a lack of consensus in the Kremlin—that there was dissent to the Soviet Afghan policy within the politburo, but that such dissidents were in the minority. The question was: was Gorbachev one of them or not? There was a split of views on Gorbachev's position within the Western intelligence community. It was decided that the best way to test this premise was to present a proposal for a face-saving Soviet withdrawal, hoping to be able to read something from the Soviet reaction to the proposal.

The tense relationship between the White House and the Kremlin at that time effectively precluded an American approach. As Bandar explained, "The Americans and the Soviets were playing chicken at that time. Who was going to blink first on the deployment on the Pershing missiles into Europe? The Russians were saying, 'If you deploy them, we will escalate matters and break off all weapons negotiations.' The Americans were saying, 'We will continue—we will deploy.' Meanwhile, most of the Europeans were saying, 'Please hold off—we don't want this to escalate.' Finally, Mrs. Thatcher was saying, 'We will deploy and to hell with it!' Against this backdrop, it was not an opportune time for the Americans to offer the Soviets a way out in Afghanistan. That was when it was decided that Saudi Arabia would make the move."

The prince later confided that King Fahd always looked at all the options to see how it would benefit Saudi Arabia. He recalled that Fahd strategized that he could go to all the Arab allies of the Soviet Union and explain that Saudi Arabia was trying to help the Soviets by trying to convince the Americans to give the Soviets a way out of the conflict. Fahd charged Bandar with meeting the Soviet president—an unusual exercise because at that time Saudi Arabia had no diplomatic relations with the Soviet Union.

Before Bandar met with Gorbachev, he contacted Anatoly Dobrynin,* who revealed to him that some of the Soviet leaders did question whether the U.S.S.R. could win the war in Afghanistan. However, Dobrynin would not disclose if Gorbachev was one of them or not. Nonetheless, at the end of their meeting, Bandar felt that Gorbachev might be persuaded to make a deal.

Bandar next traveled to Moscow. He was not to meet with Gorbachev alone, however, for the Soviet president was accompanied by several hard-line members of the politburo. His reception was acutely chilly. Gorbachev immediately lambasted him, accusing the kingdom of interfering in the internal affairs of Afghanistan. Bandar thought to himself, "My God, he has chutzpah—he is occupying a country with an army and he thinks *we* are interfering!" Gorbachev continued his tirade, arguing that the Americans were going to let the Saudis down and started talking about the situation in South Yemen and Ethiopia, arguing that Riyadh had a very unwise policy toward these nations.

The Soviet president didn't give the prince a chance to say a word. As a further complication, the interpreter only spoke Algerian Arabic and Bandar could barely understand him. Knowing that the Soviets didn't have any interpreters who spoke Saudi Arabic, he stopped Gorbachev and asked for an interpreter who spoke English. However, after they changed interpreters, Gorbachev immediately continued his verbal onslaught.

Seeking some respite from the blitz, Bandar politely asked for a drink. He was, however, becoming very angry as Gorbachev's attack continued. Bandar said, "He has a great personality, very full of life, dynamic, emotional, and gesturing—and after a while it got to me." He asked for a coffee because it would take more time to prepare. This tactic gave him time to explain to Gorbachev that they did not think it was in their interests for the Soviet Union to be seen to be occupying a Muslim country. Bandar drew a

---

*Anatoly Dobrynin was Moscow's ambassador to the United States for an unparalleled twenty-four years and became a channel for secret back-door negotiations. In a striking parallel to Prince Bandar, he had an engaging personality that enabled him to develop enviable access to the White House, State Department, and leading figures of six administrations. Dobrynin was privy to American high-level thinking, but astonishingly, the Kremlin frequently failed to keep him informed of major developments. For example, Moscow did not inform him of its plans to position nuclear missiles in Cuba. He was similarly not advised in advance of the Soviet Union's plans to invade Czechoslovakia. Moreover, although Dobrynin was in Moscow when the decision was made to invade Afghanistan, he was not consulted. Nonetheless, he was held in high regard in Washington, and when a crisis loomed, six presidents asked for his counsel.

parallel with what happened with the Americans in Vietnam, stressing that this was a war the Soviet Union could not win, a war of attrition and heavy losses.

Having made his point, Bandar diplomatically praised the Soviet Union and suggested that as a great nation, it should be promoting peace around the world; it should not be waging wars. He added that if the president was interested, he felt certain that they could come to an arrangement whereby the Soviet Union could withdraw honorably from Afghanistan through a solution that would allow the U.S.S.R. to save face.

Gorbachev merely redoubled his attack, saying, "You have no interest in Afghanistan and I know everything you are doing there. You are spending $200 million a year in Afghanistan."

Bandar interjected, "Stop! It's dangerous when a superpower leader has the wrong information!" Gorbachev immediately responded, "No. I can prove it: we have the evidence."

"Listen to me please, Mr. President," Bandar countered. "We are not spending $200 million a year; we are spending $500 million!" He then added, "And we are willing to spend more!"

That was the Saudis' trump card. Not only were Soviet and Afghan government forces incurring horrendous military losses in Afghanistan, but the Soviet Army had effectively lost control of the countryside to the Mujahideen. The Soviet Union was losing the war, and the prospect of its forces facing a stronger, better armed, and even more heavily financed resistance was abhorrent.

"You are losing people; we are losing money!" Bandar said, "But we can always print more; we can always sell more oil." He stressed that the Saudis and the Americans were losing nothing except money, while the Soviet Union was losing material, lives, and prestige.

At this, Gorbachev quietly said, "I need to talk to you alone."

Gorbachev and Reagan. "Trust but verify."

Bandar and Gorbachev retired to the Soviet premier's office, where Gorbachev said resignedly, "If we are not pushed or humiliated or taken advantage of, we will leave. You can tell King Fahd that by next March we will be out of Afghanistan."

Bandar was stunned. In hindsight, he believed that the earlier diatribe had been for local consumption, designed entirely for the benefit of the politburo members and party officials in attendance. During their private meeting, there were only three people in Gorbachev's office—Bandar, Gorbachev, and Dobrynin. The hardliners in the Kremlin believed that if the Soviets hung in long enough, the Saudis would back off, feeling threatened by Soviet satellite countries around them. They also believed that the Americans could not sustain the war in a Muslim country without the Saudis and Pakistanis, and that Pakistan would not stay in the fight if the Saudis withdrew. However, understanding Bandar's blunt message that the Soviet Union could not win, Gorbachev blinked. The meeting ended with the Soviet president thanking the prince for his candor and saying, "You have a deal, let's work it out." All that remained was to broker the formal agreement.

As an aside to his story of his meeting with Gorbachev, Bandar recalled, "One of the funniest stories of that war was that the CIA and Saudi intelligence became the largest buyers of donkeys in the world." Laughing, he explained, "We used to have shiploads of donkeys. Why? Because you could not send trucks and tanks and airplanes into Afghanistan. So we got all these donkeys, which were loaded with munitions and were sent over the mountains into Afghanistan. In this vast country there were hundreds of donkeys going everywhere. We used to joke that donkeys were beating Soviet T-72 tanks and helicopters—but guess what? It was an effective way of getting the munitions, the weapons, and the communications systems to places that nobody could reach."

Reflecting on a sequel to his meeting with Gorbachev, Bandar related how within a couple of weeks of his meeting, the Soviet premier called the president of Afghanistan, Mohammad Najibullah, to the Soviet Union; they met in Samarkand. American intelligence information later confirmed that Gorbachev told the Afghan president, "Look, I will give you whatever you need to fight your fight—but by March I am gone. If you can't take care of yourself after that, it's your problem. Between now and March, I'll give you weapons and everything you want, but then I am gone.'" Bandar said sanguinely, "And the rest is history."

*   *   *

Following his intervention with Gorbachev in early 1988, Bandar would again be called upon to act, this time closer to home. In the fall of 1980 Iraq had invaded Iran, igniting a war that would continue for eight bloody years and claim the lives of more than one million people. Considering the conflict to be one between a modern, if brutal, secular state (Iraq) and a volatile, hard-line, fundamentalist Islamic state, run in essence by the mullahs (Iran), America backed Iraq. The Pentagon and the CIA provided Hussein with intelligence reports and funneled billions of dollars of arms into Iraq. If Iraq had won the war, however, Saddam Hussein would have emerged as the most powerful leader in the Gulf, an unsavory proposition to the United States, as conceded much later by a Reagan administration official, who said, "We wanted to avoid victory by both sides."[1]

By 1983, Iraq's foreign reserves had fallen from $30 billion to $3 billion, the cost of living had risen sharply, and the dinar was devalued; it quickly became almost totally dependent on loans from Saudi Arabia and the Gulf states.

It was reported that during the run-up to the war, Saudi leaders had urged Saddam Hussein to take the fight to Iran's fundamentalist regime, intimating that President Carter, following frustration at his inability to secure the release of the fifty-two Americans imprisoned by Iran, had given a "green light" for the invasion. During a trip to the Middle East in April 1981, Secretary of State Alexander Haig was advised by senior Arab leaders, including King Fahd, of Carter's green light; it has been alleged that Haig made note of this in talking points that he prepared for a post-trip briefing for President Reagan.[2] However, far from encouraging Saddam Hussein to strike against the new fundamentalist regime, King Fahd cautioned Saddam Hussein against any attack.

Setting the stage, Bandar explained that before the war started, "King Fahd consulted directly with Saddam Hussein and Saddam had told him that he planned to teach the Iranians a lesson. Fahd told him, 'If you want my advice, stay away from that fight. Iran is in chaos after the revolution—leave them alone. They are busy fighting each other. Let them. Let's see how it settles out in the end and then we can deal with whoever wins that fight. They will be so busy with their own problems that, yes—there will be a lot of rhetoric, but they are not going to bother us.' However, Saddam Hussein insisted that he would go all the way to Tehran and 'pull Khomeini by his beard.' "

An irate Bandar exclaimed, "Talk about arrogance and delusions of grandeur. So King Fahd said to Saddam, 'If I cannot talk you out of it, for God's sake, keep it to border clashes; under no circumstances enter Iranian territory. Right now they are in chaos, their army is in chaos, and their politics is in chaos. But if you enter their land, you are going to unify the Iranians and then you will be fighting a country that has sixty million people and a lot of assets and can afford a long war of attrition; that is not in your interests or in our interests.'"

Continuing his summation of exchanges between Fahd and Saddam Hussein, Bandar said, "Needless to say, three years later Saddam told King Fahd, 'I wish I had listened to your advice, because I want to disengage.' King Fahd had told him at the first meeting, 'Saddam, going to war is your decision; disengaging will not be your decision: the other side will have to agree. So, yes, you can go in by your own decision, but when you decide that you have had enough and you want to stop, you cannot guarantee that the other side will agree. They might want to continue the fight, so then you will become hostage to the other side's decision to quit or not to quit.'"

Bandar observed, "So they ended up with almost eight years of war. And during the last couple of years, the balance was tipping towards the Iranians. Although the Iraqis were occupying large areas of Iran, they were being driven out of it and the cost was mounting. Infrastructure was being destroyed; national assets were being wasted; the human cost was extraordinarily high; casualties, both dead and wounded, were high. The entire infrastructure that Iran and Iraq had developed during the previous twenty or thirty years was demolished in front of our eyes." Bandar stressed, "If you don't understand that, you won't understand why in 1990 Fahd asked for support from the world to avoid a war that would destroy everything we had built

Saddam Hussein

in our nation—infrastructure, schools, hospitals, ports, airports—to do what? To spend eight years at war and we end up in a draw."

Bandar has said that an understanding of Saudi Arabia's position during the Iran-Iraq War and its root causes is essential for any appraisal of the kingdom's foreign policy and strategic ambitions. He argued that the war happened during a period when there were tremendous changes happening in the Middle East starting with the collapse of the Shah of Iran and the revolution in which Ayatollah Khomeini took over. Bandar perceived it to be ironic, because for the Saudis the Shah was not a friend—he was an antagonist.

Bandar explained, "At that time, the Americans were arming [the Shah] to the hilt and I believe that they thought that he would be a stabilizing factor in a volatile region. However, he began to have territorial ambitions. In the early 1970s he claimed that Bahrain (a small island nation situated adjacent to Saudi Arabia in the Persian Gulf) was Iranian; that was taboo for us!"

As a consequence, Bandar said, "Our relationship with him was always proper; however, there was mutual suspicion." In an observation that was analogous to the position of the Saudi royal family today, he remarked, "The Shah led a very secular revolution and it was one of his biggest mistakes because he forgot that he was the king of a Muslim Iran, not the king of France or Sweden. Although modernization and liberalization is healthy and good, he just took it to the extreme—just like Khomeini took the revolution to an extreme Islamic way." The Shah's push for secularism had deeply worried Saudi Arabia, Bandar said, noting that there was a difference between giving a woman a choice to cover her face or not, and banning her by law from covering her face. The Shah "unnecessarily antagonized the farmers, the laborers, the less educated people, and gave the religious mullahs a way to fight him and get public support."

Bandar observed that in theory, with an Islamic revolution taking place next door, it would be reasonable to suppose that it would have brought Saudi Arabia closer to Iran because the kingdom was a conservative country at the heart of Islam. Bandar said, "The old idiom that says a wise enemy is better than a foolish friend applied here. Instead of the victors of the Iranian revolution extending the hand of friendship to their neighbors and therefore winning recognition and support while they handled dramatic changes in their country, Khomeini made an announcement that put together Iraq and all Gulf countries—including Saudi Arabia—as enemies, as sacrilegious and nonbelievers. He believed that the revolutionary winds would sweep through Iraq and go all the way down into the Gulf." Bandar explained that Khomeini's belligerence forced the Gulf countries to take a position against Iran and to look at it as a real threat. He said, "I think that if Khomeini had not threatened to export the Islamic revolution to the Gulf countries and had not taken an anti-Saudi/Arab/Gulf countries attitude in his sermons and language, then Saudi Arabia and the Gulf countries would not have supported Iraq during the Iran-Iraq War."

"Unless people understand this fact," he said, "they could not begin to understand why Saudi Arabia spent $25 billion supporting Saddam Hussein and Iraq. It was in our national interest to stop Iran on the Iraqi borders, rather than to fight them at our borders. And we didn't choose that; they forced it on us." In an observation of the dangers of autocracy, Bandar added, "Again, this was a miscalculation—where you have individuals making decisions through emotions, rather than thinking through institutions and through wisdom."

Recalling the differing perspectives from which he observed the events unfolding in the Gulf, Bandar noted that he had been in the Air Force when the revolution took place and that for over a year he had been involved in defending Saudi Arabia's eastern province. As a fighter pilot, he had been deployed there as a contingency—just in case things turned for the worst. He recalled, "I remember when the war broke out between Iran and Iraq, we went on full alert on my base in Saudi Arabia. We thought for a week or so that it was just border clashes; but fifty-five days later, without having left the base, the squadron was still on alert. That was when we realized that it was really going to be a long war." He continued, "I remember we worked with the Iraqis to give them AWACS information, as they [the Iraqis] were going to hit targets in the southern part of Iran. I remember them landing in Saudi Arabia where we refueled them so that they could go back home. They didn't have a refueling capability and they didn't have the range."

Bandar added reflectively, "Of course, within a couple of years of that war and seeing it from my military vantage point in the Air Force, I went to Washington, initially for the AWACS deal, and then to become military attaché there. I then became ambassador and had to handle the Iran-Iraq war that I first had been exposed to as a military man. So from '82 until early

'88 my role was, 'How can we support Iraq and make sure that we galvanize and maintain the support of the U.S. and the West for it, so that we can checkmate Iran.'" Bandar observed, "In 1987, you had what was called the war of the tankers, when the Iranians began to threaten the passage of oil through the Gulf of Hormuz. We came up with the reflagging idea, whereby tankers would be reflagged under U.S. flags, which then gave America the legal rationale to protect them going in and out of the Gulf—it was a joint U.S.-Saudi idea."

"In an ironic way," Bandar continued, "I think this starkly highlights the lie of bin Laden or al-Qaeda or Muslim extremists who allege that they were there because Saudi Arabia brought in the Americans and the Western influence. The truth of the matter is that there was no American military presence before that. By attacking international waters and the international lifeline of oil, the Iranians forced people to defend their interests. The Iranians were the cause of the international presence and the international naval fleets in the Gulf. We just happened to benefit from it. That oil, the world needed it and they were going to have it, particularly if the source—Saudi Arabia—wanted to sell it."

Reiterating the root cause of an increased Western naval military presence in the Gulf, Bandar stressed, "You cannot now discuss that and forget how it all started. Saudi Arabia didn't bring them although we are their allies. The Americans came because of the Iranian threat." He added swiftly, "The same thing occurred with ground forces when Saddam Hussein invaded Kuwait. Had Saddam Hussein not invaded Kuwait, there would not have been half a million Americans in Saudi Arabia to fight against him."

Bandar shook his head and observed, "This propaganda, this fallacy, that the troubles we have today, that the Saudis brought in these people and the result was terrorism and destabilization, is incorrect. It is other people's failed policies that forced the situation."

Few modern conflicts have been so long, so bloody, and so ineffectual. The Iran-Iraq war left a distressing legacy. The fighting was extremely costly—in the neighborhood of $1.2 trillion—and was disastrous for both Iran and Iraq, stalling economic development and disrupting oil exports. An estimated 1.7 million people were wounded and one million were killed. Iraq was left with serious debts to its former Arab backers, including $14 billion loaned by Kuwait, a debt that would contribute to Saddam's 1990 decision to invade Kuwait. Much of the oil industry in both countries was damaged in air raids, yet the war left the borders unchanged.

The horrors of war were visited on both populations. Iraq's use of chemical weapons, Khomeini's decision to send thousands of young Iranians to their death in "human-wave" attacks, which allegedly included the use of children to clear minefields, and the indiscriminate use of missiles in the War of the Cities, decimated civilian populations on either side of the border.

The cause of this conflict can be traced to a border dispute in the mid-1970s. In 1974, Iran had supplied weapons to Kurdish nationalists in northern Iraq, enabling them to stage a revolt against the Iraqi government. In order to halt the rebellion, in 1975, Iraq reached a compromise with Iran over the border on the Shatt al-Arab estuary, the waterway that forms the boundary between the two countries, transferring ownership to Iran. In exchange, Iran stopped supplying arms to the Kurds. But in doing so, Iraq had lost access to the Persian Gulf. In 1980, Saddam Hussein invaded Iran, hoping to reverse the border settlement, while also hoping to curtail the religious propaganda directed against Iraq's secular regime by the Islamic government of Iran.

Believing Iran's military strength had been greatly weakened by the revolution, Hussein expected an easy victory. However, Iraq's initial military successes were short lived, and by 1982, Iraqi troops had been cleared from most of Iran. Saddam had seriously miscalculated Iranian resolve and military capabilities. Between 1982 and 1987 the fighting escalated and attacks on shipping in the Persian Gulf indirectly drew other countries, including the United States, into the conflict.

United Nations efforts to curtail the Iran-Iraq war were surprisingly muted. When Iraq attacked Iran on September 22, 1980, the U.N. Security Council waited four days before holding a meeting. Two days later, it passed Resolution 479, which called for an end to the fighting, but was rejected by Iran as being one sided.

In 1984, Iraq and Iran accepted a U.N.-sponsored moratorium on the shelling of civilian targets. But still the fighting continued.

In 1985, the Security Council issued a quiet "statement" condemning the use of chemical weapons, but not until March 1986, a full two years after Iraq's use of chemical warfare had been confirmed by a U.N. team, did a Council statement explicitly denounce Iraq.[3]

According to Bandar, by 1987 the Iraqis were looking for a way out, but they could not disengage. Once the Iranians had overcome their initial losses, they had pushed the Iraqis back and had begun to enter Iraqi territory. The Saudi belief at that time, Bandar explained, was that the Iranians had no interest in ending the conflict.

One day in late 1987, Bandar got a call from King Fahd, who told him that Saddam Hussein had called him personally. Saddam had asked Fahd if Bandar could be instructed to dedicate his time to support an Iraqi delegation led by Iraqi Foreign Minister Tariq Aziz, who was then in New York trying to close a deal for a ceasefire. Bandar agreed and contacted Aziz, who explained that he was having difficulty getting serious support from the permanent members of the U.N. Security Council. It transpired that what he really needed was the support of the United States and Britain, as China and Russia were somewhere in the middle and France already was supporting Iraq.

At that time, the Americans and the British were becoming weary of Saddam's actions: he had been caught red-handed trying to develop a super gun,* had arrested Westerners in Iraq, including a British nurse, and had had an Iranian-born British citizen shot. Later, they discovered that Iraq had been trying to buy nuclear triggers. Information also came to light about his use of chemical weapons in Hallabjah.

Bandar has confessed to a feeling of personal guilt about his country's complicity in Saddam's gassing of Kurdish civilians in Hallabjah. "Morally, we dropped the ball," he said. Bandar emphasized that he was referring to the Americans, the British, and the whole Western and Arab world—including Saudi Arabia. He explained that at that time the Iranians were at the peak of their offensive. They were getting closer to Basra and getting to Basra meant getting closer to Kuwait and closer to the Saudi border. "We were so galvanized by that fact that we *chose* not to see what was happening, not because we didn't know. That choice still burns inside of me a lot."

"In my mind," continued Bandar, "we rationalized that Saddam was a

---

*Early in the war with Iran, the Iraqi government engaged world-renowned artillery expert Gerald Bull, who was obsessed with the construction of a huge howitzer—a super gun—able to fire satellites into space or launch artillery shells thousands of miles into enemy territory. From mid-1981 until he was assassinated on March 22, 1990, he led Project Babylon, aimed at developing a massive gun with a barrel built in segments. It had a total length of five hundred twelve feet and could fire a six hundred-kg projectile, including chemical, biological, and nuclear weapons, to a range of one thousand kilometers, or a two thousand-kg rocket-assisted projectile into orbit. Iraq purchased components for Bull's super gun from a U.K.-based machine tool company, Matrix Churchill. However, British customs intercepted the final eight sections of the super gun in November 1990.

very bad man, but Khomeini was worse. So it was a choice between bad and worse. Yes, Saddam did bad things, but we were looking at some people who would do worse things. So let's first just deal with the Iranians and then we will turn around and deal with Saddam." But he acknowledged, "During that period, all of us, I believe, compromised our moral feelings and beliefs."

"I remember me and senior officials from the U.S. government going around the U.S. Congress lobbying senators not to place sanctions on Iraq for that [the chemical attacks], using the same rationale. I must say, there were a few in the U.S. Congress who were troubled by this and who wanted to go for sanctions. But I must say also that the national security argument prevailed again—for good or ill—and the majority agreed. 'Yes. What is happening is really bad, but what could happen is worse.' So in my mind, everybody is guilty. I am not proud of being part of that effort but we are all wiser after the fact."

Bandar would later be able to atone for this stain on his conscience through his role as mediator. Recalling his efforts, Bandar observed, "Saddam Hussein and Iraq suddenly found that they no longer had any influence with the U.N. permanent members. Meanwhile, U.N. Secretary General Pérez de Cuéllar was trying to get a ceasefire agreement. By that time the Iranians were getting tired, but not tired enough to quit on their own. But if there was a way out that could save face for them, that was a good deal, they would take it." Saddam's behavior, however, did little to help matters. In Iraqi propaganda he continued to act like he was victorious, which vastly complicated the task of those trying to put a compromise together. The prince observed wryly, "It also frustrated the Western powers that were saying, 'Wait a minute—we know the facts, goddammit! We know you are losing, so why are you talking to us like you are another superpower.' That's when communication broke down and the negotiations got stuck. That's when I was instructed by King Fahd—at the request of Saddam—to get involved."

The prince asked Tariq Aziz directly, "What is the most important thing for you?"

Aziz replied, "To get a meeting with the five permanent members of the Security Council."

"That's not a problem," Bandar responded. "That is all that you want? Then my mission is easy."

"Yes," the Iraqi foreign minister said. "But I invited them to come and meet me in the Iraqi embassy and they refused."

"Tariq, why are you surprised, for God's sake? You come to New York and you are the one that needs the help and you tell those people, 'Come to meet me in my embassy.' Who do you think you are?"

At that point, Bandar says, both men laughed. Sensing a break, the prince pressed Aziz, "Let's go and meet them in the secretary general's office in the U.N."

Bizarrely, Aziz again refused, saying, "No, it has to be here [at the Iraqi embassy]; that's what I want from you."

Bandar instantly replied, "If that's the only thing you want from me and that's your final position, then I had better go back to Washington because it is not going to happen. Look, I will invite them to my hotel and you can come here; then we'll have the meeting. If the meeting is what you want, who cares how and where it is?"

Only then did Tariq Aziz reluctantly agree.

After leaving the Iraqi minister, Bandar called the White House and Ten Downing Street and asked, obliquely, for their help. "I didn't ask them to meet with Tariq Aziz," he said, "just with me." The Saudi ambassador to the U.N. had permanent accommodation in the Waldorf Astoria, as did the American permanent representative to the U.N.; Bandar planned to hold the meeting in the Saudi ambassador's suite. He instructed Saudi Arabia's U.N. representative to invite the Chinese, the French, and the Russian representatives for a meeting. All agreed to come. The five ambassadors all arrived at the same time and were enjoying English tea and sandwiches when the Iraqi foreign minister appeared. The prince smiled as he announced, "And now we have the five permanent members meeting with Tariq Aziz."

"It turned out," Bandar recalled with anger, "that all Tariq Aziz wanted was to tell Saddam Hussein, 'I got the five permanent members to meet with me,' because in the meeting he did not give an inch; he was dictating a tough position." Tariq Aziz had undermined any chance of an agreement, and after this meeting, Bandar began to work directly with the U.N. secretary general.

Expanding on his role, Bandar explained, "Of course, I had no direct contact with the Iranians. I was using de Cuéllar to talk with the Iranians, and I was talking with the Iraqis." He added, "When the U.N. got frustrated with the Iraqis, I would take over and speak on their behalf and get a deal or compromise done. We went back and forth, back and forth for about two or three weeks, and then negotiations broke down because both sides were still bargaining—or thinking that they would wait for the other side to back down."

In a revealing exposé of how the U.N. operates, Bandar explained, "You have to understand that the U.N. culture diminishes the national lines between delegates. They live, they work, they eat all in one building. After a while even hostile nations' representatives will have a drink together or meet in the lounges. So there are no secrets you can keep as far as tactics. The Iranians began to suspect that the attitudes of the Americans, the British, and the French were hardening against Hussein and they felt, 'Why give in now?' So they took a tougher position. When talks broke down, they broke down on symbolism: Tariq Aziz said, 'I am too busy to stay in New York, I am going to go home. If you want a meeting, bring it to the Middle East and we'll meet there.' The Iranians said, 'That's fine, bring it to Tehran.' So—no meeting."

After repeated attempts at negotiation, in a protracted back-and-forth exercise, de Cuéllar and Bandar decided that the best way to achieve progress was to hold the talks in Geneva. It was done quietly, without any announcement, so that they could have a few days without an intrusive media presence. Bandar stayed in his father's house in Geneva, and the meetings between de Cuéllar, Tariq Aziz, and Bandar took place there and at the Iraqi embassy. Slowly, they began to thread together a ceasefire agreement.

Bandar recalled, "We got about 98 percent done and Pérez de Cuéllar started to express frustration—he felt hurt by the arrogance of the Iraqis, describing how they talked big and how they were rude and so on." Bandar worried that de Cuéllar might quit the discussions and calmed him down. The prince recalled, "In all fairness to the man—and he was a very capable and wise man—he said, 'I'm not going to quit. I'm going to continue with this.' Though I used to say to the Iraqis, 'He might really quit.' " Bandar admitted, "I used that to get the Iraqis to continue."

Despite the Iraqi bad grace and bluster, they finally had constructed a draft ceasefire agreement that both delegations could take back to their countries. A week or ten days later, they all met in New York. Aziz arrived with an agreement from Saddam Hussein to go ahead with the draft, as is. The Iranians, however, agreed to proceed with the draft only with changes—minor alterations that wouldn't change the meaning or the legal ramifications of the pact. Bandar explained that the minor changes made it "softer for the Iranians to swallow. All five permanent members of the U.N. agreed that this was not a problem."

But while Pérez de Cuéllar and the permanent members of the Security Council agreed, Aziz refused. To Bandar, it was inconceivable that after this hectic and frustrating exercise, the Iraqis would throw everything away and let the war continue. Yet the ceasefire was in serious jeopardy; Aziz would not accept any change in the words. So Bandar went to see him.

"No means no means no!" the Iraqi minister resolutely replied. "I will not accept the change." Bandar got really angry and brushed him off, saying, "Well, I guess there's not much I can do. I'm leaving. You continue the war and see how you can settle it."

And then he turned and left.

Aziz followed. He caught up with Bandar and whispered in his ear, "Can I see you in the hotel alone?"

Bandar agreed, but admitted that, "Really, I was not interested."

The Saudi ambassador to the U.N., who was with Bandar at the time, was also frustrated and said to him, "It's your mistake!"

"Why is it my mistake?" Bandar responded.

The ambassador said, "Because you convinced the Iraqis that the ambassadors representing the great powers, that when they came to meet Tariq Aziz, they came because of him or his country. He doesn't know they came because we made them come, and now he thinks he can dictate to them. So you got this into his head."

"Maybe you have a point there," Bandar conceded, "but I think there is something else to it; let's wait and see."

Bandar returned to his hotel, and Aziz followed soon thereafter. Aziz asked Bandar to turn the TV volume higher and then whispered to him, "I could not say anything to you at our embassy because we have people monitoring and recording

Iraqi Foreign Minister Tariq Aziz

everything. But I agree with you. This is a good deal. But the reason I cannot change it is because this has been agreed to by Saddam. I cannot change it until Saddam agrees."

"Tariq, what is the problem?" Bandar replied. "Call him and tell him this is what you recommend, after all, you are deputy prime minister and foreign minister."

An alarmed Aziz responded, "Are you crazy? I don't care if the war continues for ten years. I don't want to lose my life. Crossing Saddam means death!"

"All right," Bandar said. "I will call King Fahd and ask His Majesty to call Saddam about the changes."

"On one condition," Aziz responded. "You don't tell him that we talked."

Bandar agreed and said, "Okay. Give me Saddam's phone number."

But again Aziz refused, paranoid that Saddam might ask how Bandar got the number. So Bandar called Fahd and explained the situation. The frustrated king told the prince to call Saddam Hussein himself.

Bandar said to Aziz, "My boss has told me to call your boss, and I'm going to call him right now. But I am only an ambassador and you are foreign minister. Why don't you call him?"

Aziz retorted, "Never mind—just call him please."

So the prince called Saddam.

Bandar recalled that when he spoke with Saddam, "He answered in his arrogant, eloquent way, 'Hello, Abu Khalid.' Instead of calling me Bandar, he called me by my son's name." They exchanged pleasantries and then Bandar said, "We are almost done, but I have a complaint. We are stuck on a couple of words. They really need changing and your foreign minister will not agree."

The prince explained, "Tariq Aziz was sitting listening to me. His face lit up—he was so happy. I'm telling Saddam that he didn't agree."

The prince recalled how Saddam gave an arrogant cocky laugh and said, "Yes, Tariq Aziz is a good man; sometimes difficult, but a good man."

Bandar said, "I really need your support, Mr. President. Can you please tell him to agree with me so we can close the deal?"

Saddam replied, "Bandar, you don't just represent Saudi Arabia; you represent Iraq and Saudi Arabia. Anything you agree to, I accept."

"That's fine," Bandar responded, "but your man is being very stubborn."

Saddam replied, "We'll send a word to him."

Bandar confided, "Of course, I didn't tell him Tariq was listening. I hung up and thought to myself, 'If this wasn't a serious life-and-death issue, it would be a comedy show.'"

Bandar concluded, "By the next day we had an agreement, which was signed by everyone, and the rest is history."

SEVEN

THE GULF EXPLODES

"Remember, George, this is no time to go wobbly."*

MARGARET THATCHER,
AUGUST 3, 1990

On August 2, 1990, as President Saddam Hussein watched his Iraqi troops invade Kuwait, a stunned world wondered whether Saudi Arabia and its vital oil fields would be next.[1] On August 3, having just returned from London, Prince Bandar bin Sultan was called to the White House to be briefed on the Iraqi threat by U.S. national security advisor, Gen. Brent Scowcroft. During that meeting, President Bush offered the Saudis immediate military support and gave his personal assurance that if American forces were sent to Saudi Arabia, the United States would see it through.[2]

During the buildup to the first Gulf War, Bandar's work would be of vital strategic importance to the United States. It would reinforce his unique role, which, by Brent Scowcroft's own admission, was so much more than

---

*President Bush praised Margaret Thatcher for her courage and for helping forge a great coalition against the aggression that brutalized the Gulf. He recalled one special phone conversation with the prime minister in the early days of the Gulf crisis. The president called her to say "though we fully intended to interdict Iraqi shipping, we are going to let a single vessel heading for Oman enter port down at Yemen— let it enter port without being stopped." Thatcher "listened to my explanation, agreed with the decision, but then added these words of caution—words that guided me through the Gulf crisis, words I'll never forget as long as I'm alive. 'Remember George,' she said, 'this is no time to go wobbly.'" Taken from the address by President Bush during the presentation of a Presidential Medal of Freedom to Lady Margaret Thatcher on March 7, 1991.

that of a diplomat. "Bandar was a trouble-shooter for King Fahd, with the equivalent rank of minister in the Saudi government. The king frequently turned to him for advice. For these reasons we knew he was a special conduit from the U.S. to Fahd."[3] So special, in fact, it was said that the "dispatch of American troops was subsequently linked to the personal friendship between George Bush and Saudi Prince Bandar."[4]

Bandar's trouble-shooting was not limited to the White House. Prime Minister Margaret Thatcher's private secretary, Lord Charles Powell, recalled, "In the ensuing months, he was frequently in Number Ten conveying Saudi views about the preparations for war and everything that went with it. It was a particularly active time in their relationship."[5]

Remembering those difficult times, Powell said that the British prime minister knew that when Bandar said, "this is what King Fahd wanted or what he would agree to—then it was so. That's the thing you value most in any envoy or intermediary: that they can speak with authority on behalf of the one person on the other side. Especially, I might add, during the preparations for war and periods of hostility."[6]

Brent Scowcroft admitted in my interview with him that the prince's role in those early days was essential and that it was necessary that he be drawn into the very heart of the administration. Scowcroft also confirmed that the prince had been involved in the military planning at a very early stage.[7] It was observed that during the first Gulf War "Bandar would become a de

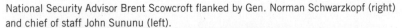

National Security Advisor Brent Scowcroft flanked by Gen. Norman Schwarzkopf (right) and chief of staff John Sununu (left).

facto member of the National Security Council."[8] From the outset, he was kept abreast of the administration's plans and thinking on a regular basis.[9] That access was unquestionably a function of his unparalleled rapport with the Saudi king. Of Bandar's relationship with Fahd, Scowcroft said, "There was almost nobody else—we couldn't use our ambassador." Almost as an afterthought, he added, "In fact, our ambassador just did not have the access that we needed. We needed somebody to get to the king right away and Bandar was the obvious choice."[10]

The vacuum between Middle East and Western diplomacy escalated the Gulf crisis. During a conference with Saddam Hussein on July 25, 1990, the U.S. ambassador to Iraq, April Glaspie, said, "As you know, we [the United States] don't take a stand on territorial disputes." Glaspie's declaration was simply and grossly misconstrued by the Iraqi president to imply that the United States would turn a blind eye to the forced acquisition of Kuwait.

In an ambiguous statement that would have colossal consequences, Glaspie told Hussein, "President Bush is an intelligent man. He is not going to declare an economic war against Iraq . . . we have no opinion on Arab-Arab conflicts like your border disagreement with Kuwait."[11] The American dog, Saddam assumed, would bark but never bite.[12] Eight days later, Saddam unleashed his army into Kuwait, launching an invasion that would require five hundred thousand U.S. troops and cost thousands of lives to reverse.[13]

Ambassador Glaspie's words had been prefaced just a day earlier by a similar statement from Margaret Tutweiller, U.S. State Department spokeswoman, who on July 24, 1990, just nine days before Iraq's invasion of Kuwait, said, "We do not have any defense treaties with Kuwait, and there are no special defense or security commitments to Kuwait."[14]

Yet despite these formal statements, throughout July 1990, U.S. intelligence had been closely monitoring Iraqi forces massing on the Kuwaiti border, apprehensive that an attack on Kuwait might be imminent. There was a history of animosity between Iraq and Kuwait, a legacy of the partition of the Arab world by Western superpowers soon after World War II. This partition significantly restricted Iraqi access to the coast and sparked boundary disputes over the division of the rich Rumaila oil field and ownership of, among other areas, the island of Bubiyan, which strategically blocked the Iraqi port and naval base of Umm Qasr. Tensions were heightened further as the eight-year Iran-Iraq war ended.

Kuwait had been a great supporter of Iraq during the Iran-Iraq war, and the $14 billion war debt Iraq had accumulated with Kuwait was now being called in, at a time when Saddam Hussein was already complaining bitterly about the constraints of OPEC and the falling price of oil. He blamed this latter event primarily on Kuwait and the United Arab Emirates, accusing them of overproduction.

Watching the Iraqi military deployments tensely, when asked by Secretary of Defense Dick Cheney for his assessment of the movement of Iraqi troops, Gen. Norman Schwarzkopf replied, "I think they [the Iraqis] are going to attack. But they are going to take Rumaila and Bubiyan and then stop." Later, when asked what action the United States should take if this should happen, he said, "Not a damn thing. The world will not care. It will be a fait accompli."[15]

News of Iraqi unrest and Saddam Hussein's increasingly threatening stance toward Kuwait led Saudi Arabia, Kuwait, and the United Arab Emirates to put their military forces on alert. Saudi Arabia and Kuwait were reluctant to ask for assistance from the West. The Emirates, however, requested and was granted U.S. aerial tankers to participate in joint military action. When pressed, the Emirates insisted that the tankers were part of a routine training exercise, pointedly stressing Arab determination to play down any outside involvement in what they saw as a private backyard dispute. Operation Ivory Justice—as the U.S. deployment of the aerial tankers became known—annoyed Bandar, who, despite finding comfort in the U.S. response to a request for help from its Arab allies, felt that the Emirates should not have asked for such involvement, which potentially threatened U.S. diplomacy in the region and irritated the conservative Arab states.

Despite the West's growing unease, President Mubarak and King Fahd both gave repeated assurances that Iraq would not attack Kuwait. In Washington, "Prince Bandar was telling everyone that there was nothing to worry about. The Kuwaitis had not asked for help."[16] The firm belief was that whatever form Saddam Hussein's grievances took they could be handled within the Arab family. This utter miscalculation would form the backdrop to the invasion that took the Arab world by storm.

Like Glaspie, Bandar had been duped. Taking Saddam Hussein at his word was an extraordinary error of judgment, one that totally misinterpreted the Iraqi leader's plans. Moreover, it was not just to Washington that he denied concern; he had also reassured Margaret Thatcher that Saddam was merely posturing and that there would be no invasion.[17]

Speaking of Bandar's misreading of the situation on the ground, Colin Powell said, "He swore it wouldn't happen; they were all telling us they [Iraq] wouldn't do it. And I kept telling him, 'Bandar, you ought to see the intelligence; there's something screwy here.' And they kept insisting they could control it."[18] But they couldn't.

Recounting the run-up to the war, Bandar said, "Two weeks before the invasion, Iraq started a verbal conflict with Kuwait about oil prices. Then it mobilized. Saudi Arabia moved immediately, starting talks with both Iraq and Kuwait." In an attempt to defuse an escalating problem, Saudi foreign minister Prince Saud was sent to see Saddam.

"You are mobilizing your forces and you have a hundred thousand troops on the Kuwaiti border," Saud said. "That's ominous."

A cocky Saddam replied dismissively, "Prince Saud, if I need to invade Kuwait, I don't need a hundred thousand; twenty thousand would be enough. This is just our annual exercises, don't worry about it."

King Fahd then arranged for a summit between the Kuwaitis and the Iraqis in Jeddah, but they couldn't come to a resolution. The Kuwaitis agreed to go to Baghdad and talk to the Iraqis separately. If they came to an agreement, great; if not, Saudi Arabia would call for a summit in the kingdom that would have Saddam Hussein, the emir of Kuwait, President Mubarak, King Hussein, PLO Chairman Yasser Arafat, and the Saudis attempt to solve the conflict.

Bandar, who had been elated when the Iraqis and the Kuwaitis had agreed to meet in Jeddah for talks, was not alarmed by Saddam's saber rattling. Instead, on July 31, 1990, he departed for England and the start of a planned, well-earned vacation to China, secure in the belief that the circumstances in the Gulf were manageable and under control. He was blithely unaware that within hours of his landing in London, Iraq would launch a full-scale attack on Kuwait. The fate of the kingdom—its very survival—was in peril. And with the loss of the Saudi and Kuwaiti oil fields, so too went the world economy.

"In all my public life," Bandar confessed, "I always felt, with all the differences I saw and had to work with in the Arab world, always, the bottom line, it was salvageable. That if the national call comes to stand together, [the Arab] people would forget their differences. But what happened to Kuwait is unique—so blatant, so arrogant, so violent, so deceiving that it makes pause to question the whole Arab situation in a way I have never questioned before."[19]

Saddam had deceived and deliberately lied to his fellow Arab nations; he could no longer be trusted. Bandar was shocked by this treachery. Indeed, the entire Arab world was shaken by the invasion and later annexation of Kuwait; to the leaders of the Middle East, the attack itself was less significant than Saddam Hussein's blatant duplicity and disregard for the Arab brotherhood.

In his many interviews given during the buildup to the Gulf War, Bandar consistently stressed the arrogance of Saddam's actions, emphasizing how his deliberate abuse of Arab leaders' trust accentuated the danger he already posed. "President Saddam Hussein invaded a brother Arab independent nation, a member of the United Nations Arab League: he told us before he would not invade; he told King Fahd, personally, he would not invade; he told President Mubarak and King Hussein he would not invade; he told President Bush and President Gorbachev he would not invade. And then he did. And then he told us he would withdraw and he didn't. Then he said he's not going to move his forces south and he did. Then he said he had no territorial ambitions against Kuwait and then he annexed it."[20]

Summing up the upshot of Saddam's utter dishonesty, Bandar told John McLaughlin, "What the man has done defies all logic or all Arabic and Islamic behavior; therefore, I don't put anything beyond this man."[21] He expanded on this comment in an interview on CNN's *Larry King Live*, saying, "If you asked me one hour before Saddam Hussein invaded Kuwait and gave me the scenario that has unfolded, I would have laughed at you and said that it is a preposterous scenario. Nevertheless, it happened."

Explaining further, Bandar said, "I was with him only four months ago, and I spent four hours with him."[22] Bandar was referring to a meeting on April 5, 1990, when, following a particularly fierce rhetorical broadcast by the Iraqi leader against Israel, he undertook a diplomatic mission to Baghdad to meet with President Hussein at the personal request of King Fahd. In a gambit designed to obfuscate and gain time, but in part perhaps because he suspected that his threats had been excessive,[23] Saddam Hussein had asked King Fahd to send a special envoy to Baghdad.[24]

During his attempt to mediate, Bandar had been reassured by Saddam that his words—"By God, we will make fire eat half of Israel if it tries to do anything against Iraq"—were not indicative of any potential Iraqi nuclear attack against Israel. In what was to mark the beginning of misconstrued rhetoric on both sides, Saddam admitted to Bandar that he wished his speech had been phrased differently, but insisted that the United States was overreacting and he hotly denied any aggressive intent behind his words.[25]

Citing a vulnerability, Saddam told the prince, "If I am attacked now [by Israel], I would not last six hours," and he entrusted the ambassador with a personal message saying, "I want to assure President Bush and His Majesty King Fahd that I will not attack Israel."[26] As well, Hussein was anxious that the prince should secure a similar agreement from the Israeli side not to attack Iraq.[27]

At the request of King Fahd, Bandar set about convincing President Bush of Saddam's sincerity. After a second interview with the president, Bandar secured Israeli assurances, via the United States and Saudi Arabia, that they would not preemptively strike Iraq. Despite Bandar's efforts, President Bush remained wary of the Iraqi leader's rhetoric, saying, "If this guy doesn't mean it, why the heck does he go around saying these things?"[28]

Without an appreciation of the subterfuge lurking behind Saddam's ardent assurances, Bandar's actions were, in theory, a textbook example of Middle Eastern/Western diplomatic negotiations. However, his achievement would only add salt to the wounds when Saddam later broke faith and launched an unprovoked invasion of Kuwait.

In unwittingly conveying Saddam's deliberate lie, Bandar was suckered into misleading not only President Bush and Prime Minister Thatcher, but also his mentor and uncle, King Fahd. With hindsight, Bandar would draw the bitter conclusion that Saddam had used him, and his unique position, to secure Iraq's position with Israel, leaving him free to engage in operations to the east on the Kuwaiti border. Indeed, it was discovered, later, that when the invasion occurred, Iraq did not have a single soldier active on its western flank.[29]

Reflecting on his diplomatic undertakings in the prelude to the Gulf War, specifically recalling the meeting when Hussein had asked him to convince Thatcher and Bush that he had no intention of fighting Israel, Bandar said, "So we went to tell the Americans and British that this guy was quoted out of context and that he was stupid." Bandar said that at the end of his meeting with him, Saddam made an off-the-cuff comment: "Oh, by the way, tell King Fahd to please assure the Gulf countries that I have no intention of invading them."

He instantly asked, "What?"

Saddam responded, "Don't believe the Zionist imperialist propaganda."

"Hold it," said Bandar. "Did we accuse you of that?"

"No."

"Do you have any intention?"

"No."

"I don't understand why you're telling me this," said Bandar.

"Because the Zionist imperialist colonialist media is trying to poison the small Gulf countries' minds."

"Don't worry about that," replied Bandar. "I just hope that you don't have any intentions."

At this point in his dialogue, Bandar shook his head and said, "And that bothered me and I made note of it, just one sentence in an eighteen-page memorandum that I wrote for King Fahd. In my memorandum I surrounded that sentence with stars and doodles as I spent the whole of that flight back to Saudi Arabia reading the sentence over and over, again and again."

When Bandar saw the king to debrief him, Fahd asked the prince to read out the whole memorandum, saying, "Don't give me your impressions, just read what you wrote."

Recalling his meeting with the king before he had left for Baghdad, Bandar explained that the king had said to him, "I'm suspicious about why he wants to see you. So when you go there, make sure you take good notes."

Bandar observed, "So I was taking notes; our ambassador in Baghdad was also taking notes. My chief of staff was taking notes. I consolidated all of them into an eighteen-page memorandum. I read those eighteen pages to His Majesty and he did not make a single comment until he came to this sentence."

"Stop," the king interrupted. "Repeat it."

Bandar repeated it three times, at which point Fahd reached for the memo and said, "Give it to me."

Having studied it, he asked, "Why did you scribble around it?"

The Prince replied, "Because it bothered me, sir, and I just kept putting stars around it."

"I hope the devil is not playing with his mind," the king observed prophetically. "This sentence bothers me."

Although the Saudis thought they had matters under control, they were suspicious. King Fahd sent Prince Saud one more time to see Saddam. But Hussein was antagonistic, saying, "Prince Saud, if you were not from Saudi Arabia, I would not receive you. How can you doubt my word? I gave my word of honor to King Fahd not to make a military move to scare the Kuwaitis. So don't even think about it."

That assurance was persuasive. After this meeting, Bandar went to see Mrs. Thatcher and President Bush to reassure them about Saddam Hussein's intentions. Bandar remembers their reactions.

"I don't trust him," Mrs. Thatcher said. "We must go and rein him in and attack him."

Bush, however, said, "I don't want anyone to attack anyone."

Two months later, believing the situation to be under control, Bandar asked Fahd, "Well, Your Majesty, since [these assurances from Saddam] have defused the crisis, can I go on my holiday?" The prince was to go to China on vacation; Princess Haifa and the children were waiting for him in Paris. The plan was to spend an extended two-week vacation with friends and family in China and another two weeks in Hong Kong, Singapore, and Thailand. Bandar reminded King Fahd that he had previously agreed that he could have the whole of August off.

The king said, "All right. Go ahead with your plans, but stop in London and brief Mrs. Thatcher on the deal that we have made with Kuwait and Iraq and then go on your vacation."

Soon after, Gen. Colin Powell called Bandar and said, "The White House tells me that you guys have got a deal. Are you sure?"

He replied, "Well, I'm sure insofar as I have been briefed."

"I had planned to take a couple of weeks off," Powell replied. "Do you think I can go?"

Bandar laughed and said, "I was planning to take four weeks off to go to China."

And so a decision was reached. "Well, you go to China," Powell responded, "I'm just going to South Carolina."

Bandar arrived in London on August 1, 1990. He went straight to see an anxious Mrs. Thatcher, who was very suspicious of Saddam's intentions. According to those close to the prince, she listened and, at the end of the briefing, asked, "Anything else?"

Bandar said, "No."

Thatcher inquired, "What does George think?"

Bandar replied, "Well, George hopes that we are right."

"That's not good enough," she replied. "I believe that we should attack him today before he attacks. I believe that he is going to attack. He is an evil man."

The prince responded, "Look, we don't want to have war."

"Well, I'm just telling you what I think," said Mrs Thatcher, backing off. "However, if George and King Fahd think we should wait and see, I'm willing to go along with it. I just want His Majesty to know that's what I feel and I'm going to call George and tell him."

With nothing further to do in London, Bandar decided to have an early night. He told his staff not to disturb him unless he had a call from the White House or from King Fahd. As was his custom, he checked CNN before retiring and then went to sleep. It was 11:30 P.M. in London. At 11:45 P.M. the phone rang. It was the prince's security staff advising him that Gen. Scowcroft was on the line from the White House.

Concerned, Bandar took the call, saying, "Hi, how are you Brent?"

Scowcroft was blunt. "I'm okay," he said. "However, the president asked me to inform you that we believe that the Iraqis have just crossed the border into Kuwait."

"Wait a minute, wait a minute," a stunned Bandar said. "Can you say that again?"

Scowcroft repeated his message. The prince, after a moment, said, "Brent, I don't believe this is an invasion. If I know Saddam Hussein well enough, he has crossed the border and he is taking over some of the border guard posts; he might go one or two kilometres in and stop, hoping that tomorrow morning King Fahd will fly to Baghdad and then fly to Kuwait and settle this between them."

Scowcroft responded, "That's your analysis. I'm just telling you what the

The Iraqi army rolls into Kuwait.

president told me to tell you. I have to rush now for a national security meeting."

Bandar asked Scowcroft to keep him updated and then put down the phone. He was now wide awake, thoroughly alert, and troubled. A compulsive news channel hopper, Bandar again checked CNN and other news channels: there were no reports of any invasion. He wondered whether he should contact King Fahd and relay the information from the White House. Explaining his decision not to rush into things, he said, "I guess inside of me, I was in denial; I just didn't want to believe that this was happening. Second, part of me was saying I want to go to China with my family. Third, it was such a suicidal move, it cannot happen—it was so dumb." After a little reflection, he clarified this latter comment, saying, "Well, the definition of strategic surprise is if you do something that is thoroughly stupid and is very clearly against your own interests, you can achieve strategic surprise. Nothing that Saddam did before the invasion was unknown to us—we saw everything—it was just the conclusion that was different. What we wanted to believe was, yes, he has done all these things, but the conclusion was that he wouldn't do it, because it just didn't make sense."

By the time Bandar was ready to make a call to King Fahd to inform him of the call from the White House, the phone rang again: it was Sandra Charles, a National Security Council staffer who worked for Scowcroft and who looked after Middle East affairs.

"Look," she said, "I have been instructed by Scowcroft to tell you that the Iraqis are halfway across Kuwait heading for Kuwait City."

Bandar was dumfounded. "What?"

Charles repeated her message.

Shaken, Bandar ended the conversation and then picked up the phone and asked a member of his security staff to put a call through to the king.

The aide's instantaneous reply was ominous. "His Majesty is actually on the other line," he said, "and he is looking for you."[30]

Bandar took the call immediately. "Hello, sir."

"What the hell is going on?" the king thundered. "I had a call from a friend, who told me that some of his friends had told him that the Iraqis had invaded Kuwait. Could that be true? Can you contact the White House?"

Bandar related his conversations with the White House, to which Fahd replied, "I can't believe it."

"Well, sir," said Bandar, "apparently this is true."

Fahd told Bandar, "You go and see President Bush right now and find out what his intentions are and let me know."

"All right, sir," Bandar responded. "I'll see him tomorrow."

Forgetting that Bandar was no longer in Washington, the king retorted, "I told you right now."

"But I'm in London," Bandar explained.

"What the hell are you doing in London at such a time?" Fahd demanded.

"Sir," said Bandar, "you cleared me to go on holiday."

"Bandar, a holiday—at this time?"

The prince diplomatically reminded the king that he had asked him to meet with Mrs. Thatcher.

"Well," Fahd said, "go and see her again. Brief her on the latest developments."

But that wouldn't happen, at least not that night. Bandar explained, "When I left Mrs. Thatcher this evening, she was flying to Aspen—and Bush is also heading to Aspen."

Unsure, in the end, where to send Bandar, Fahd eventually said, "Well get your royal ass out of there and get back to Washington!"

The prince quickly instructed his crew to prepare his aircraft. Then he rang his wife in Paris to tell her that she should return to Washington—the vacation was canceled.

Jim Baker. "Never let them diddle you!"

Bandar was certainly not the first nor the last to fall foul of Saddam Hussein's deceit. However, as a result of being duped, Bandar refused to be deceived again. As the rhetoric got thicker and as negotiations broke down among Iraq, the moderate Arab states, and the West, the one man with the necessary skills to broker the gap and decipher the misread signals was now grounded in a harsh cynicism; it was a changed reality that would have considerable bearing on the Saudi acquiescence to the deployment of U.S. troops on Saudi soil. Indeed, one of Bandar's favorite expressions during interviews concerning the Gulf War was, "Diddle me once, shame on you—diddle me twice, shame on me, and I am here to tell you we will not be diddled again by Saddam Hussein."[31]

The "diddle me once" adage was to surface again in the run-up to Operation Desert Storm. Beneath a portrait of James Baker owned by Bandar are the words, "To Bandar, my colleague and friend. Remember—never let them 'diddle' you—because it CAN be done."

It turned out that as the situation worsened, James Baker had met with the foreign minister of Egypt. Accompanying the minister was a close friend of Bandar's, Dr. Osama El-Bas. After their meeting, El-Bas called Bandar to say that the Egyptian delegation was on its way to the prince's residence.

When they arrived, El-Bas said to him, "Our meeting with Jimmy Baker was excellent; the problem is, when we got to the bottom line of the meeting, he said something we don't understand and we were too embarrassed to ask him; so we just decided to come to you because you are the one who might explain it."

"What did he say?" Bandar asked.

Dr. El-Bas replied, "He told us that the bottom line for me and for the United States of America was, 'You diddle me once, shame on you; you diddle me twice, shame on me' and we said, 'Okay, we understand—thank you' and we left. What does that mean?"

Bandar laughed, "Well, this is the way Jim Baker speaks. In Texan English it means, 'If you fool me once, shame on you; if you fool me twice, shame on me.'" Bandar then gave them a synonymous quote in Arabic: "The faithful cannot be stung from the same hole twice."

They said, "Oh! Now that puts everything into perspective."

Hearing this story later, Baker laughed and then scolded Bandar for explaining it, saying, "You should have let them go home and try and figure it out there."

Bandar has often referred to James Baker as "the ultimate political animal: a great friend and extraordinarily shrewd." Interestingly, Bandar has often commented that James Baker and Colin Powell fit in the same mold—it takes one to know one—and they all knew each other very well.

"When I first met him," Bandar said of Baker, "he was the chief of staff for President Reagan. In that context, obviously he was either aware of, or was present during many of the things that I did with the White House."

On one such occasion, Bandar was called to the White House to meet with President Reagan. When he got there, Adm. Poindexter and Bud McFarlane were also there, as was Jim Baker. The president asked Bandar to take McFarlane secretly to Syria to meet with President Assad during the height of the Lebanon war. Bandar explained, "I was to bring him back without it being made public. So I took McFarlane in my aircraft and we flew to Saudi Arabia secretly and changed aircraft there. We were so cautious we put him in a guest villa in the king's palace. He then met with the king and briefed him, listened to some advice from King Fahd on how to present the message to President Assad, went to Syria, met with Assad, came back to Saudi Arabia, debriefed King Fahd, and then I took him back to Washington to the White House. All of this took place between Friday and Sunday, so that nobody would miss him during the week."

During that meeting at the White House, Bandar asked, "Does Secretary Shultz know?"

He was told, "Secretary Shultz will be told by us; do not tell anyone about this trip."

"When Jim Baker became secretary of state," Bandar continued, "he asked me to come and meet him on his first day in office. And I thought, 'Jimmy is really a true friend; he wanted to give me the distinction of being the first foreign ambassador to meet with him as secretary of state.'"

After they talked generalities, Baker said to Bandar, "I would like to see you alone." When everybody had left the room, Baker looked Bandar straight in the eye and said, "Bandar, I want you to know that I was, once upon a time, chief of staff in the White House."

Bandar immediately understood what he meant. His response was, "Mr. Secretary, you should not forget that once upon a time *you* were a chief of staff in the White House." Bandar explained, "My understanding of that comment was, 'Bandar, do not go around me as secretary of state because I have been there and I've seen it done.' And my answer to him was, 'Remember Jimmy, I didn't go around the secretary of state; you told me not to tell him.'"

In the immediate aftermath of the Iraqi invasion, Saudi Arabia took in four hundred thousand Kuwaiti refugees, including the emir and his royal family. A testament to the world's support for the sovereignty of Kuwait was the failure of an Iraqi attempt to assemble a puppet regime: the Iraqis were unable to find eight Kuwaitis willing to cooperate. In spite of this, in a strategy designed to divide the mounting international Muslim and Christian collaboration against him, Saddam launched a peace initiative, comparing his occupation of Kuwait with the Israeli occupation of Arab lands. It was an unashamed ploy designed to deflect attention from his own actions and to exploit Muslim hostilities toward Israel and the West, and the Arab world quickly saw through it.

Speaking privately, Bandar gave a clear-cut explanation of King Fahd's view of this matter. "During the occupation, Saddam Hussein said that he was willing to withdraw from Kuwait if the Israelis were willing to withdraw from the West Bank, Gaza, and the Golan Heights. King Fahd took a very strong position on that. He said, 'That is unacceptable to us because what Saddam Hussein did was an aggression. We are not going to reward that aggression with a benefit. We, the Saudis, are going to fight for the Palestinian cause and peace in the Middle East. This is nothing to do with you [Iraq]; you must leave Kuwait unconditionally.' "

Bandar would later explain that Saddam Hussein's invasion of Kuwait, of one Muslim country against another, undermined the Palestinian cause and complicated the already fragile peace process. "One of the tragedies that Saddam Hussein has created for us is we've got the whole world united, and again, it is the principle that occupying land by force is wrong—and that applies to what the Israelis are doing in the West Bank and Gaza and the Golan Heights. But what he [Saddam] did is say that it's okay if an Arab does it to another Arab. That really weakens our position and posture."[32] That Yasser Arafat and the PLO also sided with Saddam was the ultimate irony and the cause of considerable Saudi ire. It was cynically observed that Saudi publicists had celebrated Arafat over the decades; but their true feelings came out after the Iraqi invasion of Kuwait.[33] Bandar simply described Arafat as "that clown."[34]

The West's reaction to Iraq's aggression, although seriously miscalculated by Saddam himself, was not unexpected. As President Carter stated, "The world was aroused immediately, and took dramatic and unprecedented action together against this invasion of Kuwait; we wouldn't have done a thing, the same thing, probably, if Nepal or Malaya or Sri Lanka had been invaded."[35] Senator James McClure followed up with a similar focus on the impact of oil, saying, "Certainly, the whole world wouldn't have reacted in concert as they did here. . . . energy is absolutely essential to a modern industrialized society and to our economy and we all know that."[36]

"Saddam Hussein was a tough, ruthless, and even paranoid dictator with little exposure to, and deep suspicion of, the West," said Bush.[37] His assessment of Hussein's shielded perception of the outside world may shed light on how the Iraqi dictator managed to underestimate so completely the West's determination to protect its assets in the oil-rich Middle East. Margaret Thatcher was frank about British interests in the Gulf when she told the U.S. president, "Losing Saudi oil is a blow we couldn't take."[38] The threat to Saudi Arabia was an even more convincing reason than the invasion of Kuwait for the United States to play a leading role in the conflict.[39] As the Gulf crisis continued, Bush successfully appealed to Fahd via Bandar to make up for lost Iraqi and Kuwaiti production; the Saudi response was to raise output from 5.2 million barrels per day to over eight million barrels.[40]

Although President Bush was only too aware of the United States's intrinsic interest in the region's oil, upon which the world's economies at large were (and still are) precariously balanced, the relentless media machine was keen to berate such morally weak motivation for military action. A *Washington Post* journalist wrote, "Nobody wants to say that petroleum is the reason that hundreds of Americans will spend Christmas far from families."[41] Lawrence Korb, former U.S. assistant secretary of defense, observed more cynically that, "If Kuwait grew carrots, we wouldn't give a damn."[42]

The global impact of Saddam's misadventures in the Middle East was immediate; within twenty-four hours, petrol prices had began to rise by as much as fourteen cents a gallon, increasing the price of jet fuel and consequently the cost of flying; electricity had to be rationed in Bulgaria; in Taiwan stocks fell by 65 percent. The Brazilians launched an initiative to subsidize vehicles powered by ethanol and the financial markets of Japan and Portugal were seriously disrupted. In the Middle East, the Israeli government seriously considered issuing the population with gas masks, while Egypt's $7 billion arms debt was canceled by the United States and thousands of foreign workers poured out of Kuwait to return to Egypt, Pakistan, and Bangladesh.[43]

When asked by Larry King why American blood should be spilled for oil, Bandar adopted an open and pragmatic approach in his answer, saying, "I don't think you should be apologetic for protecting your national interests, because oil affects the economies around the world."[44] America was genuinely concerned that the safety of the Saudi oil fields, without a large number of external troops on the ground, would be compromised.

Though his massing of Iraqi troops along Kuwait's border with Saudi Arabia was ominous, Saddam's territorial intentions toward the desert kingdom have never been clearly established. The concern was not that oil would cease to flow should Iraq succeed in achieving control over the vast Saudi oil fields, for it would then fall within Saddam's interests to work quickly to stabilize the oil markets. But that scenario would gift Saddam with a virtual monopoly and hence significant strategic influence over the industrialized world's most vital resource. He was a threat to Western and Arab interests alike. As Saudi General Prince Khalid bin Sultan phrased it, "He threatened the vital interests of every major player in the region. . . . None could tolerate his bid for regional hegemony, because that is what his aggression amounted to."[45]

Saddam Hussein's increasing sense of isolation was becoming acute. On August 2, 1990, the day of the Iraqi invasion, the U.N. Security Council had voted 14–0* in favor of Resolution 660 condemning the Iraqi action, demanding their withdrawal from Kuwait, and insisting upon a negotiated outcome. The Soviet Union's compliance with this resolution was especially important. Since the beginning of the Cold War, the world never had united behind one cause with the conviction illustrated by the U.N. vote. Twenty-eight countries in all, including the Soviet Union and China, voted unanimously against the invasion of Kuwait and in support of sanctions against Iraq: it was indeed a changing world, and perhaps even the beginnings of a "new world order," a phrase coined by Brent Scowcroft. "What we meant by it—and it subsequently got distorted in a number of ways," Scowcroft said, "is that one of mankind's biggest scourges over the centuries had been interstate warfare. We tried the League of Nations and it didn't work; we set up the U.N. and immediately it got frozen because of the U.S.-Soviet problem. So, come the Gulf War, we got U.S.-Soviet cooperation and that opened the prospect that we could deal with this scourge in a way which would really open up a new world order—it didn't mean much beyond that. But the security council of the U.N. could really play the role that was designed by its founders, dealing with interstate conflicts."[46]

Bandar's invitation to the White House on the day after the invasion, August 3, 1990—he had just arrived from London—spoke to the American resolve to place U.S. forces in the Gulf and the strategic importance of Saudi collaboration in this aim. Meeting in Scowcroft's office a little after 11:00 A.M. on August 3, 1990, Bandar was given an overview of the situation as the Americans saw it and was informed directly that the United

*Yemen abstained.

States was prepared to defend the kingdom and was willing to send troops in order to do so. Immediately taken aback, Bandar's blunt response was, "Why would we want to be defended by you?"

A surprised Scowcroft replied, "What on earth do you mean?"[47]

Bandar would later explain the reasons for Fahd's silence and his apparent reluctance to accept Bush's offer of help. These would include President Carter's hollow gesture in 1979, after the fall of the Shah of Iran, when the United States sent a squadron of F-15s as a show of support for Saudi Arabia only to announce, while the planes were still in the air, that they were unarmed. So too was U.S. intervention in Lebanon in 1983, when President Reagan, after a vicious terrorist attack on U.S. barracks, which killed two hundred forty-one Americans, quietly ordered them loaded back onto their ships and returned home.[48]

To the Saudis, these incidents demonstrated a lack of resolve on the part of the United States. The real question with which King Fahd and his advisers were wrestling was not whether to summon American military support, but rather would the Americans be reliable? Would they come in sufficient strength and with sufficient resolve to complete the task? The past examples of U.S. indecision or lack of resolve were seen as a test of American commitment.

Explaining simply, Bandar said, "Saudi Arabia could not afford to be left twice as vulnerable as it already was, should America decide to cut and run." He did not want to see America lending a temporary hand against Saddam and then "pull it back," thereby leaving Saddam on the Saudi border, "twice as mad as he is now."[49]

Scowcroft's response to Bandar's equivocation was equally simple, "I can tell you we won't do that; if we come, we'll stay."[50]

The importance of the meeting between Bandar and the president on August 3, 1990, is significant. It would persuade Bandar that this president had the resolve and courage to meet the challenge Saddam had presented to the world.

"When George Bush came into the room," Bandar recalled, "he said, 'Hi, Bandar!' With arms folded, he said, 'You know Bandar, it hurts when your friends don't trust you.'"

Bandar said to him, "Mr. President, we trust you. This is nothing personal. The survival of my country probably depends on this. It's very simple. If you tell me what you can do, then I can tell you our position. We need to know how far you are willing to go."

At this point, Bush extended his hand and said, "If you ask for help from the United States, we will go all the way with you."

"In that moment," recalls Bandar, "the hair on my hands stood up—you really felt the weight of the moment. After all, this was the president of the United States of America making this commitment."

The oath to protect Saudi Arabia for as long as was necessary had a crucial impact on the prince's assessment, convincing him of America's genuine concern for his country and determination to protect it. In that handshake, there was a commitment between friends that would have a profound impact on the Middle East.

The next day, August 4, Bush telephoned Fahd personally and pledged his solemn word that America would support Saudi Arabia for as long as it took.

Without his ambassador's commitment to the proposed deployment of American ground forces within Saudi Arabia's borders and his belief in the need to do so quickly, it is questionable as to whether King Fahd would have consented to their presence in the time frame that he did. Once he had been convinced of American resolve and commitment, Bandar needed to know exactly what was being proposed. Scowcroft arranged for him to be briefed at the Pentagon by Secretary of Defense Dick Cheney, Paul Wolfowitz, Richard Haas, and the chairman of the Joint Chiefs of Staff, Colin Powell.

"Bandar played his usual Americanized, jaunty fighter-pilot role, drink-

Bandar and President George H. W. Bush

ing coffee from a foam cup and stirring it with a gold pen," Powell wrote later.[51] Throughout the briefing, Bandar remained quiet, clenching his cigar between his teeth. He was shown the satellite reconnaissance photos showing Iraqi troops crossing Kuwait, approaching the Saudi Arabian border. Dick Cheney, authorized by the White House, showed the prince the United States Central Command's (CENTCOM's) defensive plan, information expressly for the U.S. government only and rather ironically labeled "NORFORN," meaning "not for release to foreign nationals." Bandar was impressed by the scale of Operations Plan 90-1002.[52] After hearing the estimated expectation of between one hundred thousand and two hundred thousand troops on the ground, he said to Powell, "Now I know you are not bullshitting me—now you know why we did not want a tactical fighter squadron."[53]

Talking about how they could best get a positive decision from King Fahd, Scowcroft said, "Actually, the first idea was that a Saudi team would come here." However, Scowcroft went on to advise strongly against this, countering, "No, no—we'll send somebody over."

At this juncture, Bandar asked, "Who would you send?"

Scowcroft responded, "I don't know."

Bandar suggested, "How about you and I do it?"[54]

In the end Scowcroft agreed that a joint U.S. team would travel to meet with King Fahd.

In his ensuing conversations, Bandar recommended that Fahd see the reconnaissance photos personally. As an alternative to sending a low-level technical team to Washington, he suggested that the king accept a senior U.S. team who would fly to the kingdom in order to outline American plans firsthand.

That the threat was real was no longer in doubt. American intelligence concerning the movement of Iraqi divisions from Basra to Kuwait and out toward the Saudi border, as well as the equipping of these divisions with Frog ground-to-ground missiles along with other offensive equipment, suggested that an invasion of the kingdom was imminent.[55] As Secretary Cheney admitted in December 1990,[56] "as of August 2, the only thing between Saddam Hussein and those oil fields [in eastern Saudi Arabia] was a battalion of the Saudi Arabian National Guard. There was no significant military obstacle to his further move south."[57] It was even suggested that the Iraqis probably could have reached Riyadh in as little as three days.[58] With a national armed forces totaling only seventy thousand men, the Saudis would need help—even if it meant the placement of "infidel" troops on their soil. But such a choice would be hugely controversial. Fahd, however, agreed to receive the U.S. briefing—and he was keen that it happen quickly.

On Saturday, August 4, 1990, Bandar flew to Saudi Arabia so that he could provide the Saudi leadership with essential briefings prior to Dick Cheney's arrival.[59] On August 4 and 5, three minor border incursions into a so-called neutral zone adjoining the kingdom and Kuwait had been instigated by Iraqi troops. These actions prompted the activation of a hotline installed six years previously between the Saudi and Iraqi armies during the Iran-Iraq war.[60] At first, the Iraqis apologized for their "mistake," promising to remain inside Kuwait's borders. Following the second infringement, the Iraqi general who had first spoken with the Saudis suddenly became unavailable and a junior officer denied any knowledge of the encroachment. After the third incursion, which had taken place within twenty-four hours of the first, there was no answer forthcoming from the Iraqi side; they simply didn't bother to answer the hotline.

Throughout the Gulf War, complications—sometimes catastrophic in nature—arose not simply as a result of the language barrier, but due to cultural barriers virtually impenetrable to all but a few. As noted by Michael Gordon at the *New York Times*, "The Saudis (and the Arab world at large) were accustomed to operating on the basis of promises and signs; the Americans on the basis of legal contracts and treaties."[61] A highly influential factor in the American approach to the Middle East crisis was President Bush himself. He felt for the Kuwaiti people and their leadership on an emotional level and was particularly affected by the constant flow of reports coming out of Kuwait of human rights violations, torture, and brutality on the streets. Saddam Hussein's unashamed use of hundreds of hostages and his siege of the U.S. embassy, in an attempt first to deter the use of sanctions, and second, to shield key Iraqi sites from aerial attack, were costly public relations errors. Hussein's action of hiding behind helpless civilians was described by an angry Bandar on U.S. television as "un-Islamic and un-Arabic."[62]

Writing in his diary, President Bush commented, "I've just read a horrible intelligence report on the brutal dismembering and dismantling of Kuwait. Shooting citizens when they are stopped in their cars. . . . This just hardens my resolve."[63] The president, aside from America's national security interests, viewed the situation with Reagan-like simplicity. "This was not a matter of shades of gray," he said, "or of trying to see the other side's point of view. It was good versus evil, right versus wrong."[64]

By August 5, Bush was so strongly committed to the twin objectives of deterring Iraqi aggression against Saudi Arabia and expelling Iraq from Kuwait that he had given his word of honor to Bandar that the United States would not desert Saudi Arabia. He also pledged to Sheikh Jabir al Ahmed al Sabah of Kuwait that the United States would free his country and reinstate him as ruler. In unambiguous terms, he told the world that Iraqi aggression "will not stand."[65] Upon his return from Camp David, where the secret planning to oust Saddam Hussein had begun, Bush astounded the U.S. Joint Chiefs of Staff by openly stating his intention that America would undertake to overturn the Iraqi attack on Kuwait.[66]

Bush's moral conviction and steadfast attitude on the invasion of Kuwait were unshakeable. His preference for an intimate approach to diplomacy, as witnessed in his personal friendships, not only with Bandar, but also with Margaret Thatcher, François Mitterrand, and many other critical figures during this period, is but one example of how he helped forge a clear policy for the challenge ahead. His personal resolve was honest and simple, and by securing the support of Arab leaders, he gained broad authority when he came to direct the conflict. The Arab world responded to George H. W. Bush's emotional reaction to the treatment of Kuwait and her citizens, seeing it as a reassuring humanity in a leader whose position, as dictated by Western politics, often necessitated harsh objectivity.

That such nuance is essential to a successful partnership with the Arab world was recognized also by Gen. Schwarzkopf, commander of the coalition forces during the Gulf War: "In the Arab world, your position gets you through the door, but your personal relationships get you commitments from the Arabs. That way of conducting affairs had evolved from the Bedouin tent in the desert, where business discussions were followed by long hours of storytelling at night."[67]

When assailed by a predatory Western media, however, President Bush's personal and emotional involvement in the traumatic events unfolding in the Middle East often created stumbling blocks; he was not an accomplished orator in Reagan's style, and his genuineness, and its bearing during the war, would cause Brent Scowcroft to say, "He was deeply sincere, but the impact of some of his rhetoric seemed a bit counterproductive, or at least it inflamed the press."[68] Bush's flights of rhetoric, while received by

Middle Eastern parties as testimony to American resolve, were often interpreted in the West as a personal vendetta against Saddam.

In Western accounts, it is often recorded that King Fahd's momentous decision to accept American troops was made during his August 6 consultation with Cheney and Gen. Schwarzkopf.* During this conference, Bandar acted as translator as Schwarzkopf presented the King with the aerial intelligence pictures showing Iraqi tanks on the Saudi border and, in some cases, over the border. Schwarzkopf explained that Saddam's intentions were unclear, but that the situation looked ominous. He then set out the U.S. proposals for defending the kingdom.

This military briefing was followed-up by Cheney, who delivered a personal message from President Bush to King Fahd, "We are prepared to deploy these forces to defend the kingdom of Saudi Arabia. If you ask us, we will come. We will seek no permanent bases. And when you ask us to go home, we will leave."[69]

After a brief discussion with his council,† the king said, "The Kuwaitis did not rush into a decision, and today they are all guests in our hotels!"[70] At this point, Fahd turned to Secretary Cheney and said simply, "Okay."

Schwarzkopf later wrote of that historic occasion, "If someone had snapped a picture at that moment, it would have shown me with my mouth wide open. Fahd had made one of the most courageous decisions I'd ever witnessed."[71]

Contrary to Saudi Arabia's habitual dithering, this time the decision was fast and unambiguous. The Americans were to be welcomed onto sacred Islamic territory—into the heart of Saudi Arabia.

Saddam Hussein had seriously miscalculated the world's reaction to his invasion of Kuwait. He also had failed to anticipate Saudi Arabia's decision to allow United States troops to be stationed on Saudi soil. His indignation was stridently apparent on August 10, 1990, when he made his declaration of a Holy War against Israel and the United States, claiming that by their actions the Saudis had surrendered as hostages to those countries, the holy places of Mecca and Medina. The prince's response to these charges was blunt and to the point, "That's poppycock and he

---

*Members of the U.S. delegation present: Secretary Cheney, Gen. Schwarzkopf, Bob Gates, Paul Wolfowitz, Pete Williams, Art Hughes, Gen. Horner, Maj. Brandter.

†Saudi Officials present: King Fahd, Crown Prince Abdullah, Prince Abd al-Rahman bin Abd al-Aziz, Prince Saud al-Faisal, Othman al-Humayd, Gen. Muhammad al-Hammad, Prince Bandar bin Sultan.

knows it. Mecca and the holy places are one thousand miles away from where all these troops are."[72]

Working hard in the United States to counter the fear generated in the media, and answering Saddam's accusations of American imperialism, Bandar laid bare the Iraqi leader's hypocrisy, by pointing out Hussein's allegiance with the United States during the eight-year Iran-Iraq War. He intensified the insult by likening Hussein to his long-term rival the Ayatollah Khomeini saying, "The truth of the matter is that President Saddam Hussein did not find the American help for him during the [Iran-Iraq] war to be either offensive or imperialist. He used to think that the greatest thing we could do to help him was getting the Americans to help him and coordinate with him during the war. . . . it almost sounds [now] like he's reading a page from Khomeini. That's the last thing I thought Saddam Hussein would do."

Replying to questions about the proposed Holy War called for by Saddam, Bandar answered with a resounding sense of realism, "To call for a Holy War you have to be holy yourself—in the sense that you do the right thing. How can you call for such a war if you've invaded an Arab brother Moslem country and devastated it the way he did?"[73]

The Saudi decision to collaborate with U.S. forces was historic; it marked the end of the perception of a passive Saudi Arabia as the turtle of the desert, always ready to withdraw its head within its shell. Because of the religious ramifications, Fahd's decision brought with it considerable risks. As a globally recognized Islamic leader, King Fahd was known by the title Custodian of the Two Holy Mosques and was very conscious of the public outcry of the presence of infidels on Islamic soil; the reaction of Saudi citizens, and indeed, international Muslims, would be severe. There was a prevailing fear within Saudi Arabia that should the forces be allowed in, they might not be eager to leave. Politics and religion are so intrinsically entwined inside the desert kingdom—the Saudi Constitution being taken from the Koran—that King Fahd had far more to consider than simply the territorial situation at hand; he had his religious responsibilities to his people constantly in the foreground of his thoughts.

In addition to the secular pressure, along with a rapidly ticking clock, King Fahd had another consideration: the American delegation. Originally to be headed by Gen. Scowcroft, the decision to send Secretary of Defense Dick Cheney had altered the situation considerably. As Brent Scowcroft himself said, "If I go over, I can go over privately, quietly, and if the king doesn't want to do it, fine; no loss of face; no one even has to know. If Cheney goes [though], he's got to come back with something—otherwise, it would be a terrible thing for both of us."

It fell to Bandar to break this news to his king—news that equated to the message, "If you accept this delegation headed by Dick Cheney, you must be prepared to agree to something." It was terribly blunt information for any subject to deliver to his monarch, and as Scowcroft recalled, "Prince Bandar gulped, but he did it . . . and I give him enormous credit; he simply took the bull by the horns and said [to King Fahd], 'This is what you have to do.'" Scowcroft smiled broadly as he explained that they then knew it was going to be an okay. In essence, as early as August 3, prior to the briefing team's leaving America, Scowcroft had known that the prince had secured a positive decision from Fahd to support a U.S. deployment into Saudi Arabia; it was essentially a "done deal."

The security and sovereignty of the kingdom were at stake. "After Cheney met with the king," Scowcroft said, "he called and he said, 'Okay,' and we started people moving there; we had troops there [in Saudi Arabia] within forty-eight hours. We got a battalion over there very rapidly—and that's all we could get over there rapidly. But again, what we really wanted to do as a first step was to put forces in his [Saddam's] way immediately that he would have to run over; so we did that and then we continued the buildup."[74]

Given the implausibility of King Fahd's making a snap decision on such an important issue, many people—and specifically, Brent Scowcroft—believe that Bandar had already secured a clear-cut pronouncement from Fahd. Others believe that a final telephone conversation between President Bush and Prime Minister Margaret Thatcher, while both were in Aspen, was at the root of the king's agreement. According to Lord Powell, Bandar was one of the first to contact the British prime minister at Aspen, and he personally arranged for her a direct line with King Fahd.[75]

Reflecting on the coincidence of Mrs. Thatcher's visit to the United States immediately prior to the outbreak of the Gulf War, Sir Richard Evans, chairman of British Aerospace Systems, highlighted the fact that Prime Minister Thatcher was thus able to meet with President Bush very quickly, speculating that the conduct of the war at the outset might well have been very different if the dialogue between Bush and Thatcher had been conducted over the red telephone, as opposed to a face-to-face meeting.[76] Certainly, Mrs. Thatcher later stated that President Bush impressed her: "He was firm, cool, showing the decisive qualities which the commander-in-chief of the greatest world power must possess."

George Bush had made his decision; he was not going to go wobbly.

"I always liked George Bush," Thatcher wrote. "Now my respect for him soared."[77]

Asked how he would characterize the prince's role in facilitating the American response to the invasion of Kuwait, Gen. Scowcroft affirmed, "I would say it was essential—and I have no idea whether Saddam had planned an attack south or not, but it [the deployment] could have been too late." Speculating on Saddam's intentions, he suggested, "All the indications were that the Iraqi forces would have continued their advance into Saudi Arabia once they had regrouped. After Kuwait fell—and it took all of about two days—we were not at all sure. We were watching, but we couldn't tell for sure, that after a slight amount of regrouping, they would not continue down the east coast to Saudi Arabia to try to seize the oil fields."

Scowcroft then stressed, "If they did that, then that would be a disaster, because they would take the ports in the area and we'd have a terrible time getting back in. In my view, Saddam was clearly contemplating it, but whether he would have done it or not, I don't know. We needed to get some forces in there quickly so that Saddam would realize that he would have to run over some American forces and that in itself might give him some thought. So we had to tell the Saudis we wanted to help and we were prepared to send forces."[78]

Those sentiments were echoed by Sir Richard Evans when he observed, "It seemed entirely possible that Saddam intended to move quickly to capture the Dhahran and the Saudi oilfields." If Saudi Arabia had fallen, the impact on the whole world economy would have been catastrophic. "There was a huge macroeconomic issue," Evans said. "Prince Bandar was one of the guys that actually understood that. Thus, Prince Bandar's role in facilitating rapid decision making by the Saudi royal family, something that is traditionally anathema to the Saudi psyche, was fundamental."[79]

Having been deceived and lied to by Saddam, there can be no doubt that Bandar was determined to repair the damage. To some extent the acute resolve that the prince demonstrated at the outset of the Iraqi invasion stemmed from his personal disappointment at being misled by Saddam.

Writing in his book, *The Politics of Diplomacy,* James Baker recalled that before seeing King Fahd in Jeddah, he met for two hours with Prince Saud and Bandar, who pressed him for an early start to the war against Saddam.

According to Baker, Bandar was particularly insistent on moving swiftly. "He goes," he quipped, "or we go by January."

During a meeting set up between James Baker and King Fahd, three important questions concerning the orchestration of the war were discussed. First, the U.S. needed Saudi permission to put a further two hundred thousand U.S. troops on the ground; Fahd nodded his approval. Second, U.S. commanders, not Saudi generals, must have full control of the field of war, to which Fahd replied, "This agreement is only natural." And third, a U.S. request for more financial aid, to which Fahd replied, "Nothing is impossible to discuss between partners."

Having asked Fahd for a contribution of $15 billion toward the cost of the U.S. deployment, Baker recalled that at a breakfast meeting with Foreign Minister Prince Saud and Bandar, they bluntly surfaced their own concept of burden sharing, saying, "Don't ask us for $15 billion unless you get $15 billion from the Kuwaitis." Bandar exhorted, "They can afford it, too. They have all these assets. What good are they if they don't have their country? So ask as much from them as you ask from us. You'll find that you'll get it."

Baker did just that and he got it.[80]

Sir Richard Evans emphasized that Bandar had assumed a lead role during the Gulf War, "because of his recognition of the severity of the threat presented by Saddam Hussein. He was perceptive enough to see that it was imperative that Saudi Arabia secure support from the United States and put troops on the ground rapidly to counter the Iraqi threat and subsequently to reverse the invasion of Kuwait."[81] Scowcroft also reinforced the value of the prince's assistance, which enabled American forces to deploy quickly enough to challenge the Iraqi advance. He recounted with some amusement, "Bandar went pale when I said what he had to do—and I think that Bandar will confirm that—because that was a big one. To tell the king he had to make a decision—like right now!"

Scowcroft laughed aloud, recalling the prince's discomfort at the prospect of the task ahead, and he repeated, "He'll remember that conversation—but he did it, and he said to the king, 'This is what you have to do.'" The general observed that in doing this Bandar was putting himself absolutely on the line, because as he put it, "The king's notion was to take time—let's go slow—we'll send a team over and then the Americans will send a team back. The sort of Arab way of doing things." Scowcroft now leaned forward and very deliberately said, "I think without Bandar, it just couldn't have been done—and it would have been a very different history."[82]

The enormity of the Saudi decision to stand against a brother Muslim country with the aid of the American superpower cannot easily be expressed. To many, it symbolized a dangerous alliance that put at the risk the Muslim faith. Saudi Arabia is the protector of the two holy mosques in Mecca and Medina; Fahd's decision shocked the hell out of Saddam, who was almost certainly relying on the Al-Saud predisposition for caution and drawn-out deliberation. As Bandar said, "The desert, it forces that kind of pragmatism on its people. You have to distinguish between a mirage and the real thing in the desert. Your survival depends on it."[83]

However, contrary to the perception that King Fahd was put on the spot about the surprise Iraqi invasion of Kuwait and the sudden White House determination to protect the Saudi kingdom and its oil fields, the king was well placed to take decisive action. When your kingdom covers an area of nearly two million square kilometers and holds the largest reserves of petroleum in the world, yet has a population of fewer than eighteen million people* and a military force of only seventy-thousand men, defense is more than a priority—it is an ever-present concern. It was a concern for which Saudi Arabia had been preparing for years.

Sharing borders with seven separate countries in a dramatically unstable region, it is not surprising that Saudi Arabia has always favored a cautionary rather than an active stance. However, the Saudis have never underestimated the region's volatility. For decades, Defense Minister Prince Sultan has been working to increase Saudi Arabia's defensive capabilities, particularly its airborne defenses. Bandar's constant, worldwide efforts on behalf of his father reflect this only too clearly. The battle for F-15s and AWACS, the Al-Yamamah deal with the United Kingdom, the Chinese missile deal—all are prime examples of the kingdom's continuous determination to defend itself. Nevertheless, given the size and strength of the Iraqi army, estimated at a million strong and described as "formidable" by the Defense Intelligence Agency's Middle East specialist Walter Lang, Saudi Arabia could not afford to take chances.

Bandar's brother and joint force commander, Prince Khalid bin Sultan, has stated unequivocally that among the Saudi elite there has always been

---

*Population as of July 1990: 17,115,728.

the assumption that if the "security and the integrity of our territory were threatened, and our own forces were in danger of being overwhelmed, then we would not hesitate to request assistance from any friendly nation with which we had common interests—including the United States."[84]

The question then was not whether or not to collaborate with the United States. The Al-Saud tradition of pragmatism and realism established that should it be necessary, it would be done. What was in debate was the reality and extent of Saddam's threat and just how far the Americans could be trusted not to abandon the kingdom should the going get tough. On these issues the Al-Sauds appeared divided. It was rumored that the younger generations and Western-educated princes—the clique around Bandar—was in favor of calling upon American assistance; however, the senior royals, including Crown Prince Abdullah and Defense Minister Prince Sultan, had reservations, exacerbated by America's increasingly proprietary stance throughout the 1970s and 1980s toward the country's oilfields.[85]

In a revealing insight into Saudi strategy during the previous several decades, Bandar was to explain that "King Fahd thought that the worst part of the Iran-Iraq War was that Iran and Iraq had equal forces. Because they had equal forces, when the rest of the world took sides, what did it have to provide? Arms! Neither side needed troops; they had those. What they needed were the tools to fight!"

Comparing that with Saudi Arabia's position, answering a question posed by the Western world, "How is it that Saudi Arabia has spent millions of dollars arming, and then when the Gulf War started in 1990, they had to bring in outside forces?" Bandar explained the strategy behind that philosophy, setting out a lesson learned from NATO during the Cold War. Although Europe had the technology, the money, the people, and strong economies, there was no reason should it have wanted to match the Soviet Union military threat—taking Europe collectively in relation to the Warsaw Pact—that it could not have done so unaided. Bandar observed, "But Europe had an ally—the United States—which already had that military capability, and which was willing to take on the role of facing off the Soviets."

Expanding on that logic, Bandar cited the legacy of World War II. Europe had just emerged from a devastating war and although the individual nations eventually had the capability to stand on their own feet, the western European countries had decided to use that ability to rebuild their nations. So, the Europeans built armed forces large enough to be effective, but not large enough to face off the Soviet Union alone, because that need was off-set by the Americans providing their nuclear umbrella and putting their forces on the line.

The logic was inescapable. Bandar asked, "Why was it wise for the Europeans to do it and stupid for Saudi Arabia to do it?" Making an analogy between Europe and Saudi Arabia, Bandar argued that if the kingdom had someone who could contribute to its military burden, thereby freeing assets that it could channel into projects such as education, health, development, and so on, doing so makes eminent sense. His view was that this provided stability and security. "Life is about trade-offs; you cannot have it both ways," said Bandar.

The prince reasoned that if Europe had decided to match the Soviet Union, Europe would probably still be a collection of third-world countries insofar as their economies and social development was concerned. "Why?" Bandar asked, "Because the billions of dollars that were spent to make Europe what it became after World War II would have been used to build a nuclear force and standing armed forces to match the Soviet Union and the Warsaw Pact."

Drawing the correlation to Saudi Arabia, Bandar concluded that Saudi rationale and strategy were based on that reasonable precept. The kingdom would put in place sufficient armed forces to deter a potential adversary of similar size. In the case of Iraq, however, with its one-million-strong army, seven thousand tanks, and eight hundred airplanes, Saudi Arabia was not going to be able to match it weapon for weapon. "Instead," Bandar reasoned, "Saudi Arabia chose to match them with alliances and a foreign policy strategy, which, when the chips were down, could enable it to win a war in one month, instead of embarking on a war that would last eight years and end in a draw." Thus, while Saudi Arabia could have bought seven thousand tanks and eight hundred airplanes, and put a million men under arms, it would have been a third-world country, because its economy would have been wasted in creating military forces to match those of Saddam Hussein or the Iranians.

As Bandar explained, "We looked across the borders and saw one million Iraqi troops and we saw five thousand tanks and we saw one thousand planes and we saw ten thousand armored personnel carriers. The question is not whether we had the quality or the will to oppose them; but we didn't have the quantity to stand up to this threat."[86] In reality, the decision had actually been made three days earlier.

Bandar was to affirm that the disparity in force between Saudi Arabia and the Iraqis was not a mistake—it was a deliberate policy that said, "I will concentrate most of my wealth and capabilities on civil activities and development. I will secure the kingdom by having a good foreign policy that creates alliances so that when force is necessary, it will offset my deficiencies. And since I don't plan to have wars every other week, it's just an insurance policy." The conclusion to this exposé on Saudi strategy was that when it came to the crunch, when Saudi Arabia had to cash in that insurance policy in the one war that counted, the kingdom came out of the war with its infrastructure intact, with all of its economic structures intact, and with its human social structure intact. As Bandar observed, "I don't think that's such a dumb policy."

Once the decision had been made to allow U.S. troops into Saudi Arabia, the problem was principally one of logistics. The number of U.S. troops to be deployed initially was said to be fifty thousand: a far cry from the two hundred thousand to two hundred fifty thousand predicted by Gen. Schwarzkopf at a Camp David meeting with the president on August 4. Yet deploying even the lesser of these figures presented a massive logistical challenge. Air power was straightforward enough, but getting real numbers of troops on the ground would take time. Should the Iraqi army choose to attack during this period, the United States would have insufficient numbers on the ground to mount an adequate defense. It became vital that Saddam Hussein remain unaware of this Achilles heel. Furthermore, the size of the eventual force the United States intended to send needed to remain a tightly guarded secret. American jet fighters and the 82nd Airborne Division were deployed immediately. However, according to Gen. Schwarzkopf's estimation, full implementation would take up to seventeen weeks to complete. Moreover, it would be approximately twenty days before there would be sufficient aircraft and carrier battle groups in place to deter the Iraqi army, already massed in Kuwait.

The day after talks with King Fahd, Prince Sultan and Bandar met with Secretary Cheney in Jeddah. They all agreed that no announcement should be made about the proposed operation until two days later, when the first U.S. troops would already be on the ground. The timing and sensitivity of the issues at stake, however, proved more difficult back in Washington, where security issues ran up against the freedom of the American press.

It has been said that "no American president has thrust the United States into a major war so swiftly and massively."[87] The rapid pace of events was matched almost instantaneously by the media; headlines rolled off the press hour by hour, minute by minute. Amid accusations of deliberately playing down the scale of U.S. troops to be sent to the Middle East, the Bush administration came under heavy fire from the media as the crisis was still unfolding.

It has been written that "truth is the first casualty not just in war, but equally in preparation for war, for both rely heavily on secrecy, evasion and deception."[88] Such a sentiment would be viewed as detrimental to public rights by the Western press, yet too much freedom of the press, particularly during a time of war, puts the lives of servicemen and servicewomen at risk. In his many interviews, Bandar has marveled at the American failure to recognize this military fact, saying, "You have the luxury in America of treating military operations like Boy Scout camps. Well, it's not that way; people cannot push for, and should not push for, details of military operations. People's lives are on the line in the Gulf; you cannot afford to talk about it like it was a football game."[89]

Despite this, the media remained a constant thorn in the president's side. It fought savagely for even more free rein—columnist Anthony Lewis labeled television "the most egregious official lap dog during the war,"[90] and Murrey Marder claimed, "The Bush administration achieved a level of control over the American print and broadcast press and public opinion that Presidents Johnson and Nixon would have given anything to have had during their turbulent years of the Vietnam War."[91]

Such negativity, perhaps, overlooked the need for national solidarity in the face of external aggression and sensitive matters of foreign policy. The president vented his frustration with the U.S. press, writing, "For those who think I'm paranoid about the press, they ought to look at the *ABC-Washington Post* poll . . . it looks to me like they don't want to print the news they don't want to read. Typical!"[92] The president was angry about a poll, sponsored in part by the *Washington Post,* that had been buried at the back of the edition because it showed the public largely in favor of the president's initiatives.

In conjunction with the deployment of U.S. forces, it was crucial to both the Al-Saud family and to the Bush administration that the supporting Arab nations and other international forces take an active role in the defense of Saudi Arabia. At the emergency Arab League Summit held in Cairo on August 9, orchestrated by President Mubarak, twelve of the twenty-one members voted in support of a pan-Arab force to defend Saudi Arabia. Those countries were determined that a motion should be passed empowering the dispatch of pan-Arab troops. Such action was deemed to be not only defensive, but one that also provided an international umbrella of support under which the American forces could operate. The summit also highlighted the rift that had opened up between those Arab states seen to be supportive of Saddam Hussein and those who opposed him. Libya and the PLO opposed the creation of a pan-Arab defense force; Bahrain, Djibouti, Egypt, Kuwait, Lebanon, Morocco, Oman, Qatar, Saudi Arabia, Somalia, Syria, and the United Arab Emirates voted in favor; Yemen and Algeria abstained; Jordan, Mauritania, and Sudan all expressed reservations; Tunisia did not attend. By August 11, Egyptian and Moroccan troops already had begun to arrive in Saudi Arabia.

The presence of international forces was a keynote point made by Bandar as he worked the U.S. media circuit. On *Larry King Live*, he said, "In sending troops to our country you are not alone. The British are there, other Muslim and Arab countries; Egypt, Morocco, Syria, Pakistan, Bangladesh. So this is a cause for the whole world to rally round."[93] In another interview, he stressed, "What I'd like our American friends and the public to know is you are not alone, the whole world is together. Can the whole world be wrong and Saddam Hussein right?"[94]

Behind the seeming steadfast unity, Bandar had been working hard with King Fahd to keep the anti-Saddam Arab states unified, as well as bring along the fence-sitters. At the king's request, the prince flew to Syria to attempt to persuade President Assad, who had been expressing concern over America's commitment. After reassuring the Syrian president of his own personal trust in the U.S. president and the strength and size of the U.S. forces being deployed, he succeeded in gaining Assad's support; however, Assad held off announcing his decision to support Saudi Arabia for another forty days.[95]

A far greater obstacle to Arab unity, one that was particularly painful to Fahd, Bandar, and the entire Saudi royal family, was King Hussein of Jordan's support for

King Hussein of Jordan—Bandar's mentor and friend, but Bandar could never understand his backing for Saddam Hussein after the invasion of Kuwait.

Saddam Hussein. Geopolitically, Jordan was in a perilous position. However, even though they were conscious of Jordan's predicament, the House of Saud found it impossible to justify the remarks made by King Hussein, essentially calling for the removal of foreign forces from Saudi Arabia on the grounds that the Kuwaiti-Iraqi border had been constructed by the colonial British.

On September 19, 1990, the Kingdom of Saudi Arabia cut all ties with Jordan, citing nonpayment of bills; it also stopped all Jordanian imports and expelled the diplomats of Jordan, Palestine, Yemen, and Iraq. Most powerfully, perhaps, Bandar was to write a personal letter—a stinging public rebuke[96]—to the Jordanian king, a man with whom he had shared a close personal friendship.

Your Majesty,

•••

Would it not be more honorable and honest to speak to the Iraqi people over the head of your other friend, Saddam, and tell them what he has dishonorably done in invading and annexing a brother Arab and Moslem country—and of horrifying acts of rape and destruction which are unprecedented in Arab history.

That is fact, and facts are stubborn things.

You say, Your Majesty, that the holy places in Saudi Arabia have been desecrated by friendly forces and that those forces must leave immediately. But those forces are actually hundreds of miles away, and there are tens of thousand of Moslem and Arab forces (your forces not among them) between those friendly forces and the holy places. And all those forces are dedicated to help defend Saudi Arabia and are respectful of its custodianship of the holy places. They will not leave until your friend Saddam leaves Kuwait, which we hope will be peacefully and immediately.

Tell us, Your Majesty, what you have done to safeguard the Al-Aqsa Mosque and the Church of the Holy Sepulchre that you lost to the Israelis in 1967, almost a quarter of a century ago? Is that the kind of protection that you want us to give to the holy places in Saudi Arabia?

•••

And, Your Majesty, you claimed to defend the Palestinian people's right to self determination and a state of their own. And I support you in that. But you were responsible for the Palestinian homeland on the West Bank from 1948 to 1967. Why in all that period did you not give them their rights and statehood? And how would the occupation of Kuwait give our brother Palestinians their homeland?

You talk of "haves" and "have-nots." Saudi Arabia's record as one of the "haves" is clear in helping the "have-nots," and we are proud of it. Just turn to the records of your finance minister, and see how much has been given to you and your country for many years by Saudi Arabia, willingly and happily, as brothers.

•••

You are a very intelligent man, Your Majesty. And you have a fine memory. You say the Kuwait-Iraqi border is disputed and based on a historical record created by the colonial British.

Your Majesty, you should be the last one to say that. Not only all your borders, but your whole country was created by the same colonial British. And do you remember when the British troops were invited by you into your country in 1958? We did not object or question your motives and judgment over that.

Your brother King Fahd is proud to have as friends Presidents Mubarak and Assad, King Hassan and the presidents of Pakistan, Bangladesh and Senegal, the leaders of the Mujahideen, Presidents Gorbachev, Bush and Mitterrand and Prime Minister Thatcher, and so many more heads of state and their people who have joined in the worldwide consensus at the United Nations arrayed against the naked aggression and annexation of our brother state Kuwait.

I hope you are proud of your new friends—Saddam Hussein, Abu Abbas, Abu Nidal, Habash, Hawatmeh and the rest of that unholy crowd.

You tell us, your majesty, that the situation today is like 1914, when the world was going to a war it did not want but could not stop, which led to World War I. That is not true. Your Majesty, the situation today is like the 1930s, when a madman decided to annex his neighbor and the world did nothing, which led to World War II.

Your Majesty, please remember what caused this entire crisis in our region—it was the invasion of the Arab and Moslem state of Kuwait by Saddam Hussein. And only after that and because of that were Moslem Arab and friendly forces invited. They will all leave when this aggression is turned back or when we ask them to leave. These are facts.

Your Majesty, I long had great respect and affection for you, and I continue to have deep respect and affection for your people. But I no longer can feel that you are the same man I knew. I hope that I am wrong. And if I am wrong, please accept my sincere apologies, Your Majesty. But facts are stubborn things.[97]

Bandar's controversial open letter written to King Hussein was submitted as an op-ed piece by Fred Dutton simultaneously to the *Washington Post*, *New York Times*, and *San Francisco Chronicle*. All ran the piece. The letter caused an outcry among the U.S. press. Bandar would later tell friends, "as much publicity as that letter got, and as much praise as I got from everybody who was against Saddam—in the kingdom, in America, in Europe, in the Arab world—it was the most painful letter that I have ever written to anybody, because I was writing it with a split personality. On the one hand, I really wanted to be mean; on the other hand, I really didn't want to be mean to the same guy whom I had such an affection for, but he gave me no room to maneuver."

In a subsequent discussion on John McLaughlin's PBS television show *One on One*, Bandar repeated his disappointment in Hussein's position, but reiterated his esteem for the king, saying, "I have great respect for King Hussein; after all, other than being one of my Arab leaders, he is a fellow fighter pilot. It hurts what he has done because Saudi Arabia had troops there for ten years in Jordan at his command, and when we extended them there at his request, there was no 'ifs' or 'buts' or 'whys' and I hope he doesn't forget that."[98]

Col. Bob Lilac was later to reveal to me the real foundations of that letter, explaining, "Prince Bandar, Princess Haifa, and some friends were sitting watching King Hussein giving this talk on CNN. As he was making his speech, the prince was making comments, sentence by sentence, reacting to him." When Hussein had finished, Princess Haifa looked at Bandar and said, "Well, why don't you write that down?"

Not even conscious of what he had been doing, Bandar said, "Write what down?"

Princess Haifa said, "Your answers to the king need to be heard."

"Even if I wanted to write it down, I can't remember what I was saying. I was just responding."

"Okay," said Haifa. "So let's get all the people here in the room, who heard both of you, to try and help your memory."

As they had taped King Hussein's interview, they now replayed it. After they had exhausted everyone's collective memory, Bandar devised the motif: 'Facts are stubborn things, Your Majesty.' It was something Reagan used to say, and it was to be continually repeated throughout the paragraphs of Bandar's letter.

Lilac recalled that years later the pain of writing that letter still lingers with Bandar, who has said, "It's amazing—what looks to people as being someone's finest hour—to that person it might be their worst hour, because I really had no joy in writing it."

Speaking to the relationship between Bandar and King Hussein, Dr. Said Karmi said, "Hussein was a man whom he loved, liked, and greatly respected; he was a king, a mentor in some ways, a friend, a fellow pilot, a down-to-earth guy, sharp, intelligent, the ultimate survivor. He totally confused Bandar by his position during the Gulf War and during the invasion of Kuwait. King Hussein stood by Saddam Hussein's position, [for reasons] more complex than people understood. The Saudi Arabian leadership and Prince Bandar personally were hurt by his position, not for what he did and said, [but] because this man was so close to them that they had absolutely no doubt where his heart was and they had been through tough times before. The big difference, that people really don't understand and appreciate in the sharp Saudi reaction toward this man whom they all loved, from the king downward and forgetting the personal feelings they had, was that in the past when he was put in such a position, he would consult with them in advance. He would let them know why he's going to do something that they wouldn't like, like when he was with Nasser and so on, and then the Saudis would agree that it was the best course for him, knowing that they understood each other and that he had not changed."

Over the years, the relationship between Saudi Arabia and Jordan would mend and strengthen. Shortly before King Hussein's death, his aides contacted Bandar at his home in England. "His Majesty cannot talk with you," they said, "but he has a message for you. 'My son (who later became King Abdullah) is your son; please look after our son and take care of him.'"

Bandar quickly responded, "Tell King Hussein that he is our son and we will take care of him."

The king passed away a short while later. Bandar was among many members of the Saudi royal family to attend the funeral.[99]

The extension of U.S. support to the Middle East was not confined to the deployment of troops. One outcome of the collaboration between the United States and Saudi Arabia was the American enhancement of the Saudi defense capabilities. The Bush administration worked hard to send what was deemed desperately needed military equipment to Saudi Arabia.

Brent Scowcroft explained, "Iraq had a far larger military than did Saudi Arabia and enjoyed a qualitative advantage in that the Saudis had no ammunition that could defeat Iraq's Soviet-made tanks."[100] As with so many Middle East arms transfers, though, there were difficulties. First, the administration was prohibited from selling certain specification munitions to non-NATO countries; second, a thirty-day waiting period was required between the notification of Congress and actual shipment of arms, which extended the Saudis' already vulnerable exposure.

Yet, by August 26, President Bush had won signed waivers authorizing the immediate transfer of one hundred fifty older tanks, twenty-four aircraft, and limited munitions to Saudi Arabia. Congress, however, rejected a second package proposed in September comprising modern tanks and equipment worth an estimated $17 to $20 billion. To meet congressional conditions, the package was broken in two. The first shipment was to be made upon determination of immediate need and availability; the second was to follow at a later date.

Throughout October and November 1990, despite an overwhelmingly hectic schedule divided between the two disparate time zones of Washington, D.C., and Saudi Arabia, Bandar also managed to channel his energy into the formation of the Committee for Peace and Security in the Gulf.[101] In essence, this was a lobbying organization working to support President Bush's initiatives during the crisis and comprised of such prominent Democrats as Senator Stephen Solarz (D-NY), and Democratic National Committee (DNC) political director Ann Lewis,* as well as former Reagan officials including Richard Perle, former assistant secretary of defense; Frank Carlucci, former U.S. secretary of defense; Jeane Kirkpatrick, U.S. ambassador to the United Nations; and other members of Congress.† The Committee advocated the use of force within the Middle East to protect U.S. interests in the region predicated on the condition that Congress was to be consulted before any action was taken. The president described the Committee as "a big help in giving the other side of the issue."[102]

Despite the efforts of the Committee, influential powers inside Congress were bent on opposing any change from the United States's defensive stand. Though U.S. troops were already mobilizing, the official position of the

---

*Media guru and former political director to the DNC.

†These included John McCain, Dick Lugar, Jack Murtha, and Bob Torricelli.

United States remained defensive. Two congressional letters of opposition were sent to President Bush, objecting to any action being taken to remove Iraqi forces from Kuwait by force; the first, delivered October 9, contained the signatures of thirty-three Democrats. A clear indication of the momentum gathering among the antiwar bloc is that a second letter delivered to the president on October 30, less than three weeks after the first, contained the signatures of eighty-one Democrats. The growing opposition stemmed from fears about the continued buildup of forces, the lack of a rotation policy in operation, and the distinct sense that decisions were being made without their involvement. Congress clearly was becoming anxious. The second letter stated plainly, "Under the U.S. Constitution, only the Congress can declare war" and "We are emphatically opposed to any offensive military action."[103]

Despite the strength of feeling pulsing through Capitol Hill, and notwithstanding stern calls from Congress for greater participation in the decision-making process, Bob Dole hit upon the crux of the issues at stake when he said, "How do we have an open debate without sending the wrong signal to Saddam? If we in Congress want to participate, then we owe our boys and the president support for [White House] policy."[104]

Beyond rhetoric, the presence of foreign, non-Moslems on Saudi soil proved thorny. Issues that were nonexistent in the American military suddenly required careful consideration, attention, and action.

"I kidded him once during the buildup to the Gulf War," Secretary Powell says of Bandar. "We used to spend an enormous amount of time together [working] through lots of issues. He said to me, 'Colin, the troops can't come into the kingdom wearing their crosses and Stars of David.' 'Bandar, you've got to be nuts,' I responded. 'Do you think that I can tell the American people that we're coming over to save you guys and they can't wear their crosses and Stars of David?'" But this was a true concern for Saudis, and an accommodation was reached that allowed personnel to wear their religious symbols, but only if they were under a T-shirt.

The issue of where Jewish soldiers might be able to observe the Sabbath was also raised. "How are you going to handle that?" Powell had asked Bandar. "And the answer was: put them on an aircraft carrier off the coast. So we rounded up all the Jewish kids and put them out to sea." Though, he confided, "We finally ignored that as long as they were quiet and did not show anything."

And again, "What are we going to do about Bibles coming into the kingdom? I said, 'Bandar; I can't have a situation where we can't send Bibles into the kingdom. So I tell you what; I'll tell you when planes are coming into the kingdom so your customs inspectors can be off having a cup of tea. So they know when they're coming in and they don't want to see them.' "[105]

Foreseeing difficulties should any romantic liaison strike up between American military personnel and Saudi women, Powell and Bandar also struck a gentleman's agreement: any American involved would be flown directly back to the United States to be disciplined before Islamic law could intervene. Thankfully, though, this proved an unnecessary precaution.

For the United States, dealing with issues like these required not only an Arab counterpart who had a profound understanding of the two cultures, but a personal relationship between the key players. Powell said, "It had to be a 'go-to' guy who understood my needs, and who knew I understood his needs. You don't get that just by title; you get that by knowing someone for a long period of time, and we were able to work through almost every problem like that as it came along—and there were dozens of them."[106] For Bush, for Powell, and for Fahd, Bandar was that 'go-to' guy.

However, one disruption, which could not have been preempted, was the presence of U.S. women in the Gulf. As Powell recalled, "Our servicewomen provoked a mini social revolution; Saudi women saw them driving, and some started driving themselves. Since they were violating Islamic law, the women were arrested."[107] In the United States, the media stirred up outrage at the hard-line regulations international forces were expected to abide by. A scathing article printed in the *Washington Post* directed particular venom at Bandar, saying, "Our American soldiers, who are waiting in the sand to defend Prince Bandar's country and who want to celebrate the central event on the Christian calendar, are required to do so 'discreetly.' We mustn't upset the Saudis, you see, while we are saving them. Our poor servicemen and women are bearing the brunt of the involvement with this touchy people [the Saudis]."[108]

Urged repeatedly by Congress to give the U.N.-imposed sanctions time to work within the framework of an international coalition, President Bush was growing increasingly convinced that offensive action was becoming the only proper course of action to pursue. He anxiously awaited the Security Council's decision on the use of force to evict Saddam Hussein from Kuwait. However, unbeknown to Bush, former President Jimmy Carter, in an unprecedented undermining of a sitting president, sent a letter to members of the Security Council, urging the international community not to vote in favor of Resolution 678, which authorized the use of force in Kuwait. The former president argued that the price of destabilizing the region and the cost in human lives would be too high.

President Bush was said to be furious, but instructed his staff to let the matter drop. It was a wise decision. On November 29, 1990, the U.N. Security Council recorded a conclusive and resounding vote of support for Resolution 678.* In the words of President Bush, "The Security Council had voted to go to war."[109]

It was widely hoped that Resolution 678† would convince Saddam Hussein of the resolve of international parties to remove his forces from Kuwait by force if necessary. Given that early on in the crisis countries such as France, Russia, Germany, and Japan were all rigorously opposed to the use of military force, it was hoped that their vote in favor of 678 would correct Saddam Hussein's presumption that the world would let him keep Kuwait. The implementation of the six-week deadline of January 15, 1991, was crucial to convincing Saddam that the world was serious and that he should withdraw from Kuwaiti territory immediately.

It was more than unfortunate, therefore, that after such success within the coalition, President Bush then made the potentially catastrophic move on November 30, 1990, to go "an extra mile for peace." Partly in response to public and congressional opposition, and partly for his own peace of mind, President Bush proposed to send James Baker to Baghdad and to proffer an invitation to Iraqi Foreign Minister Tariq Aziz to visit Washington, D.C.

The timing was disastrous. The president's actions shocked the coalition to its core. Just as the world had authorized the use of force, America was seen to be backtracking. A few days after the president's November 30 proposal, Bandar called James Baker, who recalled that the prince "suggested that Baghdad was the last place I should consider visiting. You've got to be crazy to go there," Bandar had said. "This guy is going to hold you as a

---

*All twelve participating countries voted in favor, with Yemen, Cuba, and China abstaining.

†U.N. Security Council Resolution 678 stated: "All member states cooperating with the government of Kuwait, unless Iraq on or before January 15, 1991, fully implements (the resolutions), to use all necessary means to uphold and implement (all those resolutions) and restore international peace and security to the area."

hostage." Baker thought that Bandar was convinced that "if Saddam were really persuaded we were coming after him, he wouldn't abide by any rules." In a telling comment about Saudi intentions toward Saddam Hussein, Baker also said, "Bandar, of course, didn't want me to go in the first place. The Saudis had no desire for a compromise solution that would leave Saddam's military intact."[110] Bandar had become a vociferous hawk. Frustratingly trying to explain the difference between Americans and Arabs, he said to Scowcroft, "The peace offering, twenty-four hours after the United Nations victory, [sent] precisely the wrong message to Saddam: a message of weakness. To you sending Baker is goodwill; to Saddam it suggests you're chicken."[111]

In his last-ditch attempt to avoid war, Bush had unwittingly undermined the work of the coalition and convinced the already delusional Saddam that the outside world was spineless. The effect was instantaneous. From Baghdad, a BBC crew reported, "There's no mistaking the feeling here that President Saddam Hussein has got the Americans on the run." Disastrously, President Bush had given Saddam the reason he needed to sit out the deadline set by the coalition.

Scowcroft himself admitted that the dates proposed were a mistake; Tariq Aziz was invited to Washington during the week of December 10, but Baker's invitation to Baghdad was specified only as some date between December 15, 1990, and January 15, 1991. This gave Saddam the opportunity to barter for time right up until the U.N. deadline. However, Scowcroft confessed to Bandar that the meeting was, in fact, "all exercise" and affirmed that the plans for war were going forward; Bush simply wanted to show the world—and particularly America—that he was a man of peace and that the choice for war was Saddam's.[112]

Nonetheless, Saddam was ecstatic and America's allies in the Arab world became anxious that the United States was weakening. Baker reported that it was the prince's opinion that King Fahd and the other Arab allies were too polite to confront the president on this, but nevertheless they were worried.[113]

Saddam Hussein immediately set to work manipulating America's goodwill by insisting that Baker's visit be set for January 12—just three days prior to the Security Council's deadline. Bush insisted on a date before January 3; finally, Baker and Aziz met in Geneva on January 9. During this meeting, the Iraqi foreign minister invited himself to the United States and Baker to Iraq. Infuriated by what he described to the president as "absolute total bullying," Baker replied, "*No!* We gave you fifteen days—you said no. Now you are trying to manipulate the deadline."[114] Bandar later reflected that "Bush and Baker had given Saddam great comfort during what should have been the Iraqi leader's moment of greatest distress."[115] However, in Geneva, Baker presented Tariq Aziz with a final ultimatum. If he agreed to the terms proposed, there would be no war. If he disagreed, there would be war. On January 11, Baker flew to Saudi Arabia to explain to the Royal Court that, "The Iraqis have refused, so now we are going to go to war, but we can't go to war until King Fahd approves it." That permission was quickly granted.

The allies began their final preparations for a war to oust the Iraqi dictator from Kuwaiti territory by force.

Before leaving for Washington to deliver his full report to George Bush, James Baker asked King Fahd, "How do we communicate with you about D-day H-hour? It is sensitive and lives are at risk. I need a code word between us, Your Majesty."

King Fahd told him, "That's all right, I will work it out with Bandar, and Bandar will have the code word. You just tell him and he will communicate to me."

Bandar had planned to leave Saudi Arabia right after Baker, so as to be in position in Washington for the planned offensive. However, Fahd had other plans for the prince.

"Figure out a code between you and I that nobody can break," he directed Bandar, "and tell me about it tonight." Over the prince's objections, Fahd repeated, "Tonight."

The actual code used by Bandar and Fahd to confirm the proposed start of Desert Storm has been a source of some debate. According to Bob Woodward, Bandar used the phrase in a general conversation with the king, "Our old friend Suleiman is coming at 3 A.M. He's sick and I'll ship him out, and he'll get there at 3 A.M."[116] Baker also corroborated that version.[117] However, other accounts say that the tip-off was, "How is my favorite uncle?"[118] According to Bandar, neither is correct. The code specifying that the coalition offensive against Iraqi forces was to be launched and at what time, Bandar says, was the name of Suleiman al-Helee.

Driving through Riyadh, desperately trying to think of a code the king would remember easily, Bandar remembered an Air Force saying: "KISS—keep it simple, stupid!" Thinking back to his early life with his grandmother, the prince recalled a man named Suleiman al-Helee who came from his grandmother's family on her mother's side. He was a funny man who used to tell jokes and make his grandmother and many of Bandar's family laugh, including King Fahd. Suleiman al-Helee, who had died about twenty-five years before, was a figure that no intelligence service in the world would know, as he had no place in history.

Returning to see the King, Bandar said, "I've got it—the code!"

"What is it?" asked Fahd.

"Suleiman al-Helee."

"What?! He's dead!" retorted the king.

"I know," said Bandar. "I'll bet you that neither the KGB nor the CIA nor MI6 combined could figure out who the hell was Suleiman al-Helee."

"I see," replied Fahd. "That makes sense—go ahead."

"When I know the time of the attack," the prince continued. "I will call you and tell you the family of Suleiman al-Helee—"

Fahd interrupted, "Why the family?"

Bandar explained, "Just in case someone figured out who he is and they say, 'He has been dead twenty-five years—why are they talking about him?'"

The story concocted by Bandar was that King Fahd had sent one of Suleiman al-Helee's family members to the United States for medical treatment, but that the doctors had called Bandar and told him that there was no hope. To Fahd, he said, "I would then recommend to you that we send him back home, so that if he had to die he would die at home. Then you should ask me, 'What time are they going to get home, so I can get someone to receive them?' I will then give you a time, and that will be the time of the attack." The king readily agreed to the prince's idea.*

Seven days later at a morning meeting with James Baker at the State Department on January 16, 1991, Bandar was informed of the U.S. decision to strike Baghdad that evening. The Prince duly notified King Fahd by phone using the Suleiman al-Helee code.

On January 16 at 8 p.m. Washington, D.C., time (3 a.m. in Baghdad), the United States launched Operation Desert Storm. The air offensive began without a hitch. Considering the mélange of confusion and misunderstanding that had dogged U.S.-Iraqi dialogue from the outset, and the

---

*The Americans thought that Suleiman was the prophet Solomon and that the Saudis were using a biblical reference.

deluge of mixed messages pouring from both countries across the Atlantic, it is perhaps not surprising that Saddam was unable to second guess or pre-empt U.S. action.

As the allied campaign against Iraq intensified, Saddam Hussein played yet another card. Scud missiles began to hit targets in Israel. Gen. Schwarzkopf recalled how after three Scuds hit Israel (two landed in Tel Aviv and one in Jerusalem), his operations director handed him a message advising him that "the Israelis wanted to launch their own massive counter-strike into western Iraq: one hundred planes the following morning, one hundred more planes the following afternoon, attacks by Apache helicopters the following night, and commando raids—all to enter Iraq through Saudi Arabian airspace."

Powell told Schwarzkopf curtly, "The Saudis will never buy this, and you can't sneak it by them. They have people up in our AWACS and they're gonna know." However, while the administration expressed outrage at the Scud attacks, every effort was made to persuade the Israelis to hold off with any retaliatory action or, if this was impossible, to limit any action to those airbases in western Iraq from which the Scud missiles had been fired. The administration argued, "We had already knocked out all known Scud sites; we were continuing our attack with more aircraft and more firepower than the Israelis could muster, and Israeli intervention would strain and perhaps fracture the coalition we had worked so hard to build."[119]

Expecting a rejection, Powell and Baker nonetheless duly approached

Operation Desert Storm—a U.S. Humvee and a Saudi tank head for Kuwait City.

Bandar, asking him to obtain the king's permission for Israeli overflights of Saudi Arabia, a less risky option than an Israeli attack using Jordanian airspace, which might have seen a new dimension to the conflict. "I told Bandar that the Israelis wanted permission to overfly his country to attack Iraq." Bandar immediately responded, "King Fahd is a generous man, but it would be a waste of time to pass along such a request."[120] The prince gave no hint of flexibility on the Israeli retaliation and insisted that Israel should not be allowed to enter the war.[121] Soon after, Powell confirmed, Israel had again agreed to hold off and the crisis was defused.

On February 24, 1991, the land offensive was initiated. Lasting exactly one hundred hours, Operation Desert Storm was terminated at midnight on February 27–28, a remarkable victory for coalition forces. Iraqi troops had been pushed back over the Iraqi border with ease. Despite Congress's worst fears, the final number of U.S. fatalities pronounced at the time of the ceasefire was seventy-nine, with two hundred twelve wounded in action, and forty-five missing in action. Although tragic, such minimal casualties were impressive considering that in conjunction with the ground offensive, a total of one hundred ten thousand combat sorties had been flown during the campaign. Fewer American lives were lost during Operation Desert Storm than in the Beirut bombing of U.S bases in 1983.

Bandar was more than frustrated at the U.S. decision to suspend the offensive, thereby leaving Saddam Hussein in power with much of his Republican Guard intact. Having been personally deceived by Saddam—deliberately lied to by a fellow Arab—the prince had adopted a hard-line position, something that Secretary Baker stressed to me during an interview in his Houston offices. He provided me with his own notes taken from a meeting that was held after the invasion, and during the preparation for a possible offensive to retake Kuwait. Baker's notes showed that Bandar had argued for an overwhelming military response to the Iraqi invasion saying, "If there's a military engagement, it must be total and complete. We can't generate support for a measured response. We worry about a standoff."[122]

Bush, however, agreed to a ceasefire after a significant element of the Iraqi forces had been destroyed or annihilated. The Saudis, who wanted to see the destruction of more of Saddam's army, especially the elite Republican Guard, were unhappy with that decision, deeply unhappy.[123] Contributing to the Saudi feeling of discontent with the termination of the offensive was the highly moral and conciliatory stance adopted by the

United States toward Iraq after the ceasefire, one Bandar described as "American Puritanism in its worst form."

Speaking directly about the timing of the ceasefire, Bandar says, "I believe militarily we stopped too soon, and I believe politically we did the right thing. Although, now, two years later, I think even politically it would have paid off had we continued that war."[124]

His half-brother, Prince Khalid also struck this chord in his recollections of Desert Storm and particularly highlighted the Arab view when he said, "Aggression had to be punished, not rewarded, or the whole Arab system would fall to the law of the jungle."[125]

Bandar was gravely disappointed that the allies had unilaterally suspended military operations, implementing a ceasefire without simultaneously making it conditional on Saddam Hussein's surrender. He argued that while the allies had undoubtedly won the war, the Iraqi dictator was still in power. Yes, Kuwait had been liberated. But the slaughter of the Iraqi army in the face of overwhelmingly superior U.S.-led allied forces that introduced a media-induced call for a humanitarian ceasefire resulted in something less than a satisfactory victory.

Years later, President Bush continued to justify his decision to cease hostilities at that point, saying, "The question is understandably asked, did we stop too soon? My answer is and will always be, no. We had defined the mission: it was not to kill Saddam Hussein; it was certainly not to occupy an Arab nation; it was to end the aggression against Kuwait."[126] However, despite the arguably positive outcome of the first Gulf War, Saddam remained in power. In what proved to be a reversal of fortune, the allies had fundamentally miscalculated Saddam's ability to survive. Speaking to then British Prime Minister John Major, Bandar explained that the Arab world expected the Iraqi military to remove Saddam from power; this would surely be the inevitable result of another embarrassing international military defeat. Instead, Saddam ruthlessly tightened his hold on power and the expected coup never took place.[127]

In yet another development, the Saudis advocated providing covert weapons support to the Iraqi Shiites in the hope that this would eventually lead to Saddam's downfall.[128] However, despite Saudi reassurances that the Iraqi Shiites were a world apart from the Iranian Shiites, who both the United States and the Iraqis had been fighting in the Iran-Iraq war, the Americans rejected the scheme out of hand.

This rejection had catastrophic consequences for the Iraqi people. Bush had dangerously encouraged the Iraqi military and the Iraqi people to "take matters into their own hands" and called for Saddam Hussein to "step aside," and then had turned the other way.

Bandar's attitude to Saddam Hussein and the conditions imposed on him after the ceasefire was unambiguous. Speaking to an Air Force Association Symposium some eighteen months later about the use of helicopters by the Iraqis, he said, "General Schwarzkopf agreed to allow the Iraqis to fly helicopters with the understanding that they would not misuse it. When they did misuse it in the south, my feeling personally was that we should just tell them quit flying tomorrow. The American response was, 'We told them they may and that would be breaking our word,' or 'you know, it's not fair; we tell them yes . . .' so I said, 'of course it's fair, they must not forget that we—goddamm it—won the war! We can tell them okay, we changed our mind, don't fly tomorrow!' "[129]

As with many of Bandar's international endeavors, the Western, and specifically the American press, played a fundamental role in events. Through prolific television interviews and press releases during the Gulf War, the prince worked relentlessly to interpret for Western audiences the truth behind the often disturbing images broadcast by the Middle East media. In one instance, he explained that, "The media here in the United States of America are giving the impression that fifty thousand demonstrators in Jordan are representing the Arab world. All that I would like to tell you is that there are fifty million people in Egypt who are supporting the U.S."[130]

As well as maneuvering on King Fahd's behalf during the run-up to the king's decision to accept the deployment on U.S. forces, Bandar also labored tirelessly to convince both the American public and Capitol Hill that U.S. intervention in the Gulf was a positive step that would not incur the dire consequences many experts feared. "It was amusing for me to watch quote-unquote 'Middle Eastern experts' or so called 'Arabists' tell me what will happen if America sends troops to the Middle East—how the Middle East would rise in a revolution from the Gulf to the Atlantic. Then when that didn't happen, they would say, 'But you see there are demonstrations in Nigeria, Tunisia, and Jordan. And I used to enjoy debating with those people and say, 'Could you tell me what happened in July 1990 in Nigeria, Tunisia, and Jordan? Demonstrations! In January 1991? Demonstrations! So what happened in August? Nothing has changed, they had their own problems, their own reasons, just one more banner was added."[131]

There can be no doubting the significance of the first Gulf War in defining a "new world order." Alliances were formed, and coalitions and resolutions put in place that hitherto had never been contemplated. Regardless of the motivation of national interests, East and West, Muslim and Christian, countries united together against one tyrant and succeeded, if to a limited extent. As former President Bush explained it, "This vision was not fully achieved while I was president—though we went a long way toward it—but the world order today is in fact completely new. The 'new world order' we strove for does not mean putting everything under the United Nations or surrendering an ounce of sovereignty; it means working cooperatively with other countries so there would be more democracy, more market economies, more freedom."[132] In Bandar's words, "I believe the Middle East has changed dramatically since the invasion of Kuwait and the Gulf War; the Middle East I knew before the 2nd of August is not the Middle East that exists today."

At his heart a pilot before becoming a diplomat, the prince is proud of the impressive demonstration of the Saudi and U.S. air forces capabilities. "I think the air forces for the first time in warfare history, have won decisively this war . . . and this is not an anti-marine or army comment; this is just to say, 'Let's take advantage of these new capabilities that we have.' "[133]

Bandar's views were reinforced by Sir Richard Evans, who stated emphatically that the RSAF had been largely ignored by the media and its contribution has subsequently been forgotten. He stressed, "I believe that it was a pivotal campaign for the Royal Saudi Air Force. In the context of the early raids in 1991, the Saudis were the first guys to operationally deploy a number of Tornado weapons, including the JP233, the advanced runway crater munition. Their Air Force has never had the credit that was due to it in the context of the contribution it made to the operational phase of the War." Evans added, "That was the time when the [Saudi] Air Force came of age. There was a huge amount of pride within the RSAF for their operational conduct and achievements during that war."

Reviewing the RSAF's performance during the Gulf War, Evans observed, "Bandar was certainly not an impartial bystander, nor indeed were many of the senior members of the royal family who also had extensive flying experience during the sixties and seventies. They all took immense pride in the achievements of these young guys flying operational sorties into Iraq. Indeed, the Prince would have trained many of them when he was officer commanding an operational conversion unit." He concluded,

"A lot of those early raids were hugely successful; it was quite a bloody watershed."[134]

Shortly after I completed the final paragraph of this chapter, I uncovered a startling detail that throws new light on Bandar's role as a hawk during the Gulf War. As the coalition forces built up on Saudi soil in anticipation of Desert Storm, the decision by President Bush to send James Baker to meet with Tariq Aziz was met with disbelief by the Saudis, and particularly by Bandar. Their intelligence sources confirmed that Saddam had reacted with the words, "Bush has blinked." It begged the question, "Has America got the resolve to see through a military engagement with Iraq?" For the Saudis, Saddam's treachery had to be met with a military response that would once and for all destroy the Iraqi dictator.

At this juncture, Fahd and Bandar perceived a nightmare scenario. What if, at the eleventh hour, Saddam decided to accept the U.N. resolution and withdraw from Kuwait? The coalition forces would be rendered impotent; they had no remit to attack Iraqi forces except for in Kuwait. How long could a force of 750,000 men be kept ready for action?

In Bandar's eyes, Saddam could then play the long game and sit it out on the Kuwaiti border waiting for the coalition forces to melt away. He now knew how long it would take for the United States to reinforce Saudi Arabia and when the time was right, he could strike out through Kuwait once again. However, the Saudis believed that Saddam would not make the same mistake again. Iraqi forces could brush aside Saudi forces, even with some residual American military support, and seize the oilfields, enabling him to hold the world economy ransom. To Bandar and Fahd, it was imperative that the coalition engage militarily and destroy Saddam.

To the Americans, the concern that Saddam might strike back with bio-logical and chemical weapons became a real issue. The risk of massive American casualties from a chemical or biological attack had to be diminished.

Bush therefore decided to write an uncompromising letter to Saddam Hussein, threatening the Iraqi dictator with the strongest possible response—interpreted by many as threatening a nuclear response—if weapons of mass destruction were employed by Iraqi forces. That letter, which was dated January 5, 1991, also unambiguously stressed American resolve—unless Iraqi forces pulled out from Kuwait absolutely, the coalition forces would attack. The text of the letter is set out below:

Mr. President:

We stand today at the brink of war between Iraq and the world. This is a war that began with your invasion of Kuwait; this is a war that can be ended only by Iraq's full and unconditional compliance with UN Security Council Resolution 678.

I am writing you now, directly, because what is at stake demands that no opportunity be lost to avoid what would be a certain calamity for the people of Iraq. I am writing, as well, because it is said by some that you do not understand just how isolated Iraq is and what Iraq faces as a result. I am not in a position to judge whether this impression is correct; what I can do, though, is try in this letter to reinforce what Secretary of State Baker told your Foreign Minister and eliminate any uncertainty or ambiguity that might exist in your mind about where we stand and what we are prepared to do.

The international community is united in its call for Iraq to leave all of Kuwait without condition and without further delay. This is not simply the policy of the United States; it is the position of the world community as expressed in no less than twelve Security Council resolutions.

We prefer a peaceful outcome. However, anything less than full compliance with UN Security Council Resolution 678 and its predecessors is unacceptable. There can be no reward for aggression. Nor will there be any negotiation. Principle cannot be compromised. However, by its full compliance, Iraq will gain the opportunity to rejoin the international community. More immediately, the Iraqi military establishment will escape destruction. But unless you withdraw from Kuwait completely and without condition, you will lose more than Kuwait. What is at issue here is not the future of Kuwait—it will be free, its government will be restored—but rather the future of Iraq. This choice is yours to make.

The United States will not be separated from its coalition partners. Twelve Security Council resolutions, 28 countries providing military units to enforce them, more than one hundred governments complying with sanctions—all highlight the fact that it is not Iraq against the United States, but Iraq against the world. That most Arab and Muslim countries are arrayed against you as well should reinforce what I am saying. Iraq cannot and will not be able to hold on to Kuwait or exact a price for leaving.

You may be tempted to find solace in the diversity of opinion that is American democracy. You should resist any such temptation. Diversity ought not to be confused with division. Nor should you underestimate, as others have before you, America's will.

Iraq is already feeling the effects of the sanctions mandated by the United Nations. Should war come, it will be a far greater tragedy for you and your country. Let me state, too, that the United States will not tolerate the use of chemical or biological weapons or the destruction of Kuwait's oil fields and installations. Further, you will be held directly responsible for terrorist actions against any member of the coalition. The American people would demand the strongest possible response. You and your country will pay a terrible price if you order unconscionable acts of this sort.

I write this letter not to threaten, but to inform. I do so with no sense of satisfaction, for the people of the United States have no quarrel with the people of Iraq. Mr. President, UN Security Council Resolution 678 establishes the period before January 15 of this year as a "pause of good will" so that this crisis may end without further violence. Whether this pause is used as intended, or merely becomes a prelude to further violence, is in your hands, and yours alone. I hope you weigh your choice carefully and choose wisely, for much will depend upon it.

George Bush[135]

President Bush informed Bandar about the letter that was to be handed to Tariq Aziz during his meeting with James Baker in Geneva. Determined to box Saddam in and offer him no face-saving option, Bandar advised Bush that not only should his letter be couched in uncompromising terms, but he agreed to translate the letter into Arabic for the president. Bandar explained that Arabic is a flowery language in which words could be expressed in many different ways. He admitted, however, that his rendition was designed to be as hardnosed and as aggressive as possible. In this way, Bandar believed that Saddam's anger and pride would compel him ignore the U.N. resolution and keep his forces in place in Kuwait, thus making war a certainty. And that war, in Bandar's eyes, would see the Iraqi military machine destroyed and Saddam overthrown.

In his meeting on January 9 in Geneva with Iraqi Foreign Minister Tariq Aziz, Baker was under instruction not to negotiate in any way from the requirement set out in the Security Council Resolution. He later confirmed, "I was going with absolutely no intention or willingness to negotiate down from the U.N. resolutions." However, he was conscious of the effect it had within the coalition, saying, "The only downside to it was that it caused some of our Allies to question our resolve."[136] However, at the outset of their meeting, Baker handed Tariq Aziz the letter from President Bush to Saddam Hussein. Aziz asked for a copy of that letter which he then read. Recalling that meeting, Aziz said, "I read it very carefully and then when I ended reading it, I told him, 'Look, Mr. Secretary, this is not the kind of correspondence between two heads of state. This is a letter of threat and I cannot receive from you a letter of threat to my president,' and I returned it to him." Aziz could not be persuaded to accept the letter.

When Bandar learned from Baker that Tariq Aziz had refused to take the letter, he immediately departed for London. Here he contacted Andrew Neil, then editor of the *Sunday Times*, whom he had been in regular contact with in the run-up to the Gulf War. Confirming their meeting, Neil observed, "Prince Bandar did not trust the efficiency of the Iraqi regime—Saddam did not react well to bad news and had a tendency to blame the messenger. So Bandar asked me to publish a copy of President Bush's letter to Saddam."

For Andrew Neil, once he was convinced that the letter was authentic, it was a news coup that made the front page. However, the fact that the letter had been leaked to him by Bandar was to be kept secret by Neil for a further fifteen years. He confided, "I thought it was so sensitive that I never even included it [Bandar's role] in my memoirs."[137] Once the British press published the letter, it was taken up by all the media, obliging White House Press Secretary Marlin Fitzwater to release the full text of the letter, a departure from White House protocol in which it was believed that it was inappropriate as a general matter to release diplomatic correspondence. The president's letter could not now have escaped Saddam's attention.

The motivation behind Bandar's leak was his intention to offer Saddam no face-saving formula, paradoxically the antithesis of Bandar's usual approach to Middle East issues. He had been lied to by Saddam, who assured him that he would not invade Kuwait. Having been deceived by the Iraqi dictator, he now set aside the mantle of peacemaker and became the arch hawk, as Baker revealed when he showed me a copy of minutes he had taken during a meeting prior to Desert Storm. These minutes confirmed that Bandar had stressed the need to go all the way and destroy Saddam. Having persuaded his king to accept military support from America in the days immediately following the invasion of Kuwait, Bandar wanted nothing less than an overwhelming coalition victory, the destruction of the massive Iraqi military machine, and the removal of Saddam Hussein. Bandar perceived that the risk to Saudi Arabia posed by Saddam demanded that any escape routes be closed off. Having helped design President Bush's uncompromising letter, Bandar knew full well that it would not only anger the Iraqi dictator, but would also cause Saddam enormous loss of face should he withdraw from Kuwait. It was vital, therefore, that the letter be seen by him. Bandar's leak achieved that objective. It not only guaranteed that the coalition offensive would proceed, it also closed the door on any Iraqi withdrawal.

At a stroke, and entirely covertly, Bandar had surely led America into war.

Prince Bandar the Jet Jockey in his prime

A.k.a. the Red Baron

Bandar surprised his father when he took part in the Tornado aircraft display at Wharton—a flight authorized by Margaret Thatcher.

King Fahd and his protégé, Prince Bandar, in a rare shot of the king in Western dress.

A personal photograph from Ronald and Nancy Reagan to Bandar. In time, the prince would develop a very close friendship with Nancy that enabled him to influence the ousting or selection of cabinet members.

A grim President Reagan attempts to take Prince Bandar to task over the Chinese missile deal.

The essence of the Chinese missile deal: Bandar's meeting with Prime Minister Zhao Ziyang, who became General Secretary of the Party. He was subsequently removed from power when he took the side of the students in Tiananmen Square.

The first Saudi AWACS took off with a full Saudi crew and one American officer. However, it flew in USAF colors until it landed in the Kingdom.

At an AWACS meeting. *Clockwise from left:* Deputy Chief of Staff Michael Deaver, Chief of Staff Jim Baker, Senate Republican Leader Howard Baker, President Reagan, Bandar, Vice President Bush *(par-*

President Mohammad Khatami of Iran meets Prince Bandar during an Islamic summit meeting.

A meeting of the respective delegations during King Fahd's state visit in 1985.

Prince Sultan represented the King at the fortieth anniversary of the United Nations. The meeting with Yasser Arafat took place in one of the cubicles set up for one-on-one meetings. Prince Saud and Prince Bandar are at right.

President Reagan called a special unscheduled breakfast meeting during King Fahd's visit, attended by *(clockwise from left)* U.S. Secretary of State George Shultz, King Fahd, National Security Adviser Bud McFarlane, Saudi Foreign Minister Prince Saud, President Reagan, and Bandar *(back to camera)*. Prince Saud and George Shultz were the only two people in the picture who did not know about Iran-Contra.

It was a terrific fight, but you managed to land this "giant" fighting fish. Congratulations Ambassador – Friend

Geg Bush

"Gone Fishing" with Vice President Bush—the beginning of a lifelong friendship.

Thanksgiving Day, 1990. After the official meetings in Jeddah with the King and the Emir of Kuwait, the president went to the Eastern Province to meet with Saudi Royal Air Force crews, before attending Thanksgiving services on an aircraft carrier. Bandar escorted George and Barbara Bush as they met with the pilots in Dhahran.

Bandar, who always knew it COULD be done— and WOULD be done! With esteem and friendship—Jim Baker

Secretary of State Jim Baker gives the thumbs up to American troops in the Gulf War. He added a personal tribute to Prince Bandar—"who always knew it COULD be done—and WOULD be done!"

Following the Gulf War, President Bush thanks Prince Bandar while Gen. Norman Schwarzkopf looks on

Before the start of the 1992 Madrid Peace Conference. Bandar was late for the opening of the conference, and President Bush delayed the start so he could publicly thank Bandar for his help in making it happen.

President Bush's last function at the White House—a farewell dinner for twenty of his closest friends

Famed *Sunday London Times* cartoonist Gerald Scarfe captures the essence of Nelson Mandela, Prince Bandar, and President George H. W. Bush.

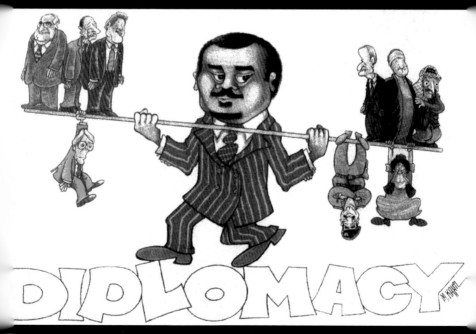

Controversial Arab cartoonist M. Kahil's pictorial impression of the political arena in the 1990s. On the left, Bill Clinton, Jacques Chirac of France, and Helmut Kohl of Germany are secure politically; Britain's John Major is hanging on with one hand and lost his bid for reelection. Balancing the West is the East

"The meeting that was not supposed to happen"—President Clinton and Prince Bandar in the waiting area at the White House on January 26, 1993. The photograph was dated by Bandar for his personal records.

Bandar and his great friend and mentor Nelson Mandela; together they brokered a deal with Qaddafi to have the Pan Am 103 bombers brought to justice and have economic sanctions lifted from Libya.

Work hard and play hard—Bandar enjoys a cruise on the Red Sea off Jeddah, and shows his stuff on the slopes at Aspen.

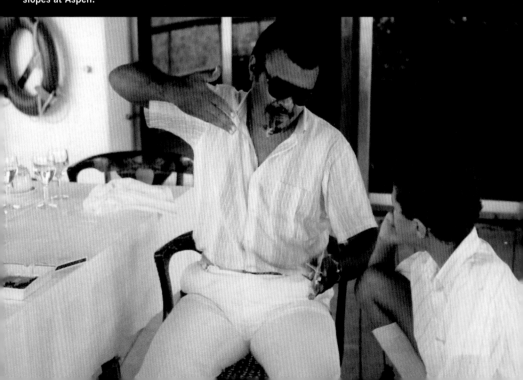

Bandar and his grandson, Prince Turki. The youngster always wanted to have a moustache, so Bandar drew one on him when they were together in Aspen.

Bandar shows his boys, Khalid and Faisal, around the kitchen, armed with spatulas and ready for action

EIGHT

PEACE IN THE
MIDDLE EAST

"Prince Bandar's achievements deserve international recognition.

I unconditionally applaud him as . . . one of the great peacemakers of our time."

NELSON MANDELA

In 1972, twenty years before the conclusion of Operation Desert Storm, Saudi Arabia's oil minister, Zaki Yamani, met with President Nixon and made him an offer to meet all of America's oil needs in exchange for American support in reaching a just and equitable solution to the Palestinian problem. Nixon declined.[1]

His rejection of the astounding Saudi offer would prolong indeterminately one of the world's long-standing problems. Following Nixon's rebuff, six successive U.S. presidents would labor to achieve a breakthrough in the intractable Israeli-Palestinian peace process. To this day, no answer has been found.

Reflecting on his efforts over more than two decades to bring a settlement to the Palestinian issue, Bandar said poignantly, "I've spent 70 percent of my time for the last twenty years on the peace process in the Middle East and the Israeli-Palestinian issue. And I had my heart broken time and time again, when we were this far from making the breakthrough and then things collapsed." In a statement that characterizes the frustrations of the process and allots shared responsibility for the failure to arrive at a solution, Bandar added, "I believe there is a leadership failure in the Middle East between Palestinians and Israelis, and I believe that the solution is as clear to my eyes as the sun. There will never be a Palestinian state that can exist in dignity unless Israel has its security met. But there will never be security for Israel unless the Palestinians are assured of their state and their dignity to be preserved. Now, in my mind, once you accept that, then filling in the details should be easier."

The prosecution of the first Gulf War in 1990 saw the Middle East peace process sidelined as the coalition countries focused on the defeat of Saddam Hussein. The successful conclusion to that conflict—and its impact on the region's political hegemony—provided a new and promising climate for a resumption of negotiations that might move forward the Palestinian question.

Peace in the Middle East is a common aspiration. While feeling great empathy for the Palestinian people and the plight of their Muslim neighbors, the Saudi monarchy paradoxically fears the strengthening of radical extremists who pose a direct threat to the House of Saud. For decades, the royal family had worked to restrain the violence between Palestine and Israel, and other warring factions in the area. At the end of Operation Desert Storm, the kingdom again pressed the United States to undertake a new initiative. On October 18, 1991, the White House agreed and sent to Fahd a letter written by James Baker, which said, "The United States will act as an honest broker in trying to resolve the Arab-Israeli conflict."[2]

Bandar would become the facilitator for this new stimulus for peace.

Convened in October 1991 in the immediate aftermath of the Gulf War, the Madrid Peace Conference would become a landmark in Arab-Israeli, Palestinian-Israeli history. It was the first time that a wide-ranging peace conference was attended by all parties concerned with the Arab-Israeli conflict, and the first time Palestinians participated in peace negotiations at any level. Until the 1991 Madrid Conference, only Egypt had accepted Israel's offer to negotiate face to face. Now, there would be multilateral negotiations conducted between Israel, Syria, Lebanon, Jordan, and the Palestinians on key regional issues. It was an unprecedented step forward.

The Madrid Conference was hosted by the Spanish government and cosponsored by the United States and the Union of Soviet Socialist Republics. Although America clearly played the dominant role at the Conference, the fact that Moscow also joined the United States in cosponsoring the Conference was a sign of the growing superpower cooperation between the United States and the Soviet Union.[3] Though the Conference has largely—and rightly—been attributed to the efforts of the Soviet Union, the United States, and, in particular, Secretary of State James Baker's enthusiastic efforts in shuttle diplomacy, Bandar's role was pivotal.

The purpose of the Madrid Conference was that it serve as an opening forum for the participants; it had no power to impose solutions or to veto agreements. In short, though without formal binding goals, the Conference was to focus on U.N. Security Council Resolutions 242 and 338, which were passed in 1967 and 1973, respectively, and called for all parties to terminate military conflict and negotiate a settlement. The resolutions anticipate, but do not specify, Israel's withdrawal from the territories taken in the 1967 and 1973 conflicts in exchange for security guarantees. Such negotiation would become known as "Land for Peace."

The Madrid Conference established negotiations on both bilateral and multilateral tracks, involving a pastiche of members of the international community. These first-ever public talks between Israel and its neighbors (except Egypt, with whom Israel had signed the Camp David Accords in 1978), were aimed at achieving peace treaties among three Arab states— Syria, Jordan, and Lebanon—and Israel. There can be no doubt, however, that the crucial significance of the Madrid Conference was its jump-starting of an Israeli and Palestinian bilateral dialogue. Talks with the Palestinians were based on a two-stage formula: the first consisted of negotiating interim self-government arrangements, to be followed by permanent status negotiations, which commenced immediately, followed by over a dozen formal rounds in Washington, D.C., from December 9, 1991, to January 24, 1994.

After four major Arab-Israeli conflicts in 1948, 1956, 1967, and 1973 left thousands dead, a deep-rooted intolerance on both sides had been inflamed still further by Palestinian support for Saddam Hussein. With this legacy, neither the Israelis nor the Palestinians were prepared to negotiate simply because the Western superpowers thought it a good idea. But persuasion and preparation was under way within the Arab world long before Madrid.

Of the kingdom's pressure for a peace initiative and Bandar's role in making Madrid a reality, Brent Scowcroft said, "In the lead-up to the war, Saddam kept bringing in the Israelis, and so on and so forth. Our position was: we are focusing on Iraq; we're not focusing on the problems in the region." However, Scowcroft confided, "But what we did was say quietly to King Fahd, and to Mubarak and others, 'You stick with us here—let's focus on this; after this is over, we'll move on the Palestinian-Israeli issue. We refuse to link this latter issue with the war, but we'll give you our private word that we'll move after this is over." Scowcroft added, "While this gave an assurance that the U.S. would support a peace initiative after the current conflict had ended, Prince Bandar had nonetheless to convince the king to trust us."[4] The prince's special relationships with both Fahd and Bush made this task immeasurably easier.

With this whisper of compromise on the table, it fell to Bandar to convince the House of Saud that the Americans' private word could be relied upon. The success of the Madrid Conference depended on Saudi Arabia's support—the backing of this leading regional power constituted an authoritative and influential signal to the rest of the Arab world.

Referring to the unspoken agreement that peace talks would be held after the Gulf War, Bandar said, "Madrid was a conference that started as a result of war. When Kuwait was invaded and war was imminent, President Bush and King Fahd began to discuss the aftermath: "What do we do after the war?" But while Fahd was eager to make plans for a peace conference that would address the Israeli-Palestinian issue through a groundbreaking new initiative, which he believed was an essential stimulus for peace in the Middle East, the Bush administration, while endorsing those aspirations, insisted on focusing on the prosecution of the war.

Unsurprisingly, the successful coalition-led prosecution of Operation Desert Storm considerably weakened Yasser Arafat's position in the Arab world. He had cheered Saddam Hussein's invasion of Kuwait, and Arab leaders retaliated by cutting subsidies to the PLO.[5]

Dr. Said Karmi

The first tangible political sign of just how weak Arafat was at that time, and the pragmatism that this induced, was his grudging decision to accept the Bush administration's terms for the Madrid

Peace Conference, which included the exclusion of Arafat from that conference.[6] Dr. Said Karmi, the late Palestinian transplant specialist and a close
friend of Bandar, recalled, "After we won the Iraq War in 1991, Bandar
called me, saying, 'There is a big movement by James Baker and the United
States government for peace talks.' As you know, we are not speaking to
Arafat now—I will need to talk to him, but not right now. But I need to talk
to three top Palestinians."

Dr. Karmi listed these men as "Professor Edward Said,* professor of history at Columbia University in New York, a very famous man who passed
away recently; he was with Arafat at that time; professor Walid Khalidi, professor of politics at Harvard University†; and Sharabi Hisham‡ of the contemporary Arab studies program at Georgetown University. All three
professors were involved in the Palestinian cause on an intellectual level,"
Dr. Karmi explained, "and could work to advise Yasser Arafat. Prince Bandar talked to the three professors and advised them on the background to
the proposed talks. He told them, 'Listen, things are going to move in the
Middle East, whether you like it or not. There is a conference coming up
that everyone is going to be involved in except for Arafat because of his
stand with Saddam Hussein, so please relay a message to all your people
that the Madrid Conference is on, and you have no way of stopping it. We
might talk with Arafat later on, but for the moment he can't be there.' Bandar also explained that one of them would have to go back to Gaza to confirm that they were not going to talk to Arafat now, but whether they [the
Palestinians] liked it or not, they were going to have to get a team to
Madrid." Karmi concluded, "Prince Bandar was also instrumental in getting
the Syrians to the table."[7]

Effectively, the U.S. secretary of state had offered Chairman Arafat a

---

*Edward Said was one of the leading literary critics of the last quarter of the twentieth century. A pro-
fessor of English and comparative literature at Columbia University, New York, he was the most articulate and visible advocate of the Palestinian cause in the United States.

†Walid Khalidi was born in Jerusalem and educated at Oxford and the University of London, and has
also been a research fellow at Princeton University. He has taught at Oxford, the American University
of Beirut, and Harvard, where he was senior research fellow at the Center for Middle Eastern Studies.
He is cofounder of both the Royal Scientific Society in Amman and the Institute for Palestine Studies,
of which he has been general secretary since 1963, and is a fellow of the American Academy of Arts and
Sciences.

‡Dr. Hisham Sharabi, professor emeritus of history at Georgetown University and chairman of the
Palestine Center in Washington, D.C.

diplomatic parole from the doghouse he found himself in after the Gulf War. Realizing that the Israelis would accept a Palestinian presence at the talks only if they were part of the Jordanian team, and not an independent PLO delegation, Baker then had to convince Arafat to accept these terms and agree to keep the official PLO out of the Madrid talks. Arafat consented, doubtless helped by the Palestinian scholars Bandar had consulted with in Washington. A Palestinian representative group was therefore assembled, composed of nonmembers of the PLO, and was sent to Madrid, loosely cloaked under the flag of Jordan.

From past dealings with Yasser Arafat and the Palestinians, Baker knew that a truly independent Palestinian delegation, detached from the PLO, was impossible. He fully realized that everything said in Madrid would be instantaneously relayed to Arafat in Tunis. Dr. Karmi confirmed that the Palestinian representation was still able to maintain dialogue with Arafat, who was in Tunisia at the time, so the PLO was indirectly represented through the Palestinian delegation. With the help of Bandar, however, Secretary Baker had circumnavigated Israel's refusal to deal with the PLO, and achieved something that had never been done before: Israelis and Palestinians sitting together around the same negotiating table.

The Bush administration also was quick to recognize and capitalize on the fall of the cards after the war. George H. W. Bush recalled, "Our new credibility (coupled with Yasser Arafat's need to redeem his image after backing the wrong side in the war) had a quick and substantial payoff in the form of the Middle East Peace Conference the following year in Madrid."[8] However, the chance to apply pressure on the Palestinians was not the only opportunity identified by Bush and Jim Baker. "They recognized what few other politicians did—that the political climate would support an effort to lean not just on the Palestinians, but also on Israel for the concessions necessary to begin peace negotiations."[9] A mix of financial and political pressure by the United States on Israel would overcome Israeli unwillingness to talk with the PLO terrorists, who had agreed to attend the Conference as part of the Jordanian delegation.

A chance moment in time and circumstance had been provided by fate, and progress in the Palestinian-Israeli conflict seemed to be attainable. America, nudged from behind by Saudi Arabia, was not going to let it slip by. In private, Bandar has given his own views on the true importance of the Madrid Peace talks, saying, "I worked very hard with Secretary Jim Baker to set up the Madrid Peace Conference—I and others. The significance of that

Peace Conference was that it was the first time that Israel sat down since the Rhodes Conference in '63. At Madrid, Israel sat down, not only with the neighboring countries to negotiate peace (i.e., Syria, Egypt, and Jordan and the Palestinians), but it was the first time that 98 percent of the Arab countries sat down together." He explained, "The GCC (Gulf Cooperation Council) countries were represented by the U.N. Secretary General and me. The Moroccan and African countries were represented by their general secretary; there was somebody from the Arab League, and then the foreign ministers from the surrounding countries. It was significant that we were really beginning to have a peace conference that was looking at the whole region having a peace together and not just the warring parties."

It has been critically observed of the Madrid talks that in the absence of any specific goals or clear objectives, the Conference was relatively ineffective in securing any tangible legislation for peace. However, what did happen, over the course of three days, is that the Conference laid the foundations for progress, and planted the seeds for the 1993 Oslo Accords. In addition, although the presence of the Palestinians was tolerated only as a result of a certain distortion of the rules, their attendance, combined with the international coverage of the multinational talks, altered the perceived image of the Palestinians and seeded a growing recognition of Palestinian rights, the legitimacy of their cause, and a clearer understanding of Palestinian concerns and aspirations.

Although Yasser Arafat was not present in person, he had an unspoken and tolerated influence in the corridors of Madrid, with one commentator saying, "Of all the peace conferences I have attended, this one was definitely the most exciting, not because of what was happening at the peace table, but what was happening in the corridors."[10] Everyone, including Israel, was aware of the flood of faxes and phone calls exchanged between Madrid and Tunis at every available opportunity; yet the charade was permitted to continue, making Madrid the beginning of the first-ever constructive dialogue, be it only relayed, between Israel and the PLO.

Yet, before any of this had transpired—before the Israelis sat down with the Syrians, before they sat down with the delegation from Lebanon, before they sat down with the Jordanians, and certainly before the Palestinians emerged onto the global consciousness as a wounded people, deserving of world action—it almost all fell apart.

Continually thwarted by Israeli tactics and demands over plans for the Madrid talks, in an echo of the Saudi position, James Baker succeeded in persuading George Bush to resort to financial pressure in order to loosen Yitzhak Shamir's seemingly unshakable position. In an unprecedented American move, in September 1991, President Bush withheld $10 billion in loan guarantees from Israel, money that was intended mostly for its settlement expansion program. It worked: Shamir was outmaneuvered and agreed to attend Madrid based on the terms Baker had dictated.[11]

Speaking of the implications of the Conference, President George H. W. Bush said, "It was an historic occasion. Up until that time the Israelis had not sat down with Arab leaders—it was a real bridge." He then continued, "The idea in getting support in the Gulf was: this is not going to be the end of this—we are going to try to address the problem that plagued every Gulf Cooperation Council country, which is the differences between Israel and the Arab states. I remember walking on [to the stage] with Gorbachev and the wonder of Arabs sitting across from Israelis; I mean it was big, it was huge, and I wish like hell they would do more of it." Bush didn't hesitate to testify to Bandar's help in nudging reluctant Arab nations toward the negotiation tables, saying, "Bandar, in encouraging people to attend and seeing that vision of something very important, did have an important role."[12]

The highly respected and articulate diplomat and Arabist Ambassador Ed Djerejian* reinforced Bush's tribute to the prince when he said, "I had the privilege of working with him when I was in the first Bush administration. And I can tell you that we truly depended on Bandar as one of the most valuable players in the construction of an Arab-Israeli peace. I really don't think the Madrid Peace Conference, which remains the framework for Arab-Israeli peace to this day, could have been accomplished without his tremendous diplomatic skills in bringing our Arab partners into the equation."[13]

During the run-up to the Madrid Peace Conference, King Fahd and President Mubarak of Egypt had had to develop a strategy to persuade Syrian President Assad to attend the Conference. It was decided by Mubarak and Fahd agreed that Bandar should convene a tripartite meeting: Egyptian, Saudi, and American—Amr Moussa, Bandar, and James Baker. The gather-

---

*Ambassador Edward P. Djerejian, the founding Director of the James A. Baker III Institute for Public Policy at Rice University, is one of the United States' most distinguished diplomats with his career spanning the administrations of eight U.S. Presidents. A leading expert on the complex political, security, economic, religious, and ethnic issues of the Middle East, Ambassador Djerejian has played key roles in the Arab-Israeli peace process, the U.S.-led coalition against Saddam Hussein's invasion of Kuwait, successful efforts to end the civil war in Lebanon, the release of U.S. hostages in Lebanon, and the establishment of collective and bilateral security arrangements in the Persian Gulf. As such, he had frequent contact with Prince Bandar and holds him in exceptional regard.

ing was held in Egypt and was intended to synchronize their respective governments' positions as to the plan to convince Assad to send a delegation to Madrid.

Amr Moussa, the Egyptian prime minister, however, was known to be a prima donna. "He began giving us a hard time," Bandar said. "While we were trying to get to the bottom line, he insisted on delivering nationalistic diatribes; he wanted to go on the record for saying certain things."

Before that meeting, the Americans had learned that Amr Moussa was likely to adopt a nationalist stance. Since Baker and Bandar were staying at the same hotel, they met before Amr Moussa arrived.

Baker asked the prince, "Do you think that Amr Moussa will attempt to lecture us after I have met with his boss?"

Bandar laughed and said, "Amr Moussa is capable of doing anything— even if it is the wrong thing."

"Would that change the policy?" Baker asked.

"No," replied the prince. "Whatever President Mubarak told you is what's going to happen. However, you have to be patient and give Amr Moussa a chance to do his dance, at the end of which he will agree with you."

The prince told Baker that he should be ready for Amr Moussa's usual tactics, and that he should be prepared with something to counter it.

Bandar chuckled, "We sat down in Jim Baker's suite, and sure enough we didn't have to wait long before Amr Moussa gave us his usual song-and-dance show. He gave a long lecture that was neither here or there; he just enjoyed doing it."

Baker had a leather folder in front of him, and in the middle of the meeting he slammed it closed in a very deliberate way and said, "Mr. Foreign Minister, I did not come here to negotiate with you. I have met with your boss and he approved the plan of President Bush and King Fahd. I'm not going to sit here and listen to a lot of bullshit. I cannot want peace more than you Arabs and Israelis. I have other important things to do. Thank you very much for the meeting; I'm going."

Bandar knew Baker was acting, but he was confident that Moussa didn't know that. Suddenly, Moussa became was panicky, believing Baker had made a deal with his boss and perhaps now had changed his mind. So Amr Moussa asked for a few minutes' delay so that he could speak to his president. After Moussa left the room, Baker sat down and, giggling, said to Bandar, "What do you think?"

"Well," Bandar said, "I think it's going to work."

A few minutes later Amr Moussa came back and announced, "I discussed this with the president and convinced him that we have a deal."

Bandar later observed, "I don't think he even spoke with President Mubarak, but he had to save face. That became a joke between Baker and me: 'Are you going to do your folder slam or not?' In my mind that shows that Jim Baker was a great statesman. Being a statesman you have to be an actor, and he did it very well."

Bandar's role in keeping the Syrians at the table was noted by the media, which reported, "Prince Bandar's behind-the-scenes arm-twisting was pivotal in finally getting Arab negotiators to sit down with the Israelis." Those same accounts described how the "flamboyant diplomat with a zest for intrigue and skills as a public speaker and stand-up comic" had seen the prince provide Baker with "valuable cards to play" as the process unfolded.[14] He was praised as being a trusted friend of Secretary Baker with an adept gift at bridging the Arab-Israeli gap. Bandar also was to apply significant financial arm-twisting to proceedings by subtly threatening to withdraw $5 billion in Saudi economic aid to Syria unless Syria participated in the talks. Both Jordan and the PLO were also kept in check by the prospect of receiving again the generous Saudi subsidies that were removed following their support for Saddam Hussein during the Gulf War. Even the Soviet Union was offered financial incentives to the tune of $2.5 billion in Saudi aid.[15]

The difficulties finally settled, it seemed the Conference could begin. However, the inaugural ceremony on October 30, 1991, with Presidents Bush and Gorbachev, almost didn't come off at all. At the moment Bush was to open the ceremonies with Gorbachev, as the world's media stood poised, Bush retreated from the stage. "Where is Prince Bandar?" he asked an aide. "Is he here yet?"

Bandar was not there: he had been blocked from attending the Conference by security, and it was all George Bush's fault.

At two o'clock in the morning, on the day of the Conference, Bandar got a call from Brent Scowcroft. Knowing that Bush and Scowcroft were early sleepers—usually in bed by ten o'clock—the timing of the call alarmed Bandar. It had to be a crisis.

"Hey Bandar," Scowcroft said. "Can you come tomorrow and see the president?"

"Sure," replied Bandar. "It would be my pleasure. I'll come after the Conference."

Scowcroft replied, "No, he wants to see you before he goes to the Conference at seven o'clock in the morning."

Bandar hates breakfast meetings but could not decline this summons from the president. He didn't sleep that night, worried that something was falling apart. Early that morning, he duly arrived at the American embassy, anxious to hear why Bush wanted to see him before the Conference.

As he walked in, Bush said, "We woke you up?"

"No," Bandar replied. "I haven't been to sleep yet."

After they exchanged pleasantries, Bush asked, "Do you know why I asked you to come?"

"No," Bandar replied.

"Well," Bush explained, "I wanted to thank you for your efforts in setting up this Conference, and I wanted to do that personally before we start."

Surprised, Bandar responded, "That's kind of you."

President Bush had arranged for a formal photograph to be taken of himself and Bandar, and then he invited the prince to join him in meeting the press. As they walked out to the garden together in front of all the press, Bush asked him, "Are you going to the Conference?"

Bandar replied with a shrug, "Not anymore."

"Why?" asked Bush.

"For security reasons. Madrid has been turned into an armed camp and all the delegates have to be there one hour before the two main principals arrive. Now that I am with you, I am told I cannot be there in time."

"Well, try to be there," Bush said.

George H. W. Bush thanks Bandar for his efforts just before the Madrid Peace Conference.

Bush then left in his presidential motorcade. But as Bandar expected, his own security team explained that he couldn't go to the Conference, as everything was already sealed off. So Bandar returned to his car for the drive back to his hotel. En route, however, his motorcade reversed course and headed toward the Conference. Bandar was told by the Spanish security officer, "I have been ordered by headquarters to take you to the conference hall immediately."

Live CNN commentary on the Conference was reporting, "In a couple of minutes, President Bush and President Gorbachev will walk from different directions to the door, meet at the door, and then they will walk into the hall together and then take their seats on the stage." But at the expected time, nothing happened.

Backstage, Bush had walked out from his side of the corridor and Gorbachev was beginning to walk out from his side when Bush turned and asked James Baker, "Do you think Bandar made it?"

"I don't know," replied Baker, who then checked with the Spanish protocol staff who confirmed that if Bandar wasn't there already, then he wasn't going to make it.

Bush promptly turned around and went back into his holding room. Seeing this, a bemused Gorbachev also retired to his room. Referring to his retreat, Bush said, "Goddammit, this guy worked his royal rear end off for this Conference, and the reason he's not here is because I asked him to come and see me. I'm not going to go in there and make him miss it. I want him here or else I'm not going to go in."

So Bandar was escorted back to the Conference. As he walked into the hall, Bernie Shaw from CNN said, "Wait a minute, somebody's coming. Who's this? It looks like Prince Bandar. Yes, it is Prince Bandar—what's he doing? He is the last guy to come. This shows you the role that Saudi Arabia is playing."

The prince later observed that the whole Conference stood up as he arrived. Bandar was surprised, as it wasn't as though he was joining the principals on the stage; his seat was in the main auditorium because he was simply a delegate within a delegation. Kuwaiti Secretary General Abdullah Bishara was already in attendance as the official representative of the Gulf Cooperation Council, but as Bandar later confided, "I was running the whole goddamn thing; the secretary general of the GCC was just a facade."

Bush's gesture "reinforced the role that I played in setting up the Conference," said Bandar. "Had I just come there for protocol reasons, why would they wait for me? I was not head of state or foreign minister. But, in the scheme of things, it confirmed the importance of the work that I had been doing up to that point." In a direct reference to his relationship with Bush, Bandar added, "It also shows you the caliber of the man and his loyalty."

Bandar continued to play the role of facilitator and mediator throughout the Conference. After the opening speeches and before the working session began, the Israelis announced they wouldn't allow one of the Palestinian delegation to attend because he was wearing his black and white Arafat-style headgear. Bandar asked the Palestinian who had been turned away, "What's the problem?"

"Sir," he responded, "the Israelis are trying to humiliate us. They won't even allow us to wear our national costume."

Bandar was irate. After so much hard work, for the Conference to be jeopardized because of who wears what was simply stupid. He told Dennis Ross,* "Dennis, this is what happened, and this is my position. If the Palestinians are not allowed to go in wearing what they want, I am not going to go in there and I am going to recommend that all Arab delegations withdraw."

Ross promptly went to see Baker, who said, "Goddammit, Bandar. This is a stupid argument. Who cares who wears what?"

"I agree with you, Jim," Bandar responded. "We are not complaining; it's the Israelis."

Baker turned to Ross and asked, "What do you think, Dennis?"

Ross replied, "Shamir insists that the Israelis are not going to come in if this guy wears his headgear."

"All right," Bandar said with a grin. "If you tell the Israelis to take off their skull caps, I will tell this guy to take off his headgear and I will take off my headgear too. We will all have bare heads."

"Shit," Baker exclaimed. "Goddammit, I don't care who wears what. Let's get on with the meeting." Baker quickly intervened with the Israelis and the crisis soon blew over. A member of the Palestinian delegation thereafter said, "Bandar saved our arses and our dignity."

The Madrid Conference led to a stabilization of Israel's relations with other Arab states. James Baker continues to draw reassurance from his knowledge that "the Madrid Peace initiative formed the basis for ongoing

*As Special Middle East Coordinator (1988–2000), Ambassador Dennis B. Ross played a major role in determining U.S. involvement in the Middle East peace process. For over twelve years, Ross helped the Israelis and Palestinians to attain the 1995 Interim Agreement, facilitated the Israeli-Jordan peace treaty, and endeavored to achieve a rapport between Israel and Syria.

negotiations and established parameters which are valued even today."[16] Bandar would certainly concur. "After the Madrid Peace Conference, a lot of taboos were broken," Bandar later remarked. "The Arab world has made a strategic choice for peace."[17] By actively encouraging American participation in the Middle East peace process, openly supporting the initiative, and persuading other Arab states to do the same, Bandar justly could claim, "Madrid would not have succeeded had we not been there."[18] Talking about Madrid five years later, in a statement that underpinned his pragmatic, ecumenical beliefs, Bandar said, "There can be no real and lasting stability and peace in the region without regard for the dignity and future of all its people—Muslims, Christians, and Jews." He concluded with the simple tenet that, in his mind, formed the basis for any solution to the Palestinian problem, "Number one, there is never going to be a solution that will satisfy the Palestinians if there is no guarantee for the Israeli people's security." He paused and with open hands continued, "Two, there will never be security for the Israeli people if there is no satisfaction for the national aspiration of the Palestinian people. Whichever way you take the Middle East and turn it around, these are the permanent pillars."[19]

Additional Israeli-Palestinian talks were hosted in Washington in December 1991, only months after Madrid, but after ten rounds of agonizing discussions, these talks concluded without agreement. However, unknown to the United States, in the corridors of Madrid, while the Conference work was progressing, a parallel track of negotiations was secretly planned by Israel and the Palestinians.[20] Believing the loose framework of the Madrid Conference to be less than conducive to real progress, the Israelis and Palestinians quietly agreed to future private discussions. Norway agreed to mediate. The Oslo Declaration of Principles resulted.

In the Oslo Declaration, both sides recognized the rights of the other to exist as a people within the borders of Israel and the Palestinian territories. Both parties also committed themselves to negotiating a permanent settlement, and to improving relations between the two peoples. Ultimately, it would pave the way for a peace treaty between Israel and Jordan in 1995. The Oslo agreement represented a major breakthrough in the Israel-PLO conflict, made possible by the consummate pragmatism of the leaders on both sides.[21]

The Oslo talks cast aside the formalities and posturing of Madrid to facilitate direct negotiation between Israel and the PLO. They astounded the world, especially the United States, which had been completely blindsided. In August 1993, the newly inaugurated Clinton administration was reportedly stunned by the revelation of this agreement between Israel and the PLO, following the secret talks in Norway.[22] Dr. Said Karmi later confided, "Whereas the U.S. administration had been initially unaware of the Oslo meeting, Prince Bandar was made aware of it from the beginning and fully supported it."

Under the Oslo Declaration, Israeli forces agreed to withdraw from unspecified areas in the Gaza Strip and a small area around Jericho, in preparation for Palestinian elections. In return, Yasser Arafat promised to change the PLO Charter calling for destruction of Israel. Finally, Israeli Prime Minister Yitzhak Rabin proclaimed Israel's intent to permit normalization of life in the occupied territories. As America reengaged in the peace process, the world was soon to be treated to the unlikely spectacle of Yasser Arafat and Yitzhak Rabin shaking hands, of Palestinians and Israelis talking of peace for the first time.

America's engagement in the Oslo Accords, combined with keen support for the peace effort, changed Yasser Arafat's position on the international stage from terrorist to politician, virtually overnight. When Arafat flew into the United States, it was Ambassador Ed Djerejian who greeted him on his arrival. As he got off his aircraft, the ambassador shook Arafat's hand. Djerejian smiled as he recalled, "This was the famous handshake; the first official handshake between an American official and Arafat on American soil." However, behind that handshake was a concern that Arafat might have greeted the ambassador with the traditional Arab embrace—the kiss on both cheeks. Djerejian feared that many Americans might think that such a greeting was inappropriate. Believing any confusion or embarrassment in front of the press could have overshadowed the importance Arafat's stay, Djerejian sought Bandar's help to ensure that the correct protocol was observed, and the initial greeting stopped at a handshake. The prince's discreet diplomatic intervention guaranteed that Arafat's arrival proceeded without incident.[23]

During Arafat's official visit, at a formal White House dinner, which was also attended by Bandar, there was a lull in the conversation, which, Djerejian observed, "is something Prince Bandar never tolerates."

At Djerejian's expense, Bandar said to Arafat, "How do you make an Armenian omelet?"

Arafat looked confused.

"Well," said Bandar, "first you steal two eggs."

Djerejian recalled that everyone started laughing, "Except Arafat, who thinks I am insulted."

The ambassador laughed at Arafat's self-induced predicament and explained, "Here he is trying to be on his best behavior; it was hilarious. Everyone is laughing and Arafat launches into a five-minute monologue on the importance of the Armenians to the Palestinians and that there are very prominent Armenian Palestinians. He just went on and on. He never got it [the joke]."

"Meanwhile, Bandar sat back and looked at me and winked."[24]

The Oslo Accords culminated in the historic handshake between Yasser Arafat and Yitzhak Rabin on the White House lawn on September 13, 1993. This handshake was a symbolic acknowledgment of both nations' official political recognition of the other, and of Arafat's acknowledgement of Israel's right to exist. President Clinton lauded it as a "great occasion of history." Yasser Arafat called it a "historic event, inaugurating a new epoch." Foreign Minister Shimon Peres of Israel discerned in it "the outline of peace in the Middle East."[25] Hopes were high for real progress at last. As in Madrid, Bandar was present at the White House to mark this important move toward peace and shook hands with Yitzhak Rabin after the meeting.[26]

Although the Oslo initiative operated outside the framework of the Madrid Conference, both peace efforts were predicated upon U.N. Resolutions 242 and 338, and little was resolved given the ambiguous nature of the U.N. stance. Pro-Arab interpretations of resolution 242 expect no less than Israel's complete withdrawal from the West Bank, Gaza, and other prime areas. Oslo's adherence to the "Land for Peace" formula adopted in

The Arafat-Rabin handshake on the White House lawn.

Madrid suggested to the PLO the prospect of a Palestinian state. When this failed to materialize, Palestinian views of the Accords became tainted with disappointment and discontent. However, the exact United Nations wording of 242 very deliberately states that Israel may wish to withdraw from "territories" as opposed to "*the* territories," in exchange for peace and security. Regardless of the division of territories, both 242 and 338 remain resolute on the need for a peaceful and negotiated solution, which both Madrid and Oslo sought to stimulate. The optimist's view is that although neither set of talks produced a lasting solution to the Israeli-Palestinian problem, they at least brought both sides together in discussion. Arguably, half the battle had been won.

Even so, the hope generated by these pragmatic efforts toward peace in Madrid and Oslo soon faded. The PLO remained disillusioned with the outcome of negotiations; Israel continued to occupy the held territories and refused to deal further or discuss withdrawal until Arafat took decisive steps to bring about the end of Palestinian violence and terror attacks.[27] Once again, it turned out to be a false dawn.

When the Democrats clinched the 1992 election, Bill Clinton was handed the baton of Middle East peace from President George H. W. Bush. The Republican president's loss was keenly felt by Saudi Arabia. Bush was highly respected by the House of Saud; a workable friendship and understanding had flourished between them. Bandar, who was a close friend of the Bush family, found the Republican defeat particularly difficult to accept. During a dark period in his career, a dispirited Bandar came very close to tendering his resignation as ambassador to the United States; it was only a deeply felt sense of duty to his country and his king that kept him in the post.

President Clinton's two terms in office heralded an unsteady period in the Middle East peace process characterized by long periods of stalemate, broken intermittently by sudden and historic drives for peace. For Bandar, the 1990s was a period of relative quiet. It has been speculated that his previous level of access to the White House, enjoyed under the Republicans, was diminished by the Democrats' attempts to keep him at arm's length. Despite media conjecture, however, the prince's access to the White House continued to far outstrip the accepted level of contact and influence wielded by other ambassadors. Nevertheless, Bandar was sensitive to the change in the political climate and acknowledged, "I was getting completely bored."[28]

November 1996 saw the Cairo Economic Conference, hosted by Egyptian President Hosni Mubarak and cosponsored by the United States and the Russian Federation.* The resulting Cairo Declaration reaffirmed the commitment to a lasting peace in the Middle East with particular reference to the Palestinian-Israeli conflict. All parties agreed to continue to strive for a negotiated peace and to build upon the achievements of Madrid and Oslo. Disappointingly, this united effort was followed by a two-and-a-half-year period of stasis. Nevertheless, the Clinton administration continued to work to revive the Palestinian-Israeli peace track. In mid-October 1998, Clinton held a Middle East summit conference at the Wye River Plantation in Maryland. The Israeli delegation was headed by Prime Minister Benjamin Netanyahu; Yasser Arafat headed the Palestinian group. As a result of the negotiations, the Wye River Memorandum was signed by Netanyahu and Arafat on October 23, 1998, witnessed by President Clinton and King Hussein of Jordan.[29]

The Wye River Memorandum was intended to clarify mutual responsibilities for executing the Interim Agreement on the West Bank and Gaza Strip (Oslo II) signed on September 28, 1995, the purpose of which was to make it possible for the Palestinians to negotiate as an independent party, without, in itself, determining the final status of any territories that might be ceded to the Palestinians in exchange for peace and security. The agreement also called for the redeployment of the Israeli army from parts of the West Bank and Gaza, thus enabling free elections to take place. However, the Wye agreement was so riddled with ambiguities that some of its critics compared it to Swiss cheese and immediately after signing the Wye River Memorandum, violations occurred on both sides and Israel began to evade and postpone its implementation.

Bandar, however, was determined to maintain pressure on the Clinton administration for a continued American lead in the peace process and observance of the provisions of the Wye River memorandum. At a press briefing following a meeting with Clinton in the White House, Bandar told the media, "We expressed our anxiety on how sensitive and dangerous the situation in the Middle East is at the moment. The Middle East and the Arab world are looking for the continued leadership of President Clinton and the United States of America, because that is an essential element to having peace in our region."[30]

---

*Japan, the European Union, and Canada also gave their support to the Cairo Economic Conference.

Asked whether the administration was paying enough attention to the deterioration of the peace process, Bandar said that the president and his administration had invested a lot of effort and prestige, and that the blame for the current concern "falls squarely on the lap of the reckless behavior of Prime Minister Netanyahu. It is not a question of Netanyahu being, or not being, a hardliner, because Begin, and Rabin, and Shamir were not pussy-cats, either." Reinforcing that message, he stated unequivocally, "This prime minister is unique. He is not constructive and he's reckless in his be-havior. I think the Israeli and Arab people may pay a heavy price if that reckless behavior does not stop."[31] Bandar's concern was prophetic. On De-cember 20, 1998, the Israeli government suspended implementation of the Memorandum.

The suspension of Wye, accompanied by a freeze of negotiations on the final settlement, created a very dangerous situation in the Middle East. Israel continued with its settlement activities in occupied Palestinian territory, as well as the confiscation of land, the building of so-called bypass roads, ac-tions against Palestinian Jerusalemites, and economic suffocation.[32] Mean-while, the media began to grow skeptical of Clinton administration efforts. The Washington Report on Middle East Affairs caustically wrote, "Increas-ingly the signing ceremonies, three times in the White House, and others at Taba and Sharm el-Sheikh in Egypt, have been nothing but reiterations of the unfulfilled pledges from the previous signings. At this point that's all the Clinton administration will look for in upcoming photo opportunities."[33]

Bandar and Clinton. The president was often blindsided by his own administration.

Despite media skepticism, Clinton hosted a summit at Camp David on July 11, 2000—an initiative described by Dr. Henry Kissinger as "doomed to failure." Justifying his view, Kissinger said, "How can you develop a peace initiative in your final days in office? It was a vain attempt by President Clinton to establish his place in history."[34] Whatever his motives, the president's determination to find a resolution coincided with Ehud Barak's fight to stay in office and his need to offer Israelis the chance of tenable security. Fate's fortuitous timing had once again breathed new life into the quest for peace in the Middle East.

Unlike the peace initiatives conducted in the early 1990s in Madrid and Oslo, the significance of the Camp David summit resided not in who came to the table, but the offer that was laid upon it. Between them and their various systems of government, Clinton and Barak had seized the opportunity for peace with both hands and had developed what was arguably one of the fairest, most workable deals for peace and security ever presented to the Palestinians.

Under the Clinton-Barak proposal, a Palestinian state would be formed of 95 percent of the West Bank and 100 percent of the Gaza Strip; Jewish settlements would be withdrawn, save for just three that were contiguous to Israel; Jerusalem would be run under dual sovereignty; a limited number of refugees would be allowed to return; and a compensation package of thirty billion dollars would be paid.[35] Washington was abuzz. Peace and the possibility of a favorable resolution were once again on the horizon. Never before had an Israeli government, backed solidly by a U.S. administration, been willing to make such concessions in favor of the Palestinians.

President Clinton threw everything he had into these negotiations. His Special Middle East Coordinator Dennis Ross met with his Palestinian counterpart, Ahmed Korei,* to make sure that Arafat understood the consequences of rejection.

Dr. Said Karmi recalled the hype and excitement the offer caused, affirming that during the last few days of Clinton's administration, Bandar

---

*Also known as Abu Ala, Ahmed Korei (or Qouri) served as speaker of the Palestinian Legislative Council from 1996, when Palestinians voted to install the eighty-eight-member lawmaking body. Korei was one of three PLO leaders who met secretly with Israelis in Norway to hammer out the Oslo Accords, paving the way for the first interim peace deal in 1993. He was also involved in the peace talks at Camp David in July 2000, and was later engaged in the Taba talks in January 2001. In early September 2003, after the resignation of Abu Mazen, Yasser Arafat appointed Korei as prime minister of the Palestinian Authority.

was in regular dialogue with Arafat and his aides about acceptance of the deal. Here, at last, was a potentially viable solution that accommodated the future and dignity of both nations. Bandar enthusiastically and unreservedly encouraged Arafat to accept the arrangement.[36]

On January 2, 2001, just weeks before the end of Clinton's term, Bandar picked Arafat up at Andrews Air Force Base and reviewed with him the Barak proposal. Afterward, he said to Arafat, "Could you ever get a better deal? Would you rather negotiate with Sharon?"

As Arafat vacillated, the prince issued a stern warning, "I hope you remember, sir, what I told you. If we lose this opportunity, it is going to be a crime. You have only two choices. Either you take this deal or we go to war."[37]

Walking away from the Camp David proposal without explanation or counteroffer, Arafat chose to go to war.

In a last-ditch effort, Clinton sent one of his officials, who had a particularly good relationship with Arafat, to speak with him directly. The envoy made an impassioned plea, "Make a deal, get a state, help your people, and do not lose the best opportunity for the Palestinians since 1948."

Arafat simply replied, "I can't."[38]

The shock at his betrayal was palpable. Bandar reflected mournfully, "That decision broke my heart; it was a crime against the Palestinians; in fact, against the entire region."[39]

It was not only Bandar that viewed Arafat's refusal to accept the deal with despair; the Egyptians tried to get Arafat to reengage, but could not budge him. Privately, one of Mubarak's top lieutenants admitted, "Arafat should have accepted the deal as a basis for negotiations. We Arabs have to learn how to compromise."[40] Reflecting in his biography on the ramifications of Arafat's rejection, Clinton correctly surmised, "I would be gone. Ross would be gone. Barak would lose the upcoming election to Sharon. Bush wouldn't want to jump in after I had invested so much and failed. I still didn't believe Arafat would make such a colossal mistake."[41]

Arafat returned to Palestine and days later launched the second Intifada. Three thousand Palestinians and one thousand Israelis lost their lives as a result. The impact on Palestine was calamitous: the economy collapsed, schools closed, the country's infrastructure lay in ruins. The Israelis were dumbfounded. Arafat defended his decision, saying, "If I do what you want, Hamas will be in power tomorrow."[42]

Five years after rejecting the historic offer of a Palestinian state, Yasser

Arafat would be dead. Ehud Barak and Bill Clinton would no longer be in power. Ariel Sharon, Barak's successor, would emerge, in an extraordinary reversal, to lead the campaign for peace between the Israelis and Palestinians, before being felled by a massive stroke. Only Hamas would remain.

On January 26, 2006, the Palestinian people, rejecting the utter corruption of Arafat's Fatah Party, would vote overwhelmingly for a Hamas government. With Hamas's record of terror and suicide bombing, and a political platform that denies the right of the state of Israel to exist, prospects for peace in the region and a Palestinian state seem bleak at the present time.

James Baker had speculated that the fruits of the Madrid Peace Conference would continue to be harvested only "when there is an Israeli prime minister who is looking for peace and a leader of the Palestinians to succeed Arafat that is prepared to negotiate properly for peace."[43] Continuing with this sentiment and reflecting with insight on the failure of the Camp David Summit, Lord Charles Powell said, "It was one of the world's greatest missed opportunities, but you could guarantee that Arafat would always miss an opportunity; Arafat only exists to be what he is, basically an opposition leader. He's quite incapable—if there ever is a settlement to the Israeli-Palestinian problem, Arafat will become instantly irrelevant." Powell continued, "Bandar was very disillusioned with Arafat—if you hand Arafat most of what he was demanding on a silver plate, he would still turn it down—he is incapable of accepting anything."[44]

This viewpoint has been reiterated frequently. Contemporaneously, Hendrick Hertzberg wrote, "Neither Arafat nor Sharon has the political will to make the necessary compromises."[45] However, there is also the possibility that the problem lies in the compromise. As was evident during America's dealings with Saddam Hussein, especially in the run-up to the Gulf War, Western attempts at reasonable mediation through concessions and goodwill were often interpreted by Saddam as weakness in his opponent and an ideal reason to dig his heels in. This rift in Arab and Western thought perhaps explains Yasser Arafat's rejection of the "too good to be true" offer on the table at Camp David. Reading Ehud Barak's compromise as evidence of Israeli weakness, it is possible that Arafat gauged the situation as an opportunity to attack rather than talk. Perhaps he was so sure of this assumption that, to the world's amazement, he turned his back on the negotiation table and launched the second Intifada.

"President Clinton's personal efforts in producing the framework agreement for Palestine were mind-boggling," observed Bandar. Clinton also praised Bandar, saying, "Bandar not only tried to get Arafat to take the deal—Arafat led Bandar to believe that he was going to take the deal—none of us really know what happened when Arafat left Washington the last time." The former president recalled, "About six weeks before I left office, I told Arafat, 'I'm going to make this deal better for you.' And we finally got it hammered out in early December in Taba; it was a good deal and gave Arafat about 98 percent of what he wanted. We thought for sure that he was going to take it because he had led Bandar to believe that he was going to take it; he led the Moroccans to believe that he was going to take it, and the importance of that was that Morocco was the head of the committee on Jerusalem."[46]

Despite Clinton's hard work, Arafat got on his aircraft for Egypt, and by the time he got there, he had backed off again. Clinton shook his head and reflected, "Many people have speculated why, or who or what, and I'm not entirely sure anybody knows. There may have been a lot of reasons; they may have decided that they would get the worst of both worlds—they would give up the right of return, and then Barak would be defeated, which would, in effect, be a referendum against it, so they would get the grief for having compromised without getting the benefits."

The president observed that at the time, Barak could have passed the resolution in Israel with his support. He speculated that Barak could have come back and won the election. "I'd tried to tell Arafat that," he continued. "Barak was down to a 38 percent approval rating in the polls; he kept giving and giving and getting nothing in return, so the Israelis thought they might as well have Sharon if they're not going to have a peace process, which was horrible for all concerned."

"Bandar really tried to get Arafat to take the deal. Actually, he went way beyond the call," he said. The president mused that the problem he had with some of the Arab leaders was that they would tell him that they were encouraging Arafat to take the deal, but Arafat was never sure that they would stand behind him publicly; he was afraid that they were going to wait to see which way the wind was blowing. "But Bandar was a stand-up guy," Clinton stressed. "He said [to Arafat], 'This is the best deal you are ever going to get and I would take it now because it will take years and years if you don't.'"

In a final review of his personal efforts to achieve a successful outcome to the abortive peace process, Clinton recalled that before Arafat left the

White House, he had said to Arafat, "If you're not going to do this, tell me—because, if so, I'm going to go to North Korea and end this mess we've got over there."

The president confided that, in hindsight, he wished that he had visited North Korea instead of continuing to make headway with Arafat, as he had a deal "just about worked out with them [the Koreans]." Clinton decided to stick with the peace process, however, after Arafat, with tears in his eyes, said to him, "Oh God, don't go; you can't do that."

In an attempt to secure a promise from Arafat that he would conclude a deal, the president said to him, "Are you going to do it?"

"Yes," responded Arafat.

Clinton now observed on Arafat's subsequent failure to make any agreement and, instead, to launch the Intifada, saying acidly, "And you know the rest—we had four thousand Palestinians dead in the Intifada. It was tragic."

As an optimistic afterthought, Clinton suggested that with Arafat's death, an opportunity may have been presented for the peace process, saying, "The good news is, we know what the final deal has to look like. We know that we have to go to Geneva and basically take the Taba agreement and fill in the blanks."[47]

But the moment was lost; fate's wormhole of opportunity had closed. Bandar encapsulated the thoughts of many on Capitol Hill when he said about Arafat, "Every time we try something, he does something the opposite; I don't trust that guy, he lied to me so many times."[48] Bandar later said that to criticize Arafat publicly at the time would have damaged the Palestinian cause. In a critical comment on the PLO chairman's failure to accept the deal presented by Barak and Clinton, however, Bandar claimed to have said to Arafat privately, "Since 1948, every time we've had something on the table we say no, [and] then we say yes. When we say yes, it's not on the table anymore. Then we have to deal with something less. Isn't it about time we say yes?"[49]

In fact, Bandar's disillusionment with Yasser Arafat ran far deeper that simple mistrust; he held the PLO leader directly responsible for the carnage that followed and the unnecessary deaths of thousands of Palestinians and Israelis. Speaking to Elsa Walsh* in 2003, he said, "I still have not recov-

---

*Elsa Walsh is an author and writer for The New Yorker and is married to Bob Woodward, the renowned political analyst, journalist, and author.

ered, to be honest with you, inside, from the magnitude of the missed opportunity that January, sixteen hundred Palestinians dead so far and seven hundred Israelis dead. In my judgment, not one life of those Israelis and Palestinians dead is justified."[50] However, despite this massive setback, Bandar's determination to find a solution to the peace process is undiminished. Explaining why he continues to pursue that solution, Bandar said, "My wife and I have eight children and two grandchildren. And I just cannot imagine my grandchildren leaving high school, or going to college, and asking me, 'Grandpa, why did you fail solving the damn thing?' "[51]

Since Arafat's dramatic refusal of the Clinton-Barak proposal, many have speculated on its implications. An article in the *Washington Times* raised the question, "If that offer could not persuade Mr. Arafat to choose peace, it is hard to see what would, short of Israel's destruction."[52] Speaking to that refusal by Arafat to conclude a deal, Henry Kissinger argued, "I doubt that the Palestinians actually want a settlement; they would only be content with the destruction of Israel." He went on to say that he understood why the Palestinians had developed such a hard-line position. This admission of understanding of the Palestinian position was a surprising comment from a Jewish former secretary of state. Kissinger pragmatically observed, however, that the PLO had unrealistic ambitions in terms of a deal with Israel, noting that they had idealistic expectations and nothing to offer the Israelis in return.[53]

In a subsequent interview, Ambassador Murphy threw additional light on Kissinger's bleak projections on the Israeli-Palestinian issue. He pointed out that while Kissinger might have reservations about the Palestinian desire for peace, his belief that perhaps the best that can be hoped for is a protracted armistice has merit. Murphy explained, "He [Kissinger] does present a pragmatic and realistic hypothesis—although both nations may never sign a full-peace treaty, a long-term truce could suffice." Murphy argued that a hundred-year armistice would be of real value in healing the emotive wounds and misery felt on each side, factors that continue to smother the peace efforts. "Peace was asking too much," Murphy suggested, "because of the humiliation and the history ever since 1948." Regarding an extended truce, Murphy ventured, "The Israelis have always held that this line is extraordinarily dangerous and we can settle for nothing less than full openhearted committed peace." Dismissing the belief that in reference to peace, both parties are intent on achieving security, Murphy observed wryly, "Well, they don't think quite that way; there is only one party's security that matters—Israel." Murphy expressed some sympathy for Kissinger's views, concluding that Kissinger's concept of what might realistically be achievable—a long-term truce rather than a proper peace treaty—wasn't "all bad."

In a final attempt to explain Arafat's rejection of the Barak deal, Murphy said resignedly, "It was the same hangover and the same attitude that the Palestinians brought to the U.N.'s offer way back in 1948 for partition. 'No way! Why should we partition? They are a very small number of people on our territory, however they got there, and you are asking that we allot them 'x' percent? Well, then came the war and they [the Israelis] got 'x, y and z' percent. So I guess that there are some Palestinians that will argue down to the wire that Israel is illegitimate. And so it might well be easier to settle for a long-term peace."[54]

Brent Scowcroft was remarkably candid in his opinions on the failure of the Camp David initiative and Chairman Arafat's rejection of the proposal. He observed, "This failure, which promised much but delivered nothing, clearly hurt Bandar, who had, in the shadows, been trying to achieve a breakthrough for several decades." He emphatically disagreed with Kissinger's belief that the Palestinians did not really want peace and that they wanted nothing short of the complete removal of the state of Israel, saying, "Henry and I disagree on this issue."

In a remark that was analogous to comparing Bandar's efforts as a peace-maker as being akin to the quest for the Holy Grail, Scowcroft said unequiv-ocally, "I think that the fact of it is that Bandar can never actually make a peace settlement—it is beyond him." He explained, "Prince Bandar has spent his career maneuvering among conflicting groups, and for Arafat to sit down and sign his name to something that fixes things in stone, I don't think he'll ever do it." He shook his head in resignation, adding as an afterthought, "Unless Arafat is pressured by his Arab colleagues and he can say 'they made me do it,'—then I think we'd get peace."[55] However, Arafat's death would close that option.

As the one person who had the credibility as an Arab, a peacemaker, and a statesman who, arguably, was best placed to persuade Arafat to take the Camp David Clinton-Barak deal, Bandar had good reason to reflect harshly on the nature of the PLO chairman. When Arafat would not go along with the proposals, Bandar said to him, "Listen to me. This is not going to be a tragedy; this is going to be a crime if you don't do this."

Reflecting on that missed opportunity of almost unparalleled proportion, Bandar has said, "I still believe that from January 4/5, 2001, when we had that final meeting with Arafat in Washington, and he rejected the proposal, two weeks before Clinton handed over to Bush, any"—he paused and again stressed, "any—this is probably too strong, but that is my conviction—any Palestinian, man, woman, or child who died in Gaza or West Bank from January 2001 until today did not have to die. And that's a lot, if you value human life."

Drawing a parallel between his own role in the Lebanon ceasefire with the choice facing Arafat at Camp David, Bandar observed, "When we finally came up with the Lebanese ceasefire agreement, before that time there had been about ten or fifteen ceasefires, and they lasted two hours or twenty-four hours or a week, whatever. I remember a Western reporter asking me then, 'What's the big deal about this ceasefire? Lebanon has had so many ceasefires and then the fighting started again and people got killed.'"

Bandar's sheer exasperation was transparent, "I got so angry with this reporter, I said, 'Listen to me. I don't know that for you, but for me, if I could get a ceasefire for five minutes which saved one or two lives, that's a lot! My hope is that this will last long enough to save many more people than that." With a barbed emphasis, the Prince continued, "But don't give me this crap about what good is a ceasefire if it's going to break later. Any time that you can save human lives—that is a big deal. The fact that it only saves one, or a hundred, or a thousand to me is irrelevant, because during a ceasefire agreement people are not dying."

Addressing Arafat's rejection of the Clinton-Barak offer, Bandar quietly confessed, "In this context, I was really hurt both emotionally and intellectually in a way that I just can't believe." Shaking his head, he stressed, "If I was the leader of 'x' tribe or 'x' nation, and I really cared about my people, and I was offered what Clinton and Barak offered to Arafat, I would have to have a hell of a reason to turn it down. I still, five years later, cannot find that reason."

Asked why Arafat walked away, Bandar speculated, "An honest answer, based on the way I think? I don't know. But I cannot judge Arafat based on the way I think; I have to judge Arafat based on the way I think he thinks." He added philosophically, "I believe that Arafat's biggest problem was that he could not make the transition from revolutionary leader to statesman. He always reached that point and backed off. A revolutionary is someone who is just fighting for the revolution. A statesman is a man who says, 'All right, the revolution is over now. I am now in charge and I'm going to make the transition from revolutionary to world leader.'"

Repeating that same assessment, but using the contrasting leadership styles of Egyptian Presidents Nasser and Sadat to illustrate Arafat's character, Bandar emphasized, "Arafat could not make that transition from being a militia leader or a revolutionary to be a statesman. I think that's the difference between Sadat and Nasser. Nasser was the revolutionary leader; he precipitated a misguided war—gave the enemy a chance to fight him in 1967 in the Six Days War, lost a lot of his country—Sinai—and never managed to figure out how he could regain it by being a statesman. However, Sadat came into power and looked at the whole situation and said, 'I have to be a statesman. The only way I can regain this land is being a statesman. I cannot use the lingo, the rhetoric, the behavior of Nasser, who lost the land, if I am to regain that land.'"

"So Sadat became a statesman, and being a statesman, he created the environment to have a war that had an objective and that objective was to move the political landscape forward, not to win or lose the war. So he prepared for a war; he initiated a war; and then agreed immediately to a cease-fire to preserve his gains, which were, in the big scheme of things, limited. But on the other hand, they were big, because they changed the equation. And then went to the negotiating table and through that negotiation he got back all his land."

"Arafat never managed to cross the line between a revolutionary leader and a statesman, and hence, every time he got the chance to make that breakthrough, he just backed off because it didn't figure in his mind set. And for whatever it is worth, my prediction is that Abu Mazen,* who is now the president of the Palestinians—if my assessment is accurate, we're seeing a replay of what happened in Egypt. Arafat is Nasser and Abu Mazen is Sadat. And Abu Mazen might lose his life in this process, like Sadat did. How-

---

*Mahmoud Abbas, also known as Abu Mazen, was a founding member of Fatah and was elected as the PLO Committee's secretary general in 1996, informally confirming his position as Yasser Arafat's deputy. Abu Mazen is considered one of the leading Palestinian figures devoted to the search for a peaceful solution to the Palestinian-Israeli conflict. He advocated negotiations with Israelis and initiated a dialogue with Jewish and pacifist movements in the 1970s. He also coordinated the negotiation process during the Madrid Conference, and he headed the Palestinian negotiating team at the secret Oslo talks. Mazen was the first PLO official to visit Saudi Arabia after the Gulf War in January 1993 and apologized to the Gulf countries for the PLO's stand during the crisis.

ever, although he doesn't have the same charisma and the same popularity of Arafat, he is going to deliver a Palestinian state that at the end of the day, regardless of what you say about Arafat's qualities, he couldn't deliver. And regardless of what you say about Abu Mazen's lack of charisma, he will deliver." Interestingly, when asked whether he would play a part in that process, Bandar neatly sidestepped the issue, saying, "We'll wait and see."

NINE

THE INVISIBLE
AMBASSADOR

"His character, his moral courage and his honesty in this issue
[the Khobar bombing] was stronger than any other player in
this whole thing. He said to me, 'I will help you with this and
we will do the right thing here' and he never wavered from
that, even though I think he put himself in great jeopardy."

FORMER FBI DIRECTOR LOUIS FREEH

When George H. W. Bush lost the election to Bill Clinton in 1992, there
could be no mistaking the change in the political climate, not just within
the Beltway and the United States, but in the world at large. It could be argued that in the vulnerable and volatile years immediately after the first
Gulf War, President Bush threw a highly complex and unstable foreign policy ball to the Clinton administration, which promptly dropped it.

The character of the new administration was revealed by Bandar in an
anecdote that exposed a great deal about President Clinton's early years in
office. He recalled, "One of the first things that his staff announced was
that the new president was not going to meet with any foreign leaders or officials for two months." This decision by the White House to close its doors
to foreign policy for the first few months immediately following the president's inauguration was in keeping with Democrat campaign slogans and
Clinton's belief that George H. W. Bush had lost the election due to his

neglect of domestic policy. The Clinton era began with a distinctly intro-spective focus.

The new administration policy stance announcement was deliberately credited to the president's staff—not to the president himself. This suspi-cion of a gap between the administration and President Clinton at this early stage, especially in the terms of crucial international policy, exposed a po-tential Achilles heel and presented a negative message to the outside world.

Despite the new policy of the Clinton White House, Bandar said, "Pres-ident Clinton did call; he had heard that I might be leaving because Bush had lost, and I told him it depended on King Fahd. One of the things he told me when he was president-elect was, 'As soon as I get to Washington, I need to sit down with you and we'll talk.' I said, 'Fine' but I thought it was just politics and being nice. However, Clinton got elected and was sworn in on January 20; on January 25, five days after he became president, I got a call from Tony Lake, the new national security adviser, who said to me, 'Could you come tomorrow at eleven o'clock?'" Despite the pronounce-ments of his staff, it seemed that Bill Clinton had every intention of devel-oping contacts outside the domestic United States.

On arriving at the White House and being informed that the president wanted to meet with him, a perplexed Bandar recounted how he hung around patiently, "I waited ten minutes, fifteen minutes, twenty minutes; I saw people go back and forth, back and forth; then I was told that the pres-ident's domestic advisers were fighting with the president, telling him, 'Wait a minute, you cannot meet with him, because we have told the world that you are not going to meet with any foreign representatives; the president of Turkey is here and you didn't meet with him.' Clinton argued, 'But I prom-ised Prince Bandar that I would meet with him and we called him to come and meet with me. I cannot *not* meet with him.'" A pragmatic Bandar ex-plained his position, saying, "So when I found that out, I said, 'Look, I didn't ask to come here; you asked me to come here. If the president cannot see me, but there is something that he needs to pass to me, then he can tell his national security adviser; he can tell me and then I'll go. I have no prob-lem with that.' They said, 'No—please wait.'"

Bandar said, "Eventually, they came up with a compromise. They asked me to stand close to where I had been sitting. Then the president walked in and we shook hands and said hello; with him was the vice president. Clin-ton took me to one side and we spoke for a few minutes before he said, 'Look, let's set up another time to meet so that we can discuss a few things.'" Bandar recounted, "What surprised me was that they had a photographer with them. They took a photo of our meeting and sent me a copy, but it had no date on it." He laughed, saying, "This was clever of the Clinton administration; so I put the date on it myself. It just shows how political and how smooth the Clinton administration was." He added, "It also shows you that Clinton had great political instincts. I believe personally that he was let down many times by the people around him, who were not as smart as he is."

When I was told of this story, I was amused by its similarity to another of Bandar's anecdotes, except in that case the shoe was on the other foot; on that occasion, Bill Clinton was the one to wait. Years earlier, Bandar had received a call informing him that the governor of Arkansas wanted to come and see him. He explained that this was in early 1990; by this time he had been to all of the lower forty-eight states, except for Arkansas, and couldn't imagine why the governor of Arkansas wanted to see him. He was told that Governor Clinton wanted to talk about the relationship between Saudi Arabia and the United States. However, Bandar had to cancel the meeting three times, the first time before the invasion of Iraq. At the third attempt at a meeting, Clinton had actually arrived at the embassy. However, Bandar suddenly had to leave; Clinton simply asked to come and meet Bandar again. Bandar recalled, "If I had had any brains at the time, I would have thought, 'This guy doesn't give up; that should have told me that he would succeed politically.'"

Bandar's relationship with the White House during President Clinton's time in office was something of an anomaly. The prince publicly acknowledged that "Clinton and I are friends; I would go and watch a movie with him." He has also explained that there was a difference between business and personal visits; whether he met with the president in the Oval Office as ambassador or in his private quarters as a friend. The perception that Bandar's sentiment had been growing increasingly bored under Clinton's leadership was in fact more a reflection on the administration and its attitude toward foreign policy, rather than the president himself. Similarly, although the media alleged that his contact with the White House was much reduced during Clinton's presidency, or had even been emasculated, the reality was that the Prince still retained amazing access.

Yet, while he did enjoy a relationship with the Clinton White House, it cannot be denied that Bandar had nowhere near the rapport he had enjoyed with President George Bush and his team. As Sir Richard Evans, former chairman of British Aerospace, explained, "I don't think that Bandar ever had the intimacy with the Clinton administration that he had with Bush." He noted that this was not due to animosity between Clinton and the prince, but rather that he had less empathy with some of the individuals within the new administration. Interestingly, Sir Richard also opined that the State Department operated differently under Clinton than it had during the first Bush administration.[1]

During a conversation with Bettina Gilbert, Bandar's private secretary for many years, Gilbert also confirmed that his access was probably at its height during the administration of George H. W. Bush, and was much quieter during the Clinton administration.[2] Gilbert's replacement as the prince's secretary, Sherry Cooper, also shed light on the Bandar-Clinton relationship, when she related a story that had been recounted to her by several Saudi diplomats. She said, "President Clinton, then Governor Clinton, turned up at the embassy wanting to meet Bandar during the primaries; he was looking for funding for a library and he came without any appointment. I heard that the prince asked one of his advisers, 'What are this guy's chances of the presidency?' and he was told, 'No chance whatsoever.'" Sherry grinned broadly and continued, "And so Mr. Clinton didn't get his appointment and went on to become president." She concluded, "I guess he never forgot that."[3]

From Bandar's reflections on the Clinton era, it is clear that in his opinion there was a distinct division between Clinton and his cabinet, and it was this factor that presented the prince with a problem. It has been said of Bandar that "he loved the gamesmanship of Washington and considered Bill Clinton his only equal at it."[4] Joe Ramsey, a long-standing friend of Bandar's and a lifetime Democrat, joked at the similarities between the U.S. president and the Saudi prince, saying, "He and Bill Clinton should have been as tight as thieves; they are alike in so many ways. Like Clinton, Bandar believes that if he talks to anyone for long enough, he can bring them around to his point of view. He prides himself on that, and that is the way Bill Clinton is." Suppressing a laugh, Ramsey observed, "There would probably be no room big enough for the two egos, but apart from that we thought it would be the perfect marriage."[5]

While foreign policy was quieter during the Clinton administration, it could not altogether be silenced. Just before 10 P.M. on June 25, 1996, three sentries posted on a rooftop at Khobar Towers in Saudi Arabia observed a tanker truck draw up alongside a perimeter fence next to the high-rise compound. The complex housed two thousand American military personnel and service people from the United Kingdom and France enforcing the U.N.-sponsored "no-fly" zone in Iraq and working at the King Abdul Aziz Airbase in Saudi Arabia. Their suspicions were immediately aroused when they saw two men jump out of the truck into a car and speed away. The area had already been identified as a likely target for a terrorist attack; they quickly realized that it must be a bomb.

One of the sentries radioed a warning to the U.S. Air Force's Central Security Control.[6] They then began pounding on the doors of sleeping airmen, frantically trying to clear the building. Only four minutes later, the truck, carrying a massive five-thousand-pound bomb of military-grade explosives, reinforced by an incendiary bomb, exploded with a force so violent that it left a crater eighty-five feet wide and thirty-five feet deep. The detonation was heard twenty miles away in Bahrain. This terrorist attack resulted in the deaths of nineteen American airmen and injured five hundred Americans and Saudis.[7]

There is far more to the Khobar bombing than the perversion of justice. It is a sobering thought that the atrocities of terrorism, pervasive in today's society, did not simply materialize out of the ether when President George W. Bush entered office. Extreme unrest in the form of religious and political intolerance, and the framework for funded, organized terror attacks, was fermenting not so quietly beneath the surface in the Middle East and in the face of U.S. foreign policy during the 1990s. Rich Lowry spoke to this real-

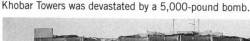

Khobar Towers was devastated by a 5,000-pound bomb.

ity in his book *Clinton & Khobar*: "If Clinton was as vigilant against terrorism as he says—handing over a wondrous counterterrorism policy to an in-
ept and inattentive Bush administration—it should be clear in cases like
that of Khobar. Instead, the Clinton administration deliberately looked the
other way after the Khobar bombing and made a near-apology to the perpetrator of the attack."[8]

In the wake of the Khobar bombing, President Clinton appeared in
public vowing to "make sure those responsible are brought to justice."[9] He
announced that the FBI would be assigned to investigate the bombing in
conjunction with Saudi authorities and that it would be headed by FBI Director Louis Freeh. As Freeh recalled, Clinton's instructions in those first
raw days of shock were unambiguous. "The president used the phrase
which the prince and I often remarked upon later on to 'leave no stone unturned.' That was my instruction."[10]

One hundred twenty-five FBI agents were immediately dispatched to
Saudi Arabia. Hard on their heels was Freeh, for whom the bomb was to
have a profound and lasting impact. He described how he visited this horrific scene soon after the attack, "I watched dozens of dedicated FBI agents
combing through the wreckage in one-hundred-twenty-degree heat, rever-
ently handling the human remains of our brave young men. More than four
hundred of our Air Force men and women were wounded in this well-
planned attack, and I was humbled by their courage and spirit. I later met
with the families of our lost Khobar heroes and promised that we would do
whatever was necessary to bring these terrorists to American justice. The
courage and dignity these wonderful families have consistently exemplified
has been one of the most powerful experiences of my twenty-six years of
public service."[11]

What resulted from this determined beginning was a vicious three-way
battle among Saudi Arabia, the FBI, and the Clinton administration as politics, public relations, and foreign policy converged to complicate what
should have remained a simple matter of retribution and justice.

In June 1996, U.S. Attorney General Janet Reno publicly criticized
Saudi officials for their failure to cooperate. Secretary of State Madeleine
Albright told Bandar in no uncertain terms, "The United States expects the
full assistance of the Saudi government on this matter." In response, Bandar
suggested that the attorney general was interfering in foreign policy matters,
to which Albright replied curtly, "Make no mistake about it, Mr. Ambassador, the United States government is completely unified on this matter.

Janet Reno and Louis Freeh are in charge of the investigation, and we expect your full cooperation in completing the investigation. Period."[12]

Secretary Albright did not realize that she was preaching to the converted. Freeh, who worked closely with the Saudi leadership, was to say of Bandar and his role in opening doors to the investigation, "His character, his moral courage, and his honesty in this issue was stronger than any other player in this whole thing. He said to me, 'I will help you with this and we will do the right thing here,' and he never wavered from that; even though I think he put himself in great jeopardy."[13]

Speaking of the Khobar bombing and the decision to support the FBI investigation, Bandar explained Saudi rationale in cultural terms, saying, "If the attack had been on a Saudi installation, we would have been angry but we would have treated it differently. Attacking our guests, who were there at our request, who were in uniform—and a uniform in Saudi Arabia means a lot; it represents a sovereign nation—was just like a thousand years ago, if you had a nomad coming to your tribe asking for protection and you gave it to them, and then another tribe came and killed him—that is an immediate cause for war—it is a matter of honor. So we were angry; therefore, normal political and legal barriers whereby people would spend weeks negotiating the parameters of the investigation were dropped right there and then. We didn't care about who got involved doing what and where; we just wanted to get the people who had violated our hospitality and had violated our honor with our guests. That was the bottom line."

The deployment of the FBI to Saudi Arabia was a controversial issue. Under standard U.S. procedure, the FBI is forbidden from operating outside of the United States without executive approval from the State Department. However, the president's public statement immediately after the bombing named FBI director Freeh as the overseer of the investigation, with the personal responsibility and authority to see it through to its conclusion.

Despite working closely with both the U.S. Embassy and the State Department, the unusual level of authority granted to the FBI in this case, was, if nothing else, a source of discomfort to the State Department. By Freeh's own admission, "We were very far out in front of where our domestic law enforcement agencies, and even our security agencies, would be in a similar circumstance." He observed, "The State Department was concerned about that, and it was important that we worked very closely with them, which we did, primarily through the embassy there. So I think there was a little friction with the State Department: why is the FBI playing such a large role? And the answer to that is the president wanted it done and the Saudis agreed that the Bureau would be permitted to conduct this investigation and do it in conjunction with the Mabaheth."*

One of the challenges for the FBI in Saudi Arabia was the development of a working relationship with their Saudi counterparts, the Mabaheth. Freeh explained that at that time no concrete relations had been established between them, saying, "The FBI representative that dealt with them was based in Rome. Every year he would visit Riyadh for a few days, shake a few hands and return to Rome, so we had no relationship; we had no liaison there . . . which was our fault, not their fault."[14] Despite this poor start, the FBI and the Mabaheth worked in close collaboration and created a firm working relationship. This process was helped by basing Arab-speaking agents in the kingdom and by flying members of the Mabaheth to America to witness firsthand the FBI's forensic and laboratory activities.

Freeh was highly respectful of the Arab culture. Bandar had been known to mock the Clinton administration's ignorant perspective of the Arab world as "just a bunch of ragheads who torture people to get a confession."[15] However, in Freeh the prince discovered views on foreign policy and the Middle Eastern allies in line with those of Bush and Reagan—scarcely surprising, as Freeh was an avowed Republican. For his part, Freeh was highly appreciative of the Saudis' open-minded approach to the demands made upon them by the Americans, "I thought it was very presumptuous to assume that because an American was killed that we would immediately take complete jurisdiction, sending our agents there to roam around the streets. We would never permit any country to do that here and I thought the fact that they did that was really quite significant. My point is that they were actually providing extraordinary cooperation with us, and I think that Americans sometimes look at the world a little differently than others."[16]

In contrast, the American media vehemently disagreed with Freeh; Saudi Arabia was openly criticized in the press for its lack of cooperation. Proclaimed the *National Review*, "Saudi reaction to every terrorist attack against the U.S. to which the kingdom has had a connection in recent years had been a mixture of avoidance, dishonesty, and passive aggression. They frustrated the U.S. investigation into the 1996 Khobar Towers bombing, al-

---

*The Mabaheth are the kingdom's antiterrorist police.

most certainly to cover up evidence of Iranian involvement—the Saudis wanted to keep the U.S. from retaliating against Iran, at a time when the kingdom was cozying up to the mullahs."[17]

In countering that media criticism, Freeh was to use the following analogy: "The criticism that they were not cooperative, as I told many people, was not well founded, because in the counterpart situation—say it happened in England, and say Americans were killed in England—we would certainly have a couple of agents sitting somewhere in New Scotland Yard. But we would not be out doing interviews, doing forensics—so I think the standard that they [the press] set was an unreasonable one and unfair."[18]

A year before the Khobar bombing, in November 1995, seven people had been killed, including five Americans, in the OPM Sang bombing, an explosion at the Saudi National Guard facility in Riyadh.[19] The Saudi authorities arrested, tried, and executed four men responsible for the attack who had admitted that they had been inspired by Osama bin Laden. This sparked an uproar in the U.S. press which accused the Saudis of deliberately beheading these men before the United States could interview them in order to subvert an American investigation.[20] This allegation would surface again after the 9/11 atrocity when the media pointed an accusing finger at Saudi Arabia. The kingdom was accused of apathy in the fight against terrorism, a point illustrated by the factually incorrect statement quoted in the *New York Times* that they refused "to allow U.S. personnel to interrogate the Khobar Towers bombing suspects before beheading them."[21] It was the individuals that were convicted of carrying out the OPM Sang bombing that were executed, not the Khobar suspects—but as Bandar often says, lies can quickly become facts when spread by the media.

Freeh, who studied the Saudi debriefing of these men, called their execution "swift justice," explaining that the OPM Sang bombing was a Saudi-based attack carried out by wealthy Sunni Muslims. He stressed that as there was no foreign sponsor of the attack, it was therefore a Saudi domestic matter and thus there was

Louis Freeh, ex-Director of the FBI.

no U.S. jurisdiction. He concluded that it was a Saudi crime, carried out by Saudis within Saudi Arabia, in which, sadly, U.S. Department of Defense personnel working with the Saudi National Guard were caught up. He added, "So although we had an interest in speaking to them, it was not the kind of interest that should have precluded them from conducting their own justice." Freeh explained that the key difference between the Khobar and OPM Sang bombings was that the latter had no foreign links or outside sponsor and was entirely an internal matter. Khobar was an Iranian operation and therein sat the difficulty.[22]

Freeh later testified that the FBI had forged an "effective working relationship" with the Saudis after the 1996 Khobar Towers bombing.[23] Moreover, he testified positively at least four times about Saudi cooperation during the Khobar investigation and has given countless speeches in which he reaffirmed his belief that Saudi support "was really quite extraordinary and I don't think they got the proper credit for it."

Amplifying these comments, Freeh observed, "Two things were extraordinary about Saudi Arabia's cooperation with the United States; firstly, the discovery of high-level Iranian involvement placed Saudi Arabia at far greater risk of retaliation for any action taken against Iran than the United States. Secondly, the extent to which, despite the Iranian threat, the Saudis consented to help—they agreed to Rule 15, an American legal procedure whereby testimony and evidence from witnesses provided in Saudi Arabia, in the presence of American prosecutors, the defendant's attorney and a U.S. magistrate, could be recorded and taken back to the U.S. and used as evidence in an American trial."

Freeh's comments express the magnitude of this consent. "I had been a prosecutor for twelve years, and the only other time I had done that successfully was in a drug case where the Swiss government approved of that procedure. The Saudis went well beyond cooperation; they were actually going to support our prosecution." He continued that if that were not surprising in itself, "It was even more extraordinary that by doing that, they were placing themselves, placing their country in very serious jeopardy in respect to the Iranians." Freeh added, "As I am sure you have heard, this wasn't a Saudi Hezbollah attack, it was an externally funded and executed attack by the senior leadership of the Iranian government."[24] He reinforced that view later when he said, "By making these witnesses directly available to the FBI, the Saudis understood that they would be helping to provide evidence that senior officials of the government of Iran were responsible for the Khobar attack. Despite these extremely sensitive and complex issues, the Saudis put their own interests aside to aid the FBI in the United States."[25]

Despite this risk, Bandar's commitment to justice in this case was undiminished, and Freeh was quick to acknowledge his role, saying, "We thought that was a great act of courage by the Saudis and by Bandar in particular. Bandar was exposing himself on both sides; he was exposing himself to the [Clinton] administration and to his own superiors and family, and the reason, I still believe, was because he thought it was the right thing to do. He said many times, because he talked, not directly, but he talked through other people to the families and he promised the families that they would fully cooperate. He was true to his promise; he thought that was a very serious promise to have made and was going to abide by it."[26]

Proof of Bandar's efforts to see justice achieved was confirmed by Freeh when he said, "From time to time, a road block or legal obstacle would occur, which was expected, given the marked differences between our legal and procedural systems. Despite these challenges, the problems were always solved by the personal intervention of Prince Bandar and his consistent support for the FBI."[27] He went on to explain, "Thanks to Prince Bandar's intervention, we were allowed to have FBI agents to go over into a prison in Saudi Arabia and interview one on one, without Saudi witnesses, Saudi nationals who had committed a crime against Americans in Saudi Arabia, which to me was absolutely extraordinary. We needed direct access to these subjects, because their admissions and testimony were critical to support our prosecution."[28] No FBI agent had ever been given such unprecedented access to a detained Saudi national, which access could potentially taint their prosecution under Islamic law.[29]

This is not the only difference between the respective American and Saudi responses to the Khobar bombing. The promise Bandar upheld was also made by Clinton to the American people and the families of those killed. There was but one obstacle for the administration to overcome in the quest for justice in this case: to present the Saudi leadership with an official request for the evidence. This was vital in order for Saudi Arabia to be able stand up to Iran: if the information was officially requested of them by the Americans, it would look better to the Iranians than if Saudi Arabia were to be seen freely indicating Iran as the perpetrator. Freeh stressed, "I was being told by both Bandar and Prince Nayef that the Iranians were behind the bombing—that 'the Iranians did this.'" According to Freeh, they were telling him that they had witnesses in custody who would confirm it. "They were telling us that we can have access to those witnesses, but we have to make a request and be serious about the consequences of getting that information, which ironically would be more adverse to the Saudis than to us."

Freeh observed, "The Americans say that Americans were killed, but a lot of Saudis were killed too, and families lost loved ones. The point that Bandar frequently made during this period, which I think he made better than many other people, was, 'Louis, you know that the Iranians did this, we know the Iranians did this, and your government knows. The Iranians know that they did this, so they are looking to see what we are all going to do about it, and if we say we know what happened here but we're not going to pursue it, we are sending an extremely dangerous message to the sponsors in that country. Not just this attack, but all the other Hezbollah attacks, what's going on in the West Bank, in Gaza."

Freeh said, "Bandar was very shrewd and completely brilliant in his analysis when he said, 'The Iranian government is a threat to King Fahd— a military threat, and a nearby one at that. By giving you the evidence that will allow you to go after the Iranians, we are putting ourselves in great jeopardy, politically and otherwise, because of what we have done. However, by not responding and ignoring this threat, you are putting everybody in jeopardy, not just the Saudis, but everybody.' That was really astute, a very broad view, a worldview of terrorism."[30]

Right from the start the Saudis made it extremely clear, "We will tell you and we will tell Mr. Freeh's agents and make available to you this evidence, but if you want this evidence you have to ask for it: if you ask for it we will provide it." Freeh's body language showed his considerable frustration as he said emphatically, "The big problem we had in making this case was not the Saudi end of it; it was the U.S. end of it, because we could not get our leadership, the president or vice president, to ask for the evidence."

Freeh continued, "In fact, they never asked for the evidence; we could not get them to press our case with the Saudis, and it didn't need any pressing; it just needed a request that the witnesses be made available to the FBI. We would write talking points for the president and give them to National Security Adviser Sandy Berger. But," he said, "what we would hear back from Bandar and others was that there was a meeting with the crown prince, but they never formally asked to have access to those witnesses, which was extremely frustrating."[31]

Freeh's professional judgment was largely ignored by the U.S. media, which continued to report, "The FBI team in Saudi Arabia complained about the lack of access to the key Saudi evidence,"[32] omitting that the evidence was in fact being blocked indirectly for release to the FBI by the U.S. administration.

The allegation that the Saudis were holding up the Khobar investigation stemmed from a series of White House press releases that gave the impression that all that could be done was being done by the administration, but couched in very specific language. In the following quote from Elsa Walsh's article, "Louis Freeh's Last Case," when she interviewed Sandy Berger about the Khobar investigation, the italics are my own and intended to highlight how even within this very rosy picture of U.S. efforts, they never officially asked for the evidence: "Samuel R. Berger, who became the Clinton administration's National Security Adviser, told me that Clinton wrote to King Fahd and met with Fahd's half brother, Crown Prince Abdullah, in New York, *personally urging* them to cooperate. 'The Secretaries of Defense and State,' Berger added, 'made *personal appeals* to the Saudi hierarchy.' "[33]

Bandar was caught in the crossfire in this game of false jargon. As Freeh explained, "Prince Bandar was in the middle; he was telling the crown prince that the president and vice president are going to make this request, but then they would have a meeting and they wouldn't make the request. I'm sure the crown prince would be saying to him, 'What's going on here?!' "[34] The prince has made his irritation in this matter very clear, intimating that duplicity on the part of Clinton's advisers was an ever-present obstacle.

George Tenet, former director of the CIA, said of Freeh, "With Khobar, you can see all of Louis's values right on his sleeve."[35] Indeed, Freeh struggled under the strain of such setbacks. Realizing that the implication of Iranian involvement in the Khobar bombing would have dramatic impact on U.S. foreign policy, Freeh said to Sandy Berger, "Look, if you want us to stop investigating because we shouldn't be interfering with foreign policy, that's fine. The only thing I have invested in this investigation is that you told me to investigate and I told the families I was going to do everything I could. Now if that's changed, then I accept that, but then I have to go to the families and I have to tell them I can't do this any more. . . . I'm not going to tell them why, but I have to tell them because I sat with them for two days while they were crying and . . . I told them I would do everything I can. Now if that's changed on the American side, that's fine, but you have to tell me that."[36]

However, Freeh was never given a direct order to terminate the Khobar investigation and Bandar noticed that whenever Freeh's name came up, Sandy Berger became distinctly uneasy, saying at one point that in his opinion Freeh had a tin ear for politics, that "he didn't know a thing about foreign affairs and could lead the United States into war."[37]

In his dealings with Sandy Berger, Bandar was all too aware of the foreign policy minefield the Khobar investigation presented. During one of Freeh's early visits to the desert kingdom, Bandar had taken him to one side and very bluntly explained, "Listen, we have the goods, goddammit, but I'll be honest with you; politically, we don't want to pursue this—we don't want to be accused of pushing you to go to war." The prince clearly recognized that in the Khobar case, the law-enforcement approach itself risked creating pressure for a military strike, as did the White House, which "was therefore angered when Freeh—the head of its lead agency in the fight against terror, whose job it was to pursue the facts—pursued the facts."[38]

Given that Pentagon officials were anonymously saying that a group outside the kingdom or a foreign government was behind the explosion, and that they were investigating ties to Iraq or Iran, Berger would have been wary of establishing a direct link to Iran, especially since U.S. Secretary of Defense William Perry had stated, "If we identify another nation as the source of the bombing, we should retaliate."[39] As early as August 2, 1996, when talking to the media, Perry eluded to Iranian involvement in the attack and stated that the size and sophistication of the bomb indicated international involvement in the atrocity.[40] By Berger's own admission, "Bandar would always ask, 'Tell me what you are going to do with the information if we share it with you?' "[41] Evidently, the Saudis were concerned as to the extent of America's thirst for justice and the implications if it became public knowledge that prominent members of the Iranian leadership were behind the bombing of an American airbase.

This situation was not unfamiliar to Bandar; in the lead-up to the Gulf War, he had been tasked with determining American resolve before King Fahd would consent to allow U.S. troops into Saudi Arabia. The kingdom could not afford to upset Iran, neither then nor over Khobar, without 100 percent backing from the United States. As he pointed out in one interview and in reference to the many attacks carried out within Saudi Arabia, "They are not attacking Westerners. They are attacking us for being your friend."[42] However, whereas during the Gulf War the Bush administration had rallied uniformly around their Saudi allies, the Clinton administration turned their back on them.

In sheer frustration Freeh took matters into his own hands. Without Clinton's prior knowledge,[43] he asked former President George H. W. Bush to intercede with the Saudis, and a Saturday luncheon was arranged at Bandar's McLean home between the former president and Crown Prince Abdullah. Remembering the event and the prior briefing of his former president, Freeh recalled George Bush's words, "He said, 'Look, I am happy to do this,' but he said to me, 'Is this going to get you into trouble?' I replied, 'It doesn't really matter—I have to make this request and I can't get anybody else to make it.' "[44]

On the Monday after this luncheon, the crown prince summoned Freeh, Ambassador Wyche Fowler, and Dale Watson, the FBI's counterterrorism chief, to a meeting with him at McLean. Here Freeh again explained what was being requested, stressing that the FBI needed not only the information, but also Saudi permission to use it as evidence. He told Crown Prince Abdullah, "My intention is to use that information ultimately to indict people, including whoever in Iran I can indict, for these murders." According to Freeh, the crown prince then simply turned to Bandar and said, "Call my brother and tell him to make these witnesses available to the FBI."[45] Just like that, after being tied up for two years in red tape, the FBI finally got what the Saudis had offered and had been trying to give them since the attack.

As a result of this collaboration, the Department of Justice returned a criminal indictment on June 22, 2001, charging thirteen Saudi defendants with the murder of the nineteen U.S. servicemen killed by the Khobar explosion.[46] The indictment also contained a total of thirty-eight references to the Iranian government.[47] That same day, Louis Freeh served his last day as director of the FBI. Days later, the statute of limitations on most of the criminal charges expired.

Throughout the investigation, Bandar had repeatedly asked the administration if it really wanted the information Freeh so desperately sought. Bandar made the consequences of obtaining such information and doing nothing with it very clear: action would have to be taken or it would be better for all parties to leave it hidden. However, for its part, and not without a certain irony, U.S. foreign policy was busy courting Iran. The Clinton administration's eagerness to repair relations with Iran emerged largely in the form of small signs and discreet but clearly identifiable differences in rhetoric and official language. Moreover, to the public, the American officials played down their suspicions that Iran was implicated in the Khobar bombing.[48]

A strong indication of the administration's softness on the Khobar investigation was evident when a big break occurred for the FBI investigation in March 1997. The Canadians arrested Hani el-Sayegh, a Saudi Shiite and suspected lookout, who had been implicated by others in Saudi custody. Freeh was keen to bring him over to Washington to question this first human link in a chain that could lead back to the perpetrators. However, in September 1997, the U.S. Justice Department dismissed the indictment, citing the suspect's refusal to cooperate and lack of corroborating witnesses. Bandar reportedly told an acquaintance that this development was received in the White House as if it were a "gift from heaven."[49]

By 1997, the Saudis were increasingly convinced that the administration had deliberately set the Khobar investigation adrift as it concentrated its efforts on cultivating its ties to a more moderate government in Iran, in spite of the fact that anti-Americanism was a fundamental rallying point with the Iranian regime and that Iran repeatedly ignored U.S. overtures.

"The cowards who committed this murderous act must not go unpunished."[50] These were President Clinton's words immediately after learning of the Khobar bombing. It was also claimed that "an attack against American servicemen abroad was not merely a crime. It was an act of war."[51] Yet despite the strength of these public statements and the mounting evidence that Iran was the foreign sponsor of the Khobar bombing, the administration chose to relax its warning on travel to Iran, to waive sanctions against foreign oil firms operating in Iran, and, finally, to remove Iran from the list of major exporters of illegal drugs.[52]

Bandar stressed the difference between previous Republican administrations and the highly political "will o' the wisp" attitude of the Clinton administration. "I tell you, if George H.W. Bush or Reagan were president when this event took place, and if they insisted like the Clinton people insisted, for us to show all our cards based on everything we have, and if the evidence that they got independently was available, Iran would have been invaded. I am confident of that."

In a cutting assessment of what happened inside the White House during that time, the prince caustically remarked, "Clinton's administration wanted to have it both ways. I said, 'We can cut off this investigation at a certain point and we can handle the rest of it. We have people we caught; we also have people that we believe were involved but they are not available to us as they have escaped, and based on what we know now, we will punish the people that we caught and we will look for the people that escaped. If we capture them, we will know definitely who's behind it and then we will take political or military action and close the affair.' " But aside from the occasional press statement, the Clinton administration remained silent.[53]

In April 1999, President Clinton issued a statement overtly reaching out to Iran. Freeh's reaction to this cozying up to the architects of the Khobar bombing was predictable. He shook his head as he said, "The message we were sending to Iran was that we would tolerate them sending in their agents, who were operationally capable agents, because we wanted to establish a better relationship with them, or that we would tolerate a bombing where these young men were killed, because we want to have a better relationship. It didn't make any sense to me and it didn't make any sense to Bandar, either morally or politically. And yet that was what we were fighting for a whole period of time." Freeh was referring to the FBI's belief, backed up by good evidence, that the Iranians were sending over active Ministry of Intelligence and Security (MOIS) agents to the United States by assigning them nominal positions as coaches or trainers on Iranian wrestling teams. It was alleged that the fingerprinting and photographing of these teams was ordered to cease because the United States wanted to develop better relations.[54]

After two years, Freeh was convinced that the administration had abandoned all interest in the Khobar bombing investigation. The only constant in the Khobar bombing seemed to be a White House policy of tilting toward Tehran. During the investigation, FBI agents interviewed eight Saudi citizens that the Saudi government had identified as being the bombing's perpetrators. Talking about those interviews, Freeh said, "They admitted they were members of Saudi Hezbollah. They admitted complicity in the act, and they implicated senior Iranian officials in the funding and planning of the attack." Freeh also affirmed that their stories were corroborated by other witnesses and evidence. Finally, he advised that the suspects had also named those Iranian military and informa-

Sandy Berger, National Security Adviser during the Clinton administration.

tion agency individuals who helped select Khobar as the target and who paid for the group's training and explosives.[55]

Bandar felt that Sandy Berger's surprising reaction to the information uncovered by Freeh that there was an Iranian finger on the trigger was an unambiguous indicator of how the administration was really handling the Khobar case. Those suspects not only confirmed their own involvement in the attack, but also described how the Iranians had ordered, supported, and financed the attack.[56] "Freeh and I saw the worst of power misuse!" Bandar recalled. "When they were pushing and pushing, and then we gave them what they were pushing for, Sandy Berger, instead of saying, 'Hurray! You've got the information; you've got the smoking gun, let's go for it,' said, 'Who else knows about this?' Think about this in historical terms, 'Who else knows about this?' In other words, if nobody else knows about it, keep your mouth shut. And what are we talking about? American lives being lost. And politicians are saying we want to avenge this, let the chips fall where they may! And telling it to whom—to the families of those who were killed?" How could the White House position be reconciled with President Clinton's words on learning of the bombing, "The cowards who committed this murderous act must not go unpunished. Let me say again: We will pursue this. America takes care of our own."[57]

Bandar stressed that Freeh "was fuming." Bandar has since made it unambiguously clear that Berger wanted Freeh to keep the information to himself, essentially saying, "If nobody else knows about it [Iranian complicity], keep your mouth shut." Bandar commented that this was in diametrical contravention to Clinton's first reaction to the Khobar bombing. "Clinton's specific words were, 'Let the chips fall where they may; we don't care, it's not politics.' Then when we did let the chips fall where they may, they say, 'Who else knows about this?' " Bandar was to reinforce this comment time and again as during a CNN interview, when he stated categorically, "Things broke down because when we got to a critical moment where Washington was telling us, 'Give us everything and let the chips fall where they may.' We were telling them, 'Maybe you won't like what you see?' Finally, when they saw what we had, they dropped the ball and that's where we are now."[58]

The fear of terrorism so prevalent in Western society today did not simply climb out of a cave in Afghanistan in 2001. It had been brewing under the surface in the Middle East for a very long period and the Khobar bombing was a blatant indication of this threat. In fact, at the time, Osama bin

Laden described the killing of nineteen U.S. airmen as "praiseworthy." However, the Khobar bombing was in many ways swept neatly under the carpet, the blame conveniently placed by the U.S. media on a lack of Saudi cooperation. "Khobar provided the keys that unlocked the new terror world," said one terror expert. "Everything you needed to know about the new terror network, the cooperation between all the different sects and factions, the rise of Wahhabi radicalism in Saudi Arabia, the changing dynamic of the Middle East—it all was present in that case."[59]

Freeh said about Bandar's role in the Khobar investigation, "I was particularly fortunate to gain the trust and cooperation of Prince Bandar bin Sultan, who was critical in achieving the FBI's investigative objectives in the Khobar case. Due to Bandar's support and personal efforts, the FBI was able to establish an FBI office in Riyadh." Freeh stressed, "On the basis of that relationship and my observations and judgments that I made during that period, I think I have a very strong and very accurate description and ability to characterize him and what significance he played in that result. I think he was pivotal in getting justice and also in ensuring that the relationships between our countries on that matter particularly were really kept on the right track."[60]

Freeh's generous praise of Saudi cooperation and the uncompromising role of Bandar contrasts with the accusations in *The Sacred Age of Terror*, a book by Daniel Benjamin and Steven Simon, both of whom worked for Clinton's national security adviser, Sandy Berger. They allege that Bandar conned Freeh into believing that the White House wasn't much interested in Freeh's frantic attempts to solve the Khobar Towers bombing and repeatedly misled Freeh. Moreover, they claimed, "the Khobar Towers case exacerbated the rancor between Freeh and Clinton's national security team, hobbling the government's efforts to combat terror."[61] Finally, they concluded that the prince's misleading of Freeh was meant to 'sow dissension within the government,' and this misinformation led Freeh to deduce that the White House had little interest in the case to which he was deeply committed.[62]

In practice, the badly sagging Khobar Towers investigation eventually became the most conspicuous example of the enduring mistrust and acrimony between Clinton and Freeh, a deep-rooted animosity that was characterized by Sidney Blumental in his book, *The Clinton Wars*: "Louis Freeh had for years treated the White House as his enemy" and "Freeh and his deputies seemed to have a visceral antagonism against Clinton."[63] During the investigation, the bad blood between the White House and the FBI was transparent. It was reported that Freeh's dislike of the president turned into a deep rift and that his "mistrust of the White House grew so strong that it seems to have blinded him and made him susceptible to manipulation."[64] That acrimony stemmed in part from Freeh's personal support for an independent counsel to investigate Democratic fund raising following the 1996 Clinton-Gore campaign finance scandal. Not surprisingly, it was reported that the White House loathed its FBI director and was lukewarm about pursuing the Khobar case.[65]

When I told President Clinton of Freeh's caustic allegations about the lack of White House cooperation with the Khobar investigation, there was a momentary silence before he responded emphatically, "Did you see Danny Benjamin's* response on that—I think I have it right here." In a letter to the editor of the *Wall Street Journal* about the Khobar bombing and the White House, Benjamin suggested that in relation to the Khobar bombing and Freeh's criticism of President Clinton and the White House, Freeh was embarking in a "slow-rolled case of personal animus" and that the former FBI director was disingenuous in suggesting that the Clinton administration refused to support a prosecution [of Iran as a sponsor of the Khobar bombing] pointing out that the prosecution and criminal indictment for these murders had to wait for a new administration.[66]

President Clinton then launched into a cold and deliberate personal rebuttal of Freeh's claims, saying, "I personally asked the crown prince to allow the FBI to interview the suspects. Louis Freeh is lying." Clinton angrily slammed his fist down on his desk. "He is a right wing, Republican fanatic and he messed up the FBI. Two of his great agents called the FBI in the lead-up to 9/11 and said, 'I've got Arabs out here flying airplanes and they are not taking off or landing,' and nothing was done about it at central headquarters of the FBI. It has all been in the press, and this was Louis Freeh's way of deflecting it [criticism]."

"Louis Freeh is the single worst appointment I ever made and I wouldn't believe anything he said," Clinton said, stressing that the way Freeh treated him, once the Republicans won the Congress, was purely a diversionary tactic. The former president alleged that Freeh "was being harshly criticized by

---

*Daniel Benjamin was director for Transnational Threats, National Security Council, during 1998–1999 and cowrote *The Age of Sacred Terror* (New York: Random House, 2002).

them [the Republicans] because they never solved the Atlanta bombing; they lost cash money, huge amounts of cash in a drug bust; they messed up a lot of things in their forensic labs; they totally blew some other major cases." Clinton now reasoned that Freeh decided once the right-wing Republicans won the Congress that the best way to curry their favor and get them off his back "was to attack me from the FBI and that's what he proceeded to do. What he said to you is simply not true!"

Clinton went on to explain that neither his administration nor the Bush administration ever indicted any Iranians. He did admit that both administrations knew that the Iranians supported the Saudi Hezbollah, and said, "The Saudis disposed of the people who were involved in it. And I think frankly they [the Saudis] were probably somewhat reluctant to see this [Khobar] become the cause of a war between the United States and Iran. But it is simply not true that we didn't try to facilitate that investigation—I personally asked the crown prince and here is Danny Benjamin's response to Louis Freeh's article. Danny Benjamin has written a very highly regarded book on terrorism, and he was one of our national security administration personnel who was working on it." Clinton then handed me a copy of the Benjamin response and said, "What he says in there is the truth. Anything he says in there you can attribute to me."[67]

Looking back on the frustrations and injustice of the Khobar bombing investigation and the way in which Freeh was treated by his political masters, Bandar cynically observed that Clinton, who had been stonewalled in his first two nominations for FBI director, selected Freeh as director of the FBI only because he thought it would appease the Republicans. "He picked him up for political reasons; here is a former FBI agent who was appointed as a judge by George H. W. Bush. He had a problem with his first two FBI director appointments and could not get them confirmed, so he thought he would appoint someone that would show that he had nothing to hide. Louis Freeh let the chips fall where they may and Clinton hated him for that. With both the Whitewater investigation and the Monica Lewinsky investigation, Judge Louis Freeh did not go out of his way to screw Bill Clinton, but he sure did not use any influence to interfere in the investigative process."

Of the investigation, Bandar said, "Clinton's advisers were advising him saying, 'No, we must look to the Congress, to the families, to the public,' but what hurt Freeh more than anything else was that they made him go and give his word to the families of those who died, that no stone would be left unturned—that they would go all the way. Then he realized that they had been lying to him because they didn't want to go that far. Okay, we are all big boys in politics, but we gave them the way to stop it where it was, before it escalated into a major world crisis, and they refused." In a damning indictment to the games played by Clinton's staff, the prince said, "They wanted it both ways; they wanted it to look like they were prepared to take it all the way, but then when the chips fell where they may, they said, 'Oops! Louis Freeh is crazy! He has no political sense—why is he doing this?' He was not doing it; they pushed it."

Summarizing his view of how the Clinton administration handled Freeh, Bandar said, "They used him. They thought he had credibility, he was a Republican, he was a judge; he was FBI director. But they used him, saying, 'You go to the families and look them straight in the eye and say, 'The president told me let the chips fall where they may and we are going to pursue this until we get to the criminals.'" Bandar concluded, "Louis believed that and then he discovered that he was lying to those people because the decision maker did not intend to do that. And that is where the clash comes—Louis is hurt because he was used. He felt that this was the ultimate responsibility of a government—to protect its people." Left unsaid was the charge that the Clinton administration failed in its duty to the American people.

Bandar's reduced profile in Washington during the Clinton era left him free to undertake perhaps one of the greatest feats of his diplomatic career: to bring to justice the Lockerbie bombers* and to facilitate the consequent withdrawal of U.N. sanctions against Libya,† an accomplishment that was achieved despite the deep suspicion of both the U.S. and U.K. governments. Bandar's work on the Lockerbie case has been lauded as an exemplary exercise in creative diplomacy. The prince was swimming against the currents of a political climate that had prevented any progress in ten years and achieved success in an intimidating task that had been avoided by many other statesmen.

---

*On December 21, 1988, at a few minutes after seven o'clock, a bomb exploded in the forward hull of Pan Am Flight 103 over the quiet Scottish town of Lockerbie. That explosion killed two hundred seventy people from twenty countries, and early on during the subsequent investigation, evidence tied two Libyan intelligence agents to the bombing.

†The U.N. Security Council imposed sanctions on Libya in 1992—a travel ban and certain spare parts—to press Tripoli to hand over two suspects wanted for the Lockerbie bombing.

In 1995, Colonel Muammar Qaddafi turned to the Saudi Arabians for help in resolving the long-running Lockerbie dispute, which had been locked in an impasse of immense proportion for seven years. Rehab Massoud,* who traveled extensively with Bandar and was present at all meetings between the prince and the principal actors in the Lockerbie negotiations, explained that Saudi Arabia's interests in helping Libya stemmed from frustration at the lack of progress on the Palestinian issue and noted, as a backdrop, that Crown Prince Abdullah had just taken over from King Fahd, who had been felled by a series of strokes in 1995. Talking about the Lockerbie standoff, Massoud observed, "This was a new introduction to world issues. Things were going very badly in the Middle East peace process. We needed something to work." However, he said, bringing the United States and the United Kingdom to the table proved difficult. He explained that the reluctance of both the United Kingdom and the United States to push for a resolution was prompted primarily by domestic concerns. The George H. W. Bush administration thought the issue a "hot potato," one not prudent to handle with an election on the horizon, whereas in the United Kingdom, Prime Minister John Major told the Saudis that if he got involved, the Thatcher wing of his party would devour him and the left would use it to undermine him in upcoming elections.[68] When the Saudis saw the political reality in both Washington and London, they had little option but to back away.

By 1997, the political landscape in the West had changed. In May 1997, Labour Party leader Tony Blair became prime minister and Bill Clinton was just beginning his second—and final—term of office. It was at this point, according to Massoud, that Saudi Arabia saw a chance to overcome the obstacles that had hindered earlier efforts to find a middle ground. Saudi Arabia also understood that their chances at a settled negotiation were still tenuous at best. The Saudis needed a secret weapon; a special individual who was politically unassailable. Massoud explained, "What better symbol than Mandela? He is the epitome of morality."[69]

In October 1997, during a stopover en route to the Commonwealth Heads of Government meeting being held in Edinburgh, Scotland—not far from where the ill-fated airliner had exploded—and at the risk of angering the Western superpowers, Nelson Mandela paid a highly publicized official visit to Libya.[70]

---

*Political minister, Saudi Arabian embassy, Washington, D.C.

When I spoke with Mandela about the trip to Libya, he chuckled and described how, following the announcement of his planned tour to meet with some of his old friends, including Qaddafi, Arafat and Castro, he was strongly advised by Washington that he should not go. He amplified this with a distinct sense of pride mixed with indignation in his voice, saying, "They said, 'Look, don't go to Qaddafi; if you go to Qaddafi, we will take serious action against you.' I said, 'You can do so, I am going to Qaddafi.' The Americans are arrogant, as you know, and I went and nothing happened."[71]

It was during his 1997 visit to Tripoli that Mandela first broached with Qaddafi his suggested compromise: the possibility of a trial of the Lockerbie suspects in a neutral country. In exchange for the surrender of the two Libyan suspects, Mandela told Qaddafi that the United Nations would call an end to its sanctions against Libya. Mandela had already proposed this compromise to President Clinton and Prime Minister Tony Blair, and with Qaddafi's theoretical backing, the formidable African head of state was then able to use the forum of the Edinburgh talks to encourage broader support for the initiative. As a sweetener, on his return from Edinburgh, Mandela presented the colonel with South Africa's highest honor, an Order of Good Hope medal, Gold Class, on October 29.

When Mandela had presented the Good Hope medal to Colonel Qaddafi, while also flattering him as "a moral leader against oppression," he conferred upon the Libyan leader a moral authority, effectively recognizing

Muammar Qaddafi's respect for Mandela was crucial to overcoming the Lockerbie impasse.

a principled stance from which Qaddafi could negotiate. Jakes Gerwel* later confirmed that this was part of Mandela's strategy, saying, "The mistake that many people make about Qaddafi, our government included, is that you'd rather keep him at your side than treat him as this crazy lunatic who doesn't know politics. Mandela understood that perfectly. Qaddafi has a naive side to him; his whole politics are based on this Don Quixote character. So his being decorated by Mandela meant a hell of a lot to him. He trusted us. Doing this was to let him know: we respect you, but then you must keep your word with us, and you must act honorably."[72]

However, propping up Qaddafi's trust was only part of Mandela's strategy. He frequently addressed Qaddafi harshly, demanding that he show respect for the United Nations. The "brother leader's" aides observed that he had never been rebuked like that previously and was astonished by Mandela's harshness.[73] However, in deference to a fellow revolutionary who had matured into a world-respected statesman, the colonel took the criticism on the chin.

It was evident that Mandela's understanding of the need to respect an enemy, a legacy of his time in prison, was to prompt a strategy in the Lockerbie case that was politically and morally sound. It would, in turn, greatly assist the tactical efforts of Bandar and Gerwel, resulting in a successful conclusion to what had been hitherto deemed an impossible mission.

Soon after Mandela presented Qaddafi with the Order of Good Hope medal, twin diplomatic tracks were initiated that would eventually put an end to the Lockerbie deadlock. At the suggestion of Crown Prince Abdullah, Bandar approached the South African leader to express his enthusiasm for the proposed settlement and to offer his assistance; Mandela was quick to accept. When interviewed about the Lockerbie initiative, Gerwel remarked, "We really started negotiations after Mandela's speech in Tripoli. The Saudis approached us to say they were interested, and we thought it would be good if we could work with them because the Saudis are close to the Americans. The Saudis are something of a comforting, conservative presence."

---

*Gert Johannes (Jakes) Gerwel made a significant contribution to South African politics as the Director-General in the office of former President, Nelson Mandela. He was directly responsible for administering Mandela's public life, accompanying him on state visits and serving as an advisor and decision-maker. Prof Gerwel is currently chancellor of Rhodes University, and, inter alia, is Chairperson of the Nelson Mandela Foundation. He has been awarded the Order of the Southern Cross, Gold, presented by President Mandela in 1999; King Abdulaziz Sash, Minister Rank, Saudi Arabia in 1999; Order of Good Deeds, presented by Colonel Muammar Qaddafi of Libya in 1999.

Assessing the merits of this political marriage, Massoud explained, "Looking at this from a political analyst's point of view, the U.S. and U.K. needed to cover their left side flank. That's where Mandela's strength is. Right of center is ours. So we thought between the two of us, we can then claim the political support that will allow the president of the U.S. as well as the prime minister in England to tackle this issue." As Saudi Arabia held the Arab-Islamic card and Mandela had very good relations with Britain, it was perceived that with Bandar's access inside the Beltway, this arcane combination had a good chance of working.[74]

Immediately after, Gerwel teamed up with Bandar to make a series of visits to Libya, the United States, the United Kingdom, and the United Nations—fifteen months of secret talks held without any fanfare. Working together, the prince and Gerwel pieced together the logistical arrangements for the Lockerbie deal. In exchange for the lifting of the U.N. sanctions that were then crippling Libya, the suspects Abdel Basset Ali el-Megrati and Al-Amin Khalifa Fhimah were to be tried by Scottish law in a neutral court in the Netherlands.

In March 1998, President Clinton visited President Mandela (his preferred name now is Madiba*) in Johannesburg. Gerwel recalled, "Clinton

---

*Nelson Mandela is called Madiba in South Africa. The name *Madiba* is an honorary title adopted by older male members of the Mandela clan. For South Africans, though, there is only one Madiba: Nelson Mandela.

Bandar and Nelson Mandela

was on a state visit here and Prince Bandar was in town, too. Madiba had his meeting with President Clinton and raised the Lockerbie issue with him. At one point, we invited Bandar to join that meeting. I thought that it was important for Clinton to hear the true story, as it were. Madiba was a bit surprised to discover that the president of the United States was not really totally informed about the whole thing."

Said Gerwel with a grin, "National Security Adviser Sandy Berger almost had a heart attack over having the president talk on something he hadn't been briefed on before."[75] Gerwel's account was corroborated by Massoud, who was also at the meeting and who later confirmed that the president appeared utterly unaware of the progress that had been made in the Lockerbie negotiations. Massoud explained that by the time of that meeting, Libya already had given a written pledge to accept a trial under Scottish law, and had agreed that the two accused individuals, if convicted, could be imprisoned in Scotland. He said, "The president was not even aware we had these commitments in writing."[76]

Bandar believed that President Bill Clinton may not have been made fully aware of the Mandela Lockerbie initiative by Sandy Berger until the meeting in South Africa. He had previously disclosed that he believed Clinton was not best served by his staff because they were overprotective of their president. When I interviewed Clinton and asked if he had been unaware of a letter written by Mandela to Berger several months earlier about an "in principle agreement" that had been reached with Qaddafi and to which there had been no response, the former president sidestepped the question, neither confirming nor denying. He merely said, "Qaddafi wanted to get it right, but he was in a terrible position at the time because these guys that we had to get given up for trial came from a different tribe. So it was a little bit difficult for him to give them up without him having some political grief within Libya." Clinton explained that he told Mandela that he wanted to lift the sanctions and normalize relations with Libya, assuming a resolution of Lockerbie and the weapons of mass destruction issue. He observed, "But there was no way, no matter how much he was willing to compensate the victims, that we could do it unless the guys were given up to trial."[77]

According to Mandela, in their private meeting he implored President Clinton to bury the hatchet with Cuba and Iran as well. Massoud later explained, "America's image in the region suffered from a policy of sanctions that extended from the Mediterranean to the Bay of Bengal, Lebanon, Syria, Iraq, Iran, Pakistan, and India. There were sanctions on Libya; there were sanctions on the Sudan. We told Clinton, 'For God's sake, you cannot run a foreign policy based on sanctioning people right and left, then basically waiting to see how things work out. You have to engage people; that's the whole concept of what a foreign policy is.'"[78] Clinton's reaction was never disclosed, but the tenor of his foreign policy was to embrace a more engaging style during the remainder of his administration.

The greatest threat to the success of the Lockerbie deal was the climate of suspicion and mistrust that existed between Qaddafi and the West. Although Clinton, Blair, and Qaddafi all agreed in theory to the proposed terms, Britain and America seriously doubted Libyan sincerity and commitment. For his part, Qaddafi was reluctant to risk handing over the suspects, believing the negotiations efforts to be a conspiracy to destroy Libya, convinced that the Western "imperialists" would renege on their side of the bargain.

Throughout the protracted negotiations, Gerwel and Bandar would run into many tricky situations. "I wouldn't want to live in his country; he has some strange ideas about how the world works," Gerwel said. Yet he was convinced that Qaddafi had a robust sense of dignity and pride. "Late into the night, he would call and ask if we could talk again. He was really anguishing with the matter."[79]

During the negotiations, each player applied his individual strengths. Nelson Mandela kept Clinton and Blair on track, while Bandar and Gerwel engaged in the unenviable task of pacifying the increasingly suspicious and often unpredictable Qaddafi. Evidence of that volatility was to surface unexpectedly during an interview with Tony Edwards, who had been responsible for the massive Al-Yamamah contract. Edwards explained how Bandar called him up one afternoon and during the subsequent conversation said, "Do you know where I'm going tomorrow? I'm going to Libya to see Qaddafi, the 'great leader.'" Edwards explained, "He told me all about him—what he's like, how you never know what mood he is in and what he is going to say or what he is going to do, how you have to be very patient and pick the right moment. And he actually tried out on me what he was going to say to him about why he should give up these two people."[80]

At this stage, Bandar's private jet was cutting regular tracks across the globe from South Africa to the United States, Britain, Tunisia, and, in the latter stages, Libya. Throughout this demanding schedule, President Mandela proved to be the vital linchpin that kept everyone at the negotiating table. As we discussed the frequency of visits by Bandar and Gerwel to and from Libya, Gerwel explained that because of the sanctions you couldn't fly directly to Libya. Most of the time he would fly to London, Riyadh, or Jeddah, meet up with Bandar and his aircraft, and together they would fly to Tunisia, at which point they faced a four- or five-hour drive to Tripoli. "It wasn't a fun trip," he exclaimed.[81]

Bandar's son-in-law Prince Faisal bin Turki, who accompanied him on all his trips to Libya during the Lockerbie negotiations, confirmed Gerwel's account of the early missions via Tunisia, "We would take a bus—a five-hour ride to Tripoli—because at that time, with the imposition of U.N. sanctions, the plane couldn't land in Libya." Faisal continued, "Then we would see Qaddafi, but sometimes he would not see us for two days and we just had to hang around."

Talking about Mandela's role, Faisal said, "Jakes would come into the meetings, but he didn't say much; he was in attendance as South Africa's representative in the negotiations. But it needed weight; that's why we had President Mandela; it was because of his status, because he is the elder statesman of the world." Faisal continued, "If Qaddafi tried to wiggle out of something, then Mandela would intervene—you know how outspoken he is." He concluded, "You know it's different when Mandela talks to Qaddafi. Prince Bandar would be polite, he has to be diplomatic; but you know Mandela!"[82]

Recalling the duration of the negotiations, Gerwel believes that he and Bandar must have gone to Tripoli between ten and fifteen times, explaining that most of the meetings were held in tents. On one occasion the tent stood next to the ruins of Qaddafi's official residence, unoccupied since it was hit by a U.S. bomb in an apparent assassination attempt a decade earlier. Gerwel said, "The colonel operates in strange ways. We would arrive in Tripoli and we'd sit there waiting and waiting, and we were drinking little cups of tea all the time. Then we'd suddenly get a message that we were to go to the airport in Tripoli and from there fly to the meeting point. We had various meetings in various places with the colonel, and because he was keeping us on and on late at night, Bandar once said to him, 'We must really bring this matter to a conclusion; it's not fun for Jakes and I to come here.'"[83]

This account was corroborated by Dr. Said Karmi, who recalled how, on one occasion, Qaddafi took Bandar's retinue to a run-down convention center, "It was the pits; they kept the entourage waiting there for hours before they were driven out to a tent located in the desert sometime during the afternoon." He added, "They were supposed to leave that night, but he told them to stay to finish the dialogue, so the team had to stay overnight in the same clothes."[84] Faisal revealed that the Libyans had deliberately bugged their rooms. "They would listen to everything; it was so obvious it was unbelievable. You could see the bugging devices. So Rehab and me would go out and write things down like, 'Let's leave this place,' but then Rehab would say, 'Faisal, you have to be diplomatic.' "[85]

Princess Reema, Bandar's daughter and Faisal's wife, said, "Faisal was very hot-blooded back then, very impatient, very go-go-go, whereas now, nothing fazes him."[86] Faisal confirmed, "Not anymore—that's because of Prince Bandar's influence on me." Referring to the lengthy negotiations with Qaddafi, Faisal stated, "There were more than ten trips; it was a lengthy and thoroughly frustrating process." He then shook his head in disbelief, saying about Qaddafi, "You would convince the guy; he would agree on something and we'd go back, and then he would change his mind. So we would go back again to convince him, and he would change his mind once again. It was annoying, but he [Prince Bandar] delivered in the end."[87]

That onerous process should hardly have been a surprise. Qaddafi—the "brother leader"—often has been described as a naive idealist. Gerwel describes him as "a bit of a strange Don Quixote"; others say he is mercurial, melodramatic, and a deeply religious revolutionary.[88] Yet Bandar was impressed by Qadaffi. "Negotiating with him is a tough task, but he forces you to respect him for he knows what he is talking about. He possesses an unusual ability for raising issues and details that might not be on your mind, only to discover how important they were after you discuss them. That is how he got American and British concessions that might not have been possible."[89]

For sixteen months, diplomacy among Bandar, Gerwel, Mandela, and Qaddafi continued and despite Qaddafi's reservations, Mandela, who had flown to Tripoli especially for the announcement, informed the world on March 19, 1999, that Libya would give the United Nations a firm date for the handing over of the two suspects.

Reciting the events surrounding the practical conclusion of the deal with Qaddafi, Gerwel said, "On the day that Madiba flew into Tripoli, Qaddafi announced [the agreement] to his people, in his typical style, with allegories of the Bible and the Koran, he said, 'If Mandela, Fahd, and Abdullah tell us to give our sons over to be sacrificed, we will do that, because if people do not keep their word they will be dishonoring Mandela and Fahd.' He added chillingly, 'and it will be on the shoulders of Bandar and Jakes!' " Said Gerwel, "The final meeting was after agreement had been reached and Prince Bandar and myself were invited over to Libya, to be there to hand over the two suspects to the United Nations." He recalled, "We actually walked with them to the plane. Typically, Colonel Qaddafi wasn't there," Gerwel explained. "You know, he's a proud man so you wouldn't expect him to be there. We then flew down to a place in the southern desert where we spent a delightful evening with him to conclude the whole matter."

Though Mandela insisted that Gerwel and Bandar played key roles in negotiating the solution, Gerwel was keen to stress the importance of the strength of the personal relationship between Mandela and Qaddafi. "That whole thing was dependent upon Qaddafi's trust of Madiba—nothing would have been achieved without that." He added, "You know it was that tough, because he [Qaddafi] distrusted the West as much as the West mistrusted him, and it was always Mandela's word—we said, 'We can assure you that if Blair says to Madiba he will do x and y, he will do it.' "

To confirm this point, Gerwel prompted Mandela, saying, "You had already spoken to Chirac, George Bush Senior, and Major; you remember you always told me that everybody agreed that there could be a trial in a third country, except Major, who said it would be an insult to the British legal system."[90] Mandela interjected, "Major, although he was an excellent man, was one of the opposition, but we convinced him that at that time Britain should really lead in normalizing relations with Qaddafi. The other person I discussed the matter with was President Clinton because he said to

Prince Sultan, British Prime Minister John Major, and Bandar.

me, 'You can't trust Qaddafi.' I said, 'No, perhaps *you* can't trust him. I have dealt with him, and I can tell you, when he makes a statement, he has got sufficient integrity to know that to depart from that would destroy that integrity.' "[91]

As to whether or not Col. Qaddafi would actually hand over the suspects when the time came, Mandela personally assured the U.S. president, "Yes, I have not the slightest doubt that he would deliver them," to which Clinton replied, "Well, if you think so, then I will just leave it to you."[92]

Qaddafi did deliver the suspects, and in 1999, a court in the Netherlands presided by Scottish judges, found Abdelbaset Ali Mohmed al-Megrahi guilty and sentenced him to life in prison for the 1988 bombing of Pan Am Flight 103 over Lockerbie. Libya acknowledged responsibility for the bombing and offered to pay about $10 million in compensation for each of the two hundred seventy victims.

Of the outcome, Bandar said, "Libya's agreement to hand over the suspects in the Lockerbie affair [brings] to an end a long and painful chapter for the Libyan people as well as for the families of the victims."[93]

The successful conclusion of the Lockerbie negotiations was to open up a new era in Libya's relations with the West. In December 2003, Libya declared that it would no longer pursue its nuclear, chemical or biological ambitions, and threw open its borders to international inspection.

As I delved deeper into Bandar's diplomatic involvements during President Clinton's time in office, it became clear that the flow of information concerning international developments was restricted not only by the administration, but information was also restricted within the administration itself. These internal crossed wires negatively impacted foreign relations and led to Bandar's belief, as reported in *The New Yorker* by Elsa Walsh, that the members of what he perceived as a "weak-dicked" foreign policy team, were either too political or culturally arrogant.[94]

In the final years of Clinton's presidency, the conflict between the Israelis and the Palestinians appeared stalled in a violent, dismal impasse. Anxious to set into motion some form of peace talks, Clinton turned his attention instead to Syria. In January 2000, at the invitation of the president, Israeli Prime Minister Ehud Barak and Syrian president Hafez al-Assad met in Shepherdstown, West Virginia, to resolve the border disputes between Israel and Syria and the continuing violence in Lebanon.

The Shepherdstown talks, however, went nowhere. Barak made demands unacceptable to the Syrians, while Assad asserted that the only outcome acceptable was a complete rollback of Israel territory to pre-1967 borders, the so-called Rabin deposit.

Despite the failure of the Shepherdstown talks, Clinton resolved to bring the Syrians and Israelis together one final time. This time, however, he would ask for help.

"I got a call on a Friday, in March 2000," Bandar recounted. "I was asked, 'Can you come to the White House tomorrow? The president wants to see you.'"

He wondered at the timing of the proposed Saturday morning meeting but promptly agreed. As it was to be held in the Oval Office—a formal visit—he asked who would be attending. Learning that Berger would be there, Bandar told the White House that Rehab Massoud would accompany him. The White House agreed, but stressed, "Please keep this to yourself—don't tell the State Department or anybody else."

Immediately upon his arrival, Bandar was asked by Clinton to deliver a message to Assad.

Bandar asked, "Is this a message I should give as an impression? Or as a message straight from you to Assad?"

"No," said Clinton, "from me to him."

"Okay," replied Bandar, "but if it's a message from you to him directly, please repeat the message because I don't want to freelance. If it's a general impression and I have to work my way through it, that's one thing; if it's from you to him directly, Rehab will take it down."

So Massoud took Clinton's message down. Then Berger again told Bandar, "Don't tell the State Department."

Bandar left for Riyadh that very night to confer with Crown Prince Abdullah. The message he was to deliver was designed by Clinton to persuade Syrian President Hafez al-Assad to attend a summit in Geneva as a prelude to a larger plan for peace between Israel and the Arab states. The message was that if Assad agreed to come back to the table one final time, Clinton would guarantee an Israeli withdrawal from the Golan Heights to the borders taken during the 1967 war. However, Clinton said, Barak's agreement was predicated on a cessation of the violence in South Lebanon. The choice of Bandar as message bearer was in itself strategic: Ehud Barak already had secretly endorsed the prince's involvement, and Assad was known to trust Saudi Arabia, and especially Bandar.

At his meeting with Assad, when Bandar brought the subject around to the fighting in South Lebanon, Assad smiled and said that he thought they could take care of the problem.[95] Having done as requested, Bandar conveyed Assad's consent to the U.S. terms to Berger and returned to Washington believing that perhaps the peace process was making headway at last.

Yet, despite a three-hour meeting between Clinton and Assad in Geneva, no agreement was reached: Clinton's proposals were dismissed out of hand by the Syrian leader. The talks collapsed so completely that the crown prince, fearing Assad would believe the Saudis were conspiring in some way to undermine Syria, immediately dispatched Bandar to speak with him. At that meeting, Bandar learned that he had been used by Clinton, that the message he had passed to Assad—Clinton's assurance that he had Barak's agreement to an Israeli pull-back to the pre-1967 borders—had been a ruse simply to get the Syrians back to the table. Clinton had had no confirmation that Barak would agree to such terms. Not only had he misled the Syrians, he had similarly deceived the Israelis, suggesting that Assad was ready to negotiate, knowing all along Assad's rigid position.

Assad said to Bandar, "Clinton knows what I want. God knows he knows what I want—we have spoken fifteen times!"

For his part, on returning from his meeting with Assad, Bandar said, "To hell with this administration." Yet, even at this point, Bandar had no idea quite how dramatically the channels of communication had been severed within American corridors of power.

Amazingly, Secretary Albright had been utterly unaware

Madeline Albright greets Crown Prince Abdullah during her visit to the kingdom.

of the prince's secret mission to Syria and of the message he had been tasked to deliver. Equally in the dark was her Middle Eastern special envoy Dennis Ross, who had negotiated with Barak on Albright's behalf. Nonetheless, in his book *The Missing Peace,* Dennis Ross wrote, "We asked Prince Bandar to see Assad and maybe Assad misunderstood what Prince Bandar said, or Prince Bandar misunderstood what we were saying."[96]

Reading Ross's secondhand account of the prince's remit at the meeting with Clinton and Berger, Bandar responded with aggravation, "What's this 'we' shit?! He didn't know at the time that I had been asked to do this!"

Days after the Geneva summit, Bandar met with Albright, who had just returned from London, for dinner in Washington. Bandar recalled, "During the meal we laughed as she explained that when in England to give a lecture she encountered Lord Levy, a fund raiser for Tony Blair and his personal envoy on the Middle East. He said to her, 'I am having a dinner party; I have Duke so-and-so coming to the dinner; I have Lord so-and-so coming; Minister so-and-so coming and I would like you to come, Madame Secretary.' Laughing heartily, Madeline told me, 'I thought he was obnoxious and was dropping names, and so I enjoyed telling him, 'Well, I'm very sorry your lordship, but I can't; I'm having dinner tomorrow with a prince in Washington.' "

As the meal progressed, the conversation turned to the failure of the Geneva talks, which Albright had attended. She was clearly annoyed with Assad and told Bandar that before the talks Assad had continually demanded to know what Barak's bottom line was. Eventually, Dennis Ross had been sent to find out. Bandar realized from Albright's comments that Assad had been trying to ascertain whether Clinton had been successful in putting pressure on Barak to withdraw from the Golan Heights to the June 4, 1967, borders. That is, after all, what Clinton knew Assad wanted, and it was the substance of his message to the Syrian leader conveyed by Bandar.

As the prince stressed, "The core of my message from Clinton to Assad was that Clinton said, 'I know what you want. I am going to work with Barak. If I get from Barak what I think will meet your needs, I will ask for a summit between you and me.' So the code was, either I would get a call to say, 'Okay, let's have a summit,' and I would get the Syrians to come, or to say, 'Let's not have a summit, let's talk some more.' The message I got was, 'Let's have a summit,' which meant to Assad we have a deal. So Assad came to the meeting in Geneva thinking that he had a deal with Clinton."

It was not difficult to deduce from Assad's actions in Geneva that the original offer was no longer on the table, due to whatever failed negotiations had taken place between Barak and the United States. However, what stunned Bandar was the fact that Albright appeared oblivious to the fact that Clinton's explicit promises had been delivered to Assad as an incentive to him to attend the Geneva summit.

Secretary Albright explained that the decision had been made to send Ross to Israel to secure Barak's agreement to adhere to the Rabin deposit. Yet it was evident to Bandar that Albright was completely unaware of his assignment in Syria. When he informed her of his trip, her response was one of utter shock: "That fucking Sandy Berger lied to me. I am gonna crucify him!" she exclaimed. "I can't believe it—you mean, you went to see Assad?"

Bandar replied, "Yes."

"This explains to me Assad's reaction," Albright responded. Referring to Assad's refusal to negotiate at all, she said, "I was so angry at him because his reaction was so stupid—that he fooled the president."

Bandar called Ross the next day to explain what had happened at his meeting with Albright. Bandar insisted that after his conversations with Albright and Ross, both of them confirmed to him that only then did they understand why that summit failed.

As note taker during Bandar's meeting with President Clinton and Sandy Berger, Rehab Massoud confirmed that he had written a contemporaneous note confirming the president's explicit assurance that he would confirm that Barak's promise to agree to the June 4, 1967, line—the Rabin deposit—referred to by President Clinton as "the Rabin pocket commitment."[97]

Rehab Massoud at a press conference in the Saudi Embassy in Washington, D.C.

The New Yorker reported, however, that "A spokesman for the Clinton administration said that neither Clinton nor Berger could specifically recall the Oval Office meeting, saying, 'It is true that we asked for Bandar's help on this with Assad, but it is not true that Clinton said he could deliver the 1967 borders.'"[98] In contrast, Bandar's assessment of the administration's stance was blunt. "The Clinton people decided to have it both ways. They say they have tried and that the failure was because of the other side; what I'm saying is that it failed because they did not coordinate their message, and that was not the first time."

During my interview with President Clinton, I asked him why the State Department had been shielded from knowledge of this initiative, he responded, "I don't remember that. Sandy and Bandar might remember it, but I don't remember that."

According to Clinton, the Geneva summit failure was far more banal. "What really happened," he said, "was that everybody's timing was off. We had a chance to make a peace in January 2000 when Barak wanted to meet. He basically dictated the time and he decided that he wasn't going to get anything done with Arafat and wanted to do Syria first." The president was referring to Barak's plan to secure peace with Syria—a move that has been interpreted as a way, if successful, of isolating the PLO leader and buying yet more time that would delay the implementation of the Oslo Accords "Land for Peace" deal that Israel had repeatedly attempted to renegotiate.

While assurances had been given to Assad by both Barak and Secretary Albright that the Rabin deposit would be tabled at the January 2000 talks in Shepherdstown, West Virginia, Barak had reneged on his assurances and introduced modifications that seriously undermined the peace talks.

With regard to those events, Clinton was highly critical of Barak, explaining how he told him that they were running

Israeli Prime Minister Ehud Barak

out of time because Assad wasn't going to help him. Clinton believed that Assad wouldn't endanger his son's succession. By the time Barak arrived at Shepherdstown, he was under a lot of pressure in Israel. Clinton observed, "He [Barak] decided that he had to stay there a week before he could make any concessions, which was a terrible insult to the Syrians, who had agreed to come during Ramadan to this cold town in West Virginia. They [the Israelis] just mishandled it. Then, [in Geneva] when Barak was finally willing to make what I thought was a pretty credible offer which could quickly have led to a solution, he [Assad] wouldn't even hear of it. But I could tell then that it was more a question of timing than anything else."

In a final attempt to explain Assad's rationale for withdrawing from the Geneva summit, Clinton explained that Assad died about ten weeks later, and ventured that Assad was afraid that if he died leaving a compromise agreement that only he would have been strong enough to pull off, his son, Bashir al-Assad, would barely have been in power. The president suggested that the dying Assad saw unacceptable risks for his son, "as the Alawite tribe was in the minority and they depended upon the military for their support. It was really tragic because they could have done that deal but both of their timings were off."[99]

Bandar was more specific. Clinton had given Assad an unequivocal assurance that Barak would agree to an Israeli withdrawal from all Syrian land held by Israel since 1967 and then failed to deliver.

With the election of George W. Bush in November 2000, Bandar was optimistic that there again would be a White House dedicated to an active foreign policy. An administration populated by many of President George H. W. Bush's cabinet promised a return to a sound working relationship between the United States and Saudi Arabia. However, the character of George W. Bush's administration was to present new challenges for Bandar.

There can be no denying that the Saudi-U.S relationship is tethered securely to oil and security, and that these factors have had an inherent impact on peace in the Middle East. As a citizen of both cultures, Bandar has played a fundamental role in the various peace initiatives that have emerged during his time as ambassador to the United States. However, late in August 2001, the prince's position made him the messenger for perhaps one of the most dangerous and challenging episodes in the history of U.S.-Saudi relations.

In response to President Bush's frequent meetings with Prime Minister Ariel Sharon and his refusal to meet with Yasser Arafat, Crown Prince Abdullah had refused repeated requests to visit the White House. In a June 2001 interview with *The Financial Times*, Abdullah castigated the Bush administration, suggesting that the American role in resolving the Middle East crisis had become so passive that it was now up to the Saudis to provide leadership.[100]

Abdullah had been incensed by President Bush's statement that "The Israelis will not negotiate under terrorist threat, simple as that; and if the Palestinians are interested in a dialogue, then I strongly urge Mr. Arafat to put 100 percent effort into . . . stopping the terrorist activity. And I believe he can do a better job of doing that."[101]

The acting Saudi head of state construed these remarks as a pardon for Israel and an unfair censure of the Palestinians. His anger mounted after viewing the distressing footage of the Israeli incursion into the West Bank on August 23, which showed an Israeli soldier holding a Palestinian woman to the ground by putting his boot on her head.

Abdullah's reaction was emotive, immediate, and severe. He called Bandar, who was at home in Aspen watching the same televised report.[102] The crown prince instructed him to deliver personally a twenty-five page letter of ultimatum to the president. It said, "We believe there has been a strategic decision by the United States that its national interest in the Middle East is 100 percent based on [Israeli Prime Minister Ariel] Sharon. This is America's right, but Saudi Arabia cannot accept the decision. Starting from today, you're from Uruguay, as they say. 'You [Americans] go your way; I [Saudi Arabia] go my way. From now on, we will protect our national interests, regardless of where America's interests lie in the region.' "[103]

The Bush administration was knocked sideways by Abdullah's message. It threatened to destroy the valuable friendship between America and Saudi Arabia, because of what Abdullah felt was, at worst, disinterest and, at best, bias toward Israel. The crown prince threatened the termination of law enforcement and intelli-

Like brothers—George W. and Bandar Bush.

gence cooperation with the United States, as well as the rethinking of their active military agreements. The change of climate was immediate: the Saudi chief of staff returned to Riyadh only a day after landing in Washington, and without meeting with any U.S. officials and forty senior Saudi officers canceled a trip to Washington, which had been set up to discuss the annual review of military relations.

An invitation to Abdullah to visit the United States was immediately rebuffed. Prince Turki Al-Faisal* said pithily, "That got their attention."[104]

The Bush administration was forced to rapidly rethink its approach to the Middle East peace process. So severe had been the rupture between the U.S. administration and the House of Saud that the *New York Times* reported that President George H. W. Bush—himself much revered in Saudi Arabia—spoke to Abdullah in an attempt to assure him that his son, the president, would do the right thing because "his heart is in the right place."[105]

Within thirty-six hours of delivering Abdullah's letter to Bush, Bandar returned to Riyadh to deliver Bush's response to the crown prince, a two-page letter promising movement on the Middle East.[106] The letter's contents were precisely what the Saudis had long been seeking—evidence of a humane American president with an even-handed approach to the Israeli-Palestinian crisis. Moreover, the letter promised a workable vision of peace that supported the creation of a Palestinian state and decried all acts of violence against both Israelis and Palestinians.

Bush's businesslike letter was said by Saudi officials to include the statement: "I reject this extraordinary, un-American bias whereby the blood of an Israeli child is more expensive and holy than the blood of a Palestinian child. I reject people who say when you kill a Palestinian, it is defense; when a Palestinian kills an Israeli, it's a terrorist act."[107]

The letter was pure dynamite to the top echelons of Saudi society, and Bush's credibility rocketed within the kingdom. Reading between the lines, Bandar was convinced that the position of the Bush administration in the letter to Abdullah could not have been developed in just thirty-six hours. He said, "This must have been something the administration was thinking about, that they just didn't share with everybody [but] were waiting for the right time."

---

*Former ambassador to London and current Saudi ambassador to the United States. He is also Bandar's brother-in-law.

Abdullah showed the president's response to other Arab leaders, including the Egyptian and Syrian presidents, and the king of Jordan, and he summoned Arafat to Riyadh to read Bush's letter. Bandar was immediately directed to reconstruct U.S.-Saudi relations, a welcome task after the fire he had been ordered to light under his friends in the White House. Sources recall that when officials told him, "Hey, you guys scared us," the prince quipped, "The hell with you—we scared ourselves!"

Bandar also carried with him from Riyadh Abdullah's hope that the president would say in public that which he had put in his letter. He was expecting that the letter's contents would be converted into policy. By way of reassuring the president as to the strength of his letter and the Arab world's support for his sentiment, a written pledge from Arafat to satisfy Bush's demands to revive the peace talks also was sent back to Washington.

According to the *Washington Post*, Bandar was euphoric and declared, "Suddenly I felt the same feeling I had as we were going to Madrid, that we really were going to have a major initiative here that could save all of us from ourselves, mostly, and from each other."[108]

Days later, fifteen Saudi hijackers, together with four other members of al-Qaeda, flew two airliners into the twin towers of the World Trade Center in New York.

Along with 2,752 American lives, so too died the chance of peace in the Middle East. Any hopes of a freshly backed Middle East peace process were buried in the rubble of Ground Zero. Bandar mourned, "I cannot imagine a way to do more damage or worse damage to Islam or to Saudi Arabia."

TEN

9/11: CATACLYSM

I will surely cast him [the unbeliever] into the Fire.
Would that you knew what the fire is like!
It leaves nothing, it spares no one; it burns the skins of men.
It is guarded by nineteen keepers.

QUR'AN, SURA 74:30–31

Fact: fifteen of the nineteen terrorists who carried out the cataclysmic and heinous attacks of September 11, 2001, were Saudis.

The established dynamics of international relationships were set aside at a stroke as America felt a pain that is still tangible today. Bandar and Saudi Arabia were suddenly in the dock, facing media accusations about their alleged involvement in the odious crime.

At news of the attacks, Bandar and the Saudis reeled in shock. Their first reaction was that it was inconceivable that any of the nineteen hijackers might have been Saudis.[1] Once the devastating truth was confirmed, the kingdom responded with stunned disbelief to their possible involvement in a horrendous act of terrorism. The Saudis even resorted to pointing out that the 9/11 hijackers were men from "the South" and from a tribal grouping with strong Yemeni connections; they were not "good Saudis."[2] That incongruous defense was derisively brushed aside.

The Saudis metaphorically circled their wagons and, having ceded the initiative to a suddenly and understandably hostile Western press, attempted to defend themselves from wave after wave of criticism. As point man in Washington, Bandar tried to fend off the media while devising a Saudi strategy to meet the increasing threat facing U.S.-Saudi relations. But the climate of mistrust continued to grow.

As accusations of complicity and blame exploded in the media, the cultural divergences between the desert kingdom and the United States were thrown into sharp relief. As *Time* magazine reflected, "the absence of democracy, freedom of speech, women's equality, and religious diversity in the kingdom don't endear it to Americans as a lovable ally."[3] Even supporters of the kingdom wrote, "It's an authoritarian regime. Its human rights record is abysmal. It has no freedom of religion. It treats women abominably. It punishes criminals with amputations and beheadings. The government is sometimes cooperative, sometimes not, in assisting the United States in fighting terrorism."[4] The inflamed climate in the United States, the horror of 9/11, the desire for revenge for almost three thousand dead Americans— all now focused on Saudi participation in this outrageous attack.

That fifteen of the nineteen hijackers were Saudis instantly painted the kingdom as a hotbed of terrorism, and the American public demanded an apology. It would fall to Bandar to express Saudi outrage at the al-Qaeda attack and condolences for those lost in this monstrous act of terrorism. He was explicit in his condemnation, saying, "In twenty years, I have never had a more painful and shocking event that happened in my life compared to 9/11. And 9/11 was a tragedy by all measures, but it also was evil."[5] Bandar's comments, however, were quickly lost in a widespread American sense of shock and a desire for retribution.

The perception that Saudi Arabia had a case to answer, that it had been complacent in addressing the terrorist threat, that it wasn't doing enough, had quickly taken root in the United States. A lawsuit filed by over six hundred families of victims of the September 11 attacks attempted to link two leading members of the Saudi royal family to

Saudi hijackers crashed two planes into the World Trade Center on September 11, 2001.

9/11. Affidavits and testimonies included in that lawsuit stated that the Saudis had paid off bin Laden, following attacks against U.S. forces in Saudi Arabia, including the Khobar bombing. In London, the *Sunday Times* claimed that this amounted to $300 million in "protection money," paid to Osama bin Laden's al-Qaeda terror network and the Taliban government in Afghanistan.[6]

On September 13, 2001, only two days after the attacks, President George W. Bush smoked a cigar on the Truman balcony of the White House with Bandar. The press went wild. Bush was excoriated for speaking with the Arab ambassador. Hints of a conspiracy abounded. Most assumed that the subject of discussion on the Truman balcony that evening was the imminent departure of the flights that extracted 148 Saudi nationals so soon after 9/11—some of whom were members of the bin Laden family— an operation initiated by Bandar at the request of King Fahd.

Bandar subsequently rejected speculation that he had discussed this evacuation with the President that night on the Truman balcony. During an interview with Tim Russert on *Meet the Press*, Bandar explained that he made the request to evacuate Saudi nationals directly to the FBI. Once he had its permission, he made a call to the National Security Council's national coordinator on counterterrorism, Richard Clarke, who said, "I have no problem if the FBI has no problem," and so it was authorized.

While this Saudi move may have been well intentioned, it was quickly interpreted as not merely being insensitive, but potentially criminal in character, whisking out potential terrorists before they could be interrogated by the security services. At Crown Prince Abdullah's behest, in organizing the removal of the bin Laden family members, Bandar unwittingly had spawned a series of spurious conspiracy allegations.

Justifying the removal of the Saudi nationals, Bandar explained, "We had those people in the country; a lot of them were relatives of the bin Laden family going to school, some teenagers, some people in college. We asked the FBI [for permission to evacuate them]. Those people were scattered all over America and with tempers high at that time, rightly so, we were worried that someone getting emotional would hurt them. The other airplanes were for Saudi officials who were here on vacation. After this disaster took place, they all had to go back home to official positions."[7]

Reacting to press speculation that these flights in some way signaled a complex Bush-Saudi conspiracy, Bandar argued, "Think about it logically. Do you think we are in a 'banana republic,' where I could take 148 Saudis and put them in an aircraft and smuggle them out and nobody would know?" Nonetheless, his denial of any conspiracy fell on deaf media ears.

Bandar would later take comfort in the findings of the 9/11 Commission on the bin Laden flights, saying, "The 9/11 Commission released a statement that says the FBI concluded that nobody, *nobody* was allowed to depart on these six flights who the FBI wanted to interview in connection with 9/11 attacks, or who the FBI later concluded had any involvement in the attacks. The statement also says that the Saudi flights were screened by law enforcement officials primarily, but also by the FBI to ensure that people on these flights did not pose a threat to the national security."

"Nobody of interest to the FBI with regard to the 9/11 investigation was allowed to leave the country," Bandar stressed. "The tragedy . . . is that the 9/11 Commission says this, the FBI says this, and you still get people coming up with books that say that they smuggled them."[8]

Reinforcing this message, Bandar set out in a press release how Saudi Arabia had been exonerated by the Commission, "Despite accusations by Craig Unger, Michael Moore, and others, the post-9/11 flights that repatriated Saudi citizens, including members of the bin Laden family, were investigated by the FBI and 'no one with known links to terrorism departed on these flights.'"

The release continued, "According to the 9/11 Commission: 'First, we found no evidence that any flights of Saudi nationals, domestic or international, took place before the reopening of national airspace on the morning of September 13, 2001. To the contrary, every flight we have identified occurred after national airspace reopened. Second, we found no evidence of

A somber Bandar and Foreign Minister Saud al-Faisal at a press conference on 9/19/01.

political intervention. . . . None of the officials we interviewed recalled any intervention or direction on this matter from any political appointee. Third, we believe that the FBI conducted a satisfactory screening of Saudi nationals who left the United States on charter flights. The Saudi government was advised of and agreed to the FBI's requirements that passengers be identified and checked against various databases before the flights departed. The Federal Aviation Administration representative working in the FBI operations center made sure that the FBI was aware of the flights of Saudi nationals and was able to screen the passengers before they were allowed to depart.' "

The press release emphasized, "The FBI interviewed all persons of interest on these flights prior to their departures. They concluded that none of the passengers was connected to the 9/11 attacks and have since found no evidence to change that conclusion. Our own independent review of the Saudi nationals involved confirms that no one with known links to terrorism departed on these flights."[9]

As to what was said between Bandar and the president, the prince replied that in line with diplomatic convention, "unless and until the president of the United States gave his permission to release the content, I am unable to talk about it."[10]

The climate of U.S.-Saudi relations had been severely damaged. On Capitol Hill, to praise Saudi Arabia was to invite criticism. As Ambassador Freeman said when commenting on the current state of affairs in the United States, "To say anything kind about Saudi Arabia is to invite a reprimand. To say anything unkind about it is to win points."[11] The U.S. "Saudi bashing" by Congress and the U.S. media, and the reciprocal "U.S. bashing" by Saudi opinion leaders and media, was largely destructive in character. Exaggerated reporting and biased conspiracy allegations hurt both countries and helped the extremists.[12] There was impatience with Saudi Arabia, and a compulsion to somehow hold it accountable for terrorism worldwide and, in particular, for the events of September 11.

Ambassador Richard Murphy noted that the attacks had sparked a steady stream of accusations against Riyadh, as long-harbored Washington resentment against Saudi Arabia bubbled to the surface.[13]

But following Bandar's formal condemnation of the terrorist atrocities of 9/11 and statement that not only was the kingdom not involved in those attacks, but that Saudi Arabia would do whatever it took to defeat al-Qaeda and terrorism, came a damaging statement from the Saudi Minister of Interior Prince Nayef. Nayef claimed that Zionists were responsible for the 9/11 terrorist attacks, saying, "We put [up] big question marks and ask who committed the events of September 11 and who benefited from events of 9/11? I think [the Zionists] are behind these events."[14] This astonishing allegation incensed the United States. In an interview about 9/11, Tim Russert reminded Bandar that Crown Prince Abdullah, too, had said on Saudi television that Zionists were behind the attacks. Bandar stated categorically, "The Zionists were not behind it. 9/11 shook us to the roots. It's an evil work done by evil people who were targeting your country but also targeting the relationship between our two countries."

But the damage had been done.

Allegations about Saudi complicity in 9/11 continued to be made. Had members of the Saudi family supported the attack by al-Qaeda? Had Saudi Arabia bought off al-Qaeda to protect the kingdom from terrorist attacks?[15] Were charitable donations within Saudi Arabia reaching terrorists? Were Saudi-funded Madrassas (the Islamic educational establishments) preaching an anti-Jewish culture of hate and providing a fertile breeding ground for terrorists? Was the kingdom failing to cooperate with the CIA and FBI? The tenor of the media coverage emitted the ugly scent of intolerance—both cultural and religious.

Bandar repeatedly sought to distance the Islamic faith from Osama bin Laden, al-Qaeda, and 9/11, saying, "I can assure you those nineteen evil human beings who committed that crime on 9/11 do not represent Islam."[16] The suggestion of Saudi complicity in September 11 was sharply countered by Bandar, who said, "The idea that the Saudi government funded, organized, or even knew about September 11 is malicious and blatantly false."[17] Bandar also stated, "On September 9 or 10, 2001, the people that Saudi Arabia called 'terrorists,' the United States and European countries generally called 'dissidents.' On September 12, 2001, the United States and Europe called those same people 'terrorists' and asked, 'Why aren't we doing anything about it?' "[18] In a belated explanation of the challenges facing the Saudis, Bandar asked, "The priority became: where do we concentrate? Fighting the terrorists, or trying to grab their money, or explaining to the American people our position, etc."[19]

Conspiracy theories were given additional credence when a congressional report on 9/11, while exonerating Saudi Arabia and stating, "We found no evidence that the Saudi government as an institution, or senior officials within the Saudi government, funded al-Qaeda," had pages blanked out. Senator Pat Roberts (R-KS), chairman of the Senate Select Committee on

Intelligence, said that twenty-eight pages in the nine-hundred-page report were redacted to avoid embarrassing Saudi Arabia.[20]

Asking that the White House reveal the content of these pages, Bandar said, "First we were criticized by 'unnamed sources.' Now we are being criticized with blank pieces of paper. In a nine-hundred-page report, twenty-eight blanked-out pages are being used by some to malign our country and our people. Saudi Arabia has nothing to hide. We can deal with questions in public, but we cannot respond to blank pages."[21]

At the heart of the twenty-eight pages was believed to be a discussion about the links between the fifteen Saudi hijackers and the Saudi government and its agents. It was speculated that the pages probably referred to the financial backing that senior Saudi princes were reported to have given Osama bin Laden from the mid-1990s—funding that presumably contributed in some measure to al-Qaeda's choice of U.S. rather than Saudi targets. It was also believed that the pages contained intelligence gathered clandestinely, perhaps through another foreign intelligence service. To reveal the information might have compromised ongoing operations. In refusing to disclose this information, President Bush simply said that publishing the pages "would help the enemy."[22]

Suspicions about the Gulf kingdom simply intensified.[23] When *Agence France-Presse* revealed that the top-secret pages related to a Saudi policy of supporting fundamentalism, apathy toward al-Qaeda's terror network despite U.S. warnings, and a suggestion that Omar al-Bayoumi, an associate of two of the hijackers, could have been a Saudi government agent, the kingdom took another hit.[24] Yet Bandar insisted, "al-Qaeda is a cult that is seeking to destroy Saudi Arabia as well as the United States. By what logic would we support a cult that is trying to kill us?"[25] Despite the apparent exoneration of Saudi Arabia in the Commission report, conspiracy theories would not disappear.

One U.S. official said, "It's really damning. What it says is that not only Saudi entities or nationals are implicated in 9/11, but the [Saudi] government as well." This would seem to be confirmed by Adel al-Jubeir, a chief Saudi spokesman, who said in an interview that there were thousands of members of the royal family, and that while an internal government investigation has uncovered "wrongdoing by some," such lapses are certainly not part of any government conspiracy.[26] *New Republic* took it further, saying the blanked section outlines "connections between the hijacking plot and the very top levels of the Saudi royal family." It also quoted an anonymous official as saying, "There's a lot more in the twenty-eight pages than money. Everyone's chasing the charities. They should be chasing direct links to high levels of the Saudi government. We're not talking about rogue elements. We're talking about a coordinated network that reaches right from the hijackers to multiple places in the Saudi government. If the twenty-eight pages were to be made public, I have no question that the entire relationship with Saudi Arabia would change overnight."[27]

But that relationship already had changed. As Bandar said, "I saw everything I've done in this country for eighteen years collapse right in front of my eyes."[28]

Despite exoneration from the bipartisan 9/11 Commission, the shock waves resulting from the horrific al-Qaeda terrorist attacks that destroyed the World Trade Center in New York and damaged the Pentagon in Washington, D.C., continued to reverberate, with the U.S. media at its epicenter, stirring up a sandstorm of anti-Saudi sentiment. In a widely read Seymour Hersh expose in *The New Yorker*, he alleged, supported by leaks from an anonymous U.S. "intelligence official" that the Saudi regime had "gone to the dark side."[29]

On op-ed pages in newspapers all over the country, indignant pundits picked up the refrain.[30] Stories about Bandar's moment on the Truman balcony, conspiracies conceived from Bush-Saud business links, notably via the Carlyle Group,* and the exodus of the bin Laden family members triggered a wave of denunciations about the alleged perfidy of the Saudi royal family in the war on terrorism.[31]

In his film, *Fahrenheit 9/11*, Michael Moore hammered on the relationship between Bandar and the Bush family. Moore's film and its perceived suppression prior to the upcoming election campaign, smacked of media sensationalism. President Bush, it was said, and his good friend, Bandar, "the ambassador known to the family as Bandar Bush, have tried to cover up the extent of Saudi involvement in terrorism. But the reality, revealed by Mr. Moore, is that Mr. Bush . . . is deeply enmeshed, financially and personally, with foreign elites—with the Saudis in particular."[32]

The Bandar-Bush relationship was repeatedly portrayed in the U.S. media as an obstacle to justice and the war on terrorism. "As long as the Bushies are in control, no one will call a spade a spade or a fig a fig. The Saudi royal family sponsors and spreads terrorism and that must end."[33]

---

*The Carlyle Group is a global private equity firm. As of 9/11, former Secretary of State James Baker was the senior counsel, and George H.W. Bush was a senior adviser.

In the raft of publicity that followed his film, Moore was to state that he did not set out to make a political movie. However, he let his guard down when interviewed by a hostile Matt Lauer on NBC's *Dateline*. When asked, "Isn't this film a direct attack on George W. Bush?" Moore admitted with a chuckle, "Well, if you put it that way, yes, of course it is."

At this time, a lone voice of sanity endeavored to make itself heard in an increasingly strident anti-Saudi climate. In an e-mail exchange with the committed anti-Bush, House of Saud opponent, Craig Unger,* Rachel Bronson attempted to explain the background to the meeting between the president and Bandar on the Truman balcony immediately after 9/11: "Let's just make sure the facts are right. The 9/13 meeting was planned before 9/11. Over the summer of 2001, the Saudi and American governments were engaged in a rip-roaring fight over Bush's policy toward Israel. In August 2001, the Saudi crown prince threatened to sever relations. Bush responded with a letter to the crown prince stating that he believed the Palestinians should have a state. . . . The Sept. 13 meeting was set up to talk about Israel/Palestinian issues. That agenda was obviously scrapped after 9/11. There were more immediate problems to speak about."[34]

The media plays an immense role in developments on the world stage. It is largely responsible for the exploitation of the cultural chasm and resulting ignorance and misinterpretation between Saudi Arabia and the United States. Bandar reflected on this complex situation in a lighthearted way when he said, "We're different cultures; the president drops his dog—it's headline news everywhere in America. Then at night it's analyzed—did he drop it intentionally? Was he grabbing its ears? Did he kick it? I have no problem with that. After twenty years, I enjoy listening to these things." The reporting styles in the United States and Saudi Arabian media are very different. Whereas the Western media examined the measures taken post-9/11 in great detail, highly significant items of news are fleetingly reported in the kingdom and can escape the attention of the Western media altogether. Bandar explained, "In Saudi Arabia, did we catch the 5 percent who were really doing the bad things, the 5 percent who were the rotten 5 percent? Yes. End of discussion, it's no more news. Let's just get on with our

---

*In his article, "Saving the Saudis," for *Vanity Fair* in October 2003, Craig Unger had been highly critical of, among other things, the removal of the Saudi nationals immediately after September 11. He is also the author of *House of Bush, House of Saud: The Secret Relationship Between the World's Two Most Powerful Dynasties* (New York: Scribner, 2004).

lives; whoever needs punishment should get it; whoever repents should be brought back into society. My point is: we express ourselves differently."

The danger arises when the media becomes biased and begins reporting solely on what it wants to hear. A frustrated Bandar commented on the impact of this upon his country, "What kills us is that the president of the United States of America says, 'They are our friends and they cooperate.' The secretary of state, the secretary of defense, the national security adviser, director of the CIA, director of the FBI, secretary of the treasury [say the same] and that's not news. A senior official in the FBI said, 'The Saudis are not cooperating,' and that is news. You ask yourself sometimes, 'Who's running this goddamn government?' "[35]

This point was succinctly reinforced by Robert Jordan, the U.S. ambassador to Saudi Arabia, who expressed his frustration at the media, saying he was "tired of reading misleading U.S. news reports about a lack of Saudi cooperation in the war on terrorism." He described those reports as untrue and accused some American reporters of seeking a fall guy.[36]

What the media got, instead, was a fall woman. It was revealed that checks signed by Bandar's wife, Princess Haifa, and delivered as charitable aid to Jordanian mother of six, Majida Ibrahim Ahmad, were in fact cashed and used to finance two of the 9/11 terrorists—Khalid Almihdhar and Nawaf Alhazmi.[37]

The unearthing of this bombshell caused uproar. This money, which was intended to defray the costs of treatment of Ahmad's thyroid condition, had apparently been diverted to al-Qaeda "advance man" Omar al-Bayoumi via Osama Basnan,[38] Saudi husband of the designated receiver. Bandar sent the initial cost of the operation as a $15,000 gift of aid in April 1998, and Haifa covered the cost of follow-up treatments with checks of $2,000 a month starting in November 1999 and ending in May 2002.[39] Neither Bandar nor his wife had ever met the woman.

It may sound extraordinary to Western ears that such sums might change hands so arbitrarily. However, as one critic explained, "Charitable contributions to the needy are an admirable obligation of Muslims, enshrined in the Qur'an; and Princess Haifa and her husband have dumpsters of money to hand out."[40] A devout Muslim, Haifa explained, "Our religion tells us to donate to the needy, and it is the kind of thing you don't announce; you just help, and it counts for you."[41]

At the time, Saudi embassy secretary Mimi Burke reflected, "Haifa was dragged through the press—it was horrible."[42] A mother of eight and grandmother of two, she was perhaps one of the most vulnerable targets the press could have preyed upon. Contrary to her husband's larger-than-life persona, Haifa chooses not to attend state dinners and avoids being photographed for cultural reasons; Victor Shipley, editor of the *Washington Diplomat*, reported that Saudi officials traditionally requested that the Princess not be photographed by his paper at public events.[43]

Severely shaken by the all-too-public events surrounding her charitable work, Haifa told the *New York Times*, "The least I can say is that I am outraged when people think I can be connected to terrorists, when all I wanted to do was give some help to someone in need."[44] Haifa had good reason for her deeply felt indignation. In a statement, she explained, "I find accusations that I contributed funds to terrorists outrageous and completely irresponsible. My father, King Faisal, was killed in a terrorist act.* This is a time for people to come together to combat the scourge of terrorism so that others will not suffer the loss of loved ones."[45]

Despite Haifa's protestations, the press remained obdurate and brutal. In a typical vitriolic outburst, Matt Welch wrote in Canada's *National Post*, "I hereby nominate the first candidates for expulsion from the country: Prince Bandar bin Sultan, Saudi ambassador to the United States, and his wife, Princess Haifa al Faisal."[46]

Of Haifa's pain at the episode, Mimi Burke recalled, "It was so difficult to get through that one year, but she really kept at the Mosaic Foundation's charitable interests; she really turned that around and made it such a great platform for all the Middle East after 9/11." Princess Haifa heads the Mosaic Foundation, which was founded in 1998 by the wives of Arab ambassadors. It raises funds for U.S. and international causes. Burke added, "Everyone rallied behind her and showed their support; it just meant so much to her."[47] Yet even this was to have negative repercussions in the press, when it was discovered that Barbara Bush and Alma Powell, both close friends of Haifa, had called to express their support and sympathy. These acts of friendship were interpreted by the *New York Post* this way: "The most embarrassing display by the administration, however, came from the distaff side."[48]

Colin Powell also publicly defended Haifa and her husband, saying, "They are old friends of mine; I think it's most unlikely that either Prince Bandar or Princess Haifa would knowingly provide money for individuals

---

*The late King Faisal was shot and killed by a nephew in 1975.

or organizations that are conducting terrorist activities." Adding a cautionary note clearly directed at the intense media coverage, he continued, "I
think this matter should be looked into and heard from all sides, and see
what information and evidence there is before people rush and jump to conclusions as to whether or not something wrong has transpired or not."[49]
Powell's advice went unheeded; despite the *New York Times* report in late
2002 that the FBI had found no evidence that the money went to the hijackers,[50] and despite the 9/11 Commission as well, which specifically
cleared Princess Haifa al-Faisal, saying it found no evidence she provided
money "directly or indirectly" to the September 11 conspiracy,[51] the damage had already been done. The harm to U.S.-Saudi relations was severe.
The negative publicity fundamentally altered American public opinion of
the kingdom. The *Washington Post* reported that 54 percent of Americans
viewed Saudi Arabia as a state supporting terrorism, compared with a mere
35 percent who had a similar perception of Syria, a country which until
2006 had sat on the U.S. State Department's "Terrorism List" since December 29, 1979.[52] The *Post* also declared that Saudi bashing has reached a lu-
dicrous stage, writing that Haifa's link to 9/11 terrorists was "so tenuous, so
virtually nonexistent, that it amounts to a parody of guilt by association." It
then argued that the prevalent anti-Saudi frenzy was "just the latest example
of Congress and the federal bureaucracy doing their irresponsible thing—
and the media merely taking it all down."[53]

During a speaking tour designed to put across Saudi views on September
11, Bandar stressed, "The tragedy and the crime of 9/11 had one objective:
to drive a wedge between the U.S. and Saudi Arabia."[54] Months later, following the release of the 9/11 Commission report, the prince stated, "The
9/11 Commission has confirmed what we have been saying all along. The
clear statements by this independent, bipartisan commission have debunked
the myths that have cast fear and doubt over Saudi Arabia."[55]

Former U.S. ambassador to Saudi Arabia Chas W. Freeman neatly encapsulated what the media had been so quick to exploit, a problem that lies
in the structural body of the U.S.-Saudi relationship, when he said, "There
is a great disconnect between popular mood and national interest."[56] In
what can best be described as the pyramid effect, the sphere of Saudi influence in the United States—greatly increased and amplified by Bandar during his time as ambassador—in many respects, before 9/11, was generally
limited to the upper echelons of U.S. society; influencing from the top
down, so to speak.

Put another way, "Saudi Arabia has a need to influence the few that in-fluence the many, rather than the need to influence the many to whom the few must respond."[57] This comment was taken from J. Crawford Cook's proposed public relations and media strategy for Saudi Arabia in the United States written several decades earlier, a strategy that in the months following 9/11 Bandar followed with aplomb. Cook's comments accurately reflected the nature of the Saudi-U.S. relationship—energy for security—which, in general, encompasses only the key players in foreign policy.

The impact of 9/11 was to shatter this fragile pyramid system—to take the legs out from under Saudi Arabia and in many respects turn the Ameri-can people's ignorance of Saudi society and the Islamic religion, as well as its long maintained friendship with the U.S. leadership, against it. It there-fore became vital for Saudi Arabia to reach out to the American people and explain the real nature of Islam and Arab culture, before dangerous stereo-types began to answer the many questions raised in the public consciousness by September 11.

Those questions, coupled with Saudi Arabia's previous lack of connec-tion with the American people, opened the door to damning and often ma-licious media speculation. As Ambassador Chas Freeman pointed out, "Saudi Arabia has been successfully vilified in the eyes of the American public. . . . This has come about because the U.S.-Saudi relationship was es-sentially really rather narrowly based and did not have a mass media or broad public dimension to it . . . 9/11 took this rather narrowly based rela-tionship and suddenly made the people in both countries intensely inter-ested in it."[58]

Marc Perelman of *The Forward* observed that before 9/11, "the king-dom was essentially known as one of the United States' 'moderate' Arab al-lies and its primary source of oil. Now, it is being portrayed as a breeding ground for would-be terrorists and a financial conduit for Islamic terror-ism."[59] Similarly, the *Los Angeles Times* noted that "the strongest attacks [against the Saudis] have been carried out by lawmakers and media, includ-ing the editorial pages of the *Wall Street Journal, Washington Times*, and the *Weekly Standard*, as well as the columns of prominent neo-conservative commentators such as Gaffney and Charles Krauthammer of the *Washing-ton Post*, with close ties to Israel's Likud Party, which has long seen Riyadh's alliance with Washington as a strategic threat."[60] Both press comments am-plified Saudi fears that their growing, yet still perilous, public relations posi-tion in the United States was being manipulated for Israel's benefit. The

Israeli lobby undeniably benefited from the media-fueled anti-Arab aftermath of 9/11; its greatest opponent, the Arab lobby, had been critically undermined in the public eye and the previously steadfast, and in Israeli eyes strategically dangerous, U.S.-Saudi relationship was under tremendous strain.

In the face of such intense negativity resonating throughout the U.S. press, and with the long-simmering belief among Arabs that the American media is controlled by the Jewish community and their representatives in press organizations, this seed of discontent germinated the theory that the Jewish lobby and its supporters had been orchestrating a media blitz against Saudi Arabia.[61] Many Saudi officials felt that "groups hostile to the kingdom and others who have links with the Zionist lobby in Washington are seeking to harshen American public opinion against Saudi Arabia, the Arabs and Muslims."[62]

Former U.S. ambassador to Saudi Arabia Richard Murphy explained how the U.S. press was creating a climate of mistrust within Saudi Arabia, highlighting the level of irritation that the Saudis felt for the sustained assault in the press since the 9/11 attacks. He explained that because the Saudis are absolutely convinced that Jews control the Western media, the onslaught confirmed their worst fears.[63] Whatever the truth, 9/11 has proved to be the catalyst for the weakness and misunderstanding of the two very different partners in the U.S.-Saudi relationship.

As Bandar observed sadly, "The most dangerous and evil thing of what happened on 9/11 is that for the first time it shook the trust between the Saudi people and the American people."[64]

Former President Jimmy Carter commented on the rising feeling within the United States that "the Saudis have not been as reliable as we had previously thought in protecting themselves and us from the threat of terrorism. Indeed, there is still a sense that the Saudi government is still surreptitiously financing elements in Saudi Arabia that do support

Ambassador Richard Murphy

some terrorist groups."[65] The press has even speculated that the Saudis may have paid off radical groups to leave Saudi Arabia alone. When I discussed this with Dr. Henry Kissinger, he spoke of the media's pivotal role in the general lack of confidence in U.S.-Saudi relations. He sourced much of this concern to the ultraconservative Madrassas and the flow of Saudi money that had found its way to al-Qaeda; however, he also acknowledged that the Saudi government had significantly tightened its financial controls and that the Saudi regime was working to correct the prime issues. Kissinger believed that the Saudis were "getting their act together" and "honestly endeavoring to improve matters."[66]

When questioned during an interview about possible Saudi protection money paid to al-Qaeda, Bandar simply answered, "That is a lovely story. And I think it's very colorful story. But it's not true." He went on to explain categorically, "It's not true because we have never worried about the effect of these organizations on our country. We might have paid people for other reasons. For example, when the Palestinians were having problems with the Jordanians, we might have just said, 'Take this, take that. Just disengage, leave each other alone.' We might've paid some people to switch from being revolutionaries to be nice citizens. But we have never paid in the sense of 'protect me; leave me alone.' "[67]

Addressing the role that the House of Saud is undertaking in the war on terror, Adel al-Jubeir, foreign policy adviser to Crown Prince Abdullah, released a statement saying, "We are not only going after the terrorists, but also the money and the mindset that support them or condone their actions."[68] As proof of this and of Kissinger's assertions that the Saudis are indeed taking decisive and effective action, thousands of imams who have violated prohibitions against preaching intolerance have been suspended or referred for training, and educational textbooks and curricula have been updated.

Faced with continued allegations regarding Saudi terrorist funding, Bandar reminded his interviewers, "A year, two years ago, it was Saudi Arabia that came and banged on the tables in Washington, saying, 'We tracked money supposedly to go to charity, but we don't know where it's going. We can track it to Europe, to Switzerland, but once it arrives in America we lose track.' [But] they tell us, by law, they cannot look into these accounts."[69]

The climate since 9/11 has revolutionized both the Saudi and American approaches to tracking money, and both countries are collaborating closely.

An employee of the U.S. Department of the Treasury confirmed, "We have created a close agent-to-agent working relationship with the Saudis to deal with terrorist financing specifically."* In fact, a report by the international Financial Action Task Force noted that the new Saudi implemented regulations to crack down on abuses at Saudi-based charities "probably go further than any country in the world."[70]

Such sentiment was echoed by James Baker, who, pointing out that he had worked with the Saudis during four administrations in various capacities, stressed that the Saudis have been "good friends of ours," and was keen to emphasize the strong links that were created during the first Gulf War and the support that was received from Saudi Arabia. Nonetheless, in light of the antipathy shown toward Saudi Arabia by the American public and media post-9/11, Baker emphasized that the Saudis needed to improve their projection and public profile.[71]

Former President Carter, when asked how he felt about the tenor of U.S.-Saudi relations in the wake of the appalling events of 9/11, observed candidly, "Well, I think that the relationship between the Saudi Royal family and the U.S. government—that is, the president, the vice president, and the secretary of defense—is quite sound." He then observed, "I see us and the Saudis as having a common justifiable reason to fight against terrorism, but I also see the fact that some of the more radical Islamicists are connected to the terrorist acts. Then, of course, the fact that fifteen of the nineteen men that caused 9/11 were from Saudi Arabia, is still remembered by many people." Having outlined the common concerns raised following 9/11, the former president concluded, "But my own sense of friendship and allegiance, in gratitude to the Saudi government, has not been diminished."[72]

In an exoneration of claims that Saudi Arabia had helped fund the al-Qaeda attack, the 9/11 Commission said, "We have found no evidence that the Saudi government as an institution or senior Saudi officials individually funded the organization."[73] Al-Qaeda's figurehead, Osama bin Laden, as a former member of an extremely wealthy and influential Saudi family, is a founding cause of American suspicion of Saudi Arabia. The U.S. press frequently overlooks the fact that this international icon of hatred and intolerance was expelled from Saudi Arabia in 1991 because his controversial beliefs were neither welcomed nor well received.

---

*Juan C. Zarate, deputy assistant secretary, Executive Office for Terrorist Financing & Financial Crimes, U.S. Department of the Treasury.

In 1994, bin Laden was legally disowned by his family and stripped of his Saudi nationality. All of his assets were frozen in Saudi Arabia from that date forward. As Bandar explained, "His family had meetings with him, and he just told them they all are sacrilegious, they all are corrupt, they are all infidels . . . so they legally disowned him. Once they did that, the government then stripped from him his nationality." Neither the bin Laden family nor Saudi Arabia endorse Osama bin Laden. What is more, they are ashamed of his fanatical cult ideology. Yet in the West, there is an inherent link by association that presumes guilt.

The fact that Osama bin Laden had a connection with the Royal House of Saud in the past cannot be denied; however, what the American public generally is unaware of is that the U.S. administration was equally involved with this future extremist leader. As Bandar explained in a *Frontline* interview, "Bin Laden used to come to us when America—underline *America*—through the CIA and Saudi Arabia, was helping our brother Mujahideen in Afghanistan to get rid of the Communist, secularist Soviet Union forces, to liberate them. Osama bin Laden came and said, 'Thank you. Thank you for bringing the Americans to help us to get rid of the secularist, atheist Soviets.' "[74]

At a time when Communism was considered the greatest evil, Osama bin Laden was overlooked. To the Saudis he was little more than an unwelcome embarrassment. "We never gave him the weight that now everybody is giving him," says Bandar "We just thought he was a nuisance, and he was bad for the image of Saudi Arabia, of Islam, his family. We never thought of him as the bin Laden who is doing all of this." Bandar has met with bin Laden. "He didn't impress me as somebody who could be a leader of anything. Actually, at that time, I thought he couldn't lead eight ducks across the street."

In interviews, Bandar tries frequently to disillusion the American public about the authority and following of Osama

Osama bin Laden

bin Laden in the Middle East, saying, "You are making this man twenty feet tall. . . . If I was as powerful as bin Laden, and my message was as strong as bin Laden, and my followers were as great as bin Laden, why would I hide in a cave in Afghanistan? I would go where it counts. I'd come to Saudi Arabia. Lead the revolution . . . let my followers take over!"[75]

September 11 led to America's vilification of that country rather than extending to it the backing it needs to fight a common enemy. Before 9/11, Saudi Arabia was under attack for its human rights and freedom-of-speech policies, an incongruity pointed out by Bandar, who said, "I am told every now and then by some smart alecks in the media here [America] that 'if only you gave the people the freedom to speak then they would not go and bomb people.' My friends, it is true, those people, we did not allow them to speak because we knew what they were speaking, and when you heard them speak, 9/11 was the answer. We had a reason why—we didn't want people who spout hate and violence—those people have no rights to express those views, if then they act on them or get some gullible people to act on them."[76]

In the post-9/11 era, it quickly became evident that the slow pace of reform in Saudi Arabia was no longer acceptable to Washington, particularly in light of the negative public attitude toward Saudi Arabia. Ambassador Richard Murphy confirmed that even after 9/11, the Saudis were reluctant to cooperate with U.S. authorities, and even insisted on denying the existence of a terrorism problem within the kingdom. They were slow to recognize *jihadist* Islam as a threat. But then Saudi Arabia received its own wake-up call.[77]

Only after a terrorist suicide attack on May 12, 2003—three cars packed with bombs were exploded in a residential compound in Riyadh, killing thirty-five people and wounding two hundred—did the Saudi government radically shift its policy and agree to cooperate more closely with the United States. Only then, after years of inaction and obfuscation, did the Saudi regime begin to move forcefully against terrorism. In a remarkable admission, one young Saudi acknowledged, "9/11 meant nothing in Saudi Arabia. Some didn't believe that any Saudis were involved in it; others thought it was a conspiracy or was deserved because of America's support for Israel. May 12 was our 9/11. Since then Saudis have had to recognize that al-Qaeda is not a fantasy. It is here."[78] The May 12 bombings shook people out of their complacency.[79] Crown Prince Abdullah declared, "There is no place for terror" and vowed to destroy the group responsible.[80]

After the May 2003 bombings, Saudi Arabia finally began to address areas of concern, and the war on terror within the kingdom took on a new momentum. Saudi Arabia came around to the painful acknowledgment that there had been Saudis involved and there just might be al-Qaeda cells in the kingdom.[81] These cells were now aggressively hunted down by the security forces. Some two thousand of the most radical clerics were either dismissed or put through reeducation programs. Religious leaders began to argue that al-Qaeda was against Islamic precepts. The kingdom also cracked down on terrorist financing; it now strictly complies with most international laws regarding financing. Saudi Arabia closed down some of its most suspect charities and made it illegal for charities to fund outside the kingdom. They began cooperating with the FBI and CIA to a greater extent than ever before.[82] These initiatives prompted Thomas Lippman to write, "Saudi Arabia is now clearly a dynamic society. There's more open debate. The Saudis have gotten the message about the need to crack down. There's been substantial curriculum reform. There are more channels for political openness. The Saudis are working with the outside world. People have more information."[83]

A defining moment in the Saudi approach to terrorism was provided by Bandar in 2004. In a brave and highly critical statement on the war on terrorism, one that appeared to express a harsh, if thinly veiled censure of some of those responsible for Saudi Arabia's security, he demanded all-out war on al-Qaeda. In a surprisingly forceful article in the reformist Saudi newspaper *Al-Watan*, Bandar argued that neither Saudi society nor the state had fully mobilized itself for this struggle.[84]

Bandar wrote, "War means war. It is a war that does not mean delicacy, but brutality." The prince clearly defined the enemy, saying, "If we deal [with them] hesitantly, in hope that [the terrorists] are Muslim youths who have been misled, and that the solution is that we call upon them to follow the path of righteousness, in hope that they will come to their senses—then we will lose this war, and this means that we will lose everything that this state and this people have accomplished over the past six hundred years." Explicitly dismissing the tendency at the highest levels of the Saudi ruling family to blame terror attacks in the kingdom on outsiders, Bandar demanded, "Enough blaming others when the reason lies within our own ranks!"[85]

This radical statement by Bandar was to presage change in Saudi Arabia, not least his own appointment by King Abdullah on October 16, 2005, as secretary-general of the National Security Council (NSC), with the rank of cabinet minister. The Saudi NSC has a mandate that covers the kingdom's national security in its broadest sense, and the restructured NSC has been therefore transformed into the most powerful policy-making body in the kingdom.[86] As ambassador, Bandar could only attempt to respond to criticisms levied at the kingdom following 9/11; as secretary-general of the NSC responsible for security policy, he could now directly engage on the much-needed transformation of Saudi Arabia. It is now possible that Bandar's influence could precipitate much-needed change in the kingdom.

Even so, the U.S. media was cynical about the kingdom's commitment in the crusade against al-Qaeda and terrorism. Pointing out that Saudi Arabia had hitherto indulged in unofficial tolerance of al-Qaeda, it was observed, "Lax government monitoring of charitable foundations and the money they sent overseas allowed large sums to flow into terrorist training and operations. Saudi rulers winked at the terrorist operations as long as they were directed outside their borders." The *New York Times* concluded that the kingdom only began cracking down on terrorist cells within the kingdom "when al-Qaeda expanded its targets to include sites and people within Saudi Arabia itself."[87] Nonetheless, the Council on Foreign Relations issued a report noting that the Saudi government's new laws monitoring money laundering and donations met or exceeded international standards in many respects.[88]

Change is taking place within Saudi Arabia, but this must be necessarily slow for the sake of keeping pace with its people. As Bandar explained, "We are the only country in the world where the government is avant-garde and the people are more conservative. And most of the trouble we had is because we wanted to move forward. But we are not arrogant enough to think we will move forward regardless of what our people think."[89]

Clearly, there are extremist elements within the staunch brand of Saudi Islamic conservatism. Bandar agrees, "Saudi Arabia, in fact, has its own brand of extremists and zealots, and even hatemongers. It is not unique in this. . . . This indigenous form of ultraconservatism was, and still is, isolationist in nature. Their major concern is to keep Saudi Arabia outside the movement towards modernity, which they perceive as a threat to the moral purity of Islamic society. Their preaching is not the global expansionist ideology of al-Qaeda, but rather an isolationist, anti-modernity ideology."[90]

These minorities are not to be confused with al-Qaeda, whose ideology poses as great a threat to Saudi Arabia as it does to the Western world. The Saudi foreign minister, Prince Saud al Faisal, endeavored to explain this when he said, "The ideology espoused by al-Qaeda can be summarized by its belief in the negation of the legitimacy of all the governments of the Islamic countries, and especially Saudi Arabia, for the purpose of reestablishing the Islamic caliphate with al-Qaeda as its vanguard. The latest version of this plan calls for the destruction of the Saudi state."[91]

The complex religious and political situation in the Middle East often perplexes the Western world. Carol Devine-Molin clarified the uncertainty of many Americans when she said, "The religion of Islam represents an enigma to most Americans, especially in the aftermath of the atrocities perpetrated by radical Islamists. There are just too many conflicting statements being disseminated that only add to the confusion. Is Islam really a 'religion of peace' as consistently asserted by President Bush, or is it a vehicle for violent jihad?"[92]

It is not just 9/11, but also the resulting war on terror which has led to a questioning of the Islamic faith in the media, with contradictory and often derogatory representations. The director of research for the Council on American-Islamic Relations stated bluntly, "The war on terrorism is equated with a war on Islam. Although the White House keeps saying this is not the case, a lot of people who support the White House cannot think of it in any other terms."[93] The isolationist and bellicose attitudes within the administration are certainly not contributing to the positive education of the U.S. people in regard to current dangerous misconceptions about Islam.

It is important that the West understands that Saudi Arabia owes its staunch conservative values to its role as the keeper of Islam. In recognition of this role, the nation's king has assumed the title "Custodian of the Holy Places of Mecca and Medina" and therefore present-day negativity toward Islam engendered in the West is felt sharply in Saudi Arabia. In a passionate speech made to the World Affairs Council in Houston, Bandar maintained that more than airplanes were hijacked on September 11. "I am here to tell you as a proud Saudi, a proud Arab and a great believer in my religion, Islam—those people decided to hijack a great religion and we will not let them succeed."[94]

Al-Qaeda's militant actions and attitudes, which are opposed to alternative beliefs, are in practice considered highly sacrilegious. Bandar phrases this very simply, explaining, "When people [al-Qaeda] talk about the infidels coming, that is sacrilegious in Islam, because Islam believes in the people of the Book. You have to believe in Judaism, Christianity, Moses, and

Jesus. I, as a Muslim, if I don't recognize Christianity or Judaism as God's religion, and the prophets of God, I am automatically excommunicated."

Continuing in defense of his faith and the poisonous slur al-Qaeda has attached to it, Bandar said emphatically, "The truth of the matter here is Islam is a good religion. It's a religion of peace and tolerance. . . . What I'm saying is you cannot judge either Islam or Arabs or Saudi Arabia by bin Laden or fifteen people—or one hundred people, for that matter."[95]

Soon after Saudi Arabia's response to the May 12, 2003 attacks, Bandar launched a massive public relations campaign headed by the Washington, D.C.–based PR firm Qorvis Communications, centered on the theme "The Values We Share." This was a multimillion-dollar TV ad that ran in twenty major cities across the country, the first of which was headlined, "America, We Grieve with You."[96] In addition, Bandar engaged in a series of high-profile speaking engagements across America that addressed issues raised by 9/11. It allowed him to admit to audiences that 9/11 left the Saudis reeling. He confessed, "It took us a long time to come out of that shock."[97] He would also point out that since September 11, Saudi Arabia had questioned over one thousand individuals, arrested more than five hundred suspects, and succeeded in extraditing al-Qaeda members from other countries to face justice. He also confirmed that the bank accounts of suspect individuals had been frozen and stringent banking regulations had been implemented, and he concluded, "Saudi Arabia today has one of the toughest counterterrorism laws and regulations in the world."[98] Bandar stressed that cooperation between the kingdom and U.S. financial authorities and security services had accelerated, adding, "9/11 was an evil work done to destroy the image and the truth of a great religion. Islam is a great religion, and we are proud to be Muslim."[99] Bandar also highlighted measures taken in the kingdom to address concerns about its education curriculum. He advised that 85 percent of the curriculum was no problem, but the 10 percent that was borderline and the 5 percent that was unacceptable were removed.[100]

It is within the highly charged atmosphere of fear and ignorance resulting from 9/11, that the vital significance of the current multimillion-dollar Saudi PR offensive becomes apparent. Neil Bush* despondently summarized the Saudi PR predicament in 2002 when he said, "American public opinion sees Arabs as terrorists and has the desert-man image about them. I

---

*Neil Bush is the younger brother of President George W. Bush and Governor Jeb Bush. He is a businessman based in Texas.

wish Americans would see Arabs and Muslims the way I see them. Arabs are losing the public relations battle in the United States. . . . Public opinion shapes public policy dramatically. It's true in the U.S., in this part of the world and elsewhere."[101]

Speaking to the *Washington Times*, Bandar said, "I believe the Saudi relationship with America will fail or continue, based on how successful we are to reach the Americans in their homes and villages. If we fail there, everything we do with the American body politic, with the elites, government to government, will be irrelevant."[102] The task is to do just that—grassroots lobbying, targeting the average American, and dispelling the myths surrounding Islam and Saudi Arabia.

Watching the Saudi PR campaign unfold, analysts have commented, "The Saudis were largely disinterested in their public image abroad—there was little reason to be seriously concerned. Buoyed up by 25 percent of the world's known oil reserves, they were able to brush aside criticisms of their foreign and domestic policies with impunity."[103] With the media assault on Saudi Arabia and the lack of a broad base of support for the [U.S.-Saudi] relationship, there was no general understanding of Saudi Arabia. "The kingdom, at the time, was a largely closed society,"[104] The failure to educate the West about the intricacies of Saudi culture and religion, together with the fallout from 9/11, forced the House of Saud to reimage itself in the Western world.

Given the dramatic cultural divide between Saudi Arabia and the United States, the Saudi PR offensive has been an uphill struggle from the outset. However, in relation to the daunting task, Michael Petruzzello, managing partner of Qorvis Communications, said, "They've got two things going for them. The first is the Bush administration, which has placed the Saudis off limits from criticism. And the second is Bandar, the un-Saudi Saudi."[105]

The Saudi desire for privacy and evasion of either public appraisal or censure has been understandably interpreted in the West as proof of something to hide. Bandar discussed the disunity between the kingdom and the media—a situation America has a hard time coming to terms with, concluding, "You all remember Somalia? When the Marines landed on the beach they were met by a CNN crew. That is the culture. Just because we don't roll with that culture, just because you don't see us identifying with it, please don't make the deadly mistake that we are not doing anything. We are."[106]

*   *   *

While the horrendous events of 9/11 altered—possibly forever—the tenor of U.S.-Saudi relations, undermining Bandar's diplomatic efforts of the previous two decades, a tangential effect was its impact on intractable Palestine-Israel problem. Immediately prior to September 11, Bandar had been engaged in devising a new peace formula with the Bush administration that offered the prospect of headway in the seemingly stalled peace process. Relaxing at his home in McLean, Virginia, Bandar prepared for his planned meeting with the president on September 13, 2001, content that this new initiative could again offer hope in the Middle East. He watched horrorstruck on live TV as two aircraft slammed into the twin towers.

Any peace initiative that might have resolved the ongoing hostilities between Palestinians and Israelis was instantly eclipsed by the 9/11 attacks perpetrated by al-Qaeda. The Bush administration understandably focused on the "War on Terror," and the president's attention to peace and security in the Middle East was immediately sidelined.

Who was to blame? Who could America target in its desire for revenge? After the quick and successful Afghanistan campaign to drive the Taliban from power—although unable to capture Osama bin Laden—the Bush administration was looking for more answers. Still sensitive to the terrorist attack of 9/11 at America's commercial and military heart, the Pentagon—persuaded by evidence manufactured by the neo-con inspired Office of Special Plans— pointed an accusing finger on Iraq. In 2003, U.S. and U.K. military forces struck in a campaign of "shock and awe," and Saddam Hussein was finally toppled from power.

Three years on, while the legacy of insurrection that followed the Iraqi War showed little sign of abating, there was some movement within the administration toward a resolution of the Palestinian-Israeli situation. In many Arab eyes, however, it was a movement away from peace, away from justice. Sharon's visit to the United States in April 2004 and Bush's backing of his controversial plan to withdraw unilaterally from the Gaza Strip and parts of the West Bank, together with the president's apparent dismissal of the Palestinian right of return to lands lost to Israel in 1948, was received with mixed responses, and was met with almost universal disbelief in the Arab world.

It was reported with an air of incredulity that the Israeli prime minister met with Bush on April 14, 2004, and "came away a very happy man. At the end of the meeting, Sharon tucked away two coveted assurances that Bush's father would never have dreamed of conferring thirteen years earlier in

Madrid." George W. Bush had agreed that Palestinian refugees could return only to a new Palestinian state, not to their homes and land in Israel; and the president stated that there were some settlements that could remain, despite the long-established U.S. policy that such settlements were either illegal or obstacles to peace.[107]

It was an about-face of breathtaking proportion.

News of Bush's acquiescence caused a volcanic uproar in the Middle East, and the Bush administration quickly sought to temper the extent of its agreement with Sharon. Secretary Powell assured Jordanian Foreign Minister Marwan al-Muasher that Bush was not dictating the terms of a final peace settlement, and Bandar was told by the White House that "all final status issues between the Palestinians and Israelis must be kept exactly that—final status issues and negotiated between the parties."[108]

When asked for his views on this unexpected move by Bush, Henry Kissinger responded, "Sharon's proposal is a constructive move forward, a stepping-stone to an eventual settlement, and perhaps an opportunity for the future to resurrect of the Land for Peace formula first seriously discussed in Madrid, and taken from U.N. Resolution 242."[109] Kissinger stressed, "Security was the core issue and that was something to which a solution could not easily be found."[110] This was precisely the sentiment that Bandar had so often expressed.

"What happened, especially after 9/11," said Brent Scowcroft, "was that Sharon was very skillful—[but] whenever anything would look like it was getting started, the radicals on the Palestinian side would send a suicide

Israeli Prime Minister Ariel Sharon

squad or something. Then Sharon would crack down and move into Palestinian areas and say [to the Americans], 'I'm fighting your fight; I'm fighting the war on terrorism—you've got to support me.' And the president would say, 'Yes sir.'"

"I remember arguing with Condi," admitted Scowcroft, who told her, "What you're doing is putting control of the process in the hands of the radicals—because they can stop at any time they want, because you're listening to Sharon and letting him say you've got to have security first. Well, if security's a precondition, then you can't get anywhere." He ruefully observed, "But that is in essence the way that it has gone." Bush and his team had conceded the initiative to Sharon.

Scowcroft's criticism of the administration's stance on Sharon's machinations was far from veiled. He alleged that Bush's acceptance of the Sharon proposal was embarrassing, given that he subsequently was unable to obtain acceptance from his own cabinet. Without that support, Bush's initiative had quickly backfired. Scowcroft solemnly stressed, "But the damage has been done. We have changed a position we had taken for fifty years: that we would not prejudge the outcome."[111]

That Bandar was frustrated by the lack of movement of the peace process in the aftermath of September 11 was all too obvious. In a direct reference to the renewed violence in the Middle East and the crown prince's attempts to inject new momentum into the process at Crawford ranch only a month prior to 9/11, Bandar stated emphatically, "When the peace process is moving, people are willing to accept a lot. But when the peace process is stalled, and this is coupled with Israeli behavior that is humiliating to Palestinians, and people see this day in and day out while America takes a standoffish attitude, all of this creates a harsh reality on the streets. The answer is to get moving." Even more bluntly, he urged the United States, "If the Arabs screw up—tell us. If Israel screws up—tell it [Israel]."[112]

Ambassador Richard Murphy attempted to explain Saudi dissatisfaction with the White House, saying, "The Palestinian issue is key to understanding Saudi frustration. They were genuinely shocked when the administration decided to back away from the issue, because they took it for granted that Bush would follow in the steps of his father. I know that for [Crown Prince] Abdullah, Palestine is very much his priority, much more than Iraq."[113]

In my interview with him, former President Carter recognized Bandar's constant, behind-the-scenes efforts to promote peace. He highlighted his own attempts at Camp David to secure a resolution to the Israeli-Palestinian dispute and said with manifest pride, "Next month is the twenty-fifth anniversary of the treaty between Israel and Egypt, not a word of which has ever been violated. It's still a symbol of what can be done—we worked out very thoroughly a fair treatment for the Palestinians at the same time." It was a treatment which, Carter observed scathingly, had "been thrown into the wastebasket by Sharon and Bush."[114]

Speculating on whether Bush personally had made the decision to accept Sharon's proposal and overturn the extant U.S. policy on the Middle East, Ambassador Murphy said, "He is a president who says proudly, 'I don't do nuance!' and the White House team make the argument that never in these thirty-seven years since the Six Day War, has Israel been ready to move off its settlements." With evident disbelief, Murphy continued bitingly, "And here is the hardest nose of all, the father of settlements, saying Gaza goes and some on the West Bank—how can we say no to that?" However, Murphy now added candidly, "I don't believe Sharon; I believe the man has stood for fifty years for other things—but this? I know that he has talked about readiness for painful compromises, but he did promise to remove the so-called illegal outposts that had been put into the West Bank since he became prime minister. He promised to do that a year-plus ago and nothing has happened yet. So I am reserved, to put it mildly, as to what he might do."[115]

Surprisingly, Bandar was characteristically sanguine about Bush's endorsement of Sharon's controversial plan to withdraw from Gaza and parts of the West Bank, while also keeping some West Bank settlements. In a measured response, he stated, "I am an optimist. You cannot look at the cup as half empty; it has to be half full. What else do we have? What other options? I mean—do we go to war? We have enough innocent people being hurt now on both sides. If the Israelis leave Gaza, this is going to be a big deal in my mind because I welcome any withdrawal by the Israelis from occupied Arab territory."[116] He observed that much was still to be negotiated. However, any negotiations have since been turned on their head with the death of Chairman Arafat and the illness of Prime Minister Sharon.

It was observed six months before Arafat passed away that "Peace between Israel and its neighbors is possible; the experience with Jordan proves this beyond any doubt. The Israeli and Palestinian people desperately need Palestinian leaders who will do what Arafat has so often refused to do—to take bold steps to bring an end to the ongoing bloodshed and sorrow."[117]

There can be no questioning Arafat's achievements as a revolutionary leader; but as times changed, as was perhaps best illustrated by his refusal of the Clinton-Barak proposal, Arafat's ability as a peacemaker, and more significantly in the day-to-day governance of his country, fell wanting. As a revolutionary icon, he brought great strength to the Palestinian cause. However, he was unable to deliver basic heath care, public services, a workable infrastructure, or the foundations of a viable economy to his people. In his absence, beneath the nation's grief and amid the fears that hard-line nationalists may seize upon Palestinian vulnerability, *Time* reported, "There was also quiet intimation of hope around the world—hope that the death of the unyielding Palestinian leader might bring a fresh opportunity to break the stalemate in the Israeli-Palestinian conflict"[118]

With the reality of a Hamas government in the wake of the Palestinian election, and a new, weaker Israeli government following Sharon's stroke and coma, the prospects for peace appear to be greatly diminished.

Whether this latest status quo will herald a turtle-like withdrawal on the part of the American president, with a reversion to his early days of muted involvement in the Israeli-Palestinian issue, remains unclear. Memories of 9/11 are still too vivid. The focus of the Bush administration is still on the "War on Terror" and the need to disengage from Iraq—to bring its troops home. With Hamas in power in Palestine and Mahmoud Abbas struggling to exert his authority as president, there appears little scope for a new initiative.

From Bandar's perspective, the prospect for peace in Palestine is temporarily dormant. But his desire to find a solution has not lessened, with the outbreak of violence between Hezbollah and Israel visiting the horrors of war on Lebanon, Bandar, in his new role as secretary-general of the Saudi NSC, has again assumed the mantle of peacemaker.

Bandar's meeting with Secretary Condoleezza Rice on July 23, 2006, saw him present an earnest plea from King Abdullah for U.S. intervention to rein in Israel and broker a ceasefire to protect the innocents. For Bandar, it foreshadows a demanding and vital new challenge, as he engages in yet another diplomatic struggle to bring peace to a Middle East on the verge of all-out conflict.

ELEVEN

FRIENDS AND THE TRAVELING COURT

"If a man does his best, what else is there?"

GENERAL GEORGE S. PATTON
(1885–1945)

During his tenure as ambassador and emissary for King Fahd and Crown Prince Abdullah, Bandar has had to endure a grueling travel schedule, necessitating a pattern of transatlantic journeys between Saudi Arabia, Washington, and many other locations across the globe dictated by world events. Bandar has managed to deal with those challenges by bringing with him both family and friends. The family members—particularly his son-in-law Prince Faisal and his half-brother Prince Salman—have acted as an anchor during the prince's extensive travels. His sons Khalid and Faisal have often found themselves traveling the globe without warning. Even Fahd, who took a year's sabbatical before going to Eton College, accompanied his father for most of that year, albeit under the tutelage of a past pupil from Eton, who prepared him academically for his entry into Eton.

However, it is Bandar's traveling companions that have enabled the prince to survive the pressures of his hectic schedule, criss-crossing the globe. Bandar's eldest daughter, Princess Loulou, described this "traveling court," which until recently comprised Fred Dutton, Joe Ramsey, Bob Lilac,

Said Karmi, Tarek Shawaf, and Rob Deacon Elliott, as "his little oasis. They're like his brothers. He is very close to them."[1]

A past secretary to Bandar, Jeri Pierre, said of this group, "He liked to surround himself with a whole group of people that had job descriptions that were never put on paper—a traveling men's club."[2] This group has more often been described as Bandar's "traveling circus." These friends and confidants have provided an enduring reference point that has been very valuable to the prince during his trips away from home. Assessing their value to Bandar, Lilac insisted, "*Traveling circus* is a good term—but I think that in the case of every one of those of us have been able to travel with him, it's more that he trusts us. Trust and loyalty—it's very hard to be sure of that; for instance, when he spends time with journalists or even business-men or diplomats, he has to be cautious."

Reflecting how that traveling court has managed to keep Bandar's feet on the ground over the years, Lilac said, "I think he tries to use us somewhat as a reasonably well-informed group of people who he can use as a sounding board and can trust. He can throw out some target balloons, if you will, and let us shoot at them. And most of that crowd has no qualms at all about shooting at them. We don't quite have the same requirement of holding back just because of his position as a member of the Saudi royal family and the deference that some of the fellow countrymen give to him."

Lilac continued, "We have been with him in all sorts of situations, so we don't mind saying this is not a very good idea—it's baloney; have you thought about this end of it?" Those criticisms, opinions, and observations have been readily forthcoming, especially from Fred Dutton and Joe Ramsey. As Lilac observed, "Especially Fred, who has a very long political legacy.

USAF Col. Joe Ramsey

Joe doesn't have the same political background as Fred, but since he has retired from the Air Force, Joe has become an avid reader and I guess a student of Fred's, so Joe has become pretty astute and doesn't hold back from shooting either. Said Karmi makes more comments when it comes to what's happening in the Arab world, but he holds back a lot and lets Fred and Joe expound."[3] Talking about the traveling court and the willingness of the group to challenge Bandar on various issues, Tarek Shawaf observed, "This is what you need; you don't need 'yes men.' In my work with Bandar, which has nothing to do with politics, I have often disagreed with him; this is part of the respect that he has for me, because he knows I tell him the truth. I have known his uncle, Crown Prince Abdullah, for a long time as a friend, and he has a quotation that he always uses: 'A friend is the guy that tells you the truth, not the guy that believes you.' "[4]

Lilac's involvement with the prince—his work with Bandar began during the introduction of F-5 aircraft into the kingdom and the fight to secure AWACS aircraft—is well covered in previous chapters. What has been glossed over is that he is the group comedian. During the toasts at the traditional New Year gathering at Aspen, Lilac invariably performs a party piece, much to his wife Jan's embarrassment, when he proposes the following toast:

> *When your skiing days are over,*
> *And from this world you pass,*
> *I hope they bury you upside down,*
> *For the world to kiss your ass!*[5]

Bob then stands on his head and proceeds to drain a glass of brandy while upside down. However, in defining the relationship between Bandar and Bob and Jan, there is no better summary than the Prince's own words: "The Lilacs? They are family—definitely!"

Joe Ramsey, Bandar's instructor when he first went to Lackland Air Force Base, formed a bond of friendship that was quickly sealed and was reinforced when Ramsey was posted to the kingdom in 1971. When he retired from the

Bob Lilac performs his New Year's Eve party piece in the snow at Aspen.

military in August 1991 he became a managing consultant. Ramsey observed, "The [Saudi] embassy rapidly became my only client, as I spent
much of my time traveling the world with Bandar." Speaking to his friendship with the prince over the years, Ramsey said, "From when I first met
him till now he is the same guy. He has matured, is wiser, but he is still basically the same—friendly, alert, generous, loves to tell stories, a winning
personality."[6]

Another member of the traveling court is Dr. Tarek Shawaf. An anglophile with homes in England, the United States, and Saudi Arabia,
Shawaf is an engaging and thoroughly likeable Saudi businessman* who is
very close to Bandar. Loulou described him as "a character; an easy-going,
nice guy."[7] Tarek met Bandar briefly in June 1967 at the Dorchester Hotel
in London during an official visit by King Faisal. In 1978, however, Bandar
was invited to a dinner hosted by Shawaf in Los Angeles. "We have remained friends ever since," said Shawaf.[8]

Bandar tells the story of how Shawaf invited him to dinner in Los Angeles, along with a distinguished group of movie people. After an excellent
dinner, they had sweets and coffee and were getting ready to go. Bandar recalled, "Tarek ordered the bill. He looked at it and then began searching for
his wallet, going from pocket to pocket. I realized that he was beginning to
panic. He asked if anyone wanted more coffee. Nobody wanted any coffee,
so he told the waiter to bring more cognac."

Understanding Shawaf's predicament, Bandar excused himself as
though to go to the bathroom, paid the bill, and returned to the table. In a
moment of pure pantomime, the prince re-enacted the amusing sketch of
an increasingly desperate Shawaf searching his pockets, time and time
again, trying to find his wallet. Bandar explained that he and Shawaf were
the only Arabs at the table, so Shawaf leaned over and said to him in Arabic,
"Can I bother you?"

"What can I do for you?" Bandar asked.

"I forgot my wallet," said Shawaf. "Do you mind paying the bill and I
will pay you back later?"

---

*Tarek Shawaf is chairman, president, and founder of Saudi Consulting Services, the oldest and largest
architectural engineering firm in Saudi Arabia, employing over six hundred technical and administra-
tive staff. Headquartered in Riyadh, the firm has offices in Damman and Jeddah, and overseas branch-
es in London and Los Angeles. It also provides engineering services to various African and Asian countries.

"But you invited me, I didn't invite you," replied Bandar, playing dumb. "You go and sign with the club."

Shawaf replied, "But they won't take my signature."

"Now, of course, at that time I didn't know why," joked Bandar. "Now I know why—he never pays!"

Bandar continued to tease Shawaf, saying, "I'm sorry Tarek, I don't have my wallet with me either."

Trying to find a way out, Shawaf ordered more coffee and cognac until, finally, everybody had to leave and so they got up to go. Shawaf looked at the waiter, who said, "Thank you very much for coming."

Bandar explained, "Only then did Tarek realize that the bill had been paid! But that's the only time Tarek came close to paying; ever since then, he doesn't even attempt to pay!"[9]

As an engineer, Shawaf became involved in helping Bandar with a number of projects, such as in 1983 when he was asked to evaluate the proposed construction costs for a palace in Riyadh. Believing the bill to be considerably overpriced, Shawaf placed it to tender with five U.S. companies, including the firm that had provided the original proposal. He was amused when that latter company came in with a figure substantially below its original proposal for the same work. Later, Shawaf worked in a design management capacity for that project, as he did at Bandar's home in Aspen in 1987. He also helped with the construction of the prince's palace in Jeddah and his country house at Glympton.

A close friend and confidant of Bandar, Dr. Said Karmi, passed away on June 6, 2005, at the age of sixty-seven. Karmi was born in Acre, Palestine, and was educated at Iraq High School in Damascus and the American University of Beirut, before getting his MD at Georgetown University. He was invited to stay as a professor and a year later returned to Jordan as a fully trained urologist. For four years, he served as a major in the Jordanian army and was chief of urology at the King Hussein Medical Center. Said completed the first kidney

Dr. Tarek Shawaf—Bandar's close friend and confidant.

transplants in Jordan in 1972, but after five years, he became frustrated at the lack of facilities and joined the University of Maryland as assistant professor. In 1979, Said became a professor of both neurology and surgery at Washington University, where he performed more than six hundred kidney transplants in the Washington area. He was named professor emeritus at the university in 1995.[10]

Karmi first met Bandar in 1981, and they became friends. However, Karmi suffered serious health problems and in 1994, following a heart transplant operation, Karmi retired from medicine and began to accompany Bandar on a regular basis, saying, "I was traveling with the boss before, but not that much. So when I retired from clinical practice, the prince said, 'That's great—we can travel together.' We have been traveling since and he is a dear friend."[11]

An astute and intelligent individual with a keen legal brain and flair for handling the media, one of Bandar's closest friends, Fred Dutton, passed away on June 25, 2005, at the age of eighty-two. His relationship with Bandar, whose image he helped to mold and project, was deep and honest; Dutton never held back if criticism was needed.

In the tribute written about this gifted Washington power broker, the *Washington Post* described Dutton as a "balding, pixie-ish, poker-playing rogue." He was once described as "Fred of Arabia," and as a lobbyist he worked assiduously behind the scenes as a force multiplier who paved the way for others—notably Bandar—to take the stage. In effect, Fred Dutton was Saudi Arabia's secret weapon in Washington.

The *Post* also made note of his military career, writing, "During World War II, he served in the Army infantry and was wounded and taken prisoner during the Battle of the Bulge. He was later awarded a Purple Heart and a Bronze Star. He served in the Judge Advocate General's Corps during the Korean War, stationed in Japan."[12] Dutton also carried a pound of shrapnel close to his heart. "He was definitely the intellectual in the group," observed Jeri Pierre. "He probably knew Bandar as well as anybody."[13]

"I was special assistant to President John F. Kennedy," Dutton recounted, "and then I was made secretary of state for congressional relations and stayed there through Kennedy's assassination." Dutton later worked for Bobby Kennedy, and when he was assassinated, went back to his law practice in California. One of his clients, Mobil Oil, asked him to go to Saudi Arabia to act as King Faisal's legal adviser in the United States and manage congressional relations. Dutton became Saudi Arabia's key adviser in Washington.[14] With the sad demise of both Dr. Karmi and Fred Dutton, the nature of that traveling court has changed irrevocably.

The newest member of the traveling court, Robert Deacon Elliott, was a fellow officer cadet and novice pilot, and was very close to Bandar during their time at Cranwell. That relationship was so familiar that Bandar became a surrogate member of the Deacon Elliott family. After a satisfying career flying in the Royal Air Force, Deacon Elliott joined British Aerospace in Saudi Arabia in 1985 as a flying instructor. On his return to the United Kingdom, however, things did not go well for him in his personal life and he and his wife divorced.

Bandar had somehow got wind of Deacon Elliott's predicament and suggested they meet. "We had lunch with Ben, me, my mother, and my father," recalled Deacon Elliott, whose parents had acted as surrogate parents to Bandar during their time at Cranwell. "He presented me a pair of cufflinks. Instinctively, I took my own cufflinks off—a leaving present from the Oman Air Force—and I said, 'Well, you've given me some cufflinks; you can have these.' And to this day, he still wears them." As they were leaving, Bandar said to him, "When you finish your license,* come out and see me in America." Deacon Elliott confided, "That was all very well, but I didn't have any money for the air fare. But when the time came and we got in touch, he sent a driver around with a ticket and off I went."

Talking of that first trip, Deacon Elliott recalled, "After seven or eight days, he and I sat down by the pool at Aspen and I brought in all my log books, my CV, and letters of commendation, etc., and in quite a moving conversation we chatted about the last ten years or so—the ups and downs—and this was obviously a bit of a down for me."

Indicating to Deacon Elliott's pile of log books and letters, Bandar said, "Put all that lot on one side. I don't think we'll need any of this. Why don't you and I do some work together?"

---

*Deacon Elliott was studying for his air transport-pilot license at that time.

Rob Deacon Elliott

Deacon Elliott replied, "Well, what?"

Bandar said, "Let's get you on a retainer so you can pay your bills and look after your family and then we'll think of something to do."

"And that's how it turned out," concluded Deacon Elliott. He has since been involved in a whole series of projects over the years, including responsibility for the refurbishment of Bandar's personal Airbus 340 and the management of crews.[15]

Following that encounter at Aspen, however, Deacon Elliott was drawn into the traveling court and now travels extensively with Bandar.

During his diplomatic career, Bandar has made many friends across the globe. But no review of his friends would be complete without mention of a very special relationship that has developed during the prince's tenure in Washington—his rapport with the Bush family and with George Herbert Walker Bush in particular.

The closeness between Bandar and George Bush was also encapsulated in the frequently quoted nickname "Bandar Bush." It is thought that the term was initially devised by *New York Times* columnist William Safire[16] in a critical essay published during the first Gulf War.[17] This simple amalgamation of the names of Bandar and George H.W. Bush provides a highly apposite linguistic characterization of their friendship. It was the president himself, however, who spoke of the prince as Bandar Bush, thereby emphasizing that he was very much an adopted part of his family. "We like him," Bush said. "He is just a joy to be around. He is gregarious and vivacious. He is almost like a—you might say—a son." This emotional statement had no caveats.[18]

Yet the relationship that exists between Bandar and the Bush family has been used and abused by the media according to the political climate of the moment. Post-9/11, the term *Bandar Bush* has been por-

Bandar with his close friends George and Barbara Bush.

trayed in primarily critical exposés on the two dynasties—the Bush family and the House of Saud. Anti-Saudi rhetoric flowed thick and fast from authors and reporters such as Robert Baer, Matt Welsh, Craig Unger, Michael Moore, Maureen Dowd and Michael Isikoff. William Safire critically observed about that relationship, "When Prince Bandar says 'jump,' George Bush asks 'how high?'"[19]

Some of these members of the press have also sought to turn a positive into a negative, such as Craig Unger's tome *House of Bush, House of Saud* and Michael Moore's film *Fahrenheit 9/11*. As Thomas Lippman observed dismissively about the Unger and Moore allegations, "It's not surprising that a family that made its money in the oil business in Texas would be close to the Saudis; I'm not aware that any untoward relationship has been uncovered."[20]

On the subject of the media and its attempts to pillory Bandar and both presidents, father and son, it is perhaps appropriate to conclude a last word by George H. W. Bush and his wife Barbara about the conduct of the media. When discussing the constant criticism of the close relationship between Bandar and the Bush families, George H. W. Bush stated in a voice that was underscored with barely disguised anger, "When they [the media] got Haifa, when they went after her on some grossly unfair allegations—you know, she is a terrorist, etc.—Barbara spoke out and so did I. That was at a time when anything Saudi was considered bad, and it was grossly unfair." The president continued, "The *New York Times* still does it and I am outraged about how they treat Saudi Arabia." The phrase that he had used about Bandar earlier in the interview—loyalty to a wingman—sprang immediately to mind.[21]

Sir Richard Evans speculated that the period when George Bush was vice president, during Reagan's administration, was the initial catalyst to the Bandar-Bush friendship. "I used to have lunch with George Bush every one or two months when he was vice president," explained Bandar. "He was very interested in foreign policy and the outside world's view on what was going on in America; we became close friends. Those lunches were a two-way street; he learned from me about whatever was going on from my view and my country's perspective, and I learned a lot from him because he was someone I held in very high regard."

Evans explained that on George H. W. Bush's inauguration, the relationship was already well established and simply continued to develop from there. He also observed, "I would say that Bush Senior, more so possibly than Reagan, had almost a mentoring influence on Bandar. It's a difficult thing to describe. Indeed, he created a relationship not just with Bush Senior, but also with the entire Bush family."[22]

"The personal relationship between Prince Bandar and the Bush family is very strong," stressed Henry Kissinger. "They are very close."[23] Kissinger's comments were to be reinforced by Joe Ramsey. When speaking about the prince's Bandar Bush nickname, Ramsey told me, "Fred Dutton and I used to joke that Bandar is wedded to the Bushes; he is a Bush man through and through."[24]

Bush confirmed that when he was vice president, after his initial contact with Bandar, they stayed in touch. "I liked Prince Bandar," he added, "and I found him to be a very good representative of the Saudi view. I always felt he was well connected with King Fahd, and I feel that same way about his relationship with Abdullah—you get the straight stuff from him." Having addressed the political dimension of their relationship, Bush continued, "He is a friend and he knows our country well. And he knows our shortcomings and he knows our great strengths—and I am sure he accurately reflects those to his government."[25]

Bandar related an anecdote that ably illustrates their personal rapport. "One day when George was still vice president," said Bandar, "he called me and said, 'What are you doing tomorrow?' I said to him, 'Whatever it is I'm doing, I guess I'm not doing it now.' And that became a line I used with him when he was the president. When I got a call from him saying, 'What are you doing tomorrow?' I would always answer, 'Whatever it is, I'm not going to do it anymore.' On this occasion, he said, 'Let's go fishing.' So I came to the White House and we got in a helicopter. We flew to Southern Shores in Maryland and went to a friend's house to join his friend, his wife, and Barbara Bush."

"Fishing is not one of my strongest suits," Bandar admitted. "I'm allergic to seafood; I don't like fishing; I don't like the sea much, particularly if I have to work; and he made me work trying to fish with him." Bandar observed, "What stuck in my mind about that visit, apart from the fact that I was the only one who caught a fish that day, is that after we sat down for lunch—and this tells you a lot about George H. W. Bush—he jumped up from the dining table and hurried off. We were all surprised, but he soon came back and sat down. I asked him, 'Is everything okay?' He said, 'Yes, I just wanted to check that your security people had been fed.'"

"That tells you a lot about this man," stressed Bandar. "Because here was the vice president of America having lunch with an Arab prince, and to think that he was worried about the security people, 'Are they being fed? Are they being taken care of?' That impressed me a lot, and that goes back to loyalty."

Bandar concluded, "Take care of your people and they will take care of you."

Bandar related another event involving George H. W. Bush, which occurred in 1989, when Bush had just taken office as president. Bandar informed him that King Fahd would like to visit. During his meeting with President Bush, Bandar said, "We are having an exhibition about Saudi Arabia in Washington; can we include it in the state visit?" Bush agreed and suggested that if King Fahd came, he would attend the opening with him. That exhibition, called "Saudi Arabia: Yesterday and Today,"* was held at the Washington, D.C., Convention Center and was to display Saudi artifacts, national costumes, musical instruments, and dancers. It had already been shown in London, Paris, Madrid, and Moscow and throughout the Arab world. However, planning for the state visit was soon thrown into disarray because of events in the Middle East, and the state visit was delayed. The White House called Bandar explaining that although the president had promised to come to the exhibition's opening, it would not be appropriate for him to attend if the king could not be there.

A week before the opening, Bandar unexpectedly received a call from John Sununu, the chief of staff. "Hi, Bandar," he said, "Your friend [President Bush] was asking that if he made a surprise visit to the exhibition, would it cause a headache?"

It transpired that the president had said, "Look, I promised Bandar that I would go and see this exhibition. Now that King Fahd isn't coming, we're sending Quayle for the formal opening. However, I really would like to go to it privately and see what they have on display."

"Tell him he is welcome any time this week," Bandar suggested.

"You don't understand," said Sununu, "He's talking about tonight."

"Tonight?" said Bandar, "Give me half an hour."

---

*Hon. Dana Rohrabacher informed the House of Representatives about the exhibition on July 24, 1989. Unlike many exhibitions designed to promote trade, it was a cultural exhibition, to help the American public understand more about the culture and people of Saudi Arabia. The hundred-thousand-square-foot exhibition was held in Washington from July 29 through August 20, 1989.

Bandar rushed to the convention, but when he got there, it was a scene of chaos. The Secret Service was there in force, as the president had already arrived with Brent Scowcroft and John Sununu. Bush then spent almost forty minutes walking through the exhibition, escorted by Bandar. "This just shows the strength of the relationship between myself and President George H. W. Bush," said Bandar. "By August 1990 and the Iraqi invasion of Kuwait, we were already very close."

Princess Haifa confirmed the strength of their relationship with the Bush family when she said, "The affection is there; it does not go away."[26] Princess Loulou reinforced Haifa's comments, "When we see them, it's like going to visit an aunt or an uncle. I like the Bushes—aside from the fact that they're friends of my father's." The princess continued, "It's not a question of status with them; it's a question of who you are as a person, not who you are in the world. And if they like you, then you know they like you. The way their family works and interacts is very similar to the way our family works and interacts, because they have a great father; they have the whole traveling, social, public image issues, but as a family they are very much a unit and nobody penetrates that unit. They will stand by each other no matter what."[27]

Socially, Bandar has had a considerable impact on the Bush household over the years. Mrs. Bush talked with great affection about Bandar's visit to

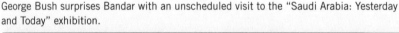

George Bush surprises Bandar with an unscheduled visit to the "Saudi Arabia: Yesterday and Today" exhibition.

Kennebunkport, where he "cooked up a storm." She related how Bandar announced that he was going to cook lunch the next day. "You can't do that," Mrs. Bush warned him. "We have a very small household and you might upset the staff—they are very sensitive about cooking meals." Bandar brushed aside her objections, saying, "No, I am doing it." President Bush explained, "Our chef was a Filipino who had cooked for me in the White House—a wonderful man." Far from being upset, their chef, Ariel, joined in the revelry that morning in the kitchen.

Mrs. Bush laughed. "And the next thing I know," she related, "the whole morning is spent, with Bandar smoking a cigar, in the kitchen. That caused a lot of excitement because I do not let the president of the United States—past or present—smoke in the house! He brought everything with him including a load of pots. They cooked and they laughed; you never heard more laughter."

Mrs. Bush continued, "They cooked so much and a big lunch was announced, and in we went. As I said, laughter for three hours out of the kitchen, and that night as he left, he said, 'The pots and pans are yours.'"[28] In her book, *Reflections: Life after the White House*, Barbara Bush writes of the visit, "When the big moment came, we all marched into the dining room to the biggest meal I had ever seen. I really can't remember what it was we ate, but he made so much that Neil [their son], at my invitation, came over that night and got pans of food, which he reheated and fed his ten guests. There was still food left over." Mrs. Bush's postscript said it all when she wrote, "Bandar stayed only twenty-four hours but made friends for life."[29]

Several seemingly insignificant anecdotes lend truth to this latter statement. Invitations to celebrate personal commemorative occasions have been frequently exchanged and appreciated between the Bush and Bandar households. However, one that particularly stuck in the president's mind was the occasion when his daughter traveled to Saudi Arabia as Bandar's guest at the marriage of their daughter Princess Reema. Bandar invited Dorothy Bush to represent the Bush family, as Mrs. Bush was unable to attend. On that occasion, he had extended an invitation to the bride's party to some three thousand mothers and daughters—friends of the family. President Bush recalled that although Bandar had all these friends from the Arab world, the United States, and elsewhere, they "tucked Doro right in with them and she stayed with Prince Bandar; we considered that a wonderful gesture."[30]

Perhaps the most widely reported story concerning the friendship between Haifa and Dorothy Bush was Haifa's invitation to Dorothy and her children in 1990. Aware of Dorothy Bush's recent divorce and move back to the White House, Haifa also knew that over Thanksgiving, President and Mrs. Bush would be reviewing U.S. troops in Saudi Arabia, shortly before the liberation of Kuwait. She therefore invited Dorothy Bush to celebrate Thanksgiving with her and her family on a farm in Virginia. This thoughtful generosity toward their daughter had a profound impact on both George and Barbara Bush. On arriving in Riyadh and seeing Bandar, the president embraced him; clearly very moved, he took the prince to one side and said with a genuinely felt emotion, "You are good people."[31]

Over his four-year term in office, President Bush amassed great respect within Saudi Arabia. Being an oil man himself immediately provided a common interest, but his unprejudiced view of the Middle East and his personal approach to leadership allowed him to make friends easily within the Arab world. As Bob Woodward wrote, Bandar felt that Bush had a balanced view of the Middle East and that he was neither emotionally nor exclusively attached to the interests of Israel.[32] This enhanced the president's standing. Most importantly, however, he had led the cavalry to defend the desert kingdom during the Gulf crisis. For all these reasons—and many more—Bandar wanted his friend George to win a second term in office.

On November 2, 1992, the night that witnessed the culmination of the Bush-Clinton election race, Bandar was surrounded by his friends, Fred Dutton, Joe Ramsey, and Dr. Said Karmi. He watched with blind optimism in the hope that Bush would somehow come from behind to clinch victory. However, Bandar's politically shrewd court saw long before he how the cards were going to fall.

Ramsey said, "Bandar was a Bush man and made no bones about it. If you could have been there that night in Houston, the writing was all over the wall; everybody knew Bush was going down the tube. But there he was, hoping against hope, grasping at any straw."[33]

Karmi recalled the energy of that night, "We were all watching the elections and boy—Bush called Bandar at six o'clock and said, 'It doesn't look good.' Bandar responded 'No, Mr. President, just wait a bit; things will be better.'" Karmi shook his head as he said, "But as the results came in, one state fell after another."[34]

"He took that very hard," admitted Dutton.[35]

In the early hours of November 3, at 12:40 A.M., and with his emotions in turmoil, Bandar wrote a passionate and poignant letter to his friend George H. W. Bush.

> You have been a great friend for the last twelve years and I feel so strongly about our friendship that I had to write to you on this very important day in your political career and share with you my feelings as a loyal friend and as an admirer and as an impartial witness to history—and whichever way today's results go, you have been an honorable human being, a loyal friend and a leader of a historical caliber where the world was very lucky to have your steady hands on the helms of statesmanship during historical times.

Bandar continued this two-page letter with his own personal thoughts and referring to another hero, Sir Winston Churchill, wrote:

> . . . Don't forget that the great leader of World War II, Winston Churchill, lost the elections two months after the great victory of World War II, but that did not diminish his greatness.

The Prince ended his letter by saying that in his heart he still believed that the President could clinch election victory, adding:

> "But if not my friend, you have done it and my family and I look forward to seeing you and your family in our little cottage in Aspen very soon regardless of what happens today. Good luck and God bless you, your lovely family and your great nation.[36]

Bandar's actions and reactions during that fateful night were unique because, as Joe Ramsey shrewdly surmised, "This was the only time in his relationship with Bush when he allowed his normal judgment and instinct to play second fiddle to his emotions. It is so uncharacteristic."[37]

Everyone in the prince's traveling court that night in Houston could see that Bandar's desire for George Bush to win went beyond a mere representation of Saudi Arabia's interests.

In a radio address delivered by George Bush on November 7, 1992, on his defeat at the polls, he started by making reference to Churchill, just as Bandar had done some three days before in his letter to the president. He began, "Way back in 1945, Winston Churchill was defeated at the polls. He said, 'I have been given the order of the boot.' And that is the exact same position in which I find myself today. I admit this is not the position I would have preferred, but it is a judgment I honor."[38]

Despite his supposedly apolitical stance, Bandar was firmly tied to the Bush camp on a personal level and to the Republican Party, a potentially dangerous position for him as a diplomat and one that certainly colored his relationship with Bill Clinton. Talking about the prince's ties to George H. W. Bush, Dutton observed, "I have been very much opposed to that. In '92, I was saying, and a number of people were saying, 'George H. W. is losing this'; Clinton definitely had it. But Bandar didn't really want to concede that; his loyalties and liking for George H. W. were so strong."[39]

Ramsey confirmed that he and Dutton were very critical of Bandar's allegiance to Bush and he has candidly said to the Prince, "The thing about you is that you have been able to disassociate your emotions from practical reality, but that all went out the window when you fell in love with Bush."[40]

Following Bush's defeat by Clinton, Bandar subsequently had a meeting with Bush at Camp David, where he said to him, "King Fahd has asked me if there is anything that we can do for you before you leave office."

"Bandar," Bush replied, "if you had asked me this the next day after the election, I would have said, 'Break diplomatic relations with America and don't work with this new president. However, thank God you're talking to me in December.'"

At the time, Bush and Bandar were taking a walk together in the woods. "You tell my friend King Fahd," Bush said, "that if there is one thing I can ask for, that I can guarantee he will do for me, please help this new president. He's young and inexperienced; if he succeeds, America succeeds, and if America succeeds, it's good for Saudi Arabia. If he fails, America fails, and if America fails, it's bad for Saudi Arabia."

"What a guy!" Bandar related. He described that at that moment he felt every hair on his body stand up. "What a great, larger-than-life, man. Here he is telling me to help the guy who defeated him because of the cause and principles." Bandar continued, "George H. W. Bush is a man of the old morality and when I told this story to Clinton when he was president, he was shaken. The moment I told him that, he made sure that his national security staff briefed Bush about everything all the time. It says a lot about the man, George H. W. Bush."

The emotion and subsequent depression that Bandar suffered following Bush's defeat stemmed from the deep friendship and loyalty they felt for each other. Speaking to that fidelity, Said Karmi said, "For Bandar, loyalty is everything, and the fact that Bush Senior was so willing to come to the aid of Saudi Arabia—the defense of Saudi Arabia in 1991—is something he will never forget. Bandar knows that was genuine, not motivated by any geographical thing. The bonding between Bandar and Bush during that buildup to Gulf War One is something that you cannot break, at least not in Bandar's mind."[41]

At a farewell dinner President Bush held in the White House before he left, he invited just twenty of his closest friends. Bandar was the only foreigner among those twenty people. Bandar recalled, "Actually, I was in Saudi Arabia when I got a call saying that the president wanted to speak to me, so I called him from there. He was unaware that I was in Saudi Arabia; this was about two o'clock in the morning Saudi time and about seven o'clock in the evening in Washington."

The president said, "Hi, Bandar."

"Hi, Mr. President," Bandar said. "How are you?"

"Look, buddy," said Bush, "what are you doing tomorrow night?"

"Well, Mr. President," Bandar replied, "whatever it is, I'm not doing it now."

"Well, look," said Bush. "Tomorrow I'm having a small group of friends, just twenty people coming for dinner to say goodbye; if you have time, I'd like you to come. Look, if you have anything else, don't worry about it."

"No, no, no, Mr. President," Bandar said, "I'll be there."

Bandar immediately picked up the phone and called King Fahd, who told him to leave that night for Washington to attend the dinner.

"Three hours later," Bandar recalled. "I flew all the way to Washington and I went straight to the White House. By then, somebody had told the president that I had been in Saudi Arabia when he had called me, so as I walked into the room he was surprised. He said, 'Goddammit.' And he put his hand on my shoulder and said, 'I thought that you were in Saudi Arabia.' I said, 'I was, Mr. President.'"

After the White House dinner, Bandar quickly went to his home in Washington to say "hi and goodbye" to Haifa before returning immediately to Saudi Arabia.

Birthdays and anniversaries in the Bush household have invariably featured invitations to Bandar Bush. "When George the elder and Barbara celebrated their fiftieth wedding anniversary," it was reported, "he [Bandar] was the only person outside the Bush family invited to the soirée."[42]

More recently, in June 2000, the prince was among the guests at Barbara Bush's seventy-fifth birthday party, which was organized by her husband, at Kennebunkport. However, while Mrs. Bush knew her family was attending—all five children and fourteen grandchildren—she was surprised to find 185 guests, including Colin Powell and Bandar.[43] Speaking about Barbara Bush's eightieth birthday party, which Bandar also attended, Mimi Burke, a secretary to the prince for many years, said, "Barbara Bush is a big fan of Prince Bandar's. It was basically a family party, with Bandar included in their family."[44]

Bandar, Haifa, and their daughter Loulou also attended the party organized in the White House by their son President George W. Bush to celebrate his mother and father's sixtieth wedding anniversary. It was an exclusive event, a black-tie White House dinner with family, former foreign leaders, and key figures in his administration. Press reports showed that about 130 guests were invited, including former Canadian Prime Minister Brian Mulroney and former British Prime Minister John Major. However, subsequent media reports failed to observe that when Bandar arrived with Haifa and their daughter Loulou, he donned a mask of Michael Moore which he had taken out from under his tuxedo. In this outrageous disguise, Bandar apologized to the president, saying, "Unfortunately, Prince Bandar is unable to attend; he asked me to come in his stead." Peals of laughter echoed around the event. Only a friend, however, could carry that prank off, given the president's animosity toward Michael Moore.

The disciplined military training Bandar and George H. W. Bush both received at a young age, their flying experiences, and their understanding of the value of camaraderie all echo in their friendship, together with their deep sense of loyalty, family, and hospitality.

Over his years as an ambassador, Bandar was to develop another particularly close friendship. Colin Powell has known Bandar for twenty-five years. He recalled, "We met in 1979 when I was a young brigadier general and I was traveling through the region with my boss at the time. We were in Saudi Arabia—Dhahran. We were with a group of Saudi military officers. Suddenly, the door opened and in comes this Saudi Air Force officer, I believe he was a major at the time, but he was clearly more than a major in terms of people quietly standing up when he walked in. That was my first exposure to Prince Bandar."

"A year or so later," Powell continued, "he came to Washington and I got to know him on a professional basis and a personal basis . . . and we always played racquetball together." Powell couldn't resist adding, "He wasn't very good." He explained simply, "We became pals. The years came and went: I came back to work for Cap Weinberger in 1983. Bandar was slowly ingratiating himself as the prime contact with the Saudi government: the mover and shaker of things Saudi. We just got to understand each other."

Continuing his account of their relationship, Powell said, "I became the deputy national security adviser in 1987, then national security adviser at the end of '87 and chairman of the Joint Chiefs of Staff in late '89. We had a lot of adventures over those years."[45] In the prince's study in Riyadh, there is a photograph of Powell clad in military combat fatigues, on which the general had written, "To my buddy Bandar. With admiration and fond memories of all our adventures together. 'It takes one to know one.'" Powell explained that most Americans would understand the reference: "It takes a bullshitter to know a bullshitter. We used to kid each other all the time." Referring to that axiom, Powell explained, "I'd say to him, 'The wonderful thing about our relationship is, Bandar, I know when you're lying to me and you know I know you're lying; the same way in reverse. You know when I'm lying to you and I know you know I'm lying.' And we would laugh about it." More seriously, Powell reflected, "We had been through a lot together, both as professional representatives of our governments, never forgetting that, but on a personal level too."[46]

No better indicator of the close friendship that Bandar and Powell have enjoyed over many years could be evidenced than when, on March 2, 2005, Bandar and Haifa hosted a glittering black-tie dinner at their magnificent

Racquetball partners Colin Powell and Bandar.

McLean home in honor of Colin L. Powell, following his retirement as secretary of state. The dinner was attended by sixty guests, friends of Bandar
and Powell, and included Richard Armitage,* Frank Carlucci,† Tom
Clancy,‡ Sam Donaldson,** Alan Greenspan,†† and a range of eminent
senators, government officials, and ambassadors, and their partners.

During this special and intimate dinner, Bandar provided eloquent testimony to his close friendship with Colin Powell, saying, tongue in cheek, "He
is the only man I know of, and the only official in the United States government, who has a prince as a secretary." As the laughter subdued, Bandar remarked, "To show you how much he abuses his power, today I had a couple of
meetings in the neighborhood here—in the State Department and the White
House—and I had to rush quickly and cut my briefings short so that I could
go to his house with the seating plan so that he could tell me what to do."

Bandar continued, "Seriously, I have met a lot of people in my life,
kings, Communist party former chiefs, presidents, heads of state, and so on,
and there are very few people whom I would really look up to with great respect and admiration, and—as much as it may hurt to say it—even affection, as I do this great man. We have seen good times and bad times
together. When the going is easy, there are a lot of people like Colin Powell,
but when the going is tough, there are very few of them, and Colin, my
friend, we will miss you, but this is a critical time and you know we will all
be coming back to you for wisdom and guidance."

In a joking accolade to Alma Powell's support for Powell, Bandar teased,

---

*Former deputy secretary of state (2001–2005), deputy assistant secretary of defense for East Asia and
Pacific (1981–1983).

†Currently chairman emeritus, and previously chairman of the Carlyle Group (1993–2003), former secretary of defense (1987–1989). He was also national security adviser to President Ronald Reagan, prior
to becoming secretary of defense.

‡Novelist, whose first book, *The Hunt for Red October*, was an international bestseller and movie. Clancy
has since written numerous bestsellers, but now that the Cold War is over, his latest novels and research
are centered around the Middle East.

**Sam Donaldson was co-anchor of *Prime-Time Live,* a regular panelist on *This Week,* and is a premier
broadcast journalist.

††The Honorable Alan Greenspan took office June 19, 2004, for a fifth term as chairman of the Board
of Governors of the Federal Reserve System. He originally took office as chairman to fill an unexpired
term as a member of the Board on August 11, 1987. Greenspan was then reappointed to the Board to
a full fourteen-year term, which began February 1, 1992, and ended January 31, 2006. Thus, Greenspan
served as chairman of the Board of Governors of the Federal Reserve System for 18 years and five
months, the second longest tenure as chairman.

"The only reason that Colin and I made it was because we married above our pay grade; we were so darn lucky." In his closing remarks, Bandar revealed the true nature of his admiration and friendship for Powell when he said, "Please raise your glasses to a great man and a great friend. I would like to remind everybody that fire warms up the body but friendship warms up the heart; you have warmed up the hearts of a lot of people around the world, Colin."[47]

In reply, Powell reminded his host that they had served together under five presidents since they met on an air base in Saudi Arabia in 1979 when a fresh young major breezed into the meeting in his flying gear together with his trademark red scarf. "We became friends that very day; it is a friendship that has continued for twenty-five years, through good times and some difficult times, through times of war and through times of peace, through times of challenge and through times of opportunity. I treasure the relationship I have with not only with you, my dear friend, but with your country and with the leaders of your country. It is a relationship that has stood the test of time and that has benefited both of our countries."

Continuing his tribute, Powell said, "The essence of our relationship is not what we do together. I don't think I would be overstating it if I were to say that Prince Bandar and I are kind of like brothers, and we have worked it for many years."

Determined to play yet another trick on Bandar, Powell recalled that he had given the prince a picture of himself to hang in the embassy, but he noted that it had disappeared. "Now one year, not too long ago," Powell explained, "Bandar gave me a gift; it was a beautiful gift and I was looking forward to it because he told me I would like it! And it showed up and it was a beautiful picture of Bandar in a beautiful silver frame, and I always thought, 'How am I going to reciprocate?'"

At this point, the prince's staff brought in an enormous portrait of Colin Powell, which he duly presented to Bandar, saying, "This is to replace the one that went missing; it should be mounted somewhere where Bandar can see it looking down on him to remind him that I am still watching over him."[48] As the laughter subsided, Powell reminded the audience that it was also the prince's birthday and he presented him with a magnificent bronze statuette of a buffalo.

After-dinner entertainment was held in the splendid drawing room, where Roberta Flack entertained the audience with a medley of her hits, including one composed especially for Nelson Mandela. A regular entertainer at Bandar's social soirées over the years, they have become great friends. Asked how she saw Bandar, Flack instantly responded, "I think he is the consummate diplomat at any level, personal or otherwise. He is a good listener. He is more than a diplomat; he is a cosmopolitan spirit. Not only is he charming, but there is something about his persona that just shines through. What you see with Prince Bandar is what you get. There are no angles to him." Flack paused and with a twinkle in her eye added, "He is a gorgeous hunk of a man; he is a hot number—very sensual, very sexy. He can't help it; he was born a hunk."

Flack then highlighted the prince's remarkable ability to make a person feel that he is totally focused on you whenever you are talking to him. "Prince Bandar is his own man," Flack stressed. "He can be counted on to be truthful and honest to the absolute best of his ability. He has tremendous dignity, integrity, and intelligence. He is a wonderful, wonderful man. He is a prince who has the ability to be down-to-earth. He genuinely loves life; he loves his children—he is a good dad and he is a good grandpa."[49]

While Bandar has enjoyed firm friendships with many world leaders, he holds Baroness Margaret Thatcher in particularly high esteem. Equally, his friendship with Prince Charles is also very close, and Charles extended a personal invitation to Bandar to his wedding to Camilla Parker Bowles in April 2005.[50] That friendship can be traced back to their experiences of Cranwell (Charles was also training at RAF Cranwell) and Charles's fascination with Islam.

Bandar's relationship with former President Nelson Mandela, however, is very special indeed. They are astonishingly close. Bandar views Mandela as a mentor and world-class statesman, while Mandela sees Bandar as an individual of extraordinary warmth, intellect, and loyalty. The depth of their friendship was perhaps best illustrated by Mandela's decision to invite Bandar to attend his wedding to Mrs. Graca Machel on the same day as he held his eightieth birthday, a day when Pretoria was filled with visiting heads of state who had been invited to attend Mandela's birthday party later that evening.

"When I married my wife and celebrated my eightieth birthday," Mandela recalled, "I invited Bandar. It was just a select group."[51] In practice, apart from President Mbeki, Archbishop Desmond Tutu, and Bandar, the wedding ceremony was a family affair.

"I got a call from Mandela," Bandar recalled. "We were in Pretoria for his eightieth birthday, and he said, 'If you have nothing else going on, I would like you to come in the morning to the presidential palace in Pretoria. I have a family gathering of my kids and grandchildren.'"

So the next morning Bandar went to spend some time with Mandela and his family.

While there, Mandela pulled Bandar aside and asked him, "What are you doing this afternoon?"

"Nothing, Mr. President," replied Bandar. "I am just going to rest and get ready for the big party."

Mandela said, "Do you think you can come and have tea with me?"

Bandar thought, "That's sweet of him, but strange—I have just had tea with him and his children and grandchildren, and I am going to have dinner with him at his party, so why does he want me to come for tea?"

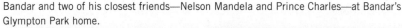

Bandar and two of his closest friends—Nelson Mandela and Prince Charles—at Bandar's Glympton Park home.

Not wishing to refuse an invitation or the opportunity to spend time with Mandela, Bandar asked, "What time?"

"Four o'clock in Johannesburg," said Mandela, "In my private house, not in the presidential palace."

Bandar said, "Fine."

"I want to tell you something," said Mandela as Bandar was leaving. "Just between you and I. Don't tell anyone, but I am getting married this afternoon."

"What?!" exclaimed Bandar. "Splendid—but is it true?"

"Yes, yes," said Mandela, who promptly extended an invitation to Bandar to attend the wedding that afternoon.

As they walked outside, Mandela said, "I want you to meet somebody—my jailer, a white man who is coming to celebrate my eightieth birthday with me. He has some presents for me. Let's go and see."

The jailer gave Mandela some shampoo and toilet soap, the same kind that he used to smuggle for Mandela when he was in jail. Bandar thought to himself, "What an individual, even his jailer has come to celebrate with him."[52]

When he returned to Pretoria, Bandar decided to go straight to his room, seeing no one, so that he could not let slip the secret of Mandela's wedding. But shortly after he arrived, he received a call from Mbeki, who told him that he had been invited to tea with the president at 4:00 P.M. that afternoon. Bandar said, "Okay, I will see you then." He made no mention of the wedding, nor did Mbeki, who was unaware of the planned ceremony.

Later that day, Bandar went to Mandela's house where there were perhaps ten reporters and photographers, taking pictures of anyone coming in or going out of his home as it was his birthday. Mandela and Mrs. Machel came out to meet him and introduced him to the family. Mandela revealed that he had to give the family thirty cows as a dowry.

Unaware that the wedding ceremony was to be a small affair, Bandar recalled, "I kept waiting for the other guests, because the town was full of who's who from around the world—and nobody came. I was waiting for the VIPs—but nobody came. I was waiting for the other officials from his government—but nobody came. There were just thirty people there, maximum. All of them were his family or her family, with just Tutu, Mbeki, and me as other guests."

Bandar was amazed at the exclusive nature of the gathering and was astounded to see that Mandela had invited a Muslim imam, a protestant minister, a rabbi, and a Hindu priestess to conduct the wedding. "It was really surreal and I was unsure what to do, Bandar observed, "I stood there thinking that perhaps I should have refused. But I suddenly realized I was one of the family."[53]

The service was conducted by the leader of the Methodist Church, Bishop Mvume Dandala, assisted by Mandela's friend and confidant, Archbishop Desmond Tutu, who gave a blessing. A reporter later recorded that Mandela was dressed in one of his characteristic shirts, and Mrs. Machel was in a long white cotton dress embroidered with gold thread. At the end of the ceremony, the happy couple exchanged rings and kissed, and were then blessed in turn by Sheik Nazeen Mohammed, the president of the Muslim Judicial Council, by Krishni Nanachand, a representative of the Hindu faith, and by Chief Rabbi Cyril Harris.[54]

Bandar recalled, "I was one of the thirty witnesses. And Madiba and Mrs. Machel were married in the Hindu faith, in the Islamic faith, in the Christian faith, and in the Jewish faith. It was the most incredible, historical, personal social scene I have ever seen in my life."[55]

When I subsequently asked Mandela to confirm that he had been married in four different faiths, he responded by saying simply, "That's true, I made sure that I didn't leave out any major religious faith because it is a way of uniting the country and to put all these religious faiths on the same basis."[56] It was an extraordinary personal gesture, but Mandela was particularly proud of the religious tolerance in his own government, which included several Muslim ministers, and he was concerned about the mounting tension between Christians and Muslims in South Africa. He is a firm believer that South Africa can help bridge the religious divide in the world today.[57]

At the end of the ceremony, Mandela turned to Archbishop Tutu and with a broad grin pointed at him and exclaimed, "This is the man who made me do this. We were happy living together and I felt I was too old to get married again. Mrs. Machel had no desire to get married. However, you nagged about my being a role model for young people and that our living together could be perceived by many as living in sin. So we have to blame you for getting married."

Mandela said to Bandar, "This man, my prince, kept nagging me, nagging me, nagging me, saying, 'You are the role model for the people and the young people—we tell them that we have AIDS [in South Africa] and you shouldn't do anything out of wedlock. What can we tell them when they say, 'Look at our president, our hero, living with his girl?' So in order to get him [Tutu] off my back, I had to get married."[58]

When I then asked Mandela why he had invited Bandar to join such an intimate wedding service, he replied, "I am out of circulation now, but whenever I am planning to have something big, I always have him in mind. Prince Bandar is my friend."[59]

As Bandar was leaving the wedding, he said, "Do you mind if I tell His Majesty and the crown prince about your marriage?"

"No, no, absolutely," Mandela responded. "You can tell them now."

"What if the press asks me questions?"

Mandela responded, "You can confirm it, but we don't want anyone to talk about the details."

Having said goodbye to Mandela, Bandar simply wanted to return to Pretoria to prepare for Mandela's birthday party later that same evening. He recalled how he was exhausted emotionally and physically, and wanted to get some sleep before the birthday party. As he left in his car, Bandar undid his tie and lit a cigar. "I thought I was walking into a zoo!" exclaimed Bandar. "The five photographers and cameramen had suddenly become hundreds. It was like a riot. They were all pushing their cameras into my face. They had waited all afternoon and the only photograph they had taken was of me."

Having escaped the media fracas as he left Mandela's wedding ceremony, Bandar returned to his hotel. As he arrived, the phone rang. "I was told it was the director of CNN calling from Atlanta," Bandar recalled.

The director said, "Look, we are hearing rumors that President Mandela has just gotten married, but nobody has confirmed it. We understand that you were there and our crew saw you leaving his house; can you help us, please?"

"Where are you hearing the rumors?" Bandar said. "On the wire?"

"No," the CNN director replied. "Everybody is running round like crazy trying to confirm it, but nobody there is daring to say anything about Mandela. We need confirmation."

"Yes," Bandar replied, "I can confirm to you that he got married."

"Will you go on air with CNN for a news flash?" asked the CNN director. When Bandar agreed, he said, "Okay, I will send a crew."

"I am not going to talk live," Bandar responded. "I am not going to talk on camera."

"Oh my God," said the deflated director. "Can you talk to a reporter on the phone?"

Bandar said, "Sure—but I can only say I was there and that he got married and who he got married to. But don't ask me who was there, their names, what happened, what ceremony, and so on."

"That's fine," responded the director. "Anything—but please talk first with us."

Bandar recalled that at this point he switched on CNN only to find that there was a caption saying, "Breaking news—President Mandela just got married and we have exclusive CNN confirmation." A reporter continued, "Bandar, Saudi ambassador to the United States, obviously a close friend of Mandela, was one of the few people at the wedding and he agreed to talk to us." With the phone line still open, he asked, "Prince Bandar, can you hear me?"

"Yes." Bandar responded.

"Is it true?"

"Yes, President Mandela got married this afternoon. I wish him and his bride well and every happiness. It is a happy day, for both his birthday and his wedding day are on the same day."

The reporter then asked, "You were there yourself?"

"Of course, I was there," Bandar responded. "Otherwise, why would I talk to you about it?"

"Can you tell us who was there?"

"No, I can't tell you who was there," Bandar said. "It was some of his friends and family."

"How was the family?" asked the reporter.

"I can't tell you," said Bandar. "If the friends and family want to talk about it, then that's their privilege, not mine."

The frustrated reporter interjected, "One last question. How many people were there?"

"About twenty to thirty people."

"That's all?"

"Yes."

"Okay, what do you know about the wedding?"

Bandar cheekily replied, "That's for me to know and you to find out! Goodbye."[60]

Since he established the Nelson Mandela Foundation in 1999, the former president of South Africa has had an endless stream of meetings, phone calls to the world's leaders, and flights around the globe organized by his loyal Afrikaner secretary, Zelda le Grange. Until recently, he has traveled frequently, particularly to Britain, the United States, and the Middle East, often in Bandar's private plane.[61] During my meeting with Nelson Mandela and Jakes Gerwel, Jakes reminded him that Bandar's aircraft had always been available to him. Mandela quickly agreed, saying, "That's true, perfectly true. He has never hesitated, and on most occasions he makes the offer; I don't know how sometimes he hears about it, but he makes the offer."[62]

This generosity on Bandar's part was confirmed by James Baker, who said, "Prince Bandar had brought over Nelson Mandela to the Rice Institute on his personal aircraft and that visit was a singular success."[63] On that occasion, Mandela was accompanied by Bandar. Taking questions from the audience, a twelve-year-old asked how he wanted to be remembered and what was in his heart. Mandela replied simply, "I never wanted to be regarded as an angel. I am an ordinary man with weaknesses—I am not a saint, unless you think of a saint as a sinner who keeps trying."[64]

Unlike many executive jets, Bandar's four-engine Airbus 340 aircraft rarely languishes on the tarmac for long. It is heavily utilized, flying an average of a thousand hours per year.[65] Examination of the aircraft log shows that it has racked up annual mileage that would take it to the moon and back every year, and still allow it to travel three times around the globe, journeys that burn almost 1.8 million gallons of fuel each year. The aircraft flight log includes destinations as diverse as Agadir, Amman, Anchorage, Cape Town, Casablanca, Honolulu, Islamabad, Rio de Janeiro, St. Lucia, Tripoli, and Xian.

Robert Deacon Elliott was responsible for supervising the refit of Bandar's aircraft before Bandar took delivery of it. He spent twelve months meticulously planning every detail of the aircraft design, an ambitious schedule that was completed within budget and on time. In a final touch of flamboyance, the delivery in Washington was timed to coincide with Bandar's birthday on March 2, 1998.[66]

While Rob Deacon Elliott has overall responsibility for Bandar's aircraft and its crews, day-to-day operations are controlled by Richie Thomas, a gifted pilot with an exceptional flying record. Arguably the most experienced ex-leader of the Red Arrows, the RAF Aerobatic Display Team, Thomas's record is superlative.* The aircraft requires two crews: one Amer-

---

*The Red Arrows has been the RAF Aerobatic Team for four decades. With a team motto of *Eclat*, meaning "brilliance," the team has created the culture of excellence, precision, and skill based on motivation, professionalism, self-discipline, and teamwork. These individual qualities provide the foundations that have enabled successive teams to represent the Royal Air Force to the highest possible standard.

ican, one British, which operate on a one-month-on, one-month-off basis. All the American crews are ex-89th or ex–Air Force One.[67]

Bandar's aircraft has also seen many distinguished visitors. The aircraft's chef, Henri Boehm, recalled, "President George Bush Senior and Mrs. Bush have been on the aircraft on several occasions, as has Secretary Baker and Secretary Powell."[68] Lead flight attendant Gina Preston showed me photographs taken on a flight from Washington to Houston. Bandar's guests on the aircraft on that occasion had been attending Reagan's funeral at Washington National Cathedral and were traveling to Houston for President Bush's eightieth birthday party. She explained, "We actually had President Gorbachev, President and Mrs. Bush, Secretary and Mrs. Baker, General Scowcroft, and Irish tenor Ronan Tynan, who performed at the church during the funeral."[69]

The aircraft was decked out with birthday congratulations, streamers, and balloons in a birthday celebration for President Bush and all of the flight staff wore cowboy outfits for the occasion. The music was Western style and lunch included, as a centerpiece, two birthday cakes—a white chocolate model of the White House and a dark chocolate Republican elephant, both of which Mrs. Bush took away with her when they arrived in Houston.[70]

Bandar's joking, wit, and appetite for fun are ever-present facets of his character; he loves to be the practical joker. An episode that occurred aboard his aircraft aptly illustrated his sense of humor.

Prince Faisal bin Turki, the prince's son-in-law, is a nervous flyer and has a particular aversion to takeoffs. As we prepared to depart during a speaking tour, there was a warning that Bandar was arriving. Shortly after, there was the usual flurry of bodyguards and other staff passing through the cabin toward the rear of the aircraft.

A broad grin and a hearty "Hello, everyone" announced the prince's larger-than-life appearance in the cabin. Everyone rose from their seats with a mixture of greetings ranging from the formal "Good evening, Your Royal Highness" to "Hello, Prince Bandar" and finally the more familiar "Hi, Boss." However, rather than taking his seat, the prince announced that he was going up to see the captain and promptly strode off toward the cockpit, turning and winking knowingly at Rob Deacon Elliott, before disappearing from view.

Just then, the aircraft began to move. As usual, Faisal looked apprehensive at the prospect of an imminent takeoff. As the aircraft trundled across the tarmac, progress was clearly visible on the giant flat screen on the forward bulkhead, since five or six strategically located external cameras provided views on all sides of the aircraft. At the end of the runway, the aircraft paused momentarily ready for takeoff.

As all aboard readied ourselves for the familiar roar of the engines and release of brakes, there was an unexpected announcement from the aircraft captain, Chief Pilot Al Turner. In his perfect English accent, he said, "Ladies and gentlemen, Prince Bandar has the controls and will be flying the aircraft until we reach cruising altitude. Prepare for takeoff—cabin crew, please take your seats." That message had barely time to sink in before the engine pitch rose and we accelerated forward down the runway. There was a look of terror on Faisal's face, and he became increasingly agitated as the aircraft gathered speed.

Now there was another announcement from the cockpit, *Steady, Your Highness—keep the stick forward until I give you the okay.* The commentary from the cockpit continued. *Ninety knots; one hundred knots—get ready to rotate, Your Highness—*(a pause)—*rotate—*(and then a cautionary) *steady, steady, that's it, Your Highness, just watch your starboard wing—easy—that's perfect!* These remarks continued from the cockpit as we gained altitude. An

From left to right: Son Fahad, son-in-law Prince Faisal bin Turki, sons Faisal and Abdulaziz (*at rear*).

anxious Faisal turned a disconcerting shade of gray—he was clearly not enjoying the experience.

At this point, Bandar's mischievous face poked into the cabin. He glanced across at Deacon Elliott and winked conspiratorially as he took his seat. It was clear that he had not been flying at all. Everyone in the cabin promptly burst out laughing and applauded, enjoying the joke. A look of relief swept across Faisal's face. Realizing that he had been the victim of a Bandar prank, he unleashed a stream of "Arab invectives," but a smile quickly reappeared as genuine relief set in. Bandar had demonstrated his appetite for fun, a trait that has often been reported in the media, as in *The Commanders*, when Bob Woodward wrote, "Working political and media circles with cigars, gifts, invitations, information, off-color stories and practical jokes, the prince was smooth and attentive. He could be both boyish and ruthless."[71]

In this brief chapter I have only been able to skim the surface of Bandar's friendships—relationships that have been forged over almost four decades, first as a fighter pilot and subsequently as a diplomat and statesman. There are also his many boyhood friends, such as one of his current Saudi retinue, Gen. Faisal Mifgai, a gifted poet and Air Force officer, and the talented and famous Arab-world singer, Mohammed Abdu. Equally, the profiled members of the traveling court comprise only a fraction of his traveling companions, as Bandar has many Saudi confidants, generals, doctors, and family members who travel with him.

Someone with Bandar's winning charisma, generosity of spirit, and genuine interest in people makes friends very easily with people from all backgrounds and all walks of life. With many of the people I have interviewed, staff and statesmen alike, a recurring facet is Bandar's ability to make everyone feel special, whatever their situation. But it is his unswerving loyalty, blended with an occasionally mischievous and often self-deprecating sense of humor, which make him not only a great friend to those who know him but also a formidable diplomat.

TWELVE

THE PRIVATE
PRINCE BANDAR

"The love of a family is life's greatest blessing."

ANONYMOUS

For Bandar, the most significant elements in his life are Saudi Arabia, his family, and his religion. All are intertwined.

In December 1972, Bandar married Princess Haifa, daughter of Saudi Arabia's ruler, King Faisal. In recalling how they met, Haifa explained, "Bandar was with my brother at Cranwell. My brother had talked about him to me, and about me to him; this was in 1966. From that time on, for some reason or other I had a feeling that this was the man I was going to marry—I really don't know why. I guess when you meet a person, you either get on or you don't get on, and we seem to get on quite well."

In part, Haifa based her decision to marry Bandar on her knowledge of his father. She explained, "His father always used to be with my father, and he traveled with him and he came to our house. Maybe it was because he resembles his father—his laughter, his sense of humor, his kindness, and his intelligence. Also the fact that he was well traveled and I was well traveled—it just clicked. I cannot say what one thing made it work, but it just clicked."

By tradition, the wedding took place in Haifa's father's home, King Faisal's palace. Although it was a splendid affair, the princess stressed that it was one of a number of weddings conducted that day. She explained,

"There were in fact five brides and grooms." After the wedding there was a large party—a party for just the women, during which the groom and part of his family would come to collect his bride and take her away. Haifa recalled, "It used to be that the first night was spent at the king's palace, and the next day, which was called in Arabic *Tehwal,* which means moving away, the bride would leave with her husband for the honeymoon. We started by going to Switzerland," Haifa recalled, "then on to France, and finally we went to Tunisia. By the time we came back to Saudi Arabia and to the Air Force base at Dhahran where Bandar was assigned, I was pregnant with my daughter Loulou."[1]

Bandar and Haifa have eight children: Loulou was born in September 1973, Reema in June 1975, Khalid in July 1977, Faisal in October 1980, Noura in September 1984, Fahad in July 1987, Hussa in April 1993, and finally, Abdulaziz in August 1994. Prince Faisal explained, "The eldest four are called 'the originals' because the top four grew up together when my father was in the Air Force in Saudi Arabia and occasionally in the United States, before we moved to Washington, D.C., so we got to see both sides of my father. The youngest four are known as 'the substitutes' or 'the replacements.' The younger ones grew up in D.C. when he was ambassador, so we [the originals] are almost more Saudi, and they [the substitutes] are more American. We are all, though, very, very Saudi—but there are little differences."[2]

Bandar relaxing with sons Khalid, Faisal, and Fahad at the family farm in Maryland.

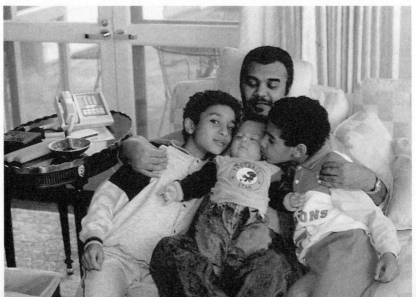

Strangely, less widely known is that Bandar and Haifa have a third set of children, for they have adopted two more. Selma is the daughter of one of Bandar's staff whose mother died while she was working for Bandar; her father also died after Bandar adopted her. Relatives asked Bandar to take care of her, and she has been a member of the family ever since. Jan Garcia, too, was adopted by Bandar, so that she could marry Bob Lilac when he was serving in Saudi Arabia.

Jan and Bob were married on May 3, 1976, but this was no ordinary wedding. It was a fairy tale wedding performed in Saudi Arabia, an event of a lifetime experienced by few, if any, Christian couples. Bandar had suggested that they marry at his home in al-Khobar. However, for that marriage to take place, the prince had to become Jan's legal guardian.

"There was a process," Bob Lilac explained, "according to the rules of the game in the kingdom, on how a wedding could take place under sharia law. A marriage, or a wedding contract, is an agreement between the father of the bride and the groom. In order for Jan to be married, she had to have a father or a legal guardian in the kingdom. But her father was in California. So in order to make it happen, which is what Ben wanted to do and we wanted to do, we went through a set of legal paperwork in which Ben became her guardian."

"In technical terms," Lilac continued, "it was as though Ben had ac-

Bandar and his "adopted daughter" Jan Lilac deliver the cake to Bob Lilac at Jan and Bob's wedding.

quired a form of limited power of attorney, so that he was able to turn her over for the purpose of her marrying me."

The couple obtained a power of attorney from Jan's father in California, who, in a certificate that was signed by the U.S. Secretary of State Dr. Henry Kissinger, and verified and legalized by both the U.S. and Saudi governments, made Bandar Jan's legal guardian. Only then were they able to have a *qadi** in Saudi Arabia officiate and authenticate the contract of marriage between Bob Lilac and Bandar. And to top it off, the *qadi* in this instance happened to be blind!

"Yes," said Lilac, "the contract was between me and Bandar."

Resplendent in his Saudi *thobe*, Lilac had to pay the bride price of ten Saudi riyals, about $3.75, to Bandar as Jan's legal guardian to complete this part of the traditional wedding process.[3] Lilac added with a smile, "And in the contract it also says that the agreement for getting into the marriage will be the same as getting out of the marriage. So I can get out of this marriage for only ten riyals."[4]

Speaking of Jan's place in the family, Reema confirmed, "Because my father adopted Jan, legally she is my older sister. This has become a family joke because on every occasion my father has done a deal or has been involved in a new project, he tells us that this will be part of Jan's inheritance." In the same way, Reema recalled that when any of the children are out of line, Bandar invariably says, "I will tell your older sister."

Describing the Bandar/Haifa brood, Reema divulged, "Loulou, the eldest, is the artist in the family, specializing in abstract paintings; she is also a keen photographer. When we were younger my sister Loulou was always more creative; I was more obtuse. I studied, I read, and I loved the museums, but I had zero artistic talent. I was always interested in archaeology. I realize now that I am creative in a different way; I look unconventionally at things." Reema went on to describe herself as a "daddy's girl" which she recognized only when she got married. Her elder sister Loulou recalled that during Reema's wedding celebration to Prince Faisal, her father very deliberately pinned a pair of Air Force wings on to Reema's dress. This had a huge personal significance for Bandar, as he subsequently confirmed that he regarded the moment when his own Air Force wings were pinned on his

*Qadi (also known as *qazi* and *kadi*) is a judge ruling in accordance with the sharia, Islamic religious law. Because Islam makes no distinction between religious and secular domains, *qadis* traditionally have jurisdiction over all legal matters involving Muslims.

chest as being one of the momentous events of his life. To echo that occasion by pinning a brooch of the Royal Saudi Air Force wings on his daughter's dress was the ultimate mark of approval. Reema cherishes those wings as a symbol of the strength of the bond between father and daughter.

The next in the family is Khalid, who Reema sees as being the image of her father. She said, "Khalid is my father as an adult." While their personalities are different, Khalid nonetheless has the presence and charisma that totally holds the conversation, much in the same way as his father does. He has a natural air of authority, is intelligent and charming. Khalid has recently been appointed chairman of Dayim Punj Lloyd Engineering, a joint venture with Indian company Punj Lloyd, and will operate in engineering, procurement, and construction of projects in the hydrocarbon, power, chemical, water, and sewage sector—civil infrastructure and industrial projects in Saudi Arabia.[5]

Reema compared her two brothers Khalid and Faisal with the two *Star Wars* characters, Luke Skywalker and Hans Solo. "They are always at each other," she said, "but they are best friends. Khalid went to Eton, then to Oxford, and finally to Sandhurst, so he is the only one with a typical English accent. He is the more serious side of my father, whereas Faisal is the American side of my father; he is a very keen Dallas Cowboys supporter.[6] As an avid Cowboys fan, Bandar even has his Airbus 340 furnished in the blue and silver colors of the Cowboys. Bandar's passion prompted Jerry Jones,

Bandar with sons Khalid and Faisal at a Dallas Cowboys game.

owner of the Cowboys, to say, "Our players have had tremendous respect for Prince Bandar for the last sixteen years—they probably feel that he owns the team."[7] Indeed, Bandar was quoted as saying, "I am their number one international cheerleader."[8]

The Dallas Cowboys website commented on a locker-room visit by Bandar and the capture of Saddam Hussein, reporting, "So how appropriate it was for a beaming Prince Bandar, Saudi Arabia ambassador and Cowboys groupie to be parading through the Cowboys locker room with an equally beaming Jerry Jones, and said to no one in particular while caught up in the moment, 'We got Saddam Hussein in the morning and beat the Redskins in the afternoon. What a great day!' "[9] Bandar's son Faisal explained what had sparked his own interest in football, saying, "When I was very young, my father used to take me to the Cowboys games. We used to watch the Cowboys on TV. It was the first thing we knew—Cowboys. But then as we got older, thank God, they got more and more successful, and so I got to like them in my own right. Now, if you see my apartment, the first thing you see when you open the door is a big shrine to the Cowboys. I've got glasses—I've even got Coca-Cola bottles for each of the Super Bowls we've won in the '70s and '90s with little helmets on them."[10]

Of Bandar's second group of four children, the "replacements," Reema said, "Noura is very, very clever with words. She is a writer and a poet." Fahad, a keen sportsman, admitted that he too likes writing—short science-fiction stories, yet Bandar explained that like Noura, Fahad is able to express himself in poetry.*

Talking to Fahad's talent as a poet, Bandar said, "I get really emotional when Fahad reads me a poem. And the fighter pilot in me, the Arab in me, and the macho in me, doesn't allow me to express my feelings and I feel sad about it. One of Fahad's poems was written after watching the war in Iraq on TV. Haifa told me about it." Bandar later asked Fahad to read the poem to him, and when Fahad finished, Bandar thought, "Jesus Christ, this man is more mature than all the world leaders." Bandar explained, "Fahad was talking about the war in an apolitical sense; he was not for the war, not against the war, not for Saddam. All that he was expressing—and it was a beautiful poem and it hurts every time I remember it—is why are we paying for the follies of older people? It was very powerful."

---

*Poetry was Arabia's principal form of literary expression in pre-Islamic times.

Fahad passed the entrance examination to Eton, and since joining the school in 2004 has shown a strong interest in architecture, something for which his father has shown a particular talent. He is going on to study architecture at a British university.

Hussa and Abdulaziz, the youngest children, appreciate all those things that every other young adult enjoys: sports, using the computer, and reading.

Bandar's frequent absences on diplomatic assignments during his time as ambassador inevitably required Haifa to act as the family anchor. In their early years as a married couple, apart from the constraints of the Air Force, Bandar and Haifa led a more or less typical family life, with Bandar going to work in the morning, returning in the evening, and often having weekends free. "When he was a fighter pilot," Reema said, recalling those years, "he came home and he could shut off from work. There was nothing that he had to carry over to home. So we would have Sunday barbecues, go swimming, and watch football together. Going on holiday, he could switch off, because he couldn't go flying when he was with us."[11]

That Haifa remained mostly at the family home at McLean, Virginia, over the two decades before Bandar resigned as ambassador provided stability, not only for the children, whose father's spontaneous absences were beyond his control, but for Bandar, too. With the incessant demands placed on him by Saudi Arabia, and his more frequent and lengthy trips to the kingdom, he was relieved of any additional pressures from home, knowing that Haifa was there for the family. Linda Weare, the palace house manager in Morocco, complimented Bandar and Haifa on the family balance they had achieved, remarking, "They have done the most amazing job with their children."[12]

That sense of balance, despite the demands of Bandar's office, was highlighted during a casual family supper evening in Washington in 2003. The phone rang and Bandar answered. He looked up from the phone and told the older children to pack their bags as they were "off to Saudi tomorrow." They merely said, "Yes, sir." It was as if it were an everyday occurrence—no big deal. A guest asked Haifa if she would be going too. She immediately responded that the little ones were at school and needed her in Washington. Jeri Pierre, Haifa's secretary, took great pains to stress that Haifa "complements Bandar in an extraordinary way" and then revealed the sense of excitement that would come over her whenever Bandar returned home from a trip away.[13]

The recurrent trips between East and West over the years, and his experience as a fighter pilot—having trained in the United Kingdom, the United States, and Saudi Arabia—enabled Bandar to develop an ability to slip into each culture with remarkable ease. His daughter Reema underscored his skill at stepping from the Saudi world into the Western world almost seamlessly, saying, "He functions perfectly in each."[14]

But despite Bandar and Haifa's best efforts to maintain a stable family unit, wherever they are located, and regardless of Bandar's calls to duty and consequent absences over the years, the family has experienced its share of distress. While the children were staying with Haifa at the family home in Jeddah, there was a horrendous car crash involving two of the children, Noura and Fahad.

"Fahad was four years old," Haifa related. "They had a very bad car accident when a station wagon ran into their car. The two children were all right, but the two nannies and the driver died. Fahad had hairline fractures in his thigh and a few scratches on his cheek; Noura had very slight concussion and cuts to her face on her eyebrows, but, thank God, they were both fine. That was a major thing for both of us; the near loss of our children."

Haifa explained that Bandar was still in the United States at the time, while she was visiting her mother in Saudi Arabia during Ramadan. The accident occurred just before the breaking of fast in the evening. "The other driver was in a hurry to get to wherever he was going because of the fast, and the children were going to the palace where my mother lives," Haifa explained. "He just slammed into them. Fahad was in hospital for ten days."[15]

"That was a horrible time," Bandar recalled when talking about the incident. "Our nanny died after she had taken the children to the curbside where they would be safe. Then she sat down and died." In an emotional account of the accident, Bandar explained, "I was in Washington; I got a phone call from Haifa telling me that the little ones had been in a car accident, but no big deal. She said that they were fine, so I asked her to keep me posted. I planned to talk to them as soon as I could and keep on top of the situation. Then my brother called me to tell me that they were fine and I thought, 'Why is he ringing me if they are fine?' That's when I got really worried. So I said to him, 'Don't fool around with me, I'm not a child; are they dead? If they are, tell me now.' I really had my doubts and worries, so I decided to leave for Jeddah immediately."

"When we got there," Bandar continued, "I went straight to the hospital. As I walked in, they were both in the same bedroom, and they were laughing and joking. I was really relieved and that's when Haifa told me that three other people were dead. If I had known that, then I would have thought that they were dead, too. It really hit me hard; it hit home how close they came to dying."

Haifa explained to Bandar that the children had been brought to a nearby military hospital by passersby and no one knew who the children were. Then Haifa said to him, "The doctor wants to say hello to you; he's really looking forward to meeting you."

The young Saudi doctor said to Bandar, "Do you remember me?"

"To be honest, no," said Bandar. "I don't remember you, but my wife says you took care of the children. Thank you very much for what you've done."

The story took on a new dimension as the doctor explained, "I have waited for this moment for a long time." He then told Bandar how he had been a government-sponsored student in America. When he finished his training as a plastic surgeon, the university wanted him to take a further course to enhance his skills. So he wrote to the Saudi education attaché, asking that he might be allowed to stay for a further year and then return to the kingdom. In what he described as "a classic case of bureaucracy," the young doctor was told that it was impossible. Although he continued to press his case, going back and forth to the embassy, he made no progress.

A few days before he was due to go home, some friends suggested that he write to the Saudi ambassador, which he did. "On the day he was leaving for the airport," Bandar recalled, "he got a call from my office telling him that I had approved his extension. So he completed his course, but I never met him. However, when I did meet him, there he was looking after my children." Bandar was stunned by this coincidence. The doctor simply observed, "I owe you so much and I am glad that I have been able to help you."

As soon as Bandar took on his diplomatic role in Washington, he was tasked by King Fahd to undertake countless missions as his emissary and often as envoy for U.S. presidents and other world leaders. His absences from home accelerated. These demands of duty precluded Bandar's giving as much time to his family as he would have wished. Speaking at a time when Bandar was still ambassador, Reema observed, "With the job now, he doesn't have the luxury of coming home and switching off. It's a continuous twenty-four-hour job, so when he does make the time and effort for us, we appreciate it more. I don't think the youngest four got the same opportunities [as the eldest four children], but in the relationship he creates for them, he is conscious of this and takes time out for them, which I think is great, because he is so busy. It's fun to see him let loose with them."[16]

But Bandar also employs humor in the upbringing of his children. "He doesn't take himself too seriously," Reema confirmed, and she added with a smile, "and whenever we get over the top he always says, 'Who do you think you are? Take ten steps back and think about it.' That makes me laugh and it puts everything back into perspective." Bandar clearly likes to try to keep his children in check and keep their feet firmly on the ground—much as his traveling court does for him.

Prince Faisal also highlighted his father's use of humor, saying, "A lot of our relationship with him has to do with humor; he is always joking with us. Even when we were kids there was always a little bit of humor attached to everything. If we were in trouble, he'd always turn it into a joke."

As an example, Faisal observed, "I remember when I was at Eton, I broke my nose playing the Wall Game.* A guy was trying to push me away, when someone elbowed me in the nose and broke it. I remember I was so nervous because I never tell my mother when I get hurt as she gets scared."

Faisal now demonstrated the difference between mother and father, saying, "I remember my mother found out and she spent an hour on the phone with me." However, contact with Bandar was markedly different. He grinned as he recalled, "I got a two-minute call from my father, and it made everything so much easier."

Bandar called his son and said, "I hear you broke your nose."

"Yes, sir," responded Faisal.

"Are you okay?" asked Bandar.

"Yes," said Faisal.

"How did you break it?" asked Bandar.

Faisal told him the story of the Wall Game.

---

*The first known occurrence of the Eton Wall Game was in 1766. It has two teams—the Collegers (students on scholarship) and the Oppidans (students paying tuition)—who play on a narrow strip of land next to a slightly curved brick wall. The field of play is about 360 feet long by 16½ feet wide. The aim is to score a goal at the opposing end of the wall. Players are not permitted to handle the ball, and only their feet and hands can touch the ground. Striking or holding opponents is also against the rules. The goal area is known as the *calx*, Latin for "chalk," and here the rules change to allow passing back. There are two forms of scoring: a shy is worth one point and a goal earns nine points. The slow-moving scrums usually lead to 0–0 scores. However, while shies are not infrequent, goals are exceptional, and none have been scored in a senior game since 1909.

Bandar said, "Is his nose broken?"

Faisal said, "Not yet, sir."

"Good," said Bandar.

"End of conversation," Faisal remembered with a laugh. "But it gave me a chance to laugh and get through it."

Before his resignation as ambassador, Bandar had frequently talked of his regrets at not being able to spend more time with his family. When I pointed out to him that his children fully understood the demands that were placed on him, he said, "That only makes it worse; that makes it even more painful—that's loyalty." Haifa's response to the demands made of Bandar and his frequent absences was uncompromising: "I am so proud of him and the children are so proud of him and admire him so much because they know what he is doing. Although he spends time away from them, they appreciate that this is his work and it has never been a problem that he is away."[17] In practice, the family adjusted well to the punishing schedule Bandar was obliged to keep, but when he was at home, he endeavored to lead a normal family life.

A glimpse of that normality was provided one evening in McLean. The phone rang every five or ten minutes, and from time to time Bandar was discreetly presented with a range of documents, notes, and papers brought in by a butler carrying a silver tray. He read and assimilated these, while still engaging in conversation and making calls out. He kept an eye on half a dozen or so news channels—Saudi, U.S., and Arab—and on Hussa, who was bemoaning the fact that no one had eaten any of the food that she had cooked with her nanny. Turki, his grandson, had climbed on him following Bandar's aside to him, "Come here, monkey head"—all while monitoring his laptop. As Faisal said, "He can be on the phone one minute to the king, and then my little niece or nephew comes into the room and he's like a kid again."[18]

In a tacit recognition of the pressures placed on her father, unremitting de-

Bandar with his granddaughter Sarah

mands that imposed a heavy workload that was exacerbated by the need to react to the working day in Riyadh as well as that of Washington, Reema reflected, "When we were younger, it was unconscious fun, whereas now I think he is more aware of when a moment is special. It's because of all the things he knows and the things he deals with all night. He doesn't carry the weight of it over to us; he keeps it into himself, and whereas the first four can see this, the replacements don't always see it in the same way. But he does attempt to make time for the youngest four whenever possible, even though there are one hundred and fifty million things going on in his mind."

Despite their large family, Reema explained that her father still treated all of them as individuals. She explained that with regard to school, Fahad and Loulou liked to be asked how they had done, whereas the other children knew that while they could approach him at any time if it were important, Bandar would not harass them about school. "After an examination," said Reema, "he will never say, 'How did you do?' It's for you to tell him. My parents would never harp on about, 'You have to have these grades, or you have to do this or you have to do that.' My father would say, 'All I ask you to do is to pass, and if you do that and you're satisfied, then I am satisfied. If you are satisfied and you get an A, then that satisfies me. But I am not doing your work and I am not leading your life—so you choose.' There was never any pressure."[19]

When asked what aspirations they had for their children, Haifa said, "I think it would be that they love what they are doing, that they excel in it, and they are happy with what they are doing. I think that if you impose your own aspirations they never excel." Haifa then set out her philosophy in life with regard to the upbringing of her children, "There are two things that are important: respect—a child's respect for their parents or the parent's for the child; and discipline—you have to have discipline in your family life and your own life. The other major thing that is important is religion. If you fear nothing in life,

Bandar at prayer

but you fear God—you have discipline. If you have no fear of God, then you are afraid of nothing and there is no accounting for anything."[20]

Haifa's comments about religion highlight the importance of the Muslim faith in the Bandar household. It is all encompassing, while never being intrusive. "What I appreciate about my father," said Reema, "particularly when it comes to religion, is that his faith is strong." Reema explained that he would often say to his children, "Your faith is *your* faith and your life is *your* life; I am giving you the skills and techniques that I know and that's it."

I was to experience that influence during the early months of writing Bandar's biography. Toward the end of 2003, my wife Wendy and I were invited to "break fast" with Bandar and his family during Ramadan. On arrival at McLean we were shown into the Moroccan Room, a long, large, very splendid room decorated in traditional Arab *majlis** style, with softly upholstered seating facing into the center of the room and half-tiled mosaic walls.

As we entered the room, I noticed some figures in the adjacent conservatory area and could see that Bandar was reading to his sons Fahad and Abdulaziz. As I waited, I cast my eyes over the many family photographs set out on tables at the head of the room. Prominent among those photographs was Bandar's father, Prince Sultan, but there was also a signed photograph of President George H. W. Bush, Barbara Bush, President George W. Bush, and Laura Bush.

Shortly after, Haifa entered the room and welcomed us. She looked relaxed and elegant in traditional Saudi dress, which she told Wendy she wears in Washington during Ramadan. Haifa explained that Bandar was reading the Qur'an, a task he liked to perform every day whenever possible during Ramadan. Haifa then led us to our seats and a butler placed a tray containing dates, a glass of water, a glass of juice, and a glass cup of traditional Arabic coffee, flavored with cardamom, on one of the tables in front of us in readiness for the breaking of the Ramadan fast.

Wendy and I had joined Haifa on the righthand side of the room as we entered, but she explained that when Bandar arrived, I should join him on the opposite side of the room, where the men would sit. A few minutes later, Bandar entered the room and his face lit up; a huge grin spread from

---

*As stated earlier, *majlis* describes a room in a private home used to entertain family and guests, the seating usually arranged around three walls of the room. In some homes, there is a women's *majlis* and a men's *majlis*.

ear to ear as he saw us. A handshake quickly became a bear hug and we moved to our appropriate places. All of the children at home had joined us in this family gathering. Suffice it to say, we exchanged pleasantries until a hungry Fahad reminded his father, "It is time!" Haifa confirmed that it was past the due time for the end of fasting, and Bandar gave his consent to start eating. Everyone duly tucked into their dates and drinks.

Bandar later drew me to one side and showed me the Qur'ans laid out on the table in the conservatory where he had been reading to his sons. He pointed out their prayer mats and explained that he was acting as an imam, leading his sons in learning to read the Qur'an and then in the traditional prayers.

As we turned to join the rest of the family downstairs, Bandar grasped my shoulder firmly and said, "Being able to read the Qur'an in this way during Ramadan makes up for the times when I am away because of official duties; it is a very special time made all the sweeter for me because I was never able to do it with my father." The emotion in his voice was all too evident and it was clear that Bandar cherished this special time with his children.

The pressures on Bandar have, over the years, taken their toll. Given his achievements on the world stage, his self-confessed tendency toward depres-

Breaking the fast at Ramadan with (*clockwise from left*) H. H. Prince Mohammed, Tarek Shawaf, Gen. Shathri, Bandar, Dr. Majid, Bandar's son Prince Khalid, and Fred Dutton.

sion can be attributed to both his success and his overachieving drive. There have been other factors at play, however, including several back operations that Bandar has had to endure following his flying accident in 1977. In the years that followed, Bandar would have recurrent back problems that were both painful and worrisome. As each year passed, his condition worsened, until in 1994, an orthopedic consultant diagnosed a calcification in the spinal column that was pinching nerves and causing him intense pain. After an operation that involved the chipping away of new bone growths surrounding the nerves, an extremely delicate and dangerous procedure, the surgeon reported that the nerves very quickly turned a healthy shade of pink from their previous gray color.

It was during this time that Bandar experienced his first period of full-blown depression, a condition he admitted he had previously thought was for wimps. During one major episode, he shut himself in his room for two weeks before he was able to shake himself out of a depressed state. Bandar suffered another episode in 1995 following the stroke suffered by King Fahd, his long-term mentor and friend. Bandar recalled how fifteen minutes before Fahd suffered the stroke, the king had tasked him with a mission to see both John Major and Bill Clinton. Reflecting on that stroke and the king's subsequent incapacity, Bandar thought to himself, "I don't have the energy or desire to work anymore." He simply wanted to be alone, but was aware that he still had a duty to his country. Nonetheless, he was unable to avoid the acute depression that he suffered as a result.[21]

On this occasion, however, Bandar wisely asked for professional help and recovered by going to Aspen with his family for a break. Shortly after arriving, in an extraordinary display of honesty, Bandar assembled his wife and children and told them all he would need their help, explaining his problem to them. This was a hard confession for Bandar to make, but he emerged refreshed after a two-month break in Glympton and Marrakech.

Speaking to his depressive tendencies, Loulou suggested that Bandar's circle of friends—his traveling court—may well have been an effective antidote to Bandar's "black dog."* Speaking about the pressures that her father

---

*Winston Churchill's struggle with depression became known only after his death, when it was revealed by his personal physician, Lord Moran. Churchill referred to such bouts as his "black dog." There is a convincing argument that suggests that Churchill's black dog and the depressive tendencies of many other great men, such as Tolstoy and Luther, may have inspired their great achievements, driving them on as they sought to escape their troubled mental states.

experienced, Loulou said, "I think with the nature of his work, he has to be remote, or thinks he has to be remote." In an oblique reference to Bandar's depression, Loulou said, "They say that it takes only one snowflake to cause an avalanche."[22]

Loulou was alluding to the acutely sensitive information presented to Bandar, who was often faced with problems for which he had to find a solution, and which he could not share with anyone. By adopting the traditional Saudi style of diplomacy—operating in the shadows—the pressure was intensified, and occasionally, that "additional snowflake" could tip Bandar into a period of despondency and self-doubt. Recognizing his father's weakness, his son Faisal said, "It's difficult for us a lot of the time, because we can tell when he is not happy, when something is wrong and we know that he can't talk about it, so we don't ask."[23]

Bandar's episodes of depression have not escaped the attention of the media. It was reported in late 2002 that after 9/11, which saw the effective destruction of all he had worked for in Washington for the previous two decades, "Not surprisingly, the prince has lowered his profile over the past year. The rumors in Riyadh have been that he has suffered from depression and spent months away from Washington."[24]

Speaking as a close friend, Colin Powell addressed Bandar's depression and insecurity when he stressed, "It's deep-rooted and you can't change it. He has an intense fear of mortality. I've been through a couple of illnesses with him." Powell amplified his comments, saying, "It has haunted him. I don't know if it is chronic depression of a medical nature, or whether it is mood swings because of events, as opposed to clinical or medical." Speaking now to the factors that he believed explained Bandar's character and tendency toward depression, Powell added, "It is mortality, insecurity, and his place in the family." When I observed that the specter of depression first appeared after Bandar's flying accident and his back problem, Powell replied, "His back problem has nagged him for years; then he had an operation not too long ago, and he won't tell me when I ask him about it."

It has been said that had he not become a fighter pilot or a royal emissary, Bandar could have excelled as an architect. That unconditional accolade was made by Tarek Shawaf, a professional engineer who has been involved in the construction of many of the prince's homes. Joe Ramsey, another close friend, was equally serious when he said, "Bandar missed his calling; he should have been an architect and a home builder."[25] From his first modest one-bedroom single-story house, which he built as a young fighter pilot in Dhahran, to the magnificent palatial residences he now owns, Bandar has taken a very personal interest in the design and construction of each. He enthuses over architects' plans, able to visualize the resulting structures. As his barber, John Veltri,* recalled, "I have a passion for architecture and Prince Bandar does, too." Veltri then related that on one occasion, discovering his interest in architecture, Bandar took out the plans of a palace he proposed building in Saudi Arabia and discussed them with him for about four hours.[26]

Bandar has luxurious homes throughout the world, and these would justify a book in itself. The very design of each of his properties affords a revealing insight into his cross-cultural background and they exemplify his cosmopolitan flair and amazing eye for detail. Each property blends into the existing landscape and uses local materials and building styles. Hence, he has a wooden lodge, Hala Ranch,† in Aspen; Arabian palaces in Riyadh, Jeddah, Marrakech, and Rabat; and a grand country mansion in Glympton in Oxfordshire.

Of Glympton Park, George and Barbara Bush were impressed by the care taken during the restoration of the main house to ensure that every stone was marked so that it could be repositioned in precisely the right place during the refurbishment.[27] "The reconstruction of the house was an immense task," recounted Peter Browne, the estate manager, "and saw the brick-by-brick demolition of the property to ensure that as much of the original material as possible, including the roof trusses, were reemployed when it was rebuilt."[28]

However, Bandar's approach to the acquisition and reconstruction of Glympton provides a revealing insight into his nature. As I interviewed former President Bush and the former first lady, Mrs. Bush recalled the story of Bandar's purchase of Glympton, saying, "When he bought it, there was a lot of criticism saying 'we don't want an Arab' and stuff like that. The first thing he did was to go in and fix up the whole village." President Bush added, "He bought the village and fixed up everybody's home." Mrs. Bush continued, "Plumbing, roofing, electricity; people who did not have jobs, he

---

*John Veltri has cut Bandar's hair across the globe, ever since the prince first arrived in Washington, D.C. Veltri cut his hair at 5 A.M. on the day Bandar became ambassador and has continued to cut it ever since.

†*Hala* means "welcome" in Arabic.

gave them all jobs and fixed their houses, so when the British papers came out and said, 'How do you like this—an Arab prince buying you?' they said, 'We think it's great.' "[29]

Each of Bandar's homes is enormous, large enough to house eight children, nannies, his adopted daughter, and guests—the main lodge in Aspen is some fifty-five thousand square feet—but the homes are not intrusive. Glympton Park and Aspen are tucked away along extensive private country roads, whereas his palaces in Riyadh and Jeddah are located behind thick, towering walls, guaranteeing privacy and enhancing security.

His sizeable estates are magnificently landscaped and are often farmed. There are some fifteen hundred date palms in Riyadh; orchards of many tropical fruits in his palace in Marrakech; and sheep, prize-winning cattle, and a shooting lodge with around sixteen thousand pheasants at Glympton Park and its twenty-five-hundred-acre estate.

Peter Browne recalled, "During one shoot at Glympton, Bandar invited Bush Senior who was accompanied by a hefty security detail." Clearly amused, Browne recounted, "Shortly after shooting commenced, President Bush hit a bird that promptly careered toward the security detail, which duly scattered. Prince Bandar dryly remarked to the president, 'I would question the coolness under fire of your security detail.' "[30]

A walk in the grounds of any of his homes might lead to the unexpected—a folly, or eccentric building. Bandar has built, for example, a mud house in the grounds of his Riyadh palace to remind himself of his roots. It is a replica of the hut in which he lived as he grew up, albeit this

Bandar's Oxfordshire retreat at Glympton Park.

one is full of modern conveniences in addition to traditional features. It has been built in the customary Arab style in that it has the appearance of a mud and straw structure. In its large entrance hall there is an abundance of Arab traditional carpets, extending into the main reception room, which is conventionally furnished in *majlis* style. This room overlooks a pool and walled enclave that has a Bedouin tent in one corner of the courtyard. Prince Charles and Camilla, Duchess of Cornwall, stayed there in April 2006 on a visit to Saudi Arabia.

However, the mud house contains a surprise. "It includes a reconstructed cowboy saloon–style room," said Barbara Bush, "complete with a large modern theater that contrasts so much with the simple style of the main house itself."[31] Here Bandar can indulge his love of old movies, though even here relaxation can never be complete. Immediately in front of his armchair in the center of the theater, cleverly positioned at floor level behind a bank of seats in front, are six TV screens streaming breaking news from both East and West.

Rob Deacon Elliott described another folly, a tiny thatched cottage situated by the lake in the grounds of Glympton Park. He recalled that many years ago, his parents lived in a cottage near Andover, a cottage visited often by the prince when he was in the United Kingdom. Theirs was a small white cottage roofed with traditional thatch. As Deacon Elliott recalled, "Ben said to me, 'One day I'm going to have one of these in my garden.'" Deacon Elliott said that when Bandar was restoring Glympton Park, the prince called him and said, "Could you send me a picture of Wild Rose Cottage?" which Deacon Elliott duly did. "The next thing I knew was that a little cottage was built by the lake at Glympton," said Deacon Elliott, "a virtual replica of my parents' home."[32]

James Baker recalled a visit to Bandar's home in Aspen where Bandar has built a log cabin away from the main house—another folly. The cabin, furnished with a wide range of authentic Indian and cowboy antiques, is appropriately named Bear Cabin since just inside the door is a brown bear, which Bandar had hunted himself. Secretary Baker joked, "I told him that he probably had it tied down before he shot it and that it was a hunt in which he had the backup of a dozen security men armed with machine guns and personal arms." He continued, "I invited the prince to my ranch in Texas, which we flew over to allow him to see it properly." As they passed over Baker's house, however, Bandar exclaimed, "It seems a little small." Baker smiled as he recalled that it was somewhat smaller than Bandar's Bear

Cabin, which was merely a small addition to his Aspen property.[33] In fact, Baker wrote tongue in cheek in Bandar's guest book, "Your gorgeous but modest little ranch reminds me of our 'shack' in Wyoming! Thanks for a spectacular time."[34]

In that same guest book, Bill Richardson, former U.S. Secretary of Energy had penned, "Thanks for:

1) All your help with oil prices.
2) Your hospitality in the *world's greatest* property.
3) Your friendship with the United States."

From the many entries in the Bear Cabin guest book, I extracted an entry by President Jimmy Carter, who wrote, "This has been another great visit—the skiing, beauty, hospitality and pleasure for our family—Thank you, again." Long after Carter had left the White House, Bandar found out that he and his wife Rosalynn had taken up skiing. Carter admitted to me, "I never saw skis until I was sixty-two years old—when I started skiing. Then Bandar sent word to me that he had a ski lodge in Aspen."

Three years later, Carter took his entire family out to Aspen, staying in Bandar's lodge. As he recalled his visit, Carter said, "We were sitting around the breakfast table one time and I had little grandchildren there who loved to ski." He grinned broadly as he said, "Every grandfather is always eager for expressions of love from one his little grandkids." The former president ex-

Bandar the bear hunter

plained how Bandar's ranch was well equipped with video game machines and big television screens—a kid's paradise. He then related a conversation with one of his grandchildren—Jeremy.

"Papa," said Jeremy. "Are you going to die someday?"

"Well, Jeremy," Carter said, "everybody has to die someday, but I hope that it will be a long time in the future."

"Jeremy," inquired his mother Annette, "why did you ask?"

"Well," replied Jeremy, "I just want to make sure that when Papa dies, that Bandar will let us come again."

President Carter promptly burst out laughing. He admitted, "It was kind of a blow to my ego."[35]

Security surrounding Bandar, his family, and his homes is paramount, as several attempts have been made on his life over the years. In an almost blasé affirmation of an assassination attempt on him in London in the late 1970s, Bandar remarked, "It was only because it was the first time that it was memorable; the other times didn't stick in my memory." The prince explained that while driving though London in 1978 or 1979, "I just looked and this car was beside me and there was a man pointing a gun at me!" A shocked Bandar repeated, "At me!" He continued, "And you just don't compute, you know; you think, 'Why would anyone want to point a gun at me?' So instinctively I ducked. When I looked up he was gone and I thought I must be seeing things! But there was the hole from the bullet going in one side of the car and out the other. So I said to the driver, 'Turn around and go the other way,' and being very English, he said, 'Pardon me, sir?' and I said, 'Don't pardon me! Turn around!' So he did and took me off somewhere else."

As a consequence, Bandar's homes embrace a host of state-of-the-art security measures preventing the unwelcome visitor from entry.

When designing the internal space of his homes, Bandar always considers the comfort of family, friends, and other visitors. Over the years he has created an appropriate formula so that there are common elements in each home. Formal rooms, where royalty, diplomats, and distinguished guests are entertained, are lavishly decorated. In his Riyadh palace there is a spectacular Chinese room full of treasures, including porcelain, sculptures, and a huge, intricately carved rosewood screen. The principal *majlis* here is beautiful, decorated in deep blue and white with a rich silk carpet on the floor.

Every home has a vast informal room for entertaining family and friends. This typically has an indoor swimming pool and is located down-stairs away from the public rooms. There is invariably a lounge area at one end and a wall of high-tech television screens and music centers, and each of them has an integral dining area. The ambassador's residence in Wash-ington, since vacated by Bandar, and his palace in Jeddah, followed this de-sign; Glympton Park is similar. The enormous space allows children, grandchildren, nannies, friends, and staff to move about freely or to relax in different areas without intruding on one another.

Bandar enjoys company, and his traveling court frequently joins him during the evening, as do members of his family. Considerable thought has therefore been given to accommodating his many guests, either within the main house or palace, or in luxurious villas within the grounds. Reema ex-plained, "My father is a frustrated architect. No building is ever complete, because he is always looking at ways of improving it to make it more com-fortable, knocking down walls and the like. He is continually rebuilding things and adding to things. And it's always—always—for other people's comfort. I find that really fascinating; he is always doing it for somebody else, and I am often tempted to say, 'Do it for you; forget all of us and do it for yourself.' "[36]

It could be argued that at Glympton Park, Bandar has done just that. For in this English manor house there is a distinct air of masculinity. The grand entrance hall is filled with antiques and period paintings. But it is the ar-mory of weapons—muskets, swords, daggers, and pikes—arrayed in perfect symmetry on every wall of the Staircase Hall that is utterly astounding.[37] Peter Browne, the estate manager, explained, "Prince Bandar had always in-tended that Glympton be a masculine house, hence the armory inside the main hall, which includes replica firearms. It is a strange quirk of law, but antique firearms don't require a certificate, whereas the replica versions, even nonworking models, require certification. However, this was only dis-covered after surplus weapons [from Glympton] were auctioned off in Lon-don and the police began to investigate the source of the illegal weapons."[38] Browne subsequently had to send all the weapons acquired for the main hall to Birmingham to confirm that they had been deactivated—a major task given the arsenal of antique and replica weapons mounted in the main foyer at Glympton.

Wherever he is in the world, Bandar likes to mix with the local commu-nity. He particularly enjoys taking friends and family to nearby restaurants. In Washington, a favorite eatery is the Peking Gourmet Inn located in a nondescript shopping mall in North Virginia. In Oxfordshire, Bandar likes to frequent a small Indian restaurant in a local village, and on one occasion when George H. W. Bush visited him in Jeddah, Bandar took him to the local pizza parlor. However, Bandar tells a story of one such visit near his Glympton home when good intentions almost led to embarrassment.

"Karmi, Ramsey, Dutton, and I were out walking around the estate at Glympton and the local area," Bandar explained. "Now, there is one pub that I was told was the most gossipy around and it would be best not to go there. But as we passed the pub, me being me, and it being a hot day, I said, 'Let's go and have a drink.'"

"There were two security guys with us," Bandar continued, "one Saudi, one British. So I said to them, 'Let us go in first, and you follow a few minutes later. We went in and sat in one corner—they then came in and sat opposite. In fact, they stood out, because they were wearing suits, white shirts, and ties, whereas we were casually dressed. Bandar explained that he went up to the bar and ordered the drinks, but when it came time to pay, 'I slapped my chest—no money!'"

Bandar looked around him, imitating his actions on the day, "Has anyone any money?" He explained that he didn't carry money and he wasn't expecting to need any. None of the prince's companions had any money either, so he thought to himself, "I can't say to the landlord, 'I haven't got any money. I'll just call Glympton and get it sent down.' It would have been in all the papers by the morning. So I went over and said to security, 'I haven't any money!'"

The British security officer immediately stood up and said, "I'll pay, my pleasure."

Bandar responded, "I'll give it back later."

The officer replied, "No, please sir, don't."

"Sometime later," Bandar recalled, "when his tour of duty was over, the security guy came to see me with a bottle of whiskey. I didn't take much notice at first, but thought, 'This is a strange gift to give to a Saudi Muslim prince.' But then I saw the House of Commons label, which was signed by lots of prime ministers including Tony Blair, Edward Heath, James Callaghan, Margaret Thatcher, and John Major."

Bandar said to the officer, "Did you buy this piece?"

"No sir," responded the police officer. "I stood with this bottle in the Houses of Parliament, and as people passed, I got them to sign it. This is a thank you from me. In all my time in Special Branch, I have always dreamed of someone saying, 'I can't pay for this,' and I would stand up and say 'allow me sir!' And for it to be a prince makes it very special."

It is Bandar who frequently does the giving, however, with many charitable institutions, establishments, and individuals benefiting from his numerous generous donations. There are those large donations that are in the public eye such as his funding of the Aspen Valley Hospital CAT scan equipment at a cost of $1 million, and the trauma unit, also at the Aspen Valley Hospital. Talking about the trauma center, William (Willy) R. Jordan III* said, "The hospital called me and said, 'Our crash room is totally inadequate; our surgeon has researched it and we have got to upgrade the equipment at a cost of some $350,000. Can Prince Bandar contribute to this?' I said, 'Let me talk to him.'"

Jordan described Bandar's response to the request for a contribution when he put it before him. Bandar said, "How much are they trying to raise?"

Jordan responded, "The whole crash room and 'state-of-the-art' equipment is $350,000."

Without blinking, Bandar said, "Buy the whole thing."

Jordan continued, "So he bought it all. You go into the hospital today, on the Board of Honors, his name is right up there. And if you go into the emergency room, right next to it is the crash room, and there is a plaque, which he never asked for, but he bought the entire crash room." Jordan confessed, "If it had been $1,350,000, he would still have said, 'Buy the whole thing.'"[39]

That gesture is, however, but one of many examples of Bandar's generosity over the years at Aspen. Among the less well publicized activities that he supports is the provision of holidays in Aspen for children suffering from cancer. He also supports another charity for children suffering from cancer called Silver Lining, run by a retired tennis professional, Andrea Jaeger.[40]

Rick Deane, the current head of the Aspen Mountain Rescue, and his wife Landon, also a volunteer, in a tribute to Bandar's support, said emphatically, "Prince Bandar is an amazing man. Without his help, the Mountain

---

*William R. Jordan III is Bandar's attorney in Aspen, Colorado.

Rescue service might not be able to function."[41] There are many more examples of Bandar's generosity, such as the Veteran's Association and its Disabled American Veterans Winter Sports Clinic in Aspen, acknowledgement of America's role during the first Gulf War. Thus, it is no surprise that the *Aspen Daily News* has reported that "Local homeowner Prince Bandar bin Sultan's philanthropic efforts run deep in Aspen. Undisputed are Bandar's generous contributions to Aspen charities and foundations."[42]

Peter Jay, a former British ambassador in Washington, related that in a similar way Bandar agreed to support Oxford Brookes University in England. Jay had been trying to raise funds for an important new development at the university that would see the creation of the University's School of Health and Social Care. This was designed to focus on all the supporting health care skills such as nurses, midwives, physiotherapists, cancer care specialists, and occupational therapists.

"I explained that I was looking for a major benefactor," Jay recalled, "and Prince Bandar immediately volunteered to provide support of 1.5 million pounds for the Professorship of Cancer Care. We then moved very swiftly on to complete the details and it was done—1.5 million pounds!"[43] In a press release, the university reported that Bandar's donation, the largest ever made to the university, had funded the *HRH Prince Sultan Chair in Cancer Care* within Oxford Brookes' School of Health and Social Care, named in honor of Bandar's father.[44]

Among other donations Bandar has made to the academic world, he funded two chairs at Johns Hopkins University in Baltimore, Maryland, one for international studies and another for environmental studies.

Bandar's gratitude to the Royal Air Force for his training at Cranwell, a formative period in his life which was to see him become a dedicated Anglophile, was to trigger a substantial donation many years later. Air Chief Marshal Sir Richard Johns, lieutenant and chief constable of Windsor Castle and chairman of the trustees of the RAF Museum, Hendon, London, recalled, "About five or six years ago, the trustees of the museum developed a vision for the future. This involved the creation of a large new hangar, which was to be called 'Milestones in Flight' that was to record one hundred years of military aviation."

Johns explained, "We went to the Heritage Lottery Fund but you have to raise a proportion of the money yourself, which was a big challenge." Tony Edwards, also a trustee, who had met Bandar during the Al-Yamamah Tornado program, took up the story. He briefed Bandar on the museum project and said, "Look, sir, can you suggest where I can go and look for this kind of money to support the RAF Museum?"

After they talked about a number of people, Bandar said, "You haven't asked me. What about me? What would it take to get this started?"

"About three hundred fifty thousand," Edwards replied.

"There was always a debate as to whether it was three hundred fifty thousand dollars or pounds," admitted Edwards, "and it was arranged for Bandar to visit the museum. And damn me, it was three hundred fifty thousand pounds and that started it—and then other sponsors from Kuwait and the Middle East stepped in. So we raised about £1.1 million and, with matching funds from the Lottery, it went ahead."

"If Prince Bandar hadn't done that," said Edwards, "it couldn't have happened. What generosity!"[45]

But while Bandar's generosity with cash is overwhelming, it is the prince's respect and care for those close to him that reveals his true compassion for others. Indeed, most examples of his generosity invariably happen quietly without the world ever becoming aware.

Mimi Burke, one of Bandar's secretaries, recalled that several years ago she met up with an ambassador's secretary from an African country, who said to her, "Do you remember when my ambassador became the dean of the Diplomatic Corps?" As a very poor country, they couldn't afford the obligations of being the dean, and although it was embarrassing, they sent out letters to all ambassadors saying, "Could you please donate a couple of hundred dollars to help us with this endeavor?"

Burke gave the request to Bandar, who said, "Oh Mimi, let's just pay for the whole thing for the whole year. I'm not just going to send a $200 check to this poor chap.'" Burke recalled that Bandar wrote a very nice letter to the ambassador, saying, "Congratulations on being the dean of the Diplomatic Corps and here is my donation." Ten years later when Burke encountered that secretary again, she said, "You know, we all started crying when we received that check—it was the nicest thing that anyone had ever done. It relieved so much of the pressure of being a very poor country and having this prestigious position—and we wanted to do it well. Prince Bandar had given us the whole thing and it made our job so much easier."

Burke concluded, "He never got any credit for it and nobody ever knew about it. But I have so many stories like that."[46]

Hearing that I was writing Bandar's biography, John Veltri, his barber, insisted that I interview him and, voice heavy with emotion, he said, "The man is truly unbelievable—he takes me to fly with him, a little common barber, can you imagine that? I've traveled with him to Switzerland, California many times, Hawaii, Saudi Arabia, and Africa—everywhere."

Veltri confided, "I want to tell you what a great person he is. I had been in business for a long time and I was getting kind of tired, so I thought I would sell the business. Anyway, I didn't do the right thing, and I was swindled and ended up with nothing. Now I never told the prince about this, but I did say I was trying to start a new business."

Veltri stressed, "A couple of days after that, I got a call from Riggs Bank; a guy told me that Prince Bandar wanted the bank to loan me the money and he was going to stand behind it. The Prince was going to give me $300,000 to get me started. How can you ever top something like that? Now I didn't use it; but you think about that—me, a little barber off the street, just think how special that was—that he had that much faith in me. I'll always remember that he offered to do that for me."[47]

But it is not just financial support that Bandar provides for those around him. It is a genuine sense of care and thoughtfulness. This was illustrated when I was a guest at his palace in Marrakech. Bandar's house manager, Linda Weare, related an incident that vividly illustrated his caring manner.

Weare recalled that her youngest daughter, Sophie, had joined her in Morocco having had a major operation for cervical cancer, but she had to go back for more surgery. Weare said, "When he [Prince Bandar] arrives, he always asks about her. She wasn't here when he arrived, and when he didn't say anything, I thought fine—I am going to leave it now."

About half an hour later, the phone rang in the pantry and Bandar said to Weare, "Lin, how is your daughter?"

"Actually, Your Highness," responded Weare, "Sophie flew back to the U.K. yesterday because she has a little health problem, but she will be back in a week's time."

"What is the problem?" asked Bandar.

Bandar's barber, John Veltri

"She has cervical cancer, Your Highness," replied Linda, "but she is see-ing an eminent surgeon and, fingers crossed, we think that it is the last treat-ment."

There was a pause before Bandar said, "I want her to have a second opin-ion."

"That is very, very kind of you, Your Highness," replied Weare. "She is going privately—we have sorted it out."

The prince interjected, "No, I want her to have a second opinion."

Clearly emotional, Weare said, "How kind is that? He is a very, very thoughtful man. For him to call and ask me about her and for him to re-member that Sophie wasn't there—that's very special."[48]

Bandar duly made the arrangements for a second medical opinion.

In another example of Bandar's thoughtfulness, one of Bandar's staff, Gen. Aseel, who has traveled widely with the prince, spoke highly of his generosity and charisma. He explained that when he was traveling with Bandar to a speaking engagement, shortly before they arrived in Houston from Washington, Aseel learned that his mother, who was in Jeddah, was very ill—she had suffered a number of strokes. Aseel informed Bandar of the situation and asked to leave for Saudi Arabia as soon as they arrived in Houston.

Bandar asked, "How do you intend to get back to Jeddah?"

Aseel explained that he would need to take a number of civil flights, and that the quickest way meant a return to Washington, another flight to Lon-don, a further flight to Cairo, and then a flight to Jeddah. Given the gravity of the condition, the prince quickly dismissed those options and rapidly made alternative arrangements.

The general took the next aircraft back to Washington from Houston, where he was escorted to a British Airways flight to London. When he ar-rived at Heathrow Airport, he was again escorted to a helicopter, which flew him directly to Stanstead Airport, where a private jet was ready to take him immediately to Jeddah. Aseel concluded, "This was only one example of Prince Bandar's human touch." The general stressed that he was not being singled out in any way—"This was simply the way that Prince Bandar looked after all his staff."[49]

This comment by Aseel was confirmed to me by many of Bandar's staff, but I was also to hear of it from Dr. Said Karmi, who observed about the prince's temperament, "He is always polite to everyone. In twenty-four years, I have never seen Bandar berate a member of staff or raise his voice to them at any time."[50]

Former FBI director Louis Freeh also gave a very penetrating appraisal of the prince when he said, "I have learned to benchmark people in power according to the way in which they treat their staff. One of the things I notice—maybe it's because I used to be an agent years ago—one of the ways you judge people, particularly people with power, is how they treat their people working for them. When I wanted to know anything about one of the people in Washington whom I didn't know, I would ask my agents, 'Talk to the guys in the detail, tell me what kind of person he is,' and the word would come back 'Good guy, considerate, kind, jerk, terrible, mean.'"

Referring now to Bandar, Freeh continued, "It's a very quick rule of thumb. My agents who dealt with him will tell you the same thing. He always looked after the needs of his security detail first, and that I thought was pretty indicative of his character."[51]

In another demonstration of Bandar's remarkable consideration and loyalty to friends, when Nelson Mandela lost his son Makgatho to AIDS in January 2005, he bravely revealed it to the world. Not only did Bandar ring Mandela and express his condolences, but he felt compelled to present them in person. During his visit, a smiling Nelson Mandela, supported by the prince's arm, said to Bandar, "It's been my honor and pleasure to work with you and for you. I consider myself to be blessed to be your friend." Mandela joked that while in the company of Bandar, he was in the presence of the most important man in the world. Bandar returned the compliment, saying, "The president is greatly admired and held in the highest esteem. He is not just the leader of Africa but of the whole world."[52]

In truth, this remarkable gesture was proof of Bandar's adage, "All my friends are loyal to me, because I am loyal to them."[53]

Another striking example of Bandar's desire to support others less fortunate than him is his financial sponsorship of the South African Ranger Life-Cycle Project. After development and successful trials in Zimbabwe, U.K. entrepreneur Mike Norman developed a motorcycle and sidecar ambulance as a simple-to-maintain, cost-effective alternative to 4 × 4 vehicles that could help rural communities in third-world countries. Robert Deacon Elliott brought the project to Bandar's attention, and he immediately saw its potential and offered his full support and sponsorship. Nelson Mandela also endorsed the humanitarian benefits of the Ranger LifeCycle and became its cosponsor.

The Ranger Production Company now has a factory in King William's Town in South Africa and a research and development unit in England. In addition to the motorcycle and sidecar ambulances, it produces mobile water purification devices, and mobile cinemas for HIV/AIDS education in rural areas. It is true to say that through Bandar's kindness, the quality of many people's lives across the third world has been improved by Ranger products.

President Carter told me another less well known story about Bandar's generosity. "Every year I make something for the Carter Center to auction off," said Carter. "I'm a fairly advanced woodworker—I make furniture. One year I carved a chess set, and I made a cherry box. My wife lined it with velvet, and it had a place for all of the chess pieces to go in. So I gave it to the Carter Center to be auctioned, and Bandar bid on that chess set. He paid $141,000 for a chess set! So he owns one of my chess sets now, the only one I've ever sold!"

Carter concluded, "This is probably the only one that has been hand carved by a former president."[54]

George H. W. Bush also talked about the prince's philanthropy, saying, "Bandar does a lot for charities. It's very easy to take a shot at him for his extraordinary wealth. So in my view it's important that he be seen as one willing to support charities—be one of what I call 'a thousand points of light' in helping others. He has this personal warmth and this generous heart." Stressed Mrs. Bush, "He tries to hide his light under a bushel, but the world should know of his generosity."[55]

When Bandar talks about his charitable activities, however, he observes that the media portray a false impression of his philanthropic record. Whereas the Western press has often reported on his charitable donations in the West, Bandar stressed that for every dollar he donated in the West, he has given ten dollars to support causes in the Arab world.

In an attempt to convey the reasons behind his philanthropy, Bandar said, "You know, when you have everything, the only high left in life is to give back to others—that's the ultimate high, to be able to give to somebody else."[56]

THIRTEEN

BANDAR: THE ENIGMA REVEALED

It matters not how strait the gate,
How charged with punishments the scroll,
I am the master of my fate:
I am the captain of my soul.[1]

"INVICTUS," WILLIAM ERNEST HENLEY
(1849–1903)

In an interview with Nelson Mandela, when asked if "Invictus" was a favorite poem, he instantly responded, "That's true—I like that poem very much, but I can no longer remember it accurately." Mandela then launched into the four lines of the verse shown above, emphasizing the last two lines, which he then repeated.[2]

Reflecting on the demands of his punishing schedule as ambassador and emissary for the king and the crown prince, Bandar, too, has often expressed a desire to be the master of his own fate and to have some time for himself. "Just to be able to have twelve months off for myself and my family—wouldn't it be great to be a 'beach bum'?" he asked. Dr. Said Karmi had used that same phrase in early 2004, when I speculated what Bandar might want to do next in life.

This yearning to be free from the incessant pressures of diplomatic intrigue was evidently a cherished aspiration of Bandar's. Though he wielded great power during his two decades as ambassador, such power came at a cost, for he was obliged to sacrifice personal freedom. As Francis Bacon so succinctly phrased it, "It is a strange desire to seek power and lose liberty."[3]

One can begin to comprehend why he envies the brave decision made by Nelson Mandela, who stood down from office after a single term and has subsequently endeavored to retire from public life. The prince has often applauded that resolve. As it became increasingly evident that Bandar wanted to escape the role he had engaged in over two decades before, it also became apparent early in 2004 that the time must come, sooner rather than later, when he would take that same daring step as Mandela—move out of the limelight and into his own personal space and the sense of freedom that retirement might bring with it. While this escape might only be temporary, it would offer him a respite, free from the pressures and challenges that accompanied an exhausting role.

That assessment was reinforced by another tête-à-tête I had with Bandar—sometime after three in the morning—when the conversation suddenly shifted from generalities to aspects of power. Without warning, Bandar said, "Money doesn't give power, but power can give you all the money you want in the world. But if you have the power and you don't exercise it, then it is worthless. And if you assume that you have the power, and therefore you can exercise it, if you are not going to exercise it in such a way that enables you to have your own freedom protected, then what good is that goddamn power? You can please everybody else except yourself."

"The complex issue here," he observed, "becomes 'duty.' You have the power to be free; you can exercise it because you have the money—and then obligation kicks in; and it's no good—whatever power and money you have, if you have a sense of duty, you will begin to sacrifice what other people will not sacrifice, who have less power than you and less money, but they want to protect their freedom." There was a hint of criticism of some of his Saudi contemporaries as he concluded, "And this goes back to two simple facts: nothing is free and nothing comes by choice."

Bandar feels an abiding sense of duty to Saudi Arabia, a sense of duty graphically illustrated by Bandar, who said, "I am convinced that I have done my duty—triple!" He then posed the rhetorical question, "People ask, 'Have you ever been in love?' Yes, I have," he answered. "My love, in a passionate way, first and last, is Saudi Arabia," he said. "And I have learned over the years that it is a heavy, heavy burden. The problem is when you are in love, you are not thinking, 'Has my lover been fair to me or not? Has my lover been good to me or not?' It's unqualified."

"But you reach a point where you say, 'Okay, for how long?' " Speculating now on what the future might hold for him, he observed, "If I stay, it's because there is something left to do, and to be honest with you I can't envisage what that might be now—what might be so important, so vital for my country, that they cannot do it without me. Then I would have to do it. But I have to be convinced of that."[4]

Bandar explained that if he were to undertake such a commitment, it must leave space for him to dedicate time to his family. In that sense, he had clearly reached a watershed in his life, determined to set clear personal objectives that better reconcile his role as a father and a husband, with his continuous devotion to duty and the needs of his beloved Saudi Arabia. More than that, I sensed that Bandar might have already spoken about that personal desire to King Fahd, Crown Prince Abdullah, and Prince Sultan. It seemed clear that Bandar was on the cusp of a change, a transformation that could see him finally step back from center stage in the world of diplomacy.

Bandar's deep-rooted sense of duty was to surface again during my interview with his barber, John Veltri. "He [Bandar] talks to me really casually, just the two of us. It's kind of a barber thing—people feel comfortable talking to their barbers. I tell him all the time, 'you are the prince—but you are the servant.' " Veltri continued thoughtfully and shook his head as he said, "Who else goes to Saudi Arabia and back in one day? No one wants that life! He is so dedicated to his country and his work; he never takes a break. He works all the time." Veltri's closing remark struck a chord, "I go to London with him and I have a great time, but he works. Now who's the servant?"[5]

Returning to his musings on power and money, Bandar said, "People think that the more powerful and the more rich you are, that you can pick and choose. The truth of the matter is that your choices become more limited because you are expected to do X, Y, and Z, and so on. It all comes as part of the package. Now, of course, you could become a Howard Hughes and lock yourself at the top of a hotel; you could be a Bill Gates and decide you want to rent an airplane when you fly and not own one, or you could be a wealthy extrovert who wants to show off everything. But really what counts is how you can mix all these together—money, freedom, old friends, way of life—it is a complex equation."

"But do you know what?" he asked. "I wouldn't want it any other way. It would just be too boring for me to live conventionally or take the easy road." Again he paused before speculating, "To be able to sit in the White House and be part of life-and-death decisions is exhilarating; but I also enjoy being with my 96 Entry [Cranwell] friends in Aspen."

"It is also true, to take the other side of the equation, 'Power corrupts; ultimate power corrupts ultimately.' And the more power you get, the harder the brakes have to work for you—in other words, you need to work harder on the brakes to stop your temptation for more power." In Bandar's judgment, power is a drug; but his recognition of the lure of power paradoxically provides him with an antidote. Reflecting on Bandar's words and the parallels struck between him and Machiavelli, I was later to recall that the only moral code followed by a Machiavellian prince was the acquisition, retention, and expansion of power, and there were no limits placed on any activity enacted in the pursuit of this goal.[6] Could this be a clue to understanding Bandar's character?

One remedy to this potential flaw in his personality became evident as Bandar discussed his circle of friends, people who are close to him and who are prepared to pull him back to earth and inject an air of reality into his life. Speaking about those friends, he said, "The question is 'Was my retention of them—was it fate or was it design?'" He instantly answered himself, saying, "I needed them, because the higher up you go, the more powerful you become and the less chance you have to hear these things."[7]

While speculation about Bandar's future has long since been quieted by his retirement and subsequent appointment only brief months later as secretary-general of Saudi Arabia's National Security Council, in October 2005, conjecture was rife. In the months that followed my enlightening conversation with Bandar in Riyadh, in an effort to discover the truth about his future, I repeatedly asked many of his friends and colleagues, "What next?" During one such conversation, Dr. Said Karmi suggested, "Perhaps he might seek to escape from the constant stress that the current role imposed. He is under a lot of stress. He has to face unrelenting pressures in his current role day in, day out."[8] However, he conceded that were it to happen, then the Prince might take on the role of adviser to the crown prince or foreign minister; or even a minister without portfolio—a special emissary. In contrast to Said's careful choice of words, Prince Faisal bin Turki was rather more forthcoming, stating, "To be honest with you, this is getting too small for him, being an ambassador for the United States. He has always done more, but he needs to do it within the context of another job. I mean twenty years in one job is too long."[9]

Asked whether a successor as Ambassador to Washington might already be in process, Said could not begin to identify a replacement should Bandar step down or be recalled to Saudi Arabia. "The most important thing to Saudi Arabia at this stage is the United States. As long as that position prevails, then I think Bandar will stay." It was evident that Karmi did not see any change in the prince's role in the near future. To support his conclusion, Karmi continued judiciously, "The Middle East is still in a mess, Iraq is still in a mess, we still don't know where we are going, the Israel/Arab problem is still unresolved and he [Prince Bandar] still has a lot of work to do."[10]

When asked what he felt Bandar might do following his extended tour as ambassador to the United States, Brent Scowcroft said, "I suspect that when a position opens up he will go into the cabinet. He is the only ambassador who has had this kind of role; his predecessors were all standard diplomats. He is unique in that sense."[11] Dr. Henry Kissinger echoed that view. Observing that not only was Bandar's access in Washington unique and his relationship with the Bush family very special, Kissinger said, "He is needed in the role of ambassador at the present time, following the events of 9/11. I cannot see who might replace him. I feel that Bandar would be the best candidate to continue in that role for the next few years." He reasoned that Bandar had so many contacts in government over five administrations that he was almost irreplaceable.[12]

In a contrasting assessment to Scowcroft and Kissinger, Louis Freeh said, "The role I see him in, if he didn't become the king—which, of course, many people over here would like to see; what a progressive, smart, and enlightened leader he would be—would be to become a sort of Mandela. An elder statesman who can intervene and help fix very serious situations that can spin out of control very easily."[13] Another view on Bandar's future was given by former President Bill Clinton, who said, "I think that he understands the two worlds in which he has lived about as well as anybody I know, and he understands what keeps them in balance, which is his job as a diplomat. When he is not a diplomat any more, he should give some thought about how to change things. . . ." Alluding to the need for change within Saudi Arabia, Clinton has said to Bandar, "Life has been good to you and you have had a great run, but you are still quite young. I think that you should spend a lot of time thinking about what you think Saudi Arabia should look like twenty years from now and what you think the Middle East would look like and what would need to be done to make it look like that, because no system is static forever."[14]

Colin Powell considered that Bandar's possible return to the kingdom could include the prospect of his undertaking a role akin to national security adviser. Powell said, "The reason that he might come up with an idea like that was he wouldn't have to run a bureaucracy or organization. He would prefer a job without portfolio. And national security adviser is kind of floating around."[15]

Postulating that albeit Bandar held a much wider remit as roving ambassador for King Fahd, and latterly Crown Prince Abdullah, Ambassador Richard Murphy agreed that he could not keep performing his current role as ambassador indefinitely. But he reinforced Powell's comments about Bandar's becoming national security adviser. "In the '80s, Bandar was pretty explicit about designing a national security council, and that he would be the national security adviser in Riyadh. He even had an artist's sketch of the national security council table and the chairs, so he had given some thought to it. Well, it has never happened. I have said to some of the royal family, 'I just don't get how you function; how decisions made by the king or the crown prince are executed. Who follows up? What is the structure there? To my knowledge, even though there are things called supreme economic councils, supreme this and supreme that, there is nothing that acts as a coordinating body, as a policeman over the government structure. At one point, that was his solution; he was trying to advance it and I think he saw himself in that role."[16] Murphy's words were prophetic.

Increasingly convinced that Bandar was preparing to retire as ambassador, I was nonetheless persuaded that there would only be a period of recuperation. There were strong indicators that he must ultimately return to the kingdom to take on a new role—despite his desire for a better work life balance. His sense of duty is just too strong. Having reviewed the comments of other Bandar watchers, I was convinced that Richard Murphy's comment about the prince adopting a sort of national security adviser function might be close to the mark. That would also dovetail with Karmi's suggestion of an appointment without portfolio, perhaps embracing the role of emissary to the crown prince.

Closer to home, in answer to my question, "Where do you see him going?" his son-in-law, Prince Faisal bin Turki* replied, "To be honest, he is

---

*Prince Faisal bin Turki, husband to Bandar and Haifa's daughter, Reema, was second secretary to the embassy of the kingdom of Saudi Arabia and travels on all Bandar's diplomatic missions. A loyal son-in-law, he is being groomed by the prince for a diplomatic career.

one of the top politicians in the world. I think Bandar would be of much more use in Saudi Arabia at this point because of what has happened in Saudi Arabia—modernizing." Faisal was keen to stress the prince's potential for leading the necessary process of change in Saudi Arabia. He continued with conviction, "He should be there because of his influence. He should be there because of the strategic relationship with the United States; it's not necessary for him to be here [Washington]." He suggested that Bandar's return to Saudi Arabia would in no way undermine the relationships he enjoys in Washington, but concluded that his move to Saudi Arabia was essential. In his view, Bandar has the ability to help Saudi Arabia right now and he could make a unique contribution to the future development of his country. On a cautionary note, Faisal observed that in pressing for the modernization of Saudi Arabia, Bandar was aware of lessons learned from the fall from power of the Shah of Iran, "or following in the footsteps of the Turks." Again Faisal emphasized that Bandar should be there "as, let's say, special adviser for the crown prince, or national security adviser for the crown prince, or a position in which he can advise."

The thrust of Prince Faisal's argument was that in assuming a role as adviser, Bandar could be in Washington one day to meet with the president and deliver a message, but could quickly be back in the kingdom working with the crown prince in a one-on-one capacity most of the time. Faisal concluded, "They know that Prince Bandar is very important for them, not because of America and so on, but because of what he has done for his country, and his experience and his knowledge. He would advise them for the betterment of Saudi Arabia."

These examples of the underlying problems faced in Saudi Arabia brought to the fore Faisal's succinct appraisal of the need for Bandar to help reshape Saudi Arabia, when he said simply "It wants modernizing."[17] Similarly, Tarek Shawaf confided that the prince was reaching a watershed in his life. "I think that the election of Bush is a beautiful and wonderful ending to the USA part of his life, but the big challenge that is coming—because they are not going to let him go as he dreams—is going to be probably the greatest of his life."

Shawaf continued, "When he returns to the kingdom now, the challenge will no longer be U.S. foreign policy; the challenge will be to interpret what we should do in our own country. And it's not just talking about the country, even if we take it from a very selfish point of view, it's the royal family and their status, and then it's the country." I was transfixed as Shawaf explained, "We can't go on like this; there are problems and there has got to be—and there is going to be—a shake-up."[18]

Shawaf's words were to be echoed by Colin Powell, who agreed that "the kingdom needs a shake-up," and added, "and Bandar and I have talked about that a lot."

Powell then related a story that succinctly illustrated that need for change in Saudi Arabia. "About three weeks ago, they [the Saudis] made a decision that was unfortunate for the municipal elections coming up; they had left open the prospect of women voting. They were being quiet about it—they didn't say anything. Then, suddenly, one of the ministers popped off at a press conference and said, 'No.'" Powell shook his head, saying, "It wasn't a considered judgment of the 'family.' And although they may have come to that judgment, they were kind of leaving it vague." Powell speculated that this might have allowed it to happen without its ever being sanctioned. "Suddenly, they might have found that women had voted. But the guy popped off and they were stuck with this decision."

"Next thing I am on television and I get asked, 'Well, your Saudi friends are supposed to be thinking about reform, but here they won't even let women vote. What do you think about that, Secretary Powell?' And my answer was, 'Well, you know, each country has to decide its own rules and blah, blah, blah. But in my own judgment, women represent an enormous resource in talent to every society and I think that they should have had the opportunity to vote.' And the family immediately criticized me. But Bandar called me and said, 'Yeah! Yeah! Yeah!'" Powell imitated Bandar punching the air as he yelled out those words. "So I said to him," said Powell, "Your guys are chewing my ass off and you're giving me a 'yeah, yeah'?"

Powell laughed, "That's happened about three times in the last six months—where I have told them [the Saudis] about things and said, 'I am going to hammer you guys. Tomorrow, I am putting out a report on religious freedom, and I am going to put Saudi Arabia on the list of countries of concern. We have never done that before Bandar, but I've got a problem. You guys aren't doing anything about it.' And he [Bandar] says, 'Go ahead, go ahead, I'll use it, I'll use it.' So I do it—they are publicly mad at it, but some of the princes are applauding it; that somebody is kicking them and is pushing them in the direction that they know they have to go."

Powell described how during his last visit to the kingdom, he met with a group of young adults. "It was wonderful to get them into an argument—these were well-educated and professional people—and they were arguing about the elections coming up and who should vote and who shouldn't. They started complaining about the elections—'we don't know what is going on'—and about the Saudi royal family and the government."

"Finally," Powell recalled, "one of these gentlemen said, 'The problem is not the royals—the problem is us! We are our own problem; we must stop blaming the Americans and stop blaming the royal family. We are the ones who for two hundred years have accepted living in this dependent relationship where we get everything we need; where we get more money than we need; where we are taken care of from cradle to grave. We just lean back and get bought by our own government. It is time for us to start pushing back.'"

Powell next recounted how a mother with two young children said, "Our textbooks, Mr. Secretary. I know you are thinking that our textbooks are Madrassa-oriented; there is too much religion in there. That's not the problem. If you read my seven-year-old son's textbook, it only has a page and a half on Islam. Only a page and a half on Islam; but how does the book start? What is Chapter One? Chapter One, Page One: Women are wonderful and dependent creatures that we must take care of." Powell said, "And so it starts her seven year-old son in a lifetime of psychological preparation for women to be held in second-class servitude. That's why when these kids are eighteen, they still think it's sensible for women not to drive."[19]

The reelection of George W. Bush in November 2004 and the continuance of a Republican administration had little impact on the timing of the Bandar's departure from Washington. But the indicators of a period of dramatic change in Bandar's life grew stronger. There was the very real expectation that a major decision might be imminent.

In early December 2004, another clue to Bandar's intent surfaced during conversation at his Glympton home. "This is the problem now," he said, "in working with world leaders. People are not as large or as colorful as they used to be. It's boring; they are thinking more about day-to-day tactical things; there is no grand vision." He continued poignantly, "Leaders were real leaders in those days."

Shifting his reflections to focus on a gnawing personal stagnation, Bandar observed, "When you've been there, you've done that, you've said this—it's the worst thing that can happen to anybody in any job or any profession; we are not excited or impressed or surprised anymore—that's the time to move on and do something else. If you still get excited and surprised, then yes, continue."

During the visit by Crown Prince Abdullah to Crawford in April 2005, the signs that Bandar was seeking to escape the demands of his office were becoming increasingly evident. Speaking with some of his staff at his home in McLean, they confided that personal items were being packed up and were concerned that the prince might be leaving Washington. When Michael Petruzzello of Qorvis Communications met with Bandar at his McLean home, he recalled, "When I saw that all his family photographs and paintings had been taken down, I said to him, 'Highness, I hope you are just redecorating!' "

Shortly after, Bandar and his family arrived at Glympton, ostensibly on summer vacation. I was to discover, however, that his younger children were now being enrolled in local schools in the Glympton area. Yet still there was no formal announcement in Saudi Arabia confirming his retirement. Bandar confided to friends that as he engaged in meetings with the crown prince, the conversation followed the traditional elaborate dance in which they exchanged greetings and talked about family, friends, and generalities, before eventually cutting to the chase. Crown Prince Abdullah and his advisers thought that Bandar was playing an elaborate hand of poker, trying to jockey for a senior role in government rather than simply resigning and moving into retirement. Bandar laughed as he recalled, "I kept thinking to myself, 'What part of "no" don't you understand?' "

A formal announcement issued by the Ministry of Foreign Affairs on July 20, 2005, confirmed that the custodian of the two holy mosques had accepted Bandar's request that he be relieved of his duties for private reasons. That official statement also highlighted the prince's more than twenty years of distinguished service wherein he demonstrated exceptional gifts and rendered outstanding services to his king and his country.[20] It also confirmed that Bandar's successor was to be his brother-in-law, Prince Turki bin Faisal, who has been Saudi ambassador to the United Kingdom for the past three years. Before taking his ambassadorial post in London, Faisal had served as head of Saudi intelligence for twenty-four years. In a comment on their respective personal styles, it was appositely reported, "If Bandar is Saudi Arabia's James Bond, Turki is the kingdom's George Smiley [of John Le Carre fame].[21]

Some of the Bandar's closest friends recalled that when he was having dinner in Riyadh with Prince Turki bin Nasser, during the negotiations with the crown prince, there was hilarity when Turki observed with a laugh about Bandar's resignation, "You should be in the Guinness Book of Records. No one has ever resigned in Saudi Arabia before. They are either reappointed, die in post, or are fired!" Certainly, disbelief at the motives behind Bandar's resignation was not only apparent within the kingdom, but also prompted intense speculation with the media.

Reaction to the news in Washington was immediate. The White House issued a statement that called Bandar "a tireless advocate for close ties, warm relations, and mutual understanding" between the two countries and complimented his advice, wit, charm, and humor.[22] Meanwhile, the press speculated about the possible reasons for his departure. Some implied poor health and depression, while others suggested that it was a political gambit by the prince as the failing health of the king was likely to see significant developments in Saudi succession. Freeing himself from the ambassadorial remit would surely allow him to jockey for power in Riyadh, and it was ventured that he had hoped to become the minister of intelligence, a post long held by Prince Turki bin Faisal.[23]

The reality, however, was captured by the reaction of Bandar's family. The formal announcement was greeted at his Glympton home by banners and balloons prepared by his family poignantly proclaiming, "Free at last!"

Before his resignation, Bandar had frequently talked of his regrets at not being able to spend more time with his family. Indeed, when it had been observed that his children fully understood the demands that were placed on him, Bandar said, "That only makes it worse; that makes it even more painful—that's loyalty. I don't want to give them my time when I'm eighty years old where they have to carry me from one place to another; I want to give them some premium time when I am there as they have been there for me all these years."

Now he had finally escaped the demands of office—or had he?

Soon after Bandar's resignation became public, he departed on a planned holiday in Morocco with family and friends. However, just three days after his arrival in Marrakech, he received word that King Fahd had passed away. Although the death of Saudi Arabia's sovereign leader caused little disruption within the kingdom—Crown Prince Abdullah quickly ascending to the throne, and his father, Prince Sultan bin Abdul Aziz, becoming crown prince—Bandar felt Fahd's loss deeply.

Although he craved a respite from the political arena in order to spend more time with his family, it seemed hardly conceivable, when the family business was politics and his father was heir to the throne, that such a goal could ever be attainable. To some extent, evidence for the assumption that Bandar would ultimately return to the service of his country—even if he would not admit it to himself—stemmed from his own comments. "With-out being cocky," he said, "there are certain things nobody else can do in this country except me. And here is the danger; the people who make the decisions know my sensitive cord. Those people know that if there was a pressing need for me to undertake a mission of paramount importance to Saudi Arabia, then my sense of duty would prevail. Deep in my heart, as much as I try to deny it, I will be there." So even after relinquishing his role as ambassador to the United States of America, Bandar could envisage that he might still be called upon from time to time to perform missions essential to Saudi Arabia. He confessed, "I know I cannot say no; although I can justify saying no, I would not do it."[24]

Speaking before the announcement of Bandar's resignation, Tarek Shawaf prophetically said, "Sooner or later the king is going to die or Abdullah is going to die or Sultan is going to die. Whichever of these three dies, it is going to shake up the kingdom. So Bandar has a role to play. That is why I am saying that his next challenge is a challenge without a job description. The USA is finished; he's done an incredible, remarkable job and now it's time to look back home."

But while Shawaf recognized that Bandar longed to be in control of his own destiny and go into retirement like Mandela, he acknowledged that "he can't. Saudi Arabia is not South Africa. Also, he has this incredible problem; he cannot say no to Prince Abdullah or to Prince Sultan."[25]

Barely two months after his resignation had been formally announced, Bandar was appointed secretary-general of the National Security Council, an office that would see him recalled to play a major role in the future of Saudi Arabia.

The Western press has often attempted to explain Bandar by attributing to him the characteristics of historical characters, tracking the parallels that they perceived existed between the Prince and such figures as Winston Churchill, Talleyrand, Gatsby, Machiavelli, T. E. Lawrence, and, to a lesser extent, Ronald Reagan and Nelson Mandela. There is some truth in each of these claims, yet ultimately they are all convenient masks—molds he can be seen to fit. They are not accurate reflections of his real character.

The factors that make Bandar what he has become today are the clues to understanding the enigma. In retrospect, I have reached the conclusion that, in addition to the insecurity that the prince developed as a youth, through lack of contact with his father until their reconciliation at the instigation of his grandmother Hassa bint Ahmed al-Sudairi, that insecurity has driven Bandar to become an "overachiever." The many female influences on his upbringing have also helped shape his character, affording him a uniquely colored perspective. Those female influences have developed in the prince an exceptional mind set, providing in him an instinctive or intuitive feeling that has honed his remarkable and incisive talent for appraising people and problems.

My personal knowledge of Bandar during the time we spent together at RAF Cranwell when we were young men, combined with the prince's explicit affection for that formative period of his life and fierce loyalty to the many friends he made whilst undergoing military training, persuades me that the shaping of the consummate statesman he is today, owes much to that rich experience. Values, standards, and discipline were instilled into that young cadet who was determined to prove himself in his own right.

Nonetheless, I am convinced that the secret to unlocking the enigma that is Bandar, despite his Western-leaning persona, lies in his national heritage.

The nation of Saudi Arabia is an extraordinary contradiction in the modern world, and it exemplifies the enigmatic Prince Bandar. Both are drawn simultaneously to Western modernization and Eastern religious tradition. Yet this dichotomy makes the Bedouin culture of Saudi Arabia, continually shifting and possessive of a wonderful fluidity, what it is. Rather than being a cursed contradiction, this fluidity is arguably a blessed gift to those living in a region that is home to three dominant faiths, and multiple races, political beliefs, and economic interests.

Bandar is a Bedouin diplomat in the truest sense, continually traveling around the globe, adrift between the tradition he belongs to and the Western culture that he works within. Judged by both Western and Eastern perspectives, he falls deceptively into the political no-man's-land between both. Yet herein lies his true Bedouin gifts; his devout faith, a loving family, and the circle of friends that form his own traveling oasis.

A personal insight into Bandar's ability to rise above the Arab/Western cultural divide was provided by the Prince himself, when in a perceptive reference to his ability to transcend cultures, he observed, "This is the difference. Very few people, I believe, can shift from that mode to this mode and go in and out of both and feel comfortable."

"I am just as comfortable in my white tie and tails, as in my *thobe*," Bandar observed. He quickly added, however, "It's not easy. I don't know how, but I made it happen and I feel comfortable with it." Adopting a more philosophical guise, he posed, "What does it take, the total sum of all my life? It's not just one thing that made it happen, it's that total sum. And I really believe, as Kennedy used to quote, 'Some people see things as they are and ask why; I imagine things and ask why not?'"

Despite his ability to slip between East and West with unconscious ease, there is still a need for Bandar to keep in touch with reality. The presence of his 'traveling court' illustrates how the prince keeps in contact with the real world. About these friends he has said, "I believe that for people with power, the fewer people like these that they have around them, the more prone to mistakes they are. You need somebody to bring you down to earth and say, 'You know what? That was a great performance but you missed this, you got that wrong.' You'd be surprised how much that contributes to one's success, because people are impressed with your performance and how down-to-earth you are, how realistic you are or how you are handling the situation."[26]

As Fred Dutton said, "He doesn't pay me to say yes."[27]

I was witness to an example of the store that Bandar puts in his friends and in particular his old colleagues from his Cranwell days, during a reunion which Bandar had arranged at his ranch in Aspen. The sixteen of us who would attend that gathering were taken aback by the extent of the Prince's warmth. Over the course of that weekend Bandar had laid on numerous daytime activities and incredible hospitality. At the end of the trip we were at a loss as to how to show our appreciation and so clubbed together to buy an original piece of Native American art—an Indian mask by a descendant of Chief Sitting Bull—which we presented to Bandar on the last night.

Clearly very moved by our gesture, Bandar's response stuck in my mind when he said, "but really, it is not necessary, if you only knew how much this has meant to me. . . ." Here he trailed off as though overwhelmed by emotion and in those few moments there was an almost palpable sense of contentment. Surrounded by old friends, free from the acute pressures that he then faced daily, Bandar was thoroughly relaxed. Here were people who liked him and knew him for who he was—and not for his political position.

Speaking at that reunion about the deep sense of affection that he has for his contemporaries from RAF Cranwell, there was a sense of bemusement in Bandar's voice as he wondered how he could be comfortable with his Cranwell peers all these years later, and yet still operate with ease in the heady world of diplomacy. In one environment, the prince is treated as an equal: he is accorded little of the protocol due to his status and is invariably addressed as Ben, the nickname bestowed on him at Cranwell. In the "real" world he is treated with enormous respect and protocol, and wields tremendous power. Analyzing himself, Bandar said, "You have to have something basic inside you that is solid and you have to be comfortable with yourself. And if you are not comfortable within yourself then you could not make the changes—the rapid transition that is required in my current role."

To better illustrate this point, Bandar came up with an anecdote. "There is a guy called George Shultz. He was in charge of the public office during Nixon's era, which is not a cabinet post. He was a professor of economics in Chicago and by the end of Nixon's term, he had become secretary of labor."

Words now spilled out in rapid time as Bandar got into his stride.

"Ford loses the election and Shultz was out into the private sector. He ended up being the president of Bechtel, which is a huge company. In dealing with Saudi Arabia, he was dealing with the government and with

Bandar hosts a Cranwell reunion at his Aspen home.

Aramco, and he developed a great friendship with Mr. Suleiman Olayan.*
He started from nothing as a truck driver with Aramco, but he was very
bright and became very rich. Mr. Olayan and George Shultz used to go on
vacation together with their wives. When Shultz came for business to Saudi
Arabia, he used to stay with Olayan and when Olayan went to San Francisco, he used to stay with Shultz. I mean, the wives were like sisters and
they were like brothers. You can't get closer than that. In 1982, Shultz became Secretary of State. Olayan was in New York when that happened, so
he picked up the phone and called his friend."

"Hi, George, how are you?" Olayan said.

"Hello, Mr. Olayan." Not Suleiman, Bandar stressed, Mr. Olayan.

Olayan was stunned by the formality in Shultz's reply, Olayan said to
him, "Congratulations. If we have time, I'll stop by in Washington and congratulate you and Bonnie."

"Actually, I was going to call you to come and see me," Shultz replied.
"Why don't you come to the house tomorrow late afternoon?"

"Fine," said Olayan, "I'll see you later."

Olayan duly went to his house, where the wives met each other like sisters; they kissed and hugged in greeting. But Shultz was stiff and remote.
Olayan thought perhaps he was out of sorts. They all sat down for tea and
sandwiches, but Shultz never warmed.

As Olayan and his wife were preparing to leave, Schultz addressed
Olayan as Suleiman. It was the first time he had called Olayan by his first
name all evening.

"We have been friends for a long time." said Shultz. "But while I am Secretary of State, I would appreciate it very much, as a sign of our friendship,
if you did not call me, neither at my home nor at my office."

There was an embarrassing silence. Stunned, Olayan said, "What the
f*** are you talking about?" At this Mrs. Shultz got up and left the room.

"George, are you joking?" Olayan asked.

---

*Suleiman Saleh Olayan died on July 4, 2002, in the United States. Although he spent more than fifty-
five years building companies in Saudi Arabia, he acted as a bridge between the United States and the
Arab world, particularly important as the Saudi-U.S. relationship was being challenged and tested. It
was said that Mr. Olayan was a proud citizen of Saudi Arabia, but, in many ways, his life was defined
by his friendship with America. He was as committed to the endurance of the Saudi-U.S. relationship
as he was to maintaining his various personal and business ties, and relations with American partners
and friends. He was not a professional diplomat, but rather, he was a statesman, someone who understood, valued, and acted to strengthen relationships that serve a greater good.

"No, I am not joking," Shultz replied. "And from now on I am Secretary of State to you, not George."

"You know what, George?" said Olayan after a longer pause. "I am not going to even shake hands to say goodbye to you. You can go to hell."

Immediately after leaving, Olayan called Bandar from his car; he had been due to go to the airport but diverted and asked if he could come and see him instead. Bandar explained, "So I'm telling you something I heard firsthand from one of the participants."

"What do you make out of this?' said Olayan to Bandar.

"Well, it's not a good sign, Suleiman," said Bandar. "I am glad that you told me so we can get ready for this bastard."

At the end of his story about Shultz, Bandar said, "This is the difference between human beings. George Bush Senior was asked when he was President, 'Is it true that Prince Bandar is considered a member of your cabinet?' George Bush said, 'Absolutely not true—but Prince Bandar is a good friend from a friendly country and I am not ashamed to call him my friend.' End of discussion." Bandar continued, "With George Bush, our friendship did come with a heavy political price. I would have been happy, understanding the politics, for him to have said only, 'He's not a member of my cabinet; this is just wrong.' End of discussion. He didn't have to go that one extra mile. Why did he do it? Loyalty! If you show loyalty, you can expect it. But don't demand it, if you're not willing to give it. Loyalty is a two-way street. And it's not just for when things are going well. What counts is that you stand by somebody when things are not going well."

A man of formidable intellect, Bandar is shrewd and calculating. Yet he has an abiding loyalty to his family, his friends, the House of Saud, his faith, and his country. Driven by personal insecurity and a desire to serve his king, he has employed his personal armory of talent—humor, likeability, charisma, poise, and a remarkable strength of character—during his service to Saudi Arabia as its ambassador in Washington. Acquiring wisdom throughout decades of single-minded focus on his role as a diplomat, Bandar has impressively played the keyboard of power, all in the pursuit of success.

As detailed in Chapter 5, after informing Secretary of State George Shultz that he was going to China to help stem the flow of Chinese arms to Iran in 1985, Bandar supervised "the most brazenly duplicitous Saudi foreign policy venture of the decade." While in Beijing, ostensibly to talk about arms control and the purchase of weapons destined for Iran, he slipped away to negotiate the purchase of the largest medium-range ballistic missiles in the Middle East. It has been succinctly alleged, "This was the Eastern Bandar, pursuing his king's secret diplomacy and hoping not to get caught by the Americans. This was the same prince who convinced the Reagan White House to share sensitive satellite intelligence with Iraq, a process that began in Bandar's living room during the Iran-Iraq War, and the same prince who was forced to go to the State Department in 1986 and excuse his government's transfer of two-thousand-pound bombs to Iraq as an oversight."[28]

The reality was something very different: to induce Iraq to carry out more bombing operations during the Iran-Iraq War, the Reagan administration had secretly authorized Saudi Arabia to transfer U.S. bombs to Iraq and encouraged the Saudis to provide Saddam with British fighter planes as well. Later that month, according to classified reports, Saudi Arabia transferred fifteen hundred two-thousand-pound bombs to Iraq. The arms transfers appeared to violate the Arms Export Control Act, a federal law that prohibits a recipient country from transferring U.S.-origin munitions to a third country without written permission from the United States. When such transfers are made, the same law requires that the president immediately notify Congress. By admitting to the oversight, the prince had effectively shielded a CIA operation, thereby winning even more friends in Washington, not the least of them CIA director Bill Casey.[29]

It is important to be aware of the disparity that exists between the application of moral standards to an individual as opposed to the applications of moral standards to a state or nation. As Alexander Hamilton expressed it, "The rule of morality . . . is not precisely the same between nations as between individuals. . . . Existing millions and future generations are concerned with the present measures of a government, while the consequences of a private action of an individual ordinarily terminate with himself."[30] That Bandar adheres to this line of thought was evidenced by his own words when he said, "I am more Alexander Hamilton ideals than Jeffersonian Democrat."[31]

Niccolo Machiavelli set out the classic handbook for this brand of political philosophy when he wrote *The Prince*. He argued, "Where the safety of the country depends upon the resolution to be taken, no considerations of justice or injustice, humanity or cruelty, nor of glory or shame, should be allowed to prevail."[32] In their revealing book, *Wilson's Ghost*, Robert S. McNamara and James G. Blight suggest that Machiavelli would have had fewer qualms than did President Truman about using the atomic bomb, an argument premised upon the greater volume of human life saved by that one destructive act.[33]

It was by sheer coincidence that I chanced upon a paper submitted by Bandar for his master's degree at Johns Hopkins University in Baltimore, Maryland. In this thesis, Bandar clearly embraced Machiavellian theory, taking particular interest in the moral standpoint, or lack thereof, and accepting the view that actions undertaken for the greater good cannot be held accountable on a moral scale. There can be no clearer evidence of this than the quote with which the young prince chose to open his paper:

> "He (the Prince) should not even concern himself about incurring infamy for those vices without which he could, with difficulty, save the state: because, if one considers everything well, it will be found that something which seems virtuous, being followed, will bring about his ruin; and something else, which seems vice, being followed, will bring security and his well-being."
>
> Niccolo Machiavelli.[34]

Bandar's backing of an ethical Machiavellian style of diplomacy can be seen in his work over two decades as a statesman and humanitarian. Accepting that the statesman had an essential and unshakable responsibility to defend the strength, security, and power of his nation, Bandar recognized that the strength required of such an undertaking was to be found in the ability to make a pragmatic decision—no matter how difficult the circumstances—and to carry it through.

Bandar's belief in that the undertaking of whatever is necessary to achieve the preferable outcome for the general good, comes with an understanding of what drives those in authority. In a reference to the pretenses and pleasantries of international diplomacy, Bandar wrote, "such assumptions of transcending morality are only dangerous facades masking the Machiavellian prescriptions for survival."[35]

Nevertheless, an optimist first and a pragmatist second, Bandar wrote, "The sheer awesome magnitude of modern power itself may force a moral code that transcends the narrow objectives of any state; the objective conditions of modern international life have taken this subject far from the quiet of the ivory towers of academia."[36]

I asked the question at the beginning of this book, "Is Prince Bandar a man of peace—a man of principle, conscience, and moral correctness?" I believe that he is, indeed, a man of peace. However, I also asked whether he should be depicted as "a Machiavellian prince—one destitute of political morality, ruled by expediency only; crafty, perfidious, and amoral in conduct and activity—a man of whom it could be argued had precipitated the first Gulf War and facilitated the Bush administration's preemptive efforts and the invasion of Iraq?"

Paradoxically, the answer must also be yes. And perhaps this can best be illustrated in the chain of events that he set in play just prior to the presidential election in November 2004.

I was a guest at an informal dinner hosted by Bandar on August 28, 2004, at his Glympton estate. Bandar and his guests were watching Kelly Holmes win her second Olympic gold medal in the fifteen hundred meters on his large-screen TV. The prince's media room features a main screen flanked by two smaller screens on each side. These smaller screens were tuned to U.S. and Arab news channels, and Bandar's attention was suddenly caught by a CNN news story. The story revealed that the FBI was investigating whether Larry Franklin, a midlevel Pentagon official, had supplied Israel, via AIPAC, with a presidential directive on U.S. policy toward Iran.[37]

A search of Franklin's office and home by FBI agents uncovered eighty-three documents classified Top Secret and Secret spanning three decades. Franklin was immediately suspended and then pressured into acting as an FBI informant against AIPAC, supporting a prior FBI investigation. He

would ultimately be charged and convicted with illegally disclosing highly classified information to employees of AIPAC and was sentenced to twelve years and seven months in prison for his actions.

It emerged that the FBI had been investigating intelligence leaks to Israel coming from the Pentagon since 2001.[38] It quickly became clear that the Franklin-AIPAC-Israel investigation was more than a simple spy case.

As he watched newsflash coverage

Larry Franklin

of the Franklin affair, Bandar became increasingly animated. When an Israeli embassy spokesman denied allegations of Israeli involvement as "completely false and outrageous," Bandar laughed and said, "They would say that—wouldn't they?"

The CNN report continued, "AIPAC has put out a statement tonight strongly denying that it has played any role in any kind of espionage. 'We take our responsibilities as American citizens seriously.' They wouldn't condone or tolerate for a second, any violation of U.S. law." Bandar dismissed that response, using a personal adage, "Make your words soft and sweet; you never know when you are going to have to eat them."

With the Republican convention planned only a few days later, the reporter continued, "Intelligence officials appeared upset that this matter had leaked out, and they also suspect a possible political motivation; they think that somebody may be trying to embarrass the administration on the eve of the Republican convention."

Bandar had a wide grin across his face. This was puzzling, given the potential damage that this story could cause President Bush. When asked if he was concerned about the political fallout for the president, Bandar countered that it could actually be beneficial.

Bandar explained that the timing of the leak could damage the Democrats in that the media might perceive it to be a Democrat-leaked story, designed to detract from the Republican convention. But it became obvious that Bandar was delighted at the prospect of a messy investigation that could hamper AIPAC's ability to operate and create concern about its links with the Israeli government.

It was apparent that Douglas Feith, Franklin's boss, and Paul Wolfowitz, deputy secretary of defense, could both catch flak for Franklin's activities, whether they had anything to do with it or not. The prospect of undermining these two individuals, both known to be strongly pro-Israel neo-conservatives, would further Bandar's interests and conceivably lead to changes in the next Republican administration, assuming President Bush was reelected.

As his guests enjoyed dinner, Bandar asked

Niccolo Machiavelli

blandly, "I wonder where that leak came from?" He then innocuously introduced one of his fellow guests—the editor of the London-based Arab newspapers *Al-Hayat* and weekly *Al-Wassat*, both owned by his father, Prince
Sultan and his half-brother, Prince Khaled.

From Bandar's comments, it became apparent that he must have known
about the FBI investigation long before the story had broken. Was Bandar
hinting that he was the source? Had Bandar deliberately seeded the Franklin
story to damage AIPAC, precipitate a shake-up in the Pentagon, and perhaps even assist President Bush in his election campaign? It certainly seemed
so. I observed, "Perhaps my analogy between you and Machiavelli was accurate after all."

Bandar merely shrugged and said, "I can't even spell Machiavelli."[39]

But, if Bandar *had* been the source of the leak, then there must be a different reason behind it—he would never harm President Bush's election
prospects.

But Bandar is an expert at playing the long game. Dr. Said Karmi reinforced Bandar's analytical strengths when he said, "He has patience and an
ability to toss an issue around in his mind, almost like playing a game of
chess, trying to anticipate the move he should make thirty-five moves from
now."[40]

These views merely reinforced suspicion that Bandar may have been the
architect of the leak about the FBI's investigation into Franklin. He had indicated that the inquiry could impact on the balance of power within the
George W. Bush administration, the hard-liners inside the Pentagon, the
Palestinian peace process, and the influence of Israel and AIPAC on U.S.
foreign policy. Changes that could work to his—and hence, Saudi
Arabia's—advantage.

Bandar had been outraged at President Bush's sudden foreign policy
about-face toward the Israeli-Palestinian peace process. Sharon's visit to
Washington resulted in a strong statement of support for his policy of unilat-
eral disengagement, including a stamp of approval on the controversial "security barrier" wall and a rejection of the Palestinians' right to return to Israel.

As the Franklin story unfolded and became public, so too did the power
struggle between the Bush administration's neo-con appointees at the Pentagon and National Security Council, and the traditionalists at the CIA and
the State Department.[41] Both Secretary of State Colin Powell and his right
hand man, Deputy Secretary of State Richard Armitage, loathed the Pentagon neo-cons who had outgunned the moderate Powell on the Iraq War and

who, it was alleged, had successfully grabbed the reins of the Middle East peace process and U.S. foreign policy after 9/11.[42]

It was undeniable that the investigation put Franklin and his neo-con bosses at the center of a swirling controversy. It made sense that Bandar would naturally be keen to damage or remove those officials.

Assuming a Republican victory—which Bandar did—changes could be expected soon after the outcome of the election, possibly enabling a pragmatic State Department to regain control of U.S. Middle East foreign policy—a consequence that would be applauded by Bandar. Privately, Bandar has often expressed frustration that during George W. Bush's first administration the neo-con cabal consistently thwarted efforts to achieve a just settlement to the Palestinian problem.

As for AIPAC, it is generally acknowledged in Congress that AIPAC is the preeminent lobbying power in the United States. The group's efficacy is light years ahead of any other political action committee, and Bandar has repeatedly been at odds with the group throughout his tenure in Washington.

The election went Bush's way, as the prince had hoped, and the president sustained no lasting damage from the leak. Damage to Israel's interests, however, was evident. The Anti-Defamation League, a leading Jewish pro-Israeli organization, called for a special prosecutor to investigate leaks into the FBI investigation because they were tarnishing Israel's image.[43] The leak also momentarily impacted U.S.-Israeli intelligence cooperation. Israeli intelligence services have worked closely with the CIA and other U.S. intelligence agencies for decades, and have provided valuable information on international terrorism. The 1985 Pollard case led to temporary disruption in that cooperation[44]; in the wake of the Franklin episode, sources reported that once again the U.S. had begun to limit intelligence exchanges with Israel.[45]

Bush administration personnel, though headed by the departure of a moderate Secretary of State Colin Powell, saw significant changes within the Department of Defense. Following the leak of the two-year FBI

Steve Rosen

probe, two of the top neo-cons moved out—Paul Wolfowitz left to head up the World Bank and Douglas Feith retired.[46]

And what of Steve Rosen and Keith Weissman of AIPAC? At the time of writing, they face trial in September 2006, with the Justice Department prosecuting the lobbyists under the World War I-era Espionage Act—a rarely used and vaguely worded law that prohibits the dissemination of classified "national defense information."[47] Moreover, in dismissing Rosen and Weissman AIPAC has, nonetheless, been unable to dissociate itself from them.[48] It has been reported that they will argue that their alleged spy activity was not a rogue operation carried out by them independently of AIPAC, but was known and approved by their bosses.[49] If Rosen and Weissman succeed in tying AIPAC to their activities, however, and if they are convicted, then it would open up the unwelcome prospect of a much larger federal investigation of AIPAC's role in aiding and abetting felonious behavior. Surely this is well beyond what Bandar could have anticipated when he decided to embark on the leak.[50]

In an apparent attempt to distance itself from any actions that might displease the FBI and the Bush administration, the Israeli media reported that AIPAC had curtailed its lobbying efforts on Israel's behalf.[51] It has also hired former Justice Department officials now working for Washington-based law firm, Howrey LLP that consults with lobbying organizations and reviews lobbying practices.

For Bandar, the impact of the leak could not have been better. What had started out as a small-scale spy trial had undermined the hitherto all-powerful pro-Israeli lobby, which had influenced the direction of U.S. Middle East policy for decades.

It seems that Bandar had a much broader and more ambitious agenda when he lifted the lid on what could emerge as the biggest Israeli spy operation against the United States since the November 1985 arrest of Pollard. I recalled Princess Loulou's words about Bandar: "I think the thing that everybody forgets is that my father does nothing by accident—nothing."[52]

Bandar had succeeded in advancing many issues on his agenda: securing a Republican victory for the Bush dynasty in the U.S. presidential election; damaging the standing of the ubiquitous AIPAC; reducing the influence of the neo-cons; and sowing the seeds of suspicion and mistrust between the United States and Israel.

Perhaps the final proof of the architect of the Franklin leak was provided by Bandar's use of the press in the past. It was Bandar who, in 1991, leaked to *Sunday Times* editor Andrew Neil, President George H. W. Bush's letter to Saddam Hussein in the weeks prior to Operation Desert Storm. Bandar's agenda was to ensure that Saddam Hussein would not withdraw from Kuwait and thus America would go to war. He succeeded in that, too.

In a similar fashion he decided to leak the information to CBS via an Arab newspaper in London owned by his father and half-brother, the editor of which I met at dinner at Glympton. Indeed, it was an action the prince all but admitted at Glympton, saying to me casually, "It's useful sometimes to have a friendly media source."

Based on the evidence uncovered since his initial observations about the Franklin affair, and his subsequent admission, Bandar was unquestionably the source of the Franklin story leak.

Having illustrated Bandar's Machiavellian traits with a contemporaneous account, I nonetheless believe that we can separate the Bandar of integrity and honesty from the amoral prince of guile and shadow diplomacy, the latter being the mask he is obliged to adopt to execute his role as diplomat and emissary on behalf of Saudi Arabi. The former recognizes the essence of a man of conscience, noble principles, humanity, and humility who believes that his role, his destiny, is to labor for the cause of peace—wherever he can in a world riven with conflict and strife.

His life has been a true fairy tale. His progress from relative obscurity within the Saudi royal family to become one of the most powerful players on the world's political stage has been remarkable.

Yet, Bandar often eschews public recognition of his work, content to know that he has achieved success.

This was echoed by his wife, Princess Haifa, who said, "I don't think he is looking for recognition in the grand sense. I think the recognition he already has for what he has achieved is having done his work very well." She then explained, "You see, he is an achiever rather than anything else. If he does his work well, that is a great recognition for himself and he is not looking for an award. He doesn't mind that he has not been recognized, that he did not get an award. The most important thing to him is that he has done his work well and to the full—and has succeeded in doing what he was asked to do."[53]

To steal a phrase from T. E. Lawrence, Bandar is a man who dreams with his eyes open, who works tirelessly behind a veil of secrecy, and who is governed by a deep-rooted sense of responsibility and a desire to "make a difference." Moreover, in his strict observance of the third pillar of Islam, the Zakat,* the prince does not look for recognition for his labors. Although his efforts as a peacemaker have been largely overlooked, he is content to have achieved his purpose.

Having talked with his peers, his family, and those who work close to or for him, I am convinced that the prince often uses his humor as a mask, disguising the anguish he feels at lost opportunities, as with the continuing failure of the Israeli-Palestinian peace process. The immense pressures that Bandar has felt and the inability to share the load due to the acute sensitivity of the work he has undertaken has often sapped his will to continue. Until his retirement in 2005, his exhaustion had become increasingly difficult to disguise.

But it was the words of his friend Tarek Shawaf that most eloquently capture the man who is Bandar bin Sultan. In a final comment on the need for change in Saudi Arabia and an indicator of the respect that is accorded to Bandar, Shawaf recalled that many years previously he had presented Bandar, then in a hospital in Dhahran being treated for his back problem, with a book about the royal family and the rule of Islam. Shawaf had written an inscription inside the front cover of the book. Years later, Shawaf came across that book in Bandar's library in Riyadh. The inscription read, "To Prince Bandar—the Prince of our hope. Because our country is in the Middle East, there are so many problems facing it. I believe that one day you will do something about that."

"Until the Gulf War, which shook his belief in Arab nationalism," Shawaf explained, "Bandar was a confirmed Arab nationalist. He is still, but in a different way now. I'm so glad that the book is still there, because I will show it to him one day. He is still the prince of our hope. In our country, and in the Arab world as a whole, we need hope—and he is the hope."[54]

---

*The third pillar of Islam—the Zakat—is a requirement placed on each individual to give to others in need—in Western terminology, to give to charity. The word *zakat* means both "purification" and "growth," and possessions are purified by setting aside a proportion for those in need, and, like the pruning of plants, this cutting back balances and encourages new growth. A pious person may also give as much as he or she pleases as Sadaqa, and does so preferably in secret. This word can be translated as "voluntary charity."

FOURTEEN

A NEW LIFE

"We seek peace, knowing that peace is the climate of freedom."

DWIGHT D. EISENHOWER (1953–1961)

Bandar insisted that his new role as secretary-general of the National Security Council (NSC) on October 16, 2005, was the furthest thing from his mind when he retired with his family to Glympton for all of three months. Asked how it had impacted on his family, Bandar admitted candidly, "Badly. You see, you can fool around with everything except the lives of your family. And the proof that I was serious when I left, and that I had no inkling that I would come back so soon—nor did I want this job—was that we decided to settle in England. We put our kids into school in England—and you don't put your kids into school knowing that you would shortly be moving to Saudi Arabia. I began thinking how I was going to keep myself busy—maybe reading, maybe writing, and traveling with the family." The family was still unpacking when King Abdullah made the call which would change Bandar's life—a return to duty.

Bandar laughed as he recalled that several months later, with the family back in Saudi Arabia, his young son, Abdulaziz, who now had been in three schools in three months—Washington, England, and Saudi Arabia—was prompted to say to Princess Haifa, "What's wrong with Daddy? Why can't he keep a job?"

This new secretary-general role saw Bandar become one of the most powerful figures in Saudi Arabia, as the Saudi press, quoting "informed sources," reported that the NSC would enjoy extensive powers, including the right to declare emergency and war, to investigate security agencies, and deal with corruption and negligence of public duty.[1] Bandar described the NSC as "a combination of national security, national economic council and homeland security." The new council's encompassing powers include direct control over "social, political, economic, military, security, media and international affairs in order to guarantee the country's comprehensive national security."[2]

The new Saudi NSC is expected to pinpoint all potential sources of economic, social, and political threats facing the kingdom now and in the future. Commenting on his new role, Bandar said, "It's been tough and totally consuming—there is no rest for the wicked, as they say." There was a fine political line to walk in dealing with so many Saudi ministries and organizations, and Bandar emphasized to his contemporaries on the NSC that his role was not a threat, but merely one of coordination and follow-up to ensure policy implementation. However, Bandar's authority is supreme; he speaks on behalf of His Majesty.

With Bandar's appointment, came changes in the kingdom's relationship with the outside world. On December 11, 2005, scarcely two months after Bandar's appointment as secretary-general, the Kingdom of Saudi Arabia joined the World Trade Organization (WTO). In his previous role as ambassador, Bandar had been active in persuading successive administrations to support Saudi Arabia's bid for WTO membership. He also worked with British Prime Minister Tony Blair and his government—particularly when Blair became chair of the EU—and could therefore influence the support for Saudi WTO accession amongst the other EU member states.

Following his appointment as secretary-general, now restructured as part of the kingdom's campaign against terrorism,* Bandar's quickly became engaged in shuttle diplomacy yet again. Bandar successfully mediated between the Americans, the French, (President Jacques Chirac), the Syrians, the Lebanese, the United Nations (Kofi Annan) and other interested parties.

One of his first tasks was to attempt to resolve the impasse then existing between the U.N. and Syria over the investigation into the assassination of Rafik Hariri by a massive bomb in February 2005. Bandar observed, "He

---

*King Abdullah is the NSC chairman, and Crown Prince Sultan is NSC deputy chairman. Other NSC members include the deputy commander of the National Guard, the ministers of interior and foreign affairs, and the head of the general intelligence.

[Hariri] was a very close friend and we had worked together all the way since '83. I was deeply hurt and offended by the way he was killed—assassinated."

The U.N. Security Council had responded to this outrage on April 7, 2005, with Resolution 1595, setting up an international commission of inquiry. However, whereas when the U.N. investigation team pointed the finger at some Lebanese security officials, who were promptly arrested in Lebanon, the Syrian government denied the U.N. access to its officials. It relented only under extreme pressure from the U.N. Security Council. The U.N. chief investigator was eventually permitted to interview the officials suspected in Hariri's death. However, those interviews proved unworkable in Syria, and Mehlis requested that they be re-interviewed in Lebanon.

Bandar explained, "The Syrians said that this was an insult."[3] The Lebanese didn't want the responsibility, in case the Syrian officials were harmed in any way, as were concerned they would be blamed for it, precipitating a war with Syria. "I wanted them to be interviewed period," Bandar stressed. "I didn't care where. So we came up with the suggestion that they do it outside the region." Geneva and Vienna were suggested and Bandar was tasked by King Abdullah with persuading President Bashar al-Assad "to see sense," as it was in Syria's own interest if there was no case to be made.[4] Bandar succeeded and Assad agreed. The investigation would be held in Vienna.

As Bandar recalled, "Nobody could have done that except Saudi Arabia and King Abdullah, as the Syrians refused [to listen] to anybody else. Of course, with my relationship with his [Assad's] father, that made it easier."

Asked if President Assad was personally implicated in the Hariri assassination, Bandar observed, "There was a question, 'How could such a major operation like this happen in a system that is very centralized without Assad being aware of it, authorizing it, or knowing about it afterwards?' But the deal was struck—leave the Assad aspect of it alone—just work on the [high level] Syrian officials who had close connections to the Lebanese security chiefs and let events run." Bandar reasoned that if those officials were convicted, then the question would become, "How could such senior officials do this without Assad being aware." Bandar continued pragmatically, "If they are not convicted, then Assad is free." Bandar concluded that if the Syrian security officials were convicted, then given their senior positions, the matter would become very serious [for Assad].

While Bandar's mission as an emissary for King Abdullah in breaking the deadlock in the U.N.'s Hariri investigation overshadowed his role as secretary-general of the NSC in his first few months in office, he was, nonetheless, thoroughly immersed in creating the infrastructure needed to support his new assignment. However, Bandar's new remit would presage change.

On December 7 and 8, 2005, leaders of Muslim nations belonging to the Organization of Islamic Conference (OIC) met in Mecca, Saudi Arabia. The OIC Summit Declaration issued at the conclusion of this Summit secures a generally positive response from the White House which welcomed the "valuable statements from the OIC regarding the common fight against terrorism and extremism. The Declaration condemns terrorism; stresses the need to criminalize all aspects of terrorism, including its financing; and rejects any justification for the deliberate killing of innocent civilians. In addition, the OIC Declaration condemns extremism and calls for developing school curricula that 'strengthen the values of understanding, tolerance, dialogue and pluralism.'"[5]

The Summit also declared a worldwide policy of religious tolerance, moderation and peaceful coexistence for the world's 1.7 billion Muslims— both within and without the Islamic world. Bandar's fingerprints in this declaration are obvious—echoing his bold statement on the need for all-out war on terrorism issued when he was ambassador in Washington, including home-grown terrorists within the kingdom. In addition, in the statement about school curricula, there is evidence of Bandar's cultural tolerance and ecumenical attitudes.

At the Gulf Cooperation Council (GCC) Summit in December 2005— referred to as the Fahd Summit in honor of the late King Fahd—Bandar's hand was again evident when GCC leaders ended their summit calling for a nuclear-free Middle East. Amid mounting international pressure on Iran over its nuclear program, GCC Secretary-General Abdul Rahman Al-Attiya urged Tehran to keep the region free of nuclear weapons.[6]

As the architect of the Al-Yamamah program in the mid-1980s, Bandar clearly derived great personal satisfaction in his first few months in office when he had to give the stamp of approval for the purchase by Saudi Arabia of the Eurofighter aircraft, known as the Typhoon. "That deal was sealed by Tony Blair visiting Crown Prince Abdullah," said Bandar. "However," he continued, "in my role as secretary-general, my job was to make sure that it was consistent with defense policy. I just had to put my stamp on it." Bandar explained that he evaluated the alternatives. The French Rafael had been rejected by the RSAF, so the only option was the U.S. F-35 (the stealth, supersonic Lockheed Martin F-35 Joint Strike Fighter—the Lightning II), and the F-22 Raptor, (the U.S. Air Force's next-generation air superiority fighter). However, Bandar dismissed the F-22 as "it was out of the question because the U.S. would not sell it to anybody, as it was their latest aircraft." On the other hand, delays with production and testing with the F-35 program, and the fact that it was a single engine aircraft, ruled out this option for the RSAF which had stipulated a twin-engine aircraft. Thus, Bandar quickly verified that the Typhoon—upgraded to provide a strike capability—was the only practical option and he authorized its purchase under the Al-Yamamah program. Bandar also explained that it was also Saudi policy to buy from a number of nations so that the kingdom could not to be held up by restrictions applied to their aircraft, as had often been the case with U.S.-supplied aircraft.

Another groundbreaking activity in which Bandar had a role is the King Abdullah Economic City. This is a $26 Billion economic project that will be located along the Red Sea, around 50 km north of Jeddah. This mega project, on which construction began on December 21, 2005, is designed to expand the economy, create employment opportunities and act as a catalyst for foreign investment, global trade, commerce and industry.

One of the most ominous threats to the region is Iran's desire to acquire a nuclear capability, highlighted during the GCC Summit. It reached crisis point during early 2006, and prompted yet another round of shuttle diplomacy by Bandar at King Abdullah's behest.

Many suspected that Iran was developing nuclear weapons, and Iran's refusal to disclose details of its nuclear program precipitated the threat of a military strike on its nuclear installations, either by Israel or by the United States. Fearing that U.S. military action against Iran would wreak further havoc in the region, Saudi Arabia asked Russia to block any bid by Washington to secure U.N. cover for an attack. Bandar met Russian Foreign Minister Sergei Lavrov in Moscow on April 4, where he "urged Russia to strive to prevent the adoption of a U.N. Security Council resolution which the United States could use as justification to launch a military assault to knock out Iran's nuclear facilities."[7]

Secretary General of Iran's National Security Council, Ali Larijani, subsequently visited Saudi Arabia on April 12, 2006, where he was hosted by Bandar—his Saudi counterpart—to discuss bilateral relations and latest developments in the region, mainly the situation in Lebanon.[8] After his meeting with Bandar, Larijani traveled to China, Russia, Washington, London and Paris in an endeavor to further defuse the situation. Bandar speculated that here again fate had intervened to place him at the centre of an international crisis, taking on the part of mediator, a role in which he thrived. Bandar would himself visit Washington to meet with Secretary of State Condoleezza Rice, after which the United States took a less aggressive stance, backtracking from expressions of military options, and stressing the desire to reach a diplomatic solution with Iran. But with the worsening situation in Lebanon linking Hezbollah's lethal armory to Iran, a complex situation presents a massive diplomatic test for Bandar.

Asked if he thought that Iranian assurances that they were not seeking to develop nuclear weapons was sincere, Bandar's pragmatic response was, "The jury's out on that one." Bandar concluded, "The region cannot stand one more military confrontation." Prophetic words perhaps, as the Lebanon conflict began to slide out of control.

With the eruption of violence in the Middle East following the kidnapping of IDF soldiers by Hezbollah on July 12, 2006, and the unleashing of hundreds of Katyusha rockets on Israel, which duly responded with a massive air, land and sea bombardment of Lebanon, the prospect of a much wider conflict seems ominously real. As I sat with Bandar at a late lunch on July 14, 2006, he was clearly appalled by the alarming media reports of surgical Israeli air attacks on Hezbollah-controlled areas in Beirut and Lebanon's infrastructure—bridges, oil installations, power stations and Beirut international airport. In response, Hezbollah's leader, Sheik Hassan Nasrallah, declared an "open war" against Israel. In a déjà vu moment for Bandar, it was a return to the brutalized Beirut of 1983 in which he succeeded in negotiating a ceasefire during the civil war.

Now it has been alleged that Hezbollah had perhaps ten thousand rockets supplied by Syria. But then came reports of a Hezbollah strike on an Israeli warship which had been shelling Beirut; the Israeli military claimed that the ship had been struck by a radar-guided C802 missile supplied by Iran. An Israeli commander, Brig. Gen. Ido Nehushtan, said ominously, "We see this attack as a very clear fingerprint of Iranian involvement."[9] Israel was concerned that Iranian-made Zelzal missiles, with an estimated range in excess of two hundred kilometers, might also be used, thus allowing Hezbollah to target the Tel Aviv metropolitan area.[10] Further, it was claimed that the IDF had destroyed one Zelzal missile as Hezbollah prepared it for a launch.[11]

At the Group of 8 meeting in St. Petersburg, President Bush said, "I call upon Syria to exert influence over Hezbollah." The Israeli ambassador to the United States charged that Iran and Syria were coordinating attacks by Islamic militia, and warned that they were "playing with fire."[12] In response, the Syrian ambassador to London, in an interview with the BBC, called on Hezbollah to stop firing missiles at Israel.[13]

Nonetheless, the spectre of a widespread regional conflict refused to disappear, as a confluence of events threatened to suck in Syria, Iran and the United States. Aside from the Hariri assassination and the Syrian arming of Hezbollah, the *Washington Post* reported, "President Mahmoud Ahmadinejad of Iran knows what he wants: nuclear weapons and the means to deliver them; suppression of freedom at home and the spread of terrorism abroad."[14]

When it was observed that the current crisis was Arafat's legacy following his rejection of the Barak/Clinton peace offer at Camp David, Bandar grimly nodded his assent. "It was a crime," he said.

In a pessimistic assessment of the current position which he recognized was beginning to spin out of control, Bandar said ruefully, "The opportunities are slipping away. There are too many players. The superpowers are players; the Palestinians are split; the Israelis are split between hardliners and those seeking peace through negotiation; Israel has a new leadership. It [the search for peace] is becoming too complex." However, it seems unimaginable that he would not engage in his role as peacemaker soon. "I just cannot imagine my grandchildren leaving high school, or going to college," he said, "and asking me, 'Grandpa, why did you fail solving the damn thing?' "

Perhaps it is not just Saudi Arabia that should consider Bandar as, "the Prince of our hope"—the whole of the Middle East needs his skills, both as a diplomat and a mediator. For Bandar sometimes seems to be the lone voice of reason seeking to be heard in the clamor of chaos.

ACKNOWLEDGMENTS

At fifty-five—an age when I would have been retiring from the Royal Air Force had I served a full career—an accident of fate triggered my latent ambitions as an aspirant writer. These aspirations owed much to a military reunion with old friends a year or so earlier and sowed the seeds for this biography. It was to spark off a three-year mission, a time laced with periods of frustration and frenetic activity, a journey that has been eventful, confusing, intensely rewarding, and fun.

What at first seemed—in my naivety as a novice author—comparatively straightforward, was in fact an immense task. I rapidly uncovered many story lines, false trails, and blind leads. Faced with that challenge, I was fortunate to receive help from many people—assistance that saw me finally produce a book I hope has done justice to the remarkable life of Prince Bandar bin Sultan.

The litany of those from whom I sought support as I attempted to coalesce the confusion of research, and medley of interviews and anecdotes, is legion—you will all know who you are. However, I must single out a number of individuals who pushed, encouraged, supported and nurtured me as my original three volumes were reduced to a single book, much of which now lies on the cutting room floor.

My research assistant, Sarah Gibbings, was remarkable; not only did she work assiduously on the many stories I would throw her way, but came back with tactful suggestions about my writing style, the direction of my observations and in truth, edited so much of those early pages as the book took shape.

I have Prince Bandar to thank for providing access to his family and friends, albeit this is an unofficial biography. And it was the support of his family—their openness, friendship, and encouragement—that enabled me to construct a truer picture of Bandar himself. It is a remarkable family unit that it has been a joy to be a part of.

Jan Lilac, a protective guardian of Bandar and his family, was understandably nervous as I delved into Bandar's life history. However, she soon became a tower of strength as she checked and rechecked my manuscript for accuracy, located long lost photographs, articles and letters, and suggested subtle changes to the script. Her Herculean efforts were thoroughly appreciated.

Equally, Bandar's "traveling court" took me into its collective confidence. Robert Deacon Elliott, an old friend from our days with Bandar at Cranwell, was supportive at every turn and quick to suggest stories that I should follow up and individuals that I should interview. Col. Bob Lilac's infectious humor and encouragement was priceless, and he astutely suggested that I should set aside the Queen's English and write in American style. Sound advice Bob! His help with photo selection and presentation was also invaluable.

Col. Joe Ramsey, another of Bandar's intimate circle of friends, encouraged me in my writing and opened his collection of photographs to illustrate Bandar's life story. In addition, he was—I suspect—the key to securing a vital interview with the late Fred Dutton, who, as a friend of many literary giants, was uncertain if I was up to the task during the early months of interviews and research. The late Dr. Said Karmi was another stalwart. A wonderful man whom I considered a true friend, Said was of immense help to me during the research phase and I miss his wisdom, charisma, and wit.

It would be remiss of me not to mention Sherry Cooper's invaluable assistance throughout; thank you Sherry. And Alice Hancock and Mimi Burke must also be commended for helping me in shaping this biography.

However, as the book's momentum picked up, my wife, Wendy, joined me as my personal assistant. The discipline she subsequently imposed on my writing was invaluable, as was her constant encouragement. Moreover, Wendy often anticipated the ruthless pencil of my editor and struck out much unnecessary material early on.

And now to my editor—Katie Hall. Ruthless she may have been, but in striking out page after page, I believe she showed vision, understanding, skill and experience. I was at times left reeling by the severity of her cruel pencil, but I now appreciate the debt I owe her. She did a superb job in giving this biography punch and focus. Katie—thank you. Her professional approach made the task of Doug Grad, Senior Editor at HarperCollins Publishing that much easier, but Doug's final finessing of the manuscript and his help in collating a suitable repertoire of photographs was also invaluable.

So, I have finally set down my pen and as I review the past three years, I am minded of the truth of Winston Churchill's words:

> "Writing a book is an adventure. To begin with it is a toy and an amusement, then it becomes a mistress, then it becomes a master, then it becomes a tyrant. The last phase is that just as you are about to be reconciled to your servitude, you kill the monster and fling him about to the public."

I can only hope that you have enjoyed my "monster." To those who have helped to create it—you have my eternal thanks.

NOTES

INTRODUCTION

1. Address by Prince Bandar to the World Affairs Council in Birmingham, Alabama, September 26, 2003.
2. Interview with former president Jimmy Carter at the Carter Center, Atlanta, Georgia, March 19, 2004.
3. Interview with former Secretary Colin Powell at the State Department, Washington, D.C., November 5, 2004.
4. Bob Woodward. *Plan of Attack.* New York: Simon & Schuster, 2004: 228.
5. *Chambers Concise Dictionary.* London: Chambers Harrap Publishers Ltd., 1997.
6. Interview with Louis J. Freeh, FBI Director (1993–2001) in Wilmington, Delaware, March 11, 2004.
7. Matt Welsh. "Is Bandar Bush Above the Law?" *National Post,* April 19, 2003.
8. Robert Baer. *Sleeping with the Devil—How Washington Sold Our Souls for Saudi Crude.* New York: Crown Publishers, 2003: 63.
9. Cynthia Dettelbach. "Saudi Ambassador's City Club Talk Sheds Little Light." *Cleveland Jewish News,* December 2, 2003.
10. Patrick E. Tyler. "Double Exposure: Saudi Arabia's Man in Washington." *New York Times,* June 7, 1992.

1. WHO IS PRINCE BANDAR?

1. T. E. Lawrence. *The Seven Pillars of Wisdom: A Triumph.* New York: Anchor, 1991.
2. Interview with Fred Dutton at the Dorchester Hotel, London, August 26, 2004.
3. Interviews with Princess Reema bint Bandar in McLean, Virginia, February 19 and March 9, 2004.
4. See note 2 above.
5. Ibid.
6. David B. Ottaway. "Been There, Done That: One of the Great Cold Warriors Faces the Dawn of a New Era." *Washington Post,* July 21, 1996.
7. Interview with Princess Haifa bint Faisal bin Abdul Aziz in McLean, Virginia, October 28, 2003.

8. Elsa Walsh. "The Prince: How the Saudi Ambassador Became Washington's Indispensable Operator." *The New Yorker,* March 24, 2003.
9. See note 2 above.
10. See note 6 above.
11. Interview with Gen. Faisal Mifgai in Marrakech, Morocco, June 26, 2004.
12. Ibid.
13. See note 8 above.
14. Interview with Sgt. Ken Adams in Leasingham, Lincolnshire, January 14, 2004.
15. Interview with John Waterfall in Brighton, Sussex, February 26, 2004.
16. Interview with Martin Shewry in Lincoln, December 2, 2003.
17. See note 14 above.
18. Ibid.
19. See note 15 above.
20. Interview with Mrs. Grace Deacon Elliott in St. Leonards-on-Sea, Sussex, January 18, 2005.
21. Interview with Robert Deacon Elliott in Jeddah, Saudi Arabia, May 2004.
22. See note 20 above.
23. See note 22 above.
24. RAF College Cranwell Report, 1968—Flight Cadet Bandar bin Sultan.
25. Telephone interview with Air Cdre Wilson Metcalfe, U.K. defence attaché, Moscow, February 12, 2004.
26. Cranwell course report on Flight Cadet Sultan prepared by his drill instructor, Sgt. Ken Adams.
27. See note 15 above.
28. Cranwell course report on Flight Cadet Sultan prepared by his flying instructor, Flight Lieutenant Tony Yule.
29. Interview with ACM Sir Richard Johns GCB, CBE, LVO, FRAeS, constable and governor of Windsor Castle, January 12, 2004.
30. RAF College graduation report for Prince Bandar Sultan, 1969.

2. FIGHTER PILOT PRINCE

1. Interview with ACM Sir Richard Johns GCB, CBE, LVO, FRAeS, constable and governor of Windsor Castle, January 12, 2004.
2. Interview with Col. Keith Phillips in Aspen, December 31, 2004.
3. Interview with Fahd Almhqani in Washington, D.C., November 4, 2004.
4. Interview with Col. Robert Lilac in Woodstock, Oxfordshire, August 27, 2004.
5. Address by Prince Bandar to the World Affairs Council, Houston, Texas, December 5, 2003.
6. Interview with Col. Joe Ramsey in Washington, D.C., October 29, 2003.
7. Address by Prince Bandar to General Dynamics, Fort Worth Division, March 31, 1989.
8. See note 6 above.
9. See note 2 above.
10. See note 6 above.
11. Interview with Dr. Henry Kissinger in New York, April 27, 2004.
12. See note 6 above.
13. James Perry Stevenson. *McDonnell Douglas F-15 Eagle.* Fallbrook, Calif.: Aero Publishers, 1978.
14. Seth P. Tillman. *The United States in the Middle East: Interest and Obstacles.* Bloomington: Indiana University Press, 1982: 99.

15. Without the sale of F-15s to Saudi Arabia, procurement schedules would have lagged. See Mitchell Geoffrey Bard. *The Water's Edge and Beyond: Defining the Limits to Domestic Influence on United States Middle East Policy.* New Brunswick, N.J.: Transaction Publishers, 1991: 37.

16. Ibid., p. 45.

17. Ibid., p. 46.

18. "The Tornados in the Desert: A Flying Piano with Resonance." *The Economist*, July 16, 1988.

19. Stephen N. Connor. *Questions and Comments on the President's Authorization of U.S. Sale of F-15 Planes for the Defense of Saudi Arabia: Pending before the U.S. Congress.* Report produced specifically for Saudi Embassy. Maryland. 1978.

20. *Washington Post*, April 21, 1978 (article title unknown).

21. Speech by President Jimmy Carter, May 5, 1978. State Department Bulletin, July 1978: 20.

22. Bard, p. 45.

23. State Department Bulletin, April 1978: 22.

24. Bard, p. 37.

25. See note 14 above.

26. Interview with former president Jimmy Carter at the Carter Center, Atlanta, Georgia, March 19, 2004.

27. Bard, p. 35.

28. *Saudi Arabia in the 1980's: Foreign Policy, Security and Oil.* Washington D.C.: The Brookings Institution, 1981: 18.

29. David Howard Goldberg and Bernard K. Johnpoll. *Foreign Policy and Ethnic Interest Groups: American and Canadian Jews Lobby for Israel.* New York: Greenwood Press, 1990: 65.

30. Hoag Levins. *Arab Reach: The Secret War against Israel.* New York: Doubleday, 1983: 10.

31. See note 26 above.

32. Address by Prince Bandar to McDonnell Douglas, January 9, 1989.

33. See note 26 above.

34. Ibid.

35. Ibid.

36. Patrick E. Tyler. "Double Exposure." *New York Times,* June 7, 1992.

37. Ibid.

38. Tillman, p. 100.

39. *New York Times,* May 8, 1978 (article title unknown).

40. Tillman, p. 101.

41. Ibid., p. 103.

42. Bard, p. 45.

43. U.S. Congress. Congressional Record—Senate S 7833 May 19, 1978; U.S. Senate. Proceedings in Closed Session. Monday, May 15, 1978, 2:04 P.M. to 4:27 P.M.

44. President's Conference, Annual Report (year ending March 31, 1979): 5.

45. Levins, p. 13.

46. David Pollock. The Politics of Pressure: American Arms and Israeli Policy Since the Six Day War. New York: Greenwood Press, 1982: 239.

3. THE TIP OF THE ICEBERG

1. Nicholas Laham. *Selling AWACS to Saudi Arabia: The Reagan Administration and the Balancing of America's Competing Interests in the Middle East.* Westport, Conn: Praeger, 2002: 90.

2. George Crile. *Charlie Wilson's War.* New York: Atlantic Monthly Press, 2003: 236–237.

3. Peter Schweizer. *Victory: The Reagan Administration's Secret Strategy That Hastened the Collapse of the Soviet Union.* New York: Atlantic Monthly Press, 1996: 26.

4. Hedrick Smith. *The Power Game: How Washington Works.* New York: Random House, 1988: 219.

5. Interview with Col. Robert Lilac in Woodstock, Oxfordshire, August 27, 2004.

6. Steven Emerson. *The American House of Saud: The Secret Petrodollar Connection.* New York: Franklin Watts, 1985: 176.

7. Rachel Bronson. "The U.S.–Saudi Love Affair Predates Bush." *Los Angeles Times.* July 9, 2004.

8. Bernard Gwertzman. "U.S. Decides to Sell Equipment to Saudis to Bolster F-15 Jets." *New York Times,* March 7, 1981.

9. Nadav Safran. *Saudi Arabia: The Ceaseless Quest for Security.* Ithaca and London: Cornell University Press, 1988: 437.

10. See note 5 above.

11. See note 7 above.

12. Rachel Bronson. "Recall, Reagan had Riyadh to Thank." *Daily Star,* June 19, 2004.

13. Schweizer, pp. 50–51.

14. Mitchell Geoffrey Bard. *The Water's Edge and Beyond: Defining the Limits to Domestic Influence in United States Middle East Policy.* New Brunswick, NJ: Transaction Publishers. 1991: 103.

15. See note 6 above.

16. Laham, p. 13.

17. Smith, p. 220.

18. Interview with Fred Dutton at the Dorchester Hotel, London, August 26, 2004.

19. See note above.

20. Interview with Ambassador Richard Murphy in New York, April 28, 2004.

21. Howard Blum. *The Gold of Exodus: The Discovery of the True Mount Sinai.* New York: Pocket Books, 1999: 13.

22. Safran, p. 436.

23. "A Fighter Pilot Turned Negotiator." *Time,* October 10, 1983.

24. See note 18 above.

25. Ibid.

26. Emerson, p. 195.

27. William D. Hartung. *And Weapons For All.* New York: HarperCollins, 1994: 97.

28. Address by Prince Bandar to General Dynamics, Fort Worth Division, March 31, 1989.

29. David E. Long. *The United States and Saudi Arabia: Ambivalent Allies.* Boulder and London: Westview Press, 1985: 65.

30. See note 5 above.

31. Laurence I. Barrett. *Gambling with History: Reagan in the White House.* New York: Doubleday, 1983: 267.

32. Ronald Reagan. *An American Life.* New York: Simon & Schuster, 1990.

33. Lou Cannon. *President Reagan: The Role of a Lifetime.* New York: Simon & Schuster, 1991: 393.

34. Laham, p. 128.

35. *Public Papers of Presidents of the United States: Ronald Reagan 1981.* Washington, D.C.: United States Government Printing Office: 867.

36. Donnie Radcliffe. "Ambassador with the Royal Touch." *Washington Post,* February 16, 1984.

37. Smith, p. 221.

38. Seth P. Tillman. *The United States in the Middle East: Interests and Obstacles.* Bloomington: Indiana University Press, 1982: 52.

39. See note 27 above.

40. See note 5 above.

41. See note 31 above.

42. Ibid., p. 274.

43. Smith, p. 231.

44. Howard M. Sachar. *A History of the Jews in America.* New York: Vintage. 1993.

45. Remarks following a meeting with former national security officials on the sale of AWACS planes and other air defense equipment to Saudi Arabia. U.S. National Archives and Records Administration, October 5, 1981.

46. Barrett, p. 275.

47. Ibid.

48. "The Arming of Saudi Arabia." Transcript of *Frontline,* February 16, 1993.

49. Ibid.

50. Smith, p. 222.

51. Ibid., p. 221.

52. Barrett, p. 445.

53. Charles McC. Mathias Jr. "Ethnic Groups and Foreign Policy." *Foreign Affairs,* Summer 1981, p. 60.

54. Blum, 14–15.

55. Barrett, p. 276.

56. S.CON.RES.35: A concurrent resolution expressing the objection of the Congress to the proposed sale of certain defense articles, together with associated spare parts and equipment and related defense services, to the kingdom of Saudi Arabia. Sponsor: Sen Packwood, Bob [OR] Introduced September 17, 1981.

    S.CON.RES.37: A concurrent resolution disapproving the proposed sales to Saudi Arabia of E-3A Airborne Warning and Control System (AWACS) aircraft, conformal fuel tanks for F-15 aircraft, AIM-9L Sidewinder missiles, and Boeing 707 aerial refueling aircraft. Sponsor: Sen Packwood, Bob [OR]. Introduced October 1, 1981.

57. Conversation with U.S. Deputy Secretary of State Richard Armitage in McLean, Virginia, March 2, 2005.

58. See note 5 above.

59. See note 18 above.

60. David Howard Goldberg and Bernard K. Johnpoll. *Foreign Policy and Ethnic Interest Groups: American and Canadian Jews Lobby for Israel.* New York: Greenwood Press, 1990: 73.

61. See note 18 above.

62. Smith, pp. 216–217.

63. Kathleen Christison. "Blind Spots: Official U.S. Myths about the Middle East." *Journal of Palestine Studies,* Winter 1988, p. 50.

64. Ibid., p. 124.

65. *New York Times,* December 2, 1982 (article title unknown).

66. U.S. Congress. Congressional Record—Senate, Robert Byrd, January 4, 1992.

67. Donald Neff. *Fallen Pillars: U.S. Policy towards Palestine and Israel Since 1945.* Washington, D.C.: Institute for Palestine Studies, 1995: 185.

68. See note 5 above.

69. Interview with Col. Keith Phillips in Aspen, December 31, 2004.

70. Smith, p. 601.

71. It is worth noting that Prince Bandar also writes personal letters when issues are dear to him, "At two in the morning, unable to sleep, he (Prince Bandar) wrote an emotional letter to Bush in which he expressed gratitude to Bush for saving his country. 'You are my friend for life, one of my family,' he wrote." See Elsa Walsh. "The Prince." *The New Yorker,* March 24, 2003, p. 52.

72. Roulah Khalaf. "The Prince Whose Fairytale Went Sour." *Financial Times,* November 29, 2002.

73. James A. Baker III. *The Politics of Diplomacy—Revolution, War and Peace 1989–1992.* New York: G. P. Putnam's Sons, 1995.

74. David Plotz. "Saudi Ambassador Prince Bandar: Why Washington's Smoothest Diplomat Is Falling from Favor." *Slate*, October 24, 2001.

75. Conversation with Prince Bandar at 96 Entry Reunion in Aspen, August 24, 2002.

76. Academy of Achievement website, www.achievement.org/autodoc/page/pow0pro-1.

4. THE YEARS OF INTRIGUE

1. Midge Decter. *Rumsfeld: A Personal Portrait*. New York: HarperCollins, 2003: 93.

2. Bob Woodward. *Veil: The Secret Wars of the CIA 1981–1987*. London: Simon & Schuster Ltd., 1987: 397–398.

3. Peter W. Wilson and Douglas F. Graham. *Saudi Arabia—The Coming Storm*. New York: M.E. Sharpe, 1994: 325–326.

4. Holly Sklar. *Washington's War on Nicaragua*. Cambridge, Mass.: South End Press, 1988: 325.

5. Lolly Weymouth. "A Prince Who Would Make Peace; Saudi Arabia's Bandar Worries about American-Israeli Ties." *Washington Post*, December 4, 1983.

6. Donnie Radcliffe. "Ambassador with the Royal Touch." *Washington Post*. February 16, 1984.

7. "A Fighter Pilot Turned Negotiator." *Time*, October 10, 1983.

8. See note 6 above.

9. Andrew E. Busch. "Ronald Reagan and the Defeat of the Soviet Empire." *Presidential Studies Quarterly*, March 27, 1997.

10. Peter Schweizer. *Victory: The Reagan Administration's Secret Strategy That Hastened the Collapse of the Soviet Union*. New York: Atlantic Monthly Press, 1996: 28.

11. Steve Coll. *Ghost Wars: The Secret History of the CIA, Afghanistan, and Bin Laden, from the Soviet Invasion to September 10, 2001*. New York: Penguin Press, 2004: 97.

12. Rachel Bronson. "Recall, Reagan Had Riyadh to Thank." *Daily Star,* June 19, 2004.

13. Ambassador Charles W. Freeman. "A Relationship in Transition—and Then 9/11." Saudi-American Forum Interview.

14. William E. Pemberton. *Exit with Honor: The Life and Presidency of Ronald Reagan*. New York: M. E. Sharpe, 1998.

15. Lou Cannon. *President Reagan: The Role of a Lifetime*. New York: PublicAffairs, 2000: 384.

16. Report of the Congressional Committees Investigating the Iran-Contra affair, p. 38.

17. Lawrence E. Walsh. *Firewall: The Iran-Contra Conspiracy and Cover-Up*. New York: W. W. Norton, 1997: 19.

18. Cannon, p. 385.

19. Oliver L. North and William Novak. *Under Fire: An American Story*. New York: Harper-Collins, 1991: 242.

20. Robert McFarlane, North Trial Testimony, March 13, 1989, p. 3933. See also Theodore Draper. *A Very Thin Line: The Iran-Contra Affairs*. New York: Hill and Wang, 1991: 81.

21. Declassified Minutes of the National Security Planning Group meeting. June 25, 1984.

22. Memorandum for the Record from Sporkin, June 26,1984, ALV 035917; and Lawrence E. Walsh. *Final Report of the Independent Counsel for Iran/Contra Matters*. U.S. Government Printing Office, Washington, D.C., August 4, 1993.

23. Cynthia J. Arnson. *Crossroads: Congress, the President, and Central America, 1976–1993*. University Park: Pennsylvania State University Press, 1993: 174. See also Declassified minutes of the National Security Planning Group meeting, June 25, 1984, p. 14.

24. Richard Reeves. *President Reagan: The Triumph of Imagination*. New York: Simon & Schuster, 2005: 221.

25. President's Special Review Board. *The Tower Commission Report*. New York: Bantam Books and Times Books, 1987: 458–459; and McFarlane hearings, p. 17. According to a Saudi

source (and confirmed to me by Prince Bandar) the money was not "offered" but rather so-licited by McFarlane. See David Hoffman and Bob Woodward. "McFarlane Said to Solicit Contra Aid from Saudis." *Washington Post*, May 14, 1987.

26. Walsh, *Final Report*.
27. Draper, p. 80.
28. Cannon, p. 335.
29. William M. LeoGrande. *Our Own Backyard: The United States in Central America, 1977–1992*. Chapel Hill: University of North Carolina Press, 1998.
30. Robert McFarlane, Select Committees Testimony, May 11, 1987, pp. 38–39; and McFarlane, North Trial Testimony, March 13, 1989, pp. 4203–4204.
31. McFarlane, North Trial Testimony, March 10, 1989, p. 3933.
32. Interview with Prince Bandar on CBS News *Nightwatch*.
33. Cannon, p. 636.
34. Sklar, p. 227.
35. Lee Michael Katz. "Prince Charming." *The Washingtonian*, November 2000.
36. Patrick E. Tyler. "Double Exposure: Saudi Arabia's Man in Washington." *New York Times*, June 7, 1992.
37. From Caspar Weinberger indictment.
38. Walsh, *Firewall*, pp. 391–392.
39. Ibid., p. 389.
40. See note 32 above.
41. Jim Lobe. "The Bewilderment of Prince Bandar." *Asia Times*, November 29, 2002.
42. Hala Jaber. *Hezbollah*. New York: Columbia University Press, 1997: 69.
43. Woodward, pp. 394–398.
44. Howard Blum. *The Gold of Exodus: The Discovery of the True Mount Sinai*. New York: Pocket Books, 1999: 151–153.
45. Sklar, p. 226.
46. William Blum. "Ronald Reagan's Legacy: Eight Years of CIA Covert Action." *Covert Action Quarterly*, Winter 1990.
47. See note 42 above.
48. Thomas Powers. "Intelligence Wars: American Secret History from Hitler to Al-Qaeda." *New York Review of Books*, December 2002, pp. 276–277.
49. Interview of Bob Woodward by Bill Moyers. *Frontline*: "Target America." October 4, 2001.
50. Paul Lashmar and Patrick Fitzgerald. "The Saudi Cesspit." *New Statesman & Society*, December 1, 1996.
51. Woodward, p. 96.
52. Interview with Fred Dutton at the Dorchester Hotel, London, August 26, 2004.
53. Woodward, p. 97.
54. See note 52 above.
55. Ibid.
56. Michael Kilian. "Nancy Reagan Noted for Style, Understated Influence." *Chicago Tribune*, July 6, 2004.
57. Nancy Reagan. *My Turn: The Memoirs of Nancy Reagan*. New York: Random House, 1989: 60.
58. Ibid., p. 61.
59. Julie Wolf. "Nancy Reagan." Public Broadcasting Service, PBS Online.
60. Dr. Peter David Beter. *Audio Letter ® No. 76*. Washington D.C.: Audio Books, Inc., June 30, 1982.
61. Ibid.

62. Sam Donaldson. ABC Evening News, June 25, 1982.

63. See note 5 above.

64. "The Power Behind the Throne: A Wife's Tale." *U.S. News & World Report*, July, 20, 1992.

65. Walsh, p. 353.

66. See note 7 above.

5. BANDAR THE ARMS DEALER

1. Address by Prince Bandar to McDonnell Douglas, January 9, 1989.

2. Ibid.

3. Farhang Rajaee. *The Iran-Iraq War: The Politics of Aggression*. Gainesville: University of Florida Press, 1993: 200.

4. Interview with Lord Powell of Bayswater at Queen Anne's Gate, London, May 26, 2004.

5. Interview with Tony Edwards, former head of the British Defense Export Sales Organization, at the RAF Club, Piccadilly, London, October 15, 2004.

6. Interview with Sir Richard Evans, chairman of British Aerospace Systems, in London, February 10, 2004.

7. David E. Long. *The United States and Saudi Arabia: Ambivalent Allies*. Boulder and London: Westview Press, 1985: 45.

8. Ibid., p. 46.

9. See note 6 above.

10. *The Observer* (London), May 10, 1992; "Saudi Arabia: Princes Fight It Out." *Indigo Intelligence Newsletter*, October 6, 1994; and Anthony Sampson, "Arms and the Middle Men." *Times Newspapers*, October 12, 1994.

11. Anthony H Cordesman. *Saudi Arabia: Guarding the Desert Kingdom*. Boulder and London: Westview Press, 1997: 157.

12. *Flight*, December 8, 1984.

13. See note 5 above.

14. *The Observer* (London), March 19, 1989.

15. Saudi Prince May Sign £3bn Arms Contract Next Week. *The Times* (London), September 9, 1985, p. 8.

16. Chrissie Hirst. "The Arabian Connection: The UK Arms Trade to Saudi Arabia." Campaign Against Arms Trade (CAAT) website: www.caat.org.uk/publications/countries/saudi-arabia.php.

17. See note 1 above.

18. See note 16 above.

19. Julie Flint. "Massive Saudi Weapons Deal Draws Unwanted Attention to BAe Systems." *Daily Star* (Lebanon), December 9, 2003.

20. "Tornado Rip-Off: Adam Raphael Investigates Britain's Biggest-ever Arms Deal and the Middlemen Who Fixed It." *The Observer* (London), March 19, 1989, p. 9.

21. *The Economist*, July 16, 1988.

22. See note 19 above; Sampson, (no page number); and Nick Cohen. "The Curse of Black Gold." *The New Statesman* June 2, 2003, p. 25ff.

23. *The Independent* (London), March 12, 1992, and June 24, 1997.

24. See note 16 above.

25. See note 10 above.

26. See note 16 above.

27. Royal Decree No. M/14, 1997; Council of Ministers Resolution No.1275, 17.9.75.

28. David Leigh and Rob Evans. "Arms Firm's £60m Slush Fund." *The Guardian* (London), May 4, 2004.

29. See note 19 above.

30. See note 11 above.

31. See note 5 above.

32. W. Seth Carus and Edward N. Luttwak. *Ballistic Missiles in the Third World: Threat and Response.* New York: Praeger, 1990.

33. Yitzhak Shichor. *East Wind over Arabia: Origins and Implications of the Sino-Saudi Missile Deal.* Los Angeles: Center for Chinese Studies, University of California Press, 1989: 26.

34. Interview with Prince Bandar. CBS News *Nightwatch.*

35. William Safire. "Those Chinese Missiles." *New York Times,* February 23, 1989; U.S. Congress. Congressional Record, 101st Cong., 1st Sess., 1989, p. S5448.

36. Interview with Ambassador Richard Murphy in New York, April 7, 2006.

37. James Mann. *About Face: A History of America's Curious Relationship with China, from Nixon to Clinton.* New York: Alfred A. Knopf, 1999: 169–170.

38. *The Independent* (London), April 2, 1988 (article title unknown).

39. Interview with Secretary of State Colin Powell at the State Department, Washington, D.C., November 5, 2004.

40. Mark Erickson Daryl, Joseph E. Goldberg, Stephen H. Gotowicki, et al. *An Historical Encyclopedia of the Arab-Israeli Conflict.* Westport, Conn.: Greenwood, 1996: 119.

41. Susanne Hoeber Rudolph. *Transnational Religion and Fading States.* Boulder and London: Westview Press, 1997.

42. Charles J. Hanlet. "Where Are the Saudis' Missiles? Saudis' Missiles Drop from Sight." Associated Press, May 12, 1997.

43. Interview with Prince Bandar bin Sultan. In "Saudis Withheld Missiles to Spare Civilians." *Washington Times,* June 10, 1991, p. 3.

44. Jim Hoagland. "The Turtle Snaps Back." *Washington Post,* April 13, 1988, p. 2.

45. Ibid.

46. Interview with Prince Bandar by Charlie Rose on CBS News *Nightwatch.*

47. Shichor, p. 30.

48. "Saudi CSS-2 Missiles Now Operational." *Flight International,* June 12, 1990, pp. 12–13.

49. R. Bates Gill. *Chinese Arms Transfers: Purposes, Patterns, and Prospects in the New World Order.* Westport, Conn: Praeger, 1992: 114.

50. Shichor, p. 41.

51. Prince Bandar in an interview on John McLaughlin's *One on One.*

52. Youssef M. Ibrahim. "Saudis Reaffirm a Right to Vary Arms Dealings." *New York Times.* July 28, 1988.

53. "Saudis Warn Iran They May Use Chinese Missiles." *New York Times,* April 28, 1988, p. 1.

54. Bill Gertz. "Saudis Withheld Missile to Spare Civilians." *Washington Times,* June 10, 1991, p. A4.

55. Akaki Dvali. *Will Saudi Arabia Acquire Nuclear Weapons?* Monterey, Calif.: Center for Nonproliferation Studies, 2004.

6. A NEW WORLD ORDER

1. Report of Congressional Committee Investigating the Iran-Contra Affair. Washington, D.C.: Government Printing Office, 1987: Vol. 1, Appendix A.

2. Robert Parry. "Missing U.S.-Iraq History." December 16, 2003. www.change-links.org/missingfacts1.htm.

3. R.P.H. King. *The United Nations and the Iran-Iraq War, 1980–1986.* New York: Ford Foundation. 1987: 19–20.

7. THE GULF EXPLODES

1. Dennis Menos. *Arms over Diplomacy: Reflections on the Persian Gulf War.* Westport, Conn.: Praeger, 1992: 3.
2. Interview with Gen. Brent Scowcroft in Washington, D.C., May 7, 2004.
3. George Bush and Brent Scowcroft. *A World Transformed.* New York: Alfred A. Knopf, 1998: 325.
4. Gregory Crane. *Thucydides and the Ancient Simplicity: The Limits of Political Realism.* Los Angeles: University of California Press, 1998.
5. Interview with Lord Charles Powell of Bayswater at Queen Anne's Gate, London, May 26, 2004.
6. Ibid.
7. See note 2 above.
8. George Crile. *My Enemy's Enemy.* New York: Grove/Atlantic, 2003: 236.
9. William Head and Earl H. Tilford. *The Eagle in the Desert: Looking Back on U.S. Involvement in the Persian Gulf War.* Westport, Conn.: Praeger, 1996: 39.
10. See note 2 above.
11. "April Glaspie–Saddam Hussein Conversation 1990: Excerpts from Iraqi Document on Meeting with U.S. Envoy." *New York Times International,* September 23, 1990.
12. Dan Goodgame. "1990: The Two George Bushes." *Time,* January 2, 1990.
13. Robert Parry. "Saddam's 'Green Light': October Surprise X-Files" (Part 5). The Consortium, www.consortiumnews.com/archive/xfile5.html.
14. William Blum. *Killing Hope: U.S. Military and CIA Interventions since World War II.* Munroe, ME: Common Courage Press, 2004; Sartre. "The Dubious U.S. State Department: State Department Running as Usual Purge the Ranks, Change the Policy." Rense .com, October 12, 2003.
15. Michael R. Gordon and Gen. Bernard E. Trainor. *The General's War.* New York: Little, Brown and Co./Back Bay Books, 1995: 26.
16. Ibid. pp. 22–23.
17. David B. Ottaway. "Been There, Done That: One of the Great Cold Warriors Faces Yawn of a New Era." *Washington Post,* July 21, 1996.
18. Interview with Secretary Colin Powell at the State Department, Washington, D.C., November 5, 2004.
19. Roxanne Roberts. "The Saudi Envoy's Supersonic Diplomatic Course." *Washington Post,* August 16, 1990.
20. Interview with Prince Bandar by Roger Mudd.
21. Interview with Prince Bandar on John McLaughlin's *One on One,* PBS.
22. Interview with Prince Bandar on *Larry King Live,* CNN.
23. James A. Blackwell Jr, Michael J. Mazarr, and Don M. Snider. *Desert Storm: The Gulf War and What We Learned.* Boulder and London: Westview Press. 1993: 29.
24. Karl Von Vorys. *American Foreign Policy: Consensus at Home, Leadership Abroad.* Westport, Conn.: Praeger, 1997: 55.
25. Turi Munthe. *The Saddam Hussein Reader.* New York: Thunders Mouth Press, 2002: 227–228.
26. Bob Woodward. *The Commanders.* New York: Touchstone/Simon & Schuster, 1991: 202.
27. Kenneth Pollack. *The Threatening Storm: The Case for Invading Iraq.* New York: Random House. 2002: 31.
28. Woodward, p. 204
29. Ibid., p. 239.
30. Interview with Sgt. Maj. Samir bin Fahd bin Turki in Casablanca, April 21, 2005.

31. See note 19 above.
32. See note 21 above.
33. Daniel Pipes. *The Hidden Hand: Middle East Fears of Conspiracy.* New York: St. Martin's Press, 1998: 354.
34. *New York Times.* February 27, 1991 (article title unknown).
35. Carter Center Briefing. "Crisis in the Gulf," segment one, 23:17.
36. Ibid.
37. Bush and Scowcroft, p. 305.
38. Ibid., p. 320.
39. Michael Watkins. *Breakthrough International Negotiation: How Great Negotiators Transformed the World's Toughest Post-Cold War Conflicts.* San Francisco: Jossey-Bass, 2001: 187.
40. Paul Aarts. "The New Oil Order: Built on Sand?" *Arab Studies Quarterly* 16(2):1; 1994.
41. Mary McGory. "A Christmas Card from Prince Bandar." *Washington Post,* December 16, 1990, p. K.01.
42. Brian Whitaker. "Saddam: Serpent in the Garden of Eden." *The Guardian Unlimited.* January 12, 2001; Lindsey Hilsum. "Cartoons and Oil." *The New Statesman,* February 13, 2006.
43. See note 35 above.
44. See note 22 above.
45. HRH Gen. Khaled bin Sultan and Patrick Seale. *Desert Warrior: A Personal View of the Gulf War by the Joint Force Commander.* New York: HarperCollins, 1995: 27.
46. See note 2 above.
47. Ibid.
48. Michael A. Palmer. *Guardians of the Gulf: A History of America's Expanding Role in the Persian Gulf, 1883–1992.* New York: Touchstone Books, 1999: 117.
49. Randall M. Miller and Steve A. Yetiv. *The Persian Gulf Crisis.* Westport, Conn.: Greenwood Press, 1997: 13; Bob Woodward. *The Commanders.* New York: Touchstone Books/Simon & Schuster, 1991: 240; Richard L. Russell. "A Saudi Nuclear Option?" *Survival* 43(2): 70; 2001.
50. See note 2 above.
51. Colin Powell with Joseph E. Persico. *Colin Powell—A Soldier's Way: An Autobiography.* London: Hutchinson, 1995: 465.
52. Gary R. Hess. *Presidential Decisions for War: Korea, Vietnam, and the Persian Gulf (The American Moment).* Baltimore: Johns Hopkins University Press, 2001: 166.
53. Gordon and Trainor, p. 40.
54. See note 2 above.
55. Judith Miller. "Saudis Tell of Iraq Hot-Line Drama." *New York Times,* October 4, 1990, p. A15.
56. Palmer, p. 168.
57. Crisis in the Persian Gulf Region: U.S. Policy Options and Implications. U.S. Congress, Senate, SASC, S. Hrg. 101-1071, sess. 101/2, p. 645; Palmer, p. 168.
58. Woodward, p. 240.
59. Dr. Nasser Rachid and Dr. Esber Shaheen. *Saudi Arabia and the Gulf War.* International Institute of Technology, 1992: 172.
60. Amatzia Baram. *Iraq's Road to War.* London: Palgrave MacMillan, 1996.
61. Gordon and Trainor, p. 49.
62. See note 21 above.
63. Bush and Scowcroft, p. 374.
64. Ibid., p. 375.
65. CNN News, August 5, 1990.

66. Daniel Pipes. "The Scandal of U.S.-Saudi Relations." *The National Interest,* Winter 2002.

67. General H. Norman Schwarzkopf and Peter Petre. *It Doesn't Take a Hero.* New York: Linda Grey/Bantam Books, 1992: 277.

68. Ibid., p. 389.

69. Schwarzkopf and Petre, pp. 302–306.

70. Peter W. Wilson and Douglas F. Graham. *Saudi Arabia—The Coming Storm.* New York: M.E. Sharpe, 1994: 112–113.

71. Schwarzkopf and Petre, pp. 304–305.

72. Interview with Prince Bandar on ABC News *Nightline* by Ted Koppel.

73. Ibid.

74. See note 2 above.

75. See note 5 above.

76. Interview with Sir Richard Evans, chairman of British Aerospace Systems, in London, February 10, 2004.

77. Margaret Thatcher. *The Downing Street Years.* New York: HarperCollins, 1995: 820.

78. See note 2 above.

79. See note 76 above.

80. James Addison Baker and Thomas M. Defrank. *The Politics of Diplomacy: Revolution, War and Peace 1989–1992.* New York: Putnam, 1995: 290.

81. See note 76 above.

82. See note 2 above.

83. "Challenges to Security in Southwest Asia." Speech by Prince Bandar bin Sultan, Tampa, Florida, May 20, 1993.

84. bin Sultan and Seale, p. 24.

85. Wilson and Graham, p. 113.

86. See note 21 above.

87. Murrey Marder. "Operation Washington Shield." *Nieman Reports* 1999; 53(4): 57.

88. Thomas A. McCain and Leonard Shyles. *The 1,000 Hour War: Communication in the Gulf.* Westport, Conn.: Greenwood Press, 1994: 39.

89. Interview with Prince Bandar on CBS News *Nightwatch.*

90. Anthony Lewis. "To See Ourselves: The Failings of the Press in the Gulf War." *New York Times,* May 6, 1991, p. A15.

91. See note 87 above.

92. Bush and Scowcroft, p. 439.

93. See note 22 above.

94. *The World Today: Crisis in the Gulf,* CNN, 1990.

95. Judith Miller. *God has Ninety Nine Names: Reporting from a Militant Middle East.* New York: Touchstone Books, 1997: 520.

96. Wilson and Graham, p. 115.

97. Prince Bandar bin Sultan al-Saud. "An Open Letter to King Hussein." *Washington Post,* September 26, 1990, p. A25.

98. See note 21 above.

99. Interview with Dr. Said Karmi in Chevy Chase, Maryland, January 27, 2004.

100. Bush and Scowcroft, p. 373.

101. Gary A. Donaldson. *America at War since 1945.* New York: Praeger 1996: 165.

102. Bush and Scowcroft, p. 427.

103. Ibid., p. 389.

104. Ibid., p. 401.

105. See note 18 above.

106. Ibid.
107. Powell and Persico, pp. 474–475.
108. See note 41 above.
109. Bush and Scowcroft, pp. 414–415.
110. Baker and Defrank, p. 354.
111. Donald Kagan. *While America Sleeps: Self Delusion, Military Weakness, and the Threat to Peace Today*. New York: St. Martin's Griffin, 2001: 252.
112. Donaldson, p. 164.
113. Bush and Scowcroft, p. 420.
114. See note 110 above.
115. See note 111 above.
116. Woodward, p. 370.
117. Baker and Defrank, p. 372.
118. Schwarzkopf and Petre, p. 408.
119. Ibid., pp. 417–418.
120. Baker and Defrank, p. 386.
121. Gordon and Trainor, p. 232.
122. Interview with Secretary James A. Baker III in Houston, Texas, March 2, 2004.
123. Wilson and Graham, pp. 115–116.
124. Address by Prince Bandar to the Air Force Association Symposium in Westford Regency Hotel, June 10, 1992.
125. bin Sultan and Seale, p. 161.
126. George W. Bush. "A Nation Blessed: Persian Gulf War as Turning Point in US Military History." *Naval War College Review*, Autumn 2001. Commencement address delivered on June 15, 2001, to the Naval War College graduating class of 2001.
127. Sarah Graham-Brown. *Sanctioning Saddam: The Politics of Intervention in Iraq*. London: I.B. Tauris. 1999: 3.
128. Gordon and Trainor, p. 454.
129. See note 124 above.
130. See note 35 above.
131. See note 124 above.
132. See note 126 above.
133. See note 124 above.
134. See note 76 above.
135. George H.W. Bush Presidential Library.
136. James Baker. The Gulf War: An In-Depth Examination of the 1990–91 Persian Gulf Crisis. Oral History: The Decision Makers. *Frontline.*
137. Telephone interview with Andrew Neil on March 21, 2006.

8. PEACE IN THE MIDDLE EAST

1. "Saudi Prince Says the Kingdom is at a Crossroads." *The Daily Star* (Lebanon), May 21, 2004.
2. Secretary of State James Baker's letter of assurance to the Palestinians, October 18, 1991. Reprinted in William B. Quandt. *Peace Process: American Diplomacy and the Arab-Israeli Conflict since 1967*. New York and Berkeley: The Brookings Institution & University of California Press, 1993: 501.
3. Robert O. Freedman. *The Middle East and the Peace Process: The Impact of the Oslo Accords*. Gainesville: University Press of Florida, 1998: 376.

4. Interview with General Brent Scowcroft in Washington, D.C., May 7, 2004.

5. Abdulaziz Bashir and Stephen Wright. "Saudi Arabia: Foreign Policy after the Gulf War." *Middle East Policy* I (1): 112; 1992.

6. Thomas L. Friedman. *From Beirut to Jerusalem*. New York: Anchor, 1990: 536.

7. Interview with Dr. Said Karmi in Chevy Chase, Maryland, January 27, 2004.

8. George Bush and Brent Scowcroft. *A World Transformed*. New York: Alfred A. Knopf, 1998: 490.

9. Kathleen Christison. *Perceptions of Palestine: Their Influence on Middle East Policy*. Berkeley and Los Angeles: University of California Press, 1999: 243.

10. Friedman, p. 537.

11. Said K. Aburish. *Arafat: From Defender to Dictator*. New York: Bloomsbury USA, 1999: p. 240.

12. Interview with former President George H.W. Bush in Houston, Texas, February 20, 2004.

13. Address by Prince Bandar to the World Affairs Council in Houston, Texas, December 5, 2003.

14. Mark Matthews. "Envoy's Madrid Role Shows Saudi's Diplomatic Muscle." *Baltimore Sun*, November 5, 1991.

15. Frank Greve. "The Politic Prince." *Philadelphia Inquirer*, November 8, 1991.

16. Interview with Secretary James A. Baker III in Houston, Texas, March 2, 2004.

17. Keynote dinner speech by Prince Bandar Sultan. U.S.-Saudi Arabian Business Council, Washington, D.C., October 2, 1996.

18. Ibid.

19. Remarks by Prince Bandar Bin Sultan to the Conference of Mayors, Washington, D.C., January 22, 2003.

20. Munther J. Haddadin. "Water in the Middle East Peace Process." *The Geographical Journal* 168 (4): 324; 2002.

21. Herbert C. Kelman. "Building a Sustainable Peace: The Limits of Pragmatism in the Israeli-Palestinian Negotiations." *Peace and Conflict* 5 (2): 101; 1999.

22. Jacinta Sanders. "Honest Brokers? American and Norwegian Facilitation of Israeli-Palestinian Negotiations." *Arab Studies Quarterly* 21 (2): 1999.

23. Interview with Ambassador Edward Djerejian at Rice University in Houston, Texas, March 2, 2004.

24. Ibid.

25. Daniel Pipes. "Why Oslo's Hopes Turned to Dust." *The New York Post*, September 9, 2003.

26. Interview with Dr. Said Karmi in Chevy Chase, Maryland, March 11, 2004.

27. John T. Rourke and Mark A. Boyer. "Palestinians: A Nation without a State." In *World Politics: International Politics on the World Stage*. New York: McGraw-Hill, 2002: 105.

28. Robert G. Kaiser and David B. Ottaway. "Saudi Leader's Anger Revealed Shaky Ties; Bush's Response Eased a Deep Rift on Mideast Policy; Then Came September 11." *Washington Post*, February 10, 2002, p. A.01.

29. Sami G. Hajjar. "The Israel-Syria Track." *Middle East Policy* VI (3) 112; 1999.

30. Prince Bandar's comments at a White House meeting with President Clinton, November 7, 1998.

31. Ibid.

32. "Israel Continuing Settlement Activities, Evading Wye River Memorandum, Palestine Observer Tells General Assembly Special Session." Science Blog. GA/9542, February 5, 1999.

33. Richard H. Curtiss. "Both Parties Now Are Waiting to Assign the Blame for Failure of the Middle East Peace Process. *Washington Report on Middle East Affairs*, December 1999.

34. Interview with Dr. Henry Kissinger in New York, April 27, 2004.

35. "Showstopper on Arafat: Prompting Reflections on Palestinian Leadership." *American Students for Israel*, September 28, 2003.

36. See note 7 above.

37. Alan Dershowitz. *The Case for Israel*. Hoboken, N.J.: John Wiley & Sons, 2003: 117.

38. Barry Rubin and Judith Colp Rubin. *Yasir Arafat: A Political Biography*. New York: Oxford University Press, 2003: 185.

39. Steve Berley. "Dual Anniversaries of Accord and Strife Point to Path of Hope." *San Francisco Chronicle*, July 25, 2004.

40. Rubin and Rubin, p. 200.

41. Bill Clinton. *My Life*. New York: Alfred A Knopf, 2004: 938.

42. Fares Al-Braizat. "Muslims and Democracy: An Empirical Critique of Fukuyama's Culturalist Approach." *International Journal of Comparative Sociology*, 2002; Fareed Zakaria. "How to Save the Arab World." *Newsweek*, December 24, 2001.

43. See note 16 above.

44. Interview with Lord Charles Powell of Bayswater at Queen Anne's Gate, London, May 26, 2004.

45. Hendrick Hertzberg. "Fade from Black." *The New Yorker*, December 17, 2001.

46. Interview with former president Bill Clinton in New York, February 10, 2005.

47. Ibid.

48. See note 7 above.

49. See note 40 above

50. "The Prince: How the Saudi Ambassador Became Washington's Indispensable Operator." *The New Yorker*, March 24, 2003.

51. See note 19 above.

52. J.D. Hayworth. "Bandar's Delusions." *Washington Times*, April 14, 2002, p. B05.

53. See note 34 above.

54. Interview with Ambassador Richard Murphy in New York, April 28, 2004.

55. See note 4 above.

9. THE INVISIBLE AMBASSADOR

1. Interview with Sir Richard Evans, chairman of British Aerospace Systems, in London, February 10, 2004.

2. Interview with Bettina Gilbert, Prince Bandar's secretary 1982–1999, in Washington, D.C., November 5, 2004.

3. Interview with Sherry Cooper, Prince Bandar's secretary, in Washington, D.C., September 4, 2004.

4. Elsa Walsh. "Louis Freeh's Last Case." *The New Yorker*, May 14, 2001.

5. Interview with Col. Joe Ramsey in Washington, D.C., October 29, 2003.

6. Gerald Posner. *Why America Slept: The Failure to Prevent 9/11*. New York: Random House, 2003; 107.

7. Louis J. Freeh. "Remember Khobar Towers: Nineteen American Heroes Still Await American Justice." *Wall Street Journal*, May 20, 2003.

8. Rich Lowrie. "Clinton & Khobar: One of the Keys to Understanding the War over the War on Terrorism." *National Online Review*, November 3, 2003.

9. See note 4 above.

10. Interview with Louis J. Freeh, FBI director, 1993–2001, in Wilmington, Delaware, March 11, 2004.

11. See note 7 above.

12. Thomas Blood. *Madam Secretary: A Biography of Madeleine Albright.* New York: St. Martin's Press, 1997: 106.

13. See note 10 above.

14. Ibid.

15. See note 4 above.

16. See note 10 above.

17. Richard Lowry. "America's Unspecial Relationship: A Cold Look at the Saudis." *National Review,* February 25, 2002.

18. See note 10 above.

19. Josh Pollack. "Anti-Americanism in Contemporary Saudi Arabia." *Middle East Review of International Affairs* (MERIA), December 2003.

20. Robert G. Kaiser and David B. Ottaway. "Oil for Security Fueled Close Ties: But Major Differences Led to Tensions." *Washington Post,* February 11, 2002; p. A01.

21. "Looking for Answers." Transcript of a *Frontline* Interview with Martin Smith and Lowell Bergman. *New York Times,* October 9, 2002.

22. See note 10 above.

23. "Furious Saudis Reject U.S. 9/11 Claims Agencies." *Guardian Unlimited,* July 25, 2003.

24. See note 10 above.

25. "Louis Freeh Praises Saudi Cooperation on Khobar Investigation." *PR Newswire,* October 9, 2002.

26. See note 10 above.

27. See note 25 above.

28. See note 10 above.

29. See note 25 above.

30. See note 10 above.

31. Ibid.

32. See note 4 above.

33. Ibid.

34. See note 10 above.

35. See note 4 above.

36. See note 10 above.

37. See note 4 above.

38. Ibid.

39. Bruce Maddy-Weitzman. *Middle East Contemporary Survey: 1996,* volume 20. Boulder and London: Westview Press, 1998: 583.

40. Alfred B. Prados. "CRS Issue Brief 93113: Saudi Arabia: Post-War Issues and U.S. Relations." *Foreign Affairs and National Defense Division,* December 2, 1996.

41. See note 4 above.

42. Transcript of Prince Bandar's interview by David Brinkley on ABC's *This Week,* July 7, 1996.

43. Cynthia Grenier. "The Last Case of Louis Freeh." *WorldNetDaily,* May 21, 2001.

44. See note 10 above.

45. See note 4 above.

46. Ronald Kessler. *The Bureau: The Secret History of the FBI.* New York: St. Martin's Press, 2002.

47. William A. Mayer. "Not Home Freeh—Clinton and the Khobar Towers Investigation." E&P PipelineNews.org, October 12, 2005.

48. Thomas Lippman. *Madeleine Albright and the New American Diplomacy.* Boulder and London: Westview Press, 179.

49. See note 4 above.

50. "Freeh Links Iran to Khobar Bombing." www.Cabalof Doom.com, December 19, 2003.

51. See note 8 above.

52. See note 50 above.

53. U.S. Department of State daily press briefing by James P. Ruben, March 31, 1998.

54. See note 10 above.

55. Ibid.

56. See note 47 above.

57. See note 8 above.

58. Interview with Prince Bandar bin Sultan by Anderson Cooper, CNN, May 14, 2003.

59. See note 8 above.

60. See note 25 above.

61. David Johnston and Thom Shanker. "Saudis Sought to Divide Clinton Team over '96 Bombing, Aides Say." *New York Times*, October 2, 2002.

62. Carl Limbacher. "Saudis Misled FBI Chief Freeh, Clinton Aides Say." FreeRepublic.com, October 1, 2002.

63. Sidney Blumenthal. *The Clinton Wars*. New York: Viking Press, 2003: 663.

64. Daniel Benjamin and Steven Simon. *The Age of Sacred Terror*. New York: Random House, 2002: 301.

65. See note 8 above.

66. Daniel Benjamin. Letters to the Editor: Khobar Bombing and the Clinton White House. *Wall Street Journal*, May 27, 2003.

67. Interview with former president Bill Clinton in New York, February 10, 2005.

68. Lyn Boyd-Judson. "Strategic Moral Diplomacy: Mandela, Qaddafi, and the Lockerbie Negotiations." *Foreign Policy Analysis* 1: 73–97; 2005.

69. Ibid.

70. Ray Hartley, "The Turning of Gaddafi." *Sunday Times* (South Africa), April 11, 1999.

71. Interview with Nelson Mandela in Cape Town, South Africa, February 2, 2004.

72. Interview with Professor Jakes Gerwel in Cape Town, South Africa, February 2, 2004.

73. See note 68 above.

74. Ibid.

75. See note 72 above.

76. See note 68 above.

77. See note 67 above.

78. See note 68 above.

79. Ibid.

80. Interview with Tony Edwards, former head of Defense Export Sales Organization, U.K., at the RAF Club, Piccadilly, London, October 15, 2004.

81. See note 72 above.

82. Interview with Prince Faisal bin Turki in McLean, Virginia, March 9, 2004.

83. See note 72 above.

84. Interview with Dr. Said Karmi in Chevy Chase, Maryland, March 11, 2004.

85. See note 82 above.

86. Interviews with Princess Reema bint Bandar in McLean, Virginia, February 19 and March 9, 2004.

87. See note 82 above.

88. See note 68 above.

89. *Asharq Al-Awsat* (London), September 4, 1998 (article title unknown).

90. See note 72 above.

91. See note 71 above.

92. See note 70 above.

93. Keynote dinner speech by Prince Bandar bin Sultan. U.S.-Saudi Arabian Business Council, Washington D.C., October 2, 1996.

94. Elsa Walsh. "The Prince: How the Saudi Ambassador Became Washington's Indispensable Operator." *The New Yorker,* March 24, 2003.

95. Ibid.

96. Dennis Ross. *The Missing Peace: The Inside Story of the Fight for Middle East Peace.* New York: Farrar, Straus & Giroux, 2004.

97. Bill Clinton. *My Life.* New York: Alfred A Knopf, 2004: 883.

98. See note 94 above.

99. See note 67 above.

100. See note 19 above.

101. Robert G. Kaiser and David B. Ottaway. "Saudi Leader's Anger Revealed Shaky Ties; Bush's Response Eased a Deep Rift on Mideast Policy; Then Came Sept. 11." *Washington Post,* February 10, 2002, p. A01.

102. David Farber. "Saudi/U.S. Relations on a Razor Edge." *Washington Post,* February 10, 2002.

103. See note 101 above.

104. "Saudi Prince Says the Kingdom Is at a Crossroads." *The Daily Star* (Lebanon), May 21, 2004.

105. "The Bush Royal Family and the Saudi Royal Family Could Hardly Be Closer." *Foreign Relations,* January 24, 2002.

106. James Heartfield. "A House of Cards." *Spiked,* May 14, 2003.

107. See note 101 above.

108. Ibid.

10. 9/11 CATACLYSM

1. "Remembering Hume Horan (1934–2004). Extract from Hume Horan, 'Saudi Arabia: A Successful Anomaly (So Far),' The American Enterprise." *Middle East Quarterly,* Fall 2004, pp. 32–35.

2. "U.S.-Saudi Anti-terror Cooperation on the Rise: An Interview with Ambassador Richard W. Murphy." *Saudi-U.S. Relations Information Service,* May 3, 2004.

3. Tony Karon. "Person of the Week: Adel al-Jubeir." *Time,* December 5, 2002.

4. Richard Cohen. "Saudi Switcheroo." *Washington Post,* November 28, 2002, p. A47.

5. Remarks by Prince Bandar bin Sultan to the Conference of Mayors, Washington, D.C., January 22, 2003.

6. Amrith Mago. "Saudis Paid Off Osama bin Laden and 9/11 Terrorists." *Jewish Institute for National Security Affairs (JINSA) Online,* September 6, 2002.

7. "Issues in Context: Prince Bandar Meets the Press." *Saudi-U.S. Relations Information Service,* April 26, 2004.

8. Ibid.

9. "Saudi Arabia in 9-11 Commission Report." *PRNewswire,* July 22, 2004.

10. See note 7 above.

11. Ahmad Faruqui. "Scapegoating Saudi Arabia for 9/11." *The Daily Times* (Pakistan), December 16, 2003.

12. Anthony H. Cordesman. "Ten Reasons for Reforging the U.S. and Saudi Relationship." *Saudi-American Forum,* February 1, 2004.

13. Khaled Dawoud. "Squeezing Saudi Arabia." *Al-Ahram Weekly Online,* December 24, 2003.

14. Transcript of interview with Prince Naif, interior minister, Kingdom of Saudi Arabia. *Al Siyava* (Kuwait), November 29, 2002.

15. Mark Steyn. "Bought-Off as We're Destroyed." *The Spectator,* November 28, 2002.

16. See note 5 above.

17. "Furious Saudis Reject US 9/11 Claims." *Guardian Unlimited* (London), July 25, 2003.

18. "U.S.-Saudi Relations: In Transition?" Address by Prince Bandar to the World Affairs Council, Los Angeles, September 22, 2003.

19. "Prince Bandar Ibn Sultan: We Were Telling You They Were Terrorists and the West Was Calling Them Dissidents." *Ain-Al-Yaqeen,* October 3, 2003.

20. "Bandar Hits 9/11 Report." *Washington Times,* July 29, 2003, p. A14.

21. See note 17 above.

22. Simon Henderson. "The September 11 Congressional Report: A Sea Change in U.S.-Saudi Relations?" *The Washington Institute for Near East Policy,* July 30, 2003.

23. "9/11 Probe Clears Saudi Arabia." BBC News, June 17, 2004.

24. "Bush Administration Censors 28 Pages on Saudi Arabia's Role from 9/11 Report." *Agence France-Presse,* July 25, 2003.

25. See note 20 above.

26. Josh Meyer. "Classified 9/11 Material Implicates Saudi Government, Officials Say." *Los Angeles Times,* August 2, 2003.

27. John B. Judis and Spencer Ackerman. 28 Pages. *New Republic,* January 8, 2003.

28. Prince Bandar interviewed by the *Los Angeles Times,* September 24, 2003.

29. Seymour M. Hersh. "King's Ransom: How Vulnerable are the Saudi Royals." *The New Yorker,* October 22, 2001.

30. Evan Thomas and Christopher Dickey. "The Saudi Game." *Newsweek,* November 19, 2001.

31. Jim Lobe. "The Bewilderment of Prince Bandar." *Asia Times,* November 29, 2002.

32. Paul Krugman. "Michael Moore's Public Service." ABS/CBS Interactive, July 2, 2004.

33. Bill Gallagher. "Saudi Connections to Bushes Make Action Highly Unlikely." *Niagara Falls Reporter,* January 22, 2002.

34. E-mail exchange between Rachel Bronson and Craig Unger. Subject: 9/11 Delayed an Attack on Iraq. July 8, 2004.

35. See note 18 above.

36. James Morrison. "Defending the Saudis." *Washington Times,* February 12, 2002.

37. Jerry Seper. "Princess's Cash Went to Al Qaeda 'Advance Man.' " *Washington Times,* November 26, 2002.

38. Craig Unger. "Saving the Saudis." *Vanity Fair,* October 2003.

39. Patrick E. Tyler. "Explaining Gift, Saudi Envoy Voices Pain for Strained Ties." *New York Times,* November 27, 2002.

40. Robert Baer. *Sleeping with the Devil—How Washington Sold Our Souls for Saudi Crude.* New York: Crown, 2003: 62–68.

41. See note 39 above.

42. Interview with Mimi Burke, Prince Bandar's private secretary, in Washington D.C., January 29, 2004.

43. Elizabeth Wolfe. "Weathering Criticism, Saudi Ambassador's Wife Questions Own Charitable History." *Detroit News,* November 28, 2002.

44. "Saudi-U.S. Ties Sorely Tested as U.S. Fails to Dampen Media Sniping." *IslamOnline & News Agencies,* November 27, 2002.

45. See note 42 above.

46. Matt Welsh. "Is Bandar Bush Above the Law?" *National Post,* April 19, 2003.

47. Interviews with Mimi Burke, Prince Bandar's private secretary, in Washington D.C., January 29 and February 17, 2004.

48. Daniel Pipes. "Government for Sale (to the Saudis)." *New York Post,* December 3, 2002.

49. See note 43 above.

50. Timothy L. O'Brien. "Inquiry at Bank Looks at Accounts of Diplomats." *New York Times*, April 2, 2004.

51. Ken Guggenheim. "Commission Finds No Evidence of Saudi Funding of Sept. 11 Hijackers." *San Diego Union Tribune*, June 16, 2004.

52. *Washington Post*, "Saudis Seen as Supporting Terror, Poll Shows." February 26, 2002; Joseph A. Kechichian. "Testing the Saudi 'Will to Power': Challenges Confronting Prince Abdallah." *Middle East Policy Council Journal*, Winter 2003.

53. Ibid.

54. Address by Prince Bandar to the World Affairs Council in Birmingham, Alabama, September 26, 2003.

55. "Facts about Saudi Arabia in 9/11 Commission Report." *PRNewswire*, July 22, 2004.

56. "A Relationship in Transition—and Then 9/11." Saudi-American Forum interview, Ambassador Chas W. Freeman.

57. J. Crawford Cook. "A Program for 1980 and Beyond." Cook, Ruef, Spann & Weiser, Inc., November 1, 1979.

58. See note 55 above.

59. See note 61 below.

60. See note 26 above.

61. Marc Perelman. "Defensive Saudis Lash Out at 'Zionist' and U.S. Critics." *Forward*, December 28, 2001.

62. See note 37 above.

63. See note 60 above.

64. See note 18 above.

65. Interview with former president Jimmy Carter at the Carter Center in Atlanta, Georgia, March 19, 2004.

66. Interview with Dr. Henry Kissinger in New York, April 27, 2004.

67. Lowell Bergman. Transcript of *Frontline* interview: Saudi Time Bomb?, November 15, 2001.

68. AboutSaudiArabia.net, March 17, 2004.

69. See note 18 above.

70. See note 67 above.

71. Interview with Secretary James A. Baker III in Houston, Texas, March 2, 2004.

72. See note 64 above.

73. *The 9/11 Commission Report: Final Report of the National Commission on Terrorist Attacks upon the United States.* New York and London: W.W. Norton & Company, 2004.

74. Prince Bandar bin Sultan. *Frontline* interview with Lowell Bergman, September 2001.

75. Ibid.

76. Address by Prince Bandar to the Houston World Affairs Council in Houston, Texas, December 5, 2003.

77. See note 13 above.

78. Fareed Zakaria. "The Saudi Trap: A Trip through the Kingdom Reveals What Really Needs to Be Done in the War on Terror." *Newsweek,* June 28, 2003.

79. See note 13 above.

80. See note 1 above.

81. "U.S.-Saudi Anti-terror Cooperation on the Rise: An interview with Ambassador Richard W. Murphy." Council on Foreign Relations, April 23, 2004.

82. "U.S.-Saudi Relations: Transcript of an Online Discussion with Rachel Bronson." *Washington Post*, June 21, 2004.

83. "U.S.-Saudi Relations: A Glass Half Empty, Or Half Full? An Interview with Thomas Lippman." *Saudi-U.S. Relations Information Service*, August 26, 2004.

84. "A Diplomat's Call for War." *Washington Post*, June 6, 2004, p. B04.

85. Tony Karon. "Saudis Wrestle with Qaeda Demons." *Time*, June 16, 2004.

86. Judith Apter Klinghoffer. "Prince Bandar Is the New Saudi NSC Secretary." George Mason University, October 21, 2005.

87. "Saudis in Terror's Shadow." Editorial. *New York Times*, June 28, 2004.

88. See note 77 above.

89. See note 73 above.

90. Remarks by Saudi Foreign Minister HRH Prince Saud al-Faisal to the Foreign Policy Association and U.S.-Saudi Business Council, April 26, 2004.

91. Ibid.

92. Carol Devine-Molin. "Understanding the Roots of Militant Islam." *GOPUSA News*, November 25, 2002.

93. Mary Beth Sheridan. "Bias against Muslims up 70%: Radio Talk Shows, Iraq War among Reasons, Study Finds." *Washington Post,* May 3, 2004, p. A12.

94. See note 75 above.

95. See note 73 above.

96. Jihane Ayed. "Saudi Arabia: Friends of America." http://nw08.american.edu/~zaharna/jihanesite/index.html, April 30, 2004.

97. See note 7 above.

98. See note 17 above.

99. Damian Guevara. "Saudi Envoy Visits Cleveland, Defends His Country's Leaders." *The Plain Dealer* (Cleveland), December 16, 2003.

100. See notes 7 and 18 above.

101. Jake Tapper. "Neil Bush Says Arab P.R Machine Not as Good as Israel's." Salon.com, January 24, 2002.

102. "Saudi Arabia Lacks Commercial Appeal as Stations Reject Ads." *Washington Times*, April 30, 2002.

103. Ibid.

104. See note 55 above.

105. Roger Franklin. "Saudis Spin Like a Well-Oiled Machine." *The Age* (Melbourne), June 23, 2002.

106. See note 18 above.

107. Michael Brown. "Bush Embraces Sharon's Vision." *Middle East International Magazine*, April 29, 2004.

108. "Bush May Offer Jordan's King Assurances on Mideast." Reuters, April 27, 2004.

109. The White House: A National Security Strategy for a New Century. October 1998: 52.

110. See note 65 above.

111. Interview with General Brent Scowcroft in Washington, D.C., May 7, 2004.

112. Patrick E. Tyler. "A Nation Challenged: The Family; Fearing Harm, bin Laden Kin Fled From U.S." *New York Times*, September 30, 2001.

113. See note 60 above.

114. See note 64 above.

115. Interview with Ambassador Richard Murphy in New York, April 28, 2004.

116. Olivier Knox. "Prince Bandar Denies Oil-Price Deal To Help Bush." *Middle East Online*, April 22, 2004.

117. Steve Berley. "Dual Anniversaries of Accord and Strife Point to Path of Hope." *San Francisco Chronicle*, July 25, 2004.

118. "Yasser Arafat 1929–2004." *Time*, November 22, 2004, p. 38.

44. FRIENDS AND THE TRAVELING COURT

1. Interview with Princess Loulou bint Bandar in McLean, Virginia, February 18, 2004.
2. Interview with Jeri Pierre, secretary to Princess Haifa, in Washington, D.C., March 9, 2004.
3. Interview with Col. Robert Lilac in Woodstock, Oxfordshire, August 27, 2004.
4. Meeting with Tarek Shawaf at Glympton, December 1, 2004.
5. See note 3 above.
6. Interview with Col. Joe Ramsey in Washington, D.C., October 29, 2003.
7. See note 1 above.
8. Interview with Tarek Shawaf en route from Marrakech to London, November 5, 2003.
9. Ibid.
10. Yvonne Shinhoster Lamb. "Transplant Specialist Said Karmi, 67, Dies." *Washington Post*, June 11, 2005.
11. Interview with Dr. Said Karmi in Chevy Chase, Maryland, March 11, 2004.
12. Patricia Sullivan. "Frederick Dutton Dies; Power Broker, Presidential Aide." *Washington Post*, June 26, 2005, p. C10.
13. See note 2 above.
14. Interview with Fred Dutton at the Dorchester Hotel, London, August 26, 2004.
15. Interview with Robert Deacon Elliott in Jeddah, Saudi Arabia May 11, 2004.
16. Lee Michael Katz. "Prince Charming." *The Washingtonian*, November, 2000.
17. William Safire. "Bandarbush" (Essay). *New York Times*, April 20, 1992.
18. Interview with President George H. W. Bush and Mrs. Barbara Bush in Houston, Texas, February 20, 2004.
19. See note 17 above.
20. Thomas W. Lippman. "Outlook: The Fall of the House of Saud?" Online discussion at *WashingtonPost*.com, June 14, 2004.
21. See note 18 above.
22. Interview with Sir Richard Evans, chairman of British Aerospace Systems, in London, February 10, 2004.
23. Interview with Dr. Henry Kissinger in New York, April 27, 2004.
24. See note 6 above.
25. See note 18 above.
26. Interview with Princess Haifa bint Faisal bin Abdul Aziz in McLean, Virginia, October 28, 2003.
27. See note 1 above.
28. See note 18 above.
29. Barbara Bush. *Reflections: Life after the White House.* New York: Scribner 2003: 233–234.
30. See note 18 above.
31. Evan Thomas and Christopher Dickey. "The Saudi Game." *Newsweek*, November 19, 2001.
32. Bob Woodward. *The Commanders.* New York: Touchstone/Simon & Schuster, 1991.
33. See note 6 above.
34. See note 11 above.
35. See note 14 above.
36. Letter from Prince Bandar to George H.W. Bush, written on November 3, 1992.
37. See note 6 above.
38. Transcript of an address delivered by President Bush, as recorded by News Transcripts Inc., Washington, D.C., November 7, 1992.
39. See note 14 above.
40. See note 6 above.
41. See note 11 above.

42. Robert Baer. *Sleeping with the Devil—How Washington Sold Our Souls for Saudi Crude.* New York: Crown, 2003: 62–68.

43. Helen Thomas. *Thanks for the Memories, Mr. President: Wit and Wisdom from the Front Row at the White House.* New York: Scribner, 2003.

44. Interview with Mimi Burke, Prince Bandar's private secretary, in Washington, D.C., February 17, 2004.

45. Interview with Secretary Colin Powell at the State Department, Washington, D.C., November 5, 2004.

46. Ibid.

47. Comments by Prince Bandar at a dinner to mark the retirement of Secretary Colin Powell in McLean, Virginia, March 2, 2005.

48. Comments by Secretary Colin Powell at dinner in McLean, Virginia, March 2, 2005.

49. Interview with Roberta Flack in New York, May 5, 2004.

50. Sarah Lyall. "Charles and Camilla, Married at Last." *New York Times*, April 10, 2005.

51. Interview with President Nelson Mandela in Cape Town, South Africa, February 2, 2004.

52. Interview with Prince Bandar at Glympton, Oxfordshire, in November 2003.

53. Ibid.

54. "Married." *Sunday Times* (South Africa), July 19, 1998.

55. See note 52 above.

56. See note 51 above.

57. "Mandela at 85." *The Observer*, July 6, 2003.

58. See note 52 above.

59. See note 51 above.

60. See note 52 above.

61. See note 57 above.

62. Interview with President Nelson Mandela and Professor Jakes Gerwel in Cape Town, South Africa, February 2, 2004.

63. Interview with Secretary James Baker in Houston, Texas, March 2, 2004.

64. Transcript of Nelson Mandela address, "The Issue of Conflict Resolution," at Rice University, Houston, October 26, 2002.

65. Interview with Richie Thomas at Dulles Airport, Dulles, Virginia, January 29, 2004.

66. Interview with Robert Deacon Elliott, October 6, 2003.

67. See note 65 above.

68. Interview with Henri Boehm, chef, Prince Bandar's A340 aircraft, in Marrakech, Morocco, June 25, 2004.

69. Interview with Gina Preston, lead flight attendant, in Marrakech, Morocco, June 25, 2004.

70. See note 68 above.

71. Woodward, p. 200.

12. THE PRIVATE PRINCE BANDAR

1. Interview with Princess Haifa bint Faisal bin Abdul Aziz in McLean, Virginia, October 28, 2003.

2. Interview with Prince Faisal bin Bandar in McLean, Virginia, February 19, 2004.

3. Interviews with Jan Lilac in Palm Springs, California, December 12, 2003, and Georgetown, Washington D.C., March 2005.

4. Interview with Col. Robert Lilac in Palm Springs, California, December 12, 2003.

5. "Punj Lloyd, S Arabian Prince Deal." *Business Standard* (Mumbai), May 15, 2006.

6. Ibid.

7. Interview with Jerry Jones, owner of the Dallas Cowboys, in Dallas, Texas, April 28, 2005.

8. William Gildea. "Saudi Prince Bandar Has Cowboy Spirit." *Washington Post*, June 20, 1994.

9. Mickey Spagnola. "Balancing Things Out." DallasCowboys.com, December 15, 2003.

10. See note 2 above.

11. Interviews with Princess Reema bint Bandar in McLean, Virginia, February 19 and March 9, 2004.

12. Interview with Linda Weare in Marrakech, Morocco, June 26, 2004.

13. Interview with Jeri Pierre, private secretary to Princess Haifa, at the offices of the Mosaic Foundation, McLean, Virginia, March 9, 2004.

14. Interview with Princess Loulou bint Bandar in McLean, Virginia, February 18, 2004.

15. See note 1 above.

16. See note 11 above.

17. See note 1 above.

18. See note 2 above.

19. See note 11 above.

20. See note 1 above.

21. Interview with Prince Bandar in Riyadh, October 13, 2004.

22. See note 14 above.

23. See note 2 above.

24. Roulah Khalaf. "The Prince Whose Fairytale Went Sour." *Financial Times*, November 29, 2002.

25. Interview with Col. Joe Ramsey in Washington D.C., October 29, 2003.

26. Interview with John Veltri, Prince Bandar's barber, in McLean, Virginia, November 3, 2004.

27. Interview with President George H. W. Bush and Mrs. Barbara Bush in Houston, Texas, February 20, 2004.

28. Interview with Col. Peter Browne at Glympton, Oxfordshire, November 4, 2003.

29. See note 27 above.

30. See note 28 above.

31. See note 27 above.

32. Interview with Robert Deacon Elliott in Jeddah, Saudi Arabia, May 11, 2004.

33. Interview with former Secretary of State James A. Baker III in Houston, Texas, March 2, 2004.

34. Entry by Secretary James Baker in the Bear Cabin guest book, Aspen, Colorado.

35. Interview with former president Jimmy Carter at the Carter Center, Atlanta, Georgia, March 19, 2004.

36. Interview with Princess Reema bint Bandar in McLean, Virginia, February 19, 2004.

37. John Martin Robinson. *Glympton Park Estate: A History*. Chichester: Phillimore & Co. Ltd., 1998.

38. See note 28 above.

39. Interview with Willy Jordan at Glympton Park, Oxfordshire, November 23, 2004.

40. Alex Markels. "Winners: A Kid Champion Champions Kids." *Tennis Magazine*, 1994.

41. Interview with Rick and Landon Deane at the T Lazy 7 Ranch, Aspen, Colorado, December 31, 2005.

42. Rick Carroll. "Prince with Aspen Ties in Delicate Situation in Terrorism War." *Aspen Daily News*, October 18, 2001.

43. Interview with Peter Jay, former British ambassador to Washington, at Woodstock, December 14, 2004.

44. Oxford Brookes University press release, January 21, 2005.

45. Interview with Tony Edwards, head of Defense Exports Sales Organization at the RAF Club, Piccadilly, London, October 15, 2004.

46. Interviews with Mimi Burke in Washington, D.C., January 29 and February 17, 2004.

47. See note 26 above.
48. Interview with Linda Weare at Al-Azziziah Palace, Marrakech, Morocco, June 29, 2004.
49. Interviews with Gen. Aseel at the embassy of the Kingdom of Saudi Arabia, Washington D.C., March 10/11, 2004.
50. Interviews with Dr. Said Karmi in Chevy Chase, Maryland, January 27 and March 11, 2004.
51. Interview with Louis J. Freeh, FBI director (1993–2001) in Wilmington, Delaware, March 11, 2004.
52. Nalisha Kalideen. "Sympathetic Saudi Ambassador Visits Mandela." *The Star* (South Africa), January 18, 2005.
53. Interview with Robert Deacon Elliott in Jeddah, Saudi Arabia, May 13, 2004.
54. See note 35 above.
55. Interview with President George H. W. Bush and Mrs. Barbara Bush in Houston, Texas, February 20, 2004.
56. See note 13 above.

13. BANDAR: THE ENIGMA REVEALED

1. Taken from Nelson Mandela's favorite poem, "Invictus."
2. Interview with former president Nelson Mandela in Cape Town, South Africa, February 2, 2004.
3. Francis Bacon. *Essays II, Of Great Place.*
4. Interview with Prince Bandar in Riyadh, October 13, 2004.
5. Interview with John Veltri, Prince Bandar's barber, in McLean, Virginia, November 3, 2004.
6. Niccolò Machiavelli. *The Prince.* New York: Oxford University Press, 1998: 145.
7. See note 4 above.
8. Interview with Dr. Said Karmi in Chevy Chase, Maryland, March 11, 2004.
9. Interview with Prince Faisal bin Turki in McLean, Virginia, March 9, 2004.
10. See note 8 above.
11. Interview with General Brent Scowcroft in Washington D.C., May 7, 2004.
12. Interview with Dr. Henry Kissinger in New York, April 27, 2004.
13. Interview with Louis J. Freeh, FBI director (1993–2001), in Wilmington, Delaware, March 11, 2004.
14. Interview with former president Bill Clinton in New York, February 10, 2005.
15. Interview with Secretary Colin Powell at the State Department, Washington D.C., November 5, 2004.
16. Interview with Ambassador Richard Murphy in New York, April 28, 2004.
17. See note 9 above.
18. Meeting with Tarek Shawaf at McLean, Virginia, November 3, 2004.
19. See note 15 above.
20. Foreign Ministry Issues Official Statement. SPA. Riyadh, July 20, 2005.
21. John R. Bradley. "Why the Saudi Envoy Really Went Home." *Asia Times,* July 29, 2005.
22. James Morrison. "Bandar Resigns." Embassy Row. *Washington Times,* July 21, 2005.
23. Paul Richter. "Saudi Ambassador to U.S. Resigns." *Los Angeles Times,* July 20, 2005.
24. See note 4 above.
25. See note 18 above.
26. See note 4 above.
27. Lunch with Fred Dutton in Washington D.C., September 14, 2004.
28. Patrick E. Tyler. "Double Exposure: Saudi Arabia's Man in Washington." *New York Times,* June 7, 1992.
29. Murray Waas and Craig Unger. "Annals of Government—How the U.S. Armed Iraq." *The New Yorker,* November 2, 1992.

30. Stanley Hoffman. *Duties Beyond Borders: On the Limits and Possibilities of Ethical International Politics.* Syracuse, NY: Syracuse University Press, 1982: 18.

31. Elsa Walsh. "The Prince: How the Saudi Ambassador Became Washington's Indispensable Operator." *The New Yorker,* March 24, 2003.

32. Niccolò Machiavelli. *Discourses,* Part 3. New York: Modern Library. 1950: 528; Hoffman, p. 24.

33. Robert S. McNamara and James G. Blight. *Wilson's Ghost.* New York: Public Affairs, 2001: 39.

34. Niccolò Machiavelli. *The Prince.* Angelo M. Codevilla. Yale University Press. 1997. Chapter 15, Pg. 58.

35. Bandar bin Sultan. "National Power and Morality." January 5, 1980.

36. Ibid.

37. "FBI Probes Pentagon Spy Case." CBS Broadcasting Inc. August 27, 2004.

38. Tom Barry. "Douglas Feith: Portrait of a neo-conservative." Antiwar.com, September 15, 2004.

39. Dinner Conversation with Prince Bandar at Glympton, Oxfordshire, August 28, 2004.

40. Interview with Dr. Said Karmi in Chevy Chase, Maryland, January 27, 2004.

41. Allen Ruff. "AIPACGate and Washington Infighting: Israel's U.S. Spy Den." *Against the Current.* Volume XIX, Number 5, November/December 2004.

42. Robert Scheer. "Israel's Albatross: US Neocons." *The Nation.* August 31, 2004.

43. James Petras. "Them or Us: AIPAC on Trial." *CounterPunch.* January 7, 2006.

44. Bill Gertz. "Pentagon Aide Draws Scrutiny from FBI." *Washington Times.* August 28, 2004.

45. The Franklin/AIPAC Spy Case Page. JonathanPollard.Org. October 4, 2004.

46. "Controversial Feith leaving Pentagon Post." *Washington Times.* January 26, 2005.

47. Michael Isikoff. "At Issue: Classified Leaks." *Newsweek.* March 20, 2006.

48. Caroline Glick. "Our World: Trial of American Jewry." *The Jerusalem Post.* January 31, 2006.

49. "Michael Saba. Pollard in Perspective." *Washington Report,* July 14, 1986, 12.

50. James Petras. "Them or Us: AIPAC on Trial." *CounterPunch.* January 7, 2006.

51. See note 48 above; Jeffrey Goldberg. "Real Insiders. A pro-Israel lobby and an F.B.I. Sting." *The New Yorker.* July 4, 2005.

52. Interview with Princess Loulou bint Bandar at McLean, Washington, D.C., on February 18, 2004.

53. Interview with H.R.H. Princess Haifa bint Faisal bin Abdul Aziz in McLean, Virginia, October 28, 2003.

54. Conversation with Tarek Shawaf at Glympton, December 1, 2004.

14. A NEW LIFE

1. Syed Rashid Husain. "Saudi NSC to Have Extensive Powers." *Dawn,* Karachi, Pakistan, October 20, 2005.

2. Dr. Ali Alyami and Micha van Waesberghe. "New NSC: Saudi Royals Vie for Power." The Center for Democracy & Human Rights in Saudi Arabia, October 24, 2005.

3. Leila Hatoum. "Mehlis, Daoudi Finalize Plans to Question Syrian Officials. Identity of Five Headed for Vienna Shrouded in Secrecy." *Daily Star,* Lebanon, November 28, 2005.

4. Jihad el Khazen. "King Abdullah: 'We Intervened to Reach the Vienna-Exit upon Assad's Insistence.'" *Al-Hayat,* November 29, 2005.

5. Statement on the Organization of Islamic Conference (OIC) Summit Declaration Issued by Office of the Press Secretary, the White House, December 12, 2005.

6. Syed Qamar Hasan. "GCC Calls for Nuclear-Free Middle East." *Arab News,* Abu Dhabi, December 20, 2005.

7. "Riyadh Seeks Russian Help to Prevent US Strike on Iran." (AFP) *Khaleej Times,* UAE, April 11, 2006.

8. "Ranking Iranian Official Visits Saudi Arabia Later Saturday." Qatar News Agency, July 15, 2006.

9. Greg Myre. "Israel Widens Scope of Attacks Across Lebanon." *New York Times,* July 16, 2006.

10. Amos Harel. "IDF Concerned Missiles Could Hit Central Israel." *Haaretz,* Tel Aviv, July 17, 2006.

11. Yuval Azoulay, Amos Harel, and Yoav Stern. "Eleven Wounded When Haifa Building Collapses Following Rocket Strike." Haaretz Service and Agencies, July 17, 2006.

12. Nicholas Kralev. "Iran, Syria Called 'Playing With Fire'." *Washington Times,* July 14, 2006.

13. Associated Press. "Syria Calls for Hezbollah Cease Fire." *Jerusalem Post,* July 14, 2006.

14. Richard Perle. "Why Did Bush Blink on Iran? (Ask Condi)." *Washington Post,* June 25, 2006; B01.

INDEX

Note: The letter *n* following a page number denotes a footnote.

Abbas, Mahmoud (Abu Mazen), 268*n*
Abdulaziz, Prince (son), 374, 379
Abdullah, Crown Prince
  Geneva Summit and, 303
  G.W. Bush and, 309–11
  Khobar bombing and, 283, 285
  Lockerbie Affair and, 293, 295, 300
  Palestinian/Israeli issues and, 334, 340
  post-9/11 issues and, 318, 330–31
Abourezk, James, 54–56
Adams, Ken, 17–21, 26, 30
ADF (Arab Defense Force), 96
AIPAC (American Israel Public Affairs
  Committee)
  arms sales to Saudi Arabia and, 81–84,
    88–90, 142–43
  Henry Kissinger and, 61
  James Abourezk and, 54–56
  Pentagon/Israel leaks and, 422–27
  purpose/influence on arms sales, 47–48,
    51–53
Airborne Warning and Control System
  (AWACS). *See* arms/aircraft sales (U.S.
  to Saudi Arabia, AWACS)
aircraft sales. *See arms/aircraft sales references*
al-Assad, Hafez. *See* Assad, Hafez
Albright, Madeleine, 276–77, 304–7
Al-Faisal, Turki, Prince (brother-in-law). *See*
  Turki, Al-Faisal, Prince (brother-in-law)
al-Hariri, Rafik. *See* Hariri, Rafik
al-Qaeda. *See* post-9/11 issues

Al-Yamamah
  British Aerospace and, 138–39, 144–48, 347
  contract structure problems/opportunities,
    149–50
  London Times article and, 146
  Michael Heseltine and, 140, 143
  National Audit Office report and, 145
  oil interests and, 146
  Prince Sultan and, 140, 144–45, 162–63
  Saddam Hussein and, 150–51
  secrecy/confidentiality/improprieties and,
    145–46, 148–49
  Tony Edwards and, 138, 141, 147–48,
    298, 397
  UK-Saudi Arabia relationship and, 144,
    150–51
  U.S. rejection of Saudi request for F-15s
    and, 142–43
American Israel Public Affairs Committee. *See*
  AIPAC (American Israel Public Affairs
  Committee)
American Jewish Congress, 7
Andreotti, Giulio, 100
Arab Defense Force, 96
Arab League (League of Arab States), 95–96
Arab League Summit, 218
Arab-Israeli peace process
  Bill Clinton and, 4–5, 258–59, 260–69,
    340
  Geneva Summit and, 303–8
  Israel/Lebanon ceasefire and, 101–10

Arab-Israeli peace process (*continued*)
  Israel/Syria talks (Shepherdstown, WV),
    303, 306
  Madeleine Albright and, 304–7
  Madrid Peace Conference and, 242–58
  North Korea and, 263
  Oslo Declaration of Principles/Accords
    and, 247, 254–58, 260, 268*n*, 303
  Wye River Memorandum and, 258–59
  See also Israeli/Palestinian issue; Madrid
    Peace Conference; Oslo Declaration of
    Principles/Accords; United Nations
    Security Council Resolutions; Wye River
    Memorandum
Arafat, Yasser
  Ariel Sharon and, 261–63
  Clinton-Barak proposal and, 4–5, 260–69
  deceit/Prince Bandar and, 263
  Gulf War and, 191, 201
  G.W. Bush, peace efforts and, 309, 311
  Madrid Peace Conference and, 153,
    244–47, 253, 257
  Oslo Declaration of Principles/Accords
    and, 255–57
  PLO rise and, 95–96, 99
  Prince Bandar and, 267–69
  revolutionary leader vs. statesman, 268–69,
    339–40, 435
  Saddam Hussein and, 245
  Wye River Memorandum and, 258
  See also Palestinian/Israeli issue; PLO
    (Palestine Liberation Organization)
Armitage, Richard, 88, 162, 360, 424
Arms Export Control Act, 72–73, 87, 87*n*, 89
arms/aircraft sales
  France to Saudi Arabia, 135, 138, 140–42
  Prince Turki Al-Faisal and, 2–3
  regulations regarding, 72–73
  UK to Saudi Arabia, 137–40, 147–48. *See
    also* Al-Yamamah
  U.S. to foreign countries, Prince Bandar
    and. *See* Bandar, Prince (career high-
    lights/achievements)
  U.S. to foreign countries, regulations
    regarding, 72–73, 87, 87*n*, 89
  U.S. to Israel, 52, 61, 90
arms/aircraft sales (China-Saudi Arabia)
  George Shultz and, 152, 155, 158
  Israel and, 162–65
  nuclear capability/Iran and, 151–58
  Prince Bandar and, 151–54

  Prince Bandar/Chao Ping deal approval,
    154
  Prince Khalid and, 158
  U.S. reaction to, 157–67
  U.S.-Saudi relationship and, 164–65
  Washington Post news story on, 157
arms/aircraft sales (U.S. to Saudi Arabia)
  AIPAC and, 47–48, 51–53, 81–84, 88–90,
    142–43
  Arms Export Control Act and, 72–73, 87*n*,
    89
  background (before Prince Bandar involve-
    ment), 46–53
  Bob Lilac and, 64, 67, 71, 77–78, 82, 88
  Camp David Treaty and, 52
  Congress and, 57, 60, 70–71, 73–77
  description/advantages, 65–66
  effort to help Saudis acquire, 45
  F-15 aircraft. *See* arms/aircraft sales (U.S.
    to Saudi Arabia, F-15)
  Fred Dutton and, 71, 81–82, 84, 88–89
  Gerald Ford and, 47–48, 50–51
  Henry Kissinger and, 61
  Iranian revolution and, 64
  Israel and, 47–49, 51, 60–61, 66–67
  James Abourezk and, 54–56
  Jimmy Carter and, 47, 49–58, 61, 62,
    64–65
  Margaret Thatcher and, 141
  Menachem Begin and, 70, 79–81
  national interests (Israel) and, 62
  national security and, support for, 62
  Nixon and, 47, 48
  oil interests and, 49, 50, 60–61, 64, 68
  OPEC and, 48
  Packwood Resolution and, 84, 87–88
  Panama Canal Treaty and, 54–56
  Prince Bandar as middleman, 63
  Prince Bandar effort to help Saudis acquire,
    45
  Prince Sultan and, 190–91
  Reagan and, 66–67, 70–75
  restrictions on, 50–51, 71–72, 78, 85, 90–91
  Robert Packwood and, 70–71, 80, 84,
    87–88
  Russell Long and, 57
  Sadat assassination and, 85
  Soviet-Afghanistan conflict and, 64
  Soviets and, 68–69
  success and Prince Bandar's career, 92–94
  tankers and, 66–67

terrorism, impact on, 62
United States Air Force study on Saudi
  needs, 64–65
arms/aircraft sales (U.S. to Saudi Arabia,
  AWACS)
aircraft, description/advantages, 65–66
AWACS. *See* arms/aircraft sales (U.S. to
  Saudi Arabia, AWACS)
Congress and, 73–77, 84, 87–88
document 81-96 (the real AWACS bill), 88
Gerald Ford and, 76
Jimmy Carter and, 64–65
LOA contract signature and, 90–92
Menachem Begin and, 80–81
Ronald Reagan and, 66–72, 80–84, 86
Saudi request and, 63–64
Saudi-Prince Bandar efforts/lobbying in
  support of, 73–79
Washington Post news story on AWACS and,
  85–86, 87
arms/aircraft sales (U.S. to Saudi Arabia,
  F-15)
background, 48–49
Congress and, 52–62
Congress vote/Reagan/Prince Bandar and,
  56–57
David Rockefeller and, 57–58
Jimmy Carter and, 50–57
Panama Canal Treaty Bill and, 54–56
Reagan-Carter and, 56–57
request rejection and, 133–37, 141–43, 151
arms/chemical weapons activities, Saddam
  Hussein and, 180
Armstrong, Scott, 85–88
Assad, Bashir, 308, 431
Assad, Hafez
anti-Saddam Arab states and, 221
Geneva Summit and, 302–8
Lebanon/King Fahd and, 95, 102–10, 200
Madrid Peace Conference and, 248–49
AWACS. *See also* arms/aircraft sales (U.S. to
  Saudi Arabia, AWACS)
Aziz, Abdul, King (grandfather), 1–2, 9, 10
Aziz, Tariq, 181–86

Baer, Robert, 6, 249
Baker, James
Gulf War and, 227–31, 238–39
Madrid Peace Conference and, 245–53, 262
The Politics of Diplomacy, 212–13
Prince Bandar and, 199–200

Bandar, Prince
character/sense of duty, 404–6, 415–22,
  427–28
charity/philanthropy, 396–402
early life and education, 1–2, 11–16
Geneva Summit and, 303–4
Gulf War invasion code and, 229–30
health, 2, 44, 387–88
Henry Siegman and, 7
homes, 390–95
U.S. intelligence leaks and, 422–27
Bandar, Prince (career highlights/achieve-
  ments)
after Ambassador, options/plans, 406
Al-Yamamah and, 3–4
ambassador, 102, 110, 406–8
ambition and, 45–46
Arab-Israeli peace efforts, 4–5
arms/aircraft sales, China-Saudi Arabia,
  151–54
AWACS proposal facilitator, 74–75
AWACS restrictions and, 78
Diplomatic Corp, dean of, 3
Gulf Cooperation Council (GCC)
  Summit, 432–33
Gulf War (Iraqi invasion of Kuwait) and,
  187–88
Israel/Lebanon ceasefire and, 3–4, 101–10
King Abdullah Economic City, 433
military attaché, 95–102
National Security Council secretary-
  general, 340, 429–30, 432–35
Organization of Islamic Conference (OIC),
  432
Panama Canal Treaty Bill, 3
resignation from ambassadorship,
  412–14
Royal Saudi Air Force Falcon Medal, 44
Royal Saudi Air Force NCOs and, xv
Soviet withdrawal from Afghanistan role,
  173
successful AWACS sale/career and,
  92–94
UN-Syria Hariri investigation, 430–31
U.S. National Security Council, de-facto
  member, 189
World Trade Organization and, 430
Bandar, Prince (military education/early
  piloting)
Peace Hawk Program, 34, 36–37, 42, 44
posts/titles, 2, 3, 38–39, 42, 44

Bandar, Prince (*continued*)
  Royal Air Force College Cranwell (England), 2, 5, 15–29, 30–31, 33
  Royal Saudi Air Force/training, 33–39, 42, 44–45
  Yom Kippur War, 40–41
Bandar, Prince (relationships)
  Alexander Haig, 74, 78–79, 96–99, 125–29, 174
  Bob Lilac, 34, 42, 341–43, 375–76, 438
  Brent Scowcroft, 369, 407
  Bush Family, 348–58
  as career asset, 46
  Casper Weinberger, 62, 130–32
  Charles Powell, 137–38, 188, 211
  Colin Powell, 162, 225–26, 358–62
  Dick Cheney, 217
  Fred Dutton, 74–75
  George Shultz, 127–28, 131–32, 165, 417–19
  G.H.W. Bush, 204–5, 419
  James Baker, 199–200
  Jimmy Carter, 3, 53–55
  Joe Ramsey, 35, 42, 274, 341–44, 354–55
  King Fahd. *See* Fahd, King
  King Hussein, 219–23
  Lord Mountbatten, 42–43
  Louis Freeh, 289, 292–93
  Margaret Thatcher, 136–38, 190–91
  Nancy/Ronald Reagan, 127–32
  Nelson Mandela, ix, 362–68
  Prince Sultan, 1, 9, 11–16, 414
  Princess Loulou, 341, 344, 374, 376
  Richard Evans, 211–13, 235–36, 349
  Richard Murphy, 159–60, 408
  Rob Deacon Elliott, 5–6, 22–24, 28, 342, 347–48, 368–71
  Robert McFarlane, 103, 117
  Ronald Reagan, 129–32
  Said Karmi, 245–47
  Tarek Shawaf, 342–45, 388, 409–10, 414, 428
  Tip O'Neill, 59
  Tony Edwards, 298, 397–98
  William Casey, 100–101, 158, 169, 420
Bandar, Prince (wife and family)
  bin Turki, Faisal, Prince (son-in-law), 408*n*
  children/family, 381–86
  Jan Garcia, 375–76
  Prince Abdulaziz, 374, 379
  Prince Fahad, (son), 374, 378, 379–80, 384
  Prince Khalid (son), 374, 377
  Princess Haifa (wife), 39, 222, 322–23, 349–59 *passim*, 373–75, 379–81
  Princess Hussa (daughter), 374, 375, 379
  Princess Loulou (daughter), 341, 344, 374, 376
  Princess Noura (daughter), 374, 378, 380
  Princess Reema, (daughter), 374, 376
  Selma (adopted daughter), 375
Barak, Ehud, 5, 260–67, 303–8. *See also* Clinton-Barak proposal
Begin, Menachem, 70, 79–81
Benjamin, Daniel, 289–91
Berger, Sandy, 282–84, 288–89, 297, 303–7
bin Abdul Aziz Al-Saud, Sultan, Prince. *See* Sultan, Prince (father)
bin Abdul Aziz Al-Saud, Turki, Prince. *See* Turki, Prince (uncle)
bin Abdul Aziz, Fahd, King. *See* Fahd, King
bin Abdul Rahman Al-Saud. *See* Aziz, Abdul, King (grandfather)
bin Abdulaziz, Abdullah, Crown Prince. *See* Abdullah, Crown Prince
bin Bandar, Abdulaziz, Prince. *See* Abdulaziz, Prince (son)
bin Bandar, Faisal, Prince. *See* Faisal, Prince (son)
bin Bandar, Khalid, Prince (son). *See* Khalid, Prince (son)
bin Ladin, Osama, 288–89, 315–20, 328–30
bin Sultan, Bandar, Prince. *See Bandar, Prince references*
bin Sultan, Khalid, Prince (brother), 158, 203, 214, 232
bin Talal, Hussein, King of Jordan. *See* Hussein, King of Jordan
bin Turki, Faisal, Prince (son-in-law), 299, 408*n*
bint Ahmed al-Sudairi, Hussa, Princess, (grandmother), 1–2, 11, 14
bint Bandar, Hussa, Princess (daughter). *See* Hussa, Princess (daughter)
bint Bandar, Loulou, Princess (daughter). *See* Loulou, Princess (daughter)
bint Bandar, Noura, Princess. *See* Noura, Princess (daughter)
bint Bandar, Reema, Princess (daughter). *See* Reema, Princess (daughter)

bint Bandar, Selma, (adopted daughter). *See* Selma, (adopted daughter)

bint Talal Faisal, Haifa, Princess. *See* Haifa, Princess (wife)

Blair, Tony, 138, 293–94, 298, 301, 305, 395, 432

Boland Amendment, 113–14, 117, 118

Brown, Harold, 77

British Aerospace, 138–39, 144–48, 347

Burke, Mimi (Saudi embassy secretary), 322–23, 358, 398

Bush, Barbara, 323, 350, 353–54, 358, 369, 385, 389–90, 402

Bush, George H.W.
    Gulf War and, 204–5, 218, 223–26
    Khobar bombing and, 285
    pledge to topple Saddam, 208–9
    Prince Bandar and, 204–5, 419
    Prince Bandar/Saudi Royals, post-9/11 and, 315, 321
    Saddam Hussein/chemical weapons letter, 236–40
    Saudi relationship and, 257

Bush, George W.
    Crown Prince Abdullah and, 309–11
    peace efforts/Yasser Arafat and, 309, 311
    Prince Bandar/Saudi Royals, post-9/11 and, 315, 321

Cairo Economic Conference, 258

Calder, Richard, 30

Calero, Adolfo, 115–16, 118

Camp David Summit/proposal (July 2000), 5, 261–62. *See also* Clinton-Barak proposal

Carter, James Earl (Jimmy)
    arms/aircraft sales (U.S. to Saudi Arabia), 47, 49–58, 61, 64–65
    F-15/Israel and, 61
    Gulf War (Iraqi invasion of Kuwait) and, 226–27
    Reagan/F-15 and, 56–57

Casey, William
    Iran Contras and, 114–15, 122–23, 125
    Prince Bandar and, 100–101, 158, 169, 420
    Reagan Doctrine and, 169
    Soviets and, 66, 68–69, 110–11

Central Intelligence Agency (CIA)
    arms/aircraft sales, China-Saudi Arabia and, 160
    Iran-Contra Affair and, 114–15, 122–25

Italian elections/U.S. anti-Communist efforts and, 99–101

Prince Bandar and, 4

Reagan Doctrine and, 169

Soviets and, 66–69, 110–12, 173–74

Chad-Libya conflict, 124–26

Chao Ping, 154

Charles, Prince, 362–63, 391

Charles, Sandra, 197

chemical-biological weapons, Saddam Hussein and, 236–40

Cheney, Dick, 190, 205–7, 209–11, 217

Chinese missile deal. *See* arms/aircraft sales (China-Saudi Arabia); CSS-2 ballistic missiles

Christian Democrats (Italian), 99–100

Churchill, Winston, 137, 355–56, 414

Clements, William P, Jr., 48–49

Clinton, William (Bill)
    Arab-Israeli peace process and, 4–5, 257–69
    foreign policy, 271–75
    Geneva Summit and, 303–8
    Khobar bombing and, 275–90
    Louis Freeh and, 289–92
    Palestinian-Israeli issue, 4–5
    Prince Bandar and, 272–74
    Wye River Memorandum and, 258–59

Clinton & Khobar, 275–76

Clinton-Barak proposal, 5, 260–69, 340

The Commanders, 371

Congress
    arms sales notification and, 72–73
    Saudi Arabia/AWACS and, 73–77, 84, 87–88
    Saudi Arabia/F-15 and, 52–62

Cooper, Sherry (Bandar's private secretary), 274

countries of concern, 111–12

Crisis: The Anatomy of Two Major Foreign Policy Crises, 41. *See also* Kissinger, Henry

CSS-2 ballistic missiles, 152, 157, 164, 166. *See also* arms/aircraft sales (China-Saudi Arabia)

Dallas Cowboys, 2, 94, 378

David Rockefeller, 57–58

de Cuéllar, Pérez, 181–84

Deacon Elliott, Robert
  Cranwell/early friendship with Prince
    Bandar, 5–6, 22–24, 28
  friend/advisor, 342, 347, 368–71, 391
Defense Export Sales Organization (DESO),
    137–38, 147–48
Dhahran Air Force Base, Royal Saudi Air
    Force training, 33–34, 37–39
Djerejian, Edward P., Ambassador, 248, 255
Dine, Tom (AIPAC executive director),
    70–71, 89
Dobrynin, Anatoly, 132, 171, 173
Dutton, Fred, 58–59, 71, 74–75, 81–84,
    88–89

Edwards, Tony, 138, 141, 147–48, 298,
    397–98
Evans, Richard, 139, 169, 211–13, 235–36,
    349

Fadlallah, Mohammed Hussein, Sheik,
    122–23
Fahad, Prince (son), 374, 378, 379–80, 384
Fahd, King
  anti-Saddam Arab states and, 219, 222, 228
  Assad/Lebanese civil war (Muslims vs.
    Christians) and, 95, 102–10, 200
  AWACS sale to Saudi Arabia and, 73–75
  F-15 aircraft, 151, 155–56
  French arms purchases and, 142–43
  Gulf War and, 191–200, 242, 244
  invasion plan/code and, 124, 229–36
  Iran-Iraq War/Saddam Hussein and,
    174–76, 180–81, 185
  Israel/Lebanon ceasefire and, 96–98, 102,
    105, 108
  Italian elections/U.S. anti-Communist
    efforts and, 99–101
  King Hussein and, 219–20
  Kuwait invasion and, 201
  LOA and, 91
  Lockerbie Affair and, 293, 300–301
  Muammar Qaddafi and, 300–301
  Reagan/Iran-Contra and, 118
  Reagan/non-U.S. weapons purchases and,
    135, 151, 154–57
  Soviets and, 170–73
  U.S. Gulf War intervention and, 204–17
  U.S. nuclear concerns and, 160–61,
    166–67

U.S.-anti-Saddam Arab intervention plans
    and, 202
Fahrenheit 9/11, 320–21
Fairbanks, Richard, 70
Faisal, King (father in law), 14, 38–39, 323,
    344, 373
Faisal, Prince (son), 374, 378
Feith, Douglas, 423, 426
Flack, Roberta, 362
Ford, Gerald, 47–48, 50–51, 76
foreign policy (Clinton), Khobar bombing
    and, 283–92
formal notification of arms sale and Congress,
    Congress and, 72–73
Franklin, Larry, 422–27
Freeh, Louis
  Bill Clinton and, 289–92
  Khobar bombing and, 271, 276–85
  OPM Sang bombing and, 280–82
  Prince Bandar and, 4–5, 289, 292–93

Garcia, Jan, 375–76. *See also* Lilac, Bob
Gemayel, Amine, 105–6
Gemayel, Pierre, 95
Geneva Summit, 303–8. *See also* Arab-Israeli
    peace process
Gerwel, Jakes, Lockerbie negotiations,
    295–301
Gilbert, Bettina, (Prince Bandar's former pri-
    vate secretary), 274
Glaspie, April, 189–90
Good Hope Medal, 294–95, 300–301
Gorbachev, Mikhail, 170–74, 192, 250–52
Gulf Cooperation Council (GCC) Summit,
    432–33
Gulf War
  Arab nations and, 218–22
  Brent Scowcroft and, 187–89, 196,
    203–13, 224, 228
  buildup, Saddam Hussein and, 189–99,
    201–17, 219–23, 227–29
  cultural issues/American soldiers in Muslim
    country, 225–26
  Dick Cheney and, 190, 205–7, 209–11,
    217
  Fahd Summit in Jeddah and, 191
  G.H.W. Bush decision to leave Saddam in
    power, 232–40
  G.H.W. Bush effort to avert, 227–28
  G.H.W. Bush/Prince Bandar and, 204–5

Hosni Mubarak and, 190–92
invasion response, 208–14
Iran-Iraq War debt to Kuwait and, 190
Iraqi invasion in, 197
Israel and, 194
James Baker and, 227–31, 238–39
Jimmy Carter and, 226–27
King Fahd and, 190–92
King Hussein of Jordan and, 219–22
Margaret Thatcher and, 187
Norman Schwarzkopf and, 190, 208–9,
    217, 231
oil/western interests and, 201–3
OPEC and, 190
Operation Desert Storm, Saddam Hussein
    and, 231–32
press and, 233
Prince Bandar and, 187–88
Prince Khalid bin Sultan and, 203, 214,
    232
Robert McFarlane and, 200
Saddam betrayal/deceit and, 190–95,
    197–98
Saudi Arabia defense needs and, 214
scud missiles and, 231–32
signal/code, Prince Bandar and, 229–30
termination/aftermath, Saddam Hussein
    and, 232–40
United Arab Emirates, 190
United Nations and, 203, 266–68
U.S. opposition to, 225
world order and, 235
Yasser Arafat and, 191, 201
See also Operation Desert Storm

Haifa, Princess (wife)
    Bush Family/Prince Bandar relationship
        and, 349–59 passim
    family/Prince Bandar and, 39, 373–75,
        379–81
    King Hussein/Prince Bandar and, 222
    post-9/11 investigation and, 322–24
Haig, Alexander, 74, 78–79, 96–99, 125–29,
    174
Hariri, Rafik, 102–7, 109, 430–31, 433, 435
Hamas, 261–62, 340
Heseltine, Michael, 140, 143
Hezbollah, 122, 280, 282, 340, 434–35
hovercraft, 42–43
Hunter, Robbie, 21, 26

Hussa, Princess (daughter), 374, 375, 379.
    See also bint Ahmed al-Sudairi, Hussa,
    Princess, (grandmother)
Hussein, King of Jordan, 39, 193, 219–23
Hussein, Saddam
    Al-Yamamah and, 150–51
    arms/chemical weapons activities, 180
    G.H.W. Bush/chemical weapons letter to,
        236–40
    Gulf War buildup and, 189–99, 201–17,
        219–23, 227–29
    Iran-Iraq War and, 174–75, 177–83
    Kuwait invasion rationale, 201
    Operation Desert Storm/aftermath and,
        231–40
    Yasser Arafat and, 245

Ibn Saud. See Aziz, Abdul, King (grandfather)
Intifada, second, 264
Iran, Khobar bombing and, 280, 282,
    285–88
Iran-Contra Affair
    Bandar and, 4
    Boland Amendment and, 113–14, 117,
        118
    Calero and, 115–16, 118
    George Shultz and, 114, 116
    National Security Council (U.S.) and,
        113–14
    North and, 82, 114–15, 117–18, 121,
        124
    Robert McFarlane and, 114–21, 128–30
    William Casey and, 114–15, 122–23, 125
Iranian revolution, arms/aircraft sales, U.S. to
    Saudi Arabia and, 64
Iran-Iraq War
    ceasefire, Prince Bandar and, 180, 183–86
    de Cuéllar and, 181–84
    debt to Kuwait and, 190
    impact on countries, 175
    oil and, 178
    Prince Bandar, mediator in, 181–86
    Saddam Hussein and, 174–75, 177–83
    Saudi position on, 176–77
    Tariq Aziz and, 181–86
    UN Security Council and, 181
    United Nations and, 179–84
Iraqi invasion, of Kuwait, 197. See also Gulf
    War
Islamic Revolution, 176–77

Israel
    arms/aircraft sales, China-Saudi Arabia
        (destined for Iran/nuclear warhead capa-
        bility) and, 162–65
    AWACS aircraft request from Saudi Arabia,
        66–67
    Geneva Summit and, 303–4
    Gulf War (Iraqi invasion of Kuwait) and,
        194
    Operation Desert Storm and, 231–32
    scud missiles and, 231–32
Israel Defense League (IDF), 434
Israeli-Arab peace process. See Arab-Israeli
    peace process
Israeli/Palestinian issue
    Bill Clinton and, 4–5
    Colin Powell and, 337
    Crown Prince Abdullah and, 334, 340
    Henry Kissinger and, 260, 265–66, 337
    Henry Kissinger/Richard Murphy and,
        265–66, 338–39
    Nixon and, 241
    post-9/11 and, 336–40
    Yamani and, 241
    See also Arab-Israeli peace process; PLO
        (Palestine Liberation Organization)
Israeli/Palestinian issue (2006 conflict)
    Hezbollah and, 434–35
    IDF and, 434
Israel's Defense Minister Sharon, Arafat and,
    261–63
Israel/Syria talks (Shepherdstown, WV),
    303–7. See also Arab-Israeli peace pro-
    cess
Italian/Communist Party, PCI (Partito
    Comunista Italiano), 99–101

Jay, Peter (former British Ambassador to the
    United States), 397
Jepson, Roger, (Senator), 86–87
John Paul II (pope), 100
Johns, Richard, 27–28
Jones, David, 64
Jones, Jerry, 377
JP233, 147–48, 235

Karmi, Said, 223, 245–47
Kennedy, John F., 74
Khaddam, Abdul Hallim, (Syrian foreign
    minister), 107, 109

Khalid, Prince (brother). See bin Sultan,
    Khalid, Prince (brother)
Khalid, Prince (son), 374
Khalidi, Walid, 245
Khizaran (mother), 1, 10–11, 13
Khobar bombing
    Crown Prince Abdullah and, 283,
        285
    FBI Director Freeh and, 276–85
    foreign policy (Clinton) and, 283–92
    G.H.W. Bush and, 285
    investigation of, 274–84
    Iranian involvement in, 282, 285–88
    Madeleine Albright and, 276–77
    media and, 278–79, 282–84
    Reno and, 276–77
    Rule 15 (evidence/testimony) and,
        282–83
    Sandy Berger and, 282–84, 288–89
    Saudi FBI (Mabaheth) and, 276–78
    Saudi-U.S. investigation of, 285–92
    terrorism and, 279, 282, 288, 291
    U.S.-Saudi response to, 280–86
Khomeini, Ayatollah, 134, 174, 176–77, 181,
    210
King Abdullah Economic City, 433
King, Larry, 192, 202, 219
Kirkpatrick, Jeane, 129, 224
Kissinger, Henry
    AIPAC and, 61
    Crisis: The Anatomy of Two Major Foreign
        Policy Crises by, 41
    Israeli/Palestinian issue and, 260, 265–66,
        337
    on U.S.-Saudi relationship, 327
    threat to Saudi Arabia, 84
    Yom Kippur War and, 40–41

Lackland Air Force Base, 34–36
Land for Peace
    Madrid Peace Conference and, 243, 256,
        307, 337
    Oslo Declaration of Principles/Accords
        and, 307
    UN Resolution 242 (1967), 337
League of Arab States (Arab League), 95–96
Lebanese Crisis, 95–99
Letter of Offer and Acceptance (LOA),
    90–91, 222–23. See also arms/aircraft
    sales (U.S. to Saudi Arabia)

Libya-Chad conflict, 124–26
Lilac, Bob
    AWACS battle and, 64–67, 71, 77–78, 82,
        88
    LOA and, 90–91, 222–23
    Prince Bandar and, 34, 42, 341–43, 375–76
Lockerbie Affair, 293
    Bill Clinton and, 296–98
    Crown Prince Abdullah and, 293, 295,
        300
    Massoud, Rehab and, 293, 296–97
    Muammar Qaddafi and, 293–95, 297–302
    Nelson Mandela and, 293–302
    Nelson Mandela/Muammar Qaddafi and,
        293–302
    Sandy Berger and, 297
    Tony Blair and, 293–94, 298
    United Nations and, 292, 294–96,
        299–301
    U.S. foreign policy and, 297–98
Long, Russell, 57
Loulou, Princess (daughter), 341, 344, 374,
        376
Lowry, Rich, 275–76

MacFarlane, Robert
    Gulf War and, 200
    Iran-Contra Affair and, 114–21, 128–30
    Israel/Lebanon ceasefire and, 103–6, 109
    suicide attempt, 120
Madrid Peace Conference
    Abbas and, 268n
    Arab-Israeli peace process and, 242–58
    Brent Scowcroft and, 243–44, 250
    Hosni Mubarak and, 248–50
    James Baker and, 245–53, 262
    Land for Peace and, 243, 256, 307, 337
    Mikhail Gorbachev and, 250–52
    United Nation Security Council,
        Resolution 242 (1967) and, 243,
        256–57
    United Nation Security Council,
        Resolution 338 (1973) and, 243,
        256–57
    Yasser Arafat and, 153, 244–47, 253,
        257
Major, John, 138, 233, 293, 358, 387, 395
Mandela, Nelson
    foreword, ix–x
    Good Hope Medal and, 294–95

    Muammar Qaddafi/Lockerbie Affair and,
        293–302, 348–58
    Prince Bandar and, ix, x, 362–68, 401–4
Maronite Party militia. See Phalange party
Massoud, Rehab, 293, 296–97, 303, 306
Maxwell Air Force Base, Alabama, Royal
        Saudi Air Force training (in U.S.), 42
McFarlane, Robert
    Gulf War, 200
    Iran-Contra Affair and, 114–21, 128–30
    Israel/Lebanon ceasefire and, 103–6
    Prince Bandar and, 103, 117
    suicide attempt, 120
media, Khobar bombing and, 278–79,
        282–84
Metcalfe, Wilson, 25
Middle East peace process, Oslo Declaration
        of Principles/Accords and, 242–55
Mifgai, Faisal, 14–15, 371
Mitterrand, François, 142, 208, 221
missiles. See CSS-2 ballistic missiles; nuclear
        missiles; scud missiles
Moore, Michael, 320–21
Mountbatten, Louis (Lord), 42–43
Moussa, Amr, 248–49
Mubarak, Hosni, 190–92, 218, 248–50,
        258
Murphy, Richard
    Israeli-Palestinian issue/Kissinger, 265–66,
        338–39
    Prince Bandar and, 159–60, 408
    Reagan view of Saudi threat, 72, 88
    Saudi purchase of Chinese missiles,
        159–60
    U.S.-Saudi relations post-9/11, 317, 326,
        330

National Association of Arab Americans,
        75–76
National Audit Office report, 145
National Security Agency (NSA), 157
National Security Council (Saudi), 331–32,
        340, 429–32
National Security Council (U.S.), 6, 64, 67,
        113–14, 189
National Security Planning Group (NSPG),
        115
Neil, Andrew (editor of Sunday Times), 239
Netanyahu, Benjamin, Prime Minister
        (Israel), 258–59

New Statesman, 123
New York Times about arms/aircraft sales,
    U.S. to Israel, 90
9/11 commission findings, 316–17, 320, 324,
    328
9/11 investigation findings, 230–32, 327–28
Nixon, Richard, 47, 48, 241
North, Oliver, 82, 114–15, 117–18, 121,
    124
North Korea, 263
Noura, Princess (daughter), 374, 378, 380
nuclear missiles, 156, 160–61, 171*n*

Office of Special Plans, 336
oil/oil interests
    Al-Yamamah and, 146
    Gulf War and, 201–3
    Iran-Iraq War and, 178
    OPEC and, 48, 70, 146, 190
    U.S. arms sales to Saudi Arabia and, 49,
        50, 60–61, 64, 68
O'Neill, Thomas (Tip), 59
OPEC (Organization of Petroleum Exporting
    Countries), 48, 70, 146, 190
Operation Desert Storm, 199, 229–33, 236,
    239
Operation Torch/U.S.-Saudi operation pre-
    venting arms to Iran, George Shultz and,
    152
OPM Sang bombing and, Saudi investiga-
    tion/adjudication, 279–80
OPM Sang bombing, FBI Director Freeh
    and, 280–82
Organization of Islamic Conference (OIC),
    432
Organization of Petroleum Exporting
    Countries (OPEC), 48, 70, 146, 190
Oslo Declaration of Principles/Accords
    Arab-Israeli peace process and, 247,
        254–58, 260, 268*n*, 303
    Land for Peace and, 307
    Middle East peace process and, 242–55
    Yasser Arafat and, 255–57

Packwood, Robert, 70–71, 80, 84, 87–88
Packwood Resolution
    AWACS opposition and, 84, 87–88
    Fred Dutton and, 88–89
Palestine Liberation Organization. *See* PLO
    (Palestine Liberation Organization)

Palestinian/Israeli issue. *See* Israeli/Palestinian
    issue
Panama Canal Treaty, 3, 54–56
PCI (Partito Comunista Italiano),
    99–100
Peace Hawk program, 34, 36–37, 42, 44
Pentagon U.S. Iran policy intelligence leaks to
    Israel, 422–27
Perrin Air Force Base, 34, 36
Phalange party, 95, 106*n*
Phalangists, 95, 102
Phillips, Keith, 37, 38, 39
pilot, Bandar ability as, 26–28, 38–39
PLO (Palestine Liberation Organization)
    Ariel Sharon and, 96–98
    Clinton-Barak proposal and, 260–66
    first Israel attack and, 62
    Gulf War/Saddam Hussein and, 201
    Madrid Peace Conference and, 246–47,
        250, 268*n*
    Oslo Declaration of Principles/Accords
        and, 254–57, 268*n*, 307
The Politics of Diplomacy, 212–13
post-9/11 issues
    Ariel Sharon and, 336–40
    Crown Prince Abdullah and, 318, 330–31
    Fahrenheit 9/11, 320–21
    G.W. Bush/Prince Bandar/Saudi Royals
        and, 315, 321
    Israeli/Palestinian issue and, 336–40
    9/11 investigation/Saudi cooperation,
        230–32, 327–28
    9/11 commission findings/Saudis, 316–17,
        320, 324, 328
    Princess Haifa and, 322–24
    Saudi public relations campaign and, 334–35
    Saudi response to, 313
    Saudi-related backlash/tension/suspicion
        and, 313–14, 317–20
    U.S.-Saudi relationship and, 317, 324–27,
        334, 335, 336
Powell, Charles, 137–38, 188, 211
Powell, Colin
    Gulf War and, 191, 195
    Israel/Palestine issue and, 337
    Pentagon and, 424
    Prince Bandar and, 62, 162–63, 225–26,
        358–62
    Princess Haifa, 323–24
    Saudi social issues and, 410–11

Prince Bandar bin Sultan bin Abdul Aziz Al-Saud. *See Bandar, Prince references*
project officer, 42, 44

Qaddafi, Muammar
  Chad and, 124–26
  Good Hope Medal, 300–301
  Lockerbie Affair and, 293–95, 297–302

Rabin, Yitzhak, and Rabin Deposit, 255–56, 259, 303, 306–7
Ramsey, Joe, 35, 42, 274, 341–44, 354–55
Randolph Air Force Base, 42
Reagan Doctrine, 4, 69, 110–13, 127, 169
Reagan, Ronald
  Al-Yamamah and, 4
  AWACS aircraft request from Saudi Arabia and, 66–67, 70–75, 82–84, 86–87
  AWACS deal importance to, 80, 82–84
  Begin vs., slogan, 84
  Jimmy Carter/F-15 and, 56–57
  Richard Murphy and, 88
Reagan, Nancy, 128, 130–33
Reema, Princess (daughter), 374, 376
Rosen, Steve, 425
Ross, Dennis, 253, 260–61, 305–6
Royal Air Force College Cranwell (England), 2, 5, 15–26, 30–31
Royal Saudi Air Force, 39, 42, 44–45, 147–48, 238
  Falcon Medal, 44
  training, 33–39, 42
Rule 15 (evidence/testimony), 282–83

Sadat, Anwar, assassination, AWACS proposal vote and, 85
Sadd, David, 75
Sampson, Anthony, 146
Sandinistas, 113, 118
Saudi Arabia
  al-Qaeda/conservative Islam and, 332–34, 335
  Chad-Libya conflict and, 124–26
  Chinese missiles/Murphy and, 159–60
  distrust of U.S. protection offer, 204, 215
  history/formation of, 10
  Iran-Iraq War position, 176–77
  OPM Sang bombing and, 279–80
  position of Khomeini on, 180–81
  post-9/11 issues, 313–14, 317–20

Shah of Iran and, 176
  social issues/Powell and, 410–11
  U.S. Air Force Peace Hawk Program with, 34, 36–37, 42, 44
  U.S. alliance after Iraqi invasion, 214, 214–17, 218
  U.S. alliance vs. communism and, 111–13. *See also* countries of concern; Reagan Doctrine
  U.S. Khobar bombing investigation and, 285–92
  U.S./UK relationship and, 139–40
Saudi Arabia (defense needs)
  background (before Prince Bandar involvement), 139–40
  Chinese arms deal and, 166–67
  distrust of U.S. protection offer, 204
  Iranian revolution and, 64–65, 70, 134, 176–77
  U.S. involvement and, 215–17
  See also arms/aircraft sales (U.S. to Saudi Arabia) references
Saudi royal family, Osama bin Ladin and, 315–20, 328–30
Schwarzkopf, Norman, 190, 208–9, 217, 231
Scowcroft, Brent
  Gulf War and, 187–89, 196, 203–13, 224, 228
  Madrid Peace Conference and, 243–44, 250
  Prince Bandar and, 369, 407
scud missiles, 134, 151, 231
Secord, Richard, 82, 85–86
Security Council, Iran-Iraq War, 181
Siegman, Henry, 7
Selma, (adopted daughter), 375
Shah of Iran, 64, 176, 204
Shamir, Yitzhak (Israeli Foreign Minister), 79
Sharon, Ariel, 96–98, 261–63, 309, 336–40
Shawaf, Tarek, 342–45, 388, 409–10, 414, 428
Shepherdstown talks, 303–7. *See also* Arab-Israeli peace process
Shewry, Martin, xv, 18
Smith, Hedrick, 93
Shultz, George
  Alexander Haig replacement, 127–28
  arms/aircraft sales, China-Saudi Arabia, 152, 155, 158
  Iran-Contra Affair and, 114, 116

Shultz, George (*continued*)
  Nancy Reagan and, 131–32
  Operation Torch/U.S.-Saudi operation pre-
    venting arms to Iran, 152
  Prince Bandar and, 127–28, 131–32, 165,
    417–19
Simpson, Bill, 6, 26*p*
Soviet Union
  arms sales to Saudi Arabia and, 68–69
  U.S.-Saudi cooperation and, 169–73
  William Casey and, 66, 68–69, 110–11
  withdrawal from Afghanistan/Prince
    Bandar and, 173
Special Situations Group (SSG), 123
Sudairi Seven, 11
Sultan, Prince (father)
  Al-Yamamah and, 140, 144–45, 162–63
  arms/aircraft sales, U.S. to Saudi Arabia,
    190–91
  Prince Bandar and, 1, 9, 11–16, 414

Taif Agreement, 109
Taliban, 315, 336
Technical Training Institute, 33–34
terrorism, Khobar bombing and, 275–76,
  279, 282, 288, 291
Thatcher, Margaret
  Al-Yamamah and, 4
  Gulf War (Iraqi invasion of Kuwait) and,
    187
  Prince Bandar and, 136–38, 190–91
  rejected Saudi request to U.S. for F-15s
    and, 136–38
Turki, Al-Faisal, Prince (brother-in-law), 53,
  310, 412
Turki, Prince (uncle), 11*n*, 43

UK-Saudi Arabia relationship, Al-Yamamah
  and, 144, 150–51
United Arab Emirates, Gulf War (Iraqi inva-
  sion of Kuwait), 190
United Nations
  Gulf War and, 203, 266–68
  Hariri assassination investigation and,
    102*n*, 430–31
  Iran-Iraq War and, 179–84

Lockerbie Affair and, 292, 294–96,
  299–301
weapons of mass destruction and, 167, 433
United Nations Security Council Resolutions
  NCS Resolution 242 (1967), Madrid
    Conference and, 243, 256–57, 337
  Resolution 338 (1973), Madrid Conference
    and, 243, 256–57
  Resolution 479, Iran-Iraq War, 179–81,
    184
  Resolution 660, Iraq Kuwait invasion,
    203
  Resolution 678, demand for Iraq Kuwait
    withdrawal, 237–38
United States Air Force study on Saudi
  defense needs, 64–65

Vatican, 100–101
Veil, 122, 371
Veliotis, Nick, 97–98

Walsh, Elsa, 264, 283, 302
Washington Post news story on AWACS,
  85–86, 87–88
Waterfall, John, 18, 21, 22, 26
weapons of mass destruction, 167, 433. *See
  also* nuclear missiles
Weinberger, Caspar, 69, 123, 130–32
Weissman, Keith, 426
Welsh, Matt, 6, 349
Williams Air Force Base, 34, 36, 42
Wolfowitz, Paul, 205, 423, 426
Woodward, Bob
  on CIA/Libya, 125
  The Commanders, 371
  Fadlallah assassination attempt and,
    122–23
  PCI/Prince Bandar and, 100
  Veil, 122
world order, Gulf War and, 235
World Trade Organization, 430
Wye River Memorandum, 258–59

Yamani, Zaki (Saudi oil minister), 241
Yom Kippur War, 40–41
Yule, Tony, 27